THE MUTUAL FUND ENCYCLOPEDIA

Fidelity • Vanguard • Twentieth Century Select • Oppenheimer • T.
we Price International • OTC Securities Fund • Acorr
green • Windsor • Fidelity • Vanguard • Twentieth Ce
• Oppenheimer • T. Rowe Price International •
s Fund • Acorn • Evergreen • Windsor • F
• Twentieth Century Select • Oppenheimer

Gerald W. Perritt

1992-1993 Edition

Fidelity • Vanguard • Twer
T. Rowe Price Internatior
Century Select • Or
C Securities Func
nguard • Tw
ce Internat
or • Fi
T.

Dearborn Financial Publishing, Inc.

While a great deal of care has been taken to provide accurate and current information, the ideas, suggestions, general principles and conclusions presented in this text are subject to local, state and federal laws and regulations, court cases and any revisions of same. The reader is thus urged to consult legal counsel regarding any points of law—this publication should not be used as a substitute for competent legal advice.

Publisher: Kathleen A. Welton
Associate Editor: Karen A. Christensen
Senior Project Editor: Jack L. Kiburz

Published by Dearborn Financial Publishing, Inc.

Printed in the United States of America

92 93 10 9 8 7 6 5 4 3 2 1

Library of Congress Cataloging-in-Publication Data

Perritt, Gerald W.
The mutual fund encyclopedia / Gerald W. Perritt. — 1992-93 ed.
p. cm.
Includes index.
ISBN 0-79310-384-3 (paper)
1. Mutual funds—United States. I. Title.
HG4530.P432 1992 92-12299
332.63'27—dc20 CIP

Contents

Acknowledgments

A task of this magnitude requires the input of a number of people. Data must be collected, verified, processed and eventually committed to paper. I was highly fortunate to have had the assistance of my staff of mutual fund analysts who normally spend their time assembling our monthly publication, *The Mutual Fund Letter*.

Return statistics and selected data were provided by Investment Company Data, Inc. (ICDI). Returns were cross-checked with other sources and the funds themselves to ensure a high degree of accuracy.

Michael Corbett supervised the collection and verification of financial statistics in addition to writing mutual fund descriptions. Mike Farmer spent many long and tedious hours summarizing mutual fund investment objectives and strategies that were frequently cryptically written in prospectuses. Carol McHugh, Allison Hearst and Gina Romagnano spent endless hours entering statistics and mutual fund descriptions on computer disks. Because of the sacrifices of these dedicated individuals, this year's edition of *The Mutual Fund Encyclopedia* was assembled in record time. To these people, my colleagues and friends, I owe a huge debt of gratitude.

Although I alone must shoulder the responsibility for errors in content, this work could not have been completed without the unselfish efforts of my colleagues and the assistance of ICDI.

Gerald W. Perritt

Preface

Although mutual funds have enjoyed unprecedented investor popularity in recent years and the mutual fund industry has responded with more product choice for the individual investor, there are still a number of obstacles encountered in surveying mutual funds. Funds are offered by more than 350 sponsors, and there are more than 3,000 funds available to individual investors. Although information is readily available, one needs to consult a variety of resources and, ultimately, each fund to compile the kind of information we provide in *The Mutual Fund Encyclopedia.*

In the pages that follow, we present information on nearly 1,300 funds, including a description of their investment objectives and the investment strategies applied by management in the pursuit of each fund's mandated objective. In addition, we supply financial statistics concerning each fund's operations and total-return data, covering several years. Thus, an investor can survey hundreds of funds and narrow the field down to a handful that merit more detailed analysis through an examination of their individual prospectuses and annual reports.

The Mutual Fund Encyclopedia is unique in that it contains descriptions of both load and no-load funds. In recent years the distinction between these two classes of funds has become somewhat blurred. Some funds do not levy a front-end sales charge but assess a fee when an investor redeems shares. A large number of funds assess an ongoing fee, called a 12b-1 charge, which is used to compensate fund salespeople and to pay for advertising. Thus, a number of other publications that profess to focus on "no-load" funds fail to deliver the goods since they ignore the fiction created by 12b-1 funds. In addition, while I have a decided preference for no-load funds, the inclusion of load funds in this book allows investors to compare their investment returns with a number of popular load funds.

Although I have taken great care to eliminate errors, in the course of assembling tens of thousands of data items a few incorrect statistics will inevitably sneak past the proofreaders. Besides, the mutual fund industry is quite dynamic. New funds appear each day, some are liquidated, a few change their names and more than a handful are acquired by other funds during the course of a year. As a result, some of the information herein will be out of date by the time copies roll off the press, a problem common to all "encyclopedic" efforts.

Gerald W. Perritt, Ph.D.
Chicago, Illinois

How To Use This Book

Individual investors can consult a number of information sources when searching for common stocks to add to their investment portfolios. In addition to *Standard & Poor's Reports* and the Value Line *Investment Survey*, investors can obtain the latest information about a company's prospects from the *Wall Street Journal, Barron's Financial Weekly, Investor's Business Daily* and a host of other weekly or monthly financial magazines. In addition, investors can call their brokers to obtain the latest research reports on dozens of companies. When it comes to analyzing a mutual fund, however, very few sources of information are available to the individual investor.

Although some financial magazines periodically list return data for mutual funds, little additional information is given. How has the fund performed in rising and falling markets? What types of stocks or bonds does the fund hold? What are its year-by-year returns? Does fund management assume a buy-and-hold posture or attempt to "time the market"? Where do you write for additional information about a fund or a copy of a fund's prospectus? These are just a few of the questions that need to be answered before investing in a mutual fund.

The Mutual Fund Encyclopedia is designed to give investors a thumbnail sketch of a large number of funds. The data presented for these funds will allow an investor to screen potential investment candidates so that a few can be analyzed further. In addition, investors can compare the performance of funds currently held with others that possess similar investment objectives and strategies.

When evaluating a fund, it is important to understand what the fund's manager will do with your money. Will management invest in blue-chip stocks or emerging growth stocks? Will they stay fully invested at all times or head for the safety of money market instruments during a stock market downturn? Most mutual fund directories merely list the fund's objective from the fund's prospectus. Since the prospectus is written to conform to SEC requirements, these statements of investment objectives are quite general and rarely give significant clues as to how your money will be invested. After reading statements such as "the objective of this fund is to seek long-term growth of capital by investing primarily in common stocks and securities convertible into common stocks," investors are left with few clues as to how their money will be invested.

The Mutual Fund Encyclopedia contains a much more detailed statement of fund objectives and strategies. It indicates what types of investments are preferred by fund management and gives some idea why the fund's historical returns are what they are. In addition, it contains a listing of a fund's key financial statistics, such as portfolio turnover rate, assets under management, current yield, returns during up and down markets, beta and year-by-year returns for the last five years. These statistics can be used to screen funds down to a handful that deserve further analysis. Furthermore, it outlines the cost of investing for a particular fund. In addition to front-end, back-end and annual 12b-1 sales charges, the fund's expense ratio is also given. Since sales fees and fund operating expenses erode investment returns, these data are critical to proper mutual fund selection.

The Mutual Fund Encyclopedia also lists the fund's portfolio manager and his or her tenure with the fund. It is important to know who is managing your money and if the fund has made a recent change in management. Finally, both the address and telephone number of funds are listed. Since the law requires that investors receive a prospectus before they invest in a mutual fund, these listings can be used to obtain a prospectus and the fund's latest annual report.

Unlike a number of other publications, every attempt has been made to ensure that this book is user-friendly. Funds are arranged by investment objective and listed alphabetically by fund name. If you are considering an investment in an international equity fund, for example, you need not wade through hundreds of funds to find what you are looking for, since these funds are presented in a single chapter. Furthermore, the general category of bond funds has been separated into the predominant type of investments in their portfolios. You can easily compare the returns of high-yield, GNMA, corporate, government, municipal and international bond funds with their peers. Finally, we have summarized several financial statistics for each class of funds. Thus, for example, you can easily compare the returns of an aggressive growth fund with the median return for the entire group. Similar comparisons can be made for a fund's turnover ratio, expense ratio and beta.

The following table lists the year-by-year returns for common stocks, long-term government bonds and Treasury bills. These returns provide benchmarks for comparing a fund's historical performance during the recent past. Furthermore, you can combine these returns to obtain a particular fund's return with the return of a portfolio with similar risk. For example, by combining the returns of common stocks with the returns of Treasury bills using a weighted average, you can produce portfolios with betas similar to those of the funds under consideration. The weighted average return for this hypothetical portfolio can be meaningfully compared with the historical return for a particular fund, since it contains the same level of risk. For example, suppose that you are considering a fund whose beta is 0.70. This level of risk could be obtained by combining a 30 percent investment in Treasury bills with a 70 percent investment in common stocks (its beta is the weighted average of the beta of the market portfolio, 1.00, and the beta of a riskless Treasury bill portfolio, 0.00). This portfolio would have produced a 24.6 percent return during 1989 (0.70 × 31.5% + 0.30 × 8.4%). Similarly, its five-year return would have been 119 percent (0.70 × 153% + 0.30 × 39%). Since the bulk of investment return is related to investment risk, risk-adjusted return comparisons more accurately indicate how well (or how poorly) a fund manager has performed.

Listed below are the definitions of the financial statistics given for the mutual funds listed in *The Mutual Fund Encyclopedia*.

Total Returns. Annual returns were computed by compounding a fund's monthly return. Monthly returns were computed by taking the difference between the fund's per share net asset value at the end of the previous month and the current month-end per share net asset value, adding any distributions paid during the month and dividing by the per share net asset value at the end of the previous month. The five-year return is the compound value of the previous five annual returns.

Bull Market Returns. These are total returns earned during the period beginning

Historical Investment Returns

Investment Category	1987	1988	1989	1990	1991	Five-Year Return
Common Stocks	5.2%	16.8%	31.5%	–3.2%	30.5%	104%
Long-term Government Bonds	–2.7	9.7	18.1	6.2	19.3	60
Treasury Bills	5.5	6.3	8.4	7.8	5.6	38

October 11, 1990, and ending October 18, 1991. During this period, the Standard & Poor's 500 Index returned a total of 33.1 percent.

Bear Market Returns. These are total returns during the period beginning July 17, 1990, and ending October 11, 1990. During this three-month period, the return for the Standard & Poor's 500 Index was -20.1 percent.

Current Yield. The fund's yield was obtained by dividing annual income distributions by the fund's year-end per share net asset value.

Turnover Ratio. This is the annual portfolio turnover ratio during the last fiscol year. This ratio is calculated by dividing the lesser of purchases or sales for the fund's fiscal year by the monthly average total assets of the fund during the year. A turnover ratio of 100 percent indicates that a fund has turned over its entire portfolio of assets during the year. The reciprocal of the turnover ratio gives an indication of the fund's average holding period. For example, a fund with an average turnover ratio of 50 percent has an average holding period of two years (1.00/0.50 = 2.00).

Expense Ratio. This ratio is the sum of the annual administrative fees and management fees divided by the average net asset value of the fund, stated as a percentage. The ratio is taken from the fund's latest annual report. Remember, however, that an increase in a fund's total assets generally will be accompanied by a decline in the fund's expense ratio.

Beta. This statistic is a measure of the relative systematic (market) risk of the fund's investment portfolio. Beta illustrates the volatility of the per share net asset value of a mutual fund relative to that of the market as a whole (the S&P 500 Index is assigned a beta of 1.00). The per share net asset value of a fund whose beta is less than 1.00 tends to vary by less than the market, whereas the per share net asset value of a fund whose beta is greater than 1.00 will vary by more than the market. Beta most accurately describes the relative risk of a fund when it is a *well-diversified equity fund*. If a mutual fund's portfolio is not well diversified, as in the case of a sector fund or a precious metals fund, then nonmarket risks may affect the fund's volatility, and these risks are not reflected in the fund's beta. Therefore, a low beta does not necessarily imply low total risk. Betas were determined by the least squares regression line (the slope of the line) of best fit for 36 pairs of monthly returns represented by the fund in question and the Standard & Poor's 500 Index (a proxy for the stock market as a whole).

Risk per Unit of Return. This statistic, known as the "Sharpe Ratio," allows direct performance comparisons between funds of varying levels of risk. In effect, it adjusts each fund's average monthly return for its average monthly risk. The ratio is calculated by dividing the difference between the fund's average monthly return during the previous 36 months and the average monthly Treasury bill yield by the fund's standard deviation of return. The greater the value of this ratio, the greater is the fund's risk-adjusted return. Thus, when comparing the ratios of two funds, the fund with the higher ratio performed best on a risk-adjusted basis. "NA" indicates that the fund either experienced a negative average return during the previous 36 months, or that the fund was not in existence during the entire period.

The objective of this book is to enable mutual fund investors to make more informed decisions. To this end, we have presented financial statistics that academic research suggests affect a fund's future return. These include: investment objective and strategy, risk, sales charges, portfolio turnover rate and annual fund expenses. In Part 1 of this book, we outline the benefits of mutual fund investing and summarize recent research that points to the variables influencing a fund's return potential. While financial forecasting is at best an inexact science, we believe that like all of life's decisions, an individual can do little more than gather data, weigh the facts and select the alternative that is expected to generate the greatest level of satisfaction. *The Mutual Fund Encyclopedia* is one of the tools that can assist individuals in making rational, informed investment decisions.

PART 1

Introduction to Mutual Funds

1991—YEAR IN REVIEW

The year 1991 was one heck of a volatile year—for the world and for the financial markets. The year began on a discordant note. Saddam Hussein was occupying tiny Kuwait and was telling the world that if anyone tried to dislodge him, he would fight "the mother of all wars." The Dow Jones Industrial Average, too, was in the doldrums. Once flying above the 3,000 level in mid-1990, this popularly quoted stock market average began the year at 2,635, about 400 points below its year-earlier highwater mark. And the U.S. economy? The nation's gross national product had just notched its first decline in nearly nine years, ending a peacetime record economic expansion. It would later add two successive down quarters as the economic recession, which began in late 1990, continued through the first half of 1991.

However, things changed quickly. On January 16, a U.S.-led air attack aimed at Saddam Hussein's military forces in Kuwait and Iraq met with early success. It quickly became apparent that Iraq would be solidly defeated in a matter of days. Jubilant investors set the stock market off like a Roman candle. On January 17, the Dow Jones Industrial Average rocketed skyward 144 points. The Dow quickly erased its earlier January losses and poked its head above the 3,000 level in early March. In the 34 trading days following the initial Allied air attack, the Dow Jones Industrial Average advanced a total of 550 points! Although the advance in blue chip stock prices would stall during the next nine months, a year-end rally propelled the Dow Jones Industrial Average to a closing level of 3,169, a gain of 536 points for the year.

While the appreciation of blue chip stock prices during 1991 was impressive, the performance of small firm stocks was the big equity story of the year. During the past 65 years, small firm stocks have returned an average of about 5 percent annually more than large firm, blue chip stocks. With the exception of 1988, however, small firm stocks had underperformed the blue chip–dominated Standard & Poor's 500 Index in every year since 1983—that is, until the past year when they returned an average of 44.5 percent (versus 30.6 percent for the Standard & Poor's 500 Index). Leading the way were the stocks of small companies in the health-care, technology and biotechnology industries. As one would expect, sector funds that concentrated their investments in one of these industries were stellar performers. For example, the Financial Strategic Health Sciences Fund returned 91.8 percent, the Financial Strategic Technology Fund returned 76.9 percent and the Oppenheimer Global Biotechnology Fund returned a whopping 121 percent during 1991.

While most equity fund investors were enjoying smooth sailing during the past year, bond fund investors were being treated to a pretty rough roller coaster ride. The yield on the Treasury 30-bond began the year at about 8.2 percent. It then rose modestly before the Federal Reserve Board unleashed an economic stimulus package that drove the yield on the long bond down to 7.6 percent by year-end. As a result, most bond fund investors who hung on all year earned handsome double-digit returns on their investments.

Precious metals investors were one of the few groups to lose money the past year. An economic recession gets part of the blame as industrial demand for silver and platinum sank along with economic growth. With inflation under control, there was little incentive to acquire precious metals as a hedge against inflation. As a result, the prices of gold, silver and platinum all ended 1991 much lower than a year earlier: Gold declined 10.2 percent, silver 7.4 percent and platinum 17.1 percent. On average, precious metals mutual funds returned minus 4.4 percent the past year.

While the domestic stock and bond markets were forging ahead during the past year, international stocks were providing shareholders with highly divergent returns. The European, Australian and Far East (E.A.F.E.) index rose 6.8 percent in local currencies and 10.2 percent in U.S. dollars, thanks to a slight decline in the value of the dollar against most foreign currencies.

The top rung on the performance ladder was occupied by the Hong Kong stock market, which rose 42.5 percent in local currency terms and 42.8 percent in U.S. dollars. Australian stocks stood one rung down with a return of 31.2 percent in local currency and 29.1 percent in U.S. dollars. The better-performing stock markets in Europe included Switzerland (+21.4 percent), France (+18.0 percent) and Denmark (+17.9 percent). The bottom rungs on the performance ladder were occupied by stocks traded in Japan, Italy, Finland, Austria and Norway, which all lost ground during 1991. On balance, international bond investors fared reasonably well the past year as international bond funds returned an average of about 12 percent for the year.

Houdini, the master magician, once made an elephant disappear right in front of an audience's eyes. However, Houdini's disappearing act pales when placed beside those mastered by economic forces. During the past year, the market economy pulled off some terrific disappearing acts. The Bank of New England, which at one time had an unbroken history of paying cash dividends every year for more than 200 years, disappeared in a wash of red ink. NCR disappeared with a wave of AT&T's magic wand (and a purchase offer of $7.5 billion). These acts, however, qualify as mere warm-ups for the master disappearing act of all time. Of course, I'm speaking of the disappearance of the Soviet Union.

One nice thing about getting older is that you can do some things that you couldn't do before. There are a few things, however, that I can't do today that I could do a year ago, such as: travel on Pan American, Eastern or Midway Airlines; buy a few shares of NCR common stock; bank at Security Pacific; watch the ticker tape on the Financial News Network (FNN); or buy a "guaranteed investment contract" from Executive Life. With the exception of flying Midway Airlines occasionally, I never really wanted to do any of those things in the first place.

What would a year be without a few financial scandals? However, there were relatively few the past year. Perhaps scoundrels were frightened by the jail terms handed down to Mr. Milken and his cronies a year or two earlier, but I doubt it.

Robert Maxwell "fell" off his yacht shortly before it was revealed that Maxwell Communications was stealing pension fund money from other companies controlled by him. The president of Cascade International, a Florida-based distributor of cosmetics, disappeared shortly before his company's board of directors announced that most of the company's retail cosmetic boutiques never really existed. Former Vernon Savings & Loan owner, Don Dixon, was sentenced to five years in prison for misusing S&L funds. Charles Keating, former head of Lincoln Savings & Loan, was convicted on 17 counts of securities fraud and was indicted by a U.S. grand jury for fraud and racketeering. The presidents of both Nikko and Nomura Securities resigned after it was learned that the firms periodically reimbursed favorite clients for losses on their investments. Salomon acknowledged that it had been illegally transacting business in the U.S. government bond market. And, of course, BCCI Holdings was exposed as nothing more than a grand international fraud.

Table 1 United States Equity Markets

Index	1991 Close	Percentage Change
Dow Jones Industrial Average	3,169	+20.4%
Standard & Poor's 500 Index	417	+26.4
New York Stock Exchange Index	229	+27.2
American Stock Exchange Index	395	+28.3
NASDAQ OTC Index	586	+56.7
Wilshire 5000	4,041	+30.3
Russell 2000	190	+43.9

Table 2 World Equity Markets (1991)

	Percentage Change	
Country	Local Currency	U.S. Dollars
Australia	+31.2%	+29.1%
Canada	+ 7.9	+ 8.3
France	+18.0	+15.8
Germany	+ 7.9	+ 6.3
Hong Kong	+42.5	+42.8
Italy	− 2.1	− 4.1
Japan	− 0.5	+ 8.3
Spain	+12.9	+11.6
Sweden	+10.3	+12.1
Switzerland	+21.4	+14.0
United Kingdom	+15.3	+11.6

An old adage proclaims: "The more things change, the more they stay the same." While this may apply to some things in life, it certainly is not true in the mutual fund industry. In 1970, investors could choose from 361 open-end funds. Today, investors can cull their selections from a list of more than 3,200 open-end funds. (Investors can choose from 1,200 equity funds, 1,300 bond funds and nearly 800 money market and short-term municipal bond funds.)

Not only are there now more mutual funds than stocks listed on the New York Stock Exchange, activity in the mutual fund industry is beginning to parallel that normally reserved for the common stock arena. For example, of the mutual funds contained in the last edition of *The Mutual Fund Encyclopedia,* 19 merged their assets with other funds, 3 were liquidated, more than 50 changed their names, more than a dozen changed their investment objectives and 4 funds ceased selling shares to new investors. Tables 1, 2, 3 and 4 highlight a number of items we came across while assembling this year's edition. We can hardly wait to see what changes next year will bring.

RETROSPECT AND PROSPECT OF MUTUAL FUNDS

The origins of the modern-day mutual fund can be traced back to nineteenth-

Table 3 Highlights of 1991 Mutual Fund Changes

Name Changes

Old Name	New Name
AFA National Aviation & Technology	John Hancock Technology National Aviation & Technology
Alliance Bond US Government	Alliance Bond US Government A
Alliance Fund	Alliance Fund A
Alliance Growth & Income	Alliance Growth & Income A
American Capital Federal Mortgage Trust	American Capital Federal Mortgage Trust A
Axe Houghton Funds	USFG Axe Houghton
Composite Northwest 50 Index	Composite Northwest 50 Fund
Delaware Government Income Series	Delaware Government Income II
Delaware Treasury Reserve Investors	Delaware Treasury Reserve Investors II
Fidelity Michigan Tax Free	Fidelity Michigan Tax Free High Yield
Franklin Option	Franklin Premier Return
Growth Industry Shares	William Blair Growth Shares
IAI Apollo	IAI Value
IDS Insured Tax Exempt	IDS Special Tax Exempt Insured
IDS Massachusetts Tax Exempt	IDS Special Tax Exempt Massachusetts
IDS Michigan Tax Exempt	IDS Special Tax Exempt Michigan
IDS Minnesota Tax Exempt	IDS Special Tax Exempt Minnesota
IDS New York Tax Exempt	IDS Special Tax Exempt
IDS Ohio Tax Exempt	IDS Special Tax Exempt Ohio
Investment Portfolio Funds	Kemper Investment Portfolios
Lexington Growth	Lexington Worldwide Emerging Growth
Lexington Research	Lexington Growth & Income
Merrill Federal Securities	Merrill Federal Securities A
Merrill Lynch Retire/Income	Merrill Lynch Federal Securities B
PaineWebber California Tax Exempt	PaineWebber California Tax Exempt A
PaineWebber Classic Atlas	PaineWebber Classic Atlas A
PaineWebber Classic Growth	PaineWebber Growth A
PaineWebber High Yield	PaineWebber Municipal High Income A
PaineWebber High Yield	PaineWebber High Income
PaineWebber Investment Grade Bond	PaineWebber Investment Grade Bond A
PaineWebber Master Growth	PaineWebber Master Blue Chip B
PaineWebber Master Income	PaineWebber Master Income B
PaineWebber Tax Exempt Income	PaineWebber National Tax Free A
Pilgrim Corporate Investors	Pilgrim Corporate Utilities
Pilgrim Short Term Multi-Market	Pilgrim Global Short Term Multi-Market
Putnam Corporate Cash Trust	Putnam Corporate Assets
Putnam GNMA Plus Trust	Putnam Federal Income
Putnam U.S. Government Guaranteed Securities	Putnam U.S. Government Income Trust
Putnam Vista Basic Value	Putnam Vista
Salem Growth Trust	Salem Value Trust
Seligman High Yield: Bond	Seligman Hi Inc: Bond
SunAmerica Aggressive Growth	SunAmerica Emerging Growth
SunAmerica High Yield	SunAmerica High Income
SunAmerica Total Return	SunAmerica Balanced Assets
TransAmerica Growth & Income	TransAmerica Growth & Income A
TransAmerica Special Emerging Growth	TransAmerica Special Emerging Growth B
TransAmerica Technology	TransAmerica Capital Appreciation
Weiss Peck Greer—WPG Fund	WPG Growth & Income

Mergers

Fund Name	Merged Into
ABT Security Income	ABT Growth & Income
Alliance Convertible	Alliance Growth & Income
AMA Classic Growth	Quest For Value Fund
AMA Global Growth	Quest For Value Global Equity
AMA Global Income	Quest For Value Global Income

Table 3 Highlights of 1991 Mutual Fund Changes (Continued)

Fund Name	Merged Into
Eaton Vance Sanders Special	Eaton Vance Growth
Monitrend Value	Monitrend Summation Index Fund
Oppenheimer Directors	Oppenheimer Target
Oppenheimer Premium Income	Oppenheimer Asset Allocation
Oppenheimer Regency	Oppenheimer Target
Pacific Horizons High Yield	T. Rowe Price High Yield
Royce Income	Royce Equity Income
Royce Total Return	Royce Equity Income
Scudder Equity Income	Scudder Growth & Income
TransAmerica Lowry Market	TransAmerica Special Emerging Growth A
TransAmerica Special Convertible Securities	TransAmerica Growth & Income B
TransAmerica Special Global Growth	TransAmerica Special Emerging Growth B
TransAmerica Sunbelt Growth	TransAmerica Special Emerging Growth A
Vanguard High Yield Stock	Vanguard Windsor
Liquidations	
Geico Qualified Dividend	Vanguard Adjustable Rate Preferred
Kemper Gold	

Table 4 Top Performing Mutual Funds by Objective

Aggressive Growth Funds
Ranked by 3-Year Return

Fund	Percent Return	Fund	Percent Return
Twentieth Century Ultra Investors	179.3	AIM Constellation Fund	125.5
Alger Small Capitalization Portfolio	171.7	AMEV Growth Fund	124.1
Berger 100 Fund	164.3	Twentieth Century Vista Investors	122.9
Robertson Stephens Emerging Growth	151.0	Pacific Horizon Aggressive Growth	121.3
Kaufmann Fund	147.3	Pasadena Growth Fund	120.3
Hartwell Emerging Growth Fund	145.5	Sit New Beginning Growth Fund	119.3
CGM Capital Development Fund	138.3	Fidelity Growth Company Fund	117.6
Oberweis Emerging Growth Fund	134.8	American Capital Emerging Growth Fund	111.2
Twentieth Century Growth Investors	132.6	United New Concepts Fund	108.4
MFS Lifetime Emerging Growth Trust	132.1	Seligman Capital Fund	107.7
Twentieth Century Giftrust Investors	130.5	Janus Venture Fund	104.2
Kemper Growth Fund	126.8	Founders Special Fund	104.2
ABT Investment Emerging Growth	126.6		

Asset Allocation Funds
Ranked by 3-Year Return

Fund	Percent Return	Fund	Percent Return
MIMLIC Asset Allocation Fund	57.7	Oppenheimer Asset Allocation Fund	35.6
AMEV Advantage Asset Allocation	56.9	North American Mod. Asset Allocation	30.7
Vanguard Asset Allocation Fund	54.0	USAA Cornerstone	28.6
Fidelity Asset Manager	50.6	National Global Allocation Fund	20.8
Stagecoach Asset Allocation Fund	47.2	Blanchard Strategic Growth Fund	19.9
Shearson Multiple Opportunities Portfolio	46.1	BB & K Diversa Fund	18.3
PaineWebber Asset Allocation B	36.6	Permanent Portfolio	10.5

Table 4 Top Performing Mutual Funds by Objective (Continued)

Growth Funds
Ranked by 3-Year Return

Fund	Percent Return	Fund	Percent Return
Janus Twenty Fund	156.7	IDS Growth Fund	107.3
Fidelity Contrafund	130.5	Kemper Investment Portfolios Growth	102.8
Idex Fund	129.3	Kemper Summit Fund	102.0
Idex II Fund	128.3	Monetta Fund	100.1
Idex Fund 3	126.8	Stein Roe Stock Fund	99.6
Enterprise Capital Appreciation Portfolio	121.7	Eaton Vance Special Equities Fund	99.3
Mainstay Capital Appreciation Fund	121.1	MFS Managed Sectors Trust	99.1
Fidelity Blue Chip Growth Fund	118.2	Mutual of Omaha Growth Fund	98.7
Vanguard World U.S. Growth Fund	111.4	Alger Growth Portfolio	98.4
AIM Weingarten Fund	110.8	IDS Managed Retirement Fund	96.9
IDS New Dimensions Fund	109.2	T. Rowe Price New America Growth Fund	96.7
Piper Jaffray Investment Value Fund	108.3	Composite Northwest 50 Fund	96.4
Janus Fund	107.5		

Growth and Income Funds
Ranked by 3-Year Return

Fund	Percent Return	Fund	Percent Return
AIM Charter Fund	105.9	Baird Blue Chip Fund	70.8
Financial Industrial Income Fund	94.7	Phoenix Balanced Fund Series	68.7
CIGNA Value Fund	92.3	Security Equity Fund	68.7
Twentieth Century Balanced Investors	87.1	IDS Stock Fund	68.3
Berger 101 Fund	78.2	Vanguard Quantitative Portfolios	67.9
Kemper Total Return Fund	74.8	Putnam Investors Fund	67.4
Founders Blue Chip Fund	74.7	PaineWebber Dividend Growth Fund A	66.9
Massachusetts Investors Trust	73.6	American National Income Fund	66.7
CGM Mutual Fund	73.4	Pax World Fund	66.5
Kemper Investment Portfolios—Total Return	71.5	Mainstay Total Return Fund	65.3
Fidelity Growth & Income Portfolio	71.3	Eaton Vance Total Return Trust	65.3
Sit New Beginning Income/Growth Fund	71.1	IDS Equity Plus Fund	65.3
		Lutheran Brotherhood Fund	64.9

International Funds
Ranked by 3-Year Return

Fund	Percent Return	Fund	Percent Return
G.T. Global Health Care Fund	78.6	G.T. Worldwide Growth Fund	44.8
Oppenheimer Global Fund	70.8	Founders Worldwide Growth Fund	43.8
New Perspective Fund	51.1	First Investors Global Fund	41.5
Scudder Global	50.5	Fidelity Canada Fund	41.3
Templeton Foreign Fund	49.8	Templeton Smaller Companies Growth	38.6
G.T. Pacific Growth Fund	48.9	T. Rowe Price International Discovery	38.2
Europacific Growth Fund	47.2	Sogen International Fund	36.4

Table 4 Top Performing Mutual Funds by Objective (Continued)

Fund	Percent Return	Fund	Percent Return
Lexington Worldwide Emerging Markets	36.2	DFA Continental Small Company Portfolio	32.9
Financial Strategic European	34.9	Fidelity Europe Fund	31.5
G.T. International Growth Fund	34.5	Merrill Lynch International Holdings A	31.3
Templeton World Fund	33.8	T. Rowe Price International Stock Fund	30.6
Putnam Global Growth Fund	33.5	Ivy International Fund	30.5
Templeton Global Opportunities Trust	33.2		

Precious Metals Funds
Ranked by 3-Year Return

Fund	Percent Return	Fund	Percent Return
Franklin Gold	20.6	Bull & Bear Gold Investors Limited	-8.1
Van Eck International Investors	13.3	United Services Gold Shares	-8.5
Vanguard Spec. Gold & Precious Metals	9.0	Shearson Precious Metals & Minerals	-10.9
United Services Global Resources	7.8	Financial Strategic Gold	-13.3
Fidelity Select Precious Metals and Min.	5.9	IDS Precious Metals	-13.4
Enterprise Precious Metals Portfolio	5.6	Scudder Gold	-14.1
Keystone Precious Metals	-0.6	Van Eck Gold Resources	-16.1
Oppenheimer Gold & Special Minerals	-1.2	USAA Gold	-17.1
Mainstay Gold and Precious Metals	-4.9	Blanchard Precious Metals Fund	-18.6
Fidelity Select American Gold	-5.1	United Service World Gold	-18.9
Benham Gold Equities Index Fund	-7.0	Shearson Precious Metals Portfolio	-19.0
Sherman Dean	-7.6	Strategic Investments	-24.7
Lexington Goldfund	-7.9		

Sector Funds
Ranked by 3-Year Return

Fund	Percent Return	Fund	Percent Return
Fidelity Select Biotechnology	313.2	United Science & Energy	95.8
Financial Strategic Health Science	284.8	Financial Strategic Leisure	88.0
Fidelity Select Medical Delivery	226.7	Franklin Dynatech	81.2
Fidelity Select Health Care	225.4	Kemper Technology	80.9
Oppenheimer Global Bio-Tech	207.2	Seligman Communications & Information	79.4
Putnam Health Sciences Trust	144.5	Putnam Information Sciences	74.4
Financial Strategic Technology	133.2	Fidelity Select Brokerage & Investment	74.3
Vanguard Specialized Health Care	127.3	Century Shares Trust	71.7
T. Rowe Price Science & Technology	122.5	Fidelity Select Insurance	69.9
Financial Strategic Financial Services	121.1	Flag Telephone Income	69.7
Fidelity Select Retailing	106.8	Fidelity Select Utilities	69.2
Fidelity Select Technology	105.6	Fidelity Select Regional Banks	66.5
Fidelity Select Food & Agriculture	103.6		

Table 4 Top Performing Mutual Funds by Objective (Continued)

Convertible Bond Funds
Ranked by 3-Year Return

Fund	Percent Return	Fund	Percent Return
Fidelity Convertible Securities Fund	70.1	Value Line Convertible Fund	37.2
AIM Convertible Securities	57.5	Putnam Convertible Income-Growth Trust	35.7
Calamos Convertible Income Fund	52.7	Lord Abbett Bond-Debenture Fund	34.5
Mainstay Convertible Fund	47.8	Rochester Convertible Fund	27.4
American Capital Harbor Fund	46.7	Dreyfus Convertible Securities Fund	27.2
Vanguard Convertible Securities Fund	42.8	Sun America Income Portfolio Convertible Securities	20.6
Phoenix Convertible Fund	41.0	Thomson Convertible Securities B	16.1
Seligman Income Fund	37.3		

Taxable Bond Funds
Ranked by 3-Year Return

Fund	Percent Return	Fund	Percent Return
Scudder International Bond Fund	58.6	Princor Government Securities Income	47.1
Benham Target Maturities 2015	58.0	Kemper U.S. Government Securities	46.7
Van Eck World Income Fund	56.9	Federated GNMA Trust	46.5
Benham Target Maturities 2005	56.0	Vanguard Fixed Income Long Term U.S. Treasuries	46.4
Benham Target Maturities 2010	55.5	Shearson Investment Grade Bond	46.3
Benham Target Maturities 2000	53.2	Lexington GNMA Income Fund	46.1
Kemper Global Income Fund	51.5	Investors Preference Fund for Income	45.9
Scudder Target Zero Coupon Bond 2000	51.1	IAI Bond Fund	45.6
USAA Mutual Income	50.3	Benham Target Maturities 1995	45.5
IDS Global Bond	50.2	American Capital Gov't. Sec. A	45.3
Scudder Target Zero Coupon Bond 1995	49.8	Benham GNMA Income Fund	45.1
Vanguard Investment Grade Bond	47.9	First Trust Fund U.S. Government Series	44.9
Vanguard Fixed Income GNMA	47.9		

Tax-Exempt Bond Funds
Ranked by 3-Year Return

Fund	Percent Return	Fund	Percent Return
Dreyfus General Municipal Bond Fund	37.6	Lord Abbett California Tax-Free Income	32.8
Vanguard Municipal Bond Long Term	35.2	Vanguard Pa. Tax Free Insured Long Term	32.8
Vanguard Municipal Bond High Yield	35.1	First Investors Multi-State Ins. TF Oh	32.7
Financial Tax Free Income Shares	34.6	Kemper California Tax-Free Fund	32.5
Eaton Vance Municipal Bond Fund	34.3	USAA Tax Exempt High Yield Fund	32.5
Kemper Municipal Bond Fund	34.0	SteinRoe Managed Municipals	32.4
Nuveen Tax-Free Bond Ohio Portfolio	33.7	Spartan Penn Municipal High Yield	32.4
SAFECO Municipal Bond Fund	33.7	Shearson Managed Municipals	32.4
Scudder Managed Municipal Bond	33.3	Vanguard Mun. Bond Int.-Term	32.3
Fidelity High Yield Tax-Free Portfolio	33.2	AARP Insured Tax Free General Bond	32.3
Nuveen Insured Tax Free Bond National	33.1	Vanguard New York Insured Tax Free	32.3
Alliance Municipal Income National	32.9	T. Rowe Price Tax Free High Yield	32.2

Table 4 Top Performing Mutual Funds by Objective (Continued)

Aggressive Growth Funds
Ranked by 5-Year Return

Fund	Percent Return	Fund	Percent Return
Twentieth Century Ultra Investors	237.6	Columbia Special Fund	155.4
Alger Small Capitalization Portfolio	214.3	Sit New Beginning Growth Fund	153.8
Berger 100 Fund	211.0	Delaware Group Delcap Concept I	153.7
Hartwell Emerging Growth Fund	203.4	Pacific Horizon Aggressive Growth	148.8
Twentieth Century Giftrust Investors	178.4	Fidelity Growth Company Fund	148.3
CGM Capital Development Fund	175.2	Keystone America Omega Fund	147.8
Twentieth Century Growth Investors	170.3	Thomson Opportunity Fund B	146.9
AIM Constellation Fund	169.9	Kaufmann Fund	146.5
Oppenheimer Discovery Fund	166.9	Putnam Voyager Fund	143.7
Kemper Growth Fund	165.5	Founders Special Fund	143.1
Pasadena Growth Fund	165.1	New England Growth Fund	142.1
MFS Lifetime Emerging Growth Trust	162.5	Twentieth Century Vista Investors	141.9
Janus Venture Fund	157.0		

Asset Allocation Funds
Ranked by 5-Year Return

Fund	Percent Return	Fund	Percent Return
MIMLIC Asset Allocation Fund	81.5	USSA Cornerstone	52.0
Stagecoach Asset Allocation Fund	75.2	Blanchard Strategic Growth Fund	49.9
North American Moderate Asset Allocation	55.4	BB & K Diversa Fund	36.9
PaineWebber Asset Allocation B	54.0	Permanent Portfolio	26.6

Growth Funds
Ranked by 5-Year Return

Fund	Percent Return	Fund	Percent Return
Idex II Fund	199.0	Brandywine Fund	130.8
Idex Fund	192.3	Thomson Growth Fund B	130.2
Fidelity Contrafund	173.7	Fidelity Destiny Plan II	129.1
Janus Twenty Fund	170.1	IDS Managed Retirement Fund	127.9
IDS New Dimensions Fund	160.8	Eaton Vance Special Equities Fund	126.1
AIM Weingarten Fund	157.6	Fidelity Magellan Fund	124.7
Janus Fund	151.9	Mainstay Capital Appreciation Fund	121.7
Monetta Fund	149.9	IAI Regional Fund	121.2
Composite Northwest 50 Fund	147.0	MFS Managed Sectors Trust	120.5
MFS Lifetime Managed Sectors Trust	145.3	IDS Growth Fund	120.2
Kemper Investment Portfolios Growth	136.5	New York Venture Fund	119.7
Mutual of Omaha Growth Fund	136.1	Kemper Summit Fund	118.2
FPA Capital Fund	132.8		

Table 4 Top Performing Mutual Funds by Objective (Continued)

Growth and Income Funds Ranked by 5-Year Return

Fund	Percent Return	Fund	Percent Return
CIGNA Value Fund	145.7	Ivy Growth with Income Fund	97.9
AIM Charter Fund	136.4	Investment Company of America	97.0
Financial Industrial Income Fund	135.7	IDS Equity Plus Fund	96.4
FPA Paramount	126.2	Founders Blue Chip Fund	96.0
Fidelity Growth & Income Portfolio	122.9	Kemper Invest. Port.—Total Return	94.4
Security Equity Fund	109.5	IAI Stock Fund	92.3
Massachusetts Investors Trust	105.9	Dreyfus Capital Value Fund	92.0
Vanguard Quantitative Portfolios	103.8	Pax World Fund	90.6
CGM Mutual Fund	103.3	Phoenix Balanced Fund Series	90.6
IDS Stock Fund	102.9	PaineWebber Dividend Growth Fund A	90.5
United Income Fund	100.9	American National Income Fund	90.3
Oppenheimer Total Return Fund	98.9	General Securities	89.9
Baird Blue Chip Fund	98.3		

International Funds Ranked by 5-Year Return

Fund	Percent Return	Fund	Percent Return
DFA Japanese Small Company Portfolio	145.5	Sogen International Fund	77.2
Templeton Foreign Fund	127.8	MFS Lifetime Global Equity Trust	74.1
First Investors Global Fund	111.0	G.T. International Growth Fund	70.4
G.T. Japan Growth Fund	106.4	T. Rowe Price International Stock Fund	66.3
Oppenheimer Global Fund	102.8	Templeton World Fund	65.6
Ivy International Fund	102.5	DFA United Kingdom Small Company	62.1
G.T. Pacific Growth Fund	94.1	Fidelity Europe Fund	59.9
EuroPacific Growth Fund	91.3	Templeton Smaller Companies Growth	57.9
New Perspective Fund	89.4	Putnam Global Growth Fund	56.0
Scudder Global	85.0	Scudder International Fund	55.0
Merrill Lynch Pacific Fund A	83.7	Kleinwort Benson International Equity	55.0
Nomura Pacific Basin Fund	80.3	PaineWebber Atlas Global Growth Fund A	54.9
Vanguard Trustees Commingled Int'l.	79.0		

Precious Metals Funds Ranked by 5-Year Return

Fund	Percent Return	Fund	Percent Return
Oppenheimer Gold & Special Minerals	83.9	Sherman Dean	16.2
Franklin Gold	62.8	Lexington Goldfund	14.4
Vanguard Spec. Gold & Prec. Metals	29.8	IDS Precious Metals	13.4
Keystone Precious Metals	19.9	Fidelity Select Precious Metals and Min.	10.9
Van Eck International Investors	19.0	Bull & Bear Gold Investors Limited	3.6
United Services Global Resources	17.0	Shearson Precious Metals Portfolio	0.1
Fidelity Select American Gold	16.7	Van Eck Gold Resources	-2.7

Table 4 Top Performing Mutual Funds by Objective (Continued)

Fund	Percent Return	Fund	Percent Return
Shearson Precious Metals & Minerals	-4.4	United Services Gold Shares	-22.7
United Service World Gold	-13.5	Strategic Silver	-34.2
Financial Strategic Gold	-19.6	Strategic Investments	-46.9
USAA Gold	-20.2	Strategic Gold & Minerals	-63.4

Sector Funds
Ranked by 5-Year Return

Fund	Percent Return	Fund	Percent Return
Financial Strategic Health Science	378.0	Seigman Communications & Information	121.5
Fidelity Select Biotechnology	316.1	Franklin Dynatech	119.1
Fidelity Select Health Care	251.9	Fidelity Select Chemicals	116.5
Fidelity Select Medical Delivery	232.5	Putnam Information Sciences	107.4
Vanguard Specialized Health Care	190.3	Flag Telephone Income	106.5
Putnam Health Sciences Trust	184.0	Fidelity Select Broadcast & Media	105.1
Fidelity Select Food & Agriculture	177.5	Fidelity Select Regional Banks	103.0
Fidelity Select Retailing	165.8	Kemper Technology	99.4
Financial Strategic Technology	152.3	Fidelity Select Software & Computer	96.7
Financial Strategic Leisure	143.4	Alliance Technology Fund	90.0
Fidelity Select Telecommunications	143.0	Vanguard Specialized Energy	82.8
United Science & Energy	140.4	Century Shares Trust	82.7
Financial Strategic Financial Services	130.5		

Convertible Bond Funds
Ranked by 5-Year Return

Fund	Percent Return	Fund	Percent Return
American Capital Harbor Fund	64.7	Value Line Convertible Fund	49.5
Phoenix Convertible Fund	62.9	Mainstay Convertible Fund	48.5
Lord Abbett Bond-Debenture Fund	55.9	Vanguard Convertible Securites Fund	47.8
Calamos Convertible Income Fund	55.0	Seligman Income Fund	45.9
Dreyfus Convertible Securities Fund	53.3	Putnam Convertible Income-Growth Trust	43.7
Aim Convertible Securities	52.8	Rochester Convertible Fund	29.5

Taxable Bond Funds
Ranked by 5-Year Return

Fund	Percent Return	Fund	Percent Return
USAA Mutual Income	71.0	Vanguard Investment Grade Bond	62.6
FPA New Income Fund	68.7	Benham GNMA Income Fund	61.7
Mackenzie Fixed Income Trust	68.2	Princor Government Securities Income	61.5
Dreyfus Strategic Income	67.9	Benham Target Maturities 2000	60.7
Merrill Lynch Corp. Bond High Income	64.5	Value Line U.S. Government Securities	60.6
Vanguard Fixed Income GNMA	64.3	Liberty High Income Bond	60.6
Federated GNMA Trust	64.1	Kemper U.S. Government Securities	60.1

Table 4 Top Performing Mutual Funds by Objective (Continued)

Fund	Percent Return	Fund	Percent Return
Benham Target Maturities 2005	60.0	Aegon USA High Yield	59.0
Alliance Mortgage Securities Income Fund	59.9	Lexington GNMA Income Fund	58.8
Fund for U.S. Government Securities	59.8	Lutheran Brotherhood Income Fund	58.7
Calvert Income Fund	59.7	Lord Abbett U.S. Government Securities	58.5
Federated Income Trust	59.3	IAI Bond Fund	58.1
Strong Government Securities	59.2		

Tax-Txempt Bond Funds
Ranked by 5-Year Return

Fund	Percent Return	Fund	Percent Return
SAFECO Municipal Bond Fund	52.4	Financial Tax Free Income Shares	48.7
Stein Roe High-Yield Municipals	52.2	Kemper California Tax-Free Fund	48.5
Alliance Municipal Income National	51.8	SteinRoe Managed Municipals	48.2
Eaton Vance Municipal Bond Fund	51.7	Vanguard Muni. Bond Int.-Term	47.9
Fidelity Aggressive Tax Free Portfolio	51.3	First Trust Tax-Free Bond Fund Income	47.9
Vanguard Municipal Bond High Yield	51.2	Putnam California Tax Exempt Income	47.8
Scudder Managed Municipal Bond	51.0	Nuveen Municipal Bond Fund	47.8
Nuveen Insured Tax Free Bond National	50.9	Alliance Muni. Income—Insured National	47.6
Vanguard Municipal Bond Long Term	50.1	Nuveen Tax-Free Bond Ohio Portfolio	47.5
Kemper Vunicipal Bond Fund	49.9	Shearson Managed Municipals	47.5
Lord Abbett Tax Free Income—National	49.8	T. Rowe Price Tax Free High Yield	47.4
MFS Managed Municipal Bond Trust	49.5	Vanguard Pa. TF Insured Long Term	47.2
Lord Abbett Tax free Income—New York	49.2		

century Europe. Although they gained considerable popularity in England a century and a half ago, mutual funds did not reach America's shores until 1924, when Massachusetts Investors Trust, the first open-end mutual fund, was organized. Today, there are more than 2,700 mutual funds, pursuing nearly every imaginable investment objective.

Growth in the mutual fund industry was hampered first by the stock market crash of 1929 and the Great Depression that followed and then by the outbreak of World War II. By the late 1940s, there were fewer than 100 mutual funds in existence, with combined assets totaling less than $2 billion.

During the first half-century of their existence, mutual funds primarily invested in common stocks and corporate bonds. The first money market mutual fund, The Reserve Fund, was organized in November 1971. Tax-exempt money funds made their initial appearance in 1979. Municipal bond funds made their debut in 1977, after the passage of legislation that permitted such funds to pass through their tax-exempt income to shareholders. Long-term U.S. government bond funds came on the scene the same year. International bond funds did not come into existence until 1986. The industry's newest addition, ARM funds, appeared on the scene the past year. (These bond funds invest in adjustable-rate mortgages.) Thus, although investors tend to take the widespread availability of funds of all kinds for granted, the industry is still in its infancy.

Table 5 illustrates the growth of mutual funds during the last two decades. At the end of 1970, there were 361 stock, bond and income funds, with combined total assets of $47.6 billion in 10.7 million shareholder

Table 5 The Mutual Fund Industry: An Overview (Excludes Money Market and Limited Maturity Municipal Bond Funds)

Calendar Year-end	Number of Funds	Number of Accounts (thousands)	Net Assets (billions)
1970	361	10,690	$ 47.6
1971	392	10,901	55.0
1972	410	10,635	59.8
1973	421	10,330	46.5
1974	416	9,970	34.1
1975	390	9,712	42.2
1976	404	8,879	47.6
1977	427	8,515	45.0
1978	444	8,190	45.0
1979	446	7,482	49.0
1980	458	7,325	58.4
1981	486	7,175	55.2
1982	539	8,190	76.8
1983	653	12,065	113.6
1984	820	14,471	137.1
1985	1,071	19,845	251.7
1986	1,356	29,790	424.2
1987	1,781	36,971	453.8
1988	2,111	36,012	472.3
1989	2,254	36,950	553.9
1990	2,362	39,614	570.8

accounts. By the end of 1990, 2,362 stock, bond and income funds had combined assets totaling $571 billion. At year-end, total industry assets (including money market funds) exceeded $1 trillion. And during 1991, fund assets topped $1.3 trillion!

Table 6 contains year-by-year mutual fund sales and redemptions (excluding money market and limited maturity municipal bond funds). Note that net sales (sales less redemptions) were negative during seven of ten years during the 1970s. In fact, there was a net outflow of more than $5.7 billion during that decade. The acceleration in both gross and net sales during the early 1980s was set off by two events. First, interest rates began to top out during mid-1982. Second, one of the most forceful bull markets of the twentieth century was unleashed in the fall of 1982.

Investors, who were enticed by the high yields offered by money funds during the late 1970s and early 1980s, began to liquidate their money fund holdings in early 1983. In fact, investors withdrew more than $40 billion from the money market funds during 1983. Active marketing efforts by fund groups led to a significant amount of money fund assets being diverted to equity and bond funds. And from this modest beginning, the rush was on. In 1984 sales of equity, bond and income funds fell a scant $4 billion short of total mutual fund sales during the entire decade of the 1970s! And in 1986 investors purchased more than $215 billion of mutual fund shares, with that year's sales exceeding the total of mutual fund shares sold during the previous 61 years!

Table 7 depicts the distribution of long-term mutual fund assets. At year-end 1970, the vast majority of mutual fund assets were concentrated in common stocks (80.9 percent). However, beginning with the introduction of municipal bond funds, the distribution of fund assets among categories of securities began to flatten out. And by the end of 1990, less than 40 percent of long-term fund assets were committed to common stocks. This partially explains why mutual fund net sales failed to drop into the negative column after the stock market crash of 1987 as they did after the 1969-70 bear market.

Two decades ago, mutual fund investors had virtually only two choices—invest in corporate bond funds or common stock funds.

Table 6 Mutual Fund Sales, Redemptions and Net Sales (Excludes Money Market and Limited Maturity Municipal Bond Funds)

Year	Sales (billions)	Redemptions (billions)	Net Sales (billions)
1970	$ 4.6	$ 3.0	$ 1.6
1971	5.1	4.8	0.3
1972	4.9	6.6	–1.7
1973	4.4	5.7	–1.3
1974	3.1	3.4	–0.3
1975	3.3	3.7	–0.4
1976	4.4	6.8	–2.4
1977	6.4	6.0	0.4
1978	6.7	7.2	–0.5
1979	6.8	8.0	–1.2
1980	10.0	8.2	1.8
1981	9.7	7.5	2.2
1982	15.7	7.6	8.1
1983	40.3	14.7	25.6
1984	45.9	20.0	25.9
1985	114.3	33.8	80.5
1986	215.8	67.0	148.8
1987	190.6	116.2	74.4
1988	95.3	92.5	2.8
1989	125.7	91.7	34.0
1990	149.5	98.3	51.2

Table 7 Distribution of Mutual Fund Assets

Year	Cash & Equivalents	Corporate Bonds	Preferred Stocks	Common Stocks	Municipal Bonds	Long-Term Gov't. Bonds	Other
1970	6.6%	9.0%	2.4%	80.9%	NA	NA	1.1%
1975	7.6	11.3	1.2	78.6	NA	NA	1.3
1980	9.1	11.3	0.9	71.2	4.9%	2.4%	0.2
1985	8.2	9.9	1.5	47.6	15.2	17.3	0.3
1990	8.5	7.8	0.6	38.1	20.9	22.6	1.5

And with both bond and common stock prices falling during the 1970 recession, investors chose to cash out of mutual funds and head for the safe haven provided by bank savings accounts. Since money market funds had yet to be created, investors who wanted to head for the sidelines had little choice but to abandon mutual funds.

Recent Trends in the Mutual Fund Industry

During the last two decades, the mutual fund industry has undergone significant change. Not only has the number and diversity of mutual funds expanded at an astonishing rate but the way funds conduct business has also changed dramatically. The trends described below are more than an historical curiosity. These changes have impacted shareholder returns and require that investors scrutinize a fund's characteristics more carefully before making an investment selection. Awareness of the evolving trends in the mutual fund industry could mean the difference between investment success and failure.

One of the most important changes in the mutual fund industry in recent years concerns the cost of fund investing. During the decade of the 1960s, the vast majority of mutual funds levied a front-end sales charge, or front-end load. The loads amounted to 9.3 percent of the amount of money actually invested in the fund. The loads represented commissions, primarily paid to stockbrokers. By the 1970s, only about 30 percent of all mutual fund assets were held by no-load funds—funds sold by sponsors directly to shareholders without a commission.

During the late 1970s and early 1980s, however, sales of no-load funds exceeded sales of load funds to the point where the majority of fund assets were controlled by the no-load group. But that trend began to reverse itself with the advent of so-called 12b-1 funds, which levy annual distribution fees on fund shareholders. A number of existing no-load funds added 12b-1 fees, some front-end load funds dropped their front-end charges and opted instead for a combination of 12b-1 fees and back-end loads. A number of fund families, led by Fidelity, added 2 percent and 3 percent front-end loads to funds that were previously no-load. In addition, brokerage firms, which had previously acted as distributors of mutual funds for other sponsors, launched their own fund families, nearly all of which were loaded with a sales charge of some sort. As a result, less than 33 percent of the currently available mutual funds can call themselves 100 percent no-load.

Although load funds can and occasionally do outperform no-load funds, when taken in aggregate, no-load funds, on average, outperform load funds by an amount approximately equal to the load. Thus, investors who make their selections from among no-load funds have a decided edge over load-fund investors in the long run. Of course, no-load fund investors must do their own homework. However, the extra effort can pay off handsomely. An individual who invests $10,000 annually in no-load funds over a 30-year investment lifetime can "pocket" $25,500 in commissions that otherwise would go to distributors selling 8.5 percent front-end load funds. Even so-called "modest" 12b-1 charges can mount up over an investment lifetime. For example, an individual who invests $10,000 in a fund that levies an annual 0.3

percent 12b-1 charge will pay $8,000 in distribution fees over a 30-year period (assuming the mutual fund returns 12 percent compounded annually).

In addition to sales fees, management fees also were on the rise during the last decade. Twenty years ago, the typical management fee amounted to 0.5 percent of fund assets. However, during the 1980s, management contracts of newly organized funds provided for annual advisor fees ranging from 0.75 to 1.00 percent of fund assets. Although fund assets have swelled during recent years, the average equity fund expense ratio is approximately 1.3 percent. And, of course, higher operating expenses result in lower returns to fund shareholders.

As reported earlier, mutual funds were swamped with new investor dollars during the 1980s. As a result, the net assets of popular funds grew by leaps and bounds. Many modest-size funds, which sported better than average track records, saw their assets swell into the hundreds of millions and even billions of dollars. Although this was a boon to advisors, who earn fees based on the amount of money under management, shareholders were often short-changed as fund managers found that they could not produce similar investment results because of the loss of investment flexibility that accompanied the fund's rapid growth. While one can find a few exceptions to the contrary, large funds, on average, tend to underperform smaller funds with similar investment objectives and investment strategies.

Interestingly, mutual fund portfolio turnover ratios also have been on the rise in recent years. Our guess is that competition is the culprit. Most mutual fund investors base their fund selections on recent investment performance. Thus, portfolio managers are forced to attempt to produce short-term returns that exceed those of the market. In attempting to do so, these managers jump from one "hot" stock to another. Unfortunately for investors, over the long run, rapid portfolio turnover takes its toll on investment results. Several studies indicate that funds with high portfolio turnover ratios underperform similar funds with low portfolio turnover ratios by a significant amount.

While mutual fund assets grew during the 1980s so did the Securities and Exchange Commission's concern over advertising abuses. Knowing that investors' eventual fund selections hung on performance, funds of all kinds began to advertise their "phenomenal" track records. Bond funds quoted double-digit past returns even though the current interest rate environment would allow them to earn only single-digit returns. Some income funds reported total returns (including capital gains realized in a falling interest rate environment) rather than yields. GNMA funds touted their high current yields even though most of their securities were selling above par, and sponsors knew that these returns would eventually be eroded when homeowners refinanced their existing mortgages at lower interest rates. Equity funds reported their performance for periods marked by superior returns although during other periods their performance was sub par.

As a result, a series of regulations governing fund advertising and marketing practices was adopted by the Securities and Exchange Commission. These rules required income funds to report yields and returns on a similar basis. In addition, when reporting total returns, funds were required to use one-, five- and ten-year periods rather than selecting their own period of comparison.

We and a number of others in the investment industry believe that the SEC made a large mistake when it enacted rule 12b-1, allowing funds to raid assets annually to pay for marketing and distribution expenses. In an effort to single out funds that have abused rule 12b-1, the SEC now requires funds to list all sales charges, management fees and operating expenses in a table placed in the front of the fund's prospectus. Other than the statement of the fund's investment objectives, we believe this to be the most important bit of information contained in a fund's prospectus. Contrary to what some would have you believe, the cost of mutual fund investing impacts long-term investment results more than any other factor.

The Industry in Prospect

Given the dramatic events of the past decade, what's in store for the mutual fund industry in the future? First, we believe that the mutual fund industry's explosive growth will moderate considerably over the next several years. Although a number of new funds will come to market in the years ahead, growth will be moderated by consolidation in the industry. A number of small fund families are already feeling the pinch of increased operating costs and slower sales growth. A number of these firms will be forced into mergers with larger families while some will undergo liquidation. The industry will eventually be dominated by a few very large players who have the ability and resources to market their wares. Furthermore, consolidation in the brokerage industry will place a limit on the new funds brought to market by this group. Thus, while industry assets will continue to grow, we expect to see little growth in the number of funds.

We also expect to see a continuation of the trend toward higher costs. Industry sales will be dominated by funds marketed by direct sales forces compensated by expanded sales fees. In addition, administration costs are also on the rise. Thus, expense ratios will continue to expand.

During the last decade, a number of states that had set maximum allowable expense ratios dropped their restrictions. Today, only the state of California retains an expense limitation. However, that limitation was recently raised from 2 percent of the first $10 million of fund assets to 2.5 percent of the first $30 million. Since funds must apply the most restrictive state limitation to all states, expense ratios will rise a bit as a result of California's change in its fee limitation.

Finally, we believe that the Securities and Exchange Commission will continue to increase its mutual fund regulatory efforts. Currently, the SEC is considering a proposal that would require mutual funds to disclose the names and professional backgrounds of their portfolio managers. Although the industry is heavily opposed to this requirement, we support any disclosure that assists individuals in making fund selections.

We believe the discovery of mutual funds by large numbers of investors is one of the big stories of the 1980s. Although investors tend to focus their attention on investment returns when evaluating portfolio management results, the reduction of investment risk is the single largest benefit provided by mutual funds. Investors, who otherwise might have held highly concentrated portfolios, saw the wisdom of diversification during the turbulent months of late 1987. Although the stock market crash took its toll on the value of mutual fund portfolios, most of the mutual fund investors who rode out the storm now find that their investment wealth is greater than it was before October, 1987. And long-term-oriented mutual fund investors will continue to prosper in the years ahead.

WHAT IS A MUTUAL FUND?

A mutual fund is a corporation chartered by a state to conduct business as an investment company. An investment company, in turn, is a financial institution whose sole business and reason for existing is to invest in a portfolio of assets. In general, investment companies are corporations that obtain capital by selling their own securities. The proceeds of such sales are reinvested in a variety of securities issued by governments or corporations. Thus, any income received by investment company shareholders is a function of income from the investment company's portfolio. Furthermore, the price of an investment company's shares is related to the market value of the securities in the company's investment portfolio.

The mutual fund's genealogy is illustrated in Figure 1. As can be seen, investment companies encompass three broad subclasses: face-amount certificate companies, unit investment trusts and management companies.

Face-amount certificate companies issue securities that possess a face value payable at the end of an installment period. The principal and interest are guaranteed and usually

Figure 1 Mutual Fund Genealogy

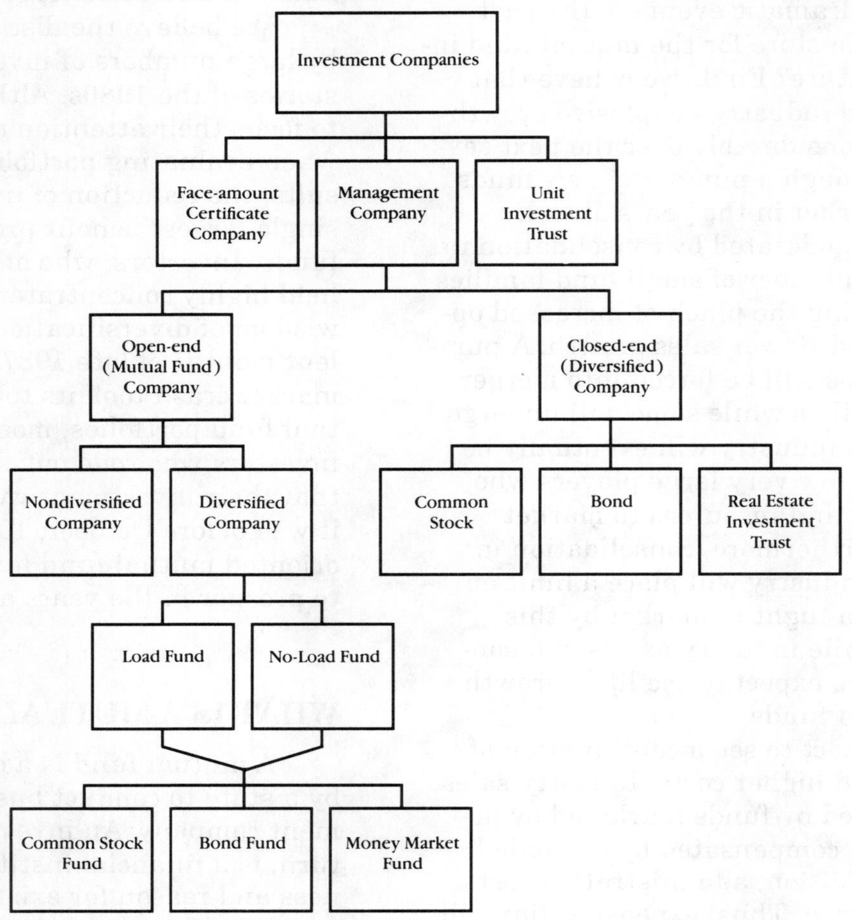

are collateralized by a specific asset such as real estate. There are only a few of these types of investment companies in existence today.

Unit investment trusts are organized under a trust indenture or contract of custodianship that issues redeemable securities, representing an undivided interest in a unit of specific securities. The trust does not have a board of directors, and since the unit, or pool of assets, is fixed at the outset, the services of a portfolio manager are not needed.

In the 1960s and early 1970s, numerous unit investment trusts were established to provide for investment in a diversified portfolio of municipal bonds. The trusts were sold with a front-end load (usually from 3 percent to 6 percent), and the proceeds were invested in "muni" bonds (tax-exempt state and local debt obligations). Interest payments from the investments were passed through to the trust participants. The principal amount of the bonds was also returned when the bonds matured. Thus, the trust was self-liquidating.

While unit investment trust participants benefit from reduced fees since the trust is essentially unmanaged, the lack of management makes the portfolio unresponsive to changing market conditions. Furthermore, unit investment trusts suffer from the absence of a viable secondary market. Trust participants must either hold their certificates until the trust is liquidated or offer large discounts from face value to attract buyers.

Management companies are the most plentiful members of the investment company family. The management company lineage includes closed-end investment companies (which include real estate investment trusts, or REITs), nondiversified open-end companies and diversified open-end companies. The latter category includes mutual funds available for public purchase and encompasses both load and no-load mutual funds.

Diversified management companies (mutual funds) can be further divided according to the types of securities held. Common stock funds are those primarily holding common stocks in their investment portfolios. Such funds follow a multitude of portfolio strategies, including: aggressive growth, growth, growth-income and specialty investments (gold funds, etc.). Bond funds generally fall into three classes, including those that hold corporate bonds, U.S. government bonds (including obligations issued by federally sponsored credit agencies) and bonds issued by states and municipalities ("munis," or tax-exempt bonds). Money market mutual funds hold securities issued by corporations, banks and the U.S. government that have short-term maturities (usually less than 360 days). Tax-exempt money market funds are actually "muni" bond funds that invest in short-term, tax-exempt securities. Thus, they are not in reality money market funds at all.

How Are Mutual Funds Regulated?

Investment companies that engage in interstate commerce are regulated by the Investment Company Act of 1940. The roots of government regulation of investment companies are found in the great stock market crash of 1929, which caused Congress to begin an extensive investigation of the U.S. securities industry. Widespread abuse was uncovered in nearly every segment of the industry. The result of these discoveries was the passage of a series of federal statutes aimed at controlling the activities of security issuers, stock exchanges, investment advisors and investment companies.

The Securities Act of 1933, often called the "Truth in Securities Act" or "Disclosure Act," attempts to ensure that the investing public has access to adequate information regarding the underlying financial condition of companies offering newly issued securities to individual investors. The Act requires that most securities offered for sale in interstate commerce and through the mail be registered with the Securities and Exchange Commission (SEC).

The objective of the Securities and Exchange Act of 1934 was to establish and maintain fair and honest markets for securities. This Act also designated the SEC as administrator of federal legislation relating to the nation's securities business.

The bulk of federal powers over the activities of investment companies is contained in the Investment Company Act of 1940, which provides for the registration and regulation of companies primarily engaged in the business of investing in securities. The major provisions of the Act are summarized as follows:

- The Act provides for registration, "full" disclosure and regulation of investment companies to prevent fraudulent abuses.
- Not more than 60 percent of the board of directors may be affiliated with the fund, its banks or brokers. (No-load funds need only one outside director.)
- Management (advisor) contracts must be approved by shareholders and the fund's outside directors.
- A company must redeem shares duly offered by shareholders within seven calendar days at per share net asset value.
- Open-end companies (mutual funds) may borrow from a bank and use the proceeds for investment purposes (leverage); such debt must be collateralized three to one.
- Shareholders must be sent complete financial reports at least semiannually, and the SEC must see such reports.
- To qualify as a registered investment company, the fund must have at least 75 percent of its total assets invested in securities, with not more than 5 percent of its assets invested in the securities of any one issuer and not holding more than 10 percent of the voting securities of any one corporation.
- A prospectus must be given to a prospective fund investor before sales can be solicited.

- The maximum load (commission) cannot exceed 9 percent of the share's offering price.
- Securities and cash must be kept by either a bank or a broker who is a member of a national securities exchange.

To qualify as a registered diversified management company under the Investment Company Act of 1940, a fund must have at least 75 percent of its assets invested such that: (1) not more than 5 percent are invested in any one security issue; and (2) not more than 10 percent of the voting securities of any corporation are held by the fund. Note that these two conditions refer to only 75 percent of the fund's assets. That is, while 75 percent of the assets of the fund must be diversified, the other 25 percent can be concentrated in a single investment if management desires. However, state "blue-sky" laws (regulations governing the offer and sale of securities) may be more restrictive than those specified in the federal act.

In addition to federal registration, a mutual fund must register in and abide by the laws and regulations of each state in which its shares are sold. In other words, unless a fund is registered in your state of residence, it cannot legally sell its shares to you. Please do not try to purchase fund shares not registered in your state. Most funds maintain a compliance staff to ensure that such purchases are not made. If you use a relative's address instead of your own in an attempt to purchase funds not registered in your home state, you could be in for a legal hassle at some point in the future. What happens if you move to another state after an initial purchase and find out that the fund is not registered in the new state? You'll be able to keep your initial investment in the fund but will be unable to make further investments. Your best strategy is to find another properly registered fund similar to the one you currently own and make all subsequent purchases in the new fund.

How Are Mutual Funds Managed?

The business affairs of mutual funds are carried out by the board of directors and officers of the fund. The fund is actually owned by its shareholders who elect board members and approve various operating policies such as changes in the fund's objective, hiring the investment advisor, the advisor's compensation contract, choice of auditor, etc.

The fund (in actuality, you, the shareholder) pays various expenses including: the advisory fee, registration fees, expenses for annual meetings, custodial bank and transfer agent fees, interest and taxes, brokerage commissions, expenses related to the fund's purchases and sales of securities and outside directors' fees and travel expenses. These fees are generally deducted from the dividend and interest income of the fund. If income is not sufficient to cover these expenses, fund management can sell some of the fund's assets and use the proceeds to pay expenses. These fees, expressed as a percentage of total assets, are limited by state statute. Expenses in excess of the statutory maximum are reimbursed to the fund by the fund's advisor.

The most important task of the fund's board of directors is the selection of the fund's investment advisor. However, since the majority of the board of directors are also principals in a fund management company, it is not surprising that their company is selected as the fund's advisor. (That's why they started the fund in the first place.) The advisor (or management company) receives a fee for its stock selection and portfolio management activities based on the average value of the assets under management. This fee was traditionally set at approximately 0.5 percent of average fund assets. However, with the costs of doing business continually increasing, the fees for newly organized funds tend to be set initially at 0.75 percent to 1 percent of average annual assets.

The management company is responsible for the day-to-day operation of the fund. In a number of cases, the management company (advisor) is responsible for and pays the cost of the following:

1. office space, facilities, personnel and supplies
2. portfolio managers and traders who execute the purchase and sell instructions of the portfolio managers

3. compliance with federal government and state registration regulations
4. preparation and distribution of prospectuses, sales material, advertising, quarterly reports and other shareholder documents
5. the transfer of shares purchased or sold by fund shareholders
6. bookkeeping, accounting services, preparation of federal, state and local tax returns and bonding and insurance

The management company profits to the extent that its management fees exceed its cost of doing business. It has been estimated that at a fee of 0.5 percent of total assets, a mutual fund must possess more than $100 million in total assets before the management company becomes profitable. However, before one becomes too concerned about the welfare of fund managers, one must recognize that many funds have organized into "families," some of which contain 30 different funds, with billions of dollars under management. Thus, mutual fund management can indeed be lucrative.

Most management companies are also engaged in other businesses closely related to fund management. Thus, the management of mutual fund investor dollars becomes quite a profitable sideline. For example, most of the front-end load funds have been organized by brokerage firms, life insurance companies and commercial banks. For the most part, no-load funds have been organized by companies engaged in private investment management, including pension fund management.

Generally, the management fee is set on a declining scale relative to fund size. A characteristic fund management agreement appears below.

> For its services, [the management company] receives a monthly fee of 1/24 of 1% (0.5% annually) of the average daily net assets of the fund up to $250 million. This monthly fee is reduced to 3/80 of 1% (0.45% annually) of the average net assets in excess of $250 million.

In a few instances, the management fee may include an incentive clause. That is, the fee is adjusted upward or downward according to how the fund performs relative to some stock market average or index.

Recently, some mutual funds have been obtaining additional dollars to pay for marketing expenses in a highly competitive market environment by adopting (either at the time the fund is formed or after, subject to shareholder approval) what is known as a 12b-1 plan. The plan is named for the SEC rule that permits such funds to raid the fund's (your) assets to cover its marketing expenses. That is, instead of paying a front-end load to cover marketing expenses, 12b-1 fund investors pay an ongoing charge for marketing. (Front-end load funds use the commissions obtained from the "load" to pay the costs associated with selling new shares.)

The SEC 12b-1 rule does not specify the maximum amount of assets that can be spent for marketing, and some 12b-1 funds are spending over 1 percent of total assets per year. Over the long run, a payment of this magnitude is much greater than the typical 8.5 percent front-end load of funds sold by brokers and financial planners. Therefore, we refer to 12b-1 funds as "hidden load funds."

Can the management of a mutual fund steal the assets and leave the country? If one tries hard enough, one can accomplish anything. However, for mutual funds registered with the SEC, the possibility of loss of assets due to theft is quite remote. The Investment Company Act of 1940 requires that all registered investment companies establish a custodial relationship with a bank otherwise unconnected with the investment company. The custodial bank holds all of the assets of the fund (cash and securities) in trust for the fund. The custodian receives the certificates for new acquisitions made by the portfolio manager, pays for securities purchased, delivers securities when sales are made, releases cash to pay fund expenses and accepts dividends and interest payments from the issuers of securities held in the fund's portfolio.

This segment of the securities business is highly specialized. The custodial business of nearly 3,000 registered mutual funds is concentrated in the hands of fewer than 20 banks. It has been estimated that one bank, State Street Bank of Boston, supplies custodial services to nearly 30 percent of all registered funds. Since employees who handle money are bonded by insurance companies, mutual fund shareholders are highly protected against theft.

The fund's transfer agent, which may be a bank or some other entity, facilitates the transfer of mutual fund shares (including new purchases and sales), disbursement of dividends and maintenance of shareholder records. Generally, the charges billed to the fund by the transfer agent range from $8 to $10 per account per year.

Distributors and wholesalers represent the sales organization of front-end load funds. The front-end load is the total commission that the investor pays when he or she buys fund shares. The distributor of a load fund is generally a separate corporation (usually owned by those with an interest in the fund) that purchases shares from the fund at net asset value and sells them to dealers (brokerage firms and large financial planning firms) at net asset value plus a commission. Wholesalers are agents of the distributor who constantly visit dealers in an attempt to get them to sell fund shares to their customers (you and me).

The front-end load commission, paid by investors, is divided up among all who participate in the distribution. The distributor receives approximately 1.5 percent of the "typical" 8.5 percent load commission. The dealer and the broker (salesperson) split the remaining 7 percent, with about 60 percent going to the dealer and 40 percent to the broker. Thus, in general, stockbrokers receive more in commissions on the sale of mutual fund shares than they do on the sale of stocks or bonds—at least on sales up to $50,000. It is of little wonder that both financial planners and stockbrokers are quick to recommend loaded mutual fund shares to the less prosperous investor. There's "no muss, no fuss" and the commission is very good.

While a number of front-end load fees begin at approximately 8 percent of the offering price and cannot exceed 9 percent of the offering price by federal law, commission percentages are usually scaled down as the size of a purchase increases. Note that these sales charges are based on the offering amount and not on the amount actually invested (since commissions are taken "up front"). This results in an increase in the percentage of sales fee when related to the amount actually invested. For example, suppose you give $1,000 to a salesman of a fund with an 8.5 percent front-end load. The 8.5 percent commission ($85) is deducted, and $915 is actually invested in the fund. The effective fee is thus 85/915 or 9.3 percent. In other words, the value of the shares purchased must rise in price by 9.3 percent before any net investment return is earned. Furthermore, since the sales commission is paid as part of the share's purchase price, its tax deductibility does not occur until the shares are sold.

No-load funds are so called because no sales commissions are paid when purchasing their shares. In most instances, the fund's sponsor is also its distributor. Since no-load funds have no sales force or method for compensating brokers, shares are purchased directly from the fund. A no-load fund's share price is identical to its per share net asset value. Thus, 100 percent of your investment is invested in no-load fund shares.

What Types of Funds Are Available?

Aggressive Growth Funds. These funds have as their objective the pursuit of maximum capital gains. They invest aggressively in speculative stocks and tend to stay fully invested over the market cycle. Frequently, these funds employ financial leverage (use borrowed funds) and may engage in trading listed stock options. Funds in this class can be highly volatile. They generally perform very well in bull markets and fare very poorly in bear markets. However, over the long run and because of the risks taken, these funds, in general, tend to outperform the market by a significant amount.

Aggressive growth funds possess relatively low current yields. That is because they tend to be fully invested in common stocks and do not earn a significant amount of interest income. Furthermore, these funds tend to invest in growth-oriented common stocks that generally do not pay cash dividends. Also, aggressive growth fund assets tend to be concentrated in particular industries (technology, health care, etc.) or in particular types of stocks (small firms, emerging growth firms, etc.) that carry increased portfolio risk. In general, long-term investors who need not be concerned with monthly or yearly variation in investment return will find investment in aggressive growth funds attractive.

Because of the extreme volatility of return (and net asset value), risk-averse investors with a short-term orientation may find that these funds lie well outside their comfort zones. However, because of the longer-term superior performance of aggressive growth funds, even highly conservative investors should consider committing some of their investment capital to mutual funds in this group. The advisable strategy is to offset the extreme portfolio variability by investing a portion of total assets in "safe" treasury bills (or money market funds). The net result is usually lower overall risk and higher long-term total portfolio return.

While we do not recommend that investors attempt to time the market on a short-term basis, aggressive growth mutual funds appear to be ideal vehicles for those who believe they possess the insight (or tools) to outguess the next market move. If one had the ability to time the market perfectly, the appropriate strategy would be to be 100 percent invested in aggressive growth funds during up markets and 100 percent invested in treasury bills (money funds) during down markets. If timing ability is less than perfect, or if four-year market cycle timing is attempted, an appropriate strategy is to be (1) fully invested in aggressive growth funds during strong bull markets; (2) partially invested in aggressive growth funds and partially invested in growth (or growth-income) funds during uncertain market periods; and (3) partially invested in growth funds and in money funds during periods of falling market prices.

Growth Funds. The primary objective of growth funds is long-term growth of capital. They generally do not engage in speculative tactics, such as using financial leverage or short-selling. However, on occasion, these funds will use stock options to hedge their portfolio positions. Growth funds tend to be more stable than aggressive growth funds since they tend to invest in growth-oriented firms that are older and larger and pay larger cash dividends than the firms sought by aggressive growth funds. One is likely to find companies such as IBM, General Motors, Xerox, DuPont, etc., in the portfolios of growth funds. Growth funds tend to diversify their portfolios across a broader range of industries than do aggressive growth funds. Additionally, these funds tend to move from fully invested to partially invested positions over the market cycle.

In general, the performance of growth funds during bull markets tends to be better than that of the Standard & Poor's 500 Index and nearly matches the performance of the S&P 500 Index during bear market periods. (During prolonged bear markets, the downside volatility of growth funds can be severe.) The overall result is that over the longer term, the average growth fund can be expected to outperform the rate of inflation (by about 5 percent to 6 percent per year) and thus lead to an increase in real wealth.

Aggressive investors should consider holding both growth fund shares and aggressive growth fund shares in their portfolios. It is an especially appealing strategy for investors who hold mutual funds that generally invest in small "emerging growth" firms. This is due to the relatively low correlation of investment returns between these two classes of investments. The combination of aggressive growth and growth funds produces an overall portfolio that possesses less variability of return than portfolios containing only aggressive growth mutual funds. Furthermore, mutual fund portfolios that combine growth and aggressive growth funds generally possess greater potential return relative to the risks taken than do portfolios consisting of a combination of aggressive growth funds and money market funds.

Since the portfolio managers of growth funds often attempt to time the market over the longer four-year market cycle rather than on a short-term basis, we do not recommend that the short-term market timer use these assets in pursuing timing strategies. However, since these funds can sustain severe declines in net asset values during prolonged bear markets, it is advisable to decrease the proportion of commitment to these funds (and increase the proportion invested in money market funds) during falling markets.

Growth-Income Funds. Generally this type of fund invests in common stocks of seasoned, well-established, cash-dividend paying companies. Portfolio managers attempt to provide shareholders with long-term growth while avoiding excessive fluctuations in net asset value. Generally, one tends to find a high concentration of public utility common stocks, corporate convertible bonds and convertible preferred stocks in the portfolios of growth-income funds.

Income Funds. These funds are generally known as equity-income funds. Portfolios usually consist of 50 percent high-yielding common stocks and 50 percent bonds and preferred stocks. These funds provide about 50 percent more current yield than the S&P 500 Index and are about half as volatile. They are ideally suited for conservative investors who prefer both current income and growth of capital.

International Funds. Strictly speaking, international funds invest exclusively in foreign securities. However, a number of these funds may also invest in U.S. securities under certain circumstances. Global funds invest in both U.S. and foreign securities. International funds may invest in a single country or a region (e.g., Europe, the Pacific Basin, etc.), or they may hold globally diversified portfolios. Although foreign investments contain additional elements of risk, such as currency risk and political risk, their returns tend to be less than perfectly correlated with the returns of U.S. stocks and bonds. Thus, they offer an opportunity to reduce overall portfolio volatility when coupled with investments in U.S. securities.

Asset Allocation Funds. These funds invest across a wide spectrum of assets such as domestic stocks, bonds, gold, international equities, real estate (usually the stocks of real estate investment trusts) and money market instruments. The goal of such funds is to produce a combination of capital appreciation and current income while reducing risk (share price volatility). Since the returns of financial assets from varying categories tend to have relatively low correlations of returns, declines in one category of assets are frequently offset by increases in the returns of other asset classes. For example, during inflationary periods, interest rates rise and bond prices fall. However, inflationary pressures tend to send the price of gold and gold stocks skyward.

Asset allocation funds either adopt a passive or active strategy. In the former, a predetermined asset class mix is initially established. Periodically (usually once each quarter), the portfolio is rebalanced to its predetermined mix. In the latter, portfolio managers continually adjust the mix of assets based on their expectations of which category or categories will perform best.

Precious Metals Funds. These funds invest in gold or silver bullion and the common stocks of gold and silver mining companies. Some of the funds limit their investments to geographical regions (e.g., South Africa or North America), while others invest globally. Precious metals funds tend to have relatively low betas; this results from the relatively low correlation between the movement in industrial stocks and gold or silver mining stocks. Thus, beta clouds the fact that precious metals funds can be very volatile during short-run periods.

Convertible Securities Funds. These funds invest in convertible bonds, convertible preferred stocks or synthetic convertibles. A convertible bond is a debenture that can be converted into common stock at the option of the holder. Thus, when the price of the underlying stock rises, these bonds tend to behave like the stock. However, their value as bonds tends to shore up their value during periods when stock prices are falling. A synthetic convertible is a combination of a bond and an equity security issued by the same company. Commonly, the "synthetics" consist of a bond plus a warrant to purchase shares of the company stock. In general, convertible bond funds possess higher than average current yields and less volatility than a diversified equity fund.

Bond Funds. Designed for income-oriented investors, these funds invest in bonds issued by corporations, the U.S. government,

government agencies, and state and local governments. Their risk depends on the types of bonds held and their average maturity. In recent years, "high yield" bond funds introduced a substantial element of risk by investing in corporate junk bonds. Some funds attempt to increase income by speculating in financial futures. Funds that invest exclusively in state and municipal issues are called tax-exempt bond funds. Although interest earned is exempt from federal taxation, investors may be subject to taxation of interest income earned on issues originating outside their state of residence. Additionally, capital gains are subject to federal, state and local taxation.

Long-term bonds have traditionally been the haven for investors requiring current income and a high degree of safety. However, this safe haven has been more fiction than fact. Investment returns from long-term corporate bonds have been illusory. Over the entire period from 1926 through 1991, long-term corporate bonds provided investors with a compound annual rate of return of 5.4 percent. While annual current yield has been greater than this rate, the interest returns were offset by declines in bond prices due to rising inflation and interest rates. The result has been an annual real (after inflation) rate of return of 2.3 percent. Furthermore, since 1945, treasury bill investors have earned about the same compound annual rate of return as long-term bond investors, even though the corporate bond return includes a whopping 44 percent return earned during 1982.

How To Invest in Mutual Fund Shares

Purchases and sales of open-end mutual fund shares are generally made between the investor and the fund itself. When an investor purchases fund shares, payment is made to the fund and new shares are issued by the fund. When investors sell their shares, the fund is usually the buyer. The fund remits cash to the buyer (using the services of the custodian and transfer agent) and cancels the shares received by the fund. This is called a redemption. Thus, most open-end mutual fund purchases are conducted in the primary market rather than the secondary market, in which share price is determined by supply and demand. In a primary market, share price is fixed by the securities issuer.

For no-load mutual funds, share price is equal to the fund's net asset value per share. Per share net asset value is determined at the close of each stock exchange business day (usually 4:00 P.M. New York time) by summing the value of cash and all securities held by the fund, subtracting outstanding liabilities and dividing the result by the number of fund shares outstanding. For example, suppose a fund with 10,000 shares outstanding has determined the value of its securities, cash and liabilities as follows:

Securities Value	$100,000
Cash	15,000
Total assets	$115,000
Less liabilities	(5,000)
Total net assets	$110,000

Net asset value per share of the fund is thus $110,000 divided by 10,000 shares, or $11.00. This amount is the price of any share purchases made by no-load fund investors during the period between the previous day's closing value and the value determined at the close of the valuation day. Note that if an investor were to make a purchase during a regular exchange business day, share price would not be known until the close of that day. (This is known as Forward Pricing.) Therefore, investor purchase orders must be stated in terms of the number of shares one wishes to purchase or by the total amount of dollar investment desired.

Also worthy of mention is the fact that if this fund sold an additional 1,000 shares at the closing price of $11.00 per share, the net asset value would remain unchanged. The amount of cash the fund holds increases by $11,000 (share price, $11.00, multiplied by 1,000 shares purchased) and total assets increase to $121,000:

Securities Value	$100,000
Cash	26,000
Total assets	$126,000
Less liabilities	(5,000)
Total net assets	$121,000

When the amount is divided by the 11,000 fund shares now outstanding, net asset value per share remains at $11.00. A similar result is obtained when shares are redeemed by the fund.

For mutual fund shares sold with a front-end load, share price is determined by the following formula. If the fund in the previous example were a load fund with an 8 percent sales charge, share price would be $11.96, determined as follows:

$$\frac{\text{Net Asset Value Per Share}}{1 - \%\text{ of Commission}}$$

$$\frac{\$11.00}{1-0.08} = \frac{\$11.00}{.92} = \text{Offering Price, or } \$11.96$$

Newspapers would report price quotations for the fund's shares at $11.00 bid and $11.96 asked. Note that when purchasing these shares, investors obtain an asset worth $11.00. The difference between the bid and ask price, 96 cents, is paid to the fund's sales organization.

When investors make an initial purchase of fund shares, they are required to complete a purchase application, which is similar to those required when opening a bank account. A check for the amount of purchase along with the application is mailed to the fund (if a no-load fund) or given to the salesman (if a load fund). At the time the application is made, the investor may apply for additional services offered by the fund. Such services may include wire transfer privileges, check writing privileges, telephone exchange privileges and a cash withdrawal plan.

According to federal regulations, all prospective fund investors must receive a prospectus from the fund and declare that they have read it before a purchase application can be accepted by the fund. Before purchase, many investors do not take the time to read the prospectus. These same investors are generally the first to complain when they learn that the fund does not provide certain services or when subsequent purchases or sales of shares are delayed because the shareholder does not understand the procedure for conducting such transactions.

Upon purchase, mutual fund shares must be registered, and there are a variety of ways to do this.

- Individual Ownership—shares are registered in your name, giving you sole ownership. Upon your death, they are placed in your estate and disposed of according to the terms of your will.
- Joint Tenancy with Right of Survivorship—registration creates joint share ownership. Both you and your joint tenant must sign when redeeming any shares. Shares revert to the sole survivor when one tenant dies.
- Joint Tenancy—registration is similar to that described above except that if one tenant dies, the shares are placed into the estate of the deceased for disposition according to the will.While both tenants are living, both must sign for redemptions, and all checks representing fund distributions are made in the names of both.

In addition to these three registration methods, fund shares may also be registered with a sole owner (either you or another entity such as an attorney or bank) as custodian, guardian or as a trust under court order.

Recently, the National Conference of Commissioners on Uniform State Laws approved the Uniform Transfer On Death (TOD) Security Registration Act. TOD registration is intended to provide an alternative to the joint tenancy form of title for shareholders who wish to arrange a nonprobate transfer upon their death but do not wish to share control and ownership during their lifetime. This act is still subject to approval by the various states.

When mutual fund shares are purchased, the fund will not send stock certificates unless requested to do so by the investor. Instead, ownership is recorded electronically, and the custodial bank keeps a record of the number of shares purchased. Since mutual fund shares can be used as collateral for bank loans (at favorable interest rates), it may be wise to order the fund to send you certificates of ownership periodically. These certificates can be stored in a safe deposit box until they are needed. If you order certificates, they will be delivered in only whole share amounts. (You can purchase fractions of mutual fund shares.)

Exchanging and redeeming shares is generally as easy as making purchases. First, if you have telephone exchange privileges, merely call the fund and request an exchange of X dollars (or the sale and transfer of Y shares) to another fund that qualifies for exchange. Most qualified exchange funds are members of the same "fund family" (i.e., are managed by the same advisor), although a few funds allow exchanges with nonfamily members. (Remember that any "switch" of fund shares, even among funds in the same family, is considered a taxable event by the IRS.) When initially requesting the telephone exchange privilege, it is wise to make initial purchases of the fund family's money market fund shares. Then, you can switch cash by telephone to the desired stock or bond fund. In this way, telephone switches can be subsequently made from the stock or bond fund to the money fund, and money fund checks can be used to withdraw cash from the fund family. (This procedure can reduce the time before cash becomes available for use by one to two weeks.)

A second method of selling fund shares is to write directly to the fund and request that shares be sold and the proceeds sent to you. (Remember that while you can request that "some" shares be exchanged by telephone, you cannot close an account [sell all shares] unless the fund receives a written and duly signed request to do so.) We suggest that when making a written request, you use a form letter similar to the following:

> Please redeem _____ shares purchased on *(date)* [or completely liquidate my holdings] in ABC Fund. My account number is __________. Enclosed is certificate number [if certificates are being held by you] for _____ shares. Please send the proceeds to (name and address) as soon as possible.
>
> Sincerely,
>
> ______________________________
> (Authorized signature(s))
>
> Date ______________________________

To avoid a delay in the redemption process, make sure that the signature(s) on the redemption letter have been guaranteed by a bank or a brokerage firm.

The proceeds of share redemptions will be sent as soon as possible. Once the transfer agent (custodial bank) receives your request, it takes an additional one or two days to effect the sale. Cash will then be disbursed by the custodial bank within seven days of sale. Allowing a total of four to six days for mail delivery, expect to receive proceeds from the sale of fund shares within 12 to 15 days after mailing the redemption request. (Remember also that your bank may not release cash to your account until the fund's check has been cleared.) If you wish to reinvest the proceeds in another fund, count on another 3 to 14 days to make the purchase.

Finally, one must read the fund's prospectus very carefully to determine the extent of all fees associated with the sale and redemption of its shares. Some funds charge a redemption fee if shares are redeemed before a specified period of time has elapsed. For example, some funds charge a fee of 0.5 percent of the value of the redemption if made within 60 days of a purchase; others may charge 4 percent on redemptions made within four years of purchase. Most funds levy a flat dollar charge on telephone exchanges that exceed some threshold number during a year. Also, most funds require that initial purchases be "on the books" for at least 30 days before allowing a telephone switch. Remember, a prospectus may be boring to read, but a lack of knowledge regarding your fund's operating procedures will invariably cost you money and/or time.

What Records Should I Keep?

The mutual fund, by law, is obligated to send all shareholders periodic statements of the shareholder's account activity, the fund's investment income and earnings during a period, proxy statements and an updated prospectus. Each fund is also required to submit a semiannual and an audited annual report to shareholders. Some funds voluntarily send unaudited quarterly investment and earnings reports as well. (With our own fund, the Perritt Capital Growth Fund, we send out monthly reports.) These documents specify the fund's investment portfolio, the income earned during the period and a statement of the fund's operating expenses. Investors must receive a prospectus before the fund can accept initial share purchases and will be sent a new prospectus each year thereafter.

It is important that the latest prospectus be kept on file so that future purchases and/or redemptions can be made in accordance with the fund's latest business procedures. It is important that shareholders retain all confirmation statements, detailing purchases and redemptions made. At year-end, the fund will send you a summary of the yearly account activity. These statements provide the backup documentation necessary for income tax filings. We suggest that you also keep an account activity summary form similar to the one illustrated in Table 8. It lists the dates of purchases and redemptions, types of transactions, dollar value of each transaction (broken down by the number of shares transacted and the appropriate share price) and a running total of the share balance. One such document should be maintained for each fund currently owned. The reasons for keeping detailed records for each fund owned is to make tax computations easier and to assist in minimizing federal and state income taxes paid on mutual fund investment profits. Attach the latest prospectus and all confirmation slips to this summary report.

The Benefits of Mutual Fund Investing

Of the dozens of benefits of investing in mutual funds, as touted by industry sources, the following are really worth mentioning.

Diversification. The greatest benefit is instantaneous portfolio diversification. To have a chance at winning the investment game, you must be around at the end. The prices of risky assets such as common stocks are highly volatile—they rise and fall. The prices of some stocks that fall may never rise again. But stock prices, when taken in the *aggregate* (i.e., the market), have always moved to higher ground—even after significant drops over prolonged periods of time.

From the academic community, we have learned that investment risk can be measured in terms of the volatility of investment return. The greater the volatility, the greater the investment risk. Modern investment theory tells us that the risk of a single investment consists of two components: systematic (market-related) risk and unsystematic (company-specific) risk. The average common stock, for example, contains 30 percent market risk and 70 percent company-specific risk. That is, 30 percent of the variability in price is related to the ups and downs of the stock market, and 70 percent of the variation in price is due to factors related to the company. This is an extremely important point since all of the company-specific (unsystematic) risk can be eliminated with proper portfolio diversification. To state it another way, an individual holding a single stock is subject to three times as much risk as is the well-diversified investor. For investors who cannot hold a well-diversified portfolio of common stocks (or bonds) due to monetary constraints, mutual fund investment is a must.

Look at it this way: the investor who holds a widely diversified portfolio of common stocks is taking only about one-third the risk of an investor holding a single stock. Since only nondiversifiable, or market, risk is rewarded in the stock market, widely diversified investors earn average rates of return nearly equivalent to investors with highly concentrated portfolios of assets—but do so at one-third the risk.

The average mutual fund, through diversification, reduces the company-specific portion of total risk from 70 percent to only 15 percent of total risk. This risk reduction is more than worth the 1 percent or 1.5 percent that we pay portfolio management to provide this extreme reduction in investment risk.

Simplified Record Keeping. A second benefit of mutual fund investment is simplified record keeping. Anyone who has held 40 or 50 common stocks in a portfolio at a given point in time knows the trouble caused by scores of dividend checks that, when received, must be cashed and reinvested in additional assets. In addition, keeping track of cash dividend payments, stock splits, interest payments, pur-

Table 8 Mutual Fund Investment Record Keeping

Name of Fund	Super Growth Shares
Minimum Investment	$1,000
Subsequent Investment	$200
Telephone Number	1-800-xxx-xxxx
Account Number	xxx-xxx-xxxx
Approximate Distribution Date(s)	December

Date	Transaction	Amount	Share Price	Shares	Share Balance
2/28/88	Initial Purchase	$5,000.00	$12.00	416.667	416.667
10/30/88	Purchase	1,000.00	13.00	76.923	493.590
12/30/88	Distribution	422.00	12.90	32.713	526.303
11/14/89	Sale (Redemption)	1,037.46	13.50	76.923	449.380

chase and sale prices and brokerage commissions and fees is demanding work. Admittedly, part of the "fun" of investing is cashing dividend and interest checks. However, lost checks can be an aggravation. Additionally, investment returns left in a drawer to collect dust are not nearly as profitable as investment returns reinvested to earn additional returns. Furthermore, at tax payment time, the requirement to document all security trades made during the year frequently becomes a paperwork jungle.

With mutual fund investments, management receives and reinvests dividends and interest payments and ultimately pays out this investment income to fund shareholders in a single check. Also, fund investors, through automatic reinvestment plans, can instantly reinvest fund distributions and thus gain the full advantage of compound growth. Finally, each mutual fund shareholder is sent a report once each year that indicates the income earned and transactions made during the year. This report can be especially convenient at tax reporting time.

Liquidity. A third benefit of mutual fund investment is that investors obtain a high degree of liquidity. That is, it is easy to become fully invested in a diversified portfolio of common stocks (or bonds) in a short period of time. Rather than placing buy (or sell) orders for 20 to 50 stocks contained in an individually managed portfolio, a fund investor can get in or out of the market with a single buy or sell order. Since many funds offer a telephone switch service with a money market fund, a 180-degree turn in investment posture can be made with a single phone call.

Professional Management. The fourth advantage of fund investment is the presence of low-cost professional management. For a management fee of as little as 0.5 percent, investors obtain management governed by a strict investment strategy as outlined in the fund's prospectus. Thus, to some degree, the investment portfolio is managed by rationality rather than emotion. Fund managers must stick to the investment objectives outlined in the prospectus.

These professional investment managers work on the behalf of shareholders. The fund's advisor (manager) determines the specific securities to be purchased, the timing of such purchases and the proportions of the various asset types held by the fund. Investors who cannot afford to hire professional analysts or portfolio managers to guide them obtain such guidance at a modest cost through mutual fund investments since management fees are divided on a pro rata basis. In addition, the fund management bears the cost of data collection, information processing and portfolio tracking. Thus, mutual fund shareholders can avail themselves of modern investment management technology at minimal cost.

On the negative side, we find two disadvantages to mutual fund investment. The first is the relatively high transaction costs borne by fund shareholders. While fund managers face lower brokerage commission charges than do individual investors, large block trades widen the spread between a market-maker's bid and ask prices, thus raising a fund's total transaction costs.

However, the biggest disadvantage is the fact that, to maintain their conduit status, funds must distribute to shareholders the bulk of the income and capital gains realized during the year. Thus, shareholders possess little control over the tax planning aspects of their investments. If a fund distributes short-term capital gains to shareholders, there is little the shareholder can do but to pay the taxes (at ordinary income rates) on the gains. While there are some precautions that a fund investor can take to minimize the tax bite, the fact remains that distributions and their tax status are determined by fund management and its portfolio strategies rather than by the needs of fund investors.

MUTUAL FUND INVESTMENT AND TAXATION

Open-end investment companies that pay out 100 percent of their realized income during the tax year are considered conduits, or pipelines, between their shareholders and the corporations whose securities the fund holds. Thus, all distributions paid by such funds create potential tax liabilities for shareholders. It is this conduit treatment, and the fact that mutual funds pay distributions rather than dividends to shareholders, that usually confuses fund investors and, in some instances, results in the payment of federal income taxes that otherwise could be avoided. The goal of this section is to clear up this confusion.

Income from Mutual Funds

Mutual funds earn income over their tax year by investing in a portfolio of securities and obtaining income in the form of cash dividends and interest paid to the fund by the security issuers. The fund can also earn capital gain income, resulting from price changes of its assets. Such capital gain (loss) income may be either realized (if the fund has disposed of securities during the tax year) or unrealized (if the securities continue to be held by the fund at the end of the tax year). Increases (decreases) in fund income, whether realized or not, are instantaneously transmitted to fund shareholders through increases (decreases) in the value of total assets and thus in the fund's per share net asset value.

Shareholders may sell fund shares at any time. At the time of sale, any gains or losses in per share net asset value become realized by the individual shareholder.

Mutual fund shareholders may also realize investment income from the distributions paid by the fund. Payments made to shareholders by mutual funds are actually distributions of realized income. On the ex-distribution date, the per share net asset value of the fund will fall by the amount of the distribution. Thus, the income received from the distribution is offset exactly by the decrease in per share net asset value. Since the income distributed to shareholders is realized by them and is taxed accordingly, the fund must indicate the source of the components of all distributions paid during the year. The various components and their tax treatments are discussed below.

Investment Income. This is the income earned by the fund from cash dividends and the interest payments it receives. This income is considered to be ordinary income and is thus taxed at the taxpayer's marginal rate.

Capital Gain Income. In trading securities, the fund may realize capital gains and losses. The gains and losses are netted, and the excess realized capital gains are paid out to shareholders. If the combination of realized capital gains and losses results in a net loss, the fund is allowed to carry the loss forward for up to eight years. These capital losses can be used to offset net realized capital gains in future periods.

Since mutual fund cash distributions result in an immediate decline in per share net asset value equal to the amount of the distribution, individuals who purchase mutual fund shares immediately before the ex-distribution date effectively have a portion of their investment capital returned to them. The distribution is considered a taxable event, and even though the distribution equals the decrease in net asset value, investors are left worse off by the amount of tax they must pay on the distribution. Therefore, under normal circumstances, taxpaying investors should wait to make their fund purchases immediately after the ex-distribution date.

The Tax Advantage of Losses

Since mutual funds can carry forward net realized capital losses, it is possible for new investors to "buy" the tax advantage of losses suffered by others. First, we must point out the fact that, whenever possible, mutual fund managers try not to distribute capital gains to shareholders; yet they cannot risk endangering their conduit status. They recognize the fact that gains in per share net asset value (rather than distributed capital gains) are more desired by shareholders since unrealized capital appreciation goes untaxed while capital gains distributions are subject to shareholder federal income taxes in the year distributed. Thus, as year-end approaches, managers with net realized capital gains positions begin to sell off assets that have declined in value and use up realized capital losses carried forward from prior periods until the total realized losses equal total realized gains. This gimmick eliminates bothersome taxable capital distributions. The advantage of buying a fund with realized capital losses being carried forward can be seen from the following example.

Suppose two mutual funds currently own exactly the same assets. Both are no-load funds with per share net asset values equal to $10.00. Fund X purchased its portfolio of securities at about one-half of today's market value, and thus the fund has a net unrealized capital gain position. Fund Y acquired the securities in its portfolio recently, after liquidating assets that had declined in value over the preceding year, and thus it has net realized capital losses to carry forward. Since both funds hold exactly the same securities, Fund Y is a more desirable investment than Fund X. To see why, consider what would happen if the assets held by both funds rise in price. If Fund Y sells some of its holdings, it can utilize the losses being carried forward to offset the realized gains. If Fund X sells some of its securities, a distribution of capital gains must be made since the fund is left with a net realized capital gains position. The fund's shares will fall in price by an amount equal to the distribution, but shareholders are at a disadvantage, compared to those holding Fund Y's shares, by the amount of personal taxes they will have to pay on the distribution.

Identifying Gains and Losses

As previously indicated, it is very important that mutual fund investors maintain adequate records of all share purchases, including shares purchased through reinvestment of distributions and redemptions. In addition to a summary report of fund purchase and sale transactions, investors should retain all statements from the fund that document specific purchases and sales.

When fund shares are sold (redeemed), a profit (or loss) may be realized by the investor. The amount of profit (loss) is determined by the difference between the price at redemption and the acquisition cost. If poor or no records of prior purchases exist, it may be virtually impossible to determine or substantiate the magnitude of the gain or loss.

For income tax purposes, the cost of mutual fund shares that have subsequently been sold can be determined by either the "first in, first out" (FIFO) method or by identifiable cost. The FIFO method assumes that the shares sold were the first ones acquired. The identifiable cost method requires that the shares sold be specifically identified as the ones acquired on a specific date at a specific acquisition cost.

When using the identifiable cost method of accounting for share costs, the IRS places the burden of proof on the taxpayer. That is, you must be able to trace a sale to a specific block of shares. The easiest method for doing that is to request, periodically, that your fund send you stock certificates that represent your holdings. When a sale is made, record the certificate number(s) and the date of acquisition along with the original cost and proceeds received. If you leave your shares on deposit with the fund (as most fund investors do), keep a record of each purchase made. When a sale is made, write to the fund and instruct it to sell a specific block of shares acquired on a specific date. Request that the fund verify the sale in writing.

Remember also that, when liquidating holdings, some of the shares may have been acquired through automatic reinvestment of distributions. Thus, the cost basis for these shares is the per share net asset value at the time of reinvestment. Since the income tax liability on these shares may have been partially satisfied in prior years, ignoring the cost of shares acquired this way could result in an overpayment of income taxes. For example, suppose that you invested $2,000 in Fund XYZ two years ago. Since the per share NAV at that time was $10, you acquired 200 shares. Recently, you liquidated your holdings in this fund and received $3,000. It might appear in this instance that you must pay taxes on $1,000 of realized capital gains. However, suppose that the fund made distributions during this period totaling $600. Since these distributions were previously subject to taxation, the investment income subject to taxation at the time of liquidation is $400, not $1,000. Thus, we cannot overstate the need to maintain good mutual fund accounting records.

MUTUAL FUND SELECTION

The process of acquiring mutual fund shares begins when a load fund is "pitched" by a salesperson or when an individual requests a purchase application from a no-load fund. According to federal law, the salesperson or the fund must deliver a prospectus to the potential investor before any money can change hands. Since the prospectus is often written in "legalese," many investors ignore the contents of the document and proceed directly to the purchase application. We believe this to be the first of a series of mistakes made by many mutual fund investors.

We strongly urge all prospective investors to obtain and read both the fund's prospectus and the latest annual report or interim financial statement. Beginning in 1984, funds were allowed to combine the annual report with the latest prospectus. Our experience indicates that some funds have chosen to combine both documents and some have not. To ensure that both these documents are sent along with a purchase application, the investor should request them. Also beginning in 1984, funds were permitted to simplify the prospectus by omitting some legal descriptions of the nature of their business. The legal descriptions were relegated to a "statement of additional information." Thus, it is important that prospective purchasers request that both the prospectus and the statement of additional information be sent with a purchase application.

Once these documents are in hand, read them thoroughly. You may become bored with the presentation, but be assured, you will also be enlightened. Here's what to look for in these documents:

- A statement of the fund's investment objective and investment strategy.
- Details concerning all sales and redemption charges (if any).
- A list of investment restrictions (e.g., can the fund use leverage, invest in letter stock, trade options, etc.).
- The fund's services and the mechanics of using them (e.g., telephone switching, automatic reinvestment of distributions, charges for excess switches, etc.).
- A statement of the fund's net realized and unrealized gains or losses. (Be especially on the lookout for funds with realized losses being carried forward since such funds can provide investors with certain tax advantages.)
- Investment advisor fee schedule.
- Dividend declaration dates.
- Condensed financial statement.

An investor should highlight or outline these specific items so that a comparison among a group of funds can be made easily.

Housekeeping Tips

Once the above items have been documented for a number of funds, the actual selection process can begin. The process of weeding out unacceptable funds should begin with the examination of a few "housekeeping" items. First, ascertain whether or not the fund is registered for sale in your state of residence. Generally, if it is not so registered, the fund will not send a prospectus. However, slip-ups can occur.

Second, check the list of services provided by the fund. Does the fund provide the services you desire (e.g., wire transfer, telephone exchanges, IRA, Keogh, etc.)?

Third, is the fund scheduled to pay a distribution in the near future? As explained previously, the answer to this question may not result in the rejection of a fund, but it may save a few tax dollars if purchases are postponed until after the distribution has been paid.

Fourth, consider all purchase and redemption fees and determine if the fees are excessive. For example, when making an IRA or Keogh purchase, all sales charges should be considered excessive since they are taken off the front end. The result is that the actual investment amount will be less than the maximum allowable retirement plan contribution for a given year. The funds that remain viable alternatives after this brief survey are then subject to a series of general screens.

General Guidelines

We recommend that investors select only those mutual funds registered with the Securities and Exchange Commission. Avoid the so-called "off-shore" or foreign-based mutual funds. While many of these unregistered funds may provide methods for hiding investment dollars and income from Uncle Sam's tax department, the funds do not offer the federal government's protection against malpractice or fraud. Remember that there is no such thing as a free lunch. The additional return promised by off-shore mutual funds is accompanied by increased investment risks (including the risk that someone will steal your money).

We also recommend that individuals only invest in mutual funds whose per share net asset values are reported in *The Wall Street Journal* or *Barron's* magazine. All funds with at least 1,000 shareholders report their daily per share NAVs to the automatic quotation services provided by the NASD and in turn are reported to the financial press. By following this rule, you may miss the "opportunity" of investing in small funds that may possess greater performance potential. However, the performance of such funds may be hindered by their small size. Furthermore, to track your overall performance over time, it is essential that you be able to obtain accurate and up-to-date share price data.

We also suggest that investors shy away from newly offered funds. Unlike so-called "hot" new stock issues, which are offered at prices set deliberately low to generate investor interest, mutual fund shares are offered at per share net asset value (plus a sales charge if a load fund). Thus, there is little advantage in getting in on the ground floor. Furthermore, when evaluating a fund, it is important to see how fund management copes with changing market conditions. A little operating history is required. We recommend not making a purchase until fund shares have been offered to the general public for at least one year. Note that we did not say "is one year old." Many new funds are started as limited partnerships. If the fund has a good track record, it is then taken public. Thus, for many new funds, the great past returns advertised in the press were available to only a few investors. The so-called "embryo" funds that do not perform well initially are never taken public. Be wary of new funds with great track records that started out as embryo funds.

In addition, avoid those mutual funds that can or do invest in letter-stock or other unregistered securities. Since these assets are infrequently traded, current value is difficult to assess. Management can easily inflate (or deflate) per share net asset value by making subjective valuations of these assets. Furthermore, since the assets are not liquid, the fund may not be able to dispose of them when market conditions or corporate fortunes change.

One of the most important screens that can be applied by the individual investor is an assessment of the appropriateness of the fund's objective. Does it correspond with the overall portfolio risk/return plan established by the investor, given his investment philosophy? The stated objective of the fund should be specific, understandable and consistent with the needs and desires of the investor.

While law requires that every prospectus contain a description of the fund's investment objectives, clarity is not mandated. The objectives contained in some mutual fund prospectuses are so garbled and nebulous that it is difficult to tell what management is going to do with your money. We suggest that if the objective is unclear, you should pass over that fund and look for another.

The investment objective illustrated in Figure 2 clearly shows what the fund will do with your money. It seeks "capital growth," invests in segments of the economy for which favorable trends are expected and seeks "smaller companies which it regards as having superior potential, although they are not yet widely recognized as growth companies." The fund invests "primarily in common stocks and in securities convertible into common stocks." What could be more clear?

If, after examining the fund's investment objectives, it appears that you have found a match between your personal objectives and the fund's investment objectives, the next step is to examine the fund's financial record. (See Table 9.) This segment of the prospectus contains a summary of the audited annual reports of the fund for the last ten years (if the fund is that old). Net asset value (for no-load funds) is synonymous with share price. Investment income consists of dividend and interest payments received by the fund plus realized short-term capital gains on its investments. Dividends from net investment income are payments made to shareholders. The ratio of net investment income to average net assets is actually the average current yield earned by the fund.

Portfolio turnover rate is a measure of the purchase and sale activity of a mutual fund. It is calculated by dividing the lesser of purchases or sales for the fiscal year by the monthly average value of the securities owned by the fund during that year. However, securities with maturities of less than one year are excluded from the calculation. A portfolio turnover of 100 percent implies a complete turnover of fund assets. All portfolio items in the accompanying table are self-explanatory.

The data provided in the statement of condensed financial information can be used for the application of several additional screens. First, examine the total assets of the

Table 9 Condensed Financial Information—Per Share Income and Capital Changes (For a Share Outstanding Throughout Each Calendar Year)

	1991	1990	1989	1988	1987	1986	1985	1984	1983	1982
Net asset value:										
End of year	$32.42	$37.27	$37.82	$30.89	$31.82	$27.35	$24.41	$29.72	$25.70	$18.73
Beginning of year	37.27	37.82	30.89	31.82	27.35	24.41	29.72	25.70	18.73	16.38
Increase (decrease) in net asset valuet	$ (4.85)	$ (.55)	$ 6.93	$ (.93)	$ 4.47	$ 2.94	$ (5.31)	$ 4.02	$ 6.97	$ 2.35
Analysis of increase (decrease) in net asset value:										
Investment income	$ 1.05	$ .98	$ .84	$ .91	$ .86	$ 1.36	$ 1.24	$ 1.14	$ .84	$ .61
Less expenses	.32	.31	.26	.24	.26	.22	.25	.24	.19	.18
Net investment income	.73	.67	.58	.67	.60	1.14	.99	.90	.65	.43
Dividends from net investment income	(.77)	(.50)	(.51)	(.55)	(1.04)	(1.03)	(.88)	(.80)	(.44)	(.38)
Net realized and unrealized gain (loss) on investments	.61	5.35	8.72	.58	5.95	2.87	(2.98)	6.26	8.09	2.30
Distributions from net realized gain reportable for federal income taxes	(5.42)	(6.07)	(1.86)	(1.63)	(1.04)	(.04)	(2.44)	(2.34)	(1.33)	—
Increase (decrease) in net asset value	$ (4.85)	$ (.55)	$ 6.93	$ (.93)	$ 4.47	$ 2.94	$ (5.31)	$ 4.02	$ 6.97	$ 2.35
Ratio of expenses to average net assets	.82%	.79%	.78%	.85%	.85%	.92%	.95%	.93%	.91%	$ 1.02%
Ratio of net investment income to average net assets	1.85%	1.71%	1.73%	2.31%	1.94%	4.82%	3.83%	3.54%	3.06%	2.39%
Portfolio turnover rate	52%	34%	32%	33%	22%	32%	16%	24%	34%	24%
Number of shares outstanding at end of year (000s) omitted	12,887	11,124	8,395	6,804	5,461	4,841	4,340	3,858	3,092	2,187

Figure 2 Example of a Fund's Written Investment Objectives Statement

The Fund invests with the objective of capital growth. Although income is considered in the selection of securities, the Fund is not designed for investors seeking primarily income rather than capital appreciation.

The Fund seeks out areas of the economy which it believes will benefit from favorable trends for a number of years. The areas of emphasis change from time to time; the dominant area at this time is the information group, with other areas of emphasis including banks, real estate and energy (see "Statement of Investments"). The Fund examines and invests in companies within the identified area. It particularly seeks smaller companies which it regards as having: superior potential, although they are not yet widely recognized as growth companies; strategic position in specialized markets because of technological, marketing or managerial skills; adequate capitalization, affording financial strength and stability. Some of the securities in which the Fund invests are available in amounts which are too limited for larger institutional holdings. The Fund also invests in securities other than those described in this paragraph, on the basis of its view of their individual merits in relation to the Fund's investment objective. There is no one area of primary emphasis.

The Fund invests primarily in common stocks and in securities convertible into common stocks. The Fund may also invest in preferred stocks and in obligations, such as bonds, debentures and notes, which in the opinion of management are depressed in price and are believed to present opportunities for capital appreciation. It may invest in corporate or government obligations or hold cash or cash equivalents if a defensive position is considered advisable. It may also invest in foreign issuers, which might involve a greater degree of risk (such as exchange rate fluctuations, exchange controls, tax provisions, expropriation of assets, other governmental restrictions and regulations and less available financial information) than does investment in domestic issuers.

fund. We recommend that aggressive growth common stock funds with total assets greater than $400 million be eliminated. It is permissible to retain growth (or growth-income) funds with assets up to $800 millon. For bonds, the greater the level of total assets, the better.

While there has been little scientific documentation of the impact of asset size on mutual fund performance, investment theory suggests that smaller funds may be in a better position to outperform the market averages than larger funds. For example, a $2 billion fund that holds 300 or 400 different stocks has literally "bought the market." As a result, its returns will, for the most part, parallel those of the market averages. Secondly, such funds generally possess large holdings of individual stocks; thus, their disposal could unfavorably affect share price and dampen the fund's return. Thirdly, some portfolio managers have candidly conceded that management of a fund becomes difficult when assets exceed $400 million to $500 million. Operational inefficiencies and increased expenses may begin to appear when the fund's assets (and number of shareholders) pass some total asset threshold. Finally, since optimal portfolio diversification can be obtained with as few as 30 to 40 different common stock issues, larger funds generally provide superfluous diversification.

As indicated earlier, portfolio turnover is the lesser of purchases or sales for the fiscal year divided by average net assets. This reflects how frequently the fund buys and sells securities. The following equation can be used to translate the turnover rate into the average holding period of the portfolio: 1 divided by the turnover rate (expressed as a decimal). For example, a fund with a 50 percent turnover rate has an average holding period of two years, calculated as follows:

$$\frac{1}{0.50} = 2 \text{ years}$$

Avoid mutual funds with historical portfolio turnover rates greater than 100 percent. These funds, on average, possess security holding periods of less than one year. Thus, it is quite possible that in periods of sustained increases in stock prices, the fund may have been caught at year-end with substantial net realized capital gains. Because funds with low portfolio turnover ratios possess long-term average holding periods (a 25 percent turnover implies an average four-year holding period), the realized gains distributed to shareholders will most likely be minimal.

In addition, investors should avoid funds with a high portfolio turnover rate because a high turnover rate results in greater brokerage costs incurred by the fund. The relatively high transaction costs borne by mutual funds could cause the net investment return of high-portfolio-turnover funds to be much smaller than would be the case if portfolio turnover were lower. Brokerage costs are directly reflected in the price of the securities a fund buys.

We also recommend that investors seek mutual funds with some degree of concentration of assets. (Remember that funds that possess widely distributed assets may have "bought the market" and thus be relegated to returns paralleling market rates of return.) This screen may already have been satisfied by application of the size screen. However, the degree of concentration of assets can be assessed directly by examining the number of common stocks held. We prefer funds with fewer than 70 stocks unless the fund is attempting to invest in small equity capitalization firms. The goal of earning a rate of return above the so-called market rate of return can only be obtained from portfolios that do not mirror the market.

A mutual fund investor may also obtain a degree of asset concentration by investing in funds that specialize in stocks of a particular industry (technology, utilities, etc.) or those funds that invest in special situations (out-of-favor companies, low P/E stocks, small equity capitalization firms, etc.). Remember, however, that along with increased concentration comes increased investment risk. Remember also that you can't beat the market if you own it. Thus, some degree of asset concentration is warranted.

We also suggest taking a cursory glance at the fund's average expense ratio and management fee schedule. Preference should be given to funds with expense ratios that average less than 1.50 percent and to management fees that average less than 0.75 percent of average annual assets. Remember that the higher the expenses, the lower will be the return to shareholders (all other things being equal).

Finally, obtain as much information as you can regarding fund management. Since it is the manager who makes portfolio purchase and sale decisions, the quality of management is frequently the determining performance factor. We like funds to possess a continuity of management. If portfolio managers have been investing for a long time, they have gained experience in trading in various types of markets. In addition, they know how they will react to a rapid change in market conditions. We also prefer to invest in mutual funds whose management possesses a well-defined investment philosophy and who can articulate their various strategies for trading in various types of markets.

For the individual investor, this data is frequently difficult to obtain. However, a number of sources endeavor to report these facts to subscribers (e.g., *The Mutual Fund Letter*). In addition, some clues to management quality and overall philosophy can be gleaned from an examination of fund price performance and distribution during bull markets, bear markets and periods of relatively flat stock prices. If old annual reports can be obtained, examine them to see what kinds of stocks were held during periods of varying market conditions. Admittedly, this is no easy task, yet such examinations generally yield additional mutual fund investment returns.

Making the Final Selections

The common stock mutual funds that remain in contention after the application of the housekeeping and general screens should then be subjected to three quantitative screens. Remember, though, that these remaining funds are all viable investment alternatives.

First, we recommend investment in growth and aggressive growth funds with betas greater than 1.00. Beta is a measure of the relative systematic risk of an asset or portfolio. It relates the volatility of the asset relative to the market as a whole (usually the S&P 500 Stock Index). The reason that we prefer investment in high beta funds is that even though stock prices rise and fall over short-term periods, over the longer term, stock prices have always moved to a higher level. Thus, long-term-oriented investors will find that their portfolios (containing high beta assets) will rise in value by more than the percentage long-term rise in stock market prices. Wealth-maximizing investors have always been better off when they have maintained long-term commitments to portfolios containing highly variable (high beta) assets.

Although some financial writers claim that an examination of the fund's portfolio of assets provides little guidance in fund selection, we strongly disagree. We believe that analysis of the individual stocks held by a growth or aggressive growth fund is a requisite in fund selection.

Before we present a method for analysis, let's look at the reasons that others believe that fund stock analysis is a frivolous activity. First, some argue that the common stock holdings of mutual funds listed in their quarterly (or annual) financial reports are not representative of current stock holdings. However, since we have suggested that fund investors select mutual funds that possess low portfolio turnover ratios, there is a high degree of probability that the financial reports of these funds will indicate very nearly the fund's current asset holdings. Secondly, some financial writers believe that nonprofessional investors lack the expertise and skill to analyze individual common stocks. This, we believe, is an insult to the average investor. Finally, some believe that the common stock holdings of most mutual funds are too extensive to allow for timely and meaningful analysis. To some extent, that is true. However, since we prefer to invest in funds with a high degree of asset concentration, the number of stocks held tends to be lower than average.

Our analytic method focuses on three variables and on only a portion of the fund's common stock holdings. The three variables are: (1) price-earnings ratios; (2) growth rate; and (3) current common stock dividend yield. (Some investors may want to add a fourth variable, the ratio of current stock price to book value per share.) A company's growth is defined as the annual growth rate in sales (or earnings per share) obtained from a variety of sources, including: *Value Line Investment Survey, Standard & Poor's Stock Guide* and *S&P's Corporate Reports*. (Most public libraries and brokerage firms are subscribers to these and other data-based investment services.)

Once the values of the three variables (P/E, annual growth and current yield) have been obtained for each of the stocks under analysis, compute the average value of each variable. To do this, merely add up the values and divide by the number of stocks analyzed. Technically speaking, one should obtain the weighted average for each variable. However, since the percentages of each stock held tend to be nearly equal, the weighted average will not yield a significantly different value than will the simple average.

We suggest that individuals confine their common stock examination to a subset of the fund's holdings. For purpose of analysis, use the data contained in the fund's most recent annual or quarterly shareholder report. Select for examination either the 10 largest common stock holdings (in terms of current market value) or a number of heavily held stocks that represents one-third of the fund's total assets. Select the larger number. For example, if the 16 largest common stock holdings equal 33 percent of the fund's assets, analyze these 16 stocks. If 9 stocks represent 33 percent of the fund's total assets, analyze the 10 highest value stocks held by the fund. Of course, the analyst must scan the other common stock holdings to see whether or not the subset chosen for analysis is representative of the entire portfolio.

The objective of this exercise is not to second guess fund management but to find out what the fund's portfolio actually contains. Many individuals, especially those who are influenced by near-term past performance figures, buy into a fund without even knowing what kind of stocks the fund holds.

If you find that a fund holds shares of stock with average P/E multiples of 30 times recent earnings, average dividend yields of 0.2 percent and average annual growth rates of 30 percent, you have found a very aggressive fund. That fact is neither good nor bad. However, if you have a very conservative investment philosophy, an investment in such a fund, regardless of past performance, is not warranted. So, to quote the Better Business Bureau, "Investigate before you invest."

Up to this point, we have carefully avoided the issue of using historical mutual fund returns as a basis for selecting funds with superior future performance potential (or avoiding those with inferior performance potential). We now address that issue. Several academic researchers have tested the ability of mutual fund managers to consistently outperform the market. The first such test was performed by Eugene Fama of the University of Chicago in 1965. He ranked 39 common stock funds on the basis of net annual return each year over the period 1951 through 1960. Of these 39 funds, he found none that consistently earned net returns great enough to place it among the top 20 funds in each of the ten years studied.

In 1966 William Sharpe analyzed the performance of 34 mutual funds over the period 1954 to 1963. He computed each fund's average annual rate of return and divided this number by the standard deviation of annual returns (a measure of the portfolio's total risk). The resulting number is the fund's average annual rate of return per unit of total risk. The average ratio of the 34 funds was below that of the Dow Jones Industrial Average. That is, on average, the returns from these funds were below the returns that an investor following a naive buy-and-hold strategy (random selection and wide diversification) could have obtained.

In 1969 Professor M. C. Jensen examined the performance of 115 mutual funds over the ten-year period of 1955 to 1964. He found that, on average, these funds earned 1.1 percent less per year than they should have earned given their level of systematic risk. Of the 115 examined, 76 funds earned less risk-adjusted return than the S&P 500 Stock Index and only 39 earned more. Thus, it appears that the funds examined in this study, on average, were not able to forecast future security prices well enough to recover their research expenses, management fees and commission costs.

The evidence provided by these studies (along with several others) strongly suggests that observations of mutual fund historical return performances alone contain very little predictive content for forecasting future return performances. A fund that "beats the market" (after risk adjustment) during a previous period has about a 50-50 chance of "beating the market" in a future period. The odds are the same for a fund that did not beat the market in a previous period. These odds imply that, on the basis of historical return alone, an investor could do just as well at selecting superior performing funds with a flip of a coin. However, if investors feel more confident basing their final choice on historical data (after screening funds on the criteria outlined earlier), we see no adverse consequences occurring. In fact, if the increase in investor confidence leads to longer holding periods than otherwise would be the case, there may be some implicit benefit in selecting only top-rated funds. That is because, time and again, it has been demonstrated that investors with longer holding periods generally obtain larger investment returns than those with shorter holding periods. Transaction costs, research costs and tax effects more than cancel out any advantage that the short-term trader may possess.

Does this discussion of fund performance mean that historical data gives little guidance in making fund selection? Quite the contrary. Many of the screens that we have outlined rely on historical financial data. However, we are suggesting that fund selections made solely on the basis of returns earned by the fund over the recent past will be less than optimal. In fact, in many instances, the overall portfolio return earned by investors conscious of historical performance will be less than should be earned given the risks taken. Remember that investment return is the reward paid for risk taking by informed investors. As in all endeavors, hard work is generally rewarded more generously than slothfulness.

THE MUTUAL FUND PROSPECTUS: READ IT BEFORE YOU INVEST

"Investigate before you invest." This motto, adopted by the Better Business Bureau, often goes unheeded by stock, bond and mutual fund investors. While an abundance of information can be obtained regarding a potential investment, many investors believe that they do not have the time or the expertise to gather and evaluate such data. While even professional investors lack perfect foresight and thus take investment losses from time to time, they rarely acquire assets that possess risk and return characteristics inconsistent with their investment needs. That is, before expectations are set regarding the outcome of an investment decision, the professionals, as well as individual investors, first evaluate the suitability of that alternative relative to their financial goals and investment philosophies.

When evaluating any investment alternative, start with the question: is this investment "right" for me? In the case of mutual fund evaluation, the answer to this question can be found by examining the goals and objectives of the fund along with fund management's ability to carry out those objectives. Additionally, one must evaluate the services provided by the fund and the costs of such services. This information is contained in the fund's prospectus, which, by law, must be sent to all potential investors before a purchase application can be accepted by the fund.

While law mandates that a prospectus be sent to all potential investors, I have found that many mutual fund investors avoid reading this important document before making an investment. These individuals are generally surprised when they incur unexpected charges for services provided or can't obtain services they thought were provided or when the value of their fund shares fluctuates abnormally.

Here are just a few examples of what can happen to those who don't take the time to read the fund's prospectus before investing. Many investors in the 44 Wall Street Fund were shocked when their fund shares took a nosedive even though the stock market as a whole was undergoing only a moderate correction. Many of these individuals were surprised to learn that fund management was using leverage in managing the portfolio. Further, they were shocked to find that the fund is characterized as nondiversified and that it held fewer than a dozen stocks in its portfolio at the time of the price plunge. This information, of course, was spelled out in the fund's prospectus. Many had ignored that document in an attempt to rush into a fund that had previously been at the top of the performance ladder.

I have seen investors quarrel with fund management when they were charged unexpected fees on premature redemptions. Others have been dismayed to learn that they could not switch their investment from one fund in the family to another until a 30-day waiting period had elapsed. Still others were dumbfounded when they received a large distribution (fully taxable) shortly after they had made a purchase. These investors all had one thing in common: they had not read the fund's prospectus.

Before making an investment in any fund, investors should request and read the following documents: annual report, latest quarterly or semiannual report, the prospectus and the statement of additional information. Here's what to look for.

How Will Your Money Be Invested?

The fund's prospectus contains three sections that spell out what management will do with your money. Begin first by reading the statement of "Investment Objectives and Policies." In this section, the fund spells out its investment objectives and the strategies that will be employed to pursue these goals. Some funds merely tell you that they are going to invest your money in stocks and bonds and that they are going to emphasize current income, capital growth or both. Others are quite specific regarding their investment philosophy. Our advice is to consider only those funds that are quite specific in spelling out their investment goals, philosophy and portfolio management strategies.

Next, look at the statement of "Risk Factors." A fundamental axiom of investing is that investment return is always accompanied by investment risk. The greater the anticipated rewards from an investment, the greater will be the risks assumed by an investor. While this is a basic tenet of the investment world, some investors who seek the largest returns possible often forget that such assets can be very risky. These individuals frequently make their mutual fund selections solely on the basis of recent performance. Since many of these individuals neglect to investigate how these short-term returns were earned, they are often perplexed when such performance fails to continue.

Next, turn to the listing of the fund's "Investment Restrictions." An example is given in Figure 3. The Investment Company Act of 1940 limits mutual funds in their investments, and these investment restrictions are repeated here. However, since many funds place additional restrictions on the activities of their investment advisors, this section is required reading by all prospective investors.

Has the Fund Conformed to Its Stated Policies and Objectives?

Once you have found out what fund management intends to do with your money, check to see how well its past actions have conformed to its policy statements. A brief review of the summary of "Income and Capital Changes," contained in the prospectus, should provide the clues. (See Table 10.)

Income refers to the dividend and interest income earned on the fund's investments. Expenses are the pro rata share of the costs borne by fund shareholders. These costs include the investment advisory fee and the costs of holding board meetings and preparing and distributing shareholder reports. Dividends from net investment income are per share distributions of income taxed at ordinary income tax rates. Open-end investment companies must distribute 100 percent of all net investment income. In addition, each tax year, a fund is required to net its realized capital gains against its realized capital losses. If a net gain results, the fund must distribute 100 percent of the gain to shareholders, which is reported as "distribution from realized gains." If a net realized loss results, the fund must carry forward the loss to offset realized gains in future tax years. Net asset value is the per share value of the fund's portfolio of assets less liabilities. For no-load funds, net asset value is synonymous with share price.

Figure 3 Investment Restrictions

1. The Fund will not purchase securities on margin, participate in a joint trading account, sell securities short, or act as an underwriter or distributor of securities other than its own capital stock.
2. The Fund will not purchase or sell real estate or interests in real estate, commodities or commodity futures. The Fund may invest in the securities of real estate investment trusts, but not more than 10% in value of the Fund's total assets will be so invested. Less than 5% of the Fund's total net assets were at risk in the securities of real estate investment trusts in the past year. The Fund does not currently intend to place at risk more than 5% of its total net assets in such investments in the foreseeable future.
3. The Fund may make temporary bank borrowings (not in excess of 5% of the lower of cost or market value of the Fund's total assets) for emergency or extraordinary purposes.
4. Not more than 5% of the total assets of the Fund, taken at market value, will be invested in the securities of any one issuer (not including United States Government securities).
5. Not more than 25% of the Fund's total assets will be concentrated in companies of any one industry or group of related industries.

When evaluating management's ability to carry out its stated investment objectives, here's what to look for. First, measure the historical net current yield of the fund. To calculate net current yield, divide the distribution from net investment income by average per share net asset value. An estimated average net asset value can be obtained by adding the net asset value (NAV) at the beginning of the year to year-end NAV and dividing by 2. Perform this calculation for the last three to five years. Compare these current yields to the yields obtainable on a broadly based market index such as the S&P 500 Index. A capital-gains-oriented fund should possess yields less than the market average while an income fund or a growth and income fund should provide higher annual current yields.

Next examine the fund's portfolio turnover rates for the last several years. A low rate indicates a long-term holding posture while an extremely high ratio indicates an aggressive trading strategy. As a benchmark, the annual turnover ratio for the average mutual fund is approximately 80 percent.

Finally, compare the annual rates of return earned by the fund each year for the past several years with those provided by the major stock market averages. Annual return can be approximated by using the following formula.

Table 10 Per Share Income and Capital Changes (for a share outstanding throughout the year)

	Year Ended March 31				
	1991	1990	1989	1988	1987
INCOME AND EXPENSES:					
Income	$ .76	$ .88	$ .84	$ .81	$ .67
Expenses	.16	.22	.16	.18	.17
Net investment income	.62	.66	.68	.63	.50
Dividends from net income	(.64)	(.64)	(.62)	(.52)	(.39)
CAPITAL CHANGES:					
Net asset value at beginning of year	24.47	25.08	17.04	19.51	12.12
Net realized and unrealized gains or (losses) on securities	6.37	.44	8.99	(1.74)	7.28
Distribution from realized gains	(1.58)	(1.07)	(1.01)	(.84)	—
Net asset value at end of year	$29.24	$24.47	$25.08	$17.04	$19.51
Ratio of operating expenses to average net assets	.82%	.87%	.95%	1.03%	1.06%
Ratio of net investment income to average net assets	3.24%	2.69%	4.05%	3.54%	3.06%
Portfolio turnover rate	13.8%	22.2%	30.5%	45.1%	51.6%
Number of shares outstanding at end of year (to nearest thousand)	10,568	6,628	5,029	3,319	2,929

$$\frac{\text{NAV (year end)} + \text{All Distributions} - \text{NAV (beginning of year)}}{\text{NAV (beginning of year)}}$$

These rates of return should be computed for at least the past five years. Check to see whether or not these returns are more or less variable than those of the general market. More variability means more investment risk.

Remember to compare the results of these analyses to the objectives stated in the prospectus. There should be general agreement between historical results and policy statements. If wide discrepancies become apparent (e.g., a fund with a buy-and-hold objective shows high portfolio turnover ratios, or an aggressive growth fund has an abnormally high current yield), pass over that fund and look for another whose investment actions and results agree with policy statements.

What Are the Costs?

When investing in mutual funds, or any asset for that matter, one must consider the costs of obtaining, maintaining and eventually liquidating the investment. Transactions and portfolio maintenance costs reduce investment returns and thus should be considered and weighed against potential returns when making any investment. Again, for mutual funds the prospectus contains the needed data to make cost evaluations.

Costs borne by mutual fund investors fall into three categories: sales commissions, management fees and general operating expenses. Until recently, some "digging" was necessary to uncover all of these various fees and expenses. However, regulations handed down by the SEC have now simplified this process by requiring mutual funds to list these items prominently in a table located within the first few pages of the prospectus. While this fee table does not relieve investors of their responsibility to read the entire prospectus, it should help reduce the time investors spend playing "detective."

Also contained in the "Investment Advisor" section of the prospectus is a description of the contract between the fund and the investment advisor. The compensation paid to the advisor is described here, along with a listing of the operating expenses borne by the advisor and those assumed by fund shareholders.

The expense ratio is the total of management fees and general operating expenses paid by shareholders divided by average total assets under management. The average expense ratio for common stock funds is around 1.3 percent and for bond funds the average expense ratio is around 0.8 percent.

Services Provided

Before making a fund decision, we suggest that you first list the services that you require. These may include any or all of the following: retirement accounts, telephone switching privileges, check writing privileges, automatic dividend reinvestment, withdrawal plans, etc. Next, refer to each relevant section of the prospectus and list the services provided by the fund, the terms and conditions and any costs associated with services provided.

Finally, refer to the "Distributions and Taxes" section of the prospectus. Note the frequency of distributions, along with the approximate distribution dates. (If a fund does not include approximate distribution dates in its prospectus, you may have to call the fund to obtain this information.) Be on the lookout for peculiarities in fund tax status. These might include tax loss carry forwards, disputes with taxing authorities and/or special tax rules applied to the fund.

The intended purpose of the mutual fund prospectus is to provide investors with information regarding the investment they are about to undertake. While the prospectus (along with the statement of additional information) is often written in legal jargon, which may be somewhat difficult to follow at times, a careful reading is requisite to long-term investment success. For those who wish to skim these documents, we have pointed out the essentials for assessing the appropriateness of a particular fund for your investment portfolio. While the prospectus does not tell you what specific return you will earn, it does point out the fund's return potential, along with the associated risks that you will be assuming. The prospectus is mandatory reading by all mutual fund investors who wish to increase the probability of earning acceptable long-term investment returns.

THE MUTUAL FUND GAME: WHAT DOES IT COST TO PLAY?

Most individuals would not buy an automobile, a television or even a pair of shoes without first knowing the price. In fact, most individuals shop around and pride themselves on obtaining the best available price for many of the things they buy. However, when investing in mutual funds, many individuals pay no attention to the cost of investing. In fact, I have met few mutual fund investors who know what they pay to invest in mutual funds. To these individuals, I say: find out first what you will pay, and shop around to get the best price available.

The Costs of Mutual Fund Investing

Sales Charges. Mutual funds come in two varieties—those with sales charges and those without. Among funds with sales charges are front-end load funds that take sales fees right off the top. For example, if you invest $1,000 in an 8.5 percent front-end load fund, you pay $85 in commission and the balance, $915, is invested in fund shares. (Note that an 8.5 percent front-end load turns out to be 9.3 percent of the money actually invested in the fund.) Not all funds charge the maximum load allowable under the law (8.5 percent). Some bill themselves as "low-loads" and carry sales charges ranging from 2 percent to 4 percent.

Some funds have opted to forgo the front-end sales charge and take their fees off the back end instead. These are so-called "contingent deferred sales charge funds," since the back-end commission is reduced in relation to the length of time you retain your shares. For example, many of these funds levy a 5 percent charge if an investment is withdrawn within one year. The fee is reduced by one percentage point for each additional year the fund shares are held. Thus, the sales charge completely disappears if the investment is held five or more years.

Some mutual funds levy an ongoing sales charge rather than either front- or back-end loads. These charges, called 12b-1 charges, typically average about 0.5 percent but can range from 0.1 percent to 1.25 percent of the value of your investment annually. Note that while these percentages appear to be lower than those applied to either front- or back-end load funds, they are levied each year instead of only once.

Finally, some funds combine 12b-1 charges with back-end loads. (In fact, most of the back-end load funds come with 12b-1 charges attached.) Note that the longer you hold the shares of such funds, the lower the contingent deferred sales charges but the greater the total 12b-1 fees. Thus, for these funds, what you gain on the one hand you tend to lose on the other.

Management and Administrative Fees. While some investors pay a sales charge when they invest in mutual funds and some do not (those individuals who invest in no-load funds), all mutual fund investors must pay the annual fund management and administrative fees. Management fees are paid to the fund's investment advisor and generally range from 0.5 percent to 1.0 percent of the fund's average assets. Typically, the management fee percentage is reduced as the total assets of the fund increase.

In addition to management fees, fund shareholders must foot the bill for such administrative items as shareholder record keeping, auditing, legal services, shareholder reports, the annual meeting, custodial fees, etc. Management and administrative fees for a typical equity fund range from 0.3 percent to 5.0 percent and average about 1.3 percent of the fund's total assets. (The combined management and administrative expenses for the typical bond fund average about 0.8 percent of total assets.)

Transactions Costs. Finally, mutual fund investors also assume the transactions costs that occur when a portfolio manager adds or deletes securities from the fund's portfolio. Transactions costs include both brokerage commissions and the dealer's bid-ask spread. These charges average about 2 percent of the value of each transaction, or about 4 percent on a round-trip trade. These expenses, of course, are related to the fund's portfolio turnover rate. For example, if a portfolio manager were to sell all of the fund's holdings and replace them with other securities once each year, portfolio turnover would equal 100 percent.

Note that the reciprocal of the turnover ratio provides a good estimate of a fund's average holding period. For example, a turnover ratio of 50 percent implies that the fund holds its investments an average of two years while a 25 percent turnover ratio indicates a four-year average holding period.

How Can You Estimate the Cost?

The best way to estimate the cost of investing in a particular mutual fund is by examining historical costs. These can be obtained by scrutinizing the fund's prospectus, statement of additional information and most recent annual report. (You should examine all three documents before making any fund investment.)

First, look at the fund's summary of per share income and capital changes presented in its prospectus. There you will find the fund's historical ratio of expenses to average net assets. This ratio equals management fees and administrative expenses divided by average net assets. Since this ratio tends to decline as the fund's assets grow, sometimes you must forecast asset size to obtain a reliable estimate of next year's ratio. For example, suppose that a fund charges a management fee of 0.75 percent and had administrative expenses of $250,000 last year. Its average net assets last year were $50 million, and its expense ratio was 1.25 percent. However, suppose that the fund ended the year with $100 million in total assets, and you expect this figure to increase to $150 million by the end of the year. Thus, you expect net assets for the fund to average $125 million and expenses to amount to about $1.24 million ($300,000 estimate of administrative fees plus $937,500 management fees). An estimate of the total expense ratio for the year turns out to be 1.0 percent ($1.24 million divided by $125 million).

Transactions charges are the most difficult to assess. While mutual funds report the amount of brokerage expenses, such expenses are only a small portion of transactions costs. The bid-ask spread paid to the market-maker is the largest component. As this figure is not reported, it must be estimated. Since brokerage commissions and the dealer's bid-ask spread combined average about 4 percent on a round-trip trade, you can estimate total transactions costs by multiplying the fund's average turnover ratio by 4 percent.

Use the average of the fund's turnover ratios for the past three years. For example, suppose that a fund's portfolio turnover ratios for the last three years were 25, 17 and 21 percent. The average ratio is 21 percent. Multiplying this ratio by 4 percent gives an estimate of transactions costs of 0.8 percent. Of course, actual transactions costs are dependent upon *next* year's portfolio turnover ratio. However, since these ratios tend to be stable over time for many funds, a three-year average of historical turnover ratios generally provides an accurate estimate of next year's ratio.

Assessing the Total Cost of Fund Investing

Before you begin an analysis of the cost of mutual fund investing, you must determine the length of your intended holding period. Since some costs are levied only once while others are assessed each year, the total cost of investing will vary according to your holding period.

Table 11 is a simplified case study of fund expense analysis. Suppose that you plan to invest in a fund and hold it for three years. You have narrowed the alternatives to four funds. Your final selection will be the fund with the lowest cost.

Fund A has a deferred contingent sales charge that begins at 5 percent but will be trimmed to 3 percent if the shares are held for three years. In addition, the fund levies an annual 12b-1 fee of 0.5 percent. The management fee is 0.75 percent annually, and you estimate that administrative fees will amount to 0.3 percent per year. The fund turns over about 25 percent of its portfolio annually ($.25 \times .04 = .01 \times 3 = .03$, or 3 percent transactions costs).

Fund B carries an 8.5 percent front-end load but no 12b-1 or back-end sales fees. Management fees are 1 percent per year, and you estimate that administrative fees will be an additional 0.4 percent annually. The fund turns over about 50 percent of its portfolio each year.

Fund C is a low-load, with a 3 percent front-end load but no 12b-1 or back-end fees. The annual management fee is 0.75 percent, and administrative fees should average 0.2 percent per year. This fund is actively managed, and portfolio turnover has averaged 100 percent per year.

Fund D is a true no-load fund and has no sales charges of any kind. The annual management fee for the fund is 0.70 percent, and administrative expenses are estimated at 0.3 percent annually. Portfolio turnover is low and averages 20 percent per year.

Table 11 illustrates the total estimated costs for the intended three-year holding period and the average annual cost for each fund. The analysis does not take the time value of money into consideration and, thus, may not be completely accurate. While the time value of money adjustments could be made (for example, a 3 percent back-end fee paid three years from now has a present worth of approximately 2.3 percent when discounted at 10 percent), an unadjusted analysis is sufficient.

Note that 12b-1 fees, management fees and administrative expenses have been multiplied by three—the intended holding period. Note also that total and average annual costs can vary substantially. Finally, note that for some funds, the average annual cost can erode return by a significant amount. For example, the management of Fund B must over-

Table 11 Determining the Cost of Mutual Fund

	Fund A	Fund B	Fund C	Fund D
Sales Charges				
Front-end	0.00%	8.50%	3.00%	0.00%
Back-end	3.00	0.00	0.00	0.00
12b-1	1.50	0.00	0.00	0.00
Expenses Ratio				
Management Fee	2.25	3.00	2.25	2.10
Admin. Expense	0.90	1.20	0.60	0.90
Transactions Costs	3.00	6.00	12.00	2.40
Total Costs	10.65%	18.70%	17.85%	5.40%
Average Annual Cost*	3.55%	6.23%	5.95%	1.80%

*Estimated holding period three years.

come a hefty burden of 6.23 percent per year or 4.43 percent more than Fund D to produce the same return for the investor.

While some funds are better managed than others and, thus, provide greater investment returns to their shareholders, over an investment lifetime, it is frequently the cost of investing that makes the difference between investment success and investment failure.

WHAT IS YOUR RISK EXPOSURE?

Many individual investors define investment success as "beating the market," or, in other words, earning above-average returns. But many investors often forget that pursuing greater-than-average returns generally means assuming greater-than-average risk. Since investment risk is defined as variability of investment return, portfolios with above-average return potential are subject to above-average swings in value relative to the stock market as a whole. These portfolios far outpace the market when the market is rising but drop faster than the market when the market falls.

However, when stock prices are rising, investors tend to forget about the negative aspects of holding a high-risk portfolio because they are "beating the market." In fact, I have found that as long as stock prices continue to rise, investors tend to increase the risk of their portfolios in pursuit of greater and greater investment rewards. These investors are generally shaken by the size of their losses when the stock market takes a sudden dip.

Proper investment management requires that individuals continually monitor the riskiness of their investment portfolios. They must periodically ask themselves if the current level of portfolio risk is consistent with their ability to weather sudden investment storms. Although they are happy with wealth expansion in up markets, they must decide whether they can live with the contraction in wealth that will surely take place during down markets.

How Risky Are Your Mutual Fund Holdings?

For diversified portfolios, such as common stock mutual funds, beta provides a useful index of investment risk. Simply stated, beta measures portfolio risk in relation to the riskiness of the S&P 500 Stock Index (i.e., the market).

Figure 4 illustrates the trade-off between investment risk and investment return with what is known as the "capital market line." This upward sloping line represents the combinations of risk and return found in well-diversified portfolios of common stocks. The return potential of a diversified common stock portfolio can be obtained by applying the following mathematical statement of the capital market line.

$$\frac{\text{Portfolio}}{\text{Return}} = \frac{\text{Risk–Free}}{\text{Return}} + \text{Beta}\left(\frac{\text{market}}{\text{return}} - \frac{\text{risk–free}}{\text{return}}\right)$$

The risk-free rate of return (RF) is approximated by the yield on short-term treasury bills while the market return (RM) is usually taken as the total rate of return on the S&P 500 Stock Index. For example, if you expect the market to return 12 percent during the next 12 months, and the risk-free rate

Figure 4 Portfolio Risk and Return: The Capital Market Line

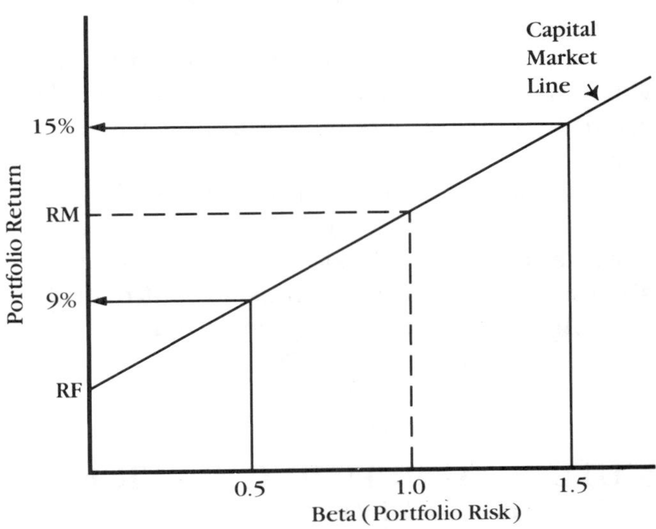

of return is 6 percent, then a portfolio whose beta is 0.5 can be expected to return 9 percent.

Portfolio Return = .06 + 0.5 (.12 – .06) = .09, or 9%

A portfolio with a beta of 1.5 would be expected to return 15 percent. These portfolios would be subject to similar declines in value if the market were to fall by 12 percent.

Although beta cannot predict the direction the stock market will take, it is an excellent predictor of the responsiveness of a portfolio's value, given changes in the stock market as a whole. For example, if the stock market were to decline by 50 percent over a prolonged period, a portfolio whose beta is 1.2 would be expected to decline in value by approximately 60 percent. Of course, if stock prices were to rise by 50 percent, the value of this portfolio would climb by 60 percent.

The purpose of this exercise is to assist investors in building investment portfolios that lie within their tolerance, or comfort zone. We have found that long-term-oriented investors earn higher returns than do those who dip in and out of the stock market over their investment lifetimes. While it is easy to maintain a long-term orientation as long as stock prices are rising, many investors abandon this strategy at the first sign of a market downturn. Usually, such panic action occurs because investors have assumed investment risk beyond their comfort zone. As a result, these investors are likely to sell out at or near market bottoms and rarely begin to participate in bull markets until much of the upward movement has already taken place. The result, generally, is suboptimal investment returns.

The moral of this tale should be clear. If you find that you are losing sleep because of worry about your investment portfolio, restructure your asset holdings so that overall portfolio risk is compatible with your sleeping point.

MUTUAL FUND TIMING SERVICES: CAN THEY DELIVER?

During the last three years, we have noticed a proliferation of the number of financial service companies offering their clients mutual fund timing services. These companies promise individual investors greater returns from their mutual fund portfolios by moving money back and forth between equity mutual funds and money market funds. The goal of such services is to get investors out of falling markets yet keep them fully invested during periods of rising prices.

All indications are that these companies are signing up clients in droves. Some firms claim to be adding more than $100 million per year to their management programs. Many of these companies use independent financial planners as agents and split the management fees with those who sign up clients. Management fees are based on the amount of money invested in the program and tend to average about 2 percent per year.

Are the Fees Worth the Results?

Most of the companies that have been in the mutual fund timing business for more than three years present fantastic claims of success. However, when one accounts for the fees being charged, one finds that while the timer may actually beat the market, the fund investor has little chance of reaping significant gains after payment of all management fees and the additional income taxes that frequently result from excessive trading.

Table 12 illustrates the total annual rates of return provided by Standard & Poor's 500 Stock Index and by treasury bills during 1971-90. A buy-and-hold approach to investing in the S&P unmanaged index over the period would have produced a compound annual return of 11.5 percent (i.e., $1,000 invested in the Index at the beginning of 1971 would have grown to $8,727 by the end of 1990, assuming the reinvestment of all cash dividends). A 20-year investment in treasury bills would have provided a 7.7 percent compound annual rate of return (i.e., a $1,000 investment in 1971 would have grown to $4,371 by the end of 1990). On the other hand, if an investor would have been able to time the market perfectly (that is, invest in stocks during those years when stock returns exceeded T-bill returns and invest in T-bills when their return exceeded the return from common

Table 12 Total Rates of Return 1971-1990

Years	S&P 500 Index	Treasury Bills
1971	14.3%	4.4%
1972	19.0	3.8
1973	–14.7	6.9
1974	–26.5	8.0
1975	37.2	5.8
1976	23.8	5.1
1977	–7.2	5.1
1978	6.6	7.2
1979	18.4	10.4
1980	32.4	11.2
1981	–4.9	14.7
1982	21.4	10.5
1983	22.5	8.8
1984	6.3	9.8
1985	32.2	7.7
1986	18.5	6.2
1987	5.2	5.5
1988	16.8	6.4
1989	31.5	8.4
1990	–3.2	7.8

stocks), an initial $1,000 investment would have grown to $23,144, and the investor would have earned a 17.3 percent compound annual rate of return. Thus, at least on the surface, mutual fund timing services have the potential to increase investment wealth by a significant amount.

However, before one jumps on the mutual fund timing bandwagon, here are a few statistics that should be considered. First, remember that the stock market return referred to above is that obtained by an unmanaged portfolio. Thus, brokerage commissions and portfolio management fees have not been included. Since these fees average more than 1 percent per year for most equity funds, a fund manager who is able to duplicate the market rate of return before these expenses would provide shareholders with an investment return that falls short of the market rate of return by approximately 1 percent per year.

Second, remember that mutual fund timing services add an additional 2 percent management fee annually. Thus, a fund manager must now outperform the market by 3 percent per year before expenses to provide fund shareholders with the market rate of return. Furthermore, most of the timing services that we have surveyed use full front-end load funds in their timing programs. (Most of the services indicated that front-end load funds were used because their sponsors were more amenable to working with them. However, we suspect that load funds are really used to provide the service and its agents with additional commission income.) Thus, in addition to the annual fund expenses and timing service fees, investors frequently pay an additional sales fee that can run as high as 8.5 percent of the initial investment.

Here's what happens to investment return when these fees are taken into account. An investor who has sold a mutual fund that possesses an 8.5 percent front-end load finds that for every $1,000 invested, only $915 finds its way into the fund. (The difference, $85, is paid to the various entities that have participated in selling the fund.) Thus, if the stock market return averages 11.5 percent a year over a 20-year period, the fund timing program must return 14.5 percent annually (before fund expenses, management fees and sales commissions) to provide an investor with a rate of return equivalent to that provided by the market. That is, the fund and the timing service must consistently beat the market rate of return by 40 percent annually just to provide a rate of return equivalent to that provided by the S&P 500 Index.

Remember also, mutual fund timing services are not infallible. Even the better ones can be invested in the wrong asset every once in a while. And these timing mistakes can reduce actual portfolio return by a considerable amount. For example, if a timing service had erred once during the 20-year period by keeping investors out of the stock market and in treasury bills during 1975 (when stocks returned 32.2 percent), the potential annual rate of return would have dropped from 17.3 percent to 15.6 percent before expenses and management fees. After the payment of fees totaling 3 percent per year, the investor's actual rate of return would have fallen to 12.6 percent. That is only 2 percent greater annually than the market rate of return. Finally, since tax payments have not been considered in this example, it is most likely that this one goof would have reduced investors' returns to approximately the market rate of return.

The Bottom Line

Remember that the stock market is a highly efficient mechanism. That means that investment returns tend to parallel the investment risks that are taken. The ability of anyone to beat the market by a significant amount without the assumption of greater-than-average investment risk is nearly impossible. Although pockets of market inefficiencies do exist, investors who exploit them rarely add more than 2 to 3 percent annually to their overall investment portfolio return. Thus, the payment of excessive fees to mutual fund timing services erodes nearly all of the potential benefit that might be obtained. In most cases, services that charge 2 percent or more annually are specifically designed to line the pockets of the promoters and not those of the mutual fund investor.

We are not suggesting that all fees charged by investment managers are unjustified. However, investors should carefully consider the cost of management advice as well as the potential benefit before they make a long-term commitment. If you believe that a mutual fund timing service is your cup of tea, we suggest that you avoid front-end load funds and invest in no-load funds and pay no more than 1 percent annually for mutual fund management advice.

ARE FOREIGN INVESTMENTS FOREIGN TO YOU?

Although equity investors around the world took it squarely on the chin during 1990, there are several reasons to invest internationally. First, investors who restrict their equity investments to U.S. stocks can miss out on explosive growth in other parts of the world. Although the United States experienced relatively strong economic growth during most of the 1980s, things were even better in Japan. It emerged from the decade as the dominant force in world trade and international banking. And Europe (especially unified Germany) could become the Japan of the 1990s. Although common stocks in the United States returned about 17 percent per year during the 1980s, an index of European, Australian and Far East stocks (the E.A.F.E. Index) grew by more than 22 percent annually during the last decade.

While the possibility of earning above-average returns may be reason enough to include international stocks in your equity portfolio, there is an even more compelling reason to globally diversify your equity portfolio. That reason is the relatively low correlation between the returns of the stocks and bonds of internationally domiciled companies and those of U.S.-based firms; that is, the returns of foreign stocks and bonds rarely move in lockstep with U.S. investment returns. Thus, losses in the value of U.S. stocks and bonds can be somewhat offset by gains in their foreign counterparts. In other words, globally diversified portfolios have lower variability than portfolios limited to a single country. In short, global diversification provides risk reduction without a sacrifice in investment return.

The relatively low correlation between returns of U.S. stocks and foreign stocks results from both the lead/lag relationships among world economies and fluctuating foreign exchange rates. Some academic studies indicate that the optimally balanced equity portfolio is one that contains 33 percent of assets allocated to foreign stocks.

International investing, while highly attractive, has long posed problems for individual investors. Information on foreign companies is difficult to obtain. Furthermore, because of varying business customs and accounting standards, foreign companies cannot be evaluated by the same methods used to evaluate the prospects and risks of U.S. companies. Finally, foreign stock investors are exposed to political and foreign exchange risks that are largely absent from U.S. stock portfolios.

However, during the last decade there has been an explosion in the number of mutual funds that invest internationally. These funds solve many of the problems faced by individuals when investing in foreign stocks. Stock valuation and selection is left to professional management. Record keeping is simplified as dividend and interest payments are collected, converted to U.S. dollars and paid to shareholders in a single payment. Finally, mutual funds are highly diversified and thereby reduce some of the risks of investing internationally.

Strictly speaking, international funds invest exclusively in foreign securities. However, a number of these funds may also invest in U.S. securities under some circumstances. Global funds invest in both U.S. and foreign securities. International funds may invest in a single country or region (e.g., Europe, the Pacific Basin, etc.), or they may hold globally diversified portfolios. Some funds specialize in investing in a single country. While single-country funds can deliver exceptional returns at times, their share prices tend to be much more volatile than geographically diversified funds.

Although this segment of the mutual funds industry is still in its infancy, one can find more than 50 funds that invest internationally. Today one can find international funds that invest in money market instruments (e.g., Fidelity Spartan and Dreyfus World Wide); bonds (e.g., Scudder International Bond Fund, T. Rowe Price International Bond Fund); small firm stocks (Dimensional Fund Advisors Small Cap Japan Fund); and even selected industries (G.T. Global Health Fund). With investor interest in investing overseas continuing to grow, we expect to see the organization of numerous international funds in the next few years. These new funds will greatly increase return potential for individual investors who opt to globally diversify their stock and bond portfolios.

Fund Alternatives for Income-Oriented Investors

If your CD is due to mature soon, my guess is that you're about to be shocked by the yields that are available in the bond market these days. Gone are the heady days when high-quality debt instruments were sporting double-digit yields. The fact is, double-digit yields prevailed for so long that most income-oriented investors forgot their history lesson and have become spoiled by the handsome yields that were being offered during most of the past decade.

Table 13 lists the average returns and average yields for long-term government bonds during each of the past five decades. As can be seen, the decade of the 1980s was the only ten-year span that provided average double-digit bond yields and total returns. In fact, for most of the past half-century, bond yields were on the rise. As a result, holders of long-term bonds fared very poorly (except for the decade of the 1980s). On average, the total annual return for long-term government bonds during the past half-century stands at a paltry 4.5 percent. And corporate bond investors fared only slightly better with a 4.9 percent average annual return. Note also, the total average returns for long-term government bonds failed to keep pace with the rate of inflation during the 1940s, 1950s, 1960s and 1970s.

So what's a fixed-income investor to do? There are three alternatives: You can live with the yields that are available; you can stretch both the maturities of your portfolios and lower the quality of your investments; or you can combine equities with bonds in an attempt to boost your total return.

Most people who are living on a fixed income can ill afford to pare their budgets any further. Thus, an investor with $250,000 invested in a CD yielding 10 percent and receiving $25,000 annually will be hard pressed if that investment is rolled over into another CD yielding 7 percent and paying $17,500 annually. Furthermore, most fixed-income investors cannot afford to assume the risk that accompanies double-digit bond yields these days. Thus, we suggest that income-oriented investors combine equity fund investments with bond fund and/or money fund investments to boost total return.

Table 13 Long-Term Government Bond Yields and Total Returns

Decade	Annual Return	Average Yield	Inflation
1940s	3.2%	2.3%	5.4%
1950s	–0.1	3.4	2.2
1960s	1.4	5.4	2.5
1970s	5.5	7.3	7.4
1980s	12.6	10.6	5.1

While the prices of equity funds are subject to the whims of the marketplace, funds that invest in stocks with higher than average dividend yields possess about 60 percent of the risk present in the typical growth fund. Furthermore, over the long run, companies that pay cash dividends tend to share their growth with investors by boosting their cash dividend. Thus, unlike a long-term bond that pays a fixed amount annually, a diversified portfolio of dividend-paying stocks provides a significant inflation hedge because of increased annual payouts. For example, if a stock has a 6 percent dividend yield that is increased by 5 percent annually, the payout doubles after 14 years, and based on the initial purchase price, so does the yield. As a bonus, the stock price usually rises along with the dividend. Thus, investors not only receive more annual income, the value of their principal expands along with consumer prices.

Here's one suggestion: Create a portfolio consisting of 50 percent allocated to government or investment-grade bond funds and 50 percent allocated to yield-oriented equity funds. (These include balanced funds, value funds, growth and income funds, utility funds and convertible bond funds.) That portfolio can be expected to provide a long-term total annual return of about 10 percent.

Table 14 lists a number of equity funds that contain higher-than-average dividend yields. While the returns of these funds have been nothing to write home about in recent years, they employ very conservative investment strategies and thus are low-risk equity funds. Most have betas less than half that of the typical equity fund.

Table 14 Equity Funds that Contain Higher-than-Average Dividend Yields

Fund Name	Policy
Growth & Income	
Bartlett Basic Value	Value Stocks
Dodge & Cox Balanced	Balanced
Dodge & Cox Stock	Value Stocks
Dreyfus Fund	Flexible
Evergreen Total Return	Balanced
Fidelity Balanced	Balanced
Fidelity Equity Income	Divid. Stocks
Fidelity Puritan	Balanced
Financial Industrial Income	Divid. Stocks
Founders Equity Income	Divid. Stocks
Lindner Dividend	Balanced
Lindner Fund	Divid. Stocks
Price Equity Income	Divid. Stocks
Price Growth & Income	Flexible
SAFECO Income	Balanced
Scudder Growth & Income	Divid. Stocks
Stratton Monthly Div. Shares	Flexible
Strong Total Return	Flexible
Value Line Income	Balanced
Vanguard Star	Flexible
Vanguard Wellesley Income	Balanced
Vanguard Wellington	Divid. Stocks
Sector Funds	
Financial Strategic Utilities	Utilities
Flag Telephone Income	Telephone
Franklin Utilities	Utilities
Convertible Bonds	
Fidelity Convertible Sec.	Conv. Bonds
Value Line Convertible	Conv. Bonds
Vanguard Convertible	Conv. Bonds

Granddaddy Funds

Excluding money market funds, more than 2,000 mutual funds have appeared on the scene during the last dozen years. Not only have the number of funds expanded geometrically, so has their variety. In addition to "plain vanilla" funds (diversified growth, growth and income and aggressive growth funds), you can invest in international equity funds (global, regional or country specific), international bond funds, sector funds, small cap funds, leveraged funds, domestic bond funds of all types, asset allocation funds, etc.

If you discovered mutual funds only recently, you may be surprised to find that mutual funds have been around for a long time (see Table 15). In fact, we counted more than 60 funds whose histories stretch back more than 50 years. A dozen funds that were initiated before the Great Crash of 1929 still are around. And one fund, the Colonial Fund, has been around since 1904. Most of these graybeards offer staid investment strategies. A large number are balanced funds (i.e., invest in a fixed ratio of stocks and bonds), a few are bond funds and the balance invest in dividend-paying common stocks (equity income funds) or seek growth of capital by pursuing "plain vanilla" asset selection strategies. Most of these funds are sold with a sales load of some kind. That's because that was the way funds were sold a half-century ago.

Mix, Don't Match

Diversification is a good thing and should be practiced by all investors. Diversification reduces risk. And believe it or not, diversification does not lower long-run rates of return. Investors who hold a portfolio of 30 or 40 stocks are exposed to about one-third the variability of return as investors who hold three or four stocks. The reason for the reduced volatility that accompanies diversification is that stocks increasing in price tend to offset the effects of those decreasing in price.

The mutual fund industry has thrived on the benefits of diversification. During the past decade, millions of investors discovered the risk-reduction benefits of mutual funds and poured billions of dollars into stock and bond funds. And during the past ten years, the mutual fund industry has accommodated eager investors by bringing to market mutual funds with nearly every investment strategy imaginable.

The plethora of new funds accompanied by intensive hype has given rise to a new kind of mutual fund investor—the mutual fund investment "junkie." This investor is addicted to mutual funds. He or she buys funds listed in the *Forbes* "Honor Roll," funds touted in *Money Magazine*, those that score high in recent performance ratings published by *Barron's* and other financial newspapers, and he or she purchases funds recommended in mutual fund newsletters. The result is that mutual fund junkies end up owning dozens of funds. Generally, little regard is given to the compatibility of a particular fund with others already held. And this can cause serious problems for these investors.

One might reason: "If some diversification is good, a lot of diversification must be better." To some extent this statement has a

Table 15 Granddaddy Funds

Fund Name	Year Began	Policy
Alliance Balanced Shares	1932	Balanced
Alliance Fund	1938	Common Stock
Alliance Growth & Inc.	1932	Common Stock
American Balanced	1932	Balanced
American Fund. Inv.	1932	Common Stock
American Invest. Co. Amer.	1933	Common Stock
Century Shares Trust	1928	Specialized
Colonial	1904	Common Stock
Composite Bond & Stock	1939	Balanced
Delaware Fund	1938	Common Stock
Dodge & Cox Balanced	1931	Balanced
Eaton Vance Investors	1932	Flexible
Federated Stock & Bond	1934	Balanced
Financial Industrial	1935	Common Stock
Founders Blue Chip	1938	Common Stock
Franklin Equity	1933	Common Stock
IDS Mutual	1940	Balanced
Mass. Investors Growth	1932	Common Stock
Mass. Investors Trust	1924	Common Stock
National Bond	1940	Bond
Nationwide	1933	Flexible
Nicholas Income	1924	Flexible
Pilgrim High Yield	1938	Bond
Pioneer Fund	1928	Common Stock
Putnam, George, Fund	1937	Balanced
Putnam Investors	1925	Common Stock
SAFECO Equity	1932	Common Stock
Scudder Growth & Income	1929	Common Stock
Scudder Income	1928	Bond
Selected Amer. Shares	1933	Common Stock
Seligman Common Stock	1929	Common Stock
Seligman Growth	1937	Common Stock
Sentinel Balanced	1938	Balanced
Sentinel Common Stock	1933	Common Stock
Sovereign Investors	1936	Common Stock
USF&G Axe-Houghton Fund B	1938	Balanced
USF&G Axe-Houghton Growth	1932	Common Stock
USF&G Axe-Houghton Income	1938	Flexible
Vanguard Wellington	1929	Balanced

ring of truth. There are limits, however, to the benefits of diversification. An investor who holds 1,000 stocks is exposed to about the same degree of risk as one who holds 200 stocks. Because the typical equity fund holds about 100 stocks, an investor who holds ten funds drawn from a single investment category (e.g., growth, aggressive growth, etc.) is exposed to about the same degree of risk as an investor who holds one or two funds. Furthermore, funds with similar investment objectives tend to hold similar common stocks. And owning shares of Philip Morris in a half-dozen portfolios can result in the assumption of redundant transactions costs that reduce overall investment return.

For example, suppose you own two funds that invest in large company, blue chip stocks. Suppose that both funds hold Philip Morris common stock. One fund manager decides to add another 100,000 shares, while the other decides to reduce his investment by 100,000 shares. As a result, *your* portfolio is unchanged, even though as a fund shareholder you assumed the costs of both trades. Multiply this example by dozens of stocks, and redundant transactions costs begin to add up.

We assembled a random sample of 16 growth funds that invest in large firm, blue chip stocks and examined the 25 largest holdings listed in each fund's most recent annual or semiannual shareholder's report. Of the 400 top investments, 112 appeared in more than one fund's portfolio. Fifteen stocks appeared in four or more fund portfolios. The most popular holding, Philip Morris, appeared in 10 of the 16 portfolios.

Remember that these results were obtained by focusing on each fund's largest investments that accounted for about one-half of each fund's total assets. On average, each of these funds held about 100 stocks. Thus, had we used the entire list of each fund's holdings, the number of redundant stocks would have expanded greatly.

While it is true that most mutual funds pay only a few cents a share in brokerage commissions to trade large blocks of stocks, payment of a market-maker's bid-ask spread and the inducement for him or her to accommodate a large block trade can add several hundred basis points to a round-trip trade. For example, the total cost of a round-trip trade for a $250,000 block of stock averages about 3 percent. Given that blue chip stocks have returned an average of about 12 percent annually during the past six decades, redundant investments could clip long-run investment return by 1 or 2 percent annually. While this appears to be a trivial amount, I assure you it is not. For example, the difference between a $10,000 investment that earns 11 percent and one that earns 12 percent over a 20-year period amounts to slightly more than $15,800!

This aside, we believe that investors should invest in more than one mutual fund. However, we recommend that investors make diverse selections to minimize portfolio duplication and the excess costs that tend to result. The simplest way to avoid duplication is to invest in different categories of funds. For example, an aggressive growth fund that focuses on rapidly growing companies with equity capitalizations below $300 million will have virtually no investments in common with a growth fund that invests in large cap, blue chip stocks.

A second way to avoid duplication is to invest in funds drawn from the same category (aggressive growth, growth, etc.) but that employ different management styles. For example, a fund whose management seeks high growth companies that possess earnings momentum will most likely have very few investments in common with a fund whose management seeks "value" investments among industries and companies that are "out of favor." The former portfolio will most likely consist of high price-earnings ratio stocks, while the latter will hold stocks with low price-earnings ratios, or even companies with no earnings at all (i.e., potential turnaround situations).

Diversification across investment styles makes good investment sense. Not only will you avoid portfolio duplication, investment styles come in and go out of vogue during various phases of the market cycle. By investing in funds with different styles of management, you avoid the near-impossible task of determining which style is the next to become "hot." Furthermore, employing this diversification strategy increases the odds that your long-run returns will be commensurate with the risks you have assumed.

Are Index Funds Your Cup of Tea?

Indexing, once considered a mere hedging device, has come into its own. Increasingly, investors are turning away from actively managed portfolios for the assurance of market-level returns offered by index funds. Of the pension funds surveyed by *Institutional Investor* in 1991, nearly 40 percent currently utilize a passive investment strategy for more than 25 percent of their equity and fixed-income assets. In turn, the number of index mutual funds has grown to more than 20 since 1974, when the first index vehicle made its debut. Simultaneously, index fund assets have swelled to approximately $5 billion. Whereas the original index funds tracked the S&P 500, the universe of index funds has since expanded to encompass an array of market segments, including the Wilshire 4500, the Russell 2000, the Morgan Stanley Europe/Pacific Index and the Salomon Brothers Broad Investment-Grade Bond Index.

Why has indexing—the investment approach that seeks to parallel the investment returns of a particular stock or bond market segment (or index)—gained such popularity? The answer has its roots in both theory and practice. The concept of indexing was first pioneered in the mid-1970s as a logical response to the Efficient Market Theory (EMH), which proposed that the stock and bond markets work with such efficiency that it is virtually impossible to beat the broad averages. If you can't beat the market, then buy it, say proponents of EMH. Forget about picking stocks.

Even for those who question the validity of EMH, the case for indexing is difficult to refute. Over long periods of time, the broad stock market averages have outperformed the majority of actively managed portfolios. Of the nearly 500 stock mutual funds in existence, less than 10 percent beat the unmanaged S&P 500 Index over the past five years, after adjusting for sales charges. As the task of beating the market becomes increasingly difficult, if not impossible for active portfolio managers, more and more investors find themselves attracted to the benefits of indexing.

To be sure, the benefits of indexing are irrefutable. First and foremost, an index portfolio offers highly predictable results in line with its benchmark in every year. While there's no guarantee of superior results, index fund shareholders can feel assured that their fund will not seriously underperform the averages. Moreover, an index—or passive—strategy involves substantially lower costs than active portfolio management. Low portfolio turnover keeps transactions costs minimal, while low trading and minimal research needs often allow fund sponsors to waive all or a portion of the management fee. The benefits of low transactions costs are particularly significant in the small company sector, where trading costs are very high.

Of course, passive investment strategies also have some drawbacks. For starters, the market doesn't always rise. As Vanguard carefully notes in its pamphlet, "Some Plain Talk about Indexing," index funds stay 100 percent invested at all times, whereas actively managed portfolios often hold at least some cash. In the prolonged bull market of recent years, index funds' fully invested stance has worked to their advantage, while cash reserves slowed the returns of many actively managed portfolios. But just as index funds can be expected to closely track the market during rallies, so, too, will they fully participate in market declines.

Of course, not all index funds are alike. Substantial differences exist, even among funds that mirror the same index. Such funds can vary with respect to the manner in which they construct their portfolios. Are they pure- or quasi-index vehicles? A pure-index vehicle attempts to exactly replicate the performance characteristics of its benchmark. It invests in every stock in its respective index, weighting each one in accordance with its market capitalization. In contrast, a quasi-index vehicle strives to achieve results relatively in line with its benchmark by investing in a representative sample of the index's stocks. Still, other funds, often identifiable by the "plus" in their name, attempt to enhance the returns available from a passively constructed portfolio by using derivative instruments (i.e., stock index futures and options). Despite their name, such funds generally subtract value, due to both the high costs associated with options strategies and the impact of derivative instruments on a fund's market exposure.

Both the impact of costs on a fund's ability to produce returns in line with its benchmark index and the narrow range of returns available from different index funds with the same objective make the degree to which a fund succeeds in minimizing transactions and operating costs critical. All else being equal, the lower a fund's costs, the better its chances of meeting its objective. As mentioned previously, one of the key advantages of indexing is reduced costs. An index fund with high expenses and/or sales charges is a contradition in terms. Investors who opt for the index route are advised to limit their selections to funds with relatively low expense ratios (see Table 16).

Table 16 Funds with Relatively Low Expense Ratios

Fund Name	Index	Year Started
Benham Gold	North Amer. Gold Equities Index	1988
Colonial Intl. Equities	EAFE	1986
Colonial Small Stock	Smallest 20% NYSE	1986
Colonial U.S. Equities	S&P 500	1986
Dreyfus People's Index	S&P 500	1990
Fidelity Spartan Market Index	S&P 500	1988
Gateway Index	S&P 500	1977
Portico Equity Index	S&P 500	1990
Rushmore OTC Index Plus	S&P 500	1985
Rushmore Stock	NASDAQ 100	1985
Vanguard Bond Market	Salomon Bros. Inv. Gr.	1986
Vanguard Index Trust: Extended	Wilshire 4500	1987
Vanguard Index Trust: 500	S&P 500	1976
Vanguard Int'l. Index: Europe	Morgan Stanley Europe	1990
Vanguard Int'l. Index: Pacific	Morgan Stanley Pacific	1990

BUYING ANNUITIES THROUGH MUTUAL FUND FIRMS

In a pitched battle to compete with other financial services enterprises, mutual fund companies are entering new fields of play. Now fund corporations are offering precious metals, coins, zero-coupon bonds, treasury bonds, a variety of insurance products and have even gone one step further—into the world of retirement vehicles such as annuities.

According to the Investment Company Institute, there are more than 300 annuity products being marketed by its members, which include everything from main-line insurance companies to the no-load products offered by mutual fund families. Once the exclusive territory of insurance firms, the annuity is being marketed as never before by fund groups such as Benham Capital Management, Colonial, Fidelity, Keystone, Massachusetts Financial, Putnam and USAA. Of course, you can also buy an annuity from a full-service stock broker. But the Merrill Lynches, Shearsons, Dean Witters and IDSs of this world will charge you more for the privilege of buying from them.

You can also shop the main-line insurance companies, which coincidentally also offer mutual funds, but here again you'll be financing the agent's new cabin cruiser. It should be noted, however, that in teaming with mutual fund companies, many insurance companies, as "underwriters" of the annuities, are offering low-cost packages.

If you know what type of annuity you want and don't want a salesperson calling you, we recommend that you take the no-load route through mutual fund groups. You'll save on fees and get only the service you request. In the case of the larger groups, however, expect follow-up phone calls.

By offering annuities, fund companies have taken a quantum leap. In a world where Individual Retirement Accounts are not tax deductible for all of their customers, Fidelity and other companies have begun to offer annuities that are pegged to mutual funds they already manage. That way, they're providing a more complete service in managing your money.

How Annuities Work

As far as vehicles go, annuities are not very exciting. You can invest a lump sum in them or varying amounts during a set period. Once you reach age 59 1/2, you can begin to withdraw the funds, or annuitize, which means you receive a fixed payment each month for a given number of years. Although annuity contributions are not tax-deductible, whatever you invest will accumulate tax-deferred until you withdraw the money, at which time it will be taxed at your marginal rate. You can, of course, take the money out sooner, but, like an IRA, you'll pay a 10 percent penalty and whatever redemption fees the issuer imposes. Many annuity issuers even allow you to withdraw less than 10 percent of your funds (per year) without nicking you for a surrender charge.

The surrender charges are designed to keep your funds in their coffers for as long as possible. The charges are based on a sliding scale that ranges from 7 to 4 percent for the first year and declines to zero by the end of a four-to-seven-year period. Or, the longer you keep your money in an annuity, the lower the surrender charge.

As long-term "accumulators" of wealth, annuities are fairly simple. If you don't need your money until a certain time after age 59 1/2, the tax-deferred compounding can work wonders. As an insurance product, annuities also pay a "death benefit" to your survivors if you have a "joint and survivor" annuity or related forms. But how much your money grows depends upon what type of annuity you buy.

Fixed-Rate Annuities. There are basically two types of annuities—fixed and variable. As you can imagine, the fixed-rate version offers an initial rate tied to some bond portfolio that is adjusted every year or so. It's a common practice for companies to entice buyers with a high opening rate and then drop the rate drastically once your money is locked in. In this regard, you should ask about the issuer's "guarantee" period. It's usually one year. The best protection against a company doing a classic "bait-and-switch" rate routine is to find a company that regularly pays competitive rates on "old" and "new" money.

Fixed annuity issuers also give you a "bailout" rate, which is an escape clause of sorts. If the issuer's bond portfolio average yield drops below the bailout rate, you can exit the annuity without being charged a surrender fee.

Variable-Rate Annuities. A variable annuity is a much more fickle beast. It's pegged to any number of mutual fund portfolios. There's no guaranteed rate because you're investing in either the stock or bond market through a portfolio manager. Naturally, you should find the managers with the best records and ask yourself how much risk you want to take.

With variables, the choice of where to put your money involves some homework. First, you'll have a choice between a fixed-income fund and an equity fund. However, long term, stocks outperform bonds by a wide margin. And when you compound dividends and capital gains tax-deferred over 20 to 30 years, you could be building a sizable nest egg. Consider $10,000 invested over 20 years and returning 10 percent a year. In a taxable account, that $10,000 would be worth about $45,000 after two decades. In an annuity, it would be worth roughly $65,000.

Another consideration in choosing your variable investment is how well the fund has performed. You can check that fairly easily by asking for five-to-ten-year returns on the fund. You may not even want to get into the fund if it has been a lackluster performer. In our research, we've found that you'll have a narrow selection of equity funds from which to choose.

When choosing a fund, keep in mind that your money won't be pooled in the same kitty as the fund of the same name. That's because by law all annuity contributions must be segregated from funds that are not tax-deferred.

In most cases, however, your funds are managed by the same people that manage the "regular" funds, so don't feel slighted.

How To Buy a Fixed Annuity

If you're ultra-conservative, we suggest you stick with a fixed-rate annuity. One of the better products in that area is USAA's Single Premium Deferred Annuity (1-800-531-8000). The company sets rates once a year, in January, based on the yield of its bond portfolio, which is standard in the industry. The elegance of USAA's annuity is that it's a no-load product without yearly administrative charges. The surrender charges are also modest: $25 and 4 percent of assets the first year and only $25 by the end of the third year. The minimum opening amount is $10,000.

How To Buy a Variable Annuity

Since a variable annuity requires some monitoring, you should also check out related services. The larger fund groups give you free switching privileges among funds as long as you don't withdraw the money, which would entail the payment of taxes and redemption fees. In other words, these annuities are self-directed.

The fact that you're entrusting your money to a manager for a long period of time doesn't mean you can leave your money unwatched until your retirement. Since you can place your funds in portfolios ranging from junk bonds to stocks, you need to select the fund first.

The Fidelity Retirement Reserves program, for example, gives you a choice of five different Fidelity funds. For safety, you can choose the money market portfolio. Income and modest growth seekers may feel comfortable with high-income or equity-income portfolios. Pure growth plays are available through the Overseas and Growth funds. As in selecting any mutual fund, you should match the risk you want to take with your investment objective. The further you are from retirement, the more you can opt for a growth portfolio. The reverse is true for those nearing retirement.

Like the other fund groups we've mentioned, Fidelity imposes a surrender charge of 5 percent the first year, sliding down to zero after five years. Additionally, Fidelity charges a fixed 1 percent per year for "administrative and risk [insurance] charges" and 0.50 to 0.82 percent for management fees.

In contrast, the Benham group charges up to 0.75 percent for management and 1.25 percent for administrative and risk charges. These products are underwritten through First Variable Life/Monarch Capital Group.

To compare Fidelity and Benham with a main-line insurer such as Kemper, consider that with Kemper you'll be paying 1.3 percent for administrative and risk charges, 0.5 percent for management fees *and* a $25 annual fee for "record keeping." This higher fee structure is typical of the full-service insurers. That's why we heartily recommend the mutual fund groups.

Annuity Pitfalls

When buying an annuity, take any "illustrations" of how much your money will be worth in 20 years with a grain of salt. Remember, these are hypothetical examples.

Although insurance companies rarely go out of business, check the underwriting company's "Best" rating, which it should provide. A rating of "A+" means that you're dealing with a quality company. Keep in mind, though, that insurers are not covered by any highly regulated federal insurance fund, although they will preach absolute preservation of principal for the fixed products. Annuity issuers do go bankrupt. Witness the case of Baldwin-United a few years ago.

Overall, though, annuities are good potential growth vehicles if you can afford to be less than liquid for a few decades. If bought through mutual fund companies, they offer relatively decent management with low front-end costs.

TAX-EXEMPT MONEY FUNDS—NOT A TAX-FREE BANK ACCOUNT

The recent volatility in the market has frightened many investors into money market funds. Traditionally, investors have viewed money market funds as a safe harbor when the stock and bond markets are choppy, and the current market environment would certainly qualify as such. But in their haste to find a safe haven for their money and to "beat" Uncle Sam out of a few tax dollars, many investors leap into tax-exempt money funds without looking. Despite what some investors may believe, a tax-exempt money fund is not a bank account, yielding tax-free interest. Understanding the characteristics of these funds is necessary before investment.

The tax-exempt money fund is a relatively new player on the financial scene, dating back a decade. However, these funds have shown good growth. The funds invest in short-term, municipal securities, the interest from which is exempt from federal income taxes. As the Tax Reform Act of 1986 eliminated many tax shelters, municipal securities are now among the last tax havens left for investors.

Compare Tax-Free and Taxable Yields

However, the attractiveness of these funds is largely contingent on the particular inves-tor's tax bracket. Investors who pay taxes in the lower tax brackets may be better off investing in a taxable fund and paying the related taxes than investing in a tax-exempt fund. Because interest on a municipal security is exempt from federal income taxes, a municipal security will offer a lower yield than a comparable taxable security. For example, a municipal security might offer a 6.5 percent yield while a taxable security might offer a 10 percent yield. For an investor in the 35 percent tax bracket, both instruments offer an equal after-tax return (i.e., after paying taxes, the 10 percent yield is reduced to 6.5 percent). However, an investor in the 15 percent tax bracket would receive 8.5 percent after taxes if he or she invested in the taxable security—a significant increase over the return offered by the municipal security. Table 17 gives the yield required from a tax-exempt fund to equal the yield from a taxable fund for investors in three different tax brackets.

Another factor that investors may overlook is that the yield quoted by a tax-exempt money fund is based on the fund's past performance and is not indicative of future results. When a bank quotes a particular interest rate for a certificate of deposit, that rate is in effect for the life of the instrument (or in the case of a savings account, for as long as the investor maintains money in the account). However, the yield on a money market fund fluctuates with changes in market interest rates, and investors are not guaranteed a particular yield.

In addition, unlike funds invested in a bank account, funds invested in a money market account are not insured against loss. The government is required to reimburse the depositors of failed federally insured savings and loans and banks up to a maximum of $100,000 per account. Many tax-exempt money market funds try to mitigate the potential problem of loss by investing in high-quality municipal securities. However, as past investors in the securities of Washington Public Power Supply System and the cities of New York and Cleveland can well attest, the risk of default is very real.

Risks of "Creative" Financing

Adding to this risk of default are the "creative" financing instruments being used by municipalities. Historically, many municipalities relied on long-term, fixed-rate instruments such as 30-year bonds to meet their financing needs. Given that many of a municipality's investments were of a long-term nature (i.e., bridges, schools, hospitals), long-term, fixed-rate instruments were attractive financing vehicles. Instruments such as tax, revenue and bond anticipation notes

Table 17 Yields Required from a Tax-Exempt Fund to Equal Taxable Yields

Tax Bracket	Taxable Yield 4%	6%	8%	10%
	Equivalent Tax-Exempt Yield			
15%	3.4%	5.1%	6.8%	8.5%
28	2.9	4.3	5.8	7.2
33	2.7	4.0	5.4	6.7

were largely used to generate temporary financing for municipalities. For example, if a city knew that it would receive a large inflow of cash in April from the receipt of property taxes, it might sell some tax anticipation notes in February to help it through the "lean" months until April tax revenues were received. Once the city received the April revenues, it would pay off the loan.

Yet, increasingly, municipalities are using so-called "short-term" instruments, such as variable-rate demand issues, that in reality may have maturities up to 30 years. The interest rate on a variable-rate demand issue is typically adjusted daily or weekly, and the holder of the security has the option to "put" (resell) the security back to the issuer at a predetermined price. For example, should the stock market soar and many investors switch out of money market funds into stocks, a fund manager may need to "put" the bond back to the issuer to generate cash to meet redemptions. The risk is that the issuer of the bond may have already spent the money and would not be able to return the security owner's investment. To avoid this problem, a municipality will typically arrange for a line of credit with a bank. However, should the bank be unable to honor its line of credit, the tax-exempt fund could incur a loss.

The variable-rate feature is another potential problem with these bonds. While this feature protects investors against a loss in the value of their principal when interest rates rise (the interest rate on the bond is adjusted upward to reflect the now higher market interest rate), the increasing interest expense could pose a heavy burden on the issuer. The municipality could potentially run into trouble meeting interest payments on the bonds and paying off the loan.

The risk of default also brings up the question of what assurances support the bonds in a tax-exempt money fund portfolio. For example, a general obligation municipal bond is backed by the full faith and credit of the municipality and is supported by the issuer's general taxing power. However, a revenue bond is supported by the revenues generated by a particular project such as a toll bridge, airport or hospital. An investor could be in for an unpleasant surprise should the revenues from the project be unable to support the interest payments on the bonds.

Changes in the tax law also have an effect on the performance of tax-exempt money funds. A future decline in the tax rate would negatively affect investors in these funds, as the value of their investment would decline. Given the whims of Congress and the controversy surrounding proposed changes in the tax law, future changes in tax rates are not unlikely.

Tax-exempt money funds offer attractive features such as safety from volatile markets and tax-free income. However, like any investment, an investor should not jump into such funds blindly. There are risks. The better an investor understands such risks, the greater are his or her chances of success with the investment.

LIFETIME PORTFOLIO MANAGEMENT: A PRIMER

History indicates that, over the long run, aggressive growth equity funds produce the highest total returns. However, these funds are highly volatile and they produce very little current income. Thus, they may not be well suited for all investors. However, for younger investors who are setting aside dollars for their retirement, aggressive growth mutual funds are ideal investment vehicles since investors with long planning horizons can tolerate a high degree of short-term price volatility.

When investing for retirement that will take place several years in the future, your investment horizon should be long term. Thus, week-to-week, month-to-month or even year-to-year variation in portfolio value can be ignored. In fact, individuals who invest equal amounts of money regularly should welcome a high degree of portfolio volatility because their regular investments will buy a larger number of fund shares when share prices decline. Furthermore, since current dividend and interest income are subject to taxation when distributed, wealth-accumulating investors' needs are better served by mutual funds that pay little or no current income. Thus, the full measure of return is left to compound over future years.

It is also no secret that bond funds provide the highest current income. In addition, these funds generally hold a large number of different issues and thus they protect investors from the default risk that they would face by holding a handful of bonds. Since retired investors generally expect their investment portfolios to provide income, bond funds are highly touted to retirees by financial planners and other security salespeople.

If investment life were that simple, wealth-accumulating investors could merely invest in a few aggressive growth mutual funds and then exchange these funds for one or more bond funds when they retire. However, life is anything but simple. And sadly to say, neither is lifetime portfolio management.

Accumulating Wealth for Retirement

Investors with more than a five-year planning horizon should adopt a highly aggressive investment posture. The goal of such investors should be to maximize investment return rather than minimize investment risk. Of course, risk management is important. Wealth- accumulating investors should avoid taking unnecessary risks by holding diversified portfolios and making regular cash contributions to their retirement programs. While all stocks fall during a bear market, a highly diversified portfolio of common stocks will eventually head for higher ground. And that statement cannot be made about a portfolio containing one or two stocks. Thus, by investing in a handful of growth and aggressive growth mutual funds, investors ensure against having temporary losses turn into permanent ones. Furthermore, by investing equal dollar amounts at regular intervals, wealth-accumulating investors benefit from dollar cost averaging. When stock prices are inordinately low, these investors accumulate more fund shares than when stock prices are inflated. Thus, when stock prices ultimately head higher, these investors magnify their investment returns. Finally, since retirement contributions will not be needed until the distant future, there is little need to hold cash reserves.

Keeping these points in mind, here is a simplified model portfolio for wealth-accumulating investors:

Aggressive Growth Funds	35%
Growth Funds	35
International Equity Funds	30

Some diversification across types of capital appreciation funds is recommended because return relationships can be unstable during the short run. For example, during the past ten years, growth funds, on average, have provided greater returns than aggressive growth funds, while aggressive growth funds provided higher returns over the last 15 to 20 years. International equity funds are suggested because of their relatively low correlation of returns with funds that invest solely in U.S. stocks. By combining international equities with domestic equities, portfolio risk can be reduced without sacrificing investment return. Furthermore, during periods marked by a weak dollar, these funds can produce handsome returns. For example, during the last ten years, international equity funds returned an average of 17 percent compounded annually, or over 2.5 percent per year return more than any other group of equity funds. Over the long run, this aggressive growth portfolio can be expected to return an average of between 11 and 14 percent annually.

It is no secret that investors who are retired generally require a balance between portfolio return and risk. First, since retirees are usually not contributing to their investment portfolios, losses cannot be tempered by dollar cost averaging. Instead of adding to their investment portfolios, most retirees are making regular withdrawals. Second, since these investors depend on income from their investments to support current consumption, predictable income streams are preferred. Finally, because of periodic withdrawals, retirees run the risk of having to sell more fund shares when prices are depressed to meet their required monthly cash flow. The result is exactly opposite that of dollar cost averaging (i.e., they gain less on market rebounds since they were required to effect inordinately large security sales when prices are depressed).

Investors who contemplate making an abrupt shift from growth funds to income funds upon retirement also suffer from temporary stock market declines that might occur shortly before the shift occurs. For example, an aggressive growth portfolio is subject to a decline of 50 percent or more during steep bear stock markets. If such a bear market were to occur shortly before retirement, income could be permanently decreased by more than one-half. Thus, years of careful planning could be undone in a few short months.

To avoid this possibility, we recommend that investors with less than five years until retirement gradually reduce the risk of their portfolios. This can be accomplished by shifting from aggressive growth funds to growth and income funds and bond funds. Here is one recommendation:

Growth Funds	20%
Growth & Income Funds	20
International Equity Funds	15
Domestic Bond Funds	15
International Bond Funds	15
Money Market Funds	15

Note that more than one-half of this portfolio is invested in equity funds. Thus, the portfolio has the potential to provide capital growth as well as income. The 45 percent allocation to bond funds and money market funds provides stability as well as current income. As a result, this portfolio could be expected to decline by one-third less than an aggressive portfolio during a steep bear market. However, over a five-year market cycle, this portfolio can be expected to return about 9 to 10 percent annually. Thus, a 40 percent reduction in investment risk is accompanied by only a 20 percent reduction in long-term total return.

A Growth and Income Retirement Portfolio

As a new retiree, you must remember that your investment portfolio will be required to support you for 20 years or more. In other words, if you have recently retired you must still invest for the long term. That means that you must continue to seek some growth of investment capital to offset the impact of inflation. For example, if consumer prices were to rise at their historical average of 3 percent annually, the prices of goods and services would be 80 percent higher 20 years from now. Thus, even a modest amount of inflation can be devasting to a retiree.

Consider the plight of a retired investor who purchased "safe" government bonds with 20-year maturities 20 years ago. If this investor had invested $200,000 in these bonds in 1970, the portfolio (then yielding 7.75 percent) would have provided an annual income of $15,000. Twenty years later, this portfolio would still be providing $15,000 in annual income. However, because of escalating consumer prices, it would have taken an annual income of $50,000 to maintain the same standard of living as when the initial investment was made. Or, to put it another way, the purchasing power of a $15,000 annual income stream would have fallen to $4,500 by the time the 20-year bond matured and the purchasing power of the initial $200,000 bond investment would have fallen to $60,000!

To protect investment income and portfolio value from the detrimental effects of inflation, an investment portfolio must be structured to provide some growth in income and capital over the long term. This, of course, requires investment in equities. Here is a model portfolio that provides both growth and a high level of current income:

Growth Funds	10%
Growth & Income Funds	10
International Equity Funds	10
Domestic Bond Funds	30
International Bond Funds	20
Money Market Funds	20

Note that this portfolio contains a 30 percent allocation to equity funds. These funds, in addition to providing some current income, can be expected to grow by an average of about 7 percent annually and thus to provide an overall portfolio growth rate of approximately 2 percent per year (about two-thirds the rate of inflation during the last 50 years). Furthermore, during periods when stock prices are advancing at a greater than average pace, the portfolio can be rebalanced by selling some equity shares and diverting the proceeds to bond and money market funds. By taking profits when stock prices are inordinately high, an investor obtains the potential to increase the portfolio's average growth rate. Furthermore, this portfolio can be expected to provide a greater current income than is generally obtainable from bank certificates of deposit, Treasury bills or money market mutual funds. Finally, because of the large allocation to fixed-income investments, the portfolio possesses less than one-third of the risk of the stock market.

Portfolios for Highly Conservative Retirees

It may come as a bit of a surprise to some investors that our recommended portfolio for very conservative retirees is not much different from the portfolio recommended for younger retirees. In fact, our recommended allocations are exactly the same: 30 percent to equity funds, 50 percent to bond funds and 20 percent to money market funds. The only difference is that we recommend the 10 percent growth fund allocation be shifted to growth and income funds (bringing the total allocation to this fund category to 20 percent). This shift will both decrease portfolio variability (risk) and increase current income. Generally, growth and income funds have betas less than 0.50 and provide about 200 basis points less yield than Treasury bills. This reduces the downside risk to less than one-fourth that of the stock market, while providing a growth potential of more than 1.5 percent annually.

Growth & Income Funds	20%
International Equity Funds	10
Domestic Bond Funds	30
International Bond Funds	20
Money Market Funds	20

Although we have attempted to provide a bare bones outline of portfolio strategies for broad groups of investors with varying income and capital appreciation needs, one can see that maintaining a lifetime investment plan can be somewhat complex. However, the proliferation of mutual funds has simplified the implementation aspect of lifetime financial planning. Individual investors can obtain a wide degree of diversification by investing in mutual funds that specialize in particular categories of financial assets. Thus, investment risk can be controlled to a much greater extent today than was possible only a few years ago. In addition, since the selection of individual stocks and bonds is left to each mutual fund's portfolio manager, investors can concentrate their decision making to allocation decisions rather than investment selection decisions. Of course, investors must still make individual mutual fund selections. However, we have addressed this topic in other selections of *The Mutual Fund Encyclopedia.*

AN "ALL WEATHER" MUTUAL FUND PORTFOLIO

The largest benefit of mutual fund investing is the risk reduction that results from portfolio diversification. By investing in a diversified equity fund, for example, rather than in one or two common stocks, investors reduce investment risk by roughly two-thirds without sacrificing any long-run return. Investors who invest in a bond fund rather than in a single bond limit capital losses that could result from default.

While the concept of not putting all your eggs in one basket is generally understood by most investors, the question of which baskets to use and how many eggs to place in each has proved to be difficult to solve for most investors.

Which Baskets?

To obtain total portfolio diversification, at least in theory, investors should purchase the "market" portfolio. This portfolio consists of all assets combined in the proportions in which they exist throughout the world. That is, the truly diversified portfolio contains a little bit of everything. Since this portfolio is impossible to construct, a truly diversified portfolio exists only in theory. However, individuals can greatly reduce investment risk by diversifying across a broad class of assets, i.e., by moving closer to the truly diversified portfolio described in theory. This portfolio should contain stocks, bonds, cash, precious metals and real estate.

The object of such diversification, of course, is to iron out the widespread fluctuation in investment wealth that can occur when only a single asset or class of assets is held. For example, the conditions that generally cause stock prices to fall (e.g., rising commodity prices and interest rates) generally cause the price of gold to rise. Thus, a decline in the value of one segment of the portfolio is offset by an increase in the value of another segment. Furthermore, a well-diversified portfolio transcends political boundaries. Thus, worldwide rather than country-specific assets should be included in the portfolio. In this way, geographical economic diversification can be obtained. Although the various economies of the world are becoming more interdependent and thus tend to expand and contract in concert, very often such movements occur with varying time lags. When one economy is contracting, another may continue to expand for a while longer. In addition, global portfolios are less risky than locally concentrated portfolios because foreign exchange risk is limited. That is, as currency values fluctuate, declines in the value of one currency are offset by relative gains in another.

Currently, Perritt Investments offers our money management clients a highly diversified portfolio called the "all weather" portfolio. It consists of mutual funds that concentrate their investments in different categories of financial assets. While far from perfect, the all weather portfolio should contain the following assets:

- U.S. Stocks—Large Companies
- U.S. Stocks—Small Companies
- International Stocks
- U.S. Bonds
- International Bonds
- Precious Metals
- Real Estate
- Money Market Assets

This all weather portfolio contains seven of these eight asset classes. Real estate has been excluded for a number of reasons. First, there are very few mutual funds that directly invest in real estate, and those that do tend to be organized as limited partnerships and thus possess limited liquidity. Second, the portfolios of most investors tend to contain a large proportion of real estate—usually their personal residences. Third, many corporations have vast real estate holdings, which affect common stock values. Thus, by investing in common stocks, investors have invested in real estate indirectly.

How Many Eggs per Basket?

One of the easiest ways to solve the allocation problem would be to spread investment capital equally across all seven asset classes (allocate about 14 percent of investment capital to each asset class). While this method is not scientific, such an allocation is relatively close to the ideal. We chose a slightly different tack. We obtained estimates of world wealth by asset class. We then excluded real estate, recomputed the percentage of world wealth in each remaining asset class and set our allocation targets to the nearest multiple of 5 percent. Thus, the long-run allocation targets for the all weather portfolio are as follows:

Small Cap Equity Funds	15%
Large Cap Equity Funds	15
International Equity Funds	15
U.S. Bond Funds	20
International Bond Funds	10
Gold Funds	10
Money Market Funds	15

Active or Passive Management?

There are two views on this question. The passive view holds that, since the goal of an all weather portfolio is risk reduction, declines in the value of one segment of the portfolio will be largely offset by gains in another. If investors knew which asset class was going to produce the greatest returns during the year, they should allocate all of their capital to that asset class. However, by actively managing the portfolio in that manner, investors increase riskiness due to forecasting errors, which the all weather portfolio was designed to limit in the first place.

A second view holds that some degree of active management can be beneficial as long as reallocations among asset classes are modest and are not made with a high degree of frequency. Thus, when it appears that one segment of the portfolio contains assets that are highly overvalued, the proportion of capital committed to that segment should be reduced. By making reallocations in this manner, investors may increase long-run returns without engaging in forecasting the short-run direction of asset prices since relative values rather than trends are used as the basis for reallocating capital. We have opted for this latter approach, which we call semi-active rather than active portfolio management.

Table 18 shows the allocation boundaries for each asset class along with our current allocations. Note that the current portfolio differs slightly from the long-run target allocations. First, the total allocated to common stocks (small firm, large firm and international stocks) is 35 percent versus a target of 45 percent. The allocation to large-firm equity funds and international equity funds was reduced from 15 percent to 10 percent due to current stock market weakness and uncertainty surrounding the direction of the dollar. Since we believe that the Federal Reserve will expand the money supply, causing interest rates to fall, we have increased the U.S. bond allocation from 20 to 30 percent. However, to reduce interest rate risk, we have selected a short-term maturity, high-quality bond fund. Finally, we reduced the allocation to gold funds and increased our allocation to money market funds due to our belief that consumer prices will increase at a moderate rate.

Long-Run Performance

Table 19 compares the returns of the all weather portfolio (using the allocation targets) with returns from treasury bills and

Table 18

Asset Class	Allocation Range	Current Allocation
Small Cap Equity Funds	10-20%	15%
Large Cap Equity Funds	10-20	10
International Equity Funds	10-20	10
U.S. Bond Funds	10-30	30
International Bond Funds	5-15	10
Gold Funds	5-15	5
Money Market Funds	5-25	20

Table 19 Investment Returns 1970-1989

Year	Treasury Bills	S&P 500 Index	All Weather Portfolio
1970	6.5	4.0	0.6
1971	4.4	14.3	14.5
1972	3.8	19.0	15.8
1973	6.9	–14.7	0.0
1974	8.0	–26.5	–1.3
1975	5.8	37.2	22.8
1976	5.1	23.8	15.3
1977	5.1	–7.2	11.1
1978	7.2	6.6	16.3
1979	10.4	18.4	18.6
1980	11.2	32.4	23.5
1981	14.7	–4.9	1.4
1982	10.5	21.4	16.1
1983	8.8	22.5	14.7
1984	9.8	6.3	3.4
1985	7.7	32.2	31.4
1986	6.2	18.5	19.7
1987	5.5	5.2	6.4
1988	6.4	16.8	8.1
1989	8.4	31.5	16.5
Compound Return	7.6%	11.5%	12.5%
Value of $10,000	$88,200	$43,300	$106,000

common stocks (the total return of the S&P 500 Index). Over the entire 1970-89 period, investment in T-bills (a riskless asset) provided a 7.6 percent compound annual return, or 1.4 percent more than the rate of inflation annually. An average risk common stock portfolio returned 11.5 percent, or 5.3 percent more than the rate of change in the Consumer Price Index. The all weather portfolio provided the greatest long-run return: 12.5 percent, or 6.3 percent more than the annual rate of inflation. And it did so while providing only minimal risk exposure. Note that the all weather portfolio lost ground during just one year (1974) versus four years for the stock market. Furthermore, while the common stock portfolio declined by as much as 26.5 percent during one year, the maximum decline in the all weather portfolio was 1.3 percent. Finally, note that during the 1973-74 bear market, common stock plunged 37.3 percent, while the all weather portfolio declined in value by slightly more than 1 percent.

At least when viewed over the period 1970-89, the all weather portfolio appears to provide the best of two worlds, greater investment returns and reduced investment risk. Although the least risky posture is investment in treasury bills, their return barely tops the rate of inflation. A $10,000 T-bill investment made at the beginning of 1970 would have grown to $43,300 by the end of 1989. On the other hand, a similar investment made in the all weather portfolio would have grown to $106,000 while exposing investors to a maximum annual decline of less than 2 percent.

During the stock market's meltdown of October, 1987, when stock prices declined by nearly 30 percent, the all weather portfolio declined by slightly more than 7 percent. And that loss was largely erased two months later. Thus, risk-conscious but growth-oriented investors should seriously consider adopting an all weather portfolio management approach. Although the return from this portfolio may roughly match the stock market's return over the long run, its variability (risk) is about one-third that of the typical equity mutual fund.

A TALE OF THREE DECADES

In Seattle, residents tell visitors, "If you don't like the weather, just wait a while and it will change." The same is usually true in the financial markets. Just when you have been conditioned to invest one way, the climate changes. On many occasions, what you have been conditioned to do based on historical analysis turns out to be exactly contrary to the strategy that ultimately could produce the best returns.

Take the decade of the 1970s, for example. Hyperinflation, a falling dollar and economic stagnation wreaked havoc in the stock and bond markets. However, those that placed the bulk of their wealth in real assets such as real estate, gold and silver bullion, collectibles, etc., obtained handsome rewards. (See Table 20.)

At the end of the decade, many blue chip common stocks were sporting about the same prices as ten years earlier. Although common stock investors earned an average of about 6 percent per year throughout the decade (largely the result of dividend payments that were reinvested in additional shares), the annual rate of return on blue chip common stocks fell 1.5 percent short of the rate of inflation. Thus, common stock investors actually experienced a decline in real wealth during the decade. Bond and treasury bill investors did only marginally better. However, small firm growth stocks returned 11.5 percent compounded annually during the decade (slightly more than 4 percent annually above the rate of inflation). Those who bought gold bullion earned more than 22 percent annually. And 30 to 40 percent annual returns from heavily leveraged real estate investments (including personal residences) were common.

By the beginning of the decade of the 1980s, most investors were convinced that the only way to survive in the investment jungle was to invest in treasury bills and other safe, interest-earning liquid assets or to hold a large investment in real assets.

Although the first two years of the 1980s proved these investors correct, the world suddenly began to change in late 1982. Interest rates came tumbling down. CD investors found that they could not obtain double-digit returns from investing in "safe" liquid assets. Gold and silver investors got burned when the inflation bubble burst and the Hunts' cor-

Table 20 Two Decades of Investment Returns

	The 1970s							**The 1980s**					
Year	Gov't Bonds	T-Bills	S&P 500	Small Stocks	Gold Bullion	CPI	Year	Gov't Bonds	T-Bills	S&P 500	Small Stocks	Gold Bullion	CPI
1970	12.1%	6.5%	4.0%	−17.4%	−12.3%	5.5%	1980	−4.0%	11.2%	32.4%	39.9%	91.7%	12.4%
1971	13.2	4.4	14.3	16.5	13.2	3.4	1981	1.9	14.7	−4.9	13.9	−32.2	8.9
1972	5.7	3.8	19.0	4.4	42.2	3.4	1982	40.3	10.5	21.4	28.0	13.9	3.9
1973	−1.1	6.9	−14.7	−30.9	66.9	8.8	1983	0.7	8.8	22.5	39.7	−16.5	3.8
1974	4.4	8.0	−26.5	−19.9	63.3	12.2	1984	15.5	9.9	6.3	−6.7	−19.2	4.0
1975	9.2	5.8	37.2	52.8	1.1	7.0	1985	31.0	7.7	32.2	24.7	7.9	3.8
1976	16.8	5.1	23.8	57.4	−22.4	4.8	1986	24.5	6.2	18.5	6.9	20.4	1.1
1977	−0.7	5.1	−7.2	25.4	18.4	6.8	1987	−2.7	5.5	5.2	−9.3	21.9	4.4
1978	−1.2	7.2	6.6	23.5	30.6	9.0	1988	9.7	6.4	16.8	22.9	−15.1	4.4
1979	−1.2	10.4	18.4	43.5	58.8	13.3	1989	18.9	8.4	31.5	10.2	−1.9	4.5
Total Return	**70.8**	**84.2**	**77.4**	**197.0**	**641.2**	**104.2**	**Total Return**	**207.8**	**134.6**	**401.6**	**333.6**	**31.7**	**64.1**
Compounded Annual Return	**5.5**	**6.3**	**5.9**	**11.5**	**22.2**	**7.4**	**Compounded Annual Return**	**11.9**	**8.9**	**17.5**	**15.8**	**3.0**	**5.0**

ner on the silver market failed. The nation's hottest real estate markets suddenly turned frigid, and the value of real estate of all kinds began to sink.

On the other hand, common stock prices rocketed skyward. In fact, after 1981, they did not experience a losing year for the remainder of the decade. During the 1980s, the Standard & Poor's 500 Index returned a total of 17.5 percent compounded annually, a full 7.5 percent per year more than the average return during the past five decades. Small firm stocks tacked on 15.8 percent annually during the decade, although a large proportion of the gain in this sector of the stock market occurred during the decade's first few years.

Income-oriented investors were rewarded handsomely, as interest rates declined for most of the decade. Long-term government bonds returned 12.5 percent annually, and treasury bills returned 8.8 percent, or about 3.8 percent more than the annual rate of inflation. On the other hand, real estate investors were lucky to break even on their investments during the decade. And gold bullion investors earned a scant 3.0 percent per year for their efforts. During the 1980s, the most rewarding investments were the least rewarding during the previous decade while the most rewarding investments of the 1970s became the laggards of the 1980s.

What Lies Ahead?

Will the 1990s surprise investors once again by reversing the investment trends of the 1980s? Will the 1990s surprise contrarian investors by continuing trends begun a decade earlier? Or will the 1990s bring the "Great Depression" predicted by many doomsayers over the last few years?

That brings us to the central point of this chapter: "What should an investor do now?" Before answering that question, here are a few things not to do. First, don't look backward. As illustrated above, the best investments during the recent past could turn into tomorrow's lemons. Second, don't panic. Invest rationally rather than emotionally. Investors who panic and those who construct extremely risky portfolios are generally those who lose the most. Books such as *The Great Depression of 1990* and *How To Prosper During the Coming Depression* are written to make the authors—not the investors who blindly follow their recommendations—rich.

Instead, begin with an assessment of your investment objectives and your tolerance and inclination to assume investment risk. If you can't tolerate a temporary 50 percent (or whatever) decline in the value of your portfolio, allocate your wealth in such a manner as to avoid a potential decline of this magnitude. For example, stock prices declined by 80 percent during the late 1920s and early 1930s (the largest decline of this century). Should that event be repeated, a portfolio consisting of one-third equity mutual funds and two-thirds money market mutual funds would decline in value less than 20 percent (assuming reinvestment of interest and dividend income). To add additional protection against the erosion of real wealth due to inflation, you could invest 5 to 10 percent of capital in a gold fund.

The point is that you can tailor your mutual fund portfolio to any tolerable risk level. Of course, since investment returns are largely tied to investment risks, relatively low-risk portfolios will provide relatively low investment returns. Which brings us to the last caution. Do not make investment decisions solely on the basis of potential return. When promised an exceptionally high rate of return, look the gift horse straight in the mouth and ask: "What's the risk?"

With the continued erosion of the barriers to international commerce and the globalization of economic trade, we believe that all investors should include international investments (stocks or bonds) in their portfolios. In addition, we believe that inflation will not be the problem it was during the 1970s.

In terms of individual sectors, we believe that the 1990s will provide significant growth opportunities for firms in the following industries: health care (including medical technology), pollution and waste control, telecommun- ications and service sector industries. Finally, we believe that small firm stocks will regain their return superiority over blue chip stocks during this decade.

We also forecast that change will be the theme of the 1990s. Economically, we believe that more and more societies will turn toward capitalism. Scientific advancement will continue at a geometric pace. Higher speed computers, space laboratories and great strides in medical technology will spawn thousands of new products. Unlike some doomsayers who believe that the 1990s will be accompanied by a return to the "Dark Ages," we believe that this decade will long be hailed by historians as an economic renaissance.

However, while periods of great change are exciting and provide a plethora of investment opportunities, they can also be highly volatile. Thus, the key to successful investing during the 1990s is to maintain a high degree of diversity in your portfolio. Income-oriented investors should maintain portfolios consisting of money market funds, international bond funds, equity-income funds and a small percentage invested in gold funds as a hedge. Equity investors' portfolios should include funds that invest in small firm stocks as well as those that invest in blue chip stocks and international equities. For long-term, growth-oriented investors, we suggest including a "sector" fund that invests in one of the growth industries described above.

Remember, also, that while the winds of economic change can blow from a number of directions, the rules of successful investing remain unbent. Maintain a diversified portfolio, invest for the longer term and avoid the urge to trade frequently, assess the risk as well as the potential rewards before you invest, maintain a level of risk no greater than you can tolerate, ease into and out of investments slowly and, if possible, continually add fresh capital to your investment portfolio. If followed unwaveringly, these easy-to-apply rules will ultimately lead to investment success, no matter what happens in the financial markets.

PART 2

Money Market Funds

Money market mutual funds invest shareholders' capital in debt securities with very short maturities. Some money market funds confine their portfolios to issues of the U.S. government. Others invest in private debt securities, which include commercial paper (short-term corporate unsecured IOUs), bank certificates of deposit, bankers' acceptances (which arise from international trade transactions) and other short-term debt.

Securities and Exchange Commission regulations restrict both the types of securities that money funds can invest in and the composition of their portfolios. Like other mutual funds, a money market fund cannot invest more than 5 percent of its assets in a single company or more than 25 percent in a single industry. In addition, SEC regulations prohibit a money market fund from investing in commercial paper below the two top grades—securities rated A1 and A2 by Standard & Poor's or P1 and P2 by Moody's. Finally, money market funds are prohibited from investing in debt with a maturity of more than one year or from holding a dollar-weighted average portfolio maturity of more than 120 days.

Money funds are the least risky of all mutual funds. Those that invest in treasury bills are nearly free of risk altogether. However, while money fund investors have never lost one dime of their assets, money funds that invest in private debt subject their shareholders to default risk. In fact, a handful of money funds suffered losses when several companies defaulted on their commercial paper. The advisers of these funds, however, assumed these losses and money fund shareholders were left whole. In addition, some "government only" money market funds invest some of their assets in repurchase agreements, or "repos."

By year-end 1991, the assets of 558 money market mutual funds had swelled to nearly $492 billion, and the number of shareholder accounts topped $22 million. These money fund assets were invested as follows: commercial paper, 43 percent; U.S. Treasury issues, 25 percent; repurchase agreements, 16 percent; certificates of deposit, 12 percent; bankers' acceptances, 1 percent; and other, 3 percent. The popularity of money market funds among savers is understandable. They generally pay a higher rate of interest than bank savings accounts, provide shareholders with free checking accounts and extend wire transfer privileges.

Money fund share prices are fixed at $1.00. Interest income earned is credited to shareholder accounts daily and reinvested in additional fund shares. While share price is fixed, interest rates fluctuate daily. Money funds report their current yields two ways—an annualized seven-day average yield and an annualized seven-day compound yield. At a particular point in time, yields among money funds will vary. These differences arise because of differences in portfolio composition, differences in average maturities and differences in fund expense ratios.

The money market funds listed here are the largest available to individual and institutional investors (in terms of total assets). Their total assets range from the giant Merrill Lynch CMA Money Fund, with $27 billion in assets, to the Reserve Government Fund, with $785 million in assets. Collectively, these funds hold more than $290 billion in total assets, which represents about 60 percent of total money market mutual fund assets.

100 LARGEST MONEY MARKET FUNDS

Fund	Assets ($ millions)	Telephone
Alex Brown Cash Prime	$ 1,208	800-767-3524
Alliance Capital Reserves	1,848	800-247-4154
Alliance Government Reserves	1,544	800-247-4154
Alliance Money Reserves	1,362	800-247-4154
American Express Daily Dividend	16,665	800-872-1166
American Express Government Agencies	3,726	800-872-1166
Automated Cash Management Trust	1,309	800-245-5000
Automated Government Money	3,134	800-245-5000
Benham Government Agency Fund	1,009	800-472-3389
Capital Preservation Fund	3,297	800-472-3389
Cash Accumulation National Money Market	2,350	800-628-1237
Cash Equivalent Fund	3,928	800-621-1048
Cash Equivalent Government Securities	3,186	800-621-1048
Cash Management Trust	1,994	800-421-9900
Cash Reserve	1,255	800-345-2021
CBA Money Fund	1,084	800-637-3863
CMA Government Securities	4,316	800-637-3863
CMA Money Fund	27,224	800-637-3863
CMA Treasury Fund	1,424	800-637-3863
Compass Capital U.S. Treasuries	916	800-451-8371
Daily Cash Accumulation	5,263	800-525-7048
Daily Money Market	1,565	800-544-8888
Daily Money U.S. Treasury	2,113	800-544-8888

Fund	Assets ($ millions)	Telephone
Dean Witter Liquid Assets	10,112	800-869-3863
Dean Witter U.S. Government Money Market	1,127	800-869-3863
Delaware Cash Reserve	924	800-523-4640
Dreyfus Cash Management	5,276	800-782-6620
Dreyfus Cash Management Plus	2,286	800-782-6620
Dreyfus Government Cash Management	3,735	800-782-6620
Dreyfus Liquid Assets	6,200	800-782-6620
Dreyfus Treasury Cash Management	3,403	800-782-6620
Dreyfus Worldwide Dollar	8,119	800-782-6620
Emerald Treasury Fund	819	800-637-6336
Federated Master Trust	1,296	800-245-5000
Federated Short U.S. Government Trust	963	800-245-5000
Fidelity Cash Reserves	10,200	800-544-8888
Fidelity Daily Income	2,722	800-544-8888
Fidelity Institutional Cash—Money	4,067	800-544-8888
Fidelity Institutional Cash—Treasuries	2,255	800-544-8888
Fidelity Institutional Cash—Treasury 2	5,620	800-544-8888
Fidelity Institutional Cash—U.S. Government	4,272	800-544-8888
Fidelity Money Retirement—Government	953	800-544-8888
Fidelity Retirement Money Market	1,283	800-544-8888
Fidelity Spartan Money	5,277	800-544-8888
Fidelity Spartan U.S. Treasury	2,722	800-544-8888
Fidelity U.S. Government Reserves	1,344	800-544-8888
Fidelity U.S. Treasury Income	1,500	800-544-8888
First Prairie Government Money Market	991	800-537-4938
Franklin Money Fund	1,329	800-342-5236
Freedom Cash Management Fund	1,161	800-225-6258
Helmsman Prime Obligation	861	800-338-4345
Heritage Cash Trust	849	800-421-4184
IDS Cash Management Fund	1,441	800-328-8300
Jones Daily Passport	2,439	800-441-2357
Kemper Money Market—Government	1,070	800-621-1048
Kemper Money Market Portfolio	6,668	800-621-1048
Kidder Peabody Premium Account	934	800-543-3377
Laurel Prime Money II	914	800-235-4331
Legg Mason Cash Reserve	806	800-822-5544
Liberty U.S. Government Money Market	1,233	800-245-4770
Liquid Capital Income Trust	790	800-321-2322
Merrill Lynch Government	1,400	800-225-1576
Merrill Lynch Institutional Fund	2,217	800-225-1576
Merrill Lynch Ready Assets	9,077	800-637-3863
Merrill Lynch Retirement Reserves	6,359	800-637-3863
Money Market Trust	946	800-245-5000
New England Cash Management	1,046	800-343-7104

Fund	Assets ($ millions)	Telephone
Oppenheimer Money Market	892	800-255-2755
Pacific Horizon Prime Fund	1,114	800-332-3863
PaineWebber Cashfund	4,143	800-762-1000
PaineWebber Retirement Managed U.S. Govt.	963	800-647-1568
PaineWebber Retirement Management Money Portfolio	3,999	800-647-1568
PaineWebber Retirement Money Fund	2,151	800-647-1568
Piper Jaffray Money Market	1,256	800-333-6000
Price Prime Reserve	4,166	800-638-5660
Prime Fund—Horizon Shares	1,661	800-332-3863
Prime Value Funds Cash	1,012	800-826-4600
Quest Cash Primary Portfolio	1,284	800-232-3863
Reserve Fund Government	785	800-637-1700
Reserve Fund Primary Portfolio	1,652	800-637-1700
Rushmore Fund For Government	797	800-621-7874
Schwab Government Securities	1,459	800-526-8600
Schwab Money Market Fund	4,867	800-526-8600
Scudder Cash Investment	1,481	800-225-2470
SEI Cash + Prime Obligation A	1,374	800-345-1151
SEI Liquid Asset Prime	1,735	800-345-1151
SEI Liquid Asset Treasury	2,115	800-345-1151
Smith Barney Money Market —Cash	1,785	800-544-7835
Smith Barney Money Market—Retirement	972	800-544-7835
Treasury Fund Horizon Share	910	800-332-3863
Treasury Fund Pacific Horizon	1,872	800-332-3863
Trust For Government Cash Reserves	1,324	800-245-5000
Trust Short U.S. Government Securities	2,701	800-245-5000
Trust U.S. Treasury Obligation	5,985	800-245-5000
USAA Money Market	961	800-531-8181
Vanguard Money Market Federal	1,976	800-662-7447
Vanguard Money Market Prime	13,068	800-662-7447
Vanguard Money Market Treasuries	2,081	800-662-7447
Vantage Money Market Cash Reserves	1,089	800-544-7835
Webster Cash Reserve Fund	1,997	800-635-1983

50 LARGEST TAX-FREE MONEY MARKET FUNDS

Fund	Assets ($ million)	Telephone
Active Assets Tax Free Trust	$1,358	800-869-3863
Alliance Tax-Exempt Reserve General	907	800-247-4154
American Express Daily Tax-Free	3,140	800-872-1166
Calvert Tax-Free Reserve—Money Market	1,421	800-368-2748
Cash Equivalent Tax-Exempt Money Market	1,250	800-621-1048
Centennial Tax-Exempt Trust	856	800-525-7048

Fund	Assets ($ millions)	Telephone
CMA California Tax-Exempt	1,004	800-637-3863
CMA New York Tax Exempt	575	800-637-3863
CMA Tax-Exempt Fund	7,090	800-637-3863
Daily Tax Free Income	617	800-221-3079
Dean Witter Tax Free Daily	829	800-869-3863
Dreyfus Municipal Money Market	1,572	800-829-3733
Dreyfus New Jersey Municipal Money Market	855	800-829-3733
Dreyfus New York Tax-Exempt Money Market	443	800-829-3733
Dreyfus Tax-Exempt Cash Management	1,763	800-782-6620
Evergreen Tax Exempt Money Market	464	800-235-0064
Federated Tax-Free Trust	1,614	800-245-5000
Fidelity California Tax Free Money Market	551	800-544-8888
Fidelity Conn. Municipal Money	406	800-544-8888
Fidelity Institutional Tax-Exempt Cash	1,991	800-544-8888
Fidelity Mass. Tax Free Money Market	692	800-544-8888
Fidelity New Jersey Tax Free Money Market	367	800-544-8888
Fidelity New York Tax Free Money Market	515	800-544-8888
Fidelity Spartan California Money Market	870	800-544-8888
Fidelity Tax-Exempt Money Market	2,659	800-544-8888
Franklin California Tax-Exempt Money Market	840	800-342-5236
General New York Municipal Money Market	580	800-829-3733
Investment Series Trust Instrument	1,278	800-245-5000
Kemper Money Market Tax-Exempt	806	800-621-1048
Kidder Peabody Tax Exempt Money	649	800-635-1983
Landmark New York Tax Free Reserves	660	800-223-4447
Merrill Lynch Institutional Tax Exempt	396	800-225-1576
Municipal Cash Series	547	800-245-2423
Nuveen California Tax Free Money	542	800-621-7227
Nuveen Tax-Exempt Money Market	1,977	800-621-7227
Nuveen Tax Free Reserves	443	800-621-7227
PaineWebber Retirement Managed Tax Free	1,085	800-647-1568
Schwab Tax-Exempt Money	1,359	800-526-8600
SEI Tax Exempt California	370	800-345-1151
SEI Tax Exempt Institutional A	440	800-345-1151
Strong Municipal Money Market	783	800-368-3863
T. Rowe Price Tax-Exempt Money	793	800-638-5660
Tax Exempt Money Horizon Shares	364	800-332-3863
Tax Free Money Fund	1,067	800-544-7835
USAA Tax-Exempt Money Market	1,463	800-531-8181
UST Master Tax Exempt Short Term	527	800-233-1136
Vanguard California Tax Free Money	756	800-662-7447
Vanguard Municipal Money Market	2,783	800-662-7447
Vanguard New Jersey Tax Free Money	554	800-662-7447
Vanguard Pennsylvania Tax Free Money	826	800-662-7447

PART 3

Aggressive Growth Funds

Aggressive growth funds have as their primary investment objective the pursuit of maximum capital gains. They invest aggressively in speculative stocks and tend to stay fully invested at all times. Some funds use financial leverage (stock market margin) in an attempt to enhance returns, others invest in small-equity-capitalization firms, while still others attempt to purchase common stocks of the fastest-growing companies regardless of whether they are large or small. Some funds in this class invest in highly concentrated portfolios, consisting of stocks in a handful of particular industries.

Needless to say, the share prices of funds in this class are quite volatile, performing very well in bull markets and faring very poorly in bear markets. The greater-than-average volatility of this group of funds is illustrated by their median beta of 1.17. And a number of funds in this group possess betas of 1.30 or more. Thus, investment in these funds is not for the faint of heart. Generally, aggressive growth funds are suitable for long-term-oriented investors who can assume above-average risks and are not bothered by short-term stock market fluctuations. However, over the long run, because of the risks assumed, these funds tend to provide the greatest investment returns.

As can be seen in the summary of statistics table, aggressive growth funds possess scant current yields (median annual current yield of less than 1 percent during 1991). In fact, more than one-third of the funds described on the following pages paid no income dividends at all the past year. In addition, these funds tend to possess very high portfolio turnover ratios (median turnover of 89 percent). Thus, on average, these funds hold their investments for approximately 13 months.

After underperforming the S&P 500 Index between 1986 and 1990, aggressive growth fund returns exploded to the upside the past year with the median fund returning nearly 50 percent versus slightly more than 30 percent for the S&P 500 Index. Leading the charge to higher ground were funds that allocated a significant portion of their assets to the small cap sector of the stock market. Small cap stocks had underperformed the large cap, blue chip–dominated S&P 500 Index during six of the seven years between 1984 and 1990. Interestingly, the performance of small cap portfolios tends to run in streaks—either good or bad. Thus, aggressive growth funds could continue to show relatively good performance numbers for the next few years.

Because of good performance numbers, a great many investors flocked to small cap funds the past year. As a result, many small cap funds were so glutted with cash that they discontinued selling shares to new shareholders. Included in this group of funds were 1991's two best-performing aggressive growth funds, CGM Capital Development and the Montgomery Small Cap Fund.

Summary of Financial Statistics (medians)

1991 Return	Five-Year Return	Current Yield	Beta	Turnover Ratio	Expense Ratio
49.9%	103.6%	0.3%	1.17	89%	1.43%

BEST AGGRESSIVE GROWTH FUNDS FOR 1991

Fund	Percent Return 1991	3-Year	5-Year
CGM Capital Development Fund	99.1%	138.3%	175.2%
Montgomery Small Cap Fund	98.7	NA	NA
American Heritage Fund	96.0	31.8	-0.6
Berger 100 Fund	88.8	164.3	211.0
United New Concepts Fund	88.3	108.4	108.3
MFS Lifetime Emerging Growth Trust	87.6	132.1	162.5
Oberweis Emerging Growth Fund	87.1	134.8	NA
Twentieth Century Ultra Investors	86.5	179.3	237.6
Twentieth Century Giftrust Investors	84.9	130.5	178.4
Kaufman Fund	79.4	147.3	146.5
ABT Investment Emerging Growth	77.2	126.6	113.8
Delaware Trend Fund	74.5	97.0	130.3
Twentieth Century Vista Investors	73.7	122.9	141.9
Hartwell Emerging Growth Fund	72.5	145.5	203.4
Oppenheimer Discovery Fund	72.3	96.2	166.9
USAA Aggressive Growth Fund	71.7	76.4	99.6
AIM Constellation Fund	70.4	125.5	169.9
Keystone Custodian Funds S4	70.3	97.9	108.2
Massachusetts Financial Emerging Growth Trust	70.2	89.5	95.2
Twentieth Century Growth Investors	69.0	132.6	170.3
Strong Discovery Fund	68.6	103.4	NA
Thomson Opportunity Fund B	68.1	103.7	146.9
Pasadena Growth Fund	67.8	120.3	165.1
AMEV Growth Fund	67.5	124.1	140.7

ABT INVESTMENT EMERGING GROWTH

ABT Financial Services
205 Royal Palm Way
Palm Beach, FL 33480
800-289-2281

Investment Objective: ABT Emerging Growth Fund makes the average aggressive growth vehicle look tame. Investing in a mix of medium- and small-sized stocks, the fund stresses top-quality growth companies with leadership positions in high-growth industries. A quick glance at a number of the fund's holdings reveals companies with 25 to 40% annual growth in earnings, and thus underscores the fund's pure growth orientation. While this patent approach can lead to chart-leading results in years such as 1989 and 1991, it also makes the fund vulnerable to big setbacks in the wake of earnings disappointments.

Portfolio Manager: Harold Ireland
Since: 1983

Minimum:
Initial: $1,000
Subsequent: $100
Telephone Exchange: Yes
Distributions:
Income: Annually
Capital Gain: Annually
Front-End Load: 4.75%
12b-1: 0.25%
Redemption Fee: None
Management Company: Palm Beach Capital Management
Ticker Symbol: ABEGX

TOTAL RETURN (%)

1987	1988	1989	1990	1991	5-year	Bull Market	Bear Market
-16.5	13.0	33.9	-4.5	77.2	113.8	86.4	-28.5

INVESTMENT PORTFOLIO

Total Assets (mil.)	Current Yield	Turnover Ratio	Expense Ratio	Beta	Risk Return
$23	0.0%	100%	1.86%	1.22	0.11

AEGON USA CAPITAL APPRECIATION PORTFOLIO

MidAmerica Management
4333 Edgewood Road N.E.
Cedar Rapids, IA 52499
800-538-5111

Investment Objective: Aegon USA Capital Appreciation fund invests in a mix of large and small stocks, with small stocks most prominent. To a lesser degree, it also invests in convertible bonds. Areas of emphasis include high-growth health care, technology and consumer staples. However, the fund also features investments in cheaper basic industry and financial stocks with above-average prospects for growth. Operating in an unfavorable environment for its small-stock orientation, the fund has produced subpar returns over the previous 5 years; however, the past year the fund chalked up a solid 55% return.

Portfolio Manager: Tom Meyers
Since: 1990

Minimum:
Initial: $1,000
Subsequent: $50
Telephone Exchange: Yes
Distributions:
Income: Annually
Capital Gain: Annually
Front-End Load: 4.75%
12b-1: None
Redemption Fee: None
Management Company: MidAmerica Management
Ticker Symbol: AEGAX

TOTAL RETURN (%)

1987	1988	1989	1990	1991	5-year	Bull Market	Bear Market
8.3	17.3	15.9	-17.1	55.0	89.3	75.9	-28.5

INVESTMENT PORTFOLIO

Total Assets (mil.)	Current Yield	Turnover Ratio	Expense Ratio	Beta	Risk Return
$15	0.4%	163%	1.00%	1.04	0.09

AFUTURE FUND

Carlisle-Asher Management
251 Royal Palm Way, Suite 601
Palm Beach, FL 33480
800-947-6984

Investment Objective: The fund has changed its strategy recently, with 50% of the fund's assets to be allocated to small- and medium-sized companies. The other half of the portfolio will consist of large, dividend-paying companies. This objective change comes in the wake of some difficult years for the fund as solid returns have been hard to come by. The past year's 10% return trailed all major market indices; however, current Portfolio Manager David Omsted took his position only this past year. Assets have fallen to a mere $6 million.

Portfolio Manager: David Omsted
Since: 1991

Minimum:
Initial: $500
Subsequent: $30
Telephone Exchange: No
Distributions:
Income: Annually
Capital Gain: Annually
Front-End Load: None
12b-1: None
Redemption Fee: None
Management Company: Carlisle-Asher Management
Ticker Symbol: AFUTX

TOTAL RETURN (%)

1987	1988	1989	1990	1991	5-year	Bull Market	Bear Market
-10.3	1.9	14.1	-12.7	10.0	0.2	8.5	-8.1

INVESTMENT PORTFOLIO

Total Assets (mil.)	Current Yield	Turnover Ratio	Expense Ratio	Beta	Risk Return
$6	0.0%	60%	1.60%	0.55	0.01

AIM CONSTELLATION FUND

AIM Distributors
11 Greenway Plaza, Suite 1919
Houston, TX 77046
800-347-1919

Investment Objective: This fund seeks capital appreciation by investing in common stocks of small to midsized companies. There is a tendency for this fund to turn its portfolio over rather quickly as management focuses on earnings momentum. Like most momentum players, any slowdown in earnings results in the stock being sold. Performance has been strong in both bear and bull markets. The fund had a positive return in 1987, lost only 4% in 1990 and returned a robust 70% the past year.

Portfolio Manager: H. Hutzler/J. Schoolar
Since: 1976

Minimum:
Initial: $1,000
Subsequent: $100
Telephone Exchange: Yes
Distributions:
Income: Annually
Capital Gain: Annually
Front-End Load: 5.50%
12b-1: 0.18%
Redemption Fee: None
Management Company: AIM Management
Ticker Symbol: CSTGX

TOTAL RETURN (%)

1987	1988	1989	1990	1991	5-year	Bull Market	Bear Market
2.9	16.3	38.0	-4.1	70.4	169.9	83.4	-35.4

INVESTMENT PORTFOLIO

Total Assets (mil.)	Current Yield	Turnover Ratio	Expense Ratio	Beta	Risk Return
$362	0.0%	192%	1.40%	1.42	0.09

ALGER SMALL CAPITALIZATION PORTFOLIO

Alger Funds
75 Maiden Lane
New York, NY 10038
800-992-3863

Investment Objective: Despite a generally unfavorable environment for small stocks, this small cap fund has whipped most rivals over the past 3 years. Its excellent results owe to both good stock selection and timing. Trading rapidly, it buys its tiny, high-growth companies when earnings growth is accelerating, selling them on any sign of a deterioration in momentum. It won't always perform so consistently as it has during its first 5 years, but it is not likely to disappoint in an earnings-driven market. Over the long haul, risk-tolerant investors can expect to be handsomely rewarded.

Portfolio Manager: David Alger
Since: 1986

Minimum:
Initial: $1,000
Subsequent: $100
Telephone Exchange: Yes
Distributions:
Income: Annually
Capital Gain: Annually
Front-End Load: None
12b-1: 1.00%
Redemption Fee: 5.00%
Management Company: Fred Alger Management
Ticker Symbol: ALSCX

TOTAL RETURN (%)

1987	1988	1989	1990	1991	5-year	Bull Market	Bear Market
-1.5	17.5	64.5	6.7	54.8	214.3	68.9	-28.5

INVESTMENT PORTFOLIO

Total Assets (mil.)	Current Yield	Turnover Ratio	Expense Ratio	Beta	Risk Return
$63	0.0%	253%	2.66%	1.34	0.07

ALLIANCE COUNTERPOINT FUND

Alliance Funds Distributor
500 Plaza Drive
Secaucus, NJ 07094
800-247-4154

Investment Objective: Led by a strategy that emphasizes consumer-growth and service stocks, this fund has enjoyed strong returns at below-market risk levels. Though it declined marginally in 1987 and 1990, the fund attained above-average performances in 1986, 1988 and 1989. Meanwhile, its beta ranks at the lower end of all aggressive growth vehicles. Low turnover and moderate expenses contribute to the attractiveness of this Alliance fund, although its 5.50% front-end load will cut into investment returns. The past year the fund returned 33.5%.

Portfolio Manager: David Handke
Since: 1985

Minimum:
Initial: $250
Subsequent: $50
Telephone Exchange: Yes
Distributions:
Income: Quarterly
Capital Gain: Annually
Front-End Load: 5.50%
12b-1: 0.30%
Redemption Fee: None
Management Company: Alliance Capital Management
Ticker Symbol: ALCPX

TOTAL RETURN (%)

1987	1988	1989	1990	1991	5-year	Bull Market	Bear Market
-1.4	19.9	34.2	-4.6	33.5	102.0	39.8	-15.1

INVESTMENT PORTFOLIO

Total Assets (mil.)	Current Yield	Turnover Ratio	Expense Ratio	Beta	Risk Return
$59	0.7%	57%	1.72%	1.02	0.06

ALLIANCE QUASAR FUND A

Alliance Funds Distributor
500 Plaza Drive
Secaucus, NJ 07094
800-247-4154

Investment Objective: Billed as a small cap growth fund, this fund has achieved much of its recent performance through rising medium to large cap stocks in technology-related industries. Concentrating its effort in explosive cellular and telecommunications stocks, which have come into their own over the past couple of years, has helped returns the most. Nonetheless, throwing assets into a few high-growth industry groups has its risks, which was demonstrated when OTC stocks took a nosedive during 1990. Although billed as a "small cap" fund, its portfolio is dotted with large-company stocks.

Portfolio Manager: Steve Barry
Since: 1988

Minimum:
Initial: $250
Subsequent: $50
Telephone Exchange: Yes
Distributions:
Income: Annually
Capital Gain: Annually
Front-End Load: 5.50%
12b-1: 0.16%
Redemption Fee: None
Management Company: Alliance Capital Management
Ticker Symbol: QUASX

TOTAL RETURN (%)

1987	1988	1989	1990	1991	5-year	Bull Market	Bear Market
-5.3	29.7	28.2	-23.4	34.3	61.8	47.3	-31.9

INVESTMENT PORTFOLIO

Total Assets (mil.)	Current Yield	Turnover Ratio	Expense Ratio	Beta	Risk Return
$306	0.0%	90%	1.66%	1.27	0.04

AMERICAN CAPITAL EMERGING GROWTH FUND

American Capital Marketing
P.O. Box 3528
Houston, TX 77253
800-421-5666

Investment Objective: This fund isn't so aggressive as it would like to be. With a portfolio filled with easily recognizable, large cap names, the fund's billing is a misnomer. In fact, in recent years, it has looked more like a regular growth vehicle that emphasizes high-growth consumer-product and service stocks while largely eschewing technology-related names. Nonetheless, this strategy worked well in 1989 and 1991, as the fund rose a strong 29% and 60.4%, respectively. Furthermore, it managed to post a small gain in 1990, which proved to be exceptionally difficult for a majority of aggressive growth funds.

Portfolio Manager: Gary Lewis
Since: 1989

Minimum:
Initial: $500
Subsequent: $50
Telephone Exchange: Yes
Distributions:
Income: Annually
Capital Gain: Annually
Front-End Load: 5.75%
12b-1: 0.16%
Redemption Fee: None
Management Company: American Capital Asset Management
Ticker Symbol: ACEGX

TOTAL RETURN (%)

1987	1988	1989	1990	1991	5-year	Bull Market	Bear Market
4.0	3.7	29.1	2.0	60.4	127.7	75.1	-29.9

INVESTMENT PORTFOLIO

Total Assets (mil.)	Current Yield	Turnover Ratio	Expense Ratio	Beta	Risk Return
$294	0.1%	47%	1.15%	1.29	0.09

AMERICAN CAPITAL ENTERPRISE FUND

American Capital Marketing
P.O. Box 3528
Houston, TX 77253
800-421-5666

Investment Objective: This fund invests in stocks of companies with established records of sales and earnings growth. Although in recent years the fund has concentrated on blue chip growth, the fund jumped on the small cap bandwagon in 1991. This small cap exposure helped the fund post a solid 39% gain the past year. Investors in the fund should see a mixture of blue chip and small cap companies with the bias being more toward the larger firms. And remember, the fund does carry a hefty 5.75% front-end load.

Portfolio Manager: Stephen Boyd
Since: 1989

Minimum:
Initial: $500
Subsequent: $50
Telephone Exchange: Yes
Distributions:
Income: Annually
Capital Gain: Annually
Front-End Load: 5.75%
12b-1: 0.13%
Redemption Fee: None
Management Company: American Capital Asset Management
Ticker Symbol: ACENX

TOTAL RETURN (%)

1987	1988	1989	1990	1991	5-year	Bull Market	Bear Market
1.1	12.1	31.2	-2.9	39.2	100.9	44.3	-22.2

INVESTMENT PORTFOLIO

Total Assets (mil.)	Current Yield	Turnover Ratio	Expense Ratio	Beta	Risk Return
$622	1.1%	105%	0.94%	1.11	0.06

AMERICAN HERITAGE FUND

American Heritage Management
31 West 52nd Street
New York, NY 10019
212-474-7308

Investment Objective: This fund seeks capital appreciation by rapidly trading a portfolio of common stocks. The fund was purchased by Heiko Thieme during 1990 after American Heritage had racked up one of the worst performances of all equity funds. Under Thieme's guidance in 1991, the fund staged a stunning reversal of fortune and returned a spectacular 96%. However, the fund's expense ratio is an astounding 6.79%, mainly because of its minuscule asset base. Also, the past year's portfolio turnover rate of 607% was one of the highest in the industry.

Portfolio Manager: Heiko Thieme
Since: 1990

Minimum:
Initial: $5,000
Subsequent: $1,000
Telephone Exchange: No
Distributions:
Income: Annually
Capital Gain: Annually
Front-End Load: None
12b-1: None
Redemption Fee: None
Management Company: American Heritage Management
Ticker Symbol: AHERX

TOTAL RETURN (%)

1987	1988	1989	1990	1991	5-year	Bull Market	Bear Market
-26.1	1.9	-2.8	-30.8	96.0	-0.6	84.3	-32.7

INVESTMENT PORTFOLIO

Total Assets (mil.)	Current Yield	Turnover Ratio	Expense Ratio	Beta	Risk Return
$4	0.0%	607%	6.79%	0.98	0.12

AMERICAN INVESTORS GROWTH FUND

American Investors Funds
777 West Putnam, P.O. Box 2500
Greenwich, CT 06836
800-243-5353

Investment Objective: This fund seeks growth of investment capital by primarily utilizing technical analysis of individual stocks, industries and the overall market. Switching in and out of issues that have fallen out of favor has resulted in a consistently high portfolio turnover rate. From 1981 to 1990, this rate has averaged more than 160% per year. One would hope that the strategic switching would have paid off, but lately, returns have been mediocre at best. Given the fund's high beta of 1.36, investors will likely experience excessive volatility for only average returns.

Portfolio Manager: Warren K. Breene
Since: 1984

Minimum:
Initial: $1,000
Subsequent: $20
Telephone Exchange: Yes
Distributions:
Income: Annually
Capital Gain: Annually
Front-End Load: 4.50%
12b-1: None
Redemption Fee: None
Management Company: D. H. Blair Advisers
Ticker Symbol: AMRVX

TOTAL RETURN (%)

1987	1988	1989	1990	1991	5-year	Bull Market	Bear Market
-2.2	18.5	33.7	-17.4	31.1	67.8	25.1	-25.6

INVESTMENT PORTFOLIO

Total Assets (mil.)	Current Yield	Turnover Ratio	Expense Ratio	Beta	Risk Return
$53	0.0%	133%	1.57%	1.36	0.04

AMEV FIDUCIARY FUND

AMEV Investors
P.O. Box 64284
St. Paul, MN 55164
800-800-2638

Investment Objective: A large cap format and a beta similar to that of the S&P 500 make this fund more conservative than its aggressive growth classification suggests. The fund pursues its capital appreciation objective by investing in large and medium capitalization growth stocks, allocating most assets to large S&P 500 names. Although the fund does not neglect any major sectors, it greatly overweighs stable growth nondurables, health care, telecommunication and retail at the expense of slower growth electric utilities and financials. This fund's willingness to pay high multiples makes it vulnerable to sharp corrections in the face of actual and/or anticipated earnings disappointments, as witnessed during 1990.

Portfolio Manager: Stephen M. Poling
Since: 1983

Minimum:
Initial: $500
Subsequent: $25
Telephone Exchange: Yes
Distributions:
Income: Annually
Capital Gain: Annually
Front-End Load: 4.50%
12b-1: 0.30%
Redemption Fee: None
Management Company: AMEV Advisers
Ticker Symbol: AMFDX

TOTAL RETURN (%)

1987	1988	1989	1990	1991	5-year	Bull Market	Bear Market
0.4	7.0	40.3	-11.1	52.7	104.5	45.1	-25.4

INVESTMENT PORTFOLIO

Total Assets (mil.)	Current Yield	Turnover Ratio	Expense Ratio	Beta	Risk Return
$38	0.4%	68%	1.44%	1.16	0.08

AMEV GROWTH FUND

AMEV Investors
P.O. Box 64284
St. Paul, MN 55164
800-800-2638

Investment Objective: Slightly more adventurous than its cousin, AMEV Fiduciary, this fund has enjoyed similar success over the past few years. With a slightly higher than average risk, the fund is pinched more by bear markets and rises more in bull markets. Management's emphasis on companies that show 25+% growth in earnings causes it to greatly overweigh high-growth industries such as retail, health care and pollution control, at the expense of sluggish sectors such as finance. The fund severely lagged 1988's value-led market but was a top performer in 1989 and 1991, when leadership turned to growth stocks. Its 6.3% 1990 loss represents good resistance to decline.

Portfolio Manager: Stephen M. Poling
Since: 1983

Minimum:
Initial: $500
Subsequent: $25
Telephone Exchange: Yes
Distributions:
Income: Annually
Capital Gain: Annually
Front-End Load: 4.75%
12b-1: 0.25%
Redemption Fee: None
Management Company: AMEV Advisers
Ticker Symbol: AMGHX

TOTAL RETURN (%)

1987	1988	1989	1990	1991	5-year	Bull Market	Bear Market
-0.3	7.8	42.8	-6.3	67.5	140.7	68.7	-29.7

INVESTMENT PORTFOLIO

Total Assets (mil.)	Current Yield	Turnover Ratio	Expense Ratio	Beta	Risk Return
$349	0.1%	58%	1.21%	1.29	0.10

BABSON ENTERPRISE FUND

Jones & Babson
Three Crown Center, 2440 Pershing Road
Kansas City, MO 64108
800-422-2766

Investment Objective: This fund seeks capital appreciation by investing in small equity cap stocks. The fund tends to maintain a fully invested position at all times; thus, its share price is more variable than the average equity fund. The past year, the fund returned 43%. The fund seeks capital appreciation by investing in small capitalization common stocks with market values generally below $100 million at the time of purchase. Management relies on a strict value discipline to identify stocks with the potential for above-average growth in earnings that isn't recognized by the market. The fund is currently closed to new investors.

Portfolio Manager: Peter Schliemann
Since: 1990

Minimum:
Initial: Closed
Subsequent: $100
Telephone Exchange: Yes
Distributions:
Income: Annually
Capital Gain: Annually
Front-End Load: Closed
12b-1: None
Redemption Fee: None
Management Company: David L. Babson & Company
Ticker Symbol: BABEX

TOTAL RETURN (%)

1987	1988	1989	1990	1991	5-year	Bull Market	Bear Market
-9.2	32.5	22.5	-15.9	43.0	77.3	49.5	-26.4

INVESTMENT PORTFOLIO

Total Assets (mil.)	Current Yield	Turnover Ratio	Expense Ratio	Beta	Risk Return
$121	0.5%	10%	1.22%	0.93	0.07

BABSON SHADOW STOCK FUND

Jones & Babson
Three Crown Center, 2440 Pershing Road
Kansas City, MO 64108
800-422-2766

Investment Objective: Timing may not be everything, but for this equity vehicle, timing certainly has affected its returns. Concentrating on the small cap, or "neglected," sector of the market, the fund holds many unknown and relatively obscure emerging growth stocks. This strategy paid big dividends in the fund's first full year (1988) of operations. After getting pounded in the October, 1987, crash, small caps made a valiant recovery in 1988, helping to lift the fund to an above-average 22.5% return. Small stocks wallowed in 1989 and plunged in 1990 and the fund's share price followed suit. However, this no-load fund is appropriate for investors anticipating a resurgence in small cap returns to continue.

Portfolio Manager: Peter Schliemann/Nick Whitridge
Since: 1986

Minimum:
Initial: $2,500
Subsequent: $100
Telephone Exchange: Yes
Distributions:
Income: Semiannually
Capital Gain: Annually
Front-End Load: None
12b-1: None
Redemption Fee: None
Management Company: David L. Babson & Company
Ticker Symbol: SHSTX

TOTAL RETURN (%)

1987	1988	1989	1990	1991	5-year	Bull Market	Bear Market
NA	22.5	11.2	-19.3	40.0	NA	42.5	-23.8

INVESTMENT PORTFOLIO

Total Assets (mil.)	Current Yield	Turnover Ratio	Expense Ratio	Beta	Risk Return
$23	0.9%	0%	1.31%	0.77	0.08

BERGER 100 FUND

Berger Associates
210 University Boulevard, Suite 900
Denver, CO 80206
800-333-1001

Investment Objective: This fund seeks long-term capital appreciation by investing in common stocks of established companies. Management generally seeks companies with at least 25% annual earnings growth potential and an historical return on equity of at least 20%. The fund enjoyed a remarkable year in 1991 as investors reaped a return of 89%. Five-year performance rankings place this fund among the leaders for all mutual funds. Although the fund comes with some volatility, longer-term shareholders should continue to be rewarded.

Portfolio Manager: William M. B. Berger
Since: 1974

Minimum:
Initial: $250
Subsequent: $50
Telephone Exchange: Yes
Distributions:
Income: Annually
Capital Gain: Annually
Front-End Load: None
12b-1: 1.00%
Redemption Fee: None
Management Company: Berger Associates
Ticker Symbol: BEONX

TOTAL RETURN (%)

1987	1988	1989	1990	1991	5-year	Bull Market	Bear Market
15.7	1.7	48.3	-5.6	88.8	211.0	99.8	-28.2

INVESTMENT PORTFOLIO

Total Assets (mil.)	Current Yield	Turnover Ratio	Expense Ratio	Beta	Risk Return
$128	0.0%	78%	2.24%	1.22	0.13

BOSTON COMPANY SPECIAL GROWTH FUND

TBC Funds Distributor
53 State Street, Exchange Place, 4th Floor - B
Boston, MA 02114
800-225-5267

Investment Objective: Boston Company Special Growth Fund seeks above-average capital growth primarily through investments in small-company common stocks. Management has traditionally pursued a value discipline, stressing stocks believed to have above-average growth prospects that sell at low price/earnings and price/book ratios. For the most part, the fund's assets are concentrated in relatively cheap industries, including energy and technology, that offer the potential for earnings surprise. While long-term returns have been disappointing, this situation may well reverse itself if the recent small-stock rally persists.

Portfolio Manager: Guy Scott
Since: 1991

Minimum:
Initial: $1,000
Subsequent: None
Telephone Exchange: Yes
Distributions:
Income: Annually
Capital Gain: Annually
Front-End Load: None
12b-1: 0.02%
Redemption Fee: None
Management Company: Boston Company Advisors
Ticker Symbol: BOSSX

TOTAL RETURN (%)

1987	1988	1989	1990	1991	5-year	Bull Market	Bear Market
-3.8	22.0	18.3	-4.8	29.2	70.8	53.2	-24.0

INVESTMENT PORTFOLIO

Total Assets (mil.)	Current Yield	Turnover Ratio	Expense Ratio	Beta	Risk Return
$37	0.0%	222%	1.62%	1.14	0.04

BULL & BEAR SPECIAL EQUITIES FUND

Bull & Bear
11 Hanover Square
New York, NY 10005
800-847-4200

Investment Objective: This fund, organized in 1986, seeks capital appreciation as its sole investment objective. It is organized as a nondiversified fund, which means that it may make investments in one or a relatively few companies to a much greater degree than diversified funds. In addition, the fund uses highly speculative means to obtain its investment objective such as investing in special situations, put and call options, short selling and short-term trading. Its portfolio turnover ratio of nearly 500% underscores the aggressive nature of the fund. Given its highly concentrated portfolio and the use of risk-enhancing strategies, investment in this fund is not for the faint of heart as can be witnessed by its highly variable investment returns.

Portfolio Manager: Brett Sneed
Since: 1988

Minimum:
Initial: $1,000
Subsequent: $100
Telephone Exchange: Yes
Distributions:
Income: Annually
Capital Gain: Annually
Front-End Load: None
12b-1: 1.00%
Redemption Fee: None
Management Company: Bull & Bear Advisers
Ticker Symbol: BBSEX

TOTAL RETURN (%)

1987	1988	1989	1990	1991	5-year	Bull Market	Bear Market
-6.4	22.7	42.3	-36.4	40.5	46.1	29.2	-48.7

INVESTMENT PORTFOLIO

Total Assets (mil.)	Current Yield	Turnover Ratio	Expense Ratio	Beta	Risk Return
$16	0.0%	475%	3.10%	1.61	0.04

CALVERT ARIEL GROWTH FUND

Calvert Securities
4550 Montgomery Avenue, Suite 1000 N.
Bethesda, MD 20814
800-368-2748

Investment Objective: John Rogers, who manages this fund, is quietly distinguishing himself as one of the mutual fund industry's superstars. During the 1987 crash, the fund enjoyed spectacular returns because of Rogers's strategy of selecting high-growth smaller capitalization securities. Many of the fund's holdings were beaten down during the crash; but Rogers jumped into the market in late 1987, capitalizing on many available bargains. Even in 1989—not a great year for small cap stocks—the fund managed a respectable 25% return. This is one of the better managed funds for investors bullish on small cap stocks in the 1990s. Unfortunately, a growing asset base forced the fund to close its doors to new investors.

Portfolio Manager: John Rogers
Since: 1986

Minimum:
Initial: Closed
Subsequent: $250
Telephone Exchange: Yes
Distributions:
Income: Annually
Capital Gain: Annually
Front-End Load: Closed
12b-1: 0.25%
Redemption Fee: None
Management Company: Calvert Asset Management
Ticker Symbol: ARGFX

TOTAL RETURN (%)

1987	1988	1989	1990	1991	5-year	Bull Market	Bear Market
11.4	39.9	25.1	-16.1	32.7	117.2	42.9	-26.0

INVESTMENT PORTFOLIO

Total Assets (mil.)	Current Yield	Turnover Ratio	Expense Ratio	Beta	Risk Return
$240	1.5%	20%	1.31%	1.00	0.05

CGM CAPITAL DEVELOPMENT FUND

New England Securities
Back Bay Annex, P.O. Box 449
Boston, MA 02117
800-345-4048

Investment Objective: Formerly known as the Loomis Sayles Capital Development Fund, CGM Capital Development Fund epitomizes high-growth investing. Longtime manager Ken Heebner is infamous for his rapid trading tactics and his tendency to concentrate assets in relatively few stocks that show good earnings momentum. His potent approach has generally produced extreme results, with the fund finishing most years near the top or bottom of the charts. Fortunately, the fund's often extraordinary years more than compensate for its periods of underperformance. Long-term results beat most rivals and the S&P 500 by a wide margin. The fund recently curtailed the sale of shares to new investors.

Portfolio Manager: Ken Heebner
Since: 1977

Minimum:
Initial: Closed
Subsequent: $50
Telephone Exchange: Yes
Distributions:
Income: Annually
Capital Gain: Annually
Front-End Load: Closed
12b-1: None
Redemption Fee: None
Management Company: Capital Growth Management
Ticker Symbol: LOMCX

TOTAL RETURN (%)

1987	1988	1989	1990	1991	5-year	Bull Market	Bear Market
15.9	-0.3	17.9	1.5	99.1	175.2	118.9	-31.8

INVESTMENT PORTFOLIO

Total Assets (mil.)	Current Yield	Turnover Ratio	Expense Ratio	Beta	Risk Return
$284	0.2%	301%	0.92%	1.52	0.12

CIGNA FUNDS GROUP AGGRESSIVE GROWTH FUND

CIGNA Mutual Funds
One Financial Plaza, 16th Floor
Springfield, MA 01103
800-572-4462

Investment Objective: The objective of this fund is to achieve long-term growth of capital. Primarily, the fund invests in companies with a market capitalization between $25 and $500 million and that are expected to approach earnings growth of 15% annually. Although the fund tends to focus on companies that are in the earlier stages of growth and development, management may invest in larger, more established companies that also exhibit strong growth potential. The past year, the fund returned a stellar 64%. Investors should, however, note the 5% front-end load.

Portfolio Manager: Dave Shinn
Since: 1989

Minimum:
Initial: $500
Subsequent: $50
Telephone Exchange: Yes
Distributions:
Income: Annually
Capital Gain: Annually
Front-End Load: 5.00%
12b-1: None
Redemption Fee: None
Management Company: CIGNA Investments
Ticker Symbol: CAGFX

TOTAL RETURN (%)

1987	1988	1989	1990	1991	5-year	Bull Market	Bear Market
-11.5	12.8	20.9	-6.5	63.9	84.9	95.9	-34.7

INVESTMENT PORTFOLIO

Total Assets (mil.)	Current Yield	Turnover Ratio	Expense Ratio	Beta	Risk Return
$14	0.0%	137%	1.25%	1.33	0.08

COLONIAL SMALL STOCK INDEX TRUST

Colonial Investment Services
One Financial Center, 14th Floor
Boston, MA 02110
800-248-2828

Investment Objective: Colonial Small Stock Index Trust seeks to provide investment results that correspond to the price and yield performance of the stocks that compose the smallest one-fifth of the stocks listed on the New York Stock Exchange. In mirroring the performance of its benchmark index, which has significantly underperformed the large cap indices in recent years, the fund has produced subpar results since its inception. With a median market cap below $100 million, one would have anticipated a strong showing in 1991, but the 19% return failed to meet expectations.

Portfolio Manager: Steve Lanzendorf
Since: 1990

Minimum:
Initial: $1,000
Subsequent: $50
Telephone Exchange: Yes
Distributions:
Income: Annually
Capital Gain: Annually
Front-End Load: 5.75%
12b-1: 0.25%
Redemption Fee: None
Management Company: Colonial Management Associates
Ticker Symbol: CSMIX

TOTAL RETURN (%)

1987	1988	1989	1990	1991	5-year	Bull Market	Bear Market
-10.8	27.2	11.8	-23.7	19.0	15.3	22.0	-27.8

INVESTMENT PORTFOLIO

Total Assets (mil.)	Current Yield	Turnover Ratio	Expense Ratio	Beta	Risk Return
$25	0.2%	79%	1.94%	0.87	0.03

COLUMBIA SPECIAL FUND

Columbia Funds Management
1301 S.W. 5th Avenue, P.O. Box 1350
Portland, OR 97207
800-547-1707

Investment Objective: Capital appreciation is this fund's primary investment objective. The fund invests in companies that are more aggressive than the market, so the fund carries an above-average beta. Started in 1986, the fund whipped most rivals for 4 straight years. Although it didn't fully resist the 1990's bear market, it still sports one of the better 5-year total return figures of any mutual fund. It owes its success to a skillful sector rotation strategy. Trading rapidly, it shifts assets among relatively few aggressive growth industries that it believes will perform well. Its skill at picking stocks and sectors and its good timing suggest it will continue to provide excellent long-term results.

Portfolio Manager: Alan J. Folkman
Since: 1985

Minimum:
Initial: $2,000
Subsequent: $10
Telephone Exchange: Yes
Distributions:
Income: Annually
Capital Gain: Annually
Front-End Load: None
12b-1: None
Redemption Fee: None
Management Company: Columbia Funds Management
Ticker Symbol: CLSPX

TOTAL RETURN (%)

1987	1988	1989	1990	1991	5-year	Bull Market	Bear Market
3.0	42.5	31.9	-12.4	50.5	155.4	69.4	-35.9

INVESTMENT PORTFOLIO

Total Assets (mil.)	Current Yield	Turnover Ratio	Expense Ratio	Beta	Risk Return
$220	0.0%	147%	1.32%	1.39	0.06

DEAN WITTER DEVELOPING GROWTH SECURITIES

Dean Witter Reynolds
Two World Trade Center, 72nd Floor
New York, NY 10048
800-869-3863

Investment Objective: This fund seeks long-term capital appreciation through investments in small- to medium-size companies. However, the portfolio is occasionally dotted with larger firms that exhibit strong growth potential. Like the small-company sector in general, the fund underperformed most market averages during the entire bull market of the 1980s. But at long last, the fund returned a solid 48% in 1991. The fund does carry a high 2.02% expense ratio.

Portfolio Manager: Robert Kimtis
Since: 1986

Minimum:
Initial: $1,000
Subsequent: $100
Telephone Exchange: Yes
Distributions:
Income: Annually
Capital Gain: Annually
Front-End Load: None
12b-1: 1.00%
Redemption Fee: 5.00%
Management Company: Dean Witter Reynolds
Ticker Symbol: DWDGX

TOTAL RETURN (%)

1987	1988	1989	1990	1991	5-year	Bull Market	Bear Market
-2.5	8.9	15.0	-3.8	48.2	74.1	78.1	-38.3

INVESTMENT PORTFOLIO

Total Assets (mil.)	Current Yield	Turnover Ratio	Expense Ratio	Beta	Risk Return
$114	0.0%	53%	2.02%	1.42	0.06

DELAWARE GROUP DELCAP CONCEPT I

Delaware Distributors
10 Penn Center Plaza
Philadelphia, PA 19103
800-523-4640

Investment Objective: Long-term capital growth is this fund's primary investment objective. Securities purchased are of companies expected to have a higher earnings-growth potential than the average stock listed on the S&P 500. Management emphasizes companies that have financial strength, management expertise and strong growth potential within their industry. Should the market warrant a temporary defensive approach, the fund may invest in fixed-income obligations issued by the government. A disciplined strategy has rewarded investors well since the fund's inception in 1986.

Portfolio Manager: Edward Antonian
Since: 1986

Minimum:
Initial: $250
Subsequent: $25
Telephone Exchange: Yes
Distributions:
Income: Annually
Capital Gain: Annually
Front-End Load: 4.75%
12b-1: 0.30%
Redemption Fee: None
Management Company: Delaware Management
Ticker Symbol: DFCIX

TOTAL RETURN (%)

1987	1988	1989	1990	1991	5-year	Bull Market	Bear Market
17.1	17.8	33.9	-3.5	42.3	153.7	55.8	-26.0

INVESTMENT PORTFOLIO

Total Assets (mil.)	Current Yield	Turnover Ratio	Expense Ratio	Beta	Risk Return
$653	0.1%	33%	1.43%	1.05	0.07

DELAWARE TREND FUND

Delaware Distributors
10 Penn Center Plaza
Philadelphia, PA 19103
800-523-4640

Investment Objective: This fund invests primarily in common stocks and securities convertible into common stocks of emerging and growth-oriented companies. To achieve its goal of long-term capital appreciation, the fund seeks dominant trends in the economy and purchases stocks that it believes will benefit from those trends. Management seeks companies with such fundamental strong points as superior management skills, product development and above-average sales and earnings growth. Because of its bent toward emerging growth stocks, the fund's annual returns are not directly comparable with blue chip indices such as the S&P 500 Index and the Dow Jones Industrial Average.

Portfolio Manager: Edward Antonian
Since: 1986

Minimum:
Initial: $250
Subsequent: $25
Telephone Exchange: Yes
Distributions:
Income: Annually
Capital Gain: Annually
Front-End Load: 4.75%
12b-1: None
Redemption Fee: None
Management Company: Delaware Management
Ticker Symbol: DELTX

TOTAL RETURN (%)

1987	1988	1989	1990	1991	5-year	Bull Market	Bear Market
-7.8	26.8	49.7	-24.6	74.5	130.3	85.3	-36.7

INVESTMENT PORTFOLIO

Total Assets (mil.)	Current Yield	Turnover Ratio	Expense Ratio	Beta	Risk Return
$92	0.0%	67%	1.30%	1.39	0.10

DELAWARE VALUE FUND

Delaware Distributors
10 Penn Center Plaza
Philadelphia, PA 19103
800-523-4640

Investment Objective: Delaware Value seeks capital growth through investments in large and medium capitalization common stocks with market values ranging from $250 million to $1 billion. Although management follows a value discipline, its flexible definition of value prevents it from focusing on a single stock profile. The fund's portfolio consists of a mix of asset plays, restructuring candidates and growth stocks with unrecognized earnings power. Major industries currently include communications, consumer nondurables and industrial products. The past year, the fund posted an above-average return of 51%.

Portfolio Manager: Edward Trumpbour
Since: 1987

Minimum:
Initial: $250
Subsequent: $25
Telephone Exchange: Yes
Distributions:
Income: Annually
Capital Gain: Annually
Front-End Load: 4.75%
12b-1: 0.30%
Redemption Fee: None
Management Company: Delaware Management
Ticker Symbol: DEVLX

TOTAL RETURN (%)

1987	1988	1989	1990	1991	5-year	Bull Market	Bear Market
NA	26.4	31.9	-13.1	51.0	NA	57.5	-22.7

INVESTMENT PORTFOLIO

Total Assets (mil.)	Current Yield	Turnover Ratio	Expense Ratio	Beta	Risk Return
$12	0.0%	99%	2.26%	1.04	0.08

DFA U.S. 9-10 SMALL COMPANY PORTFOLIO

Dimensional Fund Advisors
1299 Ocean Avenue, Suite 650
Santa Monica, CA 90401
213-395-8005

Investment Objective: This fund attempts to capture the "small-firm effect" by investing in the entire universe of small-firm stocks. The small-firm effect is the seemingly greater risk-adjusted returns provided by small-firm stocks. At year-end, the fund contained approximately 2,200 stocks, with an average equity market value of about $26 million. Stocks are selected if they have an equity market value less than that of the stock that separates the bottom 20% of NYSE-listed stocks, ranked according to size. They are sold when their equity caps grow to the point that they fall into the top 30% of NYSE stocks, ranked according to size. It is one of the few index funds that focuses solely on small cap stocks.

Portfolio Manager: Rex Singuefeld
Since: 1981

Minimum:
Initial: $50,000
Subsequent: None
Telephone Exchange: No
Distributions:
Income: Annually
Capital Gain: Annually
Front-End Load: None
12b-1: None
Redemption Fee: None
Management Company: Dimensional Fund Advisors
Ticker Symbol: DFSCX

TOTAL RETURN (%)

1987	1988	1989	1990	1991	5-year	Bull Market	Bear Market
-9.3	22.8	10.2	-21.6	44.4	39.0	45.6	-26.8

INVESTMENT PORTFOLIO

Total Assets (mil.)	Current Yield	Turnover Ratio	Expense Ratio	Beta	Risk Return
$722	0.7%	4%	0.62%	0.92	0.08

DREYFUS LEVERAGE FUND

Dreyfus Service
200 Park Avenue, 7th Floor
New York, NY 10166
800-782-6620

Investment Objective: Dreyfus Leverage is a ship that sails many seas. This fund finds its home in the aggressive growth section primarily based on the speculative investments tools it may utilize. The fund may leverage, sell short or lend its portfolio securities. Also, as high as 30% of the fund's assets may be invested in foreign markets. For those investors who associate aggressive growth with small cap stocks, this fund begs to differ. Single-year return comparisons to the S&P 500 may not appear very similar, but the fund's long-run averages closely approximate the index.

Portfolio Manager: Howard Stein
Since: 1988

Minimum:
Initial: $2,500
Subsequent: $100
Telephone Exchange: Yes
Distributions:
Income: Annually
Capital Gain: Annually
Front-End Load: 4.50%
12b-1: None
Redemption Fee: None
Management Company: Dreyfus Corporation
Ticker Symbol: DRLEX

TOTAL RETURN (%)

1987	1988	1989	1990	1991	5-year	Bull Market	Bear Market
11.2	1.8	20.4	-1.5	32.7	78.3	36.4	-17.7

INVESTMENT PORTFOLIO

Total Assets (mil.)	Current Yield	Turnover Ratio	Expense Ratio	Beta	Risk Return
$477	2.0%	89%	1.34%	0.85	0.06

DREYFUS STRATEGIC INVESTING

Dreyfus Service
200 Park Avenue, 7th Floor
New York, NY 10166
800-782-6620

Investment Objective: One of the more highly touted funds that began operations in late 1986, this nondiversified fund is able to use speculative investment techniques such as short-selling, leveraging and options transactions to boost the value of the fund. In addition, the fund is able to invest in foreign securities and lower-rated debt securities. The fund hit a home run during its first full year of operations when it returned 34% in 1987, the year of the stock market meltdown. Thus, its 5-year track record looks exceptionally good. However, it also had an exceptional year during 1989 and managed to dodge the bear market that began in the fall of 1990. Decent results were again posted in 1991.

Portfolio Manager: Richard Shields
Since: 1989

Minimum:
Initial: $2,500
Subsequent: $500
Telephone Exchange: Yes
Distributions:
Income: Annually
Capital Gain: Annually
Front-End Load: 4.50%
12b-1: 0.30%
Redemption Fee: None
Management Company: Dreyfus Corporation
Ticker Symbol: DRSIX

TOTAL RETURN (%)

1987	1988	1989	1990	1991	5-year	Bull Market	Bear Market
34.4	-5.0	32.3	0.7	41.3	140.5	35.4	-10.7

INVESTMENT PORTFOLIO

Total Assets (mil.)	Current Yield	Turnover Ratio	Expense Ratio	Beta	Risk Return
$146	0.6%	275%	2.89%	0.74	0.09

ECLIPSE EQUITY FUND

Eclipse Financial Asset Trust
144 East 30th Street
New York, NY 10016
800-872-2710

Investment Objective: One of the two portfolios in the Eclipse Asset Trust, the equity fund seeks high total returns from equity investments. In selecting issues, approximately equal weight is given to estimated relative intrinsic value, expected future earnings growth and current and expected dividend income. Thus, although characterized as an aggressive growth fund, the fund at times will exhibit characteristics of total return, value and growth and income funds. In general, the companies whose shares are purchased will sell at a total market cap less than the average total market cap of those stocks that make up the S&P 500 Index.

Portfolio Manager: W. G. McCain
Since: 1987

Minimum:
Initial: $3,000
Subsequent: None
Telephone Exchange: Yes
Distributions:
Income: Quarterly
Capital Gain: Annually
Front-End Load: None
12b-1: None
Redemption Fee: None
Management Company: Towneley Capital Management
Ticker Symbol: EEQFX

TOTAL RETURN (%)

1987	1988	1989	1990	1991	5-year	Bull Market	Bear Market
NA	12.7	16.4	-13.6	34.6	NA	38.4	-23.5

INVESTMENT PORTFOLIO

Total Assets (mil.)	Current Yield	Turnover Ratio	Expense Ratio	Beta	Risk Return
$139	4.0%	154%	1.18%	0.86	0.06

FIDELITY GROWTH COMPANY FUND

Fidelity Distributors Corporation
82 Devonshire Street, Mail Zone L7B
Boston, MA 02109
800-544-8888

Investment Objective: This fund, which began operations in 1983, seeks capital appreciation by investing primarily in the common stocks of companies believed to have above-average growth characteristics. Its investments include both smaller companies in new and emerging areas of the economy and larger companies, operating in mature industries or declining industries that have been revitalized. The fund's mix of small- and large-company stocks has allowed it to participate in the market's run up during 1988 and 1989 while sidestepping the steep bear market in emerging growth stocks that persisted during most of 1990. Its 5-year return is above average.

Portfolio Manager: Robert Stansky
Since: 1987

Minimum:
Initial: $2,500
Subsequent: $250
Telephone Exchange: Yes
Distributions:
Income: Annually
Capital Gain: Annually
Front-End Load: 3.00%
12b-1: None
Redemption Fee: None
Management Company: Fidelity Management & Research
Ticker Symbol: FDGRX

TOTAL RETURN (%)

1987	1988	1989	1990	1991	5-year	Bull Market	Bear Market
-1.7	16.1	41.6	3.6	48.3	148.3	68.0	-28.0

INVESTMENT PORTFOLIO

Total Assets (mil.)	Current Yield	Turnover Ratio	Expense Ratio	Beta	Risk Return
$1,132	0.3%	189%	1.14%	1.17	0.07

FIDELITY LOW-PRICED STOCK FUND

Fidelity Distributors Corporation
82 Devonshire Street, Mail Zone L7B
Boston, MA 02109
800-544-8888

Investment Objective: This fund seeks capital appreciation by investing in a portfolio of low-priced stocks. Generally, 65% of the fund's assets will be in stocks that were bought at below $5 or have a price per share that places the stock in the bottom 40% of the Wilshire 5000 Index. Because of these parameters, the fund is primarily invested in small cap stocks. The fund's brief 2-year history has thus far been rewarding to shareholders. For those investors looking for a new twist to stock selection, this fund might be right up your alley.

Portfolio Manager: Joel Tillinghast
Since: 1989

Minimum:
Initial: $2,500
Subsequent: $250
Telephone Exchange: Yes
Distributions:
Income: Annually
Capital Gain: Annually
Front-End Load: None
12b-1: None
Redemption Fee: None
Management Company: Fidelity Management & Research
Ticker Symbol: FLPSX

TOTAL RETURN (%)

1987	1988	1989	1990	1991	5-year	Bull Market	Bear Market
NA	NA	NA	-0.1	46.3	NA	35.5	-15.5

INVESTMENT PORTFOLIO

Total Assets (mil.)	Current Yield	Turnover Ratio	Expense Ratio	Beta	Risk Return
$280	1.1%	126%	1.92%	NA	NA

FIDELITY OTC PORTFOLIO

Fidelity Distributors Corporation
82 Devonshire Street, Mail Zone L7B
Boston, MA 02109
800-544-8888

Investment Objective: Fidelity OTC Portfolio invests primarily in securities traded on the over-the-counter market, although it may invest up to 35% of its assets in exchange-listed securities. Former manager Morris Smith, who left the fund in May of 1990 to manage Fidelity's flagship Magellan Fund, guided the fund to an outstanding record during his 5-year tenure. New manager Alan Radlo is more of a growth player than his predecessor. Although it's too soon to evaluate the long-term merits of his earnings-driven approach, it has so far served the fund well, enabling it to resist decline considerably better than most small-company vehicles. The past year, the fund posted a solid 49% gain.

Portfolio Manager: Alan Radlo
Since: 1990

Minimum:
Initial: $2,500
Subsequent: $250
Telephone Exchange: Yes
Distributions:
Income: Annually
Capital Gain: Annually
Front-End Load: 3.00%
12b-1: None
Redemption Fee: None
Management Company: Fidelity Management & Research
Ticker Symbol: FOCPX

TOTAL RETURN (%)

1987	1988	1989	1990	1991	5-year	Bull Market	Bear Market
1.6	22.9	30.4	-4.8	49.2	131.2	62.1	-21.4

INVESTMENT PORTFOLIO

Total Assets (mil.)	Current Yield	Turnover Ratio	Expense Ratio	Beta	Risk Return
$919	0.4%	198%	1.29%	0.94	0.09

FIDELITY TREND FUND

Fidelity Distributors Corporation
82 Devonshire Street, Mail Zone L7B
Boston, MA 02109
800-544-8888

Investment Objective: This fund seeks growth through early identification of new growth trends. When making individual security selections, management studies the momentum in trends of earnings and security prices of individual companies, industries and the market in general. Management believes that there are two keys to maximizing long-term investment results: diversification (spreading the fund's assets into 50 different companies and across 10 or more industries) and a fully invested position. This philosophy has served long-term shareholders well, as the fund has achieved a better than 13% average annual return over its 33-year history.

Portfolio Manager: Alan Leifer
Since: 1987

Minimum:
Initial: $2,500
Subsequent: $250
Telephone Exchange: Yes
Distributions:
Income: Annually
Capital Gain: Annually
Front-End Load: None
12b-1: None
Redemption Fee: None
Management Company: Fidelity Management & Research
Ticker Symbol: FTRNX

TOTAL RETURN (%)

1987	1988	1989	1990	1991	5-year	Bull Market	Bear Market
-4.2	24.3	31.7	-12.7	36.3	86.6	46.1	-26.1

INVESTMENT PORTFOLIO

Total Assets (mil.)	Current Yield	Turnover Ratio	Expense Ratio	Beta	Risk Return
$788	0.9%	48%	0.61%	1.17	0.05

FINANCIAL DYNAMICS FUND

INVESCO Funds Group
P.O. Box 2040
Denver, CO 80201
800-525-8085

Investment Objective: By using aggressive investment techniques, this fund seeks to attain its goal of capital appreciation. When choosing its portfolio, management looks at several factors: the growth of earnings per share, future growth of sales and current market data on the company. Because of its high beta, the fund is more suited for aggressive investors who can tolerate above-average volatility. In addition, the fund has an above-average portfolio turnover ratio, which could impair long-run returns.

Portfolio Manager: William Keithler
Since: 1989

Minimum:
Initial: $250
Subsequent: $25
Telephone Exchange: Yes
Distributions:
Income: Annually
Capital Gain: Annually
Front-End Load: None
12b-1: 0.25%
Redemption Fee: None
Management Company: INVESCO Funds Group
Ticker Symbol: FIDYX

TOTAL RETURN (%)

1987	1988	1989	1990	1991	5-year	Bull Market	Bear Market
3.9	9.1	22.7	-6.4	67.0	117.4	76.7	-28.2

INVESTMENT PORTFOLIO

Total Assets (mil.)	Current Yield	Turnover Ratio	Expense Ratio	Beta	Risk Return
$110	0.0%	243%	1.15%	1.18	0.10

FLAG INVESTORS EMERGING GROWTH FUND

Alex Brown & Sons
135 East Baltimore Street
Baltimore, MD 21202
800-767-3524

Investment Objective: Flag Investors Emerging Growth Fund seeks capital appreciation through investments in domestic and foreign emerging growth companies with revenues under $500 million that it believes are poised for rapid growth in revenues, earnings, assets and cash flow. Typically, the fund concentrates its assets in relatively few rapid growth industries. Portfolio Manager Richard Hackney likes to roll the dice often as evidenced by the fund's past 2 years. After falling by more than 20% in 1990, it rose by nearly 50% the past year. If it were not for the fund's front-end load and 12b-1 fee, this fund would be considered an excellent vehicle for aggressive investors.

Portfolio Manager: Richard C. Hackney
Since: 1987

Minimum:
Initial: $2,000
Subsequent: $500
Telephone Exchange: Yes
Distributions:
Income: Annually
Capital Gain: Annually
Front-End Load: 4.50%
12b-1: 0.25%
Redemption Fee: None
Management Company: Flag Investors Management
Ticker Symbol: FLEGX

TOTAL RETURN (%)

1987	1988	1989	1990	1991	5-year	Bull Market	Bear Market
NA	17.0	32.2	-21.1	49.6	NA	58.0	-36.3

INVESTMENT PORTFOLIO

Total Assets (mil.)	Current Yield	Turnover Ratio	Expense Ratio	Beta	Risk Return
$45	0.0%	82%	1.50%	1.48	0.01

FORTY-FOUR WALL STREET EQUITY FUND

Beckerman
26 Broadway, 2nd Floor
New York, NY 10004
800-543-2620

Investment Objective: This fund seeks capital appreciation by investing in stocks that management believes are overlooked by the market. The portfolio tends to represent more of an overall value play as price-earnings and price-to-book multiples are on the low side. Portfolio turnover has tripled in the past 2 years and although expenses have fallen by nearly 20% over this time frame, the fund's expense ratio is still an eye-popping 4.28%. The fund has returned only 9% over the past 5 years and 25.7% of that was made up the past year.

Portfolio Manager: Mark D. Beckerman
Since: 1988

Minimum:
Initial: $1,000
Subsequent: $100
Telephone Exchange: No
Distributions:
Income: Annually
Capital Gain: Annually
Front-End Load: None
12b-1: None
Redemption Fee: None
Management Company: MDB Asset Management
Ticker Symbol: FWLEX

TOTAL RETURN (%)

1987	1988	1989	1990	1991	5-year	Bull Market	Bear Market
-41.9	32.3	23.5	-8.6	25.7	9.0	33.1	-18.3

INVESTMENT PORTFOLIO

Total Assets (mil.)	Current Yield	Turnover Ratio	Expense Ratio	Beta	Risk Return
$4	0.0%	235%	4.28%	0.74	0.05

FORTY-FOUR WALL STREET FUND

Beckerman
26 Broadway, 2nd Floor
New York, NY 10004
800-543-2620

Investment Objective: Forty-Four Wall Street Fund has a checkered past. Besides incurring substantial losses from 1981 to 1987, the fund's former manager and president, David Baker, encountered severe legal problems, forcing the sale of the fund in 1988. In contrast to Baker's aggressive tactics (he bet heavily on few rapid growth stocks), the fund's current adviser stresses companies with cheap assets that appear ripe for restructuring. This approach produced decent results in 1988. However, returns have been hurt by a higher than average expense ratio as a result of the fund's small asset base.

Portfolio Manager: Mark D. Beckerman
Since: 1988

Minimum:
Initial: $1,000
Subsequent: $100
Telephone Exchange: Yes
Distributions:
Income: Annually
Capital Gain: Annually
Front-End Load: None
12b-1: None
Redemption Fee: 0.25%
Management Company: MDB Asset Management
Ticker Symbol: FWALX

TOTAL RETURN (%)

1987	1988	1989	1990	1991	5-year	Bull Market	Bear Market
-34.6	19.3	4.6	-18.7	20.5	-20.1	26.6	-19.0

INVESTMENT PORTFOLIO

Total Assets (mil.)	Current Yield	Turnover Ratio	Expense Ratio	Beta	Risk Return
$3	0.0%	194%	9.28%	0.80	0.03

FOUNDERS DISCOVERY FUND

Founders Asset Management
2930 East Third Avenue
Denver, CO 80206
800-525-2440

Investment Objective: This no-load fund seeks capital appreciation by investing in small, rapidly growing U.S. companies. Management's search for companies with rapid growth in earnings has inevitably led to large concentrations in emerging growth industries, including computer software, pollution control, technology and leisure, making the fund a highly potent vehicle. While its stocks have the potential to soar when investors' expectations run high, as was the case the past year, their high stock valuations leave plenty of room for price correction should earnings disappoint. All told, this fund offers enormous growth potential, but it's not for the risk averse.

Portfolio Manager: Investment management team
Since: 1989

Minimum:
Initial: $1,000
Subsequent: $100
Telephone Exchange: Yes
Distributions:
Income: Annually
Capital Gain: Annually
Front-End Load: None
12b-1: 0.22%
Redemption Fee: None
Management Company: Founders Asset Management
Ticker Symbol: FDISX

TOTAL RETURN (%)

1987	1988	1989	1990	1991	5-year	Bull Market	Bear Market
NA	NA	NA	13.2	62.5	NA	70.7	-19.1

INVESTMENT PORTFOLIO

Total Assets (mil.)	Current Yield	Turnover Ratio	Expense Ratio	Beta	Risk Return
$37	0.0%	271%	2.03%	1.19	0.09

FOUNDERS FRONTIER FUND

Founders Asset Management
2930 East Third Avenue
Denver, CO 80206
800-525-2440

Investment Objective: Started in 1987, Founders Frontier Fund invests primarily in small- and medium-sized companies with annual sales ranging from $25 million to $250 million. The fund may invest in large companies or foreign stocks, if management believes market conditions warrant such action. In its brief 4-year history, its returns have been excellent. High expenses are anticipated to fall with the fund's growing asset base. The fund has historically traded rapidly, adjusting its tactics to current market conditions.

Portfolio Manager: Investment management team
Since: 1990

Minimum:
Initial: $1,000
Subsequent: $100
Telephone Exchange: Yes
Distributions:
Income: Annually
Capital Gain: Annually
Front-End Load: None
12b-1: 0.25%
Redemption Fee: None
Management Company: Founders Asset Management
Ticker Symbol: FOUNX

TOTAL RETURN (%)

1987	1988	1989	1990	1991	5-year	Bull Market	Bear Market
NA	29.2	44.3	-7.5	49.9	NA	55.4	-22.3

INVESTMENT PORTFOLIO

Total Assets (mil.)	Current Yield	Turnover Ratio	Expense Ratio	Beta	Risk Return
$87	0.4%	207%	1.71%	1.26	0.07

FOUNDERS SPECIAL FUND

Founders Asset Management
2930 East Third Avenue
Denver, CO 80206
800-525-2440

Investment Objective: Above-average capital appreciation is the goal of this fund, which it attempts to achieve via investments in small- to medium-sized companies. The portfolio is dominated by companies with annual sales between $25 million and $250 million. In making stock selections, management seeks companies, foreign or domestic, that have high rates of growth and strong market positions. To hedge against a possible decline in the portfolio's value, the fund can purchase options on stock indices—but no more than 10% of the fund's assets can be used for that purpose.

Portfolio Manager: Investment management team
Since: 1990

Minimum:
Initial: $1,000
Subsequent: $25
Telephone Exchange: Yes
Distributions:
Income: Annually
Capital Gain: Annually
Front-End Load: None
12b-1: None
Redemption Fee: None
Management Company: Founders Asset Management
Ticker Symbol: FRSPX

TOTAL RETURN (%)

1987	1988	1989	1990	1991	5-year	Bull Market	Bear Market
5.2	13.2	39.2	-10.4	63.7	143.1	66.9	-24.7

INVESTMENT PORTFOLIO

Total Assets (mil.)	Current Yield	Turnover Ratio	Expense Ratio	Beta	Risk Return
$179	0.5%	146%	1.20%	1.26	0.09

FUND TRUST AGGRESSIVE GROWTH FUND

Signature Financial Group
6 St. James Avenue, 9th Floor
Boston, MA 02116
800-638-1896

Investment Objective: The Fund Trust Aggressive Fund seeks capital appreciation as its primary investment objective. The fund hopes to achieve the objective by investing in a portfolio of aggressive growth mutual funds. Further diversification may be achieved by investing in other funds, such as bond and money market mutual funds. With the exception of 1991, the fund has underperformed the S&P 500 every year since its inception in 1984. One problem with managing a "fund of funds" is the erosion of returns because of pyramiding expenses. Shareholders of this fund bear not only the cost of its operation but the operating costs of the funds in which it invests.

Portfolio Manager: Michael Hirsch
Since: 1984

Minimum:
Initial: $1,000
Subsequent: $100
Telephone Exchange: Yes
Distributions:
Income: Annually
Capital Gain: Annually
Front-End Load: 1.50%
12b-1: 0.46%
Redemption Fee: None
Management Company: M. D. Hirsch Investment Management
Ticker Symbol: FTAGX

TOTAL RETURN (%)

1987	1988	1989	1990	1991	5-year	Bull Market	Bear Market
-0.7	11.8	21.9	-7.4	38.0	72.7	41.0	-21.4

INVESTMENT PORTFOLIO

Total Assets (mil.)	Current Yield	Turnover Ratio	Expense Ratio	Beta	Risk Return
$23	1.7%	45%	1.86%	0.97	0.07

GROWTH FUND OF AMERICA

American Funds Distributor
333 South Hope Street, 52nd Floor
Los Angeles, CA 90071
800-421-9900

Investment Objective: This aggressive growth vehicle has generated above-average performance at reasonable risk levels. Despite a 5.75% front-end load, which effectively reduces long-term returns, the fund is a strong candidate for any investor's diversified portfolio. The fund's management team has shown a consistent ability to preserve capital in tough times and capitalize on rising markets. In 1987, for instance, sales of appreciated securities boosted cash to about 25% of assets, which helped protect the fund's gains during the October, 1987, crash. Then, the fund moved back into the market in late 1987 and early 1988, only to enjoy strong 1988 and 1989 returns. The past year, the fund returned a respectable 36%.

Portfolio Manager: Multiple portfolio counselors
Since: 1973

Minimum:
Initial: $1,000
Subsequent: $50
Telephone Exchange: Yes
Distributions:
Income: Annually
Capital Gain: Annually
Front-End Load: 5.75%
12b-1: 0.17%
Redemption Fee: None
Management Company: Capital Research & Management
Ticker Symbol: AGTHX

TOTAL RETURN (%)

1987	1988	1989	1990	1991	5-year	Bull Market	Bear Market
7.3	18.5	30.1	-4.1	35.8	115.3	46.9	-23.6

INVESTMENT PORTFOLIO

Total Assets (mil.)	Current Yield	Turnover Ratio	Expense Ratio	Beta	Risk Return
$2,974	1.4%	19%	0.83%	1.04	0.06

HARTWELL EMERGING GROWTH FUND

Keystone Distributors
99 High Street, 29th Floor
Boston, MA 02110
800-633-4900

Investment Objective: This fund was bought by Keystone Distributors in 1990. It seeks capital appreciation through the selection of securities with long-term growth prospects. These securities tend to sell at a high multiple of earnings relative to the market average. Thus, the fund's share price tends to be quite volatile. Nonetheless, the fund managed to post gains during both 1987 and 1990, which were both down years for emerging growth stocks. Its 5-year returns are above both the average for the market and the majority of aggressive growth funds. As evidenced by its above-average portfolio turnover ratio, the fund tends to assume an aggressive trading posture. Its 5-year results are among the best in the industry.

Portfolio Manager: John M. Hartwell
Since: 1968

Minimum:
Initial: $1,000
Subsequent: None
Telephone Exchange: Yes
Distributions:
Income: Annually
Capital Gain: Annually
Front-End Load: 4.75%
12b-1: 0.04%
Redemption Fee: None
Management Company: Hartwell Management
Ticker Symbol: HRTLX

TOTAL RETURN (%)

1987	1988	1989	1990	1991	5-year	Bull Market	Bear Market
3.7	19.2	38.6	2.7	72.5	203.4	89.0	-31.9

INVESTMENT PORTFOLIO

Total Assets (mil.)	Current Yield	Turnover Ratio	Expense Ratio	Beta	Risk Return
$85	0.0%	96%	2.50%	1.53	0.08

HARTWELL GROWTH FUND

Keystone Distributors
99 High Street, 29th Floor
Boston, MA 02110
800-633-4900

Investment Objective: This fund invests primarily in common stocks and preferred stocks. Securities are selected on the basis of fundamental research, and the fund employs a longer-term holding approach to investing as evidenced by its below-average portfolio turnover ratio. When selecting stocks, management seeks companies that have a history of sales and earnings growth of more than 30% annually, are number one or two in market position and have the ability to grow without accumulating debt. Because of its emphasis on high-growth stocks, the fund generally contains stocks with high price-earnings ratios and thus tends to be highly volatile.

Portfolio Manager: William C. Miller IV
Since: 1984

Minimum:
Initial: $1,000
Subsequent: None
Telephone Exchange: Yes
Distributions:
Income: Annually
Capital Gain: Annually
Front-End Load: 4.75%
12b-1: 0.04%
Redemption Fee: None
Management Company: Hartwell Management
Ticker Symbol: HRGRX

TOTAL RETURN (%)

1987	1988	1989	1990	1991	5-year	Bull Market	Bear Market
23.6	3.1	35.0	-15.3	62.5	136.7	51.4	-2.1

INVESTMENT PORTFOLIO

Total Assets (mil.)	Current Yield	Turnover Ratio	Expense Ratio	Beta	Risk Return
$19	0.0%	80%	3.00%	1.21	0.09

HEARTLAND VALUE FUND

Dain Bosworth
790 North Milwaukee Street
Milwaukee, WI 33202
800-432-7856

Investment Objective: As the name suggests, this fund seeks long-term capital appreciation by investing in companies that meet technical measures of value. The portfolio limits itself to companies with market capitalizations under $300 million. When looking for selections, management seeks firms selling at or below book value, price-earnings ratios below the market's and a low debt picture. The fund came into its own the past year by producing a strong 44% return. The one-two punch of small cap stocks with a value bent should provide investors with substantial returns over the long haul.

Portfolio Manager: William J. Nasgouitz
Since: 1984

Minimum:
Initial: $1,000
Subsequent: None
Telephone Exchange: Yes
Distributions:
Income: Annually
Capital Gain: Annually
Front-End Load: 4.50%
12b-1: 0.30%
Redemption Fee: None
Management Company: Heartland Advisors
Ticker Symbol: HRTVX

TOTAL RETURN (%)

1987	1988	1989	1990	1991	5-year	Bull Market	Bear Market
-8.4	28.2	6.6	-17.1	44.4	49.7	49.0	-27.7

INVESTMENT PORTFOLIO

Total Assets (mil.)	Current Yield	Turnover Ratio	Expense Ratio	Beta	Risk Return
$28	0.4%	76%	1.70%	0.80	0.07

IDS DISCOVERY FUND

IDS Financial Services
1000 Roanoke Building
Minneapolis, MN 55402
800-328-8300

Investment Objective: The IDS Discovery Fund's objective is capital appreciation. Investments are made in small companies that generally have revenues in the range of $25 million to $250 million annually. Since the arrival of the current portfolio manager, Ray Hirsch, in 1988, the fund has produced enviable returns. He has accomplished this by adding more investments in medium cap companies. Because of its movement away from a pure small cap strategy, the fund avoided the dismal market for these stocks in 1990 during which the "typical" small cap stock tumbled 22%. The past year, the fund returned a strong 53%.

Portfolio Manager: Ray Hirsch
Since: 1988

Minimum:
Initial: $2,000
Subsequent: $100
Telephone Exchange: Yes
Distributions:
Income: Annually
Capital Gain: Annually
Front-End Load: 5.00%
12b-1: 0.10%
Redemption Fee: None
Management Company: IDS Financial
Ticker Symbol: INDYX

TOTAL RETURN (%)

1987	1988	1989	1990	1991	5-year	Bull Market	Bear Market
-10.6	12.9	31.0	0.0	52.8	102.3	62.9	-28.4

INVESTMENT PORTFOLIO

Total Assets (mil.)	Current Yield	Turnover Ratio	Expense Ratio	Beta	Risk Return
$242	0.2%	95%	0.98%	1.17	0.08

IDS STRATEGY AGGRESSIVE EQUITY FUND

IDS Financial Services
1000 Roanoke Building
Minneapolis, MN 55402
800-328-8300

Investment Objective: IDS Strategy Aggressive Equity Fund pursues its sole objective of capital growth primarily through investments in common stocks of growth companies. Most of its companies—a mix of large, small and medium capitalization names—show at least 20% annual growth in earnings, a dominant niche in a growing market and financial strength. Its major industries have traditionally included high-growth retail, technology pollution control, media and health care. As seen over the past 3 years, the fund's growth-intensive approach can be expected to yield the best relative results when growth stocks lead the market.

Portfolio Manager: Ray Hirsch
Since: 1990

Minimum:
Initial: $2,000
Subsequent: $100
Telephone Exchange: Yes
Distributions:
Income: Annually
Capital Gain: Annually
Front-End Load: None
12b-1: 0.80%
Redemption Fee: 5.00%
Management Company: IDS Financial
Ticker Symbol: INAGX

TOTAL RETURN (%)

1987	1988	1989	1990	1991	5-year	Bull Market	Bear Market
-5.7	8.4	32.7	-0.7	51.2	103.5	58.7	-28.8

INVESTMENT PORTFOLIO

Total Assets (mil.)	Current Yield	Turnover Ratio	Expense Ratio	Beta	Risk Return
$422	0.1%	64%	1.61%	1.15	0.08

JANUS VENTURE FUND

Janus Group
100 Fillmore Street, Suite 300
Denver, CO 80206
800-525-8983

Investment Objective: The investment objective of this fund is capital appreciation in a manner consistent with capital preservation. In seeking common stocks, management looks for small companies listed on a national securities exchange or NASDAQ that it believes will experience strong growth in revenues, earnings and assets. Although the fund may invest in large cap stocks, the majority of its holdings tend to be common stocks of companies with less than $250 million in annual revenues. Because of management's ability to time the market, its 5-year return has far outpaced the average appreciation percent of small-firm stocks in general. The fund was forced to close its doors to new investors because of its increasing size.

Portfolio Manager: James Craig
Since: 1985

Minimum:
Initial: Closed
Subsequent: $50
Telephone Exchange: Yes
Distributions:
Income: Annually
Capital Gain: Annually
Front-End Load: Closed
12b-1: None
Redemption Fee: None
Management Company: Janus Capital
Ticker Symbol: JAVTX

TOTAL RETURN (%)

1987	1988	1989	1990	1991	5-year	Bull Market	Bear Market
5.2	19.6	38.7	-0.4	47.8	157.0	50.3	-17.9

INVESTMENT PORTFOLIO

Total Assets (mil.)	Current Yield	Turnover Ratio	Expense Ratio	Beta	Risk Return
$1,312	0.5%	184%	1.16%	0.97	0.09

KAUFMANN FUND

Hans P. Utsch
17 Battery Place, Suite 2624
New York, NY 10004
800-237-0132

Investment Objective: This fund seeks capital appreciation by investing in small-equity cap stocks. It was taken over by current management in 1986 and since then has become a top-performing small cap equity fund. Although the fund returned about 79% the past year, it took a bashing during the stock market meltdown in 1987, when its share price dropped nearly 40%. In general, management invests in small companies that are in substantial turnaround or in emerging companies capable of growing by 30% or more per year. Although it is a diversified fund, management tends to concentrate its portfolio in a handful of common stocks, a strategy that greatly increases its risk.

Portfolio Manager: H. Utsch/L. Auriana
Since: 1986

Minimum:
Initial: $1,500
Subsequent: $100
Telephone Exchange: Yes
Distributions:
Income: Annually
Capital Gain: Annually
Front-End Load: None
12b-1: 1.00%
Redemption Fee: 0.20%
Management Company: Edgemont Asset Management
Ticker Symbol: KAUFX

TOTAL RETURN (%)

1987	1988	1989	1990	1991	5-year	Bull Market	Bear Market
-37.2	58.6	46.8	-6.1	79.4	146.5	89.8	-31.4

INVESTMENT PORTFOLIO

Total Assets (mil.)	Current Yield	Turnover Ratio	Expense Ratio	Beta	Risk Return
$107	0.0%	195%	3.45%	1.28	0.11

KEMPER GROWTH FUND

Kemper Financial Services
120 South LaSalle Street, 20th Floor
Chicago, IL 60603
800-621-1048

Investment Objective: Don't expect to see many small cap stocks in this fund. With a portfolio stuffed with large cap stocks, the fund looks more like a growth and income vehicle with a growth bias. Its beta of 1.07 approximates that of the market, and except for a heavy cash position that averaged 15 to 20% in 1990, the fund would have stayed even with the S&P 500 Index. However, Kemper's many equity mutual funds are notorious for holding 10 to 20% cash stakes, which will typically limit upside potential while reducing risk and protecting capital in bear markets. The past year, though, the fund returned 67%, which would indicate a more than aggressive posture.

Portfolio Manager: S. Lewis/M. Arends
Since: 1991

Minimum:
Initial: $1,000
Subsequent: $100
Telephone Exchange: Yes
Distributions:
Income: Annually
Capital Gain: Annually
Front-End Load: 5.75%
12b-1: None
Redemption Fee: None
Management Company: Kemper Financial Services
Ticker Symbol: KPGRX

TOTAL RETURN (%)

1987	1988	1989	1990	1991	5-year	Bull Market	Bear Market
5.7	10.8	30.8	3.9	66.9	165.5	64.0	-22.9

INVESTMENT PORTFOLIO

Total Assets (mil.)	Current Yield	Turnover Ratio	Expense Ratio	Beta	Risk Return
$780	2.8%	143%	1.04%	1.07	0.11

KEYSTONE AMERICA OMEGA FUND

Keystone Distributors
99 High Street, 29th Floor
Boston, MA 02110
800-633-4900

Investment Objective: The fund attempts to maximize capital appreciation by investing in common stocks. The fund's portfolio has consisted of blue chip growth companies, but in 1991, the overall makeup of the fund shifted. Management believes that market conditions dictate a return to small and midsized companies and thus has shifted its focus toward these issues. The fund's 1991 and 5-year performances have been strong, as returns of 54% and 148%, respectively, would suggest. However, a 4.75% front-end load and a high expense ratio probably have kept assets down, despite healthy returns.

Portfolio Manager: M. Cullinane
Since: 1989

Minimum:
Initial: $1,000
Subsequent: None
Telephone Exchange: Yes
Distributions:
Income: Annually
Capital Gain: Annually
Front-End Load: 4.75%
12b-1: 0.04%
Redemption Fee: None
Management Company: Keystone Management
Ticker Symbol: OMGAX

TOTAL RETURN (%)

1987	1988	1989	1990	1991	5-year	Bull Market	Bear Market
8.3	14.0	33.2	-2.5	54.5	147.8	58.4	-23.8

INVESTMENT PORTFOLIO

Total Assets (mil.)	Current Yield	Turnover Ratio	Expense Ratio	Beta	Risk Return
$51	0.3%	108%	1.73%	1.24	0.08

KEYSTONE CUSTODIAN FUNDS S4

Keystone Distributors
99 High Street, 29th Floor
Boston, MA 02110
800-633-4900

Investment Objective: As one of the highest beta portfolios in the Keystone family of funds, this fund is suitable only for the most aggressive of investors. The fund's negligible yield indicates that many of its holdings are either emerging growth or highly volatile technology stocks. Investors should prepare for a wild ride with this fund as management purposely invests in stocks that are anticipated to have extreme price volatility. The faint of heart should steer clear of this fund, but stellar performance is attainable as 1991's 70% return indicates.

Portfolio Manager: Roland Gillis
Since: 1985

Minimum:
Initial: $1,000
Subsequent: None
Telephone Exchange: Yes
Distributions:
Income: Annually
Capital Gain: Annually
Front-End Load: None
12b-1: 1.25%
Redemption Fee: 4.00%
Management Company: Keystone Custodian Funds
Ticker Symbol: KSFOX

TOTAL RETURN (%)

1987	1988	1989	1990	1991	5-year	Bull Market	Bear Market
-5.9	11.8	23.6	-6.0	70.3	108.2	53.4	-27.5

INVESTMENT PORTFOLIO

Total Assets (mil.)	Current Yield	Turnover Ratio	Expense Ratio	Beta	Risk Return
$650	0.0%	77%	1.38%	1.48	0.12

LORD ABBETT DEVELOPING GROWTH FUND

Lord Abbett & Company
767 Fifth Avenue
New York, NY 10153
800-874-3733

Investment Objective: Lord Abbett Developing Growth Fund invests primarily in small capitalization common stocks of developing growth companies, including issues that are traded over the counter. Management has historically pursued a buy-and-hold strategy, concentrating assets in relatively few high-growth industries. With its small cap bias and large stakes in volatile sectors, the fund has severely underperformed this decade. However, the fund has sharply rebounded with the small cap market. The past year, it posted an above-average 56% gain.

Minimum:
Initial: $1,000
Subsequent: None
Telephone Exchange: Yes
Distributions:
Income: Annually
Capital Gain: Annually
Front-End Load: 6.75%
12b-1: 0.16%
Redemption Fee: None
Management Company: Lord Abbett
Ticker Symbol: LAGWX

Portfolio Manager: John Gibbons
Since: 1989

TOTAL RETURN (%)

1987	1988	1989	1990	1991	5-year	Bull Market	Bear Market
0.8	3.5	14.1	-6.4	56.4	74.1	64.5	-31.7

INVESTMENT PORTFOLIO

Total Assets (mil.)	Current Yield	Turnover Ratio	Expense Ratio	Beta	Risk Return
$140	0.2%	13%	1.24%	1.21	0.08

MACKENZIE AMERICAN FUND

Mackenzie Investment Management
P.O. Box 5007
Boca Raton, FL 33431
800-456-5111

Investment Objective: This fund seeks long-term capital appreciation by investing at least 65% of its assets in domestic stocks. Up to 35% of the fund's assets may be invested in selected debt securities. The fund has struggled for the past 3 years and returned a woeful 9% in 1991. The fund has had a few moments in the sun as 1987's 25% return would attest, but recent results have put a damper on the fund's 5-year return.

Minimum:
Initial: $250
Subsequent: $50
Telephone Exchange: Yes
Distributions:
Income: Semiannually
Capital Gain: Annually
Front-End Load: 5.75%
12b-1: None
Redemption Fee: None
Management Company: Mackenzie Investment Management
Ticker Symbol: INAFX

Portfolio Manager: Alex Christ
Since: 1985

TOTAL RETURN (%)

1987	1988	1989	1990	1991	5-year	Bull Market	Bear Market
25.3	16.3	16.3	-14.9	9.4	57.8	21.3	-21.7

INVESTMENT PORTFOLIO

Total Assets (mil.)	Current Yield	Turnover Ratio	Expense Ratio	Beta	Risk Return
$43	0.8%	5%	2.13%	0.80	0.01

MASSACHUSETTS FINANCIAL EMERGING GROWTH TRUST

Massachusetts Financial Services
500 Boylston Street
Boston, MA 02116
800-225-2606

Investment Objective: An earnings-momentum strategy that emphasizes companies with market capitalizations under $500 million guides this fund. Overall, the policy has been effective; despite a struggling small cap market over the past 8 years, the fund has enjoyed reasonable returns. Though hammered in such small cap bear markets as 1984 (-6%), 1987 (-10%) and 1990 (-12%), the recoveries that followed the losses were impressive. The fund rebounded 25.8% in 1985, rose a strong 44.4% in 1988–1989 and continued with a whopping 70% return in 1991. Like most small cap funds, its returns are not directly comparable to the more commonly used indices of market return such as the S&P 500 Index.

Portfolio Manager: Don Pitcher
Since: 1988

Minimum:
Initial: $1,000
Subsequent: $50
Telephone Exchange: Yes
Distributions:
Income: Annually
Capital Gain: Annually
Front-End Load: 5.75%
12b-1: 0.25%
Redemption Fee: 1.00%
Management Company: Massachusetts Financial Services
Ticker Symbol: MFEGX

TOTAL RETURN (%)

1987	1988	1989	1990	1991	5-year	Bull Market	Bear Market
-10.2	14.8	25.8	-11.5	70.2	95.2	72.3	-30.8

INVESTMENT PORTFOLIO

Total Assets (mil.)	Current Yield	Turnover Ratio	Expense Ratio	Beta	Risk Return
$214	0.0%	64%	1.40%	1.31	0.09

MFS LIFETIME EMERGING GROWTH TRUST

Massachusetts Financial Services
500 Boylston Street
Boston, MA 02116
800-225-2606

Investment Objective: Up until the past year, jumping aboard hot sectors had yet to produce above-market returns for this young fund. However, the fund returned a stunning 87.6% in 1991. Technology, pollution control, retail and business services have been usual fare for the fund. By stressing earnings growth above all else, the fund willingly pays high price-earnings multiples for stocks. Thus, its high beta isn't surprising, and investors should expect a volatile ride on this aggressive growth vehicle.

Portfolio Manager: John Ballen
Since: 1986

Minimum:
Initial: $1,000
Subsequent: $50
Telephone Exchange: Yes
Distributions:
Income: Annually
Capital Gain: Annually
Front-End Load: None
12b-1: 1.00%
Redemption Fee: 6.00%
Management Company: Lifetime Advisers
Ticker Symbol: LTEGX

TOTAL RETURN (%)

1987	1988	1989	1990	1991	5-year	Bull Market	Bear Market
4.7	8.0	26.9	-2.5	87.6	162.5	106.6	-36.5

INVESTMENT PORTFOLIO

Total Assets (mil.)	Current Yield	Turnover Ratio	Expense Ratio	Beta	Risk Return
$144	0.0%	86%	2.75%	1.50	0.10

MONTGOMERY SMALL CAP FUND

Montgomery Asset Management
600 Montgomery Street, 17th Floor
San Francisco, CA 94109
415-627-2400

Investment Objective: In its brief history, this fund has demonstrated the ability to perform well in bull markets. The fund returned a stunning 99% in 1991, its first full year of existence. At least 65% of its companies have market capitalizations between $100 million and $600 million. The other 35% may be invested in these same companies or larger firms that meet the fund's growth requirements. One year is not a proper time frame to gauge a fund's performance, but investors may want to closely follow this fund's performance.

Portfolio Manager: Stuart O. Roberts
Since: 1990

Minimum:
Initial: Closed
Subsequent: $1,000
Telephone Exchange: Yes
Distributions:
Income: Annually
Capital Gain: Annually
Front-End Load: Closed
12b-1: None
Redemption Fee: None
Management Company: Montgomery Asset Management
Ticker Symbol: MNSCX

TOTAL RETURN (%)

1987	1988	1989	1990	1991	5-year	Bull Market	Bear Market
NA	NA	NA	NA	98.7	NA	112.2	-24.8

INVESTMENT PORTFOLIO

Total Assets (mil.)	Current Yield	Turnover Ratio	Expense Ratio	Beta	Risk Return
$54	0.0%	195%	1.50%	1.45	0.11

NAUTILUS FUND

Eaton Vance
24 Federal Street, 5th Floor
Boston, MA 02110
800-225-6265

Investment Objective: Eaton Vance Nautilus seeks capital appreciation through investments in common stocks of small, emerging growth companies. Although the fund historically invested the bulk of its assets in technology stocks, it began diversifying into other emerging growth sectors in 1988. Technology and medical technology stocks continue to dominate the portfolio, but financial, pollution control and transportation stocks also are prominent. The fund's large exposure to volatile technology stocks suggests it will continue to show significant volatility. The fund returned an above-average 57% the past year.

Portfolio Manager: Richardson/Gardner/Goodof
Since: 1990

Minimum:
Initial: $1,000
Subsequent: $20
Telephone Exchange: Yes
Distributions:
Income: Annually
Capital Gain: Annually
Front-End Load: 4.75%
12b-1: None
Redemption Fee: None
Management Company: Eaton Vance Management
Ticker Symbol: NTLSX

TOTAL RETURN (%)

1987	1988	1989	1990	1991	5-year	Bull Market	Bear Market
-14.8	7.5	14.1	-2.5	57.0	59.9	32.9	-7.7

INVESTMENT PORTFOLIO

Total Assets (mil.)	Current Yield	Turnover Ratio	Expense Ratio	Beta	Risk Return
$13	0.0%	105%	2.50%	1.25	0.07

NEUBERGER & BERMAN GENESIS FUND

Neuberger & Berman Management
605 Third Avenue, 2nd Floor
New York, NY 10158
800-877-9700

Investment Objective: Guided by a strict value orientation, this pure small-company fund has been swimming upstream since its inception. Not only has the market favored blue chips over tiny capitalization stocks, it has focused almost exclusively on expansion and growth issues, neglecting the fund's value stocks. Particularly damaging has been the fund's considerable exposure to industrial products and consumer durables sectors that have been hurt by the market's recession fears. While its tiny companies are vulnerable to corrections, Neuberger Berman's excellent track record, its concern for quality and its value orientation suggests the fund will prove rewarding over time.

Portfolio Manager: Stephen Milman
Since: 1988

Minimum:
Initial: $1,000
Subsequent: $100
Telephone Exchange: Yes
Distributions:
Income: Annually
Capital Gain: Annually
Front-End Load: None
12b-1: None
Redemption Fee: None
Management Company: Neuberger & Berman Management
Ticker Symbol: NBGNX

TOTAL RETURN (%)

1987	1988	1989	1990	1991	5-year	Bull Market	Bear Market
NA	NA	17.2	-16.2	41.5	NA	52.2	-27.2

INVESTMENT PORTFOLIO

Total Assets (mil.)	Current Yield	Turnover Ratio	Expense Ratio	Beta	Risk Return
$36	0.1%	46%	2.00%	0.97	0.07

NEUWIRTH FUND

Wood Struthers & Winthrop
140 Broadway, 42nd Floor
New York, NY 10005
800-225-8011

Investment Objective: The fund seeks capital appreciation by investing in relatively established companies in growth industries that have product, management or similar advantages over other companies in those industries. Dividend yield is not considered in the choice of portfolio securities. Capital growth also may be sought through investment in special situations such as companies being reorganized or merged, having unusual new products or having undergone management changes. Recently, the fund has concentrated on equity securities of small to medium-sized companies.

Portfolio Manager: Gary Haubold
Since: 1989

Minimum:
Initial: $1,000
Subsequent: $50
Telephone Exchange: No
Distributions:
Income: Annually
Capital Gain: Annually
Front-End Load: None
12b-1: None
Redemption Fee: None
Management Company: Wood Struthers & Winthrop Management
Ticker Symbol: NEUFX

TOTAL RETURN (%)

1987	1988	1989	1990	1991	5-year	Bull Market	Bear Market
-10.1	31.6	14.4	-13.1	50.5	77.2	47.4	-17.8

INVESTMENT PORTFOLIO

Total Assets (mil.)	Current Yield	Turnover Ratio	Expense Ratio	Beta	Risk Return
$28	0.2%	87%	1.98%	0.89	0.09

NEW ENGLAND GROWTH FUND

TNE Investment Services
399 Boylston Street, 8th Floor
Boston, MA 02116
800-343-7104

Investment Objective: New England Growth seeks long-term capital growth. During the past decade, the fund has concentrated heavily on blue chip growth stocks and shareholders have been well rewarded. Its aggressive growth classification stems from the fund's ability to invest up to 25% of its assets in small emerging growth companies. Despite its 75% commitment to large cap stocks, the fund chalked up an outstanding 57% return in 1991. Furthermore, 5-year return figures reflect the strong performance this fund has been able to consistently deliver.

Portfolio Manager: Ken Heebner
Since: 1977

Minimum:
Initial: $1,000
Subsequent: $25
Telephone Exchange: Yes
Distributions:
Income: Annually
Capital Gain: Annually
Front-End Load: 6.50%
12b-1: 0.25%
Redemption Fee: None
Management Company: Capital Growth Management
Ticker Symbol: NELGX

TOTAL RETURN (%)

1987	1988	1989	1990	1991	5-year	Bull Market	Bear Market
18.5	1.4	22.3	5.1	56.7	142.1	58.6	-21.5

INVESTMENT PORTFOLIO

Total Assets (mil.)	Current Yield	Turnover Ratio	Expense Ratio	Beta	Risk Return
$878	0.7%	185%	1.23%	1.11	0.09

NICHOLAS LIMITED EDITION

Nicholas
700 North Water Street, Suite 1010
Milwaukee, WI 53202
800-227-5987

Investment Objective: If this small cap offering from the Nicholas group performs nearly as well as its better-known siblings, it's going to be a big winner. Investing primarily in stocks with market capitalizations below $250 million, the fund rose strongly in 1988 in conjunction with the postcrash, small cap rebound. The fund posted a small loss in 1990 as large cap growth stocks took center stage. It then followed with a robust 43% gain the past year. Nonetheless, a reasonable expense ratio, small asset base and Nicholas's tried-and-true investment philosophy should reward shareholders over the long haul.

Portfolio Manager: Albert Nicholas
Since: 1987

Minimum:
Initial: Closed
Subsequent: $100
Telephone Exchange: No
Distributions:
Income: Annually
Capital Gain: Annually
Front-End Load: Closed
12b-1: None
Redemption Fee: None
Management Company: Nicholas
Ticker Symbol: NCLEX

TOTAL RETURN (%)

1987	1988	1989	1990	1991	5-year	Bull Market	Bear Market
NA	27.3	17.4	-1.7	43.2	NA	57.1	-22.3

INVESTMENT PORTFOLIO

Total Assets (mil.)	Current Yield	Turnover Ratio	Expense Ratio	Beta	Risk Return
$164	0.7%	15%	1.07%	0.86	0.08

OBERWEIS EMERGING GROWTH FUND

Hamilton Investments
841 North Lake Street
Aurora, IL 60506
800-323-6166

Investment Objective: Small cap, high-growth guru Jim Oberweis hit the jackpot the past year. With an extraordinary return of 87%, this fund ranked near the top of all mutual funds for 1991. The fund invests in companies that demonstrate an above-average potential for growth. Management uses a strict set of investment parameters when selecting companies and this strategy has recently paid off. The fund deftly sidestepped the 1990 massacre of small cap funds and followed that up with the past year's record performance.

Minimum:
Initial: $5,000
Subsequent: $1,000
Telephone Exchange: No
Distributions:
Income: Annually
Capital Gain: Annually
Front-End Load: 4.00%
12b-1: 0.50%
Redemption Fee: None
Management Company: Hamilton Investments
Ticker Symbol: OBEGX

Portfolio Manager: James D. Oberweis
Since: 1987

TOTAL RETURN (%)

1987	1988	1989	1990	1991	5-year	Bull Market	Bear Market
NA	5.7	25.0	0.4	87.1	NA	120.1	-39.6

INVESTMENT PORTFOLIO

Total Assets (mil.)	Current Yield	Turnover Ratio	Expense Ratio	Beta	Risk Return
$18	0.0%	63%	2.15%	1.38	0.10

OPPENHEIMER DISCOVERY FUND

Oppenheimer Fund Management
P.O. Box 300
Denver, CO 80201
800-255-2755

Investment Objective: Like many Oppenheimer-managed funds, Oppenheimer Discovery Fund interprets its mandate flexibly. Although it primarily invests in small, emerging growth companies, it freely purchases large stocks that meet its growth and value parameters. Management relies on both top-down and bottom-up approaches to identify macroeconomic, industry and market trends and their potential beneficiaries. Although its approach backfired in 1990, the fund more than erased earlier losses by posting a 72% return the past year.

Minimum:
Initial: $1,000
Subsequent: $25
Telephone Exchange: Yes
Distributions:
Income: Annually
Capital Gain: Annually
Front-End Load: 5.75%
12b-1: 0.23%
Redemption Fee: None
Management Company: Oppenheimer Management
Ticker Symbol: OPOCX

Portfolio Manager: Donna Calder
Since: 1986

TOTAL RETURN (%)

1987	1988	1989	1990	1991	5-year	Bull Market	Bear Market
13.7	19.7	34.0	-15.0	72.3	166.9	68.5	-24.0

INVESTMENT PORTFOLIO

Total Assets (mil.)	Current Yield	Turnover Ratio	Expense Ratio	Beta	Risk Return
$126	0.0%	244%	1.53%	1.19	0.11

OPPENHEIMER TIME FUND

Oppenheimer Fund Management
P.O. Box 300
Denver, CO 80201
800-255-2755

Investment Objective: Oppenheimer Time Fund seeks capital appreciation by investing in common stocks of companies that are poised to benefit from unfolding macroeconomic, demographic and/or industry trends. Management relies heavily on top-down analysis to identify such trends and their potential beneficiaries. Typically, it invests approximately 65% of the fund's assets in just 4 or 5 industries in the early phase of fundamental improvement. Most recently, these have included energy, health care, cable TV and telecommunications. Remaining assets are reserved for special situations—companies with improving fundamentals irrespective of their industries.

Portfolio Manager: Donna Calder
Since: 1987

Minimum:
Initial: $1,000
Subsequent: $25
Telephone Exchange: Yes
Distributions:
Income: Annually
Capital Gain: Annually
Front-End Load: 5.75%
12b-1: 0.02%
Redemption Fee: None
Management Company: Oppenheimer Management
Ticker Symbol: OPPTX

TOTAL RETURN (%)

1987	1988	1989	1990	1991	5-year	Bull Market	Bear Market
8.2	13.8	28.0	-7.1	39.2	103.6	34.9	-15.6

INVESTMENT PORTFOLIO

Total Assets (mil.)	Current Yield	Turnover Ratio	Expense Ratio	Beta	Risk Return
$353	1.2%	107%	0.96%	0.91	0.08

PACIFIC HORIZON AGGRESSIVE GROWTH PORTFOLIO

Concord Financial Group
333 South Hope Street
Los Angeles, CA 90071
800-332-3863

Investment Objective: Though it's hard to advocate a fund that promotes high turnover, this aggressive growth vehicle deserves a lot of respect. With turnover rates that average more than 300%, the fund actively restructures its portfolio at short notice. It is searching for the hottest growth areas of the market, and when a stock or industry group begins to lag, it is sold immediately. Though this policy seems to imply high risk, the fund actually has a modest beta. Despite the aggressiveness of the fund, it was able to deftly sidestep losses in both 1987 and 1990. The past year the fund posted a strong 53.5% gain.

Portfolio Manager: Jeff Mallet
Since: 1990

Minimum:
Initial: $1,000
Subsequent: $100
Telephone Exchange: Yes
Distributions:
Income: Annually
Capital Gain: Annually
Front-End Load: 4.50%
12b-1: 0.16%
Redemption Fee: None
Management Company: Security Pacific National Bank
Ticker Symbol: PHAGX

TOTAL RETURN (%)

1987	1988	1989	1990	1991	5-year	Bull Market	Bear Market
12.0	0.4	37.2	5.1	53.5	148.8	95.6	-30.3

INVESTMENT PORTFOLIO

Total Assets (mil.)	Current Yield	Turnover Ratio	Expense Ratio	Beta	Risk Return
$146	0.0%	155%	1.55%	1.19	0.07

PARKSTONE SMALL CAPITALIZATION VALUE FUND

Winsbury
1900 East Dublin-Grandville Road
Columbus, OH 43229
800-451-8377

Investment Objective: This relative newcomer to the small cap arena has strung together an impressive track record since its inception. The fund seeks capital appreciation by investing in common stocks of small to mid-sized companies. Management attempts to maintain a minimum of 80% of its assets in common stocks and convertible securities. Although we have yet to see performance in a bear market, management lost a mere 1% in 1990, which was a brutal year for most small cap funds. The past year the fund returned a solid 44%.

Portfolio Manager: Roger Stamper
Since: 1988

Minimum:
Initial: $1,000
Subsequent: $100
Telephone Exchange: Yes
Distributions:
Income: Semiannually
Capital Gain: Annually
Front-End Load: 4.50%
12b-1: None
Redemption Fee: None
Management Company: First of America
Ticker Symbol: PKSVX

TOTAL RETURN (%)

1987	1988	1989	1990	1991	5-year	Bull Market	Bear Market
NA	NA	32.3	-1.3	43.9	NA	37.8	-24.9

INVESTMENT PORTFOLIO

Total Assets (mil.)	Current Yield	Turnover Ratio	Expense Ratio	Beta	Risk Return
$130	0.3%	83%	1.11%	1.23	0.08

PASADENA GROWTH FUND

Ascher/Decision Services
600 North Rosemead Boulevard
Pasadena, CA 91107
800-882-2855

Investment Objective: The sole investment objective of this fund is long-term capital appreciation. Portfolio Manager Roger Engemann emphasizes the purchase of common stocks of domestic corporations with equity capitalizations below $500 million. Over the past 5 years, management has done an impressive job by producing a 165% total return. This fund's success is mainly attributable to adhering to its strategy and maintaining a fully invested posture. If you can tolerate its hefty front-end load, this fund is a solid choice for an aggressive growth fund.

Portfolio Manager: Roger Engemann
Since: 1986

Minimum:
Initial: $2,500
Subsequent: $100
Telephone Exchange: No
Distributions:
Income: Annually
Capital Gain: Annually
Front-End Load: 5.50%
12b-1: None
Redemption Fee: None
Management Company: Roger Engemann Management
Ticker Symbol: PASGX

TOTAL RETURN (%)

1987	1988	1989	1990	1991	5-year	Bull Market	Bear Market
-11.4	35.8	37.6	-4.6	67.8	165.1	79.5	-32.2

INVESTMENT PORTFOLIO

Total Assets (mil.)	Current Yield	Turnover Ratio	Expense Ratio	Beta	Risk Return
$252	0.0%	32%	2.20%	1.45	0.09

PERRITT CAPITAL GROWTH FUND

Perritt Investments
680 N. Lake Shore Drive, 2038 Tower Offices
Chicago, IL 60611
800-338-1579

Investment Objective: This fund is patiently biding its time, waiting for investors to recognize the screaming values in the lower tiers of the stock market. With a median market cap of about $70 million, the fund ranks as one of the few with a proclaimed small cap strategy to actually invest only in smaller capitalization stocks. Small caps have been in the doghouse for much of the fund's 3-year history. However, patient investors were rewarded with a better-than-average 39% return the past year. This no-load fund offers investors who are bullish on small cap stocks an undiluted portfolio of high-growth, small-company securities.

Portfolio Manager: Gerald W. Perritt
Since: 1988

Minimum:
Initial: $1,000
Subsequent: $250
Telephone Exchange: No
Distributions:
Income: Annually
Capital Gain: Annually
Front-End Load: None
12b-1: None
Redemption Fee: None
Management Company: Perritt Investments
Ticker Symbol: PRCGX

TOTAL RETURN (%)

1987	1988	1989	1990	1991	5-year	Bull Market	Bear Market
NA	NA	2.0	-16.8	38.8	NA	37.3	-21.0

INVESTMENT PORTFOLIO

Total Assets (mil.)	Current Yield	Turnover Ratio	Expense Ratio	Beta	Risk Return
$6	0.0%	37%	2.50%	0.78	0.08

PIPER JAFFRAY INVEST TRUST SECTOR PERFORMANCE

Piper Jaffray & Hopwood
Piper Jaffray Tower, 222 South 9th Street
Minneapolis, MN 55402
800-333-6000

Investment Objective: This fund seeks total investment return though the use of aggressive investment techniques. The fund focuses on investing in 11 sectors of the economy. Depending on the outlook or the anticipated change in the general economy, management will decide what sectors they believe will provide the highest total return for shareholders. Competent companies in each sector are selected by earnings potential, financial condition and technical analysis. The past year the fund returned almost 41%.

Portfolio Manager: Edward Nicoski
Since: 1987

Minimum:
Initial: $250
Subsequent: $100
Telephone Exchange: No
Distributions:
Income: Semiannually
Capital Gain: Annually
Front-End Load: 4.00%
12b-1: 0.33%
Redemption Fee: None
Management Company: Piper Capital Management
Ticker Symbol: SEPFX

TOTAL RETURN (%)

1987	1988	1989	1990	1991	5-year	Bull Market	Bear Market
NA	4.2	27.8	-0.5	40.7	NA	45.3	-25.4

INVESTMENT PORTFOLIO

Total Assets (mil.)	Current Yield	Turnover Ratio	Expense Ratio	Beta	Risk Return
$9	0.3%	514%	1.49%	1.09	0.06

PRINCOR GROWTH FUND

Princor Financial Services
711 High Street
Des Moines, IA 50309
800-247-4123

Investment Objective: The most remarkable feature about this fund is its relatively low turnover ratio. Although the fund's 1.4% current yield makes it look like an aggressive growth vehicle, a turnover rate of approximately 10% is downright startling. Nonetheless, this fits with the fund's appetite for moderately priced industrial stocks, which take time to grow within a business cycle, and its penchant for consumer-growth stocks, which grow every year. Basically, management believes there is really no reason to trade away decent stocks that remain undervalued. The fund's strategy began to pay off in 1991 as reflected by its 57% return.

Portfolio Manager: Mike Hamilton
Since: 1987

Minimum:
Initial: $300
Subsequent: $50
Telephone Exchange: Yes
Distributions:
Income: Annually
Capital Gain: Annually
Front-End Load: 5.00%
12b-1: 0.15%
Redemption Fee: None
Management Company: Principal Management
Ticker Symbol: PRGWX

TOTAL RETURN (%)

1987	1988	1989	1990	1991	5-year	Bull Market	Bear Market
3.2	11.0	18.1	-1.4	56.6	108.8	59.7	-24.2

INVESTMENT PORTFOLIO

Total Assets (mil.)	Current Yield	Turnover Ratio	Expense Ratio	Beta	Risk Return
$45	1.4%	9%	1.18%	1.12	0.09

PRUDENT SPECULATOR LEVERAGED FUND

Prudent Speculator Group
4023 West 6th Street
Los Angeles, CA 90020
800-444-4778

Investment Objective: As is always the case with leverage, when the going gets tough, it often gets tougher before it gets better. This fund is a prime example of this adage, for in 1990, it sank 37.6%. A heavy stake in S&Ls and other financials took a big beating in the fourth quarter, and a penchant for struggling small cap stocks didn't help either. Add these factors to hefty interest payments on the 40 to 45% leveraged position of the fund, and this totals disaster. Nonetheless, it's far too early to write off this young fund. The leverage factor can produce spectacular results during a bull market. During the past year, for example, the fund returned almost 64%. Investments in this fund, however, are not for the faint of heart.

Portfolio Manager: Edwin R. Bernstein
Since: 1989

Minimum:
Initial: $1,000
Subsequent: $100
Telephone Exchange: Yes
Distributions:
Income: Annually
Capital Gain: Annually
Front-End Load: None
12b-1: 0.25%
Redemption Fee: None
Management Company: Prudent Speculator Group
Ticker Symbol: PSLFX

TOTAL RETURN (%)

1987	1988	1989	1990	1991	5-year	Bull Market	Bear Market
NA	12.7	-2.6	-37.6	63.8	NA	96.0	-50.0

INVESTMENT PORTFOLIO

Total Assets (mil.)	Current Yield	Turnover Ratio	Expense Ratio	Beta	Risk Return
$14	0.0%	107%	4.09%	1.70	0.06

PUTNAM OTC EMERGING GROWTH FUND

Putnam Financial Services
One Post Office Square, 12th Floor
Boston, MA 02109
800-634-1590

Investment Objective: This fund seeks capital appreciation by investing in common stocks of small- to medium-sized emerging growth companies traded in the over-the-counter market that management believes have potential for capital appreciation significantly greater than that of the market averages. In choosing investments, management seeks public companies in a relatively early stage of development with a record of profitability and a strong financial position. These companies may have a new technology, a unique proprietary product or a profitable market niche. In addition, preference is given to companies that are experiencing strong unit sales growth and in which management has a substantial equity investment.

Portfolio Manager: Richard Jodka
Since: 1982

Minimum:
Initial: $500
Subsequent: $50
Telephone Exchange: Yes
Distributions:
Income: Annually
Capital Gain: Annually
Front-End Load: 5.75%
12b-1: 0.25%
Redemption Fee: None
Management Company: Putnam Management
Ticker Symbol: POEGX

TOTAL RETURN (%)

1987	1988	1989	1990	1991	5-year	Bull Market	Bear Market
4.8	16.1	29.1	-9.8	40.8	99.4	56.4	-32.5

INVESTMENT PORTFOLIO

Total Assets (mil.)	Current Yield	Turnover Ratio	Expense Ratio	Beta	Risk Return
$237	0.0%	54%	1.48%	1.32	0.05

PUTNAM VOYAGER FUND

Putnam Financial Services
One Post Office Square, 12th Floor
Boston, MA 02109
800-634-1590

Investment Objective: The fund seeks capital appreciation primarily by investing in common stocks of small companies. It may participate in initial public offerings for such small companies. Also, up to 20% of its assets may be invested in foreign markets. Further aggressiveness is achieved by the fund's ability to leverage. The fund has an attractive 5-year record and returned 50% the past year. Portfolio turnover has been kept to a minimum, but the fund does charge a substantial 5.75% front-end load.

Portfolio Manager: Matthew Weatherbie
Since: 1983

Minimum:
Initial: $500
Subsequent: $50
Telephone Exchange: Yes
Distributions:
Income: Annually
Capital Gain: Annually
Front-End Load: 5.75%
12b-1: 0.22%
Redemption Fee: None
Management Company: Putnam Management
Ticker Symbol: PVOYX

TOTAL RETURN (%)

1987	1988	1989	1990	1991	5-year	Bull Market	Bear Market
10.8	11.7	34.8	-2.8	50.3	143.7	68.7	-26.9

INVESTMENT PORTFOLIO

Total Assets (mil.)	Current Yield	Turnover Ratio	Expense Ratio	Beta	Risk Return
$1,108	0.2%	49%	1.10%	1.21	0.07

RIGHTIME FUND

Rightime Family of Funds
218 Glenside Avenue, Suite 3000
Wyncote, PA 19095
800-242-1421

Investment Objective: Rightime Fund seeks a high total return consistent with reasonable risk primarily through investments in shares of other open-end mutual funds. Like most Rightime-managed funds, the fund actively adjusts its stock market exposure by raising cash or hedging with futures in response to market conditions. The fund's habit of retreating to cash at the least sign of uncertainty is seen in its good resistance to decline in bear markets, its low beta and its often sluggish blue chip market gains. Returns also have been slowed by the overlapping of expenses and transactions costs generally associated with a fund of funds.

Minimum:
Initial: $2,000
Subsequent: $100
Telephone Exchange: Yes
Distributions:
Income: Annually
Capital Gain: Annually
Front-End Load: None
12b-1: 1.20%
Redemption Fee: None
Management Company: Rightime Econometrics
Ticker Symbol: RTFDX

Portfolio Manager: David J. Rights
Since: 1985

TOTAL RETURN (%)

1987	1988	1989	1990	1991	5-year	Bull Market	Bear Market
19.2	-1.3	11.8	1.2	30.6	73.8	27.8	-11.2

INVESTMENT PORTFOLIO

Total Assets (mil.)	Current Yield	Turnover Ratio	Expense Ratio	Beta	Risk Return
$155	0.4%	383%	2.67%	0.62	0.07

RIGHTIME GROWTH FUND

Rightime Family of Funds
218 Glenside Avenue, Suite 3000
Wyncote, PA 19095
800-242-1421

Investment Objective: This young fund seeks growth of capital as its primary investment objective. Management hopes to achieve the fund's objective by investing in securities of companies with prospects for above-average capital growth. Investments also can be made in securities convertible into common stocks and preferred stocks. This fund has the distinction of having one of the highest turnover ratios in the mutual fund industry. On top of that, the fund has a high expense ratio that dampens the already lackluster performance of the fund.

Minimum:
Initial: $2,000
Subsequent: $100
Telephone Exchange: Yes
Distributions:
Income: Annually
Capital Gain: Annually
Front-End Load: 4.75%
12b-1: 0.90%
Redemption Fee: None
Management Company: Rightime Econometrics
Ticker Symbol: RTGRX

Portfolio Manager: David J. Rights
Since: 1988

TOTAL RETURN (%)

1987	1988	1989	1990	1991	5-year	Bull Market	Bear Market
NA	NA	19.3	-13.7	26.0	NA	21.8	-15.3

INVESTMENT PORTFOLIO

Total Assets (mil.)	Current Yield	Turnover Ratio	Expense Ratio	Beta	Risk Return
$39	1.0%	880%	2.35%	0.74	0.05

ROBERTSON STEPHENS EMERGING GROWTH FUND

Robertson Stephens
One Embarcadero Center, Suite 3100
San Francisco, CA 94111
800-766-3863

Investment Objective: This fund seeks capital appreciation by investing in emerging growth companies generally with revenues below $200 million. Investors get a double dose of aggressiveness with this fund. One, the small-company bias enhances the volatility, and two, management tends to invest over a few sectors. Primary stocks will be selected from the technology, health-care, proprietary manufacturing or service sector. These companies usually have earnings growth of at least 25% and a return on equity of 20%. Investors have been well rewarded during this fund's brief history.

Portfolio Manager: Robert Czepiel
Since: 1986

Minimum:
Initial: $5,000
Subsequent: $100
Telephone Exchange: No
Distributions:
Income: Annually
Capital Gain: Annually
Front-End Load: None
12b-1: 0.25%
Redemption Fee: None
Management Company: Robert Stephens Investment Management
Ticker Symbol: GSEGX

TOTAL RETURN (%)

1987	1988	1989	1990	1991	5-year	Bull Market	Bear Market
NA	14.1	44.5	9.6	58.5	NA	80.3	-26.4

INVESTMENT PORTFOLIO

Total Assets (mil.)	Current Yield	Turnover Ratio	Expense Ratio	Beta	Risk Return
$105	0.0%	272%	1.88%	1.28	0.08

RUSHMORE NOVA

Rushmore Funds
4922 Fairmont Avenue
Bethesda, MD 20814
800-633-4900

Investment Objective: This no-load fund seeks total returns over time that are superior to the market average as measured by the S&P 500 Index. This relatively new fund was established so investors could take advantage of market timing as management allows unlimited free switching. Despite the fund's effort to duplicate the S&P 500 Index, the fund has lagged behind the Index in both 1990 and 1991. So far, the only bright spot about this fund is its low expense ratio and lack of loads.

Portfolio Manager: Daniel Ryczek
Since: 1989

Minimum:
Initial: $2,500
Subsequent: None
Telephone Exchange: Yes
Distributions:
Income: Annually
Capital Gain: Annually
Front-End Load: None
12b-1: None
Redemption Fee: None
Management Company: Money Management Associates
Ticker Symbol: RSNVX

TOTAL RETURN (%)

1987	1988	1989	1990	1991	5-year	Bull Market	Bear Market
NA	NA	NA	-9.7	15.7	NA	NA	NA

INVESTMENT PORTFOLIO

Total Assets (mil.)	Current Yield	Turnover Ratio	Expense Ratio	Beta	Risk Return
$90	4.5%	NA	1.25%	NA	NA

SALOMON BROTHERS CAPITAL FUND

Salomon Brothers
7 World Trade Center
New York, NY 10048
800-725-6666

Investment Objective: The fund seeks capital appreciation by investing primarily in common stocks. Its historically large-company bias has been shifted somewhat to take advantage of the resurgence in the small cap market. The fund may invest 10% of its securities in foreign stocks. A stellar 1989 performance has been followed by 2 average years. This aggressive growth fund sports a high historical turnover ratio and charges a hefty 5.00% front-end load. Its 5-year return is a low 65%.

Portfolio Manager: Les Pollack
Since: 1991

Minimum:
Initial: $1,000
Subsequent: $100
Telephone Exchange: No
Distributions:
Income: Annually
Capital Gain: Annually
Front-End Load: 5.00%
12b-1: None
Redemption Fee: None
Management Company: Salomon Brothers Asset Management
Ticker Symbol: SACPX

TOTAL RETURN (%)

1987	1988	1989	1990	1991	5-year	Bull Market	Bear Market
1.7	-4.9	40.4	-9.1	33.4	64.8	31.1	-22.4

INVESTMENT PORTFOLIO

Total Assets (mil.)	Current Yield	Turnover Ratio	Expense Ratio	Beta	Risk Return
$80	1.6%	156%	1.44%	1.15	0.05

SCUDDER DEVELOPMENT FUND

Scudder Stevens & Clark
175 Federal Street, 12th Floor
Boston, MA 02110
800-225-2470

Investment Objective: This fund seeks capital growth by investing in smaller equity capitalization firms. From 1986 to 1990, the fund's returns did not keep pace with the S&P 500 Index, as small-company stocks significantly lagged their blue chip counterparts. However, in the past year, it rose by a robust 72%, far outpacing the average small cap fund. To provide a bit of stability and liquidity, the fund management invests at least 25% of the fund's assets in larger, more established companies; thus, the fund avoided losing money in 1990.

Portfolio Manager: R. MacKay/G. Morgan
Since: 1988

Minimum:
Initial: $1,000
Subsequent: $100
Telephone Exchange: Yes
Distributions:
Income: Annually
Capital Gain: Annually
Front-End Load: None
12b-1: None
Redemption Fee: None
Management Company: Scudder Stevens & Clark
Ticker Symbol: SCDVX

TOTAL RETURN (%)

1987	1988	1989	1990	1991	5-year	Bull Market	Bear Market
-1.6	10.9	22.9	1.4	21.9	133.8	50.1	-24.2

INVESTMENT PORTFOLIO

Total Assets (mil.)	Current Yield	Turnover Ratio	Expense Ratio	Beta	Risk Return
$620	0.0%	71%	1.29%	1.23	0.08

SECURITY ACTION FUND

Security Distributors
700 Harrison
Topeka, KS 66636
800-888-2461

Investment Objective: This fund seeks capital appreciation by investing in a wide range of companies. Management attempts to diversify across types of firms as well as the sizes of those companies that it chooses. Shareholders must commit themselves to either a 10- or 15-year plan where they agree to make fixed monthly contributions to their account. The fund returned a lackluster 27% in 1991 after losing 10% in 1990. The fund flexibility does allow it to move in and out of large and small companies based on management's projection of their respective prospects. Investors should be aware, however, that there is a hefty 8.50% front-end load levied on initial investments.

Minimum:
Initial: $50
Subsequent: $25
Telephone Exchange: Yes
Distributions:
Income: Annually
Capital Gain: Annually
Front-End Load: 8.50%
12b-1: None
Redemption Fee: None
Management Company: Security Management
Ticker Symbol: SACTX

Portfolio Manager: Ron Niedziela
Since: 1988

TOTAL RETURN (%)

1987	1988	1989	1990	1991	5-year	Bull Market	Bear Market
-5.5	14.9	19.0	-10.1	27.0	47.5	43.8	-31.2

INVESTMENT PORTFOLIO

Total Assets (mil.)	Current Yield	Turnover Ratio	Expense Ratio	Beta	Risk Return
$276	1.6%	65%	0.81%	1.20	0.05

SECURITY ULTRA FUND

Security Distributors
700 Harrison
Topeka, KS 66636
800-888-2461

Investment Objective: Security Ultra Fund seeks capital appreciation through investments in small capitalization common stocks. Management utilizes a fairly deep value discipline, stressing stocks that sell at low multiples to book value. The fund's rigorous value parameters have lead to a concentration of assets in cheap technology and financial stocks. These two sectors make up a large portion of the fund's assets. Coupled with its small-company focus, the fund's concentrated stakes in technology and finance (2 of the most volatile sectors in recent years) have resulted in muted returns over the past 5 years.

Minimum:
Initial: $100
Subsequent: $100
Telephone Exchange: Yes
Distributions:
Income: Annually
Capital Gain: Annually
Front-End Load: 5.75%
12b-1: None
Redemption Fee: None
Management Company: Security Management
Ticker Symbol: SECUX

Portfolio Manager: Ron Niedziela
Since: 1987

TOTAL RETURN (%)

1987	1988	1989	1990	1991	5-year	Bull Market	Bear Market
-18.1	23.0	11.9	-27.4	59.7	30.7	78.4	-45.3

INVESTMENT PORTFOLIO

Total Assets (mil.)	Current Yield	Turnover Ratio	Expense Ratio	Beta	Risk Return
$62	0.6%	96%	2.58%	1.42	0.07

SELIGMAN CAPITAL FUND

Seligman Financial Services
130 Liberty Street, 22nd Floor
New York, NY 10006
800-221-2450

Investment Objective: This fund seeks capital appreciation by investing in both blue chip and emerging growth companies. Management has done a fine job of determining which area of stocks, blue chip or small cap, would be the market leader. The past year the fund rode the emerging growth bull and returned almost 55%, while in 1990, the fund posted a slight gain as small caps were clobbered and the S&P 500 Index finished down 3%. The fund does, however, charge investors a 4.75% front-end load.

Minimum:
Initial: $1,000
Subsequent: $50
Telephone Exchange: Yes
Distributions:
Income: Annually
Capital Gain: Annually
Front-End Load: 4.75%
12b-1: None
Redemption Fee: None
Management Company: J. & W. Seligman
Ticker Symbol: SCFIX

Portfolio Manager: Doris Muzzatti
Since: 1985

TOTAL RETURN (%)

1987	1988	1989	1990	1991	5-year	Bull Market	Bear Market
-2.6	2.5	32.4	1.4	54.7	107.2	69.7	-29.1

INVESTMENT PORTFOLIO

Total Assets (mil.)	Current Yield	Turnover Ratio	Expense Ratio	Beta	Risk Return
$152	0.0%	23%	0.92%	1.20	0.08

SELIGMAN GROWTH FUND

Seligman Financial Services
130 Liberty Street, 22nd Floor
New York, NY 10006
800-221-2450

Investment Objective: This fund, one of the first growth stock funds, seeks out well-established companies poised for strong growth. While selections are based on an analysis of a company's underlying fundamentals, certain broadly defined industry groups have produced a significantly large number of issues for the fund that include: telecommunications, health care, pollution control and entertainment. Management tends to exhibit a degree of patience with its investments as evidenced by its lower-than-average portfolio turnover ratio. Despite its preference for the stocks of companies that are growing faster than the economy as a whole, the fund possesses a modest beta and has performed reasonably well during bear markets.

Minimum:
Initial: $1,000
Subsequent: $50
Telephone Exchange: Yes
Distributions:
Income: Semiannually
Capital Gain: Annually
Front-End Load: 4.75%
12b-1: None
Redemption Fee: None
Management Company: J. & W. Seligman
Ticker Symbol: SGRFX

Portfolio Manager: Suzanne Zak
Since: 1989

TOTAL RETURN (%)

1987	1988	1989	1990	1991	5-year	Bull Market	Bear Market
3.4	7.3	33.5	-5.2	38.5	94.5	47.9	-26.5

INVESTMENT PORTFOLIO

Total Assets (mil.)	Current Yield	Turnover Ratio	Expense Ratio	Beta	Risk Return
$554	0.6%	26%	0.71%	1.15	0.06

SHEARSON AGGRESSIVE GROWTH FUND

Shearson Lehman Brothers
Two World Trade Center
New York, NY 10048
212-464-8068

Investment Objective: This fund seeks capital appreciation by investing primarily in common stocks of companies that management believes have the potential to grow earnings faster than stocks included in the S&P 500 Index. These are often small- or medium-sized companies that stand to benefit from new products or services, technological developments or changes in management. Management's appetite for high price-earnings multiples, high growth companies has given the fund a relatively high beta. However, its turnover ratio is one of the lowest in the fund industry. This strategy has paid off handsomely in recent years as the fund has produced higher-than-average returns during the past 5 years.

Portfolio Manager: Richard Freeman
Since: 1983

Minimum:
Initial: $500
Subsequent: $200
Telephone Exchange: No
Distributions:
Income: Annually
Capital Gain: Annually
Front-End Load: 5.00%
12b-1: None
Redemption Fee: None
Management Company: Shearson Asset Management
Ticker Symbol: SHRAX

TOTAL RETURN (%)

1987	1988	1989	1990	1991	5-year	Bull Market	Bear Market
5.4	9.4	41.4	-6.0	42.3	118.2	63.1	-32.5

INVESTMENT PORTFOLIO

Total Assets (mil.)	Current Yield	Turnover Ratio	Expense Ratio	Beta	Risk Return
$156	0.0%	14%	1.13%	1.34	0.05

SHEARSON SPECIAL EQUITY PORTFOLIO

Shearson Lehman Brothers
Two World Trade Center
New York, NY 10048
800-451-2010

Investment Objective: This fund seeks capital growth by investing in companies believed to possess superior growth potential. Primarily, these companies would fall into the emerging growth classification, but management does purchase large capitalization stocks that it believes may be entering a period of strong growth. Portfolio turnover is extremely high, with 1990's rate reaching almost 400% (average holding period for a stock just over 3 months). Furthermore, the fund has an expense ratio exceeding 2.00%. After a whopping loss of 24% in 1990, the fund returned 44% the past year.

Portfolio Manager: George Novello
Since: 1990

Minimum:
Initial: $500
Subsequent: $250
Telephone Exchange: No
Distributions:
Income: Annually
Capital Gain: Annually
Front-End Load: None
12b-1: None
Redemption Fee: 1.00%
Management Company: Shearson Lehman Advisors
Ticker Symbol: HSPEX

TOTAL RETURN (%)

1987	1988	1989	1990	1991	5-year	Bull Market	Bear Market
-10.9	12.6	18.2	-24.3	44.0	29.4	41.7	-31.7

INVESTMENT PORTFOLIO

Total Assets (mil.)	Current Yield	Turnover Ratio	Expense Ratio	Beta	Risk Return
$74	0.2%	372%	2.30%	1.13	0.06

SIT NEW BEGINNING GROWTH FUND

Sit Investment Associates
4600 N.W. Center, 90 S. 7th Street
Minneapolis, MN 55402
800-332-5580

Investment Objective: In the pursuit of its objective of maximum capital appreciation, management invests primarily in the common stocks of small- and medium-sized emerging growth companies before they become well recognized. In recent years, it has concentrated its investments in medium cap stocks drawn from the technology, consumer growth and capital goods industries. With this strategy, the fund returned more than 65% during 1991 and managed to escape the bloodbath taken by small growth companies in 1990 when they plunged an average of more than 20%. The fund's modest asset size and below-average turnover rate are 2 additional pluses for investors seeking long-term capital appreciation.

Portfolio Manager: Doug Jones
Since: 1982

Minimum:
Initial: $2,000
Subsequent: $100
Telephone Exchange: Yes
Distributions:
Income: Annually
Capital Gain: Annually
Front-End Load: None
12b-1: None
Redemption Fee: None
Management Company: Sit Investment Management
Ticker Symbol: NBNGX

TOTAL RETURN (%)

1987	1988	1989	1990	1991	5-year	Bull Market	Bear Market
5.5	9.8	35.2	-2.0	65.5	153.8	72.4	-25.2

INVESTMENT PORTFOLIO

Total Assets (mil.)	Current Yield	Turnover Ratio	Expense Ratio	Beta	Risk Return
$173	0.4%	37%	1.03%	1.19	0.10

SKYLINE SPECIAL EQUITIES PORTFOLIO

Mesirow Investment Services
450 North Clark Street
Chicago, IL 60610
800-458-5222

Investment Objective: This fund seeks capital appreciation by investing primarily in stocks with market capitalizations below $300 million. Management has consistently stressed a value-oriented philosophy and has had strong success with it. Despite what has been an earnings-driven, high-growth bull market for small caps lately, this fund still returned more than 47% in 1991. The fund attempts to identify companies with above-average revenue and earnings growth but below-average price/earnings multiples. Also, special value situations are considered (i.e., turnaround plays).

Portfolio Manager: Bill Dutton
Since: 1987

Minimum:
Initial: $1,000
Subsequent: $100
Telephone Exchange: Yes
Distributions:
Income: Annually
Capital Gain: Annually
Front-End Load: 3.85%
12b-1: None
Redemption Fee: None
Management Company: Mesirow Asset Management
Ticker Symbol: SKSEX

TOTAL RETURN (%)

1987	1988	1989	1990	1991	5-year	Bull Market	Bear Market
NA	29.8	24.0	-9.2	47.4	NA	35.2	-22.4

INVESTMENT PORTFOLIO

Total Assets (mil.)	Current Yield	Turnover Ratio	Expense Ratio	Beta	Risk Return
$38	0.1%	98%	1.59%	1.01	0.08

STEIN ROE CAPITAL OPPORTUNITIES FUND

Stein Roe & Farnham
P.O. Box 1162
Chicago, IL 60690
800-338-2550

Investment Objective: This fund seeks long-term growth of capital by investing in a mixture of securities of smaller, emerging growth companies and well-seasoned companies of larger size that offer strong capital appreciation potential. When making individual stock selections, management looks for companies that might benefit from new products or services, technological developments or changes in management. Although it invests primarily in common stocks, the fund may invest in all types of equity securities, including preferred stocks and securities convertible into common stocks. The fund also may invest up to 35% of its total assets in debt securities.

Portfolio Manager: Bruce Dunn
Since: 1991

Minimum:
Initial: $1,000
Subsequent: $100
Telephone Exchange: Yes
Distributions:
Income: Annually
Capital Gain: Annually
Front-End Load: None
12b-1: None
Redemption Fee: None
Management Company: Stein Roe & Farnham
Ticker Symbol: SRFCX

TOTAL RETURN (%)

1987	1988	1989	1990	1991	5-year	Bull Market	Bear Market
9.4	-3.9	36.8	-29.1	62.8	66.1	66.2	-38.7

INVESTMENT PORTFOLIO

Total Assets (mil.)	Current Yield	Turnover Ratio	Expense Ratio	Beta	Risk Return
$123	0.8%	69%	1.18%	1.31	0.08

STRONG DISCOVERY FUND

Strong/Corneliuson Capital Management
100 Heritage Reserve
Menomonee Falls, WI 53051
800-368-3863

Investment Objective: This fund seeks maximum capital appreciation through a diversified portfolio of securities. It may, from time to time, emphasize equity securities of smaller companies with favorable prospects for earnings growth. In addition, it also may invest in mature companies with the potential for accelerated earnings growth because of new management, new products or changes in the economy. However, the fund will not invest more than 5% of its assets in companies with continuous operating histories of less than 3 years. The fund boasts one of the highest portfolio turnover ratios in the industry, yet this relatively new fund has performed well during its first 4 years of existence.

Portfolio Manager: Richard Strong
Since: 1987

Minimum:
Initial: $1,000
Subsequent: $200
Telephone Exchange: Yes
Distributions:
Income: Semiannually
Capital Gain: Annually
Front-End Load: 2.00%
12b-1: None
Redemption Fee: None
Management Company: Strong/Corneliuson Capital
Ticker Symbol: STDIX

TOTAL RETURN (%)

1987	1988	1989	1990	1991	5-year	Bull Market	Bear Market
NA	24.4	24.0	-2.7	68.6	NA	60.9	-16.0

INVESTMENT PORTFOLIO

Total Assets (mil.)	Current Yield	Turnover Ratio	Expense Ratio	Beta	Risk Return
$130	4.1%	494%	1.90%	0.96	0.11

SUN AMERICA EMERGING GROWTH FUND

Sun America Capital Services
10 Union Square East, 2nd Floor
New York, NY 10003
800-821-5100

Investment Objective: This fund seeks growth of capital by normally investing 80% of its assets in stocks of small to midsized companies. Larger companies may be included in the portfolio if management believes they possess the same above-average growth potential of their smaller counterparts. Management acknowledges that the fund may be aggressively traded and the consistently high turnover ratio bears this out. This fund doubles up on aggressiveness by investing in small companies as well as concentrating on select industry sectors. The fund also has abnormally high expenses.

Portfolio Manager: Harvey Eisen
Since: 1991

Minimum:
Initial: $2,500
Subsequent: None
Telephone Exchange: Yes
Distributions:
Income: Annually
Capital Gain: Annually
Front-End Load: None
12b-1: 0.86%
Redemption Fee: 5.00%
Management Company: Sun America Asset Management
Ticker Symbol: SAEMX

TOTAL RETURN (%)

1987	1988	1989	1990	1991	5-year	Bull Market	Bear Market
0.2	7.5	15.5	-14.5	43.8	53.2	53.7	-30.6

INVESTMENT PORTFOLIO

Total Assets (mil.)	Current Yield	Turnover Ratio	Expense Ratio	Beta	Risk Return
$21	0.0%	236%	2.31%	1.04	0.07

SUN AMERICA EQUITY PORTFOLIO—AGGRESSIVE GROWTH

Sun America Capital Services
10 Union Square East, 2nd Floor
New York, NY 10003
800-821-5100

Investment Objective: Formerly known as Integrated Equity Aggressive Growth Fund, Sun America Aggressive Growth invests primarily in small capitalization common stocks. Management maintains a compact portfolio of about 30 stocks. Its affinity for low price/earnings ratios typically leads it into out-of-favor industries. Industrial products, consumer durables and finance have been heavily weighted in recent years, explaining the fund's huge 1990 loss. However, its prospects have rebounded with the resurgence in the small cap market as 1991's 55% gain would attest.

Portfolio Manager: Harvey Eisen
Since: 1987

Minimum:
Initial: $500
Subsequent: $100
Telephone Exchange: Yes
Distributions:
Income: Annually
Capital Gain: Annually
Front-End Load: 5.75%
12b-1: 0.35%
Redemption Fee: None
Management Company: Sun America Asset Management
Ticker Symbol: SAGRX

TOTAL RETURN (%)

1987	1988	1989	1990	1991	5-year	Bull Market	Bear Market
NA	48.5	23.0	-27.0	54.9	NA	68.1	-34.4

INVESTMENT PORTFOLIO

Total Assets (mil.)	Current Yield	Turnover Ratio	Expense Ratio	Beta	Risk Return
$28	0.0%	27%	2.05%	1.13	0.08

T. ROWE PRICE NEW HORIZONS FUND

T. Rowe Price Investor Services
100 East Pratt Street
Baltimore, MD 21202
800-638-5660

Investment Objective: This fund seeks capital appreciation by investing in small stocks. Although more than 90 funds now claim to invest in small firms, this fund, which began operations in 1960, was the first to do so. During the 1970s and early 1980s, the fund was a stellar performer. However, small cap stocks have performed relatively poorly since mid-1983 (excluding 1991). Because small-firm stock returns tend to run in streaks that can last up to 7 years, one cannot use recent past performance as a guide to future returns. Instead, investors should examine the fund's performance relative to small-firm stock indices such as the Russell 2000—this fund's comparison is quite favorable.

Portfolio Manager: R. McNamee/J. Laporte
Since: 1987

Minimum:
Initial: $2,500
Subsequent: $100
Telephone Exchange: Yes
Distributions:
Income: Annually
Capital Gain: Annually
Front-End Load: None
12b-1: None
Redemption Fee: None
Management Company: T. Rowe Price Associates
Ticker Symbol: PRNHX

TOTAL RETURN (%)

1987	1988	1989	1990	1991	5-year	Bull Market	Bear Market
-7.2	14.0	26.2	-9.6	52.3	83.7	70.3	-32.2

INVESTMENT PORTFOLIO

Total Assets (mil.)	Current Yield	Turnover Ratio	Expense Ratio	Beta	Risk Return
$1,278	0.3%	38%	0.82%	1.23	0.07

T. ROWE PRICE SMALL-CAP VALUE FUND

T. Rowe Price Investor Services
100 East Pratt Street
Baltimore, MD 21202
800-638-5660

Investment Objective: This fund invests primarily in small companies (market value of $500 million or less), using a value approach that entails finding companies with current stock prices that do not reflect underlying value as measured by assets, earnings, cash flow or business franchise. Stocks are selected when undervalued on the basis of price/earnings ratio, estimated asset value per share and whether or not a catalyst exists that may not cause the stock's price to reflect its underlying value. Although its performance has been unattractive during the fund's brief existence, future performance potential cannot be extrapolated from recent results.

Portfolio Manager: Preston G. Athey
Since: 1991

Minimum:
Initial: $2,500
Subsequent: $100
Telephone Exchange: Yes
Distributions:
Income: Annually
Capital Gain: Annually
Front-End Load: None
12b-1: None
Redemption Fee: None
Management Company: T. Rowe Price Associates
Ticker Symbol: PRSVX

TOTAL RETURN (%)

1987	1988	1989	1990	1991	5-year	Bull Market	Bear Market
NA	NA	18.1	-11.3	34.2	NA	37.4	-21.6

INVESTMENT PORTFOLIO

Total Assets (mil.)	Current Yield	Turnover Ratio	Expense Ratio	Beta	Risk Return
$46	1.1%	33%	1.25%	0.75	0.07

THOMSON OPPORTUNITY FUND B

Thomson Investor Services
1 Station Place
Stamford, CT 06902
800-628-1237

Investment Objective: One of 4 portfolios in the Thomson Trust, this fund seeks appreciation with no consideration given to current income. When making investment selections, management gives preference to the common stocks of smaller companies in emerging industries and turnaround situations. In recent years, the fund's portfolio has contained an above-average concentration in software and biotechnology stocks that have enhanced both returns and risks. The fund has had more success than the average aggressive growth fund during the past 5 years because management has avoided the stocks of smaller companies for most of that time frame.

Portfolio Manager: Don Chiboucas
Since: 1986

Minimum:
Initial: $1,000
Subsequent: $100
Telephone Exchange: Yes
Distributions:
Income: Annually
Capital Gain: Annually
Front-End Load: None
12b-1: 1.00%
Redemption Fee: 1.00%
Management Company: Thomson Advisory Group
Ticker Symbol: TOPBX

TOTAL RETURN (%)

1987	1988	1989	1990	1991	5-year	Bull Market	Bear Market
6.4	14.0	30.7	-7.3	68.1	146.9	78.1	-26.7

INVESTMENT PORTFOLIO

Total Assets (mil.)	Current Yield	Turnover Ratio	Expense Ratio	Beta	Risk Return
$66	0.0%	68%	2.00%	1.28	0.10

TRANSAMERICA CAPITAL APPRECIATION

TransAmerica Distributors
1000 Louisiana, Suite 6000
Houston, TX 77002
800-343-6840

Investment Objective: This fund seeks capital appreciation by investing in a wide variety of common stocks. The fund intends to keep 65% of its assets invested at all times, but keeps its investment options wide open. Management may invest in foreign stocks if their outlook appears good. Investors should note that up until April of 1991, this fund was known as the TransAmerica Technology fund. The recent change has enabled the fund to expand its stock selection options and limit its sector volatility. The fund returned 38% in 1991, despite the objective change early in the year.

Portfolio Manager: Roger Young
Since: 1985

Minimum:
Initial: $100
Subsequent: $10
Telephone Exchange: Yes
Distributions:
Income: Annually
Capital Gain: Annually
Front-End Load: 4.75%
12b-1: 0.25%
Redemption Fee: None
Management Company: TransAmerica Fund Management
Ticker Symbol: TATKX

TOTAL RETURN (%)

1987	1988	1989	1990	1991	5-year	Bull Market	Bear Market
22.4	20.4	20.7	-6.4	38.0	129.9	63.1	-38.8

INVESTMENT PORTFOLIO

Total Assets (mil.)	Current Yield	Turnover Ratio	Expense Ratio	Beta	Risk Return
$80	0.0%	152%	1.54%	1.32	0.04

TRANSAMERICA SPECIAL EMERGING GROWTH FUND B

TransAmerica Distributors
1000 Louisiana, Suite 6000
Houston, TX 77002
800-343-6840

Investment Objective: This fund seeks capital appreciation by searching for high-growth companies with small- to medium-sized capitalizations. Though it is early in this fund's history, its performance has been anything but infantile. In 1988, the fund rose a strong 21.8%, while in 1989, it jumped another 29%. Even more to Ed Larsen's credit is the modest loss posted the past year when small cap stock prices declined slightly more than 20%. The past year the fund returned a better-than-average 59%.

Portfolio Manager: Ed Larsen
Since: 1987

Minimum:
Initial: $1,000
Subsequent: $50
Telephone Exchange: Yes
Distributions:
Income: Annually
Capital Gain: Annually
Front-End Load: None
12b-1: 1.18%
Redemption Fee: 6.00%
Management Company: TransAmerica Fund Management
Ticker Symbol: TSEGX

TOTAL RETURN (%)

1987	1988	1989	1990	1991	5-year	Bull Market	Bear Market
NA	21.8	28.8	-1.2	58.8	NA	83.2	-31.9

INVESTMENT PORTFOLIO

Total Assets (mil.)	Current Yield	Turnover Ratio	Expense Ratio	Beta	Risk Return
$46	0.0%	38%	1.62%	1.31	0.08

TWENTIETH CENTURY GIFTRUST INVESTORS

Twentieth Century Investors
4500 Main Street, P.O. Box 418210
Kansas City, MO 64111
800-345-2021

Investment Objective: This fund offers investors a creative method of setting aside money for children or foundations. In fact, you can't invest in the fund yourself, for it's set up as a trust for charitable or intrafamily giving and not as a retirement vehicle. There's a 10-year minimum holding period, perfect for encouraging long-term investing, and an aggressive growth strategy that has been phenomenally successful in the past. Investors should not be too wary of the fund's high beta; it's a purposeful strategy on the part of Twentieth Century that has amassed impressive returns for all its equity funds during the past 15 years. Overall, this is a great investment vehicle for certain investors.

Portfolio Manager: James Stowers
Since: 1958

Minimum:
Initial: $250
Subsequent: None
Telephone Exchange: Yes
Distributions:
Income: Annually
Capital Gain: Annually
Front-End Load: None
12b-1: None
Redemption Fee: None
Management Company: Investors Research
Ticker Symbol: TWGTX

TOTAL RETURN (%)

1987	1988	1989	1990	1991	5-year	Bull Market	Bear Market
8.7	11.1	50.2	-17.0	84.9	178.4	85.3	-38.7

INVESTMENT PORTFOLIO

Total Assets (mil.)	Current Yield	Turnover Ratio	Expense Ratio	Beta	Risk Return
$53	0.0%	137%	1.00%	1.64	0.10

TWENTIETH CENTURY GROWTH INVESTORS

Twentieth Century Investors
4500 Main Street, P.O. Box 419200
Kansas City, MO 64111
800-345-2021

Investment Objective: If you're looking for growth and have a long-term investment horizon, this is the fund for you. By keeping expenses at a modest 1.00% per annum, maintaining a no-load format and ensuring that the portfolio stays fully invested in high-growth stocks at all times, the fund offers growth potential at a low cost. This is one of the few funds that has no minimum initial investment requirements. A team of portfolio managers sifts through stocks of companies that pass a sophisticated computer screening process that emphasizes earnings momentum. Because of a full investment posture, this fund's share price is much more variable. However, this strategy has paid off handsomely during the past 15 years.

Portfolio Manager: James Stowers
Since: 1958

Minimum:
Initial: None
Subsequent: None
Telephone Exchange: Yes
Distributions:
Income: Annually
Capital Gain: Annually
Front-End Load: None
12b-1: None
Redemption Fee: None
Management Company: Investors Research
Ticker Symbol: TWCGX

TOTAL RETURN (%)

1987	1988	1989	1990	1991	5-year	Bull Market	Bear Market
13.1	2.7	43.1	-3.8	69.0	170.3	64.2	-28.1

INVESTMENT PORTFOLIO

Total Assets (mil.)	Current Yield	Turnover Ratio	Expense Ratio	Beta	Risk Return
$3,204	0.1%	118%	1.00%	1.30	0.10

TWENTIETH CENTURY HERITAGE INVESTORS

Twentieth Century Investors
4500 Main Street, P.O. Box 419200
Kansas City, MO 64111
800-345-2021

Investment Objective: Although chosen for their growth potential, securities selected for this fund must have a history of paying cash dividends or interest. Relative to the other Twentieth Century funds, Heritage's asset base is considerably smaller and, thus, the fund invests a greater portion of its assets in smaller companies. However, stocks of large companies are frequently held in the portfolio. This moderately aggressive fund returned an average 36% in 1991 after giving back 9% in 1990. As far as the Twentieth Century family goes, this fund is one of the more conservative ones.

Portfolio Manager: James Stowers
Since: 1987

Minimum:
Initial: None
Subsequent: None
Telephone Exchange: Yes
Distributions:
Income: Annually
Capital Gain: Annually
Front-End Load: None
12b-1: None
Redemption Fee: None
Management Company: Investors Research
Ticker Symbol: TWHIX

TOTAL RETURN (%)

1987	1988	1989	1990	1991	5-year	Bull Market	Bear Market
NA	16.0	35.0	-9.2	35.9	NA	23.2	-17.3

INVESTMENT PORTFOLIO

Total Assets (mil.)	Current Yield	Turnover Ratio	Expense Ratio	Beta	Risk Return
$275	1.2%	127%	1.00%	1.10	0.12

TWENTIETH CENTURY SELECT INVESTORS

Twentieth Century Investors
4500 Main Street, P.O. Box 419200
Kansas City, MO 64111
800-345-2021

Investment Objective: This fund has one of the best 15-year records in the business. When making stock selections, management seeks seasoned, dividend-paying growth stocks whose sales and earnings are on an uptrend. Unlike a number of aggressive growth funds, Select attempts to stay fully invested at all times. Usually, its shares are prone to wide swings over the market cycle. As with all funds that maintain a full investment posture, cash-allocation decisions are left to the individual investor. However, despite its highly variable share price, the fund weathered the turmoil that plagued the stock market during both 1987 and 1990. It is one of the few funds with no minimum initial investment requirement.

Portfolio Manager: James Stowers
Since: 1958

Minimum:
Initial: None
Subsequent: None
Telephone Exchange: Yes
Distributions:
Income: Annually
Capital Gain: Annually
Front-End Load: None
12b-1: None
Redemption Fee: None
Management Company: Investors Research
Ticker Symbol: TWCIX

TOTAL RETURN (%)

1987	1988	1989	1990	1991	5-year	Bull Market	Bear Market
5.7	5.6	39.5	-0.4	31.6	104.2	31.6	-19.9

INVESTMENT PORTFOLIO

Total Assets (mil.)	Current Yield	Turnover Ratio	Expense Ratio	Beta	Risk Return
$4,052	1.5%	83%	1.00%	1.06	0.05

TWENTIETH CENTURY ULTRA INVESTORS

Twentieth Century Investors
4500 Main Street, P.O. Box 419200
Kansas City, MO 64111
800-345-2021

Investment Objective: This fund, with a beta of about 1.49, is one of the most volatile equity funds in the industry. As a result, its share price soars in a bull market and plummets in a bear market. Furthermore, fund management generally maintains a fully invested posture through thick and thin. However, because the stock market has headed to higher ground over the long haul, management believes that its "full-investment" strategy will ultimately pay huge rewards for long-term-oriented investors. Stock selection for the Ultra fund follows that of the Growth and Vista funds. The difference between funds is that stocks are allocated to each fund on the basis of equity cap with medium cap company shares being allocated to Ultra.

Portfolio Manager: James Stowers
Since: 1958

Minimum:
Initial: None
Subsequent: None
Telephone Exchange: Yes
Distributions:
Income: Annually
Capital Gain: Annually
Front-End Load: None
12b-1: None
Redemption Fee: None
Management Company: Investors Research
Ticker Symbol: TWCUX

TOTAL RETURN (%)

1987	1988	1989	1990	1991	5-year	Bull Market	Bear Market
6.7	13.3	36.9	9.4	86.5	237.6	116.3	-29.3

INVESTMENT PORTFOLIO

Total Assets (mil.)	Current Yield	Turnover Ratio	Expense Ratio	Beta	Risk Return
$2,288	0.0%	141%	1.00%	1.49	0.11

TWENTIETH CENTURY VISTA INVESTORS

Twentieth Century Investors
4500 Main Street, P.O. Box 419200
Kansas City, MO 64111
800-345-2021

Investment Objective: This fund seeks capital growth by investing primarily in common stocks that are considered by management to have better-than-average prospects for appreciation. Twentieth Century's criteria for stock selection include choosing companies with above-average revenue and earnings growth. Once selected, the stocks are allocated to 1 of 3 portfolios: Growth, Ultra or Vista. Stocks with the smallest equity capitalizations are allocated to Vista. The fund stays fully invested at all times. As its beta would suggest, it is one of the most volatile funds in the industry. However, during rising markets, it has delivered exceptional investment returns. Over the long run, it should reward patient investors well.

Portfolio Manager: James Stowers
Since: 1958

Minimum:
Initial: None
Subsequent: None
Telephone Exchange: Yes
Distributions:
Income: Annually
Capital Gain: Annually
Front-End Load: None
12b-1: None
Redemption Fee: None
Management Company: Investors Research
Ticker Symbol: TWCVX

TOTAL RETURN (%)

1987	1988	1989	1990	1991	5-year	Bull Market	Bear Market
6.0	2.4	52.2	-15.7	73.7	141.9	68.5	-37.9

INVESTMENT PORTFOLIO

Total Assets (mil.)	Current Yield	Turnover Ratio	Expense Ratio	Beta	Risk Return
$626	0.0%	103%	1.00%	1.56	0.09

UNITED NEW CONCEPTS FUND

Waddell & Reed
6300 Lamar Avenue, P.O. Box 29217
Shawnee Mission, KS 66201
913-236-0000

Investment Objective: This fund seeks capital appreciation by investing in the common stocks of new or unseasoned companies in their early stages of development or smaller companies positioned in new and emerging industries where opportunity for rapid growth is above average. Although the fund invests in growth stocks, it has an above-average portfolio turnover ratio, indicating that it is not averse to taking short-term profits. Its performance, during recent years, has been significantly below average when compared with the S&P 500. However, smaller equity-cap stocks surged to the forefront the past year. As a result, the fund posted an astounding 88% return in 1991.

Portfolio Manager: Mark Seferovich
Since: 1989

Minimum:
Initial: $500
Subsequent: None
Telephone Exchange: No
Distributions:
Income: Annually
Capital Gain: Annually
Front-End Load: 8.50%
12b-1: None
Redemption Fee: None
Management Company: Waddell & Reed Investment
Ticker Symbol: UNECX

TOTAL RETURN (%)

1987	1988	1989	1990	1991	5-year	Bull Market	Bear Market
-3.8	3.9	8.5	2.0	88.3	108.3	92.5	-25.5

INVESTMENT PORTFOLIO

Total Assets (mil.)	Current Yield	Turnover Ratio	Expense Ratio	Beta	Risk Return
$118	0.2%	90%	1.36%	1.09	0.14

USAA AGGRESSIVE GROWTH FUND

USAA Investment Management
USAA Building
San Antonio, TX 78288
800-531-8181

Investment Objective: This capital appreciation–seeking fund places most of its bets on small emerging growth companies with market capitalizations below $500 million. It has the option of investing up to 10% of its assets in foreign firms. Stock selection tends to follow industry selection. However, when choosing stocks, management seeks companies with strong earnings growth, experienced management and proven product development capabilities. The fund followed 1990's 11% drop with a strong showing in 1991. The fund was formerly known as the USAA Mutual Sunbelt Era Fund.

Portfolio Manager: Stuart H. Wester
Since: 1988

Minimum:
Initial: $1,000
Subsequent: None
Telephone Exchange: Yes
Distributions:
Income: Annually
Capital Gain: Annually
Front-End Load: None
12b-1: None
Redemption Fee: None
Management Company: USAA Investment Management
Ticker Symbol: USAUX

TOTAL RETURN (%)

1987	1988	1989	1990	1991	5-year	Bull Market	Bear Market
-0.9	14.3	16.6	-11.9	71.7	99.6	89.4	-34.2

INVESTMENT PORTFOLIO

Total Assets (mil.)	Current Yield	Turnover Ratio	Expense Ratio	Beta	Risk Return
$224	0.0%	78%	0.94%	1.35	0.09

USF&G AXE-HOUGHTON GROWTH FUND

USF&G Investment Services
275 Commerce Drive, Suite 228
Fort Washington, PA 19034
800-323-8734

Investment Objective: This fund seeks long-term capital growth by investing in small and medium capitalization stocks and convertible preferred stocks. Despite fine showings in 1990 and 1991 when the fund gained 6.4% and 39.3%, respectively, the 5-year return figure is not very strong. The fund had an extremely low portfolio turnover rate of 28% in 1991 and its expense ratio is a minuscule 0.24%. However, shareholders are subjected to a hefty 5.75% front-end load and a 0.25% 12b-1 fee.

Portfolio Manager: Porter H. Sutro
Since: 1990

Minimum:
Initial: $1,000
Subsequent: None
Telephone Exchange: Yes
Distributions:
Income: Annually
Capital Gain: Annually
Front-End Load: 5.75%
12b-1: 0.25%
Redemption Fee: None
Management Company: USF&G Review Management
Ticker Symbol: AXETX

TOTAL RETURN (%)

1987	1988	1989	1990	1991	5-year	Bull Market	Bear Market
-6.0	-0.2	29.8	6.4	39.3	80.5	56.4	-17.5

INVESTMENT PORTFOLIO

Total Assets (mil.)	Current Yield	Turnover Ratio	Expense Ratio	Beta	Risk Return
$73	0.0%	28%	0.24%	0.95	0.06

USF&G OVER-THE-COUNTER SECURITIES FUND

USF&G Investment Services
275 Commerce Drive, Suite 228
Fort Washington, PA 19034
800-323-8734

Investment Objective: Portfolio Manager Binkley Shorts, who has been dogging small-firm stocks for more than a decade, has received more than his share of bruises. Beginning in late 1983, small-firm stocks began a string of dismal performances that did not end until the past year. During this period, a number of portfolio managers turned away from this sector of the market. However, Shorts has stuck to his guns. The result has been lackluster long-term performance. However, as the small-firm sector of the market rebounds (as it did in 1991), look for this well-managed fund to be among the leaders.

Portfolio Manager: Binkley Shorts
Since: 1981

Minimum:
Initial: $1,000
Subsequent: $50
Telephone Exchange: No
Distributions:
Income: Annually
Capital Gain: Annually
Front-End Load: 5.75%
12b-1: 0.13%
Redemption Fee: None
Management Company: USF&G Review Management
Ticker Symbol: OTCFX

TOTAL RETURN (%)

1987	1988	1989	1990	1991	5-year	Bull Market	Bear Market
-12.5	27.2	19.1	-20.5	38.6	46.1	42.8	-25.1

INVESTMENT PORTFOLIO

Total Assets (mil.)	Current Yield	Turnover Ratio	Expense Ratio	Beta	Risk Return
$249	0.5%	16%	1.47%	0.94	0.07

VALUE LINE FUND

Value Line Securities
711 Third Avenue
New York, NY 10017
800-223-0818

Investment Objective: This fund seeks long-term growth of capital with income as a secondary consideration. Management makes its stock selections based on the Value Line ranking system. The system ranks stocks on the basis of past and projected earnings, price momentum and historical price levels. The portfolio tends to be comprised of midsized stocks with strong earnings growth. The fund returned 48% in 1991 while almost breaking even in 1990. It sports an admirable 5-year return of 123.3% and keeps expenses to a minimum.

Portfolio Manager: Joel Goldsmith
Since: 1987

Minimum:
Initial: $1,000
Subsequent: None
Telephone Exchange: Yes
Distributions:
Income: Semiannually
Capital Gain: Annually
Front-End Load: None
12b-1: None
Redemption Fee: None
Management Company: Value Line
Ticker Symbol: VLIFX

TOTAL RETURN (%)

1987	1988	1989	1990	1991	5-year	Bull Market	Bear Market
5.2	9.7	31.4	-0.8	48.4	123.3	48.4	-22.1

INVESTMENT PORTFOLIO

Total Assets (mil.)	Current Yield	Turnover Ratio	Expense Ratio	Beta	Risk Return
$274	0.8%	84%	0.71%	1.06	0.08

VALUE LINE LEVERAGED GROWTH INVESTORS

Value Line Securities
711 Third Avenue
New York, NY 10017
800-223-0818

Investment Objective: This fund seeks capital appreciation and attempts to boost return by buying common stocks on margin. The fund stays almost fully invested in common stocks or convertible securities and also can write covered call options. Although the use of margins can boost investment returns, the fund's return has paralleled that of the market as a whole during the past 5 years. Surprisingly, the fund's beta is about average for an equity fund despite its use of financial leverage. This indicates that the fund has been judicious about the use of margins during speculative markets. Thus, it is not so risky as other leveraged funds.

Portfolio Manager: David Campbell
Since: 1988

Minimum:
Initial: $1,000
Subsequent: None
Telephone Exchange: Yes
Distributions:
Income: Annually
Capital Gain: Annually
Front-End Load: None
12b-1: None
Redemption Fee: None
Management Company: Value Line
Ticker Symbol: VALLX

TOTAL RETURN (%)

1987	1988	1989	1990	1991	5-year	Bull Market	Bear Market
2.8	6.4	32.3	-1.6	46.4	108.4	50.0	-23.0

INVESTMENT PORTFOLIO

Total Assets (mil.)	Current Yield	Turnover Ratio	Expense Ratio	Beta	Risk Return
$291	0.8%	94%	0.96%	1.12	0.08

VALUE LINE SPECIAL SITUATIONS FUND

Value Line Securities
711 Third Avenue
New York, NY 10017
800-223-0818

Investment Objective: This fund seeks capital appreciation by investing in special situations or companies believed to be ripe for merger or acquisition. Special situations are considered unique developments in a company that can lead to increased profitability and earnings growth and subsequent stock price appreciation. Currently, management has been emphasizing investment in small-company stocks across a wide range of industries. During the past 5 years, its performance has been somewhat of a disappointment. Furthermore, with the corporate frenzy now abated, Portfolio Manager Peter Schraga may find "special situations" a little more difficult.

Portfolio Manager: Peter Schraga
Since: 1987

Minimum:
Initial: $1,000
Subsequent: None
Telephone Exchange: Yes
Distributions:
Income: Annually
Capital Gain: Annually
Front-End Load: None
12b-1: None
Redemption Fee: None
Management Company: Value Line
Ticker Symbol: VALSX

TOTAL RETURN (%)

1987	1988	1989	1990	1991	5-year	Bull Market	Bear Market
-9.1	3.3	21.7	-4.4	36.6	49.3	50.8	-25.9

INVESTMENT PORTFOLIO

Total Assets (mil.)	Current Yield	Turnover Ratio	Expense Ratio	Beta	Risk Return
$116	0.3%	33%	1.11%	1.04	0.06

VANGUARD EXPLORER FUND

Vanguard Group
Vanguard Financial Center
Valley Forge, PA 19482
800-662-7447

Investment Objective: This fund seeks capital appreciation by investing in companies with small-equity market values. In recent years, the fund's management has stressed investment in smaller firms in the technology sector. In late 1990, the assets of the Explorer II fund were merged into Explorer. In addition, the portfolio manager of Explorer II joined existing management. As expected, the fund has shown lackluster performance during the past 5 years, as small cap stocks in general have languished. However, a continuation of a small cap strategy eventually could allow shareholders to reap big rewards. Small cap stock returns tend to run in streaks. For example, the past year the fund produced a sizable 56% return.

Portfolio Manager: F. Wisneski/J. Granahan
Since: 1979

Minimum:
Initial: $3,000
Subsequent: $100
Telephone Exchange: No
Distributions:
Income: Annually
Capital Gain: Annually
Front-End Load: None
12b-1: None
Redemption Fee: None
Management Company: Wellington/Granahan
Ticker Symbol: VEXPX

TOTAL RETURN (%)

1987	1988	1989	1990	1991	5-year	Bull Market	Bear Market
-6.9	25.8	9.4	-10.8	55.9	78.2	65.5	-29.4

INVESTMENT PORTFOLIO

Total Assets (mil.)	Current Yield	Turnover Ratio	Expense Ratio	Beta	Risk Return
$374	0.7%	49%	0.56%	1.05	0.09

VANGUARD SMALL CAPITALIZATION STOCK FUND

Vanguard Group
Vanguard Financial Center
Valley Forge, PA 19482
800-662-7447

Investment Objective: This fund seeks to mirror the return of the Russell 2000 Stock Index. By using a statistical sample of stocks in the Index, management hopes it can duplicate the Russell 2000 without actually buying all the stocks included in it. Expenses are kept to a minimum, as shareholders must bear only the brunt of a passively managed portfolio. The fund narrowly missed matching its benchmark the past year as it returned just more than 45%. A one-time 1% transaction fee is charged by the fund. For investors looking to index the small cap market, this fund is probably the best choice available.

Portfolio Manager: George Sauter
Since: 1989

Minimum:
Initial: $3,000
Subsequent: $100
Telephone Exchange: Yes
Distributions:
Income: Annually
Capital Gain: Annually
Front-End Load: None
12b-1: None
Redemption Fee: None
Management Company: Core Management Group
Ticker Symbol: NAESX

TOTAL RETURN (%)

1987	1988	1989	1990	1991	5-year	Bull Market	Bear Market
-7.0	24.6	10.5	-18.1	45.3	52.4	56.6	-28.2

INVESTMENT PORTFOLIO

Total Assets (mil.)	Current Yield	Turnover Ratio	Expense Ratio	Beta	Risk Return
$116	1.4%	21%	0.21%	1.08	0.07

WALL STREET FUND

Wall Street Management
230 Park Avenue, 20th Floor
New York, NY 10169
800-443-4693

Investment Objective: This fund seeks capital appreciation by primarily investing in small companies. The fund attempts to reduce some of the risk by broadly diversifying in its company selection. After years of enduring the unfavorable market for small capitalization stocks, the fund was rewarded in 1991. During the past year, the fund returned 54%, after suffering a 20% drop in 1990. Expenses remain high at 2.00% and management actively trades the portfolio, thus its high turnover ratio. Investors also should pay attention to the 4.00% front-end load.

Portfolio Manager: Robert P. Morse
Since: 1984

Minimum:
Initial: $2,000
Subsequent: $10
Telephone Exchange: No
Distributions:
Income: Annually
Capital Gain: Annually
Front-End Load: 4.00%
12b-1: None
Redemption Fee: None
Management Company: Wall Street Management
Ticker Symbol: WALLX

TOTAL RETURN (%)

1987	1988	1989	1990	1991	5-year	Bull Market	Bear Market
-2.5	18.6	22.3	-20.4	54.4	73.8	69.7	-32.3

INVESTMENT PORTFOLIO

Total Assets (mil.)	Current Yield	Turnover Ratio	Expense Ratio	Beta	Risk Return
$10	0.6%	142%	2.00%	1.23	0.08

WPG TUDOR FUND

Weiss Peck & Greer
One New York Plaza
New York, NY 10004
800-223-3332

Investment Objective: This fund seeks capital appreciation by investing in growth stocks. It may place up to 50% of its assets in "special situations" that offer prospects for appreciation in the short run. The fund managed to eke out a small gain in 1987 and returned a solid 45% in 1991. Management has shifted the fund's focus from blue chip to middle and small cap companies for they believed the smaller issues are poised for a period of sustained superior performance. Investors should note that the fund is a true no-load investment vehicle.

Portfolio Manager: Melville Straus
Since: 1973

Minimum:
Initial: $2,500
Subsequent: $100
Telephone Exchange: Yes
Distributions:
Income: Annually
Capital Gain: Annually
Front-End Load: None
12b-1: None
Redemption Fee: None
Management Company: Tudor Management Company
Ticker Symbol: TUDRX

TOTAL RETURN (%)

1987	1988	1989	1990	1991	5-year	Bull Market	Bear Market
1.1	15.2	25.1	-5.2	45.8	101.3	47.2	-22.8

INVESTMENT PORTFOLIO

Total Assets (mil.)	Current Yield	Turnover Ratio	Expense Ratio	Beta	Risk Return
$233	1.1%	73%	1.11%	1.14	0.07

PART 4

Asset Allocation Funds

Asset allocation has become a modern-day finance buzzword. It is used to describe portfolios that contain two or more different classes of assets. Even some market timers who switch their investments back and forth between stocks and cash refer to themselves as asset allocators. To us, however, an asset allocator is one who spreads investments among several asset classes whose returns are less than perfectly correlated. Thus, the objective of the true asset allocator is to reduce portfolio variability (risk).

Asset allocation funds differ widely on the selection of asset classes to be included in their portfolios. However, most include several assets from the following classes: U.S. stocks, foreign stocks, precious metals, real estate stocks, domestic bonds, foreign bonds, foreign currencies and money market instruments. Some asset allocation funds, such as the Merriman Asset Allocation Fund, invest in other mutual funds. When managing asset allocation funds, some portfolio managers apply a passive reallocation strategy, such as rebalancing the portfolio back to its initial allocation once each quarter. Others attempt to forecast returns in the various categories in which they invest. They then reallocate the fund's assets, giving more weight to those asset classes that are expected to produce the best returns. Thus, when investing in an asset allocation fund, it is very important to know which classes of assets the fund will invest in as well as whether management follows a passive or active reallocation strategy.

In theory, asset allocation funds should provide a greater rate of return than the S&P 500 Index, while at the same time being less volatile. Unfortunately, asset allocation funds are relative new additions to the investment world (the grandfather of asset allocation funds, the Permanent Portfolio Fund, commenced operations during 1982). Thus, there is insufficient data to tell how investment fact measures up to investment theory. However, if 1987 is in any way representative of asset allocation fund performance during a chaotic investment climate, these funds are all that they claim to be. By year-end 1987, all four asset allocation funds in existence at that time managed to beat the market. The group's best performer returned more than 16 percent during 1987. While their returns trailed the S&P 500 Index during the first nine months of the year, they rose to the fore during the year's final three months. During the turbulent fourth quarter when the S&P 500 Index tumbled nearly 27 percent, these four asset allocation funds declined an average of only 10 percent, with the group's best performer giving back only 3.4 percent in total return.

During recent years, asset allocation funds have been underperformers when compared to the returns provided by the S&P's 500 Index. However, before summarily dismissing the concept of asset allocation, you must remember that these funds tend to shine during periods marked by adverse conditions in the financial markets. Their return comparisons pale when blue chip stocks are performing well, consumer prices are growing at modest rates and interest rates are relatively stable. These are precisely the conditions that have prevailed in the financial markets in recent years. Thus, it is not surprising to find that the returns from asset allocation funds have been relatively unimpressive when compared to the performance of common stocks.

It also is not fair to compare the returns of asset allocation funds with those of popular stock market indices either. Most asset allocation funds invest in bonds, cash equivalents and other assets such as gold and precious metals. As a result, they tend to possess far less risk than that of the typical equity fund. In fact, their average beta (market risk exposure) is only about one-half that of the typical equity mutual fund. Because a large portion of investment returns can be explained by investment risk, lower risk funds should, in fact, return less than riskier funds over long periods of time. Thus, despite their unimpressive returns in recent years, asset allocation funds have lived up to their billing as low-risk growth and income funds.

Summary Financial Statistics (medians)

1991 Return	5-Year Return	Current Yield	Beta	Turnover Ratio	Expense Ratio
20.3%	52.0%	3.5%	0.57	78%	1.46%

BEST ASSET ALLOCATION FUNDS FOR 1991

Fund	Percent Return 1991	3-Year	5-Year
AMEV Advantage Asset Allocation Portfolio	29.3%	56.9%	NA
MIMLIC Asset Allocation Fund	27.7	57.7	81.5%
Vanguard Asset Allocation Fund	25.6	54.0	NA
Fidelity Asset Manager	23.6	50.6	NA
Stagecoach Asset Allocation Fund	22.1	47.2	75.2
North American Moderate Asset Allocation	21.6	30.7	55.4
PaineWebber Asset Allocation B	20.3	36.6	54.0
Shearson Multiple Opportunities Portfolio	19.2	46.1	NA
USAA Cornerstone	16.2	28.6	52.0
BB&K Diversa Fund	16.0	18.3	36.9
Oppenheimer Asset Allocation Fund	14.7	35.6	NA

AMEV ADVANTAGE ASSET ALLOCATION PORTFOLIO

AMEV Investors
P. O. Box 64284
St. Paul, MN 55164
800-800-2638

Investment Objective: The fund seeks maximum capital appreciation by shifting assets among stocks, bonds and money market instruments, in response to financial market conditions. The fund primarily purchases Treasury and U.S. Government Agency securities and rarely takes an aggressive interest rate stance. By contrast, the common stock portion of its portfolio (about 40% of total assets) has assumed a rather aggressive stance in recent years. While its posture of investing primarily in high-growth, blue chip stocks paid off handsomely last year (the fund was the number-one performing asset allocation fund last year), the fund could stumble during a period marked by a downdraft in growth stocks and rising interest rates.

Portfolio Manager: Stephen Poling/Dennis Ott
Since: 1985

Minimum:
Initial: $500
Subsequent: $50
Telephone Exchange: Yes
Distributions:
Income: Annually
Capital Gain: Annually
Front-End Load: 4.50%
12b-1: 0.45%
Redemption Fee: None
Management Company: Fortis Advisors
Ticker Symbol: AMAAX

TOTAL RETURN (%)

1987	1988	1989	1990	1991	5-year	Bull Market	Bear Market
NA	3.2	22.7	-1.1	29.3	NA	27.9	-13.0

INVESTMENT PORTFOLIO

Total Assets (mil.)	Current Yield	Turnover Ratio	Expense Ratio	Beta	Risk Return
$28	3.4%	112%	1.98%	0.59	0.08

BB&K DIVERSA FUND

Bailard Biehl & Kaiser
2755 Campus Drive
San Mateo, CA 94403
800-882-8383

Investment Objective: The fund seeks a high rate of total return while providing a lower-than-average level of risk by using a broadly based asset allocation strategy. It invests in stocks, bonds, foreign securities, real estate-related securities and cash equivalents. The fund has lived up to its billing as a low-risk growth and income fund. For example, it returned slightly more than 8.0% in 1987's crash-pocked market. Although it posted a 9.5% loss during 1990, all but blue chip stocks suffered significant declines that year. Its five-year return is unimpressive beside that of the S&P 500 Index, but broadly based asset allocation funds tend to perform best when financial markets are in turmoil; not the case in recent years.

Portfolio Manager: David R. Rahn
Since: 1986

Minimum:
Initial: $25,000
Subsequent: $2,000
Telephone Exchange: No
Distributions:
Income: Quarterly
Capital Gain: Annually
Front-End Load: None
12b-1: None
Redemption Fee: None
Management Company: Bailard Biehl & Kaiser
Ticker Symbol: BBKDX

TOTAL RETURN (%)

1987	1988	1989	1990	1991	5-year	Bull Market	Bear Market
8.5	6.6	12.7	-9.5	16.0	36.9	17.2	-16.0

INVESTMENT PORTFOLIO

Total Assets (mil.)	Current Yield	Turnover Ratio	Expense Ratio	Beta	Risk Return
$55	4.2%	235%	1.46%	0.60	0.03

BLANCHARD GLOBAL GROWTH FUND

Sheffield Investments
41 Madison Avenue, 24th Floor
New York, NY 10010
800-922-7771

Investment Objective: This asset allocation fund seeks capital appreciation and a low variability of return by investing in various classes of assets, including gold, bonds, blue chip common stocks, foreign equities and interest-earning liquid assets. Separate portfolio managers make asset selections within their subportfolio, while the fund sponsor makes strategic allocations of capital to each subportfolio. Although the fund is technically sold without a front-end load, a $125 start-up fee is levied on all new accounts. And aside from the stellar performance during 1987, its performance has lagged far behind that of the S&P 500 Index since then.

Portfolio Manager: Andrea Sharon
Since: 1986

Minimum:
Initial: $3,000
Subsequent: $500
Telephone Exchange: Yes
Distributions:
Income: Annually
Capital Gain: Annually
Front-End Load: None
12b-1: 0.78%
Redemption Fee: None
Management Company: Sheffield Management
Ticker Symbol: BSGFX

TOTAL RETURN (%)

1987	1988	1989	1990	1991	5-year	Bull Market	Bear Market
16.3	7.4	15.7	-6.4	10.7	49.9	12.7	-11.4

INVESTMENT PORTFOLIO

Total Assets (mil.)	Current Yield	Turnover Ratio	Expense Ratio	Beta	Risk Return
$148	3.1%	78%	2.36%	0.51	0.02

FIDELITY ASSET MANAGER

Fidelity Distributors Corporation
82 Devonshire St., Mail Zone L7B
Boston, MA 02109
800-544-8888

Investment Objective: The fund, which shifts assets among stocks, bonds and short-term fixed-income securities, restricts equities to a maximum 50% of assets. When neutral, the fund's asset mix consists of 30% stocks, 40% bonds, 30% cash. Partially offsetting the low volatility is its taste for rapid growth, small capitalization stocks. Still, the fund promises a fairly smooth ride, as its minimum 50% bond/cash component limits downside risk. In its brief history, it has yet to experience a down year despite the plunge in small firm stocks that occurred during 1990. It is a conservative alternative for investors who seek some exposure to small firm growth stocks yet wish to limit their risk.

Portfolio Manager: Bob Beckwitt
Since: 1988

Minimum:
Initial: $2,500
Subsequent: $250
Telephone Exchange: Yes
Distributions:
Income: Annually
Capital Gain: Annually
Front-End Load: None
12b-1: None
Redemption Fee: None
Management Company: Fidelity Management & Research
Ticker Symbol: FASMX

TOTAL RETURN (%)

1987	1988	1989	1990	1991	5-year	Bull Market	Bear Market
NA	NA	15.6	5.4	23.6	NA	33.2	-8.5

INVESTMENT PORTFOLIO

Total Assets (mil.)	Current Yield	Turnover Ratio	Expense Ratio	Beta	Risk Return
$898	3.5%	105%	1.17%	0.46	0.07

MERRIMAN ASSET ALLOCATION FUND

Merriman Investment Management
1200 Westlake Avenue North, #507
Seattle, WA 98109
800-423-4893

Investment Objective: This fund is unique in that it allocates its assets among the shares of other investment companies. It allocates in 4 specific areas: 50% to equities, 20% to fixed-income securities, 20% to foreign securities and the balance to precious metals securities. Also, market timing strategies and techniques are employed independently by each segment of the fund's portfolio in response to actual market trends in that segment. During its brief existence, its market timing bent has resulted in a very high percentage of assets allocated to cash equivalents. Its conservative posture allowed it to dodge the bear markets of 1990, but also capped its returns during 1991.

Portfolio Manager: Paul Merriman/William Notaro
Since: 1989

Minimum:
Initial: $1,000
Subsequent: $100
Telephone Exchange: Yes
Distributions:
Income: Quarterly
Capital Gain: Annually
Front-End Load: None
12b-1: None
Redemption Fee: None
Management Company: Merriman Investment Management
Ticker Symbol: MTASX

TOTAL RETURN (%)

1987	1988	1989	1990	1991	5-year	Bull Market	Bear Market
NA	NA	NA	0.8	12.3	NA	11.6	-4.4

INVESTMENT PORTFOLIO

Total Assets (mil.)	Current Yield	Turnover Ratio	Expense Ratio	Beta	Risk Return
$27	2.6%	415%	1.78%	0.30	0.03

MIMLIC ASSET ALLOCATION FUND

MIMLIC
400 North Robert Street
St. Paul, MN 55101
800-443-3677

Investment Objective: This fund strives to achieve a reasonable rate of return, while reducing volatility. Management relies on a dividend discount model to evaluate the relative risk of stocks, bonds and cash, striving for the best risk-adjusted rate of return. The fund's stock market exposure isn't likely to exceed a neutral 40% of assets, unless its projected rate of return is highly competitive relative to lower-risk bonds. As seen in the fund's better-than-average 1990 return, a neutral asset mix of 40% stocks, 40% bonds, 20% cash provides a degree of protection when stock prices are falling. Its emphasis on big-cap growth stocks gave the fund an edge over most rivals during the past year.

Portfolio Manager: Thomas Gunerson
Since: 1984

Minimum:
Initial: $250
Subsequent: $25
Telephone Exchange: Yes
Distributions:
Income: Quarterly
Capital Gain: Annually
Front-End Load: 5.00%
12b-1: 0.35%
Redemption Fee: None
Management Company: MIMLIC Asset Management
Ticker Symbol: MIAAX

TOTAL RETURN (%)

1987	1988	1989	1990	1991	5-year	Bull Market	Bear Market
4.4	10.2	19.4	3.4	27.7	81.5	28.0	-9.1

INVESTMENT PORTFOLIO

Total Assets (mil.)	Current Yield	Turnover Ratio	Expense Ratio	Beta	Risk Return
$19	3.6%	66%	1.35%	0.57	0.08

NATIONAL GLOBAL ALLOCATION FUND

NSR Distributors
2 Pickwick Plaza
Greenwich, CT 06830
800-356-5535

Investment Objective: This fund seeks long-term capital growth by investing in 4 individually managed categories of assets: U.S. equities, foreign securities, precious metals securities and bullion, and fixed-income securities. Although the percentage of the fund's total assets allocated into any one sector depends on management's assessment of current conditions, the fund maintains some commitment to each category of assets at all times: equities may not exceed 50% or be less than 10% of the fund's total assets, foreign stocks may not exceed 50% or be less than 10%, precious metals may not exceed 50% or be less than 10%, and fixed-income securities may not exceed 35% or be less than 5%.

Portfolio Manager: John Doney/Robert Rawe
Since: 1991

Minimum:
Initial: $250
Subsequent: $25
Telephone Exchange: Yes
Distributions:
Income: Semiannually
Capital Gain: Annually
Front-End Load: 5.75%
12b-1: 0.25%
Redemption Fee: None
Management Company: National Securities & Research
Ticker Symbol: NAGAX

TOTAL RETURN (%)

1987	1988	1989	1990	1991	5-year	Bull Market	Bear Market
NA	6.3	16.9	-6.2	10.2	NA	11.8	-12.4

INVESTMENT PORTFOLIO

Total Assets (mil.)	Current Yield	Turnover Ratio	Expense Ratio	Beta	Risk Return
$53	1.0%	52%	1.78%	0.57	0.01

NORTH AMERICAN MODERATE ASSET ALLOCATION

NASL Financial Services
695 Atlantic Avenue
Boston, MA 02111
800-872-8037

Investment Objective: The fund invests in common stocks, bonds (generally U.S. Treasuries) and money market instruments in pursuit of total return at suitable risk levels. The fund's former name, the Hidden Strength Funds Total Return Portfolio, is probably a more appropriate title as we have yet to find the fund's strength. At best, the fund's performance can be summed up as average, although this may be a kind assessment. A hefty front-end load of 4.75%, a high 2.40% expense ratio and a lagging historical performance chart make the outlook for this fund a bit dreary. However, a better indication of the fund's ability will be determined during the next significant down year for the S&P 500.

Portfolio Manager: James McCluere
Since: 1991

Minimum:
Initial: $500
Subsequent: $50
Telephone Exchange: Yes
Distributions:
Income: Semiannually
Capital Gain: Annually
Front-End Load: 4.75%
12b-1: 0.85%
Redemption Fee: None
Management Company: NASL Financial Services
Ticker Symbol: NAMAX

TOTAL RETURN (%)

1987	1988	1989	1990	1991	5-year	Bull Market	Bear Market
4.3	14.0	17.7	-8.7	21.6	55.4	17.1	-10.2

INVESTMENT PORTFOLIO

Total Assets (mil.)	Current Yield	Turnover Ratio	Expense Ratio	Beta	Risk Return
$31	2.4%	66%	2.40%	0.68	0.05

OPPENHEIMER ASSET ALLOCATION FUND

Oppenheimer Investor Services
P. O. Box 300
Denver, CO 80201
800-255-2755

Investment Objective: This fund's highly liberal charter imposes no restrictions on its asset allocation strategy; it may invest in any mix of stocks, bonds and cash. Although its growth objective usually keeps it heavily tilted toward equities, signs of an impending economic recession caused the fund to maintain a highly cautious stance during 1990, with cash and bonds claiming a full two-thirds of assets. The fund's modest returns during 1991 owe to its taste for value stocks and neglect of the pricey growth issues that were 1991's stock market leaders. During its 4-year existence, the fund has returned a respectable 12.2% compounded annually.

Portfolio Manager: Ken Oberman/Richard Rubinstein
Since: 1987

Minimum:
Initial: $1,000
Subsequent: $25
Telephone Exchange: Yes
Distributions:
Income: Quarterly
Capital Gain: Annually
Front-End Load: 5.75%
12b-1: 0.15%
Redemption Fee: None
Management Company: Oppenheimer Management
Ticker Symbol: OPASX

TOTAL RETURN (%)

1987	1988	1989	1990	1991	5-year	Bull Market	Bear Market
NA	16.8	17.2	0.9	14.7	NA	14.0	-4.4

INVESTMENT PORTFOLIO

Total Assets (mil.)	Current Yield	Turnover Ratio	Expense Ratio	Beta	Risk Return
$265	3.6%	71%	1.36%	0.41	0.04

PAINEWEBBER ASSET ALLOCATION B

PaineWebber
1285 Avenue of the Americas
New York, NY 10019
800-647-1568

Investment Objective: Asset allocation investors may not get the diversification many seek when investing in this particular fund. Although the fund seeks high total return in conjunction with low volatility, the fund's bias toward common stocks probably will give shareholders a bit of a bumpy ride. The possibility exists that all of the fund's assets may be invested in one asset class. The fund possesses a high turnover ratio and has not performed particularly well during its short life span, although there has not been a down year thus far. A recent change in portfolio management may offer some hope for the fund, but only time will tell. Also, dissatisfied investors face a stiff redemption fee.

Portfolio Manager: Michael Jamison
Since: 1991

Minimum:
Initial: $1,000
Subsequent: $100
Telephone Exchange: No
Distributions:
Income: Semiannually
Capital Gain: Annually
Front-End Load: None
12b-1: 1.00%
Redemption Fee: 5.00%
Management Company: Mitchell Hutchins Asset Management
Ticker Symbol: PASBX

TOTAL RETURN (%)

1987	1988	1989	1990	1991	5-year	Bull Market	Bear Market
1.3	11.3	10.8	2.5	20.3	54.0	18.3	-10.2

INVESTMENT PORTFOLIO

Total Assets (mil.)	Current Yield	Turnover Ratio	Expense Ratio	Beta	Risk Return
$357	4.6%	169%	2.03%	0.42	0.03

PERMANENT PORTFOLIO

Permanent Portfolio Funds
625 Second Street
Petaluma, CA 94952
800-531-5142

Investment Objective: This fund deserves some special attention. Returns have been fairly mediocre over the past 5 years for this inflation-hedging investment vehicle, as a combination of moderate inflation, lower gold prices and weakening housing prices have hurt returns. These 3 factors play major roles in determining the fund's fate because about one-third of its assets are tied up in gold and silver bullion, another 25% (or more) in real estate–related industries, with the remainder in natural resources. If the 1990s are a repeat of the low-inflation 1983–1989 period, this fund will be grounded.

Portfolio Manager: Terry Coxon
Since: 1982

Minimum:
Initial: $1,000
Subsequent: $100
Telephone Exchange: Yes
Distributions:
Income: Annually
Capital Gain: Annually
Front-End Load: None
12b-1: 0.25%
Redemption Fee: None
Management Company: World Money Managers
Ticker Symbol: PRPFX

TOTAL RETURN (%)

1987	1988	1989	1990	1991	5-year	Bull Market	Bear Market
13.1	1.3	6.4	-3.9	8.1	26.6	9.8	-6.6

INVESTMENT PORTFOLIO

Total Assets (mil.)	Current Yield	Turnover Ratio	Expense Ratio	Beta	Risk Return
$71	6.0%	32%	1.36%	0.27	0.01

SHEARSON MULTIPLE OPPORTUNITIES PORTFOLIO

Shearson Lehman Brothers
Two World Trade Center
New York, NY 10048
800-451-2010

Investment Objective: This fund attempts to balance the risks of the stock market with a healthy portion of fixed-income securities. In fact, with nearly equal pots of cash and stocks, the fund survived 1990's punishing market with barely a dent. Yet since inception, the fund's risk-return figure is below par, as its -3.9% return in 1988 and high 3.0% expense ratio have whittled its net performance. Investors may be enticed into the fund's temple without knowing the cost of the increase it levies by an ongoing 1.00% 12b-1 fee and a 3.00% redemption fee, thereby reducing returns.

Portfolio Manager: Michael Sherman
Since: 1987

Minimum:
Initial: $25,000
Subsequent: $10,000
Telephone Exchange: No
Distributions:
Income: Annually
Capital Gain: Annually
Front-End Load: None
12b-1: 1.00%
Redemption Fee: 3.00%
Management Company: Strategy Advisors
Ticker Symbol: SMOPX

TOTAL RETURN (%)

1987	1988	1989	1990	1991	5-year	Bull Market	Bear Market
NA	-3.9	22.7	-0.1	19.2	NA	16.5	-15.3

INVESTMENT PORTFOLIO

Total Assets (mil.)	Current Yield	Turnover Ratio	Expense Ratio	Beta	Risk Return
$98	1.6%	112%	3.02%	1.46	0.02

STAGECOACH ASSET ALLOCATION FUND

Wells Fargo Investment Advisors
525 Market Street, 12th Floor
San Francisco, CA 94163
800-222-8222

Investment Objective: Formerly the Wells Fargo Asset Allocation Fund, Stagecoach Asset Allocation seeks a high total return at moderate risk levels. Allocations are made to common stocks, U.S. Treasury bonds and money market funds based on the anticipated relative performance of stocks versus bonds. The unique feature of this fund is its decision to index the S&P 500 with its stock allocation while mirroring the Lehman Brothers Treasury Index with the bond portfolio. The fund has not had a down year in its 5-year history and sports one of the lower risk levels within the asset allocation group. The fund is available only to Wells Fargo customers, but this policy is being reevaluated.

Portfolio Manager: Janice Deringer
Since: 1986

Minimum:
Initial: $1,000
Subsequent: $100
Telephone Exchange: Yes
Distributions:
Income: Annually
Capital Gain: Annually
Front-End Load: 4.50%
12b-1: 0.05%
Redemption Fee: None
Management Company: Wells Fargo Investment Management
Ticker Symbol: WFAAX

TOTAL RETURN (%)

1987	1988	1989	1990	1991	5-year	Bull Market	Bear Market
8.5	9.7	11.9	7.7	22.1	75.2	20.4	-2.7

INVESTMENT PORTFOLIO

Total Assets (mil.)	Current Yield	Turnover Ratio	Expense Ratio	Beta	Risk Return
$341	0.0%	2%	0.95%	0.29	0.09

USAA CORNERSTONE

USAA Investment Management
USAA Building
San Antonio, TX 78288
800-531-8181

Investment Objective: This asset allocator has done what it set out to do. Its investment objective is the preservation of shareholders' purchasing power against inflation and the achievement of a stable net asset value with a positive real (after inflation) return. The fund divides its assets among 5 investment categories (domestic, foreign and gold equities, U.S. government bonds and real estate–related securities) to meet its objective. After performing with style from 1986 to 1989, with a strong 9.0% return in 1987, the fund tumbled 9.2% in 1990 because of its 20% gold equities and real estate position. Nonetheless, the fund remains a strong all-weather candidate.

Portfolio Manager: Harry W. Miller
Since: 1990

Minimum:
Initial: $1,000
Subsequent: $100
Telephone Exchange: Yes
Distributions:
Income: Annually
Capital Gain: Annually
Front-End Load: None
12b-1: None
Redemption Fee: None
Management Company: USAA Investment Management
Ticker Symbol: USCRX

TOTAL RETURN (%)

1987	1988	1989	1990	1991	5-year	Bull Market	Bear Market
9.0	8.4	21.9	-9.2	16.2	52.0	17.6	-11.6

INVESTMENT PORTFOLIO

Total Assets (mil.)	Current Yield	Turnover Ratio	Expense Ratio	Beta	Risk Return
$574	3.1%	41%	1.21%	0.51	0.03

VANGUARD ASSET ALLOCATION FUND

Vanguard Group
Vanguard Financial Center
Valley Forge, PA 19482
800-662-7447

Investment Objective: Looking more like a balanced fund than an asset allocation vehicle, this Vanguard vehicle contains a near-equal mix of common stocks and fixed-income securities in only U.S. government bonds. On the equity side, the portfolio appears to mirror the S&P 500, both in terms of the types of companies and the number of securities held. The fund has performed with distinction. It has provided significant returns during bull markets and limited losses during stock market declines. Like most Vanguard funds, its expense ratio is among the lowest in its class.

Portfolio Manager: Thomas Hazuka
Since: 1988

Minimum:
Initial: $3,000
Subsequent: $100
Telephone Exchange: Yes
Distributions:
Income: Annually
Capital Gain: Annually
Front-End Load: None
12b-1: None
Redemption Fee: None
Management Company: Mellon Capital Management
Ticker Symbol: VAAPX

TOTAL RETURN (%)

1987	1988	1989	1990	1991	5-year	Bull Market	Bear Market
NA	NA	23.7	-0.9	25.6	NA	30.6	-11.7

INVESTMENT PORTFOLIO

Total Assets (mil.)	Current Yield	Turnover Ratio	Expense Ratio	Beta	Risk Return
$291	4.3%	12%	0.50%	0.66	0.06

PART 5

Growth Funds

As the name implies, these funds attempt to obtain long-term growth of investment capital as their primary investment objective. The portfolio managers of these funds do not engage in speculative tactics such as using financial leverage (i.e., buying common stocks on margin) or short-selling. However, on occasion, some managers will use stock or index options to hedge their portfolio positions.

The table below summarizes some selected financial statistics for the growth funds that follow. As can be seen, returns of growth funds tend to be less variable than those of funds classified as aggressive growth (median beta of 0.98). In addition, because they tend to invest in the common stocks of larger, established companies that usually pay cash dividends, these funds also provide a modest amount of current income (median current yield of 1.2 percent). A growth fund investor is likely to find companies such as IBM, General Motors, Xerox, DuPont, etc., in these portfolios.

While a growing number of growth fund portfolio managers have adopted short-term trading strategies, the vast majority hold their investments for long-term capital appreciation. On average, these funds tend to hold their common stock investments for approximately 20 months, and one can find a large number of funds with significantly longer average holding periods.

During the past five years, these funds have provided an average compound rate of return of 13.6 percent, versus a 15.4 percent compound annual rate of return for the Standard

& Poor's 500 Index. The difference is caused by a number of factors, including both transactions costs, incurred when trading securities, and fund expense ratios. In addition, most equity funds hold some of their assets in cash equivalents, which are used to meet shareholder redemptions. Thus, when all costs are considered, growth funds adequately meet their mandated investment objective of long-term growth of capital.

Summary of Financial Statistics (medians)

1991 Return	Five-Year Return	Current Yield	Beta	Turnover Ratio	Expense Ratio
32.7%	89.4%	1.2%	0.98	62%	1.21%

BEST GROWTH FUNDS FOR 1991

Fund	Percent Return 1991	3-Year	5-Year
Janus Twenty Fund	69.2%	156.7%	170.1%
Kemper Summit Fund	69.0	102.0	118.2
Mainstay Capital Appreciation Fund	68.4	121.1	121.7
FPA Capital Fund	64.5	77.7	132.8
SAFECO Growth Fund	62.6	64.7	115.4
Mutual of Omaha Growth Fund	62.4	98.7	136.1
MFS Managed Sectors Trust	62.1	99.1	120.5
T. Rowe Price New America Growth Fund	61.9	96.7	111.1
Idex Fund 3	61.8	126.8	NA
Idex Fund	61.5	129.3	192.3
MFS Lifetime Managed Sectors Trust	59.6	92.7	145.3
Enterprise Capital Appreciation Portfolio	58.9	121.7	NA
Idex II Fund	58.7	128.3	199.0
Eaton Vance Special Equities Fund	57.3	99.3	126.1
Kemper Investment Portfolios Growth	57.0	102.8	136.5
Strong Common Stock	56.9	NA	NA
WPG Growth Fund	56.8	70.9	84.7
Monetta Fund	55.9	100.1	149.9
Fidelity Contrafund	54.9	130.5	173.7
Merrill Lynch Special Value Fund A	54.9	12.8	7.5
Fidelity Blue Chip Growth Fund	54.8	118.2	NA
Harbor Capital Appreciation Fund	54.8	88.8	NA
Parnassus Fund	52.6	23.6	62.2
Dreyfus Growth Opportunity Fund	51.5	62.4	104.5
IDS New Dimensions Fund	50.7	109.2	160.8

AARP CAPITAL GROWTH FUND

Scudder Stevens & Clark
175 Federal Street, 12th Floor
Boston, MA 02110
800-253-2277

Investment Objective: This member of the AARP family seeks to provide long-term capital growth through a broad and flexible investment program. The fund pursues its objective primarily through investments in common stocks and securities convertible into common stocks. Management purchases firms that appear to have potential to provide long-term growth greater than that of most stocks contained in the S&P 500 Index. Over the past 5 years, management has done an adequate job by matching the performance of the S&P 500 Index. While this pure no-load fund has performed exceptionally well over the past 5 years, it has done so by assuming additional risk as evidenced by its 1.25 beta.

Portfolio Manager: Steven Aronoff
Since: 1989

Minimum:
Initial: $500
Subsequent: None
Telephone Exchange: Yes
Distributions:
Income: Annually
Capital Gain: Annually
Front-End Load: None
12b-1: None
Redemption Fee: None
Management Company: Scudder Stevens & Clark
Ticker Symbol: ACGFX

TOTAL RETURN (%)

1987	1988	1989	1990	1991	5-year	Bull Market	Bear Market
0.3	27.3	33.5	-15.8	40.5	101.7	51.4	-26.2

INVESTMENT PORTFOLIO

Total Assets (mil.)	Current Yield	Turnover Ratio	Expense Ratio	Beta	Risk Return
$245	0.7%	83%	1.11%	1.25	0.06

ACORN FUND

Harris Associates
Two North LaSalle Street, Suite 500
Chicago, IL 60602
800-476-9625

Investment Objective: This well-managed fund seeks to capitalize on the small-firm effect by investing in above-average growth, niche companies with market values generally below $500,000 that sell at modest multiples to book value and earnings. Because a very large asset base would jeopardize the fund's small to midsized-company focus, the fund stopped accepting new accounts in 1990. This isn't good news for most investors, but those lucky enough to have gotten into this top-quality fund before it closed its doors can rest assured that the strategy responsible for its superb record remains in place.

Portfolio Manager: Ralph Wanger
Since: 1970

Minimum:
Initial: Closed
Subsequent: $200
Telephone Exchange: Yes
Distributions:
Income: Semiannually
Capital Gain: Annually
Front-End Load: Closed
12b-1: None
Redemption Fee: None
Management Company: Harris Associates
Ticker Symbol: ACRNX

TOTAL RETURN (%)

1987	1988	1989	1990	1991	5-year	Bull Market	Bear Market
4.4	24.7	24.9	-17.5	47.3	97.8	48.5	-27.5

INVESTMENT PORTFOLIO

Total Assets (mil.)	Current Yield	Turnover Ratio	Expense Ratio	Beta	Risk Return
$1,041	1.1%	26%	0.73%	0.97	0.08

ADDISON CAPITAL SHARES

Addison Capital Management
1608 Walnut Street, 13th Floor
Philadelphia, PA 19103
800-526-6397

Investment Objective: This value-oriented fund seeks long-term growth of capital by concentrating on out-of-favor stocks. These stocks tend to exhibit low price/earnings multiples, dividends and positive long-term growth prospects. Although billed as a growth and income fund, its scant yield of 1.2% places it in our growth category. The past year's 30.6% return fell just shy of the average growth fund's return and its 5-year record also trails that of the pack. Part of its underperformance can be attributed to the fund's 2.34% expense ratio. The fund has a 12b-1 plan and charges a 3.00% front-end load.

Portfolio Manager: Cliff Cheston
Since: 1986

Minimum:
Initial: $1,000
Subsequent: $50
Telephone Exchange: No
Distributions:
Income: Annually
Capital Gain: Annually
Front-End Load: 3.00%
12b-1: 0.65%
Redemption Fee: None
Management Company: Addison Capital Management
Ticker Symbol: ADCSX

TOTAL RETURN (%)

1987	1988	1989	1990	1991	5-year	Bull Market	Bear Market
-0.8	13.3	27.8	-6.4	30.6	75.4	36.8	-21.1

INVESTMENT PORTFOLIO

Total Assets (mil.)	Current Yield	Turnover Ratio	Expense Ratio	Beta	Risk Return
$30	1.2%	57%	2.34%	0.98	0.05

AEGON USA GROWTH PORTFOLIO

MidAmerica Management
4333 Edgewood Road N.E.
Cedar Rapids, IA 52499
800-538-5111

Investment Objective: This fund pursues its capital-appreciation objectives through a buy-and-hold discipline. Its portfolio of established, large companies stresses relatively low-priced names with good earnings prospects. With the exception of slow-growth electric utilities, the fund has representation in all major industries. Its good diversification, blue chip bias, decent dividend stream and often high cash reserves makes the fund one of the growth category's most conservative vehicles. It has traditionally lagged its average rival during bull markets, but it has shown decent resistance to decline in down markets.

Portfolio Manager: Jon Augustine
Since: 1990

Minimum:
Initial: $1,000
Subsequent: $50
Telephone Exchange: Yes
Distributions:
Income: Annually
Capital Gain: Annually
Front-End Load: 4.75%
12b-1: None
Redemption Fee: None
Management Company: MidAmerica Management
Ticker Symbol: AEGGX

TOTAL RETURN (%)

1987	1988	1989	1990	1991	5-year	Bull Market	Bear Market
7.9	8.8	17.6	-5.5	36.8	78.6	38.6	-16.9

INVESTMENT PORTFOLIO

Total Assets (mil.)	Current Yield	Turnover Ratio	Expense Ratio	Beta	Risk Return
$40	1.5%	73%	1.00%	0.82	0.08

AIM SUMMIT FUND

AIM Distributors
11 Greenway Plaza, Suite 1919
Houston, TX 77046
800-347-1919

Investment Objective: Marketed as a contractual plan, the fund requires that its shareholders make fixed monthly investments for 15 years. In return for their long-term commitment, shareholders are promised all-weather performance. Management relies on a multiple strategy approach to ensure above-average results in most markets. Each of the portfolio's 3 subsections is run in accordance with a different investment discipline: core growth, emerging growth and value. While this strategy hasn't always worked, it has been quite successful since current manager Julian Lerner's 1988 arrival, allowing the fund to beat most rivals for 4 straight years.

Portfolio Manager: Julian Lerner
Since: 1988

Minimum:
Initial: $50
Subsequent: $50
Telephone Exchange: No
Distributions:
Income: Annually
Capital Gain: Annually
Front-End Load: 8.50%
12b-1: None
Redemption Fee: None
Management Company: AIM Advisors
Ticker Symbol: SMMIX

TOTAL RETURN (%)

1987	1988	1989	1990	1991	5-year	Bull Market	Bear Market
-4.7	17.6	30.9	0.9	43.6	112.9	45.5	-19.9

INVESTMENT PORTFOLIO

Total Assets (mil.)	Current Yield	Turnover Ratio	Expense Ratio	Beta	Risk Return
$449	1.1%	143%	0.80%	1.07	0.08

AIM WEINGARTEN FUND

AIM Distributors
11 Greenway Plaza, Suite 1919
Houston, TX 77046
800-347-1919

Investment Objective: This earnings-oriented fund divides its assets between established, stable growth stocks and stocks that show extraordinarily good current earnings. Its combination of steady growers and high-momentum cyclicals has produced excellent results, keeping the fund well ahead of the average growth fund and the S&P 500 in 8 out of the past 10 years. Despite some setbacks (the fund lost money in 1981 and 1984), it has achieved one of the highest total returns of any mutual over the past 10 years.

Portfolio Manager: H. Hutzler/J. Schoolar
Since: 1969

Minimum:
Initial: $1,000
Subsequent: $100
Telephone Exchange: Yes
Distributions:
Income: Annually
Capital Gain: Annually
Front-End Load: 5.50%
12b-1: 0.29%
Redemption Fee: None
Management Company: AIM Advisors
Ticker Symbol: WEINX

TOTAL RETURN (%)

1987	1988	1989	1990	1991	5-year	Bull Market	Bear Market
9.7	11.3	36.0	5.5	46.9	157.6	49.2	-23.3

INVESTMENT PORTFOLIO

Total Assets (mil.)	Current Yield	Turnover Ratio	Expense Ratio	Beta	Risk Return
$2,631	0.4%	79%	1.30%	1.14	0.08

ALGER GROWTH PORTFOLIO

Alger Funds
75 Maiden Lane
New York, NY 10038
800-992-3863

Investment Objective: This fund seeks long-term growth of capital by investing in companies that demonstrate high historical and potential earnings growth. Given the market's recent bias toward earnings momentum, this fund has chalked up an admirable 5-year return of 110%. The past year's 44% showing also was well above average. Because of its willingness to pay up for growth issues, the fund sports an above-average beta of 1.20. However, in 1990, the fund avoided a loss even though the S&P 500 fell by more than 3%. Obvious drawbacks to the fund are its high expense ratio and its redemption fee.

Minimum:
Initial: $1,000
Subsequent: $100
Telephone Exchange: Yes
Distributions:
Income: Annually
Capital Gain: Annually
Front-End Load: None
12b-1: 1.00%
Redemption Fee: 5.00%
Management Company: Fred Alger Management
Ticker Symbol: AFGPX

Portfolio Manager: David Alger
Since: 1986

TOTAL RETURN (%)

1987	1988	1989	1990	1991	5-year	Bull Market	Bear Market
-0.4	6.4	35.0	2.2	43.8	110.3	55.1	-25.5

INVESTMENT PORTFOLIO

Total Assets (mil.)	Current Yield	Turnover Ratio	Expense Ratio	Beta	Risk Return
$10	0.0%	86%	2.41%	1.20	0.06

ALLEGRO GROWTH FUND

Chapman Company
Dows Building, 7th Floor
Cedar Rapids, IA 52401
319-366-8400

Investment Objective: Although this fund typically pursues its capital-appreciation objective through a portfolio of common stocks, management has opted to hold nearly 100% of its assets in cash during the past 3 years. Management's extreme caution reflects both its concerns over the economy's weakness and its view that stocks are overvalued. Management's extreme caution has been nothing short of disastrous. During the past 3 years, the fund has failed to keep pace with even most money market funds. The fund's scant $3 million in assets attests to shareholder dissatisfaction.

Minimum:
Initial: $1,000
Subsequent: $100
Telephone Exchange: No
Distributions:
Income: Annually
Capital Gain: Annually
Front-End Load: None
12b-1: None
Redemption Fee: None
Management Company: Chapman Company
Ticker Symbol: None

Portfolio Manager: John H. Chapman
Since: 1985

TOTAL RETURN (%)

1987	1988	1989	1990	1991	5-year	Bull Market	Bear Market
2.2	10.2	6.3	5.7	3.9	31.4	32.5	-29.4

INVESTMENT PORTFOLIO

Total Assets (mil.)	Current Yield	Turnover Ratio	Expense Ratio	Beta	Risk Return
$3	4.1%	21%	2.43%	0.30	0.04

ALLIANCE FUND A

Alliance Funds Distributor
500 Plaza Drive
Secaucus, NJ 07094
800-247-4154

Investment Objective: This fund's willingness to bet heavily on volatile industries makes it one of the growth category's riskier offerings. It high beta largely reflects its earnings orientation and its affinity for economically sensitive technology stocks, which, because of short product cycles, fierce industry competition and enormous potential for earnings disappointments makes them extremely volatile. Also enhancing the fund's risk in recent years has been its emphasis on basic industry stocks, which have suffered from the market's recession fears, and its preference for consumer growth stocks that it believes will be able to sustain growth even in a sluggish economy.

Portfolio Manager: Paul Jenkel
Since: 1984

Minimum:
Initial: $250
Subsequent: $500
Telephone Exchange: Yes
Distributions:
Income: Semiannually
Capital Gain: Annually
Front-End Load: 5.50%
12b-1: 0.18%
Redemption Fee: None
Management Company: Alliance Capital Management
Ticker Symbol: CHCLX

TOTAL RETURN (%)

1987	1988	1989	1990	1991	5-year	Bull Market	Bear Market
4.9	17.1	23.4	-4.4	33.9	94.1	45.1	-25.0

INVESTMENT PORTFOLIO

Total Assets (mil.)	Current Yield	Turnover Ratio	Expense Ratio	Beta	Risk Return
$671	0.9%	71%	0.81%	1.20	0.05

AMCAP FUND

American Funds Distributor
333 South Hope Street, 52nd Floor
Los Angeles, CA 90071
800-421-9900

Investment Objective: This fund epitomizes the all-weather performance that has become the investment signature of adviser Capital Research & Management. Unlike many growth funds, the fund doesn't strive for spectacular single-year gains, but seeks to build a superior record over time by achieving consistently moderate results in most markets. Extensive research, a long-term focus, a well-defined price discipline and an effective use of cash largely explain its ability to achieve its goals. Despite its earnings orientation—and large stakes in volatile industries such as technology—it has achieved above-average long-term total returns without excessive risk.

Portfolio Manager: Multiple Portfolio Counselors
Since: 1991

Minimum:
Initial: $1,000
Subsequent: $50
Telephone Exchange: Yes
Distributions:
Income: Annually
Capital Gain: Annually
Front-End Load: 5.75%
12b-1: 0.16%
Redemption Fee: None
Management Company: Capital Research & Management
Ticker Symbol: AMCPX

TOTAL RETURN (%)

1987	1988	1989	1990	1991	5-year	Bull Market	Bear Market
11.5	8.9	27.1	-4.0	36.9	102.9	49.1	-25.4

INVESTMENT PORTFOLIO

Total Assets (mil.)	Current Yield	Turnover Ratio	Expense Ratio	Beta	Risk Return
$2,373	1.1%	16%	0.79%	1.07	0.06

AMERICAN CAPITAL COMSTOCK FUND

American Capital Marketing
P.O. Box 3528
Houston, TX 77253
800-421-5666

Investment Objective: This full-load fund seeks capital appreciation by investing in a portfolio of securities believed to have above-average potential for capital appreciation. Over the past 3 years, the fund has managed to mirror the performance of the S&P 500 Index. Needless to say, this fund promises to do best when S&P 500 stocks lead the market. This fund has all the attributes of an excellent growth vehicle except for the fact that investors have to pay a hefty 8.50% front-end load.

Portfolio Manager: David Reichert
Since: 1989

Minimum:
Initial: $500
Subsequent: $50
Telephone Exchange: Yes
Distributions:
Income: Semiannually
Capital Gain: Annually
Front-End Load: 8.50%
12b-1: None
Redemption Fee: None
Management Company: American Capital Asset Management
Ticker Symbol: ACSTX

TOTAL RETURN (%)

1987	1988	1989	1990	1991	5-year	Bull Market	Bear Market
-0.2	14.8	30.5	-3.4	31.9	90.7	34.5	-18.5

INVESTMENT PORTFOLIO

Total Assets (mil.)	Current Yield	Turnover Ratio	Expense Ratio	Beta	Risk Return
$890	2.0%	30%	0.79%	0.98	0.06

AMERICAN CAPITAL PACE FUND

American Capital Marketing
P.O. Box 3528
Houston, TX 77253
800-421-5666

Investment Objective: Although current manager Peter Hidalgo has decorated the portfolio's fringes with a smattering of medium cap and foreign stocks, the fund's affinity to the average growth fund is still unmistakable. Classic S&P 500 growth stocks, such as Coca-Cola, Philip Morris and Pepsico, predominate. Although the fund modestly overweights growth sectors such as consumer nondurables and services at the expense of slow-growth utilities, it doesn't neglect any major industries. Such conventional tactics suggest that the fund isn't likely to severely lead or lag its average rival. It figures to do best when blue chips lead the market.

Portfolio Manager: Peter Hidalgo
Since: 1988

Minimum:
Initial: $500
Subsequent: $50
Telephone Exchange: Yes
Distributions:
Income: Annually
Capital Gain: Annually
Front-End Load: 5.75%
12b-1: 0.18%
Redemption Fee: None
Management Company: American Capital Asset Management
Ticker Symbol: ACPAX

TOTAL RETURN (%)

1987	1988	1989	1990	1991	5-year	Bull Market	Bear Market
1.5	12.1	28.6	-5.8	31.7	81.5	36.8	-20.6

INVESTMENT PORTFOLIO

Total Assets (mil.)	Current Yield	Turnover Ratio	Expense Ratio	Beta	Risk Return
$2,325	1.6%	40%	1.01%	1.03	0.05

AMERICAN NATIONAL GROWTH FUND

Securities Management & Research
Two Moody Plaza
Galveston, TX 77550
800-231-4639

Investment Objective: This fund's investment objective is to seek long-term growth by investing its assets in securities that provide an opportunity for capital appreciation. Management maintains a broad definition of the types of firms they will invest in. Over the past 5 years, this broad definition has paid off as the fund is up an impressive 97.1%, which compares favorably to the median of 89.4% for growth funds. Despite the hefty 8.50% front-end load, this fund is an excellent growth vehicle.

Portfolio Manager: Ben Hock
Since: 1987

Minimum:
Initial: $100
Subsequent: $20
Telephone Exchange: No
Distributions:
Income: Semiannually
Capital Gain: Annually
Front-End Load: 8.50%
12b-1: None
Redemption Fee: None
Management Company: Securities Management & Research
Ticker Symbol: AMRNX

TOTAL RETURN (%)

1987	1988	1989	1990	1991	5-year	Bull Market	Bear Market
12.5	6.0	24.3	-2.9	37.0	97.1	36.6	-19.4

INVESTMENT PORTFOLIO

Total Assets (mil.)	Current Yield	Turnover Ratio	Expense Ratio	Beta	Risk Return
$113	1.0%	152%	1.03%	1.04	0.06

AMEV CAPITAL FUND

AMEV Investors
P.O. Box 64284
St. Paul, MN 55164
800-800-2638

Investment Objective: This fund seeks capital appreciation by investing in the common stocks of established companies representing a cross section of American industry. Although income is a secondary objective, the fund takes pride in the fact that it has paid consecutive quarterly dividends to its shareholders since 1949. Individual stock selections are those of growth companies that have both the expectation of a higher share value and a solid record of paying cash dividends. The fund tends to invest in companies valued in the $1 billion and higher market-capitalization range. Management attempts to avoid stocks caught up in recent fads and looks to the longer term for investment results.

Portfolio Manager: Stephen M. Poling
Since: 1983

Minimum:
Initial: $500
Subsequent: $25
Telephone Exchange: Yes
Distributions:
Income: Quarterly
Capital Gain: Annually
Front-End Load: 4.75%
12b-1: 0.25%
Redemption Fee: None
Management Company: AMEV Advisers
Ticker Symbol: AMCLX

TOTAL RETURN (%)

1987	1988	1989	1990	1991	5-year	Bull Market	Bear Market
3.3	5.2	33.6	-9.5	49.4	96.2	42.4	-23.4

INVESTMENT PORTFOLIO

Total Assets (mil.)	Current Yield	Turnover Ratio	Expense Ratio	Beta	Risk Return
$194	0.8%	62%	1.25%	1.06	0.08

API TRUST GROWTH FUND

American Pension Investors
2303 Yorktown Avenue
Lynchburg, VA 24501
800-544-6060

Investment Objective: This fund seeks long-term growth of capital by investing in other mutual funds. The underlying funds in which the fund invests may vary but need not have the same investment objectives, policies and limitations as the fund itself. In addition to having an extremely high expense ratio, the fund's management invests in funds that have average or above-average expense ratios, too. This layering of expenses reduces an investor's total return.

Minimum:
Initial: $500
Subsequent: $100
Telephone Exchange: No
Distributions:
Income: Annually
Capital Gain: Annually
Front-End Load: None
12b-1: 1.00%
Redemption Fee: None
Management Company: American Pension Advisor
Ticker Symbol: APITX

Portfolio Manager: David D. Basten
Since: 1985

TOTAL RETURN (%)

1987	1988	1989	1990	1991	5-year	Bull Market	Bear Market
-7.6	26.0	15.7	-12.7	45.9	71.6	73.3	-31.2

INVESTMENT PORTFOLIO

Total Assets (mil.)	Current Yield	Turnover Ratio	Expense Ratio	Beta	Risk Return
$32	0.0%	118%	2.60%	1.30	0.06

ARMSTRONG ASSOCIATES

Armstrong Associates
1445 Ross Avenue, Suite 1490
Dallas, TX 75202
214-720-9101

Investment Objective: This fund seeks capital appreciation by investing in a diversified portfolio of common stocks. Management has an affinity for depressed stocks in out-of-favor industries. Its portfolio is relatively compact and contains less than 2 dozen different common stocks. A high degree of concentration coupled with the selection of stocks that have remained out of favor have hampered returns for more than a decade. Nearly 90% of all funds over that period have provided higher returns than this fund. The fund has protected investors during declining markets. However, because of its ultraconservatism, the fund has failed to participate fully in advancing markets.

Minimum:
Initial: $250
Subsequent: None
Telephone Exchange: No
Distributions:
Income: Annually
Capital Gain: Annually
Front-End Load: None
12b-1: None
Redemption Fee: None
Management Company: Portfolios
Ticker Symbol: ARMSX

Portfolio Manager: C. K. Lawson
Since: 1967

TOTAL RETURN (%)

1987	1988	1989	1990	1991	5-year	Bull Market	Bear Market
0.0	15.5	14.3	-6.7	18.7	46.3	20.5	-17.5

INVESTMENT PORTFOLIO

Total Assets (mil.)	Current Yield	Turnover Ratio	Expense Ratio	Beta	Risk Return
$9	2.1%	24%	1.90%	0.70	0.04

BABSON GROWTH FUND

Jones & Babson
3 Crown Center, 2440 Pershing Road
Kansas City, MO 64108
800-422-2766

Investment Objective: This growth player adheres to its discipline. Relying solely on bottom-up analysis, the fund stresses quality companies of various sizes with good management, financial strength and industry leadership. It does not attempt to time the market, forecast industry/economic trends or bet on sectors. As its low turnover rate shows, the fund invests with a view to the long term. It purchases its companies when they are out of favor and relatively inexpensive and then waits patiently for value to be realized. While its value orientation has been out of sync during the past 3 years, the fund has generally produced dependable, above-average results.

Portfolio Manager: David G. Kirk
Since: 1989

Minimum:
Initial: $500
Subsequent: $50
Telephone Exchange: Yes
Distributions:
Income: Semiannually
Capital Gain: Annually
Front-End Load: None
12b-1: None
Redemption Fee: None
Management Company: Jones & Babson
Ticker Symbol: BABSX

TOTAL RETURN (%)

1987	1988	1989	1990	1991	5-year	Bull Market	Bear Market
3.4	16.0	22.1	-9.4	26.1	67.2	33.4	-21.9

INVESTMENT PORTFOLIO

Total Assets (mil.)	Current Yield	Turnover Ratio	Expense Ratio	Beta	Risk Return
$233	1.8%	22%	0.86%	1.01	0.04

BABSON VALUE FUND

Jones & Babson
3 Crown Center, 2440 Pershing Road
Kansas City, MO 64108
800-422-2766

Investment Objective: This fund's poor relative performance highlights the difficulties that have plagued value investors over the past 2 years. Like most value players, the fund's search for undervalued stocks has led it to stress recently unpopular financials, durables and transportation stocks, which have suffered from the market's recession fears, while also preventing it from owning the pricier growth stocks that have benefited. Eventually, the market is bound to return to traditional measures of value—an event that should allow the fund to rebound sharply.

Portfolio Manager: Nick Whitridge
Since: 1990

Minimum:
Initial: $1,000
Subsequent: $100
Telephone Exchange: Yes
Distributions:
Income: Annually
Capital Gain: Annually
Front-End Load: None
12b-1: None
Redemption Fee: None
Management Company: Jones & Babson
Ticker Symbol: BVALX

TOTAL RETURN (%)

1987	1988	1989	1990	1991	5-year	Bull Market	Bear Market
3.1	19.0	18.2	-11.4	28.9	65.7	39.4	-21.7

INVESTMENT PORTFOLIO

Total Assets (mil.)	Current Yield	Turnover Ratio	Expense Ratio	Beta	Risk Return
$25	3.6%	6%	1.04%	1.00	0.05

BAIRD CAPITAL DEVELOPMENT FUND

Robert W. Baird
777 East Wisconsin Avenue
Milwaukee, WI 53202
800-792-2473

Investment Objective: This fund seeks long-term capital appreciation by investing in stocks whose future growth prospects warrant higher prices. Also, management studies a firm's financial statements and determines whether its stock price is too low relative to its underlying asset value. The fund's 5-year return trails the average by 6%, although in 1991 it bested the competition by almost 14%. Investments in medium cap stocks aided the past year's performance and may continue to provide the impetus for this fund. All in all, this fund carries a bit more risk than most growth funds but has the potential for superior returns.

Minimum:
Initial: $1,000
Subsequent: $100
Telephone Exchange: No
Distributions:
Income: Annually
Capital Gain: Annually
Front-End Load: 5.75%
12b-1: 0.45%
Redemption Fee: None
Management Company: Fiduciary Management
Ticker Symbol: BCDFX

Portfolio Manager: Kellner/Wilson
Since: 1984

TOTAL RETURN (%)

1987	1988	1989	1990	1991	5-year	Bull Market	Bear Market
-6.3	16.5	24.3	-7.8	46.6	83.4	36.2	-22.8

INVESTMENT PORTFOLIO

Total Assets (mil.)	Current Yield	Turnover Ratio	Expense Ratio	Beta	Risk Return
$27	0.4%	64%	1.70%	1.06	0.07

BEACON HILL MUTUAL FUND

Beacon Hill Mutual Fund
75 Federal Street
Boston, MA 02110
617-482-0795

Investment Objective: This fund seeks capital appreciation by investing primarily in the common stocks of established growth companies. At last count, the fund's portfolio was quite compact and contained fewer than 2 dozen different issues. The fund is designed for patient, long-term-oriented investors as evidenced by the fund's exceptionally low portfolio turnover ratio. Despite its penchant for a buy-and-hold strategy, the fund has performed quite well during turbulent markets. During the past 5 years, it has not posted a single down year. A higher-than-average expense ratio, however, has depressed returns during the past 5 years.

Minimum:
Initial: None
Subsequent: None
Telephone Exchange: No
Distributions:
Income: Annually
Capital Gain: Annually
Front-End Load: None
12b-1: None
Redemption Fee: None
Management Company: Beacon Hill Management
Ticker Symbol: BEHMX

Portfolio Manager: David L. Stone
Since: 1964

TOTAL RETURN (%)

1987	1988	1989	1990	1991	5-year	Bull Market	Bear Market
5.3	4.3	20.9	5.9	26.4	77.6	28.7	-14.3

INVESTMENT PORTFOLIO

Total Assets (mil.)	Current Yield	Turnover Ratio	Expense Ratio	Beta	Risk Return
$5	0.0%	3%	3.50%	0.87	0.05

BOSTON COMPANY CAPITAL APPRECIATION FUND

TBC Funds Distributor
53 State Street, 4th Floor
Boston, MA 02114
800-225-5267

Investment Objective: This fund seeks capital appreciation by investing primarily in the common stocks of U.S. companies. It is designed for investors who take a long-term approach to equity investing and are willing to ride out market fluctuations. Three years ago, the fund adopted a value approach to asset selection and during this period, the fund's returns have trailed those of the S&P 500 Index. In short, the recent past has been anything but a value player's dream. However, the value of investing tends to shine during periods of economic recovery when the market is lead by cyclical stocks. Despite its average performance history, this fund may surprise investors with decent returns during the next couple of years.

Portfolio Manager: David Mills
Since: 1989

Minimum:
Initial: $1,000
Subsequent: $50
Telephone Exchange: Yes
Distributions:
Income: Quarterly
Capital Gain: Annually
Front-End Load: None
12b-1: 0.20%
Redemption Fee: None
Management Company: Boston Company Advisers
Ticker Symbol: BCCAX

TOTAL RETURN (%)

1987	1988	1989	1990	1991	5-year	Bull Market	Bear Market
0.5	19.6	24.9	-13.4	22.9	59.6	32.7	-24.2

INVESTMENT PORTFOLIO

Total Assets (mil.)	Current Yield	Turnover Ratio	Expense Ratio	Beta	Risk Return
$430	1.8%	180%	1.26%	1.00	0.03

BRANDYWINE FUND

Friess Associates
3908 Kennett Pike
Greenville, DE 19807
302-656-6200

Investment Objective: This fund epitomizes high-growth investing. The fund concentrates on owning highly profitable niche companies with explosive growth potential. It features a mix of stock sizes, with medium caps from rapid-growth sectors such as technology and health care most prominent. An adept use of cash has so far kept the fund on an even keel; it has produced remarkably consistent, above-average returns since its 1986 inception. Still, the volatility inherent in its potent approach should not be ignored. This is an excellent vehicle for patient, aggressive growth investors, but it isn't for the risk wary. A $25,000 minimum-purchase requirement further limits the fund's use to investors with deep pockets.

Portfolio Manager: Foster Friess
Since: 1985

Minimum:
Initial: $25,000
Subsequent: $1,000
Telephone Exchange: No
Distributions:
Income: Annually
Capital Gain: Annually
Front-End Load: None
12b-1: None
Redemption Fee: None
Management Company: Friess Associates
Ticker Symbol: BRWIX

TOTAL RETURN (%)

1987	1988	1989	1990	1991	5-year	Bull Market	Bear Market
2.6	17.7	32.9	0.6	43.0	130.8	51.0	-25.3

INVESTMENT PORTFOLIO

Total Assets (mil.)	Current Yield	Turnover Ratio	Expense Ratio	Beta	Risk Return
$552	0.6%	157%	1.12%	1.11	0.06

BRUCE FUND

Bruce Fund
20 North Wacker Drive, Suite 2414
Chicago, IL 60606
312-236-9160

Investment Objective: This fund was acquired by Robert Bruce in 1983. Prior to that time, it was the Herold Fund, a nondiversified investment company. The fund seeks capital appreciation and income by investing primarily in common stocks. However, at times, the fund has assumed a large investment position in zero-coupon bonds. In recent years, its common stock investments generally have been in smaller companies and in so-called "turnaround situations." Despite a relatively low portfolio turnover ratio and a lower-than-average beta, the fund's shares have been highly volatile. During the past 5 years, the fund has been out of step with financial markets as evidenced by its meager 7% 5-year total return.

Portfolio Manager: Robert B. Bruce
Since: 1983

Minimum:
Initial: $1,000
Subsequent: $500
Telephone Exchange: No
Distributions:
Income: Annually
Capital Gain: Annually
Front-End Load: None
12b-1: None
Redemption Fee: None
Management Company: Bruce & Company
Ticker Symbol: BRUFX

TOTAL RETURN (%)

1987	1988	1989	1990	1991	5-year	Bull Market	Bear Market
-18.1	12.9	15.7	-1.1	1.4	7.3	15.3	-30.1

INVESTMENT PORTFOLIO

Total Assets (mil.)	Current Yield	Turnover Ratio	Expense Ratio	Beta	Risk Return
$2	2.1%	40%	2.47%	0.72	NA

BULL & BEAR CAPITAL GROWTH FUND

Bull & Bear Group
11 Hanover Square
New York, NY 10005
800-847-4200

Investment Objective: This high turnover fund tends to concentrate its assets in relatively few industry sectors that it expects will outperform the broad market. Typically, its companies are exhibiting earnings growth at a well-above-average rate, have high profitability ratios and below-average debt. So far, its rapid trading tactics have not proved fruitful. Although a huge bet on telecommunications stocks propelled the fund to an impressive 30% gain in 1989, a large stake in emerging-growth stocks and large cap technology issues saw it suffer a huge 26% decline in 1990. Such boom-or-bust results suggest the fund is suitable only for risk-tolerant investors.

Portfolio Manager: Brett Sneed
Since: 1988

Minimum:
Initial: $1,000
Subsequent: $25
Telephone Exchange: Yes
Distributions:
Income: Annually
Capital Gain: Annually
Front-End Load: None
12b-1: 1.00%
Redemption Fee: None
Management Company: Bull & Bear Advisers
Ticker Symbol: BBCGX

TOTAL RETURN (%)

1987	1988	1989	1990	1991	5-year	Bull Market	Bear Market
-4.6	13.9	30.3	-26.2	21.3	26.7	20.5	-39.8

INVESTMENT PORTFOLIO

Total Assets (mil.)	Current Yield	Turnover Ratio	Expense Ratio	Beta	Risk Return
$40	0.0%	254%	2.40%	1.38	0.02

CALDWELL FUND

Caldwell & Company
250 West Tampa Avenue
Venice, FL 34285
800-338-9476

Investment Objective: Caldwell Fund has the risk-averse investor at heart. Manager Roland Caldwell stresses stocks of companies that he believes are generating a return on investment in excess of their true cost of capital. Relying on a proprietary model, he assigns a warranted value to stocks of companies that meet the aforementioned criteria; then he looks to buy them when they are selling at a meaningful discount. His practice of increasing the fund's exposure to stocks when valuations are low and lowering it as valuations approach what he considers excessive levels has caused the fund to lag rallies but to exhibit excellent resistance to decline in bear markets.

Portfolio Manager: Roland Caldwell
Since: 1985

Minimum:
Initial: None
Subsequent: None
Telephone Exchange: No
Distributions:
Income: Semiannually
Capital Gain: Annually
Front-End Load: None
12b-1: None
Redemption Fee: None
Management Company: Caldwell & Company
Ticker Symbol: None

TOTAL RETURN (%)

1987	1988	1989	1990	1991	5-year	Bull Market	Bear Market
-0.4	7.1	18.3	-1.4	22.6	52.5	23.4	-13.5

INVESTMENT PORTFOLIO

Total Assets (mil.)	Current Yield	Turnover Ratio	Expense Ratio	Beta	Risk Return
$2	4.6%	35%	2.00%	0.63	0.05

CALVERT ARIEL APPRECIATION FUND

Calvert Securities
4550 Montgomery Avenue, Suite 1000
Bethesda, MD 20814
800-368-2748

Investment Objective: By investing primarily in small to medium-sized companies, this fund seeks long-term growth of capital. Management seeks undervalued stocks that show growth potential but have limited downside risk. These financially stable companies must show concern for the environment. For instance, this fund will not invest in any company that has a poor environmental record or that produces weapon systems, nuclear energy or equipment used to produce nuclear energy. In its brief history, this fund posted a slight loss in 1990 and returned an average 33% in 1991. Portfolio turnover has been kept to the bare minimum.

Portfolio Manager: Eric McKissack
Since: 1990

Minimum:
Initial: $2,000
Subsequent: $250
Telephone Exchange: Yes
Distributions:
Income: Annually
Capital Gain: Annually
Front-End Load: 4.75%
12b-1: 0.35%
Redemption Fee: None
Management Company: Calvert Asset Management
Ticker Symbol: CAAPX

TOTAL RETURN (%)

1987	1988	1989	1990	1991	5-year	Bull Market	Bear Market
NA	NA	NA	-1.5	33.1	NA	NA	NA

INVESTMENT PORTFOLIO

Total Assets (mil.)	Current Yield	Turnover Ratio	Expense Ratio	Beta	Risk Return
$72	0.8%	4%	0.70%	NA	NA

CALVERT CAPITAL VALUE FUND

Calvert Securities
4550 Montgomery Avenue, Suite 1000
Bethesda, MD 20814
800-368-2748

Investment Objective: This fund focuses on buying growth at a reasonable price. Most of its companies are growing earnings at a well-above-average rate but are selling near a market multiple. Like many value players, the fund underperformed during the past 2 years. However, like most value managers, Hevner stuck to her guns. Her patience could pay off handsomely during an economic rebound as out-of-favor companies return to investor favor.

Portfolio Manager: Patricia Hevner
Since: 1988

Minimum:
Initial: $2,000
Subsequent: $250
Telephone Exchange: Yes
Distributions:
Income: Annually
Capital Gain: Annually
Front-End Load: 4.75%
12b-1: None
Redemption Fee: None
Management Company: Calvert Asset Management
Ticker Symbol: CFEQX

TOTAL RETURN (%)

1987	1988	1989	1990	1991	5-year	Bull Market	Bear Market
-8.2	20.0	30.3	-11.2	24.6	59.0	31.9	-24.2

INVESTMENT PORTFOLIO

Total Assets (mil.)	Current Yield	Turnover Ratio	Expense Ratio	Beta	Risk Return
$7	0.9%	24%	1.44%	0.96	0.04

CARNEGIE-CAPPIELLO TRU S T GROWTH SERIES

Carnegie Fund Distributor
1331 Euclid Avenue
Cleveland, OH 44115
800-321-2322

Investment Objective: To be sure, the tactics of this fund are sound. Manager Frank Cappiello likes financially strong companies with increasing cash flow and low leverage that are selling at relatively low price-earnings multiples. Although he'd rather own stocks poised to benefit from economic trends, his price consciousness causes him to favor less popular sectors. Large positions in technology, basic industry, consumer durables and financials and the fund's medium-company bias explain its disastrous 1990 results. However, its patient long-term approach led to better-than-average returns the past year as the economy turned upward and smaller-company and economically sensitive stocks provided stellar returns.

Portfolio Manager: Frank Cappiello
Since: 1984

Minimum:
Initial: $1,000
Subsequent: $500
Telephone Exchange: Yes
Distributions:
Income: Annually
Capital Gain: Annually
Front-End Load: 4.50%
12b-1: 0.43%
Redemption Fee: None
Management Company: Carnegie Capital Management
Ticker Symbol: CCGTX

TOTAL RETURN (%)

1987	1988	1989	1990	1991	5-year	Bull Market	Bear Market
-9.1	34.9	31.2	-8.5	37.8	103.0	45.2	-24.6

INVESTMENT PORTFOLIO

Total Assets (mil.)	Current Yield	Turnover Ratio	Expense Ratio	Beta	Risk Return
$82	0.2%	31%	1.72%	1.14	0.05

CHARTER CAPITAL BLUE CHIP GROWTH FUND

Charter Capital Management
4920 West Vliet Street
Milwaukee, WI 53208
414-257-1842

Investment Objective: Formerly known as the Adtek Fund, Charter Capital Blue Chip Growth Fund seeks long-term appreciation. Prior to the fund's 1990 name change, it underwent several managerial/strategy changes. With the arrival of current manager Lauren Toll, the fund abandoned its market-timing tactics and switched to a blue chip, growth stock approach. It now invests primarily in established, dividend-paying growth companies rated 1 or 2 for safety by Value Line. A full 55% of its portfolio consists of the kind of consumer growth stocks that led the past year's market. Examples include Merck, Bristol Myers and Wal-Mart. Consequently, the fund has performed better than most rivals during the past 2 years.

Portfolio Manager: Lauren E. Toll
Since: 1990

Minimum:
Initial: $10
Subsequent: $10
Telephone Exchange: No
Distributions:
Income: Annually
Capital Gain: Annually
Front-End Load: None
12b-1: None
Redemption Fee: None
Management Company: Charter Capital Management
Ticker Symbol: ATKFX

TOTAL RETURN (%)

1987	1988	1989	1990	1991	5-year	Bull Market	Bear Market
-4.9	1.9	9.1	-1.7	45.8	51.5	44.1	-15.9

INVESTMENT PORTFOLIO

Total Assets (mil.)	Current Yield	Turnover Ratio	Expense Ratio	Beta	Risk Return
$11	0.0%	194%	2.07%	0.91	0.08

CIGNA GROWTH FUND

CIGNA Mutual Funds
One Financial Plaza, 16th Floor
Springfield, MA 01103
800-572-4462

Investment Objective: This fund's main strength is consistency. Rarely a top performer, it grinds out consistently moderate results year in and year out. Its steadiness owes largely to its diversified approach. Rather than focus on one stock type, the fund features a mix of high multiple, stable growth stocks and cheaper cyclicals with good earnings. Its predominately blue chip portfolio has representation in all major market segments, with growth industries such as technology, health care and retail modestly overweighted. Expect average, long-term results with moderate risk from this conventional fund.

Portfolio Manager: David Shinn
Since: 1985

Minimum:
Initial: $500
Subsequent: $50
Telephone Exchange: Yes
Distributions:
Income: Annually
Capital Gain: Annually
Front-End Load: 5.00%
12b-1: 0.25%
Redemption Fee: None
Management Company: CIGNA Investments
Ticker Symbol: CGFDX

TOTAL RETURN (%)

1987	1988	1989	1990	1991	5-year	Bull Market	Bear Market
3.6	10.1	28.9	-5.0	37.0	91.4	41.7	-26.3

INVESTMENT PORTFOLIO

Total Assets (mil.)	Current Yield	Turnover Ratio	Expense Ratio	Beta	Risk Return
$165	0.7%	61%	1.16%	1.16	0.06

CLIPPER FUND

Pacific Financial Research
9601 Wilshire Boulevard, Suite 828
Beverly Hills, CA 90210
800-776-5033

Investment Objective: An avowed value investor and asset allocator, manager James Gipson will only buy a stock if he believes it is significantly underpriced relative to its underlying earnings power and/or asset values. Moreover, he willingly adjusts the fund's asset mix when he believes the risk-adjusted return on bonds and/or cash is superior to that on common stocks. A 50% cash position explains the fund's resistance to decline during the 1987 crash. Although the fund didn't exhibit the same defensive abilities during 1990, its 7.6% decline is still better than expected given its huge stake in financial and media stocks. These tactics promise to reward patient shareholders over the long haul as witnessed by the past year's return.

Portfolio Manager: James Gipson
Since: 1984

Minimum:
Initial: $25,000
Subsequent: $1,000
Telephone Exchange: No
Distributions:
Income: Annually
Capital Gain: Annually
Front-End Load: None
12b-1: None
Redemption Fee: None
Management Company: Pacific Financial Research
Ticker Symbol: CFIMX

TOTAL RETURN (%)

1987	1988	1989	1990	1991	5-year	Bull Market	Bear Market
2.9	19.7	22.1	-7.6	32.6	84.2	40.4	-19.2

INVESTMENT PORTFOLIO

Total Assets (mil.)	Current Yield	Turnover Ratio	Expense Ratio	Beta	Risk Return
$149	2.5%	23%	1.15%	0.86	0.06

COLONIAL GROWTH SHARES TRUST

Colonial Investment Services
One Financial Center, 14th Floor
Boston, MA 02110
800-248-2828

Investment Objective: A computer-driven strategy that stresses value and earnings momentum has enabled this growth fund to produce steady, above-average results in a wide variety of markets. Like many value players, the fund got caught with too many financial stocks in 1990, which took a big hit in the face of that sector's increasingly severe asset quality problems. However, the fund rebounded smartly the past year as its relatively early commitment in financial stocks began to pay off. During the past 5 years, the fund has produced a 14% compound annual return.

Portfolio Manager: Daniel Rie
Since: 1986

Minimum:
Initial: $1,000
Subsequent: $25
Telephone Exchange: Yes
Distributions:
Income: Semiannually
Capital Gain: Annually
Front-End Load: 5.75%
12b-1: 0.10%
Redemption Fee: 1.00%
Management Company: Colonial Management Associates
Ticker Symbol: COLGX

TOTAL RETURN (%)

1987	1988	1989	1990	1991	5-year	Bull Market	Bear Market
2.0	25.6	29.4	-10.7	34.1	98.6	43.9	-25.8

INVESTMENT PORTFOLIO

Total Assets (mil.)	Current Yield	Turnover Ratio	Expense Ratio	Beta	Risk Return
$132	1.2%	37%	1.03%	1.08	0.05

COLONIAL UNITED STATES EQUITY INDEX TRUST

Colonial Investment Services
One Financial Center, 14th Floor
Boston, MA 02110
800-248-2828

Investment Objective: This index fund seeks to duplicate the performance of a portfolio of blue chip stocks by investing in most of the stocks contained in the Standard and Poor's 500 Index. Like most index funds, the fund's portfolio turnover is an extremely low 13% (versus about 80% for the typical equity fund). Its returns can be expected to rise and fall in line with common stocks generally. Although its 5-year return falls short of that produced by the S&P 500 Index, the difference is because of the fund expenses. In fact, ignoring expenses, the fund has produced a return identical to that of the S&P 500 during the past 5 years.

Portfolio Manager: Steve Lanzendorf
Since: 1988

Minimum:
Initial: $1,000
Subsequent: $25
Telephone Exchange: Yes
Distributions:
Income: Semiannually
Capital Gain: Annually
Front-End Load: 5.75%
12b-1: 0.25%
Redemption Fee: None
Management Company: Colonial Management Associates
Ticker Symbol: CLUSX

TOTAL RETURN (%)

1987	1988	1989	1990	1991	5-year	Bull Market	Bear Market
3.0	15.1	29.2	-4.2	28.1	88.1	34.8	-18.9

INVESTMENT PORTFOLIO

Total Assets (mil.)	Current Yield	Turnover Ratio	Expense Ratio	Beta	Risk Return
$44	1.5%	13%	1.57%	0.98	0.05

COLUMBIA GROWTH FUND

Columbia Funds Management
1301 S.W. 5th Avenue, P.O. Box 1350
Portland, OR 97207
800-547-1707

Investment Objective: Columbia Growth Fund succeeds where few funds do. Although it seems that the fund's rapid trading/sector rotation tactics would invite whipsaw, this hasn't been the case. Generally moderate results interspersed with an occasional banner year give it one of the best risk-adjusted return records of any growth fund. Its success owes to management's skill at interpreting macroeconomic/industry trends and identifying reasonably priced, well-run companies that are poised to benefit. That the fund features a mix of stock sizes bodes well for its continued success. Unlike pure blue chip rivals, it will participate if and when small caps lead the market.

Portfolio Manager: Columbia Management Team
Since: 1967

Minimum:
Initial: $1,000
Subsequent: $50
Telephone Exchange: Yes
Distributions:
Income: Annually
Capital Gain: Annually
Front-End Load: None
12b-1: None
Redemption Fee: None
Management Company: Columbia Funds Management
Ticker Symbol: CLMBX

TOTAL RETURN (%)

1987	1988	1989	1990	1991	5-year	Bull Market	Bear Market
14.7	10.8	29.1	-3.3	34.3	113.1	38.4	-19.6

INVESTMENT PORTFOLIO

Total Assets (mil.)	Current Yield	Turnover Ratio	Expense Ratio	Beta	Risk Return
$385	1.4%	172%	0.96%	0.95	0.06

COMPOSITE GROWTH FUND

Murphy Favre Securities
W. 601 Riverside, Suite 900
Spokane, WA 99201
800-543-8072

Investment Objective: Safety comes first for Composite Growth Fund. The fund mitigates risk though both a rigorous price discipline and often conservative asset mix. Admittedly, its emphasis on low price-earnings and low price/book value wasn't suited to the 1989–1990 recessionwary market. As investors focused on a narrow group of growth stocks with highly visible earnings, already cheap fund holdings got even cheaper. Fortunately, a 20% cash cushion and modest exposure to financials prevented the fund from declining as much as most value players during 1990. The fund then rebounded smartly the past year. Over the long haul, it offers moderate stock market participation with relatively low risk.

Portfolio Manager: Randall Yoakum
Since: 1991

Minimum:
Initial: $1,000
Subsequent: $25
Telephone Exchange: Yes
Distributions:
Income: Quarterly
Capital Gain: Annually
Front-End Load: 4.00%
12b-1: 0.30%
Redemption Fee: None
Management Company: Composite Research & Management
Ticker Symbol: CMPFX

TOTAL RETURN (%)

1987	1988	1989	1990	1991	5-year	Bull Market	Bear Market
-0.4	18.7	12.0	-6.0	27.3	58.5	37.2	-18.8

INVESTMENT PORTFOLIO

Total Assets (mil.)	Current Yield	Turnover Ratio	Expense Ratio	Beta	Risk Return
$67	2.7%	37%	1.17%	0.81	0.05

COMPOSITE NORTHWEST 50 FUND

Murphy Favre Securities
W. 601 Riverside, Suite 900
Spokane, WA 99201
800-543-8072

Investment Objective: Launched in 1986, this fund attempts to capitalize on the growth of the Pacific Northwest by investing exclusively in companies in Alaska, Idaho, Montana, Oregon and Washington. Stocks are selected and weighted solely on the basis of their weighting in the Northwest Index 50. The fund doesn't utilize traditional securities analyses. As is true of the region, the fund's major industries include economically sensitive technology, paper, transportation (mostly Boeing) and retail. Highly visible earnings have allowed most of the fund's major sectors to benefit from the market's recently narrow focus and appetite for rapid-growth stocks.

Portfolio Manager: Randall Yoakum
Since: 1991

Minimum:
Initial: $1,000
Subsequent: $100
Telephone Exchange: Yes
Distributions:
Income: Quarterly
Capital Gain: Annually
Front-End Load: 4.50%
12b-1: 0.25%
Redemption Fee: None
Management Company: Composite Research & Management
Ticker Symbol: CMNWX

TOTAL RETURN (%)

1987	1988	1989	1990	1991	5-year	Bull Market	Bear Market
2.3	22.9	38.0	-1.1	43.9	147.0	61.9	-30.5

INVESTMENT PORTFOLIO

Total Assets (mil.)	Current Yield	Turnover Ratio	Expense Ratio	Beta	Risk Return
$99	0.5%	7%	1.45%	1.24	0.06

COPLEY FUND

Copley Financial Services
315 Pleasant Street, 5th Floor
Fall River, MA 02724
508-674-8459

Investment Objective: This fund utilizes its corporate status to generate dividend income, 70% of which is exempt from federal income taxation. The remaining 30% taxable portion of income generated by the fund is used to offset operating expenses. The fund does not make taxable income distributions to shareholders; instead, dividends and capital gains are accumulated in the fund and reflected in its share price. In keeping with its income aspirations, approximately 80% of its assets are concentrated in high-paying utility stocks. Energy stocks claim most remaining assets. Because of certain unresolved legal matters, prospective buyers are advised to read this fund's prospectus carefully before purchasing shares.

Portfolio Manager: Irving Levine
Since: 1978

Minimum:
Initial: $1,000
Subsequent: $100
Telephone Exchange: No
Distributions:
Income: Annually
Capital Gain: Annually
Front-End Load: None
12b-1: None
Redemption Fee: None
Management Company: Copley Financial Services
Ticker Symbol: COPLX

TOTAL RETURN (%)

1987	1988	1989	1990	1991	5-year	Bull Market	Bear Market
-8.3	19.9	17.8	-1.5	17.1	49.5	16.2	-3.0

INVESTMENT PORTFOLIO

Total Assets (mil.)	Current Yield	Turnover Ratio	Expense Ratio	Beta	Risk Return
$31	0.0%	16%	1.50%	0.37	0.05

COUNTRY CAPITAL GROWTH FUND

Country Capital Management
1711 G.E. Road, Box 2222
Bloomington, IL 61704
800-322-3838

Investment Objective: Available only to residents of the state of Illinois, this fund pursues its capital-appreciation objective through a portfolio of dividend-paying blue chips that it believes sell at a discount to their underlying earnings power. Besides reasonable valuations, the fund's companies are characterized by their generally good-quality balance sheets and improving earnings outlook. Such tactics have allowed the fund to achieve remarkably consistent results. It rarely leads the pack, but it also rarely underperforms. Long-term total returns are highly competitive. By growth-fund standards, the fund's risk has been extremely moderate.

Portfolio Manager: Steve Miller
Since: 1979

Minimum:
Initial: $100
Subsequent: $50
Telephone Exchange: Yes
Distributions:
Income: Annually
Capital Gain: Annually
Front-End Load: 3.00%
12b-1: None
Redemption Fee: None
Management Company: Country Capital Management
Ticker Symbol: CNTCX

TOTAL RETURN (%)

1987	1988	1989	1990	1991	5-year	Bull Market	Bear Market
5.3	13.8	26.1	-4.1	27.8	85.4	33.9	-19.3

INVESTMENT PORTFOLIO

Total Assets (mil.)	Current Yield	Turnover Ratio	Expense Ratio	Beta	Risk Return
$81	2.0%	26%	0.82%	0.87	0.05

CUMBERLAND GROWTH FUND

Beckerman & Company
26 Broadway, 2nd Floor, Room 205
New York, NY 10004
800-543-2620

Investment Objective: This fund's primary investment objective is capital appreciation; current income is a secondary objective. The fund actively adjusts its asset mix in response to market conditions, raising cash and bonds in the face of uncertainty. Unfortunately, its rapid retreats to cash have made the fund vulnerable to missing bull markets. A 5-year return of 34.3% is a good example of what happens to performance if management sits on the sidelines. Further compounding the fund's problems is its high expense ratio, which is currently more than 1% higher than its average rival.

Portfolio Manager: Mark Berkerman
Since: 1990

Minimum:
Initial: $1,000
Subsequent: None
Telephone Exchange: No
Distributions:
Income: Annually
Capital Gain: Annually
Front-End Load: None
12b-1: None
Redemption Fee: None
Management Company: MDB Asset Management
Ticker Symbol: CUGFX

TOTAL RETURN (%)

1987	1988	1989	1990	1991	5-year	Bull Market	Bear Market
-15.5	11.6	9.1	3.1	26.5	34.3	30.8	-11.9

INVESTMENT PORTFOLIO

Total Assets (mil.)	Current Yield	Turnover Ratio	Expense Ratio	Beta	Risk Return
$1	0.0%	165%	2.31%	0.57	0.07

DREYFUS GROWTH OPPORTUNITY FUND

Dreyfus Service
200 Park Avenue, 7th Floor
New York, NY 10166
800-782-6620

Investment Objective: This fund's primary goal is to provide long-term growth of capital consistent with the preservation of capital. The fund is particularly alert to companies that are undervalued in terms of current earnings, assets or overall growth prospects. Although the fund may invest a large percentage of its assets in cash equivalents during periods of major market weakness, its turnover ratio has been well below that of the typical equity fund during the past 5 years. To earn additional income, the fund may write and sell covered call options contracts to the extent of 20% of the value of its net assets. Despite its stellar return the past year, its performance has been subpar in recent years.

Portfolio Manager: Richard Shields
Since: 1990

Minimum:
Initial: $2,500
Subsequent: $50
Telephone Exchange: Yes
Distributions:
Income: Semiannually
Capital Gain: Annually
Front-End Load: None
12b-1: None
Redemption Fee: None
Management Company: Dreyfus Corporation
Ticker Symbol: DREQX

TOTAL RETURN (%)

1987	1988	1989	1990	1991	5-year	Bull Market	Bear Market
6.7	17.9	14.8	-6.6	51.5	104.5	43.1	-20.3

INVESTMENT PORTFOLIO

Total Assets (mil.)	Current Yield	Turnover Ratio	Expense Ratio	Beta	Risk Return
$528	0.9%	146%	0.98%	0.94	0.09

DREYFUS INDEX FUND

Dreyfus Service
200 Park Avenue, 7th Floor
New York, NY 10166
800-782-6620

Investment Objective: This S&P 500 imitator is open only to institutional investors as the $1 million minimum investment would suggest. Since its first full year of operation, the fund has trailed its benchmark by an average of 1.25% per year. One advantage of an index fund is the low expense ratio associated with it. Although this fund does not currently have the lowest ratio of the funds with the same objective, expenses less than one-half a percent are nothing to scoff at. However, up to this time, other index funds have matched the S&P 500 more closely.

Minimum:
Initial: $1,000,000
Subsequent: $100,000
Telephone Exchange: No
Distributions:
Income: Quarterly
Capital Gain: Annually
Front-End Load: None
12b-1: None
Redemption Fee: None
Management Company: Dreyfus Corporation
Ticker Symbol: DINDX

Portfolio Manager: Geraldine Hom
Since: 1990

TOTAL RETURN (%)

1987	1988	1989	1990	1991	5-year	Bull Market	Bear Market
NA	15.8	30.6	-3.9	29.7	NA	36.5	-19.2

INVESTMENT PORTFOLIO

Total Assets (mil.)	Current Yield	Turnover Ratio	Expense Ratio	Beta	Risk Return
$96	2.6%	54%	0.49%	1.00	0.05

DREYFUS NEW LEADERS FUND

Dreyfus Service
200 Park Avenue, 7th Floor
New York, NY 10166
800-782-6620

Investment Objective: This fund invests primarily in midsized, emerging-growth companies with innovative products, services and/or processes. Management mitigates the volatility usually associated with small-stock investing by adjusting the fund's asset mix in response to market conditions and by stressing diversification. The fund features a blend of value and growth situations. This, coupled with its willingness to raise cash in the face of uncertainty, enabled it to produce consistent, above-average results from 1986 to 1989. The fund's 11.9% 1990 loss looks good compared to the average small stock's approximate 25% decline. Its return the past year paralleled that of the "typical" small-firm stock.

Minimum:
Initial: $2,500
Subsequent: $100
Telephone Exchange: Yes
Distributions:
Income: Annually
Capital Gain: Annually
Front-End Load: None
12b-1: 0.25%
Redemption Fee: 1.00%
Management Company: Dreyfus Corporation
Ticker Symbol: DNLDX

Portfolio Manager: Thomas Frank
Since: 1985

TOTAL RETURN (%)

1987	1988	1989	1990	1991	5-year	Bull Market	Bear Market
-5.0	23.3	31.3	-11,9	45.4	97.1	48.2	-22.7

INVESTMENT PORTFOLIO

Total Assets (mil.)	Current Yield	Turnover Ratio	Expense Ratio	Beta	Risk Return
$176	0.6%	129%	1.42%	0.91	0.09

DREYFUS THIRD CENTURY FUND

Dreyfus Service
200 Park Avenue, 7th Floor
New York, NY 10166
800-782-6620

Investment Objective: Designed for socially conscious investors, this fund invests in common stocks of companies that it believes contribute to the quality of life. Its companies are screened for their policies and practices regarding the environment, occupational health and safety, consumer protection and equal-opportunity employment. The fund stopped investing in companies that conduct business in South Africa in 1985. Although some "social responsibility" funds have significantly lagged the market in recent years, this fund has delivered solid returns during the past 5 years when it posted gains in each year.

Minimum:
Initial: $2,500
Subsequent: $50
Telephone Exchange: Yes
Distributions:
Income: Annually
Capital Gain: Annually
Front-End Load: None
12b-1: None
Redemption Fee: None
Management Company: Dreyfus Corporation
Ticker Symbol: DRTHX

Portfolio Manager: Thomas Frank
Since: 1990

TOTAL RETURN (%)

1987	1988	1989	1990	1991	5-year	Bull Market	Bear Market
2.6	23.2	17.3	3.5	38.1	112.0	50.0	-22.7

INVESTMENT PORTFOLIO

Total Assets (mil.)	Current Yield	Turnover Ratio	Expense Ratio	Beta	Risk Return
$309	0.9%	72%	1.04%	0.80	0.07

EATON VANCE GROWTH FUND

Eaton Vance Distributors
24 Federal Street, 5th Floor
Boston, MA 02110
800-225-6265

Investment Objective: Eaton Vance Growth Fund adheres to the tried and true. Its portfolio of large cap growth stocks features familiar household names. The majority of its companies are growing at a well-above-average rate but sell at just a modest premium to the broad market. In addition, most operate in stable—rather than cyclical—growth industries. As has been the case historically, this fund can be expected to keep returns fairly in line with the S&P 500. However, the past year the fund delivered a solid, market-beating performance.

Minimum:
Initial: $1,000
Subsequent: $20
Telephone Exchange: Yes
Distributions:
Income: Semiannually
Capital Gain: Annually
Front-End Load: 4.75%
12b-1: 0.01%
Redemption Fee: None
Management Company: Eaton Vance Management
Ticker Symbol: EVGFX

Portfolio Manager: Peter F. Kiely
Since: 1990

TOTAL RETURN (%)

1987	1988	1989	1990	1991	5-year	Bull Market	Bear Market
10.7	8.5	30.3	-5.5	39.7	106.7	39.8	-23.0

INVESTMENT PORTFOLIO

Total Assets (mil.)	Current Yield	Turnover Ratio	Expense Ratio	Beta	Risk Return
$136	0.8%	73%	0.92%	1.05	0.07

EATON VANCE SPECIAL EQUITIES FUND

Eaton Vance Distributors
24 Federal Street, 5th Floor
Boston, MA 02110
800-225-6265

Investment Objective: The fund, which invests in a mix of stock sizes, targets an annual growth rate on the order of 20% for the next 5 years. Most of its companies show top-line growth (as opposed to price increases or margin expansion), low leverage, high profitability ratios and a high reinvestment rate. Inevitably, the fund's pure growth orientation, coupled with its willingness to pay high multiples, has resulted in above-average volatility. Like many growth players, the fund lagged the broad market for most of the 1980s, but it has been a top performer during the past 2 years during which the market favored stocks with highly visible earnings-growth momentum.

Minimum:
Initial: $1,000
Subsequent: $20
Telephone Exchange: Yes
Distributions:
Income: Annually
Capital Gain: Annually
Front-End Load: 4.75%
12b-1: None
Redemption Fee: None
Management Company: Eaton Vance Management
Ticker Symbol: EVSEX

Portfolio Manager: Clifford H. Krauss
Since: 1987

TOTAL RETURN (%)

1987	1988	1989	1990	1991	5-year	Bull Market	Bear Market
2.0	11.2	23.6	2.5	57.3	126.1	69.6	-29.0

INVESTMENT PORTFOLIO

Total Assets (mil.)	Current Yield	Turnover Ratio	Expense Ratio	Beta	Risk Return
$65	0.0%	46%	1.06%	1.20	0.09

EMBLEM RELATIVE VALUE EQUITY FUND

Winsbury
1900 East Dublin-Granville Road
Columbus, OH 43229
800-543-6956

Investment Objective: This fund seeks capital appreciation by investing in common stocks and convertible securities. During the fund's first full year, 1990, it managed to avoid a loss. However, the past year the fund trailed the growth-fund average by a wide 8%. The fund does not bill itself as either a growth player or a value one, but instead it searches for stocks selling at a discount to either a growth or value model. Shareholders must pay a 4.00% front-end load. The jury is still out on this young offering.

Minimum:
Initial: $1,000
Subsequent: $50
Telephone Exchange: Yes
Distributions:
Income: Quarterly
Capital Gain: Annually
Front-End Load: 4.00%
12b-1: None
Redemption Fee: None
Management Company: Society National Bank
Ticker Symbol: ERVEX

Portfolio Manager: Larry Babin
Since: 1989

TOTAL RETURN (%)

1987	1988	1989	1990	1991	5-year	Bull Market	Bear Market
NA	NA	NA	0.8	23.9	NA	25.4	-13.1

INVESTMENT PORTFOLIO

Total Assets (mil.)	Current Yield	Turnover Ratio	Expense Ratio	Beta	Risk Return
$175	1.7%	63%	0.91%	NA	NA

ENTERPRISE CAPITAL APPRECIATION PORTFOLIO

Enterprise Funds
1200 Ashwood Parkway, Suite 290
Atlanta, GA 30338
800-432-4320

Investment Objective: This fund seeks to maximize capital appreciation by investing primarily in common stocks of large, medium and small companies with steadily increasing earnings, 5-year records of sales, earnings, dividend growth, pretax margins, returns on equity and reinvestment rates approximately 1.5 times that of the S&P 500. These strict criteria result in a high-growth portfolio with emphasis on high-momentum industries, including capital goods, communications, entertainment, health care and retail, which led the market in 1989 and again in 1991.

Portfolio Manager: Jeff Miller
Since: 1987

Minimum:
Initial: $500
Subsequent: $25
Telephone Exchange: Yes
Distributions:
Income: Annually
Capital Gain: Annually
Front-End Load: 4.75%
12b-1: 0.45%
Redemption Fee: None
Management Company: Enterprise Capital Management
Ticker Symbol: ENCAX

TOTAL RETURN (%)

1987	1988	1989	1990	1991	5-year	Bull Market	Bear Market
NA	5.9	34.3	3.9	58.9	NA	66.4	-26.3

INVESTMENT PORTFOLIO

Total Assets (mil.)	Current Yield	Turnover Ratio	Expense Ratio	Beta	Risk Return
$28	0.0%	60%	1.75%	1.06	0.10

ENTERPRISE GROWTH PORTFOLIO

Enterprise Funds
1200 Ashwood Parkway, Suite 290
Atlanta, GA 30338
800-432-4320

Investment Objective: This fund has long pursued a moderate growth strategy that has enabled it to achieve competitive returns in just about every year during the past 10 years. While this strategy will continue to guide roughly one-half of the fund's portfolio, its remaining moneys will be managed by a new comanager. Herb Ehlers, who also runs Heritage Capital Appreciation Fund, joined longtime manager Ron Canakaris in mid-1990. Unlike Canakaris, who stresses quality growth stocks, Ehlers focuses on stocks that sell at a discount to their underlying business value. His approach has considerable merit. The dual-management approach delivered smart results in its first full year of operation.

Portfolio Manager: H. Ehlers/R. Canakaris
Since: 1990

Minimum:
Initial: $500
Subsequent: $25
Telephone Exchange: Yes
Distributions:
Income: Annually
Capital Gain: Annually
Front-End Load: 4.75%
12b-1: 0.45%
Redemption Fee: None
Management Company: Enterprise Capital Management
Ticker Symbol: ENGRX

TOTAL RETURN (%)

1987	1988	1989	1990	1991	5-year	Bull Market	Bear Market
11.5	12.3	23	-2.3	41.8	113.6	42.6	-20.8

INVESTMENT PORTFOLIO

Total Assets (mil.)	Current Yield	Turnover Ratio	Expense Ratio	Beta	Risk Return
$67	0.7%	138%	1.60%	1.02	0.07

EVERGREEN FUND

Evergreen Funds
2500 Westchester Avenue
Purchase, NY 10577
800-235-0064

Investment Objective: This no-load fund was originally created as a small-company vehicle. However, a growing asset base and a desire to produce all-weather performance has caused it to feature a variety of stock sizes. Small and medium caps predominate, but blue chips also claim a sizable portion of its assets. While many of the fund's stocks were purchased for their solid underlying earnings growth, management also likes special situations—an affinity that enabled the fund to participate in the deal-driven markets of 1985, 1986 and 1988. A small cap revival, coupled with a renewed interest in value stocks, gave this fund's return a solid boost the past year.

Portfolio Manager: Stephen A. Lieber
Since: 1971

Minimum:
Initial: $2,000
Subsequent: None
Telephone Exchange: Yes
Distributions:
Income: Annually
Capital Gain: Annually
Front-End Load: None
12b-1: None
Redemption Fee: None
Management Company: Saxon Woods Asset Management
Ticker Symbol: EVGRX

TOTAL RETURN (%)

1987	1988	1989	1990	1991	5-year	Bull Market	Bear Market
-3.0	23.0	15.0	-11.7	40.1	69.7	51.0	-26.4

INVESTMENT PORTFOLIO

Total Assets (mil.)	Current Yield	Turnover Ratio	Expense Ratio	Beta	Risk Return
$705	1.2%	39%	1.15%	1.08	0.06

FAIRMONT FUND

Morton H. Sachs & Company
1346 South Third Street
Louisville, KY 40208
800-262-9936

Investment Objective: After a solid showing in the early 1980s, this growth fund proceeded to severely underperform its peer group for 4 straight years from 1987 to 1990. Its problems owe in part to its large exposure to smaller capitalization securities, which significantly underperformed large caps during the late 1980s. Also damaging has been the fund's affinity for stocks selling at historically low valuations, which has inevitably led it to unpopular companies, which unfortunately became even less popular between 1988 and 1990. However, performance soared with the resurgence of small cap stocks the past year.

Portfolio Manager: Morton H. Sachs
Since: 1981

Minimum:
Initial: $1,000
Subsequent: None
Telephone Exchange: No
Distributions:
Income: Annually
Capital Gain: Annually
Front-End Load: None
12b-1: None
Redemption Fee: None
Management Company: Morton H. Sachs & Company
Ticker Symbol: FAIMX

TOTAL RETURN (%)

1987	1988	1989	1990	1991	5-year	Bull Market	Bear Market
-7.8	3.1	6.8	-22.1	40.6	11.2	47.3	-21.5

INVESTMENT PORTFOLIO

Total Assets (mil.)	Current Yield	Turnover Ratio	Expense Ratio	Beta	Risk Return
$16	0.5%	1%	1.68%	1.10	0.06

FARM BUREAU GROWTH FUND

FBL Investment Advisory Services
5400 University Avenue
West Des Moines, IA 50265
800-247-4170

Investment Objective: Under current Portfolio Manager Roger Grefe, Farm Bureau Growth Fund has evolved into one of the growth category's most cautious vehicles. Grefe's refusal to invest in what he perceives as an overvalued stock market has kept the fund's cash position at high levels since 1987. The few common stocks the fund does own illustrate the characteristics Grefe looks for when he does buy stocks: good management, a solid niche, low leverage and a high return on assets. However, ultraconservatism has its own risks. As a result of a hefty cash position and a stock market that has continued to edge higher, this fund sports a very poor 5-year track record.

Portfolio Manager: Roger Grefe
Since: 1986

Minimum:
Initial: $250
Subsequent: None
Telephone Exchange: Yes
Distributions:
Income: Annually
Capital Gain: Annually
Front-End Load: None
12b-1: 0.75%
Redemption Fee: 5.00%
Management Company: FBL Investment Advisory
Ticker Symbol: FABUX

TOTAL RETURN (%)

1987	1988	1989	1990	1991	5-year	Bull Market	Bear Market
-10.1	11.6	13.7	5.2	14.4	37.3	13.8	-5.1

INVESTMENT PORTFOLIO

Total Assets (mil.)	Current Yield	Turnover Ratio	Expense Ratio	Beta	Risk Return
$38	4.9%	59%	1.59%	0.29	0.04

FEDERATED GROWTH TRUST

Federated Securities
Federated Investors Tower
Pittsburgh, PA 15222
800-245-2423

Investment Objective: This institutional growth vehicle stresses relatively inexpensive stocks with good earnings momentum. Inevitably, its price parameters lead it into out-of-favor sectors. Economically sensitive industrial products and consumer durables are currently most prominent. Still, the fund has representation in most major industries. Its blend of value and momentum criteria has enabled it to perform well in a wide variety of markets. Except in 1987, when it felt the full blow of that year's crash, its produced consistent above-average results in every year since its 1985 inception. It sports a good trailing 5-year total return record.

Portfolio Manager: G. M. Meluin
Since: 1987

Minimum:
Initial: $25,000
Subsequent: None
Telephone Exchange: No
Distributions:
Income: Quarterly
Capital Gain: Annually
Front-End Load: None
12b-1: None
Redemption Fee: None
Management Company: Standard Fire Insurance
Ticker Symbol: FGTRX

TOTAL RETURN (%)

1987	1988	1989	1990	1991	5-year	Bull Market	Bear Market
-3.1	28.8	29.2	-4.9	35.1	107.1	44.6	-24.6

INVESTMENT PORTFOLIO

Total Assets (mil.)	Current Yield	Turnover Ratio	Expense Ratio	Beta	Risk Return
$265	2.4%	67%	1.01%	1.04	0.05

FEDERATED STOCK TRUST

Federated Securities
Federated Investors Tower
Pittsburgh, PA 15222
800-245-2423

Investment Objective: Available only to institutional accounts, this no-load fund stresses quality, earnings and value. Its blue chip portfolio features industry leaders that sell at a relatively low multiples-to-earnings and cash-flow ratio. Most of its companies show good earnings but operate in industries, such as technology and manufacturing, that have market sentiment against them. While these industries have suffered recently from the market's recession worries, they stand to rebound sharply once the economy shows signs of improving. Still, the fund's earnings orientation and its policy of staying fully invested at all times make it a bit riskier than its otherwise cautious tactics might suggest.

Portfolio Manager: P. R. Anderson
Since: 1982

Minimum:
Initial: $25,000
Subsequent: None
Telephone Exchange: No
Distributions:
Income: Quarterly
Capital Gain: Annually
Front-End Load: None
12b-1: None
Redemption Fee: None
Management Company: Federated Management
Ticker Symbol: FSTKX

TOTAL RETURN (%)

1987	1988	1989	1990	1991	5-year	Bull Market	Bear Market
1.6	12.7	13.1	-5.0	29.0	58.9	40.3	-22.5

INVESTMENT PORTFOLIO

Total Assets (mil.)	Current Yield	Turnover Ratio	Expense Ratio	Beta	Risk Return
$357	1.9%	53%	0.98%	0.97	0.05

FIDELITY BLUE CHIP GROWTH FUND

Fidelity Distributors Corporation
82 Devonshire Street, Mail Zone L7B
Boston, MA 02109
800-544-8888

Investment Objective: This fund's affinity for rapid growth rates and good earnings momentum leads it into expensive, high-expectation stocks. The maintenance of a portfolio containing popular growth stocks worked like a charm over the past 3 years, playing into the hands of an earnings-driven market. Still, hefty price/earnings and price/book ratios make the fund extremely vulnerable to big jolts in the face of any actual or anticipated earnings disappointments. As such, it is not for risk-wary investors. Patient risk-tolerant shareholders can expect to be amply rewarded over the long haul, but they might not get a smooth ride.

Portfolio Manager: Steven Kaye
Since: 1990

Minimum:
Initial: $2,500
Subsequent: $250
Telephone Exchange: Yes
Distributions:
Income: Semiannually
Capital Gain: Annually
Front-End Load: 3.00%
12b-1: None
Redemption Fee: None
Management Company: Fidelity Management & Research
Ticker Symbol: FBGRX

TOTAL RETURN (%)

1987	1988	1989	1990	1991	5-year	Bull Market	Bear Market
NA	5.9	36.2	3.5	54.8	NA	55.4	-21.8

INVESTMENT PORTFOLIO

Total Assets (mil.)	Current Yield	Turnover Ratio	Expense Ratio	Beta	Risk Return
$262	0.3%	99%	1.26%	1.13	0.09

FIDELITY CAPITAL APPRECIATION FUND

Fidelity Distributors Corporation
82 Devonshire Street, Mail Zone L7B
Boston, MA 02109
800-544-8888

Investment Objective: In seeking growth of capital, management looks for companies in industries that have been depressed and are about to improve. Over the years, the fund has concentrated on the utility, shipping and power-generation industries. More recently, it has focused on financial, automotive and metal industries. Management generally uses a value-oriented strategy of buying the stocks of companies that are undervalued in relation to their potential for growth in earnings and book value. These stocks generally are overlooked and undervalued by researchers. However, there is a danger in investing in out-of-favor stocks, namely, that they may stay out of favor for a long period of time. Such has been the case recently.

Portfolio Manager: Thomas Sweeney
Since: 1986

Minimum:
Initial: $2,500
Subsequent: $250
Telephone Exchange: Yes
Distributions:
Income: Annually
Capital Gain: Annually
Front-End Load: 3.00%
12b-1: None
Redemption Fee: None
Management Company: Fidelity Management & Research
Ticker Symbol: FDCAX

TOTAL RETURN (%)

1987	1988	1989	1990	1991	5-year	Bull Market	Bear Market
19.3	37.6	26.9	-15.7	10.0	93.2	23.0	-21.8

INVESTMENT PORTFOLIO

Total Assets (mil.)	Current Yield	Turnover Ratio	Expense Ratio	Beta	Risk Return
$987	4.2%	56%	1.14%	0.82	0.08

FIDELITY CONTRAFUND

Fidelity Distributors Corporation
82 Devonshire Street, Mail Zone L7B
Boston, MA 02109
800-544-8888

Investment Objective: Despite a series of managerial changes, Fidelity Contrafund has whipped most rivals and the S&P 500 for 4 straight years. Its recent success owes to its moderate value orientation and its taste for healthy niche companies and turnarounds with unrecognized but solid earnings prospects. An adept use of cash, which explains the fund's resistance to 1990's severe third-quarter market downturn, also has helped. The fund is among the very few value players to have performed well in the past 3 years' growth-driven market. The fund's recent success has brought an infusion of new monies, and its assets are approaching $1 billion. However, the flood of cash has yet to impair its performance.

Portfolio Manager: Will Danoff
Since: 1990

Minimum:
Initial: $2,500
Subsequent: $250
Telephone Exchange: Yes
Distributions:
Income: Annually
Capital Gain: Annually
Front-End Load: 3.00%
12b-1: None
Redemption Fee: None
Management Company: Fidelity Management & Research
Ticker Symbol: FCNTX

TOTAL RETURN (%)

1987	1988	1989	1990	1991	5-year	Bull Market	Bear Market
-1.9	21.0	43.2	3.9	54.9	173.7	66.3	-18.4

INVESTMENT PORTFOLIO

Total Assets (mil.)	Current Yield	Turnover Ratio	Expense Ratio	Beta	Risk Return
$822	0.4%	320%	1.06%	1.00	0.10

FIDELITY DESTINY PLAN I

Fidelity Distributors Corporation
82 Devonshire Street, Mail Zone L7B
Boston, MA 02109
800-544-8888

Investment Objective: Destiny I is super. The fund, which was offered as a contractual plan, has historically achieved its goal of providing all-weather performance with admirable success, beating the growth-fund average in 9 out of the past 10 years. It is among the very few mutual funds to actually beat the market in the 1980s. Its consistently strong results owe to a discipline that stresses both growth and value. While some of the fund's companies have above-average earnings-growth potential, others offer compelling value. This fund can be expected to provide excellent long-term results.

Portfolio Manager: George Vanderheiden
Since: 1980

Minimum:
Initial: $50
Subsequent: $25
Telephone Exchange: Yes
Distributions:
Income: Semiannually
Capital Gain: Semiannually
Front-End Load: 8.50%
12b-1: None
Redemption Fee: None
Management Company: Fidelity Management & Research
Ticker Symbol: FDEXX

TOTAL RETURN (%)

1987	1988	1989	1990	1991	5-year	Bull Market	Bear Market
5.9	19.5	25.5	-3.2	39.0	113.8	56.4	-25.1

INVESTMENT PORTFOLIO

Total Assets (mil.)	Current Yield	Turnover Ratio	Expense Ratio	Beta	Risk Return
$2,034	2.7%	84%	0.50%	1.15	0.06

FIDELITY DESTINY PLAN II

Fidelity Distributors Corporation
82 Devonshire Street, Mail Zone L7B
Boston, MA 02109
800-544-8888

Investment Objective: Fidelity Destiny II follows in the footsteps of its namesake. Also organized in a contractual-plan format, the fund is run in the same manner by the same manager as Destiny I. Like its sibling, the fund features a blend of value and growth stocks; a considerable portion of the 2 funds' stocks overlap. Shareholders disturbed over the fund's disappointing 1990 showing were gratified by the fund's stellar 1991 return. Its 129% 5-year return has earned the fund a spot in the top 10% of all funds in terms of long-term performance. Patient investors can expect to be amply rewarded over the long haul by this top-quality fund.

Portfolio Manager: George Vanderheiden
Since: 1985

Minimum:
Initial: $50
Subsequent: $25
Telephone Exchange: Yes
Distributions:
Income: Semiannually
Capital Gain: Semiannually
Front-End Load: 8.50%
12b-1: None
Redemption Fee: None
Management Company: Fidelity Management & Research
Ticker Symbol: FDETX

TOTAL RETURN (%)

1987	1988	1989	1990	1991	5-year	Bull Market	Bear Market
7.1	22.8	26.4	-2.5	41.4	129.1	64.8	-26.7

INVESTMENT PORTFOLIO

Total Assets (mil.)	Current Yield	Turnover Ratio	Expense Ratio	Beta	Risk Return
$362	1.2%	129%	0.84%	1.20	0.06

FIDELITY DISCIPLINED EQUITY FUND

Fidelity Distributors Corporation
82 Devonshire Street, Mail Zone L7B
Boston, MA 02109
800-544-8888

Investment Objective: This fund seeks capital growth by investing primarily in a broadly diversified portfolio of common stocks. Management normally will invest in securities with equity capitalization exceeding $100 million. The fund will try to maintain representation in as many sectors as possible, although sector emphasis will shift as a result of changes in the outlook for earnings among market sectors. Management has followed its disciplined approach closely as the fund has outpaced the broader market since its inception in 1988.

Portfolio Manager: Brad Lewis
Since: 1989

Minimum:
Initial: $2,500
Subsequent: $250
Telephone Exchange: Yes
Distributions:
Income: Annually
Capital Gain: Annually
Front-End Load: None
12b-1: None
Redemption Fee: 0.50%
Management Company: Fidelity Management & Research
Ticker Symbol: FDEQX

TOTAL RETURN (%)

1987	1988	1989	1990	1991	5-year	Bull Market	Bear Market
NA	NA	36.3	-0.8	36.0	NA	29.3	-16.7

INVESTMENT PORTFOLIO

Total Assets (mil.)	Current Yield	Turnover Ratio	Expense Ratio	Beta	Risk Return
$185	1.3%	210%	1.19%	0.99	0.05

FIDELITY MAGELLAN FUND

Fidelity Distributors Corporation
82 Devonshire Street, Mail Zone L7B
Boston, MA 02109
800-544-8888

Investment Objective: While some investors were disturbed by the departure of legendary manager Peter Lynch in the spring of 1990, the fund was left in the capable hands of Morris Smith. Although the fund's return dipped into the red that year, most of the fund's stocks were those selected by Lynch. During 1991, Smith reduced the fund's holdings by more than 400 issues, mostly small positions in smaller stocks. In his first full year, Smith then went on to top the market by nearly 11%. And this was no small feat for the world's largest mutual fund with nearly $17 billion in assets.

Portfolio Manager: Morris Smith
Since: 1990

Minimum:
Initial: $2,500
Subsequent: $250
Telephone Exchange: Yes
Distributions:
Income: Semiannually
Capital Gain: Semiannually
Front-End Load: 3.00%
12b-1: None
Redemption Fee: None
Management Company: Fidelity Management & Research
Ticker Symbol: FMAGX

TOTAL RETURN (%)

1987	1988	1989	1990	1991	5-year	Bull Market	Bear Market
1.0	22.8	34.6	-4.5	41.0	124.7	50.4	-22.2

INVESTMENT PORTFOLIO

Total Assets (mil.)	Current Yield	Turnover Ratio	Expense Ratio	Beta	Risk Return
$16,993	1.7%	135%	1.06%	1.07	0.07

FIDELITY RETIREMENT GROWTH FUND

Fidelity Distributors Corporation
82 Devonshire Street, Mail Zone L7B
Boston, MA 02109
800-544-8888

Investment Objective: This fund's dual emphasis on value and earnings growth prevents it from producing spectacular single-year returns but allows it to grind out consistent, moderately above-average results in most years and a superior rate of return over the long haul. Like many Fidelity growth vehicles, the fund features a blend of blue chips and medium caps, including some foreign issues. Moreover, it does not attempt to mirror the market's industry weightings, but it freely concentrates its assets in industries that meet its earnings and price criteria. Formerly called the "Freedom Fund," it has delivered better-than-average returns during the past 1, 3 and 5 years.

Portfolio Manager: Stuart Williams
Since: 1988

Minimum:
Initial: $500
Subsequent: $250
Telephone Exchange: Yes
Distributions:
Income: Annually
Capital Gain: Annually
Front-End Load: None
12b-1: None
Redemption Fee: None
Management Company: Fidelity Management & Research
Ticker Symbol: FDFFX

TOTAL RETURN (%)

1987	1988	1989	1990	1991	5-year	Bull Market	Bear Market
9.3	15.5	30.4	-10.2	45.6	115.4	42.3	-25.0

INVESTMENT PORTFOLIO

Total Assets (mil.)	Current Yield	Turnover Ratio	Expense Ratio	Beta	Risk Return
$1,577	1.0%	156%	1.09%	1.09	0.07

FIDELITY SPECIAL SITUATIONS FUND

Fidelity Distributors Corporation
82 Devonshire Street, Mail Zone L7B
Boston, MA 02109
800-544-8888

Investment Objective: This fund seeks capital appreciation by investing primarily in securities that management believes are "special situations." In the case of stocks, that means searching out firms undergoing financial difficulties, restructurings or heavy regulatory pressures. A "special-situation" company may be on the brink of a renewed strength as a result of a change in management, increasing demand for its products or the introduction of a revolutionary new service. Overall, management uses a value strategy for selecting securities. Performance for this fund has been below average as value stocks have been out of favor.

Portfolio Manager: Dan Frank
Since: 1983

Minimum:
Initial: $2,500
Subsequent: $250
Telephone Exchange: Yes
Distributions:
Income: Annually
Capital Gain: Annually
Front-End Load: 4.75%
12b-1: 0.65%
Redemption Fee: None
Management Company: Fidelity Management & Research
Ticker Symbol: FSLSX

TOTAL RETURN (%)

1987	1988	1989	1990	1991	5-year	Bull Market	Bear Market
-5.7	22.7	33.0	-6.6	23.7	77.7	29.2	-8.3

INVESTMENT PORTFOLIO

Total Assets (mil.)	Current Yield	Turnover Ratio	Expense Ratio	Beta	Risk Return
$18	3.3%	114%	1.59%	0.65	0.05

FIDELITY STOCK SELECTOR FUND

Fidelity Distributors
82 Devonshire Street, Mail Zone L7B
Boston, MA 02109
800-544-8888

Investment Objective: This fund seeks growth of capital by investing in a broad range of companies both domestic and international. Management attempts to identify undervalued industries through the use of its computer models. After identifying the most attractive industries, individual stock selection is made based on product line, management, earnings momentum and historical performance. Although the fund will be volatile because of the industry concentration, no more than 25% of its total assets can be allocated to any specific one. This Fidelity offering is of a no-load format and in its first full year returned a strong 45%.

Portfolio Manager: Brad Lewis
Since: 1990

Minimum:
Initial: $2,500
Subsequent: $250
Telephone Exchange: Yes
Distributions:
Income: Annually
Capital Gain: Annually
Front-End Load: 3.00%
12b-1: None
Redemption Fee: None
Management Company: Fidelity Management & Research
Ticker Symbol: FDSSX

TOTAL RETURN (%)

1987	1988	1989	1990	1991	5-year	Bull Market	Bear Market
NA	NA	NA	NA	45.9	NA	NA	NA

INVESTMENT PORTFOLIO

Total Assets (mil.)	Current Yield	Turnover Ratio	Expense Ratio	Beta	Risk Return
$150	0.0%	210%	1.19%	NA	NA

FIDELITY VALUE FUND

Fidelity Distributors Corporation
82 Devonshire Street, Mail Zone L7B
Boston, MA 02109
800-544-8888

Investment Objective: As its name implies, this fund invests primarily in common stocks that it believes sell at discounts to their underlying asset values and/or earnings power. Undervaluation isn't its sole criteria, however. Management typically will not buy a stock unless it also can identify a potential catalyst that will cause its unrecognized value to be realized within a reasonable time frame. Like many value players, the fund recently has stressed cheap basic industry and financial stocks, which largely explain its 1990 loss. All things considered, however, this fund can be expected to provide competitive long-term returns with modest risk.

Portfolio Manager: Brian Posner
Since: 1990

Minimum:
Initial: $2,500
Subsequent: $250
Telephone Exchange: Yes
Distributions:
Income: Annually
Capital Gain: Annually
Front-End Load: None
12b-1: None
Redemption Fee: None
Management Company: Fidelity Management & Research
Ticker Symbol: FDVLX

TOTAL RETURN (%)

1987	1988	1989	1990	1991	5-year	Bull Market	Bear Market
-8.6	29.0	22.9	-12.8	26.2	59.6	35.7	-17.6

INVESTMENT PORTFOLIO

Total Assets (mil.)	Current Yield	Turnover Ratio	Expense Ratio	Beta	Risk Return
$113	2.9%	165%	1.06%	0.91	0.04

FIDUCIARY CAPITAL GROWTH FUND

Fiduciary Funds
225 East Mason Street
Milwaukee, WI 53202
800-338-1579

Investment Objective: This fund's search for companies with above-average earnings growth and relatively low leverage that sell at modest price/earnings ratios inevitably drives it into out-of-favor segments of the market. Small stocks, which have been in a bear market since 1983, claim the bulk of the fund's assets. Returns also have been slowed by the fund's large stakes in recently unpopular industries, including finance and technology, and its relative neglect of stable-growth consumer nondurables stocks, which have recently outperformed. Although this fund's relative results should improve if and when small stocks return to favor, it is unlikely to lead any charts.

Portfolio Manager: T. Kellner/ D. Wilson
Since: 1981

Minimum:
Initial: $1,000
Subsequent: $100
Telephone Exchange: No
Distributions:
Income: Semiannually
Capital Gain: Annually
Front-End Load: None
12b-1: None
Redemption Fee: None
Management Company: Fiduciary Management
Ticker Symbol: FCGFX

TOTAL RETURN (%)

1987	1988	1989	1990	1991	5-year	Bull Market	Bear Market
-8.9	18.8	17.9	-11.7	36.3	53.6	42.5	-26.5

INVESTMENT PORTFOLIO

Total Assets (mil.)	Current Yield	Turnover Ratio	Expense Ratio	Beta	Risk Return
$31	0.8%	55%	1.40%	0.98	0.06

FINANCIAL INDUSTRIAL FUND

INVESCO Funds Group
P.O. Box 2040
Denver, CO 80201
800-525-8085

Investment Objective: This fund, which began operations in 1935, is among the oldest equity funds in the industry. It seeks both growth and income by investing in the stocks of companies with greater-than-average earnings growth. Generally, these companies reside in industries that also have greater-than-average growth rates. In making individual selections, management also considers a company's record of cash dividend payments. In recent years, the fund has provided investors with exceptional returns while maintaining relatively low volatility. Despite its appetite for high-growth companies, the fund sidestepped the sharp market declines in such stocks during 1987 and 1990.

Portfolio Manager: Dalton Sim
Since: 1987

Minimum:
Initial: $250
Subsequent: $25
Telephone Exchange: Yes
Distributions:
Income: Quarterly
Capital Gain: Quarterly
Front-End Load: None
12b-1: 0.25%
Redemption Fee: None
Management Company: INVESCO Funds Group
Ticker Symbol: FLRFX

TOTAL RETURN (%)

1987	1988	1989	1990	1991	5-year	Bull Market	Bear Market
-0.1	5.9	31.2	-1.2	42.1	94.9	46.3	-23.4

INVESTMENT PORTFOLIO

Total Assets (mil.)	Current Yield	Turnover Ratio	Expense Ratio	Beta	Risk Return
$398	1.2%	86%	0.78%	1.11	0.07

FIRST EAGLE FUND OF AMERICA

Arnhold & S. Bleichroeder
45 Broadway
New York, NY 10006
800-451-3623

Investment Objective: This fund seeks growth of capital by investing in both domestic and international stocks. Management stresses a value philosophy and has shown the patience to adhere to it. Since its success in 1988, the fund has significantly trailed the returns of the S&P 500. Two reasons generally account for this. Value investing has been out of favor during the past few years, as investors have kept their focus on earnings momentum. Also, the fund keeps a relatively low amount of issues in its portfolio, which exposes it to volatile swings like 1990's 17.6% loss.

Portfolio Manager: Management team
Since: 1987

Minimum:
Initial: $25,000
Subsequent: $1,000
Telephone Exchange: No
Distributions:
Income: Annually
Capital Gain: Annually
Front-End Load: None
12b-1: None
Redemption Fee: 1.00
Management Company: Arnhold & S. Bleichroeder
Ticker Symbol: FEAFX

TOTAL RETURN (%)

1987	1988	1989	1990	1991	5-year	Bull Market	Bear Market
NA	22.6	26.6	-17.6	21.3	NA	16.1	-12.1

INVESTMENT PORTFOLIO

Total Assets (mil.)	Current Yield	Turnover Ratio	Expense Ratio	Beta	Risk Return
$74	0.8%	72%	1.10%	0.83	0.07

FLAG INVESTORS QUALITY GROWTH FUND

Alex Brown & Sons
135 East Baltimore Street
Baltimore, MD 21202
800-767-3524

Investment Objective: To be sure, Flag Quality Growth Fund was launched at the right time. Started in August of 1989, the fund's strategy of investing in top-quality, stable growth stocks has been ideally suited to the market's recently narrow focus on companies that it believes can sustain earnings growth even in a recession. Most of the fund's companies are the familiar S&P 500 names that have led the market since 1989. Also responsible for the fund's good 1990 showing was its huge 20% stake in health-care stocks—one of the few market segments to generate a positive return that year.

Portfolio Manager: Robert S. Killibrew
Since: 1989

Minimum:
Initial: $2,000
Subsequent: $500
Telephone Exchange: Yes
Distributions:
Income: Quarterly
Capital Gain: Annually
Front-End Load: 4.50%
12b-1: 0.25%
Redemption Fee: None
Management Company: Alex Brown & Sons
Ticker Symbol: FLQGX

TOTAL RETURN (%)

1987	1988	1989	1990	1991	5-year	Bull Market	Bear Market
NA	NA	NA	3.7	28.2	NA	50.4	-22.1

INVESTMENT PORTFOLIO

Total Assets (mil.)	Current Yield	Turnover Ratio	Expense Ratio	Beta	Risk Return
$58	1.1%	21%	1.25%	1.10	0.09

FLEX GROWTH FUND

R. Meeder & Associates
6000 Memorial Drive
Dublin, OH 43017
800-325-3539

Investment Objective: This fund, which relies heavily on technical analysis, readily retreats to cash when its indicators suggest that stock prices are in a downtrend. Conversely, it increases its equity exposure when its indicators are positive. When selecting stocks, the fund does not utilize traditional securities analysis. Rather, it invests in baskets of stocks designed to mirror certain market segments based on capitalization. Unsurprisingly, these tactics have produced disappointing long-term results. While the fund's extensive use of cash has given the fund an impressively low beta, it also produced one of lowest 5-year compound returns of any growth fund.

Portfolio Manager: Philip Voelker
Since: 1989

Minimum:
Initial: $2,500
Subsequent: $100
Telephone Exchange: Yes
Distributions:
Income: Quarterly
Capital Gain: Annually
Front-End Load: None
12b-1: 0.10%
Redemption Fee: None
Management Company: R. Meeder & Associates
Ticker Symbol: FLCGX

TOTAL RETURN (%)

1987	1988	1989	1990	1991	5-year	Bull Market	Bear Market
7.6	-5.8	10.2	4.3	21.5	41.5	23.8	-3.9

INVESTMENT PORTFOLIO

Total Assets (mil.)	Current Yield	Turnover Ratio	Expense Ratio	Beta	Risk Return
$30	2.8%	436%	1.46%	0.52	0.05

FLEX MUIRFIELD FUND

R. Meeder & Associates
6000 Memorial Drive
Dublin, OH 43017
800-325-3539

Investment Objective: This aggressive fund pursues its capital-appreciation objective by investing in shares of open-end mutual funds, excluding funds in the Flex-Fund family. Its 16-fund portfolio is heavily biased toward high-growth vehicles, including Twentieth Century's Select, Ultra and Vista funds. Although the fund also owns shares in tamer, large cap vehicles, including Mutual Shares and Federated Growth, its affinity for small stocks and rapid growers predominates, suggesting that it will exhibit considerable risk.

Portfolio Manager: Robert Meeder
Since: 1988

Minimum:
Initial: $2,500
Subsequent: $100
Telephone Exchange: Yes
Distributions:
Income: Semiannually
Capital Gain: Annually
Front-End Load: None
12b-1: 0.16%
Redemption Fee: None
Management Company: R. Meeder & Associates
Ticker Symbol: FLMFX

TOTAL RETURN (%)

1987	1988	1989	1990	1991	5-year	Bull Market	Bear Market
NA	NA	14.0	2.3	29.8	NA	24.2	-7.4

INVESTMENT PORTFOLIO

Total Assets (mil.)	Current Yield	Turnover Ratio	Expense Ratio	Beta	Risk Return
$38	4.3%	649%	1.52%	0.56	0.05

FOUNDERS GROWTH FUND

Founders Asset Management
2930 East Third Avenue
Denver, CO 80206
800-525-2440

Investment Objective: Founders Growth Fund features a quality growth portfolio. The fund's emphasis on established, quality companies with demonstrated records of above-average earnings growth leads it into classic growth industries. Its major sectors include health care, medical services, telecommunications, business services and retail. Although the fund's quality focus generally keeps it on an even keel, this wasn't the case during 1990. Despite a large stake in health-care stocks—one of the few market segments to actually make money the past year—the fund was unable to resist the drag of declining telecommunications and cable-TV stock prices. However, it delivered a solid return the following year.

Portfolio Manager: Investment management team
Since: 1990

Minimum:
Initial: $1,000
Subsequent: $25
Telephone Exchange: Yes
Distributions:
Income: Annually
Capital Gain: Annually
Front-End Load: None
12b-1: 0.25%
Redemption Fee: None
Management Company: Founders Asset Management
Ticker Symbol: FRGRX

TOTAL RETURN (%)

1987	1988	1989	1990	1991	5-year	Bull Market	Bear Market
10.1	4.8	41.7	-10.6	47.4	115.6	39.3	-19.7

INVESTMENT PORTFOLIO

Total Assets (mil.)	Current Yield	Turnover Ratio	Expense Ratio	Beta	Risk Return
$113	0.5%	178%	1.45%	1.12	0.07

FPA CAPITAL FUND

First Pacific Advisers
10301 West Pico Boulevard
Los Angeles, CA 90064
800-421-4374

Investment Objective: FPA Capital's unyielding value discipline has caused it to stress small capitalization stocks in recent years. Typically, its emphasis on individual stock selection keeps its portfolio concentrated in relatively few out-of-favor companies that sell at significant discounts to their underlying fundamentals. A longtime horizon ensures that the fund will profit as the market eventually recognizes its companies' true worth. Despite an unfavorable market for small stocks, this quality fund has produced highly competitive results over the past 5 years. It is an excellent choice for risk-tolerant, long-term investors who seek small-company exposure.

Portfolio Manager: Bob Rodriguez
Since: 1984

Minimum:
Initial: $1,500
Subsequent: $100
Telephone Exchange: Yes
Distributions:
Income: Semiannually
Capital Gain: Semiannually
Front-End Load: 6.50%
12b-1: None
Redemption Fee: None
Management Company: First Pacific Advisers
Ticker Symbol: FPPTX

TOTAL RETURN (%)

1987	1988	1989	1990	1991	5-year	Bull Market	Bear Market
11.0	18.1	25.3	-13.8	64.5	132.8	86.7	-35.5

INVESTMENT PORTFOLIO

Total Assets (mil.)	Current Yield	Turnover Ratio	Expense Ratio	Beta	Risk Return
$93	0.8%	22%	0.92%	1.42	0.08

FRANKLIN CUSTODIAN FUNDS INC.—GROWTH SERIES

Franklin Distributors
777 Mariners Island Blvd., 6th Floor
San Mateo, CA 94404
800-342-5236

Investment Objective: This inactively traded fund features a classic moderate-growth portfolio. Established industry leaders, most of which have been owned by the fund for at least 10 years, dominate its portfolio. Most have solid histories of annual earnings increases and strong balance sheets. The fund's major industries, which include health care, pollution control, technology and entertainment, underscore its pure growth approach, which has produced highly competitive long-term returns. A value discipline, which prevents the fund from owning speculatively priced stocks, and an effective use of cash has kept the fund's risk quite moderate.

Portfolio Manager: Jerry Palmieri
Since: 1964

Minimum:
Initial: $100
Subsequent: $25
Telephone Exchange: Yes
Distributions:
Income: Annually
Capital Gain: Annually
Front-End Load: 4.00%
12b-1: None
Redemption Fee: None
Management Company: Franklin Advisers
Ticker Symbol: FKGRX

TOTAL RETURN (%)

1987	1988	1989	1990	1991	5-year	Bull Market	Bear Market
19.8	9.0	23.7	2.0	26.6	108.6	33.5	-17.6

INVESTMENT PORTFOLIO

Total Assets (mil.)	Current Yield	Turnover Ratio	Expense Ratio	Beta	Risk Return
$359	2.4%	0%	0.73%	0.86	0.05

FRANKLIN EQUITY FUND

Franklin Distributors
777 Mariners Island Boulevard, 6th Floor
San Mateo, CA 94404
800-342-5236

Investment Objective: Franklin Equity Fund stresses growth at a price. The fund's search for large capitalization companies that show above-average earnings growth and sell at below-average price/earnings ratios makes for a highly cyclical portfolio with large concentrations in cheap growth industries. Energy, basic industry, capital goods and retail are greatly overweighted relative to the broad market at the expense of pricey consumer nondurables and slow-growth utilities and financials. This fund's disciplined approach hasn't been suited to the past 2 years' recession-wary market. Still, it promises competitive results over the long haul.

Portfolio Manager: Marvin McClay
Since: 1982

Minimum:
Initial: $100
Subsequent: $25
Telephone Exchange: Yes
Distributions:
Income: Semiannually
Capital Gain: Annually
Front-End Load: 4.00%
12b-1: None
Redemption Fee: None
Management Company: Franklin Advisers
Ticker Symbol: FKREX

TOTAL RETURN (%)

1987	1988	1989	1990	1991	5-year	Bull Market	Bear Market
-1.3	25.3	15.4	-9.1	26.6	64.3	38.7	-25.9

INVESTMENT PORTFOLIO

Total Assets (mil.)	Current Yield	Turnover Ratio	Expense Ratio	Beta	Risk Return
$359	1.7%	43%	0.69%	1.12	0.04

FUND TRUST GROWTH FUND

Signature Financial Group
6 St. James Avenue, 9th Floor
Boston, MA 02116
800-638-1896

Investment Objective: This fund seeks long-term growth of capital by investing in shares of open-end stock mutual funds. The fund's current mutual fund portfolio stresses conservative, valued-oriented vehicles, many of which stress dividend income as well as potential capital gains. While virtually all of the funds included in this portfolio have produced excellent long-term results, overlapping expenses and transactions costs have prevented this fund from achieving competitive returns. Its 5-year total return pales in comparison to the average equity mutual fund.

Portfolio Manager: Michael Hirsch
Since: 1984

Minimum:
Initial: $1,000
Subsequent: $100
Telephone Exchange: Yes
Distributions:
Income: Semiannually
Capital Gain: Annually
Front-End Load: 1.50%
12b-1: 0.50%
Redemption Fee: None
Management Company: Republic National Bank of New York
Ticker Symbol: FTGFX

TOTAL RETURN (%)

1987	1988	1989	1990	1991	5-year	Bull Market	Bear Market
-0.9	14.4	18.6	-6.2	28.8	62.5	33.3	-17.2

INVESTMENT PORTFOLIO

Total Assets (mil.)	Current Yield	Turnover Ratio	Expense Ratio	Beta	Risk Return
$26	1.6%	70%	1.92%	0.85	0.06

GABELLI ASSET FUND

Gabelli & Company
Corporate Center at Rye
Rye, NY 10580
800-422-3554

Investment Objective: This fund seeks capital appreciation by investing in common stocks with underlying assets/franchises that it believes are undervalued by the market. Strong franchise telecommunications, motion-picture and cable-TV stocks dominate its portfolio. This asset-valuation approach proved highly successful in 1987 and 1988, when the fund's large stakes in numerous deal stocks played into the hands of a takeover-driven market. While a slowing in corporate restructurings recently has hurt performance, this disciplined fund still can be expected to produce excellent results over the long haul.

Portfolio Manager: Mario J. Gabelli
Since: 1986

Minimum:
Initial: $25,000
Subsequent: None
Telephone Exchange: No
Distributions:
Income: Annually
Capital Gain: Annually
Front-End Load: None
12b-1: 0.09%
Redemption Fee: 2.00%
Management Company: Gabelli Funds
Ticker Symbol: GABAX

TOTAL RETURN (%)

1987	1988	1989	1990	1991	5-year	Bull Market	Bear Market
16.2	31.1	27.2	-5.8	18.1	115.8	25.8	-12.7

INVESTMENT PORTFOLIO

Total Assets (mil.)	Current Yield	Turnover Ratio	Expense Ratio	Beta	Risk Return
$460	2.1%	49%	1.26%	0.61	0.04

GABELLI GROWTH FUND

Gabelli & Company
Corporate Center at Rye
Rye, NY 10580
800-422-3554

Investment Objective: This fund features a mix of large and small stocks that it believes represent undervalued earnings power. Management stresses companies that show above-average growth in market share, increasing profitability and good earnings momentum. Most of the fund's major industries, which include retail, entertainment and telecommunications, underscore its high-growth aspirations. Still, a hefty stake in low-multiple basic industry stocks also reveals a sound value discipline at work. This dual emphasis on growth and value has so far proven highly successful, allowing the fund to whip most rivals in a variety of markets since its 1987 inception.

Portfolio Manager: Elizabeth Brammell
Since: 1987

Minimum:
Initial: $1,000
Subsequent: None
Telephone Exchange: No
Distributions:
Income: Annually
Capital Gain: Annually
Front-End Load: None
12b-1: 0.20%
Redemption Fee: None
Management Company: Gabelli Funds
Ticker Symbol: GABGX

TOTAL RETURN (%)

1987	1988	1989	1990	1991	5-year	Bull Market	Bear Market
NA	39.2	40.1	-2.0	34.3	NA	32.2	-15.0

INVESTMENT PORTFOLIO

Total Assets (mil.)	Current Yield	Turnover Ratio	Expense Ratio	Beta	Risk Return
$362	0.7%	75%	1.50%	0.94	0.06

GABELLI VALUE FUND

Gabelli & Company
Corporate Center at Rye
Rye, NY 10580
800-422-3554

Investment Objective: Reflecting manager Mario Gabelli's private market value methodology, the fund features a mix of strong franchise telephone, media and consumer stocks, restructuring/takeover candidates and special-situation utilities. This strategy has been out of sync with the market's taste for recessionproof earnings over the past 2 years. A slowing in deal financing also has hurt. If and when this situation reverses, however, this portfolio's significant unrecognized value surely will be realized. For patient accounts, this fund currently makes an excellent contrarian play.

Portfolio Manager: Mario J. Gabelli
Since: 1989

Minimum:
Initial: $5,000
Subsequent: $200
Telephone Exchange: No
Distributions:
Income: Annually
Capital Gain: Annually
Front-End Load: 5.50%
12b-1: 0.25%
Redemption Fee: None
Management Company: Gabelli Funds
Ticker Symbol: GABVX

TOTAL RETURN (%)

1987	1988	1989	1990	1991	5-year	Bull Market	Bear Market
NA	NA	NA	-5.6	15.3	NA	27.6	-17.0

INVESTMENT PORTFOLIO

Total Assets (mil.)	Current Yield	Turnover Ratio	Expense Ratio	Beta	Risk Return
$571	1.8%	59%	1.39%	0.70	0.02

GALAXY EQUITY VALUE FUND

SMA Equities
P.O. Box 0007
Worcester, MA 01653
800-628-0414

Investment Objective: This fund seeks capital appreciation by investing in common and preferred stocks, convertible securities and options, if necessary. Although the fund name implies a value bent, management will invest in non-value plays, often as a defensive measure. After a difficult 1989, the fund has matched the S&P 500's return the past 2 years. This offering is a pure no-load investment vehicle and sports a low expense ratio of 0.95%. Also, the fund may appeal to the small investor for there is no minimum initial subsequent investment.

Portfolio Manager: Tony Mordaci
Since: 1988

Minimum:
Initial: None
Subsequent: None
Telephone Exchange: No
Distributions:
Income: Quarterly
Capital Gain: Annually
Front-End Load: None
12b-1: None
Redemption Fee: None
Management Company: Fleet/Norstar Investment Advisors
Ticker Symbol: GALEX

TOTAL RETURN (%)

1987	1988	1989	1990	1991	5-year	Bull Market	Bear Market
NA	NA	NA	NA	30.2	NA	NA	NA

INVESTMENT PORTFOLIO

Total Assets (mil.)	Current Yield	Turnover Ratio	Expense Ratio	Beta	Risk Return
$101	1.5%	94%	0.95%	NA	NA

GATEWAY GROWTH PLUS FUND

Gateway Investment Advisers
400 Technecenter Drive
Milford, OH 45150
800-354-6339

Investment Objective: This fund seeks long-term growth of capital by investing in a broadly diversified portfolio of large and medium capitalization common stocks. Management keeps market-level representation in most major sectors, although it modestly overweights sectors, such as capital goods and consumer durables, that offer a large number of relatively cheap stocks with above-average historical earnings growth and good earnings momentum. This fund's relative results have improved significantly since the 1988 arrival of current manager Peter Williams. Looking forward, his diversified approach suggests dependable returns in most markets.

Portfolio Manager: Peter Williams
Since: 1988

Minimum:
Initial: $1,000
Subsequent: $100
Telephone Exchange: Yes
Distributions:
Income: Annually
Capital Gain: Annually
Front-End Load: None
12b-1: None
Redemption Fee: None
Management Company: Gateway Investment Advisers
Ticker Symbol: GATGX

TOTAL RETURN (%)

1987	1988	1989	1990	1991	5-year	Bull Market	Bear Market
0.7	-2.0	36.3	-4.5	34.2	72.4	44.6	-22.1

INVESTMENT PORTFOLIO

Total Assets (mil.)	Current Yield	Turnover Ratio	Expense Ratio	Beta	Risk Return
$15	1.0%	79%	1.50%	1.07	0.06

GINTEL CAPITAL APPRECIATION FUND

Gintel & Company
Greenwich Office Park #6
Greenwich, CT 06830
800-243-5808

Investment Objective: Gintel Capital Appreciation Fund prefers to bet heavily on relatively few stocks in which it has strong conviction. Its portfolio rarely includes more than 30 stocks; top holdings can comprise anywhere from 5 to 30% of its assets each. Robert Gintel's emphasis on cheap prospective earnings typically causes him to invest heavily in out-of-favor cyclicals and turnarounds. Coupled with the fund's concentrated approach, its contrarian tactics don't make for all-weather performance. Over the long haul, however, it has been a solid performer. A $5,000 minimum purchase makes this fund a lot more accessible to the average investor than its predecessor, the Gintel Fund.

Portfolio Manager: Robert Gintel
Since: 1986

Minimum:
Initial: $5,000
Subsequent: $2,000
Telephone Exchange: Yes
Distributions:
Income: Annually
Capital Gain: Annually
Front-End Load: None
12b-1: 0.06%
Redemption Fee: None
Management Company: Gintel Equity Management
Ticker Symbol: GINCX

TOTAL RETURN (%)

1987	1988	1989	1990	1991	5-year	Bull Market	Bear Market
-7.6	35.6	25.3	-9.8	18.0	67.1	30.8	-18.7

INVESTMENT PORTFOLIO

Total Assets (mil.)	Current Yield	Turnover Ratio	Expense Ratio	Beta	Risk Return
$35	6.2%	106%	2.10%	0.93	0.02

GINTEL ERISA FUND

Gintel & Company
Greenwich Office Park #6
Greenwich, CT 06830
800-243-5808

Investment Objective: Offered exclusively to certain pension and retirement plans, this fund pursues its capital-appreciation objectives through a nondiversified portfolio of common stocks. Its top 3 holdings may make up as much as 15% of the fund's assets each. Like siblings Gintel Capital Appreciation Fund and Gintel Fund, the fund is guided by a contrarian strategy that favors cheap stocks with improving earnings outlooks that haven't been recognized by the market. Particularly prominent holdings include out-of-favor cyclicals, which underperformed the overall market in 1991. However, the fund could post solid performance numbers during an economic rebound.

Portfolio Manager: Robert Gintel
Since: 1982

Minimum:
Initial: $10,000
Subsequent: $2,000
Telephone Exchange: No
Distributions:
Income: Annually
Capital Gain: Annually
Front-End Load: None
12b-1: 0.02%
Redemption Fee: None
Management Company: Gintel Equity Management
Ticker Symbol: GINTX

TOTAL RETURN (%)

1987	1988	1989	1990	1991	5-year	Bull Market	Bear Market
-1.0	22.0	15.5	-5.1	13.5	50.3	23.4	-17.5

INVESTMENT PORTFOLIO

Total Assets (mil.)	Current Yield	Turnover Ratio	Expense Ratio	Beta	Risk Return
$70	5.6%	96%	1.60%	0.83	0.02

GINTEL FUND

Gintel & Company
Greenwich Office Park #6
Greenwich, CT 06830
800-243-5808

Investment Objective: Gintel Fund invests with conviction. Specializing in companies that have temporarily suffered earnings downturns either because they are cyclical or took a large, one-time charge, the fund sees its fortunes wax and wane quite widely. In 1987, for instance, the fund took a tumble as investors dashed out of companies with weak fundamentals during the crash. However, when value investing became all the rage the following year, the fund soared 29%. Overall, the fund offers growth investors with hearty constitutions a chance to bet on winners that have recently stumbled for one reason or another. However, its performance during the past 5 years has been disappointing.

Portfolio Manager: Robert Gintel
Since: 1981

Minimum:
Initial: $100,000
Subsequent: None
Telephone Exchange: Yes
Distributions:
Income: Annually
Capital Gain: Annually
Front-End Load: None
12b-1: None
Redemption Fee: None
Management Company: Gintel Equity Management
Ticker Symbol: GINLX

TOTAL RETURN (%)

1987	1988	1989	1990	1991	5-year	Bull Market	Bear Market
-14.3	29.3	23.8	-6.7	15.6	48.1	28.9	-18.3

INVESTMENT PORTFOLIO

Total Assets (mil.)	Current Yield	Turnover Ratio	Expense Ratio	Beta	Risk Return
$78	8.8%	75%	1.50%	0.90	0.02

GIT EQUITY TRUST SELECT GROWTH PORTFOLIO

GIT Investment Services
1655 Fort Myer Drive
Arlington, VA 22209
800-336-3063

Investment Objective: This portfolio seeks capital appreciation with a secondary objective of current income by investing in established companies that management believes are undervalued. Typically, the fund's portfolio is fairly compact, consisting of about 2 dozen stocks that show solid earnings growth, industry leadership and financial strength. Management is not shy about heading for cash when it appears that the stock market is headed for a prolonged decline. This strategy trimmed losses during 1990 but inhibited returns the past year when the S&P 500 Index returned more than 30%. Even so, the fund has a remarkably low portfolio turnover ratio, which exemplifies management's patience.

Portfolio Manager: John Edwards
Since: 1988

Minimum:
Initial: $2,500
Subsequent: None
Telephone Exchange: Yes
Distributions:
Income: Semiannually
Capital Gain: Annually
Front-End Load: None
12b-1: None
Redemption Fee: None
Management Company: Bankers Finance Investment
Ticker Symbol: None

TOTAL RETURN (%)

1987	1988	1989	1990	1991	5-year	Bull Market	Bear Market
0.6	15.7	22.6	-1.7	22.9	72.5	23.6	-14.0

INVESTMENT PORTFOLIO

Total Assets (mil.)	Current Yield	Turnover Ratio	Expense Ratio	Beta	Risk Return
$5	1.5%	12%	2.00%	0.74	0.05

GIT EQUITY TRUST SPECIAL GROWTH PORTFOLIO

GIT Investment Services
1655 Fort Myer Drive
Arlington, VA 22209
800-336-3063

Investment Objective: This fund seeks capital growth by investing in small to medium capitalization stocks in high-growth industries. To achieve its objective, the fund may use certain specialized investment techniques, including writing covered call options, investing in foreign securities and "when-issued" securities and making loans of portfolio securities and repurchase agreement transactions. The fund has been an average performer during the past 5 years, which were generally marked by the underperformance of smaller-firm stocks. However, while smaller-firm stocks were producing stellar returns the past year, the fund posted a gain equal to half that of the small-stock average. This may bode poorly for future performance.

Portfolio Manager: Richard Carney
Since: 1983

Minimum:
Initial: $2,500
Subsequent: None
Telephone Exchange: Yes
Distributions:
Income: Semiannually
Capital Gain: Annually
Front-End Load: None
12b-1: None
Redemption Fee: None
Management Company: Bankers Finance Investment
Ticker Symbol: GTSGX

TOTAL RETURN (%)

1987	1988	1989	1990	1991	5-year	Bull Market	Bear Market
-1.4	24.7	25.2	-15.9	25.7	62.8	37.8	-23.0

INVESTMENT PORTFOLIO

Total Assets (mil.)	Current Yield	Turnover Ratio	Expense Ratio	Beta	Risk Return
$60	1.1%	6%	1.40%	0.80	0.05

GRADISON GROWTH TRUST—ESTABLISHED GROWTH FUND

Gradison Mutual Funds
580 Walnut Street
Cincinnati, OH 45202
800-869-5999

Investment Objective: Adhering to a rigorous value discipline, this fund emphasizes stocks that sell at depressed price/earnings and price/book ratios. Most of its cheap companies are experiencing temporary difficulties and/or are operating in out-of-favor industries. Turnarounds are prominent along with economically sensitive basic industry and capital-goods stocks. While the fund's contrarian tactics have hampered returns in the narrow, growth-stock market of the past 3 years, they could produce handsome returns during an economic rebound when out-of-favor, cyclical stocks shine. It is particularly suitable for the risk averse.

Portfolio Manager: William Leugers
Since: 1983

Minimum:
Initial: $1,000
Subsequent: $100
Telephone Exchange: Yes
Distributions:
Income: Quarterly
Capital Gain: Annually
Front-End Load: None
12b-1: 0.23%
Redemption Fee: None
Management Company: Gradison & Company
Ticker Symbol: GETGX

TOTAL RETURN (%)

1987	1988	1989	1990	1991	5-year	Bull Market	Bear Market
12.4	15.1	16.1	-8.1	22.2	68.7	30.8	-17.1

INVESTMENT PORTFOLIO

Total Assets (mil.)	Current Yield	Turnover Ratio	Expense Ratio	Beta	Risk Return
$154	2.4%	73%	1.39%	0.88	0.04

GRADISON GROWTH TRUST—OPPORTUNITY GROWTH FUND

Gradison Mutual Funds
580 Walnut Street
Cincinnati, OH 45202
800-869-5999

Investment Objective: Investing primarily in common stocks of companies with annual revenues under $500 million, this fund screens a universe of approximately 2,000 stocks—none of which are included in the S&P 500—for quality issues that show above-average growth in earnings that does not appear to be reflected in valuations. Typically, the fund's assets are concentrated in relatively few out-of-favor industries with good earnings. Finance and consumer durables, for example, claim a large portion of its assets. This fund's sound approach results in an extremely moderate risk profile, making it a good choice for conservative investors seeking exposure to small caps.

Portfolio Manager: William Leugers
Since: 1983

Minimum:
Initial: $1,000
Subsequent: $100
Telephone Exchange: Yes
Distributions:
Income: Semiannually
Capital Gain: Semiannually
Front-End Load: None
12b-1: 0.23%
Redemption Fee: None
Management Company: Gradison & Company
Ticker Symbol: GOGFX

TOTAL RETURN (%)

1987	1988	1989	1990	1991	5-year	Bull Market	Bear Market
-5.4	23.6	23.1	-13.1	35.9	70.1	52.0	-24.3

INVESTMENT PORTFOLIO

Total Assets (mil.)	Current Yield	Turnover Ratio	Expense Ratio	Beta	Risk Return
$35	1.6%	64%	1.61%	0.92	0.06

GREENSPRING FUND

Greenspring Fund
Quadrangle Village of Cross Keys, #322
Baltimore, MD 21210
301-435-9000

Investment Objective: This fund is a rather interesting offering. Management attempts to identify companies in trouble that have turnaround potential. Most of these firms are smaller companies. Despite the small-company bias, the fund possesses a high yield of 4%. The yield is the result of the convertible issues utilized by the portfolio managers in protection against bankruptcy of the firms. The fund's 5-year record trails the average growth fund by more than 30%, but its risk is one-third of the average fund. Success for this fund depends on management's ability to select turnaround plays and to patiently wait them out.

Portfolio Manager: Management team
Since: 1987

Minimum:
Initial: $1,000
Subsequent: $250
Telephone Exchange: No
Distributions:
Income: Annually
Capital Gain: Annually
Front-End Load: None
12b-1: None
Redemption Fee: None
Management Company: Key Equity Management
Ticker Symbol: GRSPX

TOTAL RETURN (%)

1987	1988	1989	1990	1991	5-year	Bull Market	Bear Market
9.3	16.0	10.5	-6.4	19.3	56.4	10.4	-7.2

INVESTMENT PORTFOLIO

Total Assets (mil.)	Current Yield	Turnover Ratio	Expense Ratio	Beta	Risk Return
$20	4.0%	90%	1.31%	0.31	0.02

G.T. AMERICA GROWTH FUND

G.T. Global Financial Services
50 California Street
San Francisco, CA 94111
800-824-1580

Investment Objective: G.T. America Growth Fund is among the most aggressive of growth funds. Management's growth-intensive strategy causes it to stress medium and small capitalization companies that show rapid 20+% growth in earnings. Its growth-intensive approach inevitably leads it into emerging industries; health care, biotechnology, retail, energy service, computers and entertainment stocks claim a large portion of its assets. As seen in its extraordinary 54.8% 1989 gain, this fund's potent approach makes for chart-leading performances. The past year's disappointing results notwithstanding, it should reward patient, risk-tolerant investors with top-notch long-term returns.

Portfolio Manager: Kevin Wenck
Since: 1991

Minimum:
Initial: $500
Subsequent: $100
Telephone Exchange: Yes
Distributions:
Income: Annually
Capital Gain: Annually
Front-End Load: 4.75%
12b-1: 0.35%
Redemption Fee: None
Management Company: G.T. Capital Management
Ticker Symbol: GTAGX

TOTAL RETURN (%)

1987	1988	1989	1990	1991	5-year	Bull Market	Bear Market
NA	11.1	54.8	-7.4	19.3	NA	31.2	-31.6

INVESTMENT PORTFOLIO

Total Assets (mil.)	Current Yield	Turnover Ratio	Expense Ratio	Beta	Risk Return
$79	0.1%	145%	2.00%	1.23	0.02

GUARDIAN PARK AVENUE FUND

Guardian Investor Services
201 Park Avenue South
New York, NY 10003
800-221-3253

Investment Objective: This fund's dual emphasis on growth and value has historically enabled it to produce highly competitive results in most markets. Most of its companies sell at low multiples-to-earnings and book-value ratios, but also show good earnings momentum. Its major industries include cyclical consumer durables, transportation, energy and industrial products, which recently have suffered from the market's recession fears. Still, the fund sports a decent 81% trailing 5-year gain. Moreover, it could benefit handsomely from any pickup in economic growth. Its mix of stock sizes also ensures that it won't be left behind if and when leadership rotates to small caps.

Portfolio Manager: Charles Albers
Since: 1972

Minimum:
Initial: $1,000
Subsequent: $50
Telephone Exchange: Yes
Distributions:
Income: Semiannually
Capital Gain: Annually
Front-End Load: 4.50%
12b-1: None
Redemption Fee: None
Management Company: Guardian Investor Services
Ticker Symbol: GPAFX

TOTAL RETURN (%)

1987	1988	1989	1990	1991	5-year	Bull Market	Bear Market
3.0	20.8	23.9	-12.3	34.7	81.8	42.9	-20.4

INVESTMENT PORTFOLIO

Total Assets (mil.)	Current Yield	Turnover Ratio	Expense Ratio	Beta	Risk Return
$252	2.6%	58%	0.69%	0.83	0.07

HARBOR CAPITAL APPRECIATION FUND

Harbor Funds
One Seagate
Toledo, OH 43666
800-422-1050

Investment Objective: Harbor Capital growth fund invests primarily in equity securities of large established companies with market capitalizations of nearly $1 billion or more. After following a conservative value orientation during its first 2 years, the fund switched to a more growth-intensive approach during 1990. It now focuses on companies that show rapid growth in earnings. Although the fund's new aggressive tactics have been in sync with the market's recent earnings orientations, shareholders should expect to see considerably greater share-price volatility from this fund in the future than they have in the past. However, that volatility was to the upside the past year.

Portfolio Manager: Spiros Segalas
Since: 1990

Minimum:
Initial: $2,000
Subsequent: $500
Telephone Exchange: Yes
Distributions:
Income: Annually
Capital Gain: Annually
Front-End Load: None
12b-1: None
Redemption Fee: None
Management Company: Harbor Capital Advisors
Ticker Symbol: HACAX

TOTAL RETURN (%)

1987	1988	1989	1990	1991	5-year	Bull Market	Bear Market
NA	15.4	24.2	-1.8	54.8	NA	60.2	-27.2

INVESTMENT PORTFOLIO

Total Assets (mil.)	Current Yield	Turnover Ratio	Expense Ratio	Beta	Risk Return
$78	0.3%	162%	0.88%	1.27	0.08

HARBOR GROWTH FUND

Harbor Funds
One Seagate
Toledo, OH 43666
800-422-1050

Investment Objective: Management focuses on companies that have the potential for future earnings to exceed investor expectations. Beginning with a universe of more than 6,500 companies, a computer screen produces a list of about 1,600 companies for further analysis. Basically, the company attempts to project future earnings on the basis of historical returns and earnings reinvestment. It then invests in those stocks that possess the lowest price-to-expected-earnings ratios. No effort is made to time the market. When selecting assets, management looks at a 2- to 5-year time horizon. Recently, this strategy has served investors well. The fund ranks among the top 20% of all funds in terms of total return.

Portfolio Manager: Bartley J. Madden
Since: 1986

Minimum:
Initial: $2,000
Subsequent: $500
Telephone Exchange: Yes
Distributions:
Income: Annually
Capital Gain: Annually
Front-End Load: None
12b-1: None
Redemption Fee: None
Management Company: Harbor Capital Management
Ticker Symbol: HAGWX

TOTAL RETURN (%)

1987	1988	1989	1990	1991	5-year	Bull Market	Bear Market
2.9	14.3	23.0	-6.7	50.5	103.1	68.3	-28.0

INVESTMENT PORTFOLIO

Total Assets (mil.)	Current Yield	Turnover Ratio	Expense Ratio	Beta	Risk Return
$199	0.3%	96%	0.94%	1.22	0.07

HERITAGE CAPITAL APPRECIATION FUND

Raymond James & Associates
880 Carillon Parkway
St. Petersburg, FL 33022
800-421-4184

Investment Objective: This fund seeks long-term capital appreciation and its low portfolio turnover history illustrates management's long-term outlook. Although not a traditional value fund, the portfolio tends to be comprised of undervalued stocks that are out of favor by the market. The fund's 5-year return is approximately 18% below that of the growth-fund average, despite a better-than-average 1991. Investors must pay a 4.00% front-end load. Also, the above-average expense ratio will hurt long-term returns.

Portfolio Manager: Herbert Ehlers
Since: 1985

Minimum:
Initial: $1,000
Subsequent: $100
Telephone Exchange: Yes
Distributions:
Income: Annually
Capital Gain: Annually
Front-End Load: 4.00%
12b-1: 0.50%
Redemption Fee: None
Management Company: Heritage Asset Management
Ticker Symbol: HRCPX

TOTAL RETURN (%)

1987	1988	1989	1990	1991	5-year	Bull Market	Bear Market
1.3	19.4	20.4	-12.9	34.9	71.1	22.0	-15.5

INVESTMENT PORTFOLIO

Total Assets (mil.)	Current Yield	Turnover Ratio	Expense Ratio	Beta	Risk Return
$60	1.7%	45%	1.96%	0.84	0.05

IAI REGIONAL FUND

Investment Advisers
1100 Dain Tower, P.O. Box 357
Minneapolis, MN 55440
800-945-3863

Investment Objective: The fund seeks growth of capital by investing at least 80% of its assets in companies located in Minnesota, Wisconsin, Iowa, Nebraska, Montana, North Dakota or South Dakota. The fund sports one of the highest 5-year total return figures of any stock mutual fund. Importantly, it owes its top-notch returns not only to spectacular single-year gains but also to its ability to produce at least moderately above-average results in most markets. Excellent stock selection, a fairly strict price discipline and an effective use of cash have made the fund one of the growth category's most consistent performers.

Portfolio Manager: Bing Carlin
Since: 1980

Minimum:
Initial: $5,000
Subsequent: $100
Telephone Exchange: No
Distributions:
Income: Semiannually
Capital Gain: Semiannually
Front-End Load: None
12b-1: 0.25%
Redemption Fee: None
Management Company: Investment Advisers
Ticker Symbol: IARGX

TOTAL RETURN (%)

1987	1988	1989	1990	1991	5-year	Bull Market	Bear Market
5.3	18.6	31.3	-0.3	35.4	121.2	42.6	-18.2

INVESTMENT PORTFOLIO

Total Assets (mil.)	Current Yield	Turnover Ratio	Expense Ratio	Beta	Risk Return
$408	1.0%	169%	1.01%	0.86	0.07

IAI VALUE FUND

Investment Advisers
1100 Dain Tower, P.O. Box 357
Minneapolis, MN 55440
800-945-3863

Investment Objective: This fund's affinity for cheap stocks with improving fundamentals leads it into a host of misunderstood cyclicals, turnarounds and venture-capital plays (the latter may not make up more than 10% of the fund's assets). Although the fund may invest freely in stocks of all sizes, it has recently favored small and medium-sized companies in view of their relatively low valuations. Nevertheless, the fund has achieved respectable results during the blue-chip-led market of the past 5 years. Should the market's recent interest in small stocks persist, this well-managed fund stands to benefit handsomely.

Portfolio Manager: Douglas Platt
Since: 1991

Minimum:
Initial: $5,000
Subsequent: $100
Telephone Exchange: No
Distributions:
Income: Semiannually
Capital Gain: Semiannually
Front-End Load: None
12b-1: None
Redemption Fee: None
Management Company: Investment Advisers
Ticker Symbol: IAAPX

TOTAL RETURN (%)

1987	1988	1989	1990	1991	5-year	Bull Market	Bear Market
14.1	24.3	22.6	-11.5	19.8	84.3	31.2	-24.3

INVESTMENT PORTFOLIO

Total Assets (mil.)	Current Yield	Turnover Ratio	Expense Ratio	Beta	Risk Return
$21	1.5%	54%	1.00%	1.06	0.03

IDEX FUND

Idex Group
201 Highland Avenue
Largo, FL 34640
800-624-4339

Investment Objective: Run by subadviser Janus Capital Management, Idex Fund has traditionally offered an excellent risk/reward profile. Superb stock selection and well-timed retreats to cash have enabled the fund to fully participate in stock market rallies, while also resisting bear market declines. Closed for several years, this quality fund recently reopened its doors. It is now the only fund in the IDEX series that is open to new accounts. The fund's return the past 5 years has been nothing short of spectacular, capped by the past year's whopping market-beating performance.

Portfolio Manager: Tom Marsico
Since: 1985

Minimum:
Initial: $50
Subsequent: $50
Telephone Exchange: Yes
Distributions:
Income: Semiannually
Capital Gain: Annually
Front-End Load: 8.50%
12b-1: None
Redemption Fee: None
Management Company: Idex Management
Ticker Symbol: IDEFX

TOTAL RETURN (%)

1987	1988	1989	1990	1991	5-year	Bull Market	Bear Market
7.6	18.5	43.3	-0.9	61.5	192.3	57.4	-22.9

INVESTMENT PORTFOLIO

Total Assets (mil.)	Current Yield	Turnover Ratio	Expense Ratio	Beta	Risk Return
$212	0.4%	159%	1.39%	1.20	0.09

IDEX FUND 3

Idex Group
201 Highland Avenue
Largo, FL 34640
800-624-4339

Investment Objective: The newest fund in the Idex series offers the same excellent risk-reward characteristics as its predecessors. Like the Idex Fund and Idex II, the fund has achieved one of the growth-fund category's best returns since its inception in 1987. Management stresses undervalued growth stocks while attempting to preserve capital. Like other Idex funds, its management does not attempt to time the market during the short term but will head for cash when it believes that the market is headed for a prolonged skid. Its portfolio generally contains popular, timely stocks that sell at reasonable multiples of earnings and dividends. Unfortunately, this fund is closed to new shareholders.

Portfolio Manager: Tom Marsico
Since: 1987

Minimum:
Initial: Closed
Subsequent: $50
Telephone Exchange: Yes
Distributions:
Income: Semiannually
Capital Gain: Annually
Front-End Load: Closed
12b-1: None
Redemption Fee: None
Management Company: Idex Management
Ticker Symbol: IDFDX

TOTAL RETURN (%)

1987	1988	1989	1990	1991	5-year	Bull Market	Bear Market
NA	17.0	42.9	-1.9	61.8	NA	58.3	-23.6

INVESTMENT PORTFOLIO

Total Assets (mil.)	Current Yield	Turnover Ratio	Expense Ratio	Beta	Risk Return
$189	0.4%	187%	1.37%	1.22	0.09

IDEX II FUND

Idex Group
201 Highland Avenue
Largo, FL 34640
800-624-4339

Investment Objective: Like all Idex funds, this fund seeks growth of capital by investing in sound, well-managed growth companies whose stock prices do not reflect their potential values. This fund seeks to achieve attractive returns in rising markets while offering a degree of protection in down markets. While its manager does not attempt to predict the short-term movements of the stock market, he may shift more than 50% of the portfolio's assets to cash in uncertain market conditions. This disciplined strategy has paid off handsomely for shareholders. The fund ranks among the top 1% of all funds since it was created in 1986.

Portfolio Manager: Tom Marsico
Since: 1986

Minimum:
Initial: $50
Subsequent: $50
Telephone Exchange: Yes
Distributions:
Income: Semiannually
Capital Gain: Annually
Front-End Load: 5.50%
12b-1: 0.25%
Redemption Fee: None
Management Company: Idex Management
Ticker Symbol: IDETX

TOTAL RETURN (%)

1987	1988	1989	1990	1991	5-year	Bull Market	Bear Market
8.7	20.4	44.6	-0.5	58.7	199	57.5	-24.2

INVESTMENT PORTFOLIO

Total Assets (mil.)	Current Yield	Turnover Ratio	Expense Ratio	Beta	Risk Return
$148	0.3%	128%	1.35%	1.23	0.09

IDS GROWTH FUND

IDS Financial Services
1000 Roanoke Building
Minneapolis, MN 55402
800-328-8300

Investment Objective: This fund epitomizes high-growth investing. The fund's affinity for rapid earnings growth leads it into expensive, high-momentum stocks. Typically, its portfolio is concentrated in relatively few high-growth industries, including retail, technology, pollution control and health care. This potent, growth-intensive approach inevitably causes extreme results. The fund tends to be among its category's best or worst performers in most years. While it has delivered highly competitive long-term rewards, it is only for risk-tolerant, long-term investors.

Minimum:
Initial: $2,000
Subsequent: $100
Telephone Exchange: Yes
Distributions:
Income: Annually
Capital Gain: Annually
Front-End Load: 5.00%
12b-1: 0.07%
Redemption Fee: None
Management Company: IDS Financial Services
Ticker Symbol: INIDX

Portfolio Manager: Gordon Fines
Since: 1989

TOTAL RETURN (%)

1987	1988	1989	1990	1991	5-year	Bull Market	Bear Market
-1.0	7.3	36.6	3.3	46.9	120.2	47.5	-26.2

INVESTMENT PORTFOLIO

Total Assets (mil.)	Current Yield	Turnover Ratio	Expense Ratio	Beta	Risk Return
$808	0.8%	49%	0.73%	1.12	0.07

IDS MANAGED RETIREMENT FUND

IDS Financial Services
1000 Roanoke Building
Minneapolis, MN 55402
800-328-8300

Investment Objective: The fund seeks to maximize total return through investment in both equity and debt securities; common stocks typically claim the bulk of its assets. Like most of its IDS siblings, the fund follows an earnings-driven strategy. Management's affinity for companies that show rapid demonstrated growth in earnings generally results in a fairly expensive collection of high-beta growth stocks. An effective use of cash, however, has helped keep the fund on a fairly even keel. Thanks to its large cap orientation and earnings bias, this fund has been a top performer over the past 3 years.

Minimum:
Initial: $2,000
Subsequent: $2,000
Telephone Exchange: Yes
Distributions:
Income: Quarterly
Capital Gain: Annually
Front-End Load: 5.00%
12b-1: 0.09%
Redemption Fee: None
Management Company: IDS Financial Services
Ticker Symbol: IMRFX

Portfolio Manager: Robert Healy
Since: 1991

TOTAL RETURN (%)

1987	1988	1989	1990	1991	5-year	Bull Market	Bear Market
10.0	5.2	34.7	0.1	46.0	127.9	41.8	-21.5

INVESTMENT PORTFOLIO

Total Assets (mil.)	Current Yield	Turnover Ratio	Expense Ratio	Beta	Risk Return
$1,007	1.6%	78%	0.90%	0.97	0.09

IDS NEW DIMENSIONS FUND

IDS Financial Services
1000 Roanoke Building
Minneapolis, MN 55402
800-328-8300

Investment Objective: This fund seeks long-term capital appreciation by investing primarily in common stocks of American companies that show the potential for significant growth. The fund also invests a portion of its assets (but not more than 30%) in foreign securities. Like most of its IDS siblings, the fund follows a growth-intensive strategy, focusing on relatively expensive, large capitalization growth stocks with significantly above-average growth in earnings. Theoretically, the fund's growth-intensive approach would involve greater-than-average risk. Management's effective use of cash, however, has prevented this from being the case for this fund. Its beta is equal to that of the market as a whole.

Portfolio Manager: Gordon Fines
Since: 1991

Minimum:
Initial: $2,000
Subsequent: $25
Telephone Exchange: Yes
Distributions:
Income: Annually
Capital Gain: Annually
Front-End Load: 5.00%
12b-1: 0.07%
Redemption Fee: None
Management Company: IDS Financial Services
Ticker Symbol: INNDX

TOTAL RETURN (%)

1987	1988	1989	1990	1991	5-year	Bull Market	Bear Market
15.3	8.1	31.7	5.4	50.7	160.8	51.0	-19.2

INVESTMENT PORTFOLIO

Total Assets (mil.)	Current Yield	Turnover Ratio	Expense Ratio	Beta	Risk Return
$1,687	1.0%	91%	0.88%	1.04	0.09

IDS PROGRESSIVE FUND

IDS Financial Services
1000 Roanoke Building
Minneapolis, MN 55402
800-328-8300

Investment Objective: IDS Progressive Fund is not the typical IDS offering. In contrast to the aggressive, earnings-driven tactics employed by most IDS-managed growth vehicles, this fund utilizes a tamer value approach. Management stresses investments in low-multiple stocks that it believes represent undervalued earnings power and/or asset values. Inevitably, these criteria have led the fund to overweight cheap industrial products, natural resources and transportation stocks, all of which suffered during 1990 from the market's preoccupation with recessionproof earnings growth. Sizable stakes in gold and financial stocks proved particularly harmful. As a result, its 5-year return has been subpar.

Portfolio Manager: Michael Garbish
Since: 1991

Minimum:
Initial: $2,000
Subsequent: $25
Telephone Exchange: Yes
Distributions:
Income: Annually
Capital Gain: Annually
Front-End Load: 5.00%
12b-1: 0.08%
Redemption Fee: None
Management Company: IDS Financial Services
Ticker Symbol: INPRX

TOTAL RETURN (%)

1987	1988	1989	1990	1991	5-year	Bull Market	Bear Market
1.9	20.5	10.8	-17.7	25.1	40.2	27.5	-21.3

INVESTMENT PORTFOLIO

Total Assets (mil.)	Current Yield	Turnover Ratio	Expense Ratio	Beta	Risk Return
$123	2.6%	86%	0.79%	0.79	0.04

IVY GROWTH FUND

Mackenzie Investment Management
P.O. Box 5007
Boca Raton, FL 33431
800-235-3322

Investment Objective: The principal investment objective of this fund is long-term capital growth primarily through conservative growth-oriented domestic common stocks. Along with the rest of the Ivy family of funds, this fund was bought out by Mackenzie Investment Management the past year. Mackenzie has decided to keep Ivy Investment as the investment adviser, but has changed the fund characteristics. The fund now carries a 5.75% front-end load and an ongoing 12b-1 plan. Investors would be wise to wait a few years to see how this fund handles its transformation.

Portfolio Manager: Michael Peers
Since: 1986

Minimum:
Initial: $1,000
Subsequent: None
Telephone Exchange: Yes
Distributions:
Income: Annually
Capital Gain: Annually
Front-End Load: 5.75%
12b-1: 0.25%
Redemption Fee: None
Management Company: Ivy Management
Ticker Symbol: IVYFX

TOTAL RETURN (%)

1987	1988	1989	1990	1991	5-year	Bull Market	Bear Market
-1.8	12.4	27.2	-3.8	30.8	76.8	37.2	-19.5

INVESTMENT PORTFOLIO

Total Assets (mil.)	Current Yield	Turnover Ratio	Expense Ratio	Beta	Risk Return
$206	1.5%	67%	1.29%	1.01	0.05

JANUS FUND

Janus Funds
100 Fillmore Street, Suite 300
Denver, CO 80206
800-525-8983

Investment Objective: Janus Fund's superb risk-reward profile is matched by few rivals. Over the past 5 years, the fund has achieved one of the highest total returns of any growth funds, while also showing one of the lowest levels of risk. Its excellent results are attributable to management's skill at adapting to market trends. Regardless of market trends, the fund usually is caught holding very timely, popular stocks. Besides excellent stock selection, this no-load fund also has benefited from extremely well-timed retreats to cash, which has enabled it to resist sharp bear market declines.

Portfolio Manager: James Craig
Since: 1987

Minimum:
Initial: $1,000
Subsequent: $100
Telephone Exchange: Yes
Distributions:
Income: Annually
Capital Gain: Annually
Front-End Load: None
12b-1: None
Redemption Fee: None
Management Company: Janus Capital Corporation
Ticker Symbol: JANSX

TOTAL RETURN (%)

1987	1988	1989	1990	1991	5-year	Bull Market	Bear Market
4.2	16.6	46.3	-0.7	42.8	151.9	43.8	-18.0

INVESTMENT PORTFOLIO

Total Assets (mil.)	Current Yield	Turnover Ratio	Expense Ratio	Beta	Risk Return
$2,581	1.0%	307%	1.02%	1.05	0.07

JANUS TWENTY FUND

Janus Funds
100 Fillmore Street, Suite 300
Denver, CO 80206
800-525-8983

Investment Objective: Janus Twenty's subpar 1986 and 1987 returns—the result of a since-abandoned value strategy—give no indication of its current capabilities. To be sure, the fund has been a top performer since the arrival of current manager Tom Marsico, who now runs this fund in accordance with the growth strategy responsible for the success of siblings Janus Fund and the three Marsico-run Idex funds. Distinguishing this fund from its siblings is its more concentrated approach; as its name implies, it invests in only 20 stocks. Its excellent results to date underscore how well suited this new, concentrated approach is to Marsico's superb stock-picking abilities.

Portfolio Manager: Thomas Marsico
Since: 1988

Minimum:
Initial: $1,000
Subsequent: $50
Telephone Exchange: Yes
Distributions:
Income: Annually
Capital Gain: Annually
Front-End Load: None
12b-1: None
Redemption Fee: None
Management Company: Janus Capital Corporation
Ticker Symbol: JAVLX

TOTAL RETURN (%)

1987	1988	1989	1990	1991	5-year	Bull Market	Bear Market
-11.6	19.1	50.8	0.6	69.2	170.1	66.4	-24.1

INVESTMENT PORTFOLIO

Total Assets (mil.)	Current Yield	Turnover Ratio	Expense Ratio	Beta	Risk Return
$1,014	0.1%	163%	1.07%	1.26	0.10

JP GROWTH FUND

Jefferson Pilot Investor Services
100 North Greene Street
Greensboro, NC 27401
800-458-4498

Investment Objective: JP Growth Fund pursues its capital-appreciation objectives through a moderate growth discipline. Although the fund owns a smattering of small growth stocks, large S&P 500 names dominate the portfolio. Most show stable moderately above-average earnings growth and sell at moderate price/earnings ratios. Besides quality and value, the fund stresses industry diversification. It typically keeps near market-level representation in most major sectors, slightly overweighting growth industries such as health care and technology. Unsurprisingly, the fund's conventional tactics have produced average results.

Portfolio Manager: Hardee Mills
Since: 1991

Minimum:
Initial: $300
Subsequent: $25
Telephone Exchange: Yes
Distributions:
Income: Semiannually
Capital Gain: Annually
Front-End Load: 5.50%
12b-1: None
Redemption Fee: None
Management Company: JP Investment Management
Ticker Symbol: JPGRX

TOTAL RETURN (%)

1987	1988	1989	1990	1991	5-year	Bull Market	Bear Market
0.8	7.4	31.2	-1.4	32.0	84.9	22.9	-14.5

INVESTMENT PORTFOLIO

Total Assets (mil.)	Current Yield	Turnover Ratio	Expense Ratio	Beta	Risk Return
$32	2.1%	31%	0.88%	0.95	0.04

KEMPER INVESTMENT PORTFOLIOS GROWTH

Kemper Financial Services
120 South LaSalle Street
Chicago, IL 60603
800-621-1048

Investment Objective: This fund seeks capital appreciation primarily from a portfolio of high-quality common stocks. While investment for long-term capital appreciation is emphasized, investment may be made for short-term capital appreciation. Although the fund does not make huge industry bets, its portfolio is skewed toward growth industries such as health care and pollution control. In 1991, the fund was in the top 10% of growth-oriented funds as growth stocks lead the way the past year. Despite a greater than 2% expense ratio, this fund is an above-average growth fund.

Portfolio Manager: Stephen Lewis
Since: 1987

Minimum:
Initial: $250
Subsequent: $50
Telephone Exchange: Yes
Distributions:
Income: Annually
Capital Gain: Annually
Front-End Load: None
12b-1: 1.25%
Redemption Fee: 3.00%
Management Company: Kemper Financial Services
Ticker Symbol: IPEQX

TOTAL RETURN (%)

1987	1988	1989	1990	1991	5-year	Bull Market	Bear Market
6.4	9.6	31.4	-1.7	57.0	136.5	50.5	-21.5

INVESTMENT PORTFOLIO

Total Assets (mil.)	Current Yield	Turnover Ratio	Expense Ratio	Beta	Risk Return
$449	0.4%	96%	2.18%	1.04	0.10

KEMPER SUMMIT FUND

Kemper Financial Services
120 South LaSalle Street
Chicago, IL 60603
800-621-1048

Investment Objective: Kemper Summit Fund seeks maximum capital appreciation by investing in a mix of large, medium and small capitalization companies with above-average earnings growth prospects that are not fully reflected in stock prices. The fund's value parameters have increasingly led it to emphasize small and medium-sized growth stocks. Major industries include high-growth retail, technology, pollution control, cable TV and telecommunications. Despite its seemingly sound approach, this fund's long-term results have been mediocre at best, that is until the past year, when small cap stocks surged to the fore.

Portfolio Manager: Beth Cotner
Since: 1987

Minimum:
Initial: $1,000
Subsequent: $100
Telephone Exchange: Yes
Distributions:
Income: Annually
Capital Gain: Annually
Front-End Load: 5.75%
12b-1: None
Redemption Fee: None
Management Company: Kemper Financial Services
Ticker Symbol: KMSMX

TOTAL RETURN (%)

1987	1988	1989	1990	1991	5-year	Bull Market	Bear Market
0.2	7.8	26.1	-5.2	69.0	118.2	64.6	-25.1

INVESTMENT PORTFOLIO

Total Assets (mil.)	Current Yield	Turnover Ratio	Expense Ratio	Beta	Risk Return
$280	2.7%	107%	0.86%	1.15	0.11

KEYSTONE AMERICA FUND OF GROWTH STOCKS

Keystone Distributors
99 High Street, 29th Floor
Boston, MA 02110
800-633-4900

Investment Objective: Keystone America Fund of Growth Stocks seeks long-term growth of capital by investing in large and medium-sized growth companies with demonstrated records of consistent growth in earnings over more than one business cycle. The fund's emphasis on consistent earnings causes it to stress stable growth industries including food, health care, retail and services at the expense of highly cyclical technology, energy and basic industry stocks; the fund neglects the latter group entirely.

Portfolio Manager: D. Dates
Since: 1989

Minimum:
Initial: $1,000
Subsequent: None
Telephone Exchange: Yes
Distributions:
Income: Annually
Capital Gain: Annually
Front-End Load: 4.75%
12b-1: 0.25%
Redemption Fee: None
Management Company: Keystone Custodian Funds
Ticker Symbol: KAGRX

TOTAL RETURN (%)

1987	1988	1989	1990	1991	5-year	Bull Market	Bear Market
NA	5.7	28.4	-2.8	48.4	NA	56.1	-24.9

INVESTMENT PORTFOLIO

Total Assets (mil.)	Current Yield	Turnover Ratio	Expense Ratio	Beta	Risk Return
$6	0.0%	71%	2.00%	1.15	0.08

KEYSTONE CUSTODIAN FUNDS—K2

Keystone Distributors
99 High Street, 29th Floor
Boston, MA 02110
800-633-4900

Investment Objective: This fund's objective is to provide growth of capital by investing in a wide range of stocks. These securities may be blue chip, mid caps or emerging-growth companies. Also, the fund may invest in foreign markets. Management favored smaller issues in 1991 and was rewarded with a 41.6% gain. The flexibility of the fund allows it to capitalize on hot markets as was the case with small caps the past year. Five-year returns are subpar for this fund, but if the small-company bull continues to run, this fund should make some ground in a hurry.

Portfolio Manager: W. McCormick
Since: 1989

Minimum:
Initial: $1,000
Subsequent: None
Telephone Exchange: Yes
Distributions:
Income: Annually
Capital Gain: Annually
Front-End Load: None
12b-1: 0.43%
Redemption Fee: 4.00%
Management Company: Keystone Custodian Funds
Ticker Symbol: KKTWX

TOTAL RETURN (%)

1987	1988	1989	1990	1991	5-year	Bull Market	Bear Market
-1.9	10.7	24.1	-7.0	41.6	77.5	43.6	-20.8

INVESTMENT PORTFOLIO

Total Assets (mil.)	Current Yield	Turnover Ratio	Expense Ratio	Beta	Risk Return
$298	0.7%	30%	1.65%	1.08	0.07

KEYSTONE CUSTODIAN FUNDS—S3

Keystone Distributors
99 High Street, 29th Floor
Boston, MA 02110
800-633-4900

Investment Objective: This back-end load fund stresses established, large and midsized companies with moderately above-average growth in earnings. In typical Keystone fashion, the fund relies heavily on diversification. Its 200-stock-strong portfolio has market-level representation in most major industries. High-growth sectors such as retail, technology and services are modestly overweighted. Inevitably, the fund's unwillingness to diverge very much from the broad index rules out extraordinary results. Long-term returns are average.

Portfolio Manager: Jill Lyndon
Since: 1987

Minimum:
Initial: $1,000
Subsequent: None
Telephone Exchange: Yes
Distributions:
Income: Annually
Capital Gain: Annually
Front-End Load: None
12b-1: 0.41%
Redemption Fee: 4.00%
Management Company: Keystone Custodian Funds
Ticker Symbol: KSTHX

TOTAL RETURN (%)

1987	1988	1989	1990	1991	5-year	Bull Market	Bear Market
0.4	14.1	24.7	-8.8	42.1	85.3	45.5	-24.3

INVESTMENT PORTFOLIO

Total Assets (mil.)	Current Yield	Turnover Ratio	Expense Ratio	Beta	Risk Return
$229	0.8%	65%	1.54%	1.14	0.07

LANDMARK EQUITY FUND

Landmark Funds
6 St. James Avenue
Boston, MA 02116
800-223-4447

Investment Objective: Unfortunately, poor timing may be this fund's greatest fault. Up until late 1990, the fund invested in small cap stocks. When Citibank became the adviser, the objective was changed to obtain blue chip returns. Although the fund returned approximately the growth-fund average, the strategy backfired as small cap stocks began their run just as the move was made. Investors only have 1991 to judge the fund's performance as previous returns were achieved under different management and objective.

Portfolio Manager: Chris Trompeter
Since: 1990

Minimum:
Initial: $1,000
Subsequent: None
Telephone Exchange: Yes
Distributions:
Income: Semiannually
Capital Gain: Annually
Front-End Load: None
12b-1: 0.20%
Redemption Fee: None
Management Company: Citibank
Ticker Symbol: LCGFX

TOTAL RETURN (%)

1987	1988	1989	1990	1991	5-year	Bull Market	Bear Market
NA	6.0	24.8	-14.0	31.8	NA	26.1	-16.1

INVESTMENT PORTFOLIO

Total Assets (mil.)	Current Yield	Turnover Ratio	Expense Ratio	Beta	Risk Return
$7	1.7%	68%	1.40%	1.04	0.08

LEGG MASON SPECIAL INVESTMENT TRUST

Legg Mason Distributor
7 East Redwood Street
Baltimore, MD 21202
800-822-5544

Investment Objective: Legg Mason Special Investment Trust seeks capital appreciation by investing primarily in equity securities of companies with market capitalizations of less than $1 billion that it believes are undervalued relative to their underlying earnings power and/or asset values. The fund's major industries—industrial products, retail, technology and business services—underscore management's affinity for inefficiently priced rapid earnings growth, which largely explains its good resistance to decline during 1990. It also explains its better-than-average return the past year.

Minimum:
Initial: $1,000
Subsequent: $500
Telephone Exchange: Yes
Distributions:
Income: Annually
Capital Gain: Annually
Front-End Load: None
12b-1: 0.95%
Redemption Fee: None
Management Company: Legg Mason Fund Adviser
Ticker Symbol: LMASX

Portfolio Manager: William H. Miller
Since: 1985

TOTAL RETURN (%)

1987	1988	1989	1990	1991	5-year	Bull Market	Bear Market
-10.4	19.7	32.1	0.5	39.4	98.5	50.8	-18.2

INVESTMENT PORTFOLIO

Total Assets (mil.)	Current Yield	Turnover Ratio	Expense Ratio	Beta	Risk Return
$144	0.2%	76%	2.30%	0.87	0.07

LEGG MASON VALUE TRUST

Legg Mason Distributor
7 East Redwood Street
Baltimore, MD 21202
800-822-5544

Investment Objective: As its name implies, this no-load fund pursues a fairly rigorous value discipline. Management's taste for stocks that sell at well-below-market price/earnings and price/book ratios has led to large industry concentrations. Financial stocks, for example, currently make up a large portion of its assets. Cheap consumer durables and transportation stocks also are heavily weighted. Like many deep-value players, the fund severely underperformed during the 1989-1990 earnings-driven market. However, it rebounded smartly the past year as the economy struggled out of recession.

Minimum:
Initial: $1,000
Subsequent: $500
Telephone Exchange: Yes
Distributions:
Income: Quarterly
Capital Gain: Annually
Front-End Load: None
12b-1: 0.93%
Redemption Fee: None
Management Company: Legg Mason Fund Adviser
Ticker Symbol: LMVTX

Portfolio Manager: William H. Miller
Since: 1990

TOTAL RETURN (%)

1987	1988	1989	1990	1991	5-year	Bull Market	Bear Market
-7.4	25.8	20.2	-17	34.7	56.7	36.8	-24.7

INVESTMENT PORTFOLIO

Total Assets (mil.)	Current Yield	Turnover Ratio	Expense Ratio	Beta	Risk Return
$670	1.4%	39%	1.90%	0.97	0.06

LEXINGTON TECHNICAL STRATEGY FUND

Lexington Funds Distributor
P.O. Box 1515
Saddle Brook, NJ 07662
800-526-0056

Investment Objective: Lexington Technical Strategy Fund seeks long-term growth of capital using proprietary quantitative techniques in security selection. Run by Lexington Management, the fund does not utilize traditional securities analysis. Its methods focus solely on analysis of stock price cycles. The fund continually screens all 500 stocks included in the S&P 500. Ideally, it will own the 50 stocks that appear to be at the most favorable point in their price cycles. The same quantitative methods also determine the fund's asset allocation, as it begins to raise cash when the number of stocks in a favorable price-cycle phase begins to decline.

Portfolio Manager: Frank Peluso
Since: 1987

Minimum:
Initial: $1,000
Subsequent: $50
Telephone Exchange: Yes
Distributions:
Income: Annually
Capital Gain: Annually
Front-End Load: None
12b-1: None
Redemption Fee: None
Management Company: Lexington Management
Ticker Symbol: LXTSX

TOTAL RETURN (%)

1987	1988	1989	1990	1991	5-year	Bull Market	Bear Market
NA	5.3	35.5	-9.5	31.8	NA	30.9	-20.9

INVESTMENT PORTFOLIO

Total Assets (mil.)	Current Yield	Turnover Ratio	Expense Ratio	Beta	Risk Return
$11	0.6%	134%	2.14%	0.96	0.05

LORD ABBETT FUNDAMENTAL VALUE FUND

Lord Abbett
767 Fifth Avenue
New York, NY 10153
800-874-3733

Investment Objective: In the Lord Abbett tradition, this fund emphasizes sectors of the market that it believes are poised to benefit from macroeconomic/industry trends. Management looks to identify industries and individual companies in the early stage of positive change that have yet to be recognized by the market. Most of the fund's large and midsized companies sell at modest price/earnings ratios despite their well-above-average growth rates. Like most Lord Abbett equity funds, major industries—capital goods, basic industry and energy—reflect management's long-term confidence in the U.S. manufacturing sector. As expected, its returns were subpar during the past 2 years' weak economy.

Portfolio Manager: Denise Higgins
Since: 1988

Minimum:
Initial: $1,000
Subsequent: None
Telephone Exchange: Yes
Distributions:
Income: Semiannually
Capital Gain: Annually
Front-End Load: 6.75%
12b-1: 0.21%
Redemption Fee: None
Management Company: Lord Abbett
Ticker Symbol: LDFVX

TOTAL RETURN (%)

1987	1988	1989	1990	1991	5-year	Bull Market	Bear Market
2.2	8.7	29.0	-0.1	19.2	70.5	28.7	-16.2

INVESTMENT PORTFOLIO

Total Assets (mil.)	Current Yield	Turnover Ratio	Expense Ratio	Beta	Risk Return
$24	1.9%	42%	1.75%	0.88	0.03

LORD ABBETT VALUE APPRECIATION FUND

Lord Abbett
767 Fifth Avenue
New York, NY 10153
800-874-3733

Investment Objective: This fund applies the same investment discipline that guides sibling Lord Abbett Fundamental Value Fund to investing in medium-sized companies with market values between $200 million and $1 billion. Fundamental Value invests in both large and midsized companies. As is also true of its sibling, the fund maintains a fairly compact portfolio of some 30-odd stocks, emphasizing industries that it believes are in the early stage of an earnings uptrend. In recent years, it has stressed basic industry, capital goods and energy. While this approach has not been rewarded in recent years, the fund's results should improve with signs of renewed economic growth.

Portfolio Manager: Denise Higgins
Since: 1990

Minimum:
Initial: $1,000
Subsequent: None
Telephone Exchange: Yes
Distributions:
Income: Annually
Capital Gain: Annually
Front-End Load: 6.75%
12b-1: 0.16%
Redemption Fee: None
Management Company: Lord Abbett
Ticker Symbol: LAVLX

TOTAL RETURN (%)

1987	1988	1989	1990	1991	5-year	Bull Market	Bear Market
-3.9	15.6	20.1	-4.6	27.4	62.1	35.8	-17.8

INVESTMENT PORTFOLIO

Total Assets (mil.)	Current Yield	Turnover Ratio	Expense Ratio	Beta	Risk Return
$150	2.0%	55%	1.12%	0.94	0.05

MAINSTAY CAPITAL APPRECIATION FUND

NYLIFE Securities
51 Madison Avenue, Room 117
New York, NY 10010
800-522-4202

Investment Objective: This fund seeks capital growth by maintaining a flexible approach to investing in various types of companies with the following investment characteristics: participation in expanding markets, increasing unit-sales volume, earnings and revenue growth greater than that of companies in the S&P 500 Index and increasing return on investment. Although it is not the fund's policy to invest or trade for short-term profits, the past year's portfolio turnover ratio exceeded 250%. However, a disciplined approach to asset selection has served investors well during the past 5 years.

Portfolio Manager: Ronald J. Worobel
Since: 1990

Minimum:
Initial: $500
Subsequent: $50
Telephone Exchange: Yes
Distributions:
Income: Annually
Capital Gain: Annually
Front-End Load: None
12b-1: 1.00%
Redemption Fee: 5.00%
Management Company: MacKay-Shields Financial
Ticker Symbol: MCSCX

TOTAL RETURN (%)

1987	1988	1989	1990	1991	5-year	Bull Market	Bear Market
-2.2	2.5	26.1	4.1	68.4	121.7	75.6	-19.9

INVESTMENT PORTFOLIO

Total Assets (mil.)	Current Yield	Turnover Ratio	Expense Ratio	Beta	Risk Return
$77	0.0%	259%	2.50%	1.11	0.10

MAINSTAY VALUE FUND

NYLIFE Securities
51 Madison Avenue, Room 117
New York, NY 10010
800-522-4202

Investment Objective: This load fund seeks maximum long-term total return from a combination of growth of capital and income. Although the fund does have income as part of its objective, it really cannot be called a growth and income fund because dividend income is minimal. The adviser considers price/book ratio, estimated liquidating value and projected cash flow as significant factors when assessing relative value. Since its inception in 1986, the fund has delivered solid returns considering its lower-than-average risk. The past year's 40+% return was the fund's best ever.

Minimum:
Initial: $500
Subsequent: $50
Telephone Exchange: Yes
Distributions:
Income: Quarterly
Capital Gain: Annually
Front-End Load: None
12b-1: 1.00%
Redemption Fee: 5.00%
Management Company: MacKay-Shields Financial
Ticker Symbol: MKVAX

Portfolio Manager: Denis La Plaige
Since: 1990

TOTAL RETURN (%)

1987	1988	1989	1990	1991	5-year	Bull Market	Bear Market
-2.6	16.1	21.4	-6.00	41.3	82.2	45.5	-15.6

INVESTMENT PORTFOLIO

Total Assets (mil.)	Current Yield	Turnover Ratio	Expense Ratio	Beta	Risk Return
$45	1.5%	117%	2.60%	0.83	0.08

MASSACHUSETTS FINANCIAL CAPITAL DEVELOPMENT

Massachusetts Financial Services
500 Boylston Street
Boston, MA 02116
800-225-2606

Investment Objective: This fund, which once pursued an aggressive, earnings-driven strategy, switched to a tamer value orientation in late 1988. Current manager Jeffrey Shames stresses large capitalization stocks that he believes sell at a discount to their cash flow and/or asset values. Since implementing the fund's current strategy, he has stressed strong franchise telephones, entertainment and consumer durables. Asset-rich integrated oils and cheap financials also have been prominent.

Minimum:
Initial: $1,000
Subsequent: $50
Telephone Exchange: Yes
Distributions:
Income: Semiannually
Capital Gain: Annually
Front-End Load: 5.75%
12b-1: 0.25%
Redemption Fee: None
Management Company: Massachusetts Financial Services
Ticker Symbol: MCDFX

Portfolio Manager: Jeffrey Shames
Since: 1987

TOTAL RETURN (%)

1987	1988	1989	1990	1991	5-year	Bull Market	Bear Market
3.9	9.0	28.5	-4.4	22.4	70.5	31.5	-17.1

INVESTMENT PORTFOLIO

Total Assets (mil.)	Current Yield	Turnover Ratio	Expense Ratio	Beta	Risk Return
$684	1.4%	89%	0.80%	0.91	0.04

MASSACHUSETTS FINANCIAL DEVELOPMENT FUND

Massachusetts Financial Services
500 Boylston Street
Boston, MA 02116
800-225-2606

Investment Objective: This fund invests primarily in large capitalization common stocks that it believes sell at a discount to their underlying book value. In addition, current manager Frederick Simmons also insists that the fund's companies show an improving return on equity. Unsurprisingly, Simmons' criteria have led to large concentrations in out-of-favor sectors, including finance and industrial products. Like many strict value players, Simmons allows cash reserves to rise when stocks meeting his criteria are scarce. This practice largely explains the fund's ability to hold up relatively well during 1990, despite its large stake in hard-hit financial stocks.

Portfolio Manager: Frederick Simmons
Since: 1988

Minimum:
Initial: $1,000
Subsequent: $50
Telephone Exchange: Yes
Distributions:
Income: Quarterly
Capital Gain: Annually
Front-End Load: 5.75%
12b-1: 0.25%
Redemption Fee: 1.00%
Management Company: Massachusetts Financial Services
Ticker Symbol: MFDFX

TOTAL RETURN (%)

1987	1988	1989	1990	1991	5-year	Bull Market	Bear Market
5.4	10.3	26.1	-6.0	32.6	82.7	31.6	-16.8

INVESTMENT PORTFOLIO

Total Assets (mil.)	Current Yield	Turnover Ratio	Expense Ratio	Beta	Risk Return
$219	1.3%	79%	0.83%	0.90	0.06

MASSACHUSETTS FINANCIAL SPECIAL FUND

Massachusetts Financial Services
500 Boylston Street
Boston, MA 02116
800-225-2606

Investment Objective: Massachusetts Financial Special seeks capital appreciation by investing in securities that it believes are undervalued. In particular, the fund stresses companies that it believes sell at a discount to their underlying asset values and cash flows. Management also likes companies with unrecognized restructuring potential. The fund's affinity for cheap assets has lead to large concentrations in strong-franchise media, asset-rich integrated oils and a host of restructuring candidates. Severely depressed financial stocks also are prominent.

Portfolio Manager: Jefrey Shames
Since: 1985

Minimum:
Initial: $1,000
Subsequent: $50
Telephone Exchange: Yes
Distributions:
Income: Annually
Capital Gain: Annually
Front-End Load: 5.75%
12b-1: 0.18%
Redemption Fee: None
Management Company: Massachusetts Financial Services
Ticker Symbol: MSFSX

TOTAL RETURN (%)

1987	1988	1989	1990	1991	5-year	Bull Market	Bear Market
2.4	26.6	22.3	-11.8	24.0	73.3	28.5	-20.7

INVESTMENT PORTFOLIO

Total Assets (mil.)	Current Yield	Turnover Ratio	Expense Ratio	Beta	Risk Return
$87	0.7%	36%	1.51%	0.85	0.04

MASSACHUSETTS INVESTORS GROWTH STOCK FUND

Massachusetts Financial Services
500 Boylston Street
Boston, MA 02116
800-225-2606

Investment Objective: Massachusetts Investors Growth Stock Fund stresses pure growth. In contrast to the moderate strategy that guided the fund prior to 1988, current manager Tom Cashman stresses above-average growth companies with strong revenue and earnings growth that stems from unit volume growth rather than price increases or margin expansion. His strict growth criteria causes the fund to concentrate its assets in a handful of high-growth industries such as technology, pollution control and retail. Needless to say, this potent approach leads to extreme results, as already seen in the fund's sharply contrasting 1989, 1990 and 1991 returns.

Portfolio Manager: Tom Cashman
Since: 1988

Minimum:
Initial: $1,000
Subsequent: $50
Telephone Exchange: Yes
Distributions:
Income: Annually
Capital Gain: Annually
Front-End Load: 5.75%
12b-1: 0.25%
Redemption Fee: None
Management Company: Massachusetts Financial Services
Ticker Symbol: MIGFX

TOTAL RETURN (%)

1987	1988	1989	1990	1991	5-year	Bull Market	Bear Market
5.8	4.1	35.7	-4.7	47.7	110.4	65.5	-32.4

INVESTMENT PORTFOLIO

Total Assets (mil.)	Current Yield	Turnover Ratio	Expense Ratio	Beta	Risk Return
$950	0.0%	44%	0.53%	1.35	0.06

MATHERS FUND

Mathers & Company
100 Corporate North, Suite 201
Bannockburn, IL 60015
800-962-3863

Investment Objective: Mathers Fund has the risk-averse investor at heart. Besides following a strict value discipline, the fund also keeps risk relatively low by retreating to cash when stocks that meet its value parameters are scarce. With a full 80 to 90% of its assets in cash, it severely trailed 1989's bull market but fully resisted 1990's debacle. When the fund does invest in stocks, it stresses fundamentally undervalued companies with good earnings/price momentum and above-average dividend yields that represent a low percentage of earnings. Of course, an ultraconservative stance comes replete with its own risks as witnessed by the past year's disappointing results.

Portfolio Manager: Henry G. Van Der Eb, Jr.
Since: 1975

Minimum:
Initial: $1,000
Subsequent: $200
Telephone Exchange: No
Distributions:
Income: Annually
Capital Gain: Annually
Front-End Load: None
12b-1: None
Redemption Fee: None
Management Company: Mathers & Company
Ticker Symbol: MATRX

TOTAL RETURN (%)

1987	1988	1989	1990	1991	5-year	Bull Market	Bear Market
27.0	13.7	10.4	10.4	9.4	92.8	6.0	0.8

INVESTMENT PORTFOLIO

Total Assets (mil.)	Current Yield	Turnover Ratio	Expense Ratio	Beta	Risk Return
$512	4.7%	190%	0.98%	0.02	0.00

MENTOR FUND

Wheat First Securities
P.O. Box 30
Richmond, VA 23206
800-999-4328

Investment Objective: This Wheat First offering stresses long-term capital appreciation through investments in primarily midsized companies. Because of the surge in medium-sized companies during 1991, the fund bested many of its growth-fund counterparts with its return of 50%. The past year's return helped offset subpar performance during the past 4 years. This growth selection should be more volatile than most, as its portfolio market capitalization will be small relative to other growth vehicles. However, should smaller issues continue their ascent, Mentor Fund should be near the top of our growth-fund list.

Portfolio Manager: Theodore Price
Since: 1985

Minimum:
Initial: $1,000
Subsequent: $500
Telephone Exchange: No
Distributions:
Income: Annually
Capital Gain: Annually
Front-End Load: None
12b-1: 1.00%
Redemption Fee: 5.00%
Management Company: Investment Management Group
Ticker Symbol: MGRTX

TOTAL RETURN (%)

1987	1988	1989	1990	1991	5-year	Bull Market	Bear Market
-10.0	16.9	17.4	-11.3	50.3	64.7	39.8	-20.9

INVESTMENT PORTFOLIO

Total Assets (mil.)	Current Yield	Turnover Ratio	Expense Ratio	Beta	Risk Return
$100	0.0%	26%	2.24%	1.18	0.08

MERRILL LYNCH BASIC VALUE FUND A

Merrill Lynch Funds Distributor
P.O. Box 9011
Princeton, NJ 08543
800-637-3863

Investment Objective: This load fund seeks capital appreciation by investing in securities that management believes are undervalued and therefore represent basic investment value. Securities are chosen that are selling at a discount, either from book value or historical price/earnings ratios, or that seem capable of recovering from out-of-favor considerations. Many of these firms have, indeed, been out of favor as evidenced by the fund's 5-year performance of 66.5%. The only year that the fund outpaced the broader markets was in 1988 when value issues were in favor. Patient investors eventually will be rewarded by this high-quality value fund.

Portfolio Manager: Paul Hoffman
Since: 1977

Minimum:
Initial: $250
Subsequent: $50
Telephone Exchange: No
Distributions:
Income: Semiannually
Capital Gain: Semiannually
Front-End Load: 6.50%
12b-1: None
Redemption Fee: None
Management Company: Merrill Lynch Asset Management
Ticker Symbol: MLBVX

TOTAL RETURN (%)

1987	1988	1989	1990	1991	5-year	Bull Market	Bear Market
4.4	22.7	17.5	-13.1	27.2	66.5	36.5	-18.5

INVESTMENT PORTFOLIO

Total Assets (mil.)	Current Yield	Turnover Ratio	Expense Ratio	Beta	Risk Return
$1,456	3.7%	20%	0.58%	0.88	0.05

MERRILL LYNCH CAPITAL FUND A

Merrill Lynch Funds Distributor
P.O. Box 9011
Princeton, NJ 08543
800-637-3863

Investment Objective: Offered in 2 share classes, this fund seeks capital appreciation by stressing stocks of well-managed companies that sell at low price/earnings and price/book ratios and that offer above-average dividend yields. Reflecting these criteria, the fund's major industries include cheap, high-yielding electric utilities, integrated oils, financials and pharmaceuticals. The latter explains its good resistance to decline in 1990's bear market. Long-term returns and risk are highly competitive.

Portfolio Manager: Ernest Watts
Since: 1983

Minimum:
Initial: $250
Subsequent: $50
Telephone Exchange: No
Distributions:
Income: Semiannually
Capital Gain: Semiannually
Front-End Load: 6.50%
12b-1: None
Redemption Fee: None
Management Company: Merrill Lynch Asset Management
Ticker Symbol: MLCPX

TOTAL RETURN (%)

1987	1988	1989	1990	1991	5-year	Bull Market	Bear Market
4.6	17.0	23.0	1.1	24.7	89.8	29.3	-11.4

INVESTMENT PORTFOLIO

Total Assets (mil.)	Current Yield	Turnover Ratio	Expense Ratio	Beta	Risk Return
$1,308	4.7%	86%	0.58%	0.66	0.06

MERRILL LYNCH FUND FOR TOMORROW B

Merrill Lynch Funds Distributor
P.O. Box 9011
Princeton, NJ 08543
800-637-3863

Investment Objective: This fund, which is offered in 2 share classes, seeks capital growth by investing in quality companies that it believes are well positioned to benefit from demographic and cultural changes, primarily as they affect the consumer sectors, with moderately priced food, health-care, household-products, entertainment, media and telecommunications stocks representing 75% of its assets. Over the past 5 years, the fund failed to keep pace with the S&P 500. It will appeal to investors seeking concentrated exposure to consumer stocks.

Portfolio Manager: Vincent Dileo
Since: 1984

Minimum:
Initial: $500
Subsequent: $50
Telephone Exchange: No
Distributions:
Income: Semiannually
Capital Gain: Semiannually
Front-End Load: None
12b-1: 1.00%
Redemption Fee: 4.00%
Management Company: Merrill Lynch Asset Management
Ticker Symbol: MRFFX

TOTAL RETURN (%)

1987	1988	1989	1990	1991	5-year	Bull Market	Bear Market
-5.1	22.1	28.9	-8.0	30.8	79.8	39.0	-18.9

INVESTMENT PORTFOLIO

Total Assets (mil.)	Current Yield	Turnover Ratio	Expense Ratio	Beta	Risk Return
$431	2.0%	26%	2.00%	1.02	0.05

MERRILL LYNCH GROWTH FUND FOR INVEST/RETIRE—B

Merrill Lynch Funds Distributor
P.O. Box 9011
Princeton, NJ 08543
800-637-3863

Investment Objective: This volatile fund seeks growth at a reasonable price. Management relies on strict value parameters to purchase quality, above-average growth stocks when they seem undervalued and to sell them as soon as they appear fully priced. Its dual emphasis on low valuations and above-average earnings causes it to emphasize out-of-favor industries that it believes have better prospects for growth than the market is willing to recognize. The fund heavily weights technology, health-care services and financials, while neglecting pricey consumer nondurables and services. Patient investors can expect competitive long-term returns with slightly higher-than-average risk.

Portfolio Manager: Stephen Jones
Since: 1987

Minimum:
Initial: $1,000
Subsequent: $50
Telephone Exchange: No
Distributions:
Income: Annually
Capital Gain: Annually
Front-End Load: None
12b-1: 1.00%
Redemption Fee: 4.00%
Management Company: Merrill Lynch Asset Management
Ticker Symbol: MRQRX

TOTAL RETURN (%)

1987	1988	1989	1990	1991	5-year	Bull Market	Bear Market
NA	16.0	31.6	-1.0	23.9	NA	52.7	-29.5

INVESTMENT PORTFOLIO

Total Assets (mil.)	Current Yield	Turnover Ratio	Expense Ratio	Beta	Risk Return
$760	0.1%	20%	1.93%	1.24	0.03

MERRILL LYNCH SPECIAL VALUE FUND A

Merrill Lynch Funds Distributor
P.O. Box 9011
Princeton, NJ 08543
800-637-3863

Investment Objective: This fund seeks capital appreciation by investing in a diversified portfolio of common stocks. Although it owns a few blue chips, most of its companies have market capitalizations below $500 million. Unsurprisingly, the fund's emphasis on small caps has not been helpful in recent years (with the exception of 1991), for small stocks significantly underperformed large stocks. Returns also have been slowed by the fund's strict value parameters, which explain its large stakes in sluggish sectors such as technology and capital goods. While a prolonged shift in leadership to small stocks may soon allow for improved results, this fund's subpar 5-year returns are not very encouraging.

Portfolio Manager: Michael Davis
Since: 1978

Minimum:
Initial: $250
Subsequent: $50
Telephone Exchange: No
Distributions:
Income: Semiannually
Capital Gain: Annually
Front-End Load: 6.50%
12b-1: None
Redemption Fee: None
Management Company: Merrill Lynch Asset Management
Ticker Symbol: MLSVX

TOTAL RETURN (%)

1987	1988	1989	1990	1991	5-year	Bull Market	Bear Market
-18.5	17.1	0.4	-27.5	54.9	7.5	57.9	-30.0

INVESTMENT PORTFOLIO

Total Assets (mil.)	Current Yield	Turnover Ratio	Expense Ratio	Beta	Risk Return
$47	0.6%	73%	1.88%	0.95	0.09

MERRIMAN BLUE CHIP FUND

Merriman Investment Management
1200 Westlake Avenue North, #507
Seattle, WA 98109
800-423-4893

Investment Objective: Merriman Blue Chip Fund utilizes technical trend analysis to pursue its objectives of growth, income and preservation of capital. Management continuously monitors a universe of blue chip common stocks in an effort to identify issues that show superior relative price strength. In addition, it looks to significantly reduce market risk by quickly retreating to cash when its models indicate that the relative price strength of a large number of stocks is deteriorating. Although this fund's resistance to decline the past year is encouraging, potential investors should be aware of the fact that few mutual funds have been consistently successful at market timing.

Portfolio Manager: Merriman/Notaro
Since: 1988

Minimum:
Initial: $1,000
Subsequent: $100
Telephone Exchange: Yes
Distributions:
Income: Quarterly
Capital Gain: Annually
Front-End Load: None
12b-1: None
Redemption Fee: None
Management Company: Merriman Investment Management
Ticker Symbol: MTBCX

TOTAL RETURN (%)

1987	1988	1989	1990	1991	5-year	Bull Market	Bear Market
NA	NA	9.8	3.8	19.2	NA	13.2	-4.6

INVESTMENT PORTFOLIO

Total Assets (mil.)	Current Yield	Turnover Ratio	Expense Ratio	Beta	Risk Return
$20	1.5%	329%	1.83%	0.44	0.05

MERRIMAN CAPITAL APPRECIATION FUND

Merriman Investment Management
1200 Westlake Avenue North, #507
Seattle, WA 98109
800-423-4893

Investment Objective: Merriman Capital Appreciation Fund pursues its objectives of growth, income and capital preservation by adjusting its asset allocation in response to technical indications of relative price. When management does seek stock market exposure, it does so by investing in shares of other open-end mutual funds with long and successful operating histories, modest expenses and good relative price strength. During its 2-year existence, the fund has shown a strong affinity for fairly small-company growth funds.

Portfolio Manager: Merriman/Notaro
Since: 1989

Minimum:
Initial: $1,000
Subsequent: $100
Telephone Exchange: Yes
Distributions:
Income: Semiannually
Capital Gain: Annually
Front-End Load: None
12b-1: None
Redemption Fee: None
Management Company: Merriman Investment Management
Ticker Symbol: MNCAX

TOTAL RETURN (%)

1987	1988	1989	1990	1991	5-year	Bull Market	Bear Market
NA	NA	NA	3.1	21.9	NA	20.0	-4.4

INVESTMENT PORTFOLIO

Total Assets (mil.)	Current Yield	Turnover Ratio	Expense Ratio	Beta	Risk Return
$46	1.9%	429%	1.84%	0.42	0.06

MFS LIFETIME CAPITAL GROWTH TRUST

Massachusetts Financial Services
500 Boylston Street
Boston, MA 02116
800-225-2606

Investment Objective: This fund relies on a diversified portfolio of low-multiple common stocks to provide all-weather performance. While some of its companies, specifically its banks, are experiencing fundamental problems, most show above-average earnings, financial strength and industry leadership. Their relatively low valuations owe primarily to market sentiment, not poor fundamentals. Also responsible for the fund's moderate risk profile is its tendency to keep representation in most major industries rather than make huge sector bets. Competitive 3- and 5-year returns and an average beta underscore the merits of this fund's moderate approach.

Portfolio Manager: Kevin Parke
Since: 1986

Minimum:
Initial: $1,000
Subsequent: $50
Telephone Exchange: Yes
Distributions:
Income: Annually
Capital Gain: Annually
Front-End Load: None
12b-1: 1.00%
Redemption Fee: 6.00%
Management Company: Lifetime Advisers
Ticker Symbol: LCGTX

TOTAL RETURN (%)

1987	1988	1989	1990	1991	5-year	Bull Market	Bear Market
12.2	15.4	29.3	-2.0	30.2	113.7	35.9	-19.0

INVESTMENT PORTFOLIO

Total Assets (mil.)	Current Yield	Turnover Ratio	Expense Ratio	Beta	Risk Return
$312	0.4%	68%	2.38%	0.94	0.05

MFS LIFETIME MANAGED SECTORS TRUST

Massachusetts Financial Services
500 Boylston Street
Boston, MA 02116
800-225-2606

Investment Objective: Run in the same manner as MFS Managed Sectors, this fund differs from its namesake primarily in its fee structure. Whereas the former is offered with a 5.75% front-end load, this fund comes with a 6.00% deferred load and a 1.00% 12b-1 fee format. Otherwise, the 2 funds are virtually identical. Both concentrate assets in relatively few sectors that meet management's fundamental criteria. The fund's major industries, which include retail, telecommunications and finance, are a residual of management's search for companies with sustainable, high-growth rates, strong franchises, undervalued assets and, most important, good earning momentum.

Portfolio Manager: George Bennett
Since: 1986

Minimum:
Initial: $1,000
Subsequent: $50
Telephone Exchange: Yes
Distributions:
Income: Annually
Capital Gain: Annually
Front-End Load: None
12b-1: 1.00%
Redemption Fee: 6.00%
Management Company: Lifetime Advisers
Ticker Symbol: LTMSX

TOTAL RETURN (%)

1987	1988	1989	1990	1991	5-year	Bull Market	Bear Market
20.7	5.4	39.9	-13.7	59.6	145.3	59.1	-29.7

INVESTMENT PORTFOLIO

Total Assets (mil.)	Current Yield	Turnover Ratio	Expense Ratio	Beta	Risk Return
$190	0.0%	79%	2.50%	1.23	0.09

MFS MANAGED SECTORS TRUST

Massachusetts Financial Services
500 Boylston Street
Boston, MA 02116
800-225-2606

Investment Objective: As its name implies, this fund pursues its capital-appreciation objectives by concentrating its assets in just a handful of industry sectors that it believes have above-average prospects for growth. In choosing the fund's major sectors, current manager George Bennett doesn't utilize top-down judgments, but relies solely on bottom-up analysis to identify companies with 20+% sustainable growth in earnings, solid franchises, undervalued assets and, most important, good current earnings momentum. In recent years, these criteria have caused him to stress retail, cable TV, cellular telephones, capital goods and financial stocks. While volatile, the fund has performed exceptionally well during the past 5 years.

Portfolio Manager: George Bennett
Since: 1988

Minimum:
Initial: $1,000
Subsequent: $50
Telephone Exchange: Yes
Distributions:
Income: Annually
Capital Gain: Annually
Front-End Load: 5.75%
12b-1: 0.35%
Redemption Fee: None
Management Company: Massachusetts Financial Services
Ticker Symbol: MMNSX

TOTAL RETURN (%)

1987	1988	1989	1990	1991	5-year	Bull Market	Bear Market
5.7	4.8	41.8	-13.4	62.1	120.5	62.1	-30.1

INVESTMENT PORTFOLIO

Total Assets (mil.)	Current Yield	Turnover Ratio	Expense Ratio	Beta	Risk Return
$119	0.0%	70%	1.77%	1.26	0.09

MONETTA FUND

Monetta Financial Services
1776-A South Naperville Road, Suite 207
Wheaton, IL 60187
800-666-3882

Investment Objective: A strict discipline has allowed this fund to post phenomenal returns over the past 5 years. In its pursuit of capital appreciation, management looks for fast-growing companies that appear to have strong 1-year earnings potential. This short-term outlook tends to result in rapid trading techniques based on capital appreciation or earnings disappointments. Despite the high portfolio turnover ratio, the fund has returned a brilliant 150% during the past 5 years including 1991's strong showing. Furthermore, a loss was avoided in both 1987 and 1990, 2 difficult years for portfolio managers.

Portfolio Manager: Robert S. Bacarella
Since: 1986

Minimum:
Initial: $100
Subsequent: $50
Telephone Exchange: No
Distributions:
Income: Annually
Capital Gain: Annually
Front-End Load: None
12b-1: None
Redemption Fee: None
Management Company: Monetta Financial Services
Ticker Symbol: MONTX

TOTAL RETURN (%)

1987	1988	1989	1990	1991	5-year	Bull Market	Bear Market
1.5	23.0	15.2	11.4	55.9	149.9	70.1	-23.3

INVESTMENT PORTFOLIO

Total Assets (mil.)	Current Yield	Turnover Ratio	Expense Ratio	Beta	Risk Return
$44	0.3%	207%	1.50%	0.92	0.10

MUTUAL BEACON FUND

Heine Securities
51 John F. Kennedy Parkway
Short Hills, NJ 07078
800-553-3014

Investment Objective: Run by the same portfolio manager as the highly acclaimed Mutual Shares Fund, this fund takes a patient, long-term approach to investing in stocks that sell at substantial discounts to their underlying asset values. Most of its cheap companies are experiencing severe difficulties, but their low valuations leave little room for further downside. Also reducing risk is the fund's enormous diversification; its portfolio consists of more than 200 stocks. While its contrarian tactics have not fared well in the narrow, earnings-driven market of the past 3 years, this fund promises excellent results with minimal risk over the long haul.

Portfolio Manager: Michael F. Price
Since: 1985

Minimum:
Initial: $50,000
Subsequent: $1,000
Telephone Exchange: No
Distributions:
Income: Annually
Capital Gain: Annually
Front-End Load: None
12b-1: None
Redemption Fee: None
Management Company: Heine Securities
Ticker Symbol: BEGRX

TOTAL RETURN (%)

1987	1988	1989	1990	1991	5-year	Bull Market	Bear Market
12.7	28.9	17.5	-8.2	17.6	84.3	20.4	-13.1

INVESTMENT PORTFOLIO

Total Assets (mil.)	Current Yield	Turnover Ratio	Expense Ratio	Beta	Risk Return
$404	3.1%	57%	0.85%	0.53	0.04

MUTUAL OF OMAHA GROWTH FUND

Mutual of Omaha Fund
10235 Regency Circle
Omaha, NE 68114
800-228-9596

Investment Objective: Given its medium to small cap focus, this fund's trailing 5-year results are much better than would be expected. At a time when small stocks greatly underperformed blue chips, the fund outgained roughly two-thirds of its growth-fund competitors. Its success owes to strong 1988, 1989 and 1991 performances, which, in turn, reflect its taste for above-average earnings, strong balance sheets and reasonable valuations. Expect the fund to continue to produce respectable long-term returns, but don't count on a smooth ride.

Portfolio Manager: Eugenia Simpson
Since: 1986

Minimum:
Initial: $1,000
Subsequent: $50
Telephone Exchange: Yes
Distributions:
Income: Annually
Capital Gain: Annually
Front-End Load: 4.75%
12b-1: 0.25%
Redemption Fee: None
Management Company: Mutual of Omaha Fund Management
Ticker Symbol: MOMGX

TOTAL RETURN (%)

1987	1988	1989	1990	1991	5-year	Bull Market	Bear Market
-3.4	23.0	33.6	-8.4	62.4	136.1	59.0	-33.4

INVESTMENT PORTFOLIO

Total Assets (mil.)	Current Yield	Turnover Ratio	Expense Ratio	Beta	Risk Return
$77	0.2%	44%	1.29%	1.39	0.08

NEUBERGER & BERMAN GUARDIAN FUND

Neuberger & Berman
605 Third Avenue, 2nd Floor
New York, NY 10158
800-877-9700

Investment Objective: This fund's dual emphasis on growth and value usually enables it to produce highly competitive results in most markets. Management's affinity for above-average growth companies that sell cheaply causes the fund to stress out-of-favor sectors, including consumer durables, transportation, energy and industrial products. The fund sports an impressive 5-year return figure. Moreover, it stands to benefit handsomely on signs of renewed economic growth. The fund's mix of stock sizes also should prevent it from being left behind if market leadership rotates to smaller stocks.

Portfolio Manager: Kent Simons
Since: 1982

Minimum:
Initial: $1,000
Subsequent: $100
Telephone Exchange: Yes
Distributions:
Income: Quarterly
Capital Gain: Annually
Front-End Load: None
12b-1: None
Redemption Fee: None
Management Company: Neuberger & Berman Management
Ticker Symbol: NGUAX

TOTAL RETURN (%)

1987	1988	1989	1990	1991	5-year	Bull Market	Bear Market
-1.0	28.0	21.5	-4.7	34.3	97.1	47.1	-21.3

INVESTMENT PORTFOLIO

Total Assets (mil.)	Current Yield	Turnover Ratio	Expense Ratio	Beta	Risk Return
$606	2.0%	59%	0.84%	1.09	0.05

NEUBERGER & BERMAN MANHATTAN FUND

Neuberger & Berman
605 Third Avenue, 2nd Floor
New York, NY 10158
800-877-9700

Investment Objective: Neuberger & Berman Manhattan Fund keeps an even keel. The fund, which stresses above-average growth at a reasonable price, has produced consistently moderate returns in almost every year this past decade. Its success owes to a number of factors, including its preference for quality companies, its price consciousness and its practice of keeping market-level representation in most major sectors. A no-load format and reasonable expenses make this well-managed fund a fine choice for moderate growth investors.

Portfolio Manager: Irwin Lainoff
Since: 1974

Minimum:
Initial: $1,000
Subsequent: $100
Telephone Exchange: Yes
Distributions:
Income: Annually
Capital Gain: Annually
Front-End Load: None
12b-1: None
Redemption Fee: None
Management Company: Neuberger & Berman Management
Ticker Symbol: NMANX

TOTAL RETURN (%)

1987	1988	1989	1990	1991	5-year	Bull Market	Bear Market
0.1	18.3	29.1	-8.0	30.9	83.9	38.2	-22.1

INVESTMENT PORTFOLIO

Total Assets (mil.)	Current Yield	Turnover Ratio	Expense Ratio	Beta	Risk Return
$402	0.9%	78%	1.10%	1.11	0.05

NEUBERGER & BERMAN PARTNERS FUND

Neuberger & Berman
605 Third Avenue, 2nd Floor
New York, NY 10158
800-877-9700

Investment Objective: Neuberger & Berman Partners Fund was designed for the cautious investor. Giving top priority to capital preservation, the fund stresses relatively inexpensive growth stocks. Most of its companies show strong underlying fundamentals but sell at depressed valuations because of negative market sentiment and/or temporary difficulties. Despite the fact that the stock market has been lead by growth stocks demonstrating earnings momentum, the fund has performed reasonably well over the long term. It ranks in the top third of all funds in terms of performance during the past 5- and 10-year periods. Although its recent returns have been modest, it offers good downside protection.

Portfolio Manager: Mike Kassen
Since: 1990

Minimum:
Initial: $1,000
Subsequent: $100
Telephone Exchange: Yes
Distributions:
Income: Semiannually
Capital Gain: Semiannually
Front-End Load: None
12b-1: None
Redemption Fee: None
Management Company: Neuberger & Berman Management
Ticker Symbol: NPRTX

TOTAL RETURN (%)

1987	1988	1989	1990	1991	5-year	Bull Market	Bear Market
4.3	15.5	22.8	-5.1	22.4	71.7	29.0	-15.7

INVESTMENT PORTFOLIO

Total Assets (mil.)	Current Yield	Turnover Ratio	Expense Ratio	Beta	Risk Return
$813	1.8%	161%	0.88%	0.86	0.04

NEW ALTERNATIVES FUND

New Alternatives Fund
295 Northern Boulevard, Suite 300
Great Neck, NY 11021
516-466-0808

Investment Objective: This fund's most interesting feature is its unusual minimum initial investment requirement. The odd amount ensures that after the 5.66% front-end load, the management company will have $2,500 left to invest—a not-so inconvenient amount. In addition, this fund invests at least 25% of its assets in alternative sources of energy, primarily solar and geothermal operations. As a result, fund returns are highly correlated to the performance of energy stocks. It is suitable only to investors willing to bet heavily on this sector.

Portfolio Manager: Maurice Schoenwald
Since: 1982

Minimum:
Initial: $2,650
Subsequent: $1,000
Telephone Exchange: No
Distributions:
Income: Annually
Capital Gain: Annually
Front-End Load: 5.66%
12b-1: None
Redemption Fee: None
Management Company: Accrued Equities
Ticker Symbol: NALFX

TOTAL RETURN (%)

1987	1988	1989	1990	1991	5-year	Bull Market	Bear Market
-3.2	23.9	26.1	-7.6	25.5	75.4	31.7	-16.1

INVESTMENT PORTFOLIO

Total Assets (mil.)	Current Yield	Turnover Ratio	Expense Ratio	Beta	Risk Return
$22	1.3%	25%	1.27%	0.79	0.05

NEW ECONOMY FUND

American Funds Distributor
333 South Hope Street, 52nd Floor
Los Angeles, CA 90071
800-421-9900

Investment Objective: This fund attempts to capitalize on the rapid growth prospects of the services sector. Neglecting manufacturing stocks, it concentrates moneys in service industries, such as broadcasting, publishing and telecommunications. Like most American Funds offerings, the fund is highly disciplined. Extensive research, strict quality/value parameters and an effective use of cash allowed it to outperform most rivals from its 1984 inception to 1989. Interestingly, the fund's value bent has caused it to underperform the S&P 500 Index during the past 2 years when growth stocks with earnings momentum were the market's best-performing issue.

Portfolio Manager: Multiple Portfolio Counselors
Since: 1991

Minimum:
Initial: $1,000
Subsequent: $250
Telephone Exchange: Yes
Distributions:
Income: Annually
Capital Gain: Annually
Front-End Load: 5.75%
12b-1: 0.16%
Redemption Fee: None
Management Company: Capital Research & Management
Ticker Symbol: ANEFX

TOTAL RETURN (%)

1987	1988	1989	1990	1991	5-year	Bull Market	Bear Market
5.2	15.7	31.8	-10.1	29.2	86.3	37.6	-25.1

INVESTMENT PORTFOLIO

Total Assets (mil.)	Current Yield	Turnover Ratio	Expense Ratio	Beta	Risk Return
$908	1.1%	17%	0.92%	1.07	0.04

NEW ENGLAND RETIREMENT EQUITY FUND

TNE Investment Services
399 Boylston Street, 8th Floor
Boston, MA 02116
800-343-7104

Investment Objective: Under the direction of new manager Jeb Bailey, this fund is beginning to merit the defensive image its name implies. In sharp contrast to the aggressive, earnings-momentum strategy employed by his predecessor, Ken Heebner, Bailey stresses a diversified portfolio of low-multiple common stocks. Although the fund's new conservative tactics backfired during 1990's earnings-driven market, they should provide an attractive risk/reward profile over the long haul.

Portfolio Manager: Jeb Bailey
Since: 1990

Minimum:
Initial: $1,000
Subsequent: $25
Telephone Exchange: Yes
Distributions:
Income: Annually
Capital Gain: Annually
Front-End Load: 6.50%
12b-1: 0.25%
Redemption Fee: None
Management Company: Loomis Sayles
Ticker Symbol: NELQX

TOTAL RETURN (%)

1987	1988	1989	1990	1991	5-year	Bull Market	Bear Market
11.7	-2.2	22.6	-13.6	27.1	46.9	39.4	-27.5

INVESTMENT PORTFOLIO

Total Assets (mil.)	Current Yield	Turnover Ratio	Expense Ratio	Beta	Risk Return
$132	1.8%	8%	1.31%	1.16	0.04

NEWTON GROWTH FUND

Newton Funds
411 East Wisconsin Avenue
Milwaukee, WI 53202
800-242-7229

Investment Objective: Newton Growth Fund seeks long-term capital growth primarily through investment in common stocks. Current management pursues a fairly cautious approach, stressing relatively cheap, large capitalization stocks with earnings prospects that it believes have been overly discounted by the market. The fund's major industries, which include industrial products, technology, services, transportation and finance, highlight the fund's emphasis on both value and growth. Although it is yet to be the case, the fund's current strategy should produce improved long-term results.

Portfolio Manager: Anthony Leszczynski
Since: 1990

Minimum:
Initial: $1,000
Subsequent: $25
Telephone Exchange: Yes
Distributions:
Income: Semiannually
Capital Gain: Annually
Front-End Load: None
12b-1: None
Redemption Fee: None
Management Company: M & I Investment Management
Ticker Symbol: NEWTX

TOTAL RETURN (%)

1987	1988	1989	1990	1991	5-year	Bull Market	Bear Market
-3.6	12.8	19.0	-4.5	25.8	55.3	28.2	-17.1

INVESTMENT PORTFOLIO

Total Assets (mil.)	Current Yield	Turnover Ratio	Expense Ratio	Beta	Risk Return
$35	4.7%	65%	1.30%	0.93	0.04

NEW YORK VENTURE FUND

Venture Advisers
P.O. Box 1688
Santa Fe, NM 87501
800-279-0279

Investment Objective: New York Venture Fund has been a consistent winner. Longtime manager Shelby Davis pursues a moderate value discipline. Trading slowly, he stresses financially strong companies with earnings prospects that he believes are unrecognized by the market. Although Davis rarely neglects any major industry group, his value parameters inevitably cause him to overweight out-of-favor sectors. Financial and consumer cyclical stocks, for example, usually claim a high percentage of the fund's assets. Nevertheless, this fund's 5-year track record is matched by few rivals.

Portfolio Manager: Shelby Davis
Since: 1969

Minimum:
Initial: $1,000
Subsequent: $25
Telephone Exchange: Yes
Distributions:
Income: Semiannually
Capital Gain: Annually
Front-End Load: 4.75%
12b-1: 0.05%
Redemption Fee: None
Management Company: Venture Advisers
Ticker Symbol: NYVTX

TOTAL RETURN (%)

1987	1988	1989	1990	1991	5-year	Bull Market	Bear Market
-1.5	21.4	34.6	-2.9	40.5	119.7	42.6	-19.1

INVESTMENT PORTFOLIO

Total Assets (mil.)	Current Yield	Turnover Ratio	Expense Ratio	Beta	Risk Return
$404	1.6%	47%	0.97%	1.03	0.07

NICHOLAS FUND

Nicholas Company
700 North Water Street, Suite 1010
Milwaukee, WI 53202
800-227-5987

Investment Objective: This no-load fund successfully achieves its objective of providing long-term capital growth and moderate risk through investments in mid-sized companies. Manager Albert Nicholas is best described as a price-conscious growth investor. Most of the fund's quality companies show above-average earnings growth, high returns on earnings, low leverage and strong franchises, but sell at low valuations. Although the fund has delivered an average performance during the past 5 years (compared to the S&P 500 Index), the fund has outperformed most other funds that emphasize smaller companies. The past year's return is illustrative of performance potential when small cap stocks began to shine.

Portfolio Manager: Albert O. Nicholas
Since: 1969

Minimum:
Initial: $500
Subsequent: $100
Telephone Exchange: Yes
Distributions:
Income: Annually
Capital Gain: Annually
Front-End Load: None
12b-1: None
Redemption Fee: None
Management Company: Nicholas Company
Ticker Symbol: NICSX

TOTAL RETURN (%)

1987	1988	1989	1990	1991	5-year	Bull Market	Bear Market
-0.8	18.0	24.5	-4.8	42.0	97.1	49.7	-22.8

INVESTMENT PORTFOLIO

Total Assets (mil.)	Current Yield	Turnover Ratio	Expense Ratio	Beta	Risk Return
$1,872	1.4%	22%	0.81%	0.99	0.07

NICHOLAS II

Nicholas Company
700 North Water Street, Suite 1010
Milwaukee, WI 53202
800-227-5987

Investment Objective: Despite its focus on small companies with market values below $500 million, the fund has held its own in the large-cap-driven market of the past 8 years. Its success owes to excellent stock selection. Manager Albert Nicholas likes highly profitable, stable growth companies that sell at reasonable valuations. Mundane industries such as finance, consumer durables, business services and retail claim a large portion of the fund's assets. The defensive characteristics inherent in this approach are seen in the fund's modest beta and its decent resistance to decline during 1990 when small cap stocks declined an average of 22%.

Portfolio Manager: Albert O. Nicholas
Since: 1983

Minimum:
Initial: $1,000
Subsequent: $100
Telephone Exchange: Yes
Distributions:
Income: Annually
Capital Gain: Annually
Front-End Load: None
12b-1: None
Redemption Fee: None
Management Company: Nicholas Company
Ticker Symbol: NCTWX

TOTAL RETURN (%)

1987	1988	1989	1990	1991	5-year	Bull Market	Bear Market
7.8	17.3	17.7	-6.2	39.6	94.7	46.5	-21.1

INVESTMENT PORTFOLIO

Total Assets (mil.)	Current Yield	Turnover Ratio	Expense Ratio	Beta	Risk Return
$502	1.0%	19%	0.71%	0.83	0.08

NORTHEAST INVESTORS GROWTH FUND

Northeast Investors Trust
50 Congress Street, Suite 1000
Boston, MA 02109
800-225-6704

Investment Objective: This fund pursues its capital-appreciation objective primarily through investments in large capitalization common stocks that management believes sell at a discount to their underlying earnings growth. Still, most of the fund's companies command well-above market multiples, evidencing management's willingness to pay up growth. Expensive, stable growth sectors, including health care, household products and foods, are most prominent. Needless to say, with its big cap, stable-growth bias, the fund has had the wind at its back for 3 straight years.

Portfolio Manager: William Oates, Jr.
Since: 1980

Minimum:
Initial: $1,000
Subsequent: None
Telephone Exchange: Yes
Distributions:
Income: Annually
Capital Gain: Annually
Front-End Load: None
12b-1: None
Redemption Fee: None
Management Company: Northeast Management & Research
Ticker Symbol: NTHFX

TOTAL RETURN (%)

1987	1988	1989	1990	1991	5-year	Bull Market	Bear Market
-3.6	12.8	32.9	1.4	37.0	100.8	33.9	-16.3

INVESTMENT PORTFOLIO

Total Assets (mil.)	Current Yield	Turnover Ratio	Expense Ratio	Beta	Risk Return
$34	1.1%	37%	1.74%	1.00	0.06

OPPENHEIMER FUND

Oppenheimer Fund Management
P.O. Box 300
Denver, CO 80201
800-255-2755

Investment Objective: This fund seeks capital appreciation primarily through investments in common stocks. Management relies heavily on top-down analysis to identify industries with above-average prospects for growth that have yet to be recognized by the market. The fund's major industries, which include energy, industrial products and insurance, underscore its affinity for relatively cheap sectors with good earnings momentum. Although the fund has delivered average returns in recent years, it has the potential to provide better-than-average returns in a value-driven market.

Portfolio Manager: Richard Rubinstein
Since: 1990

Minimum:
Initial: $1,000
Subsequent: $25
Telephone Exchange: Yes
Distributions:
Income: Quarterly
Capital Gain: Annually
Front-End Load: 5.75%
12b-1: None
Redemption Fee: None
Management Company: Oppenheimer Management
Ticker Symbol: OPPFX

TOTAL RETURN (%)

1987	1988	1989	1990	1991	5-year	Bull Market	Bear Market
-2.9	8.3	23.7	-4.5	30.3	62.0	38.4	-16.8

INVESTMENT PORTFOLIO

Total Assets (mil.)	Current Yield	Turnover Ratio	Expense Ratio	Beta	Risk Return
$211	3.0%	80%	1.04%	0.87	0.06

OPPENHEIMER SPECIAL FUND

Oppenheimer Fund Management
P.O. Box 300
Denver, CO 80201
800-255-2755

Investment Objective: This fund seeks capital appreciation primarily through investments in common stocks. Under the direction of current manager Robert Doll since 1987, the fund has pursued a moderate approach, stressing both growth and value. Most of the fund's companies show above-average profitability and growth in earnings. However, negative market sentiment toward their industries has kept valuations low. Unpopular financial, technology, basic industry and retail stocks claim a large portion of the fund's assets. Nevertheless, it showed decent resistance to decline in 1990's bear market. It then delivered a stellar return the past year as both financial and technology stocks rebounded smartly.

Portfolio Manager: Robert Doll, Jr.
Since: 1987

Minimum:
Initial: $1,000
Subsequent: $25
Telephone Exchange: Yes
Distributions:
Income: Annually
Capital Gain: Annually
Front-End Load: 5.75%
12b-1: 0.01%
Redemption Fee: None
Management Company: Oppenheimer Management
Ticker Symbol: OPPSX

TOTAL RETURN (%)

1987	1988	1989	1990	1991	5-year	Bull Market	Bear Market
-9.2	18.1	21.3	-2.5	44.0	82.7	56.5	-25.0

INVESTMENT PORTFOLIO

Total Assets (mil.)	Current Yield	Turnover Ratio	Expense Ratio	Beta	Risk Return
$579	1.3%	31%	0.94%	1.06	0.07

PAINEWEBBER BLUE CHIP GROWTH FUND B

PaineWebber
1285 Avenue of the Americas
New York, NY 10019
800-647-1568

Investment Objective: This back-end load fund seeks capital appreciation by investing at least 65% of its assets in companies with market capitalizations above $300 million. The remainder of its assets may be allocated to smaller companies or various debt instruments. The fund nailed the growth-fund average on the head in 1991 with its 32.7% return. Its 5-year return trails the industry average mainly because of its poor showing in 1987 and 1990, and the fund's 0.0% yield provides little downside protection in bear markets.

Portfolio Manager: Whitney Merrill
Since: 1988

Minimum:
Initial: $1,000
Subsequent: $100
Telephone Exchange: No
Distributions:
Income: Annually
Capital Gain: Annually
Front-End Load: None
12b-1: 0.79%
Redemption Fee: 5.00%
Management Company: Mitchell Hutchins Asset Management
Ticker Symbol: PBLBX

TOTAL RETURN (%)

1987	1988	1989	1990	1991	5-year	Bull Market	Bear Market
-2.1	17.9	30.4	-11.6	32.7	76.6	30.9	-22.7

INVESTMENT PORTFOLIO

Total Assets (mil.)	Current Yield	Turnover Ratio	Expense Ratio	Beta	Risk Return
$101	0.0%	43%	1.87%	1.01	0.05

PAINEWEBBER GROWTH FUND

PaineWebber
1285 Avenue of the Americas
New York, NY 10019
800-647-1568

Investment Objective: This fund attempts to provide long-term capital appreciation by investing at least 65% of its assets in common stocks. The fund may invest in both mature growth companies or in smaller issues. The fund returned a strong 48% in 1991, which helped boost the fund's 5-year return to almost 134%. Management looks to identify hot growth industries and then select the firms that will lead these particular areas. A deft touch, moderate expenses and low turnover has thus far rewarded shareholders. About the only knock on the fund is the 4.50% front-end load.

Portfolio Manager: Ellen Harris
Since: 1985

Minimum:
Initial: $1,000
Subsequent: $100
Telephone Exchange: No
Distributions:
Income: Annually
Capital Gain: Annually
Front-End Load: 4.50%
12b-1: 0.25%
Redemption Fee: None
Management Company: Mitchell Hutchins Asset Management
Ticker Symbol: PGRAX

TOTAL RETURN (%)

1987	1988	1989	1990	1991	5-year	Bull Market	Bear Market
4.5	22.1	34.3	-7.7	47.9	133.9	30.1	-18.9

INVESTMENT PORTFOLIO

Total Assets (mil.)	Current Yield	Turnover Ratio	Expense Ratio	Beta	Risk Return
$97	0.0%	39%	1.60%	1.02	0.05

PARNASSUS FUND

Parnassus Financial Management
244 California Street, Suite 210
San Francisco, CA 94111
800-999-3505

Investment Objective: This fund, which emphasizes investment in socially conscious companies, also seeks companies selling at depressed prices relative to both the market and their own price/earnings multiple histories. The fund's social criteria include: the quality of the company's products and services, the degree to which the company is customer responsive, the company's treatment of employees, the sensitivity of the company to the community where it operates and the company's ability to innovate and respond well to change. Management expects each stock to have a market price no more than 125% of book value per share except for smaller companies, which may have a market price of up to 175% of book value.

Portfolio Manager: Jerome L. Dodson
Since: 1985

Minimum:
Initial: $2,000
Subsequent: $1,000
Telephone Exchange: No
Distributions:
Income: Annually
Capital Gain: Annually
Front-End Load: 3.50%
12b-1: None
Redemption Fee: None
Management Company: Parnassus Financial Management
Ticker Symbol: PARNX

TOTAL RETURN (%)

1987	1988	1989	1990	1991	5-year	Bull Market	Bear Market
-8.0	42.4	2.8	-21.2	52.6	62.2	59.5	-33.6

INVESTMENT PORTFOLIO

Total Assets (mil.)	Current Yield	Turnover Ratio	Expense Ratio	Beta	Risk Return
$29	0.2%	38%	1.77%	1.11	0.08

PENNSYLVANIA MUTUAL FUND

Pennsylvania Mutual Fund
1414 Avenue of the Americas
New York, NY 10019
800-221-4268

Investment Objective: This fund invests primarily in stocks with market values between $15 million and $300 million. Manager Charles Royce invests cautiously, relying on a strict value discipline, broad diversification and an effective use of cash to mitigate the volatility normally associated with small stocks. Comprised of more than 600 stocks, the portfolio stresses financially strong, established companies that management believes are undervalued; most sell at large discounts to book value. This approach has enabled the fund to produce solid results in most years despite the market's focus on large stocks.

Portfolio Manager: Charles M. Royce
Since: 1973

Minimum:
Initial: $2,000
Subsequent: $50
Telephone Exchange: No
Distributions:
Income: Annually
Capital Gain: Annually
Front-End Load: None
12b-1: None
Redemption Fee: 1.00%
Management Company: Quest Advisory
Ticker Symbol: PENNX

TOTAL RETURN (%)

1987	1988	1989	1990	1991	5-year	Bull Market	Bear Market
1.4	24.6	16.7	-11.5	31.8	71.9	36.8	-19.9

INVESTMENT PORTFOLIO

Total Assets (mil.)	Current Yield	Turnover Ratio	Expense Ratio	Beta	Risk Return
$723	1.6%	15%	0.96%	0.69	0.07

PHOENIX CAPITAL APPRECIATION FUND

Phoenix Equity Planning
100 Bright Meadow Boulevard
Enfield, CT 06082
800-243-4361

Investment Objective: Phoenix Capital Appreciation's 2-year return of 77.1% falls just 12% below the 5-year growth-fund average of 89.4%. If one considers that the S&P 500 returned almost 62% from 1987 to 1989, this performance becomes astounding. Amazingly, the fund returned more than 20% in 1990 and followed that up with a 47% showing in 1991. The high turnover ratio can be attributed to the strict discipline the fund follows when selling stocks. The fund's fairly liberal charter allows it to invest in small or blue chip stocks, foreign securities and noninvestment grade bonds.

Portfolio Manager: R. Chesek/C. Dudley
Since: 1990

Minimum:
Initial: $500
Subsequent: $25
Telephone Exchange: Yes
Distributions:
Income: Annually
Capital Gain: Annually
Front-End Load: 4.75%
12b-1: 0.25%
Redemption Fee: None
Management Company: Phoenix Investment Counsel
Ticker Symbol: PHCPX

TOTAL RETURN (%)

1987	1988	1989	1990	1991	5-year	Bull Market	Bear Market
NA	NA	NA	20.4	47.1	NA	38.1	-9.4

INVESTMENT PORTFOLIO

Total Assets (mil.)	Current Yield	Turnover Ratio	Expense Ratio	Beta	Risk Return
$96	1.1%	445%	NA	NA	NA

PHOENIX GROWTH FUND

Phoenix Equity Planning
100 Bright Meadow Boulevard
Enfield, CT 06082
800-243-4361

Investment Objective: Investing primarily in large capitalization common stocks, this fund follows a moderate growth strategy. Management favors highly profitable industry leaders with the ability to sustain growth regardless of the economic environment. Although the fund has representation in most major industries, it overweights stable-growth consumer nondurables and services. Excellent stock selection and an effective use of cash and bonds have enabled this fund to achieve better-than-average return relative to its risk. Relative returns may slow if leadership rotates to small caps. Still, this is an excellent choice for conservative growth investors.

Portfolio Manager: R. Chesek/C. Dudley
Since: 1980

Minimum:
Initial: $500
Subsequent: $25
Telephone Exchange: Yes
Distributions:
Income: Semiannually
Capital Gain: Annually
Front-End Load: 4.75%
12b-1: None
Redemption Fee: None
Management Company: Phoenix Investment Counsel
Ticker Symbol: PHGRX

TOTAL RETURN (%)

1987	1988	1989	1990	1991	5-year	Bull Market	Bear Market
11.2	7.0	27.5	6.1	22.3	96.6	34.3	-13.3

INVESTMENT PORTFOLIO

Total Assets (mil.)	Current Yield	Turnover Ratio	Expense Ratio	Beta	Risk Return
$1,268	1.9%	203%	1.01%	0.71	0.05

PHOENIX STOCK FUND

Phoenix Equity Planning
100 Bright Meadow Boulevard
Enfield, CT 06082
800-243-4361

Investment Objective: Although this fund has an aggressive beta, a hint of its aggressive trading tactics can be gleaned from its unusually high portfolio turnover ratio, which is among the highest in the industry. Like most Phoenix-managed funds, this fund stresses expensive, rapid-growth stocks. Most of its midsized selections show at least 20% annual earnings growth and most command high price/earnings ratios. However, historically high cash and bond investment positions have enabled the fund to keep risk quite moderate. To management's credit is the fact that this high turnover fund ranks among the top 10% of all funds in terms of 10-year return.

Portfolio Manager: Michael Matty
Since: 1990

Minimum:
Initial: $500
Subsequent: $25
Telephone Exchange: Yes
Distributions:
Income: Semiannually
Capital Gain: Annually
Front-End Load: 4.75%
12b-1: None
Redemption Fee: None
Management Company: Phoenix Investment Counsel
Ticker Symbol: PHSKX

TOTAL RETURN (%)

1987	1988	1989	1990	1991	5-year	Bull Market	Bear Market
10.9	4.5	21.6	-5.6	29.6	72.5	42.6	-23.0

INVESTMENT PORTFOLIO

Total Assets (mil.)	Current Yield	Turnover Ratio	Expense Ratio	Beta	Risk Return
$118	1.5%	407%	1.07%	0.99	0.05

PINE STREET FUND

Wood Struthers & Winthrop
140 Broadway, 42nd Floor
New York, NY 10005
800-225-8011

Investment Objective: This fund seeks continuity of current income and capital growth by investing primarily in blue chip common stocks. To a lesser degree, it also invests in fixed-income securities. Equity investments stress moderately priced, dividend-paying blue chips that management believes are underpriced relative to their underlying business value. While the fund successfully achieves a market-level income stream with moderate risk, long-term total returns have been unexciting.

Portfolio Manager: Jim Engle
Since: 1986

Minimum:
Initial: $1,000
Subsequent: $50
Telephone Exchange: No
Distributions:
Income: Quarterly
Capital Gain: Annually
Front-End Load: None
12b-1: None
Redemption Fee: None
Management Company: Wood Struthers & Winthrop
Ticker Symbol: PINSX

TOTAL RETURN (%)

1987	1988	1989	1990	1991	5-year	Bull Market	Bear Market
-5.9	16.2	24.8	-3.1	23.7	63.7	26.9	-14.0

INVESTMENT PORTFOLIO

Total Assets (mil.)	Current Yield	Turnover Ratio	Expense Ratio	Beta	Risk Return
$46	2.6%	41%	1.21%	0.72	0.05

PIONEER II

Pioneer Funds Distributor
60 State Street
Boston, MA 02109
800-225-6292

Investment Objective: Investing in a mix of large and medium-sized companies, this conservative fund relies heavily on fundamental analysis to identify quality, stable growth companies that sell at reasonable valuations. Its refusal to pay high multiples prevents the fund from exposure to volatile, emerging-growth stocks. Most of its fairly mature companies operate in mundane, moderate growth industries. Management looks to further mitigate risk and ensure at least moderate returns in most markets by keeping a well-diversified portfolio with market-level representation in most major industries. It has been an average performer during the past 10 years.

Portfolio Manager: David Tripple
Since: 1979

Minimum:
Initial: $50
Subsequent: $25
Telephone Exchange: Yes
Distributions:
Income: Semiannually
Capital Gain: Annually
Front-End Load: 5.75%
12b-1: None
Redemption Fee: None
Management Company: Pioneer Management
Ticker Symbol: PIOTX

TOTAL RETURN (%)

1987	1988	1989	1990	1991	5-year	Bull Market	Bear Market
-0.3	21.8	22.2	-12.0	25.8	64.1	30.6	-20.7

INVESTMENT PORTFOLIO

Total Assets (mil.)	Current Yield	Turnover Ratio	Expense Ratio	Beta	Risk Return
$3,901	2.5%	42%	0.75%	0.87	0.05

PIONEER THREE

Pioneer Funds Distributor
60 State Street
Boston, MA 02109
800-225-6292

Investment Objective: As the "grandchild" of the consistently strong Pioneer Fund, this fund follows confidently in its footsteps. To achieve its objective of growth of capital and a reasonable amount of income, the fund invests in common stocks of small to medium-sized companies. Like most Pioneer-managed vehicles, the fund follows a buy-and-hold strategy (as evidenced by its exceptionally low portfolio turnover rate). Management invests in fundamentally sound, stable growth companies that it believes are undervalued. A broadly diversified portfolio with representation in most major market sectors further evidences this fund's affinity to its Pioneer siblings. This fund promises consistent moderate results in most markets.

Portfolio Manager: Robert Benson
Since: 1986

Minimum:
Initial: $1,000
Subsequent: $100
Telephone Exchange: Yes
Distributions:
Income: Semiannually
Capital Gain: Annually
Front-End Load: 5.75%
12b-1: None
Redemption Fee: None
Management Company: Pioneer Management
Ticker Symbol: PITHX

TOTAL RETURN (%)

1987	1988	1989	1990	1991	5-year	Bull Market	Bear Market
-7.9	30.0	20.5	-13.0	36.5	71.3	41.3	-22.3

INVESTMENT PORTFOLIO

Total Assets (mil.)	Current Yield	Turnover Ratio	Expense Ratio	Beta	Risk Return
$671	2.0%	14%	0.71%	0.89	0.07

PIPER JAFFRAY INVESTMENT VALUE FUND

Piper Jaffray & Hopwood
222 South 9th Street
Minneapolis, MN 55402
800-333-6000

Investment Objective: This fund seeks long-term capital appreciation primarily by investing in common stocks that appear undervalued relative to their earnings power. Management's taste for companies with above-average stable earnings growth causes the fund to overweight recession-resistant industries such as food, services and health care. Because these industries have led the market over the past 3 years, the fund has been a strong performer. While market conditions won't always be so favorable, the fund's mix of stock sizes and its broad industry diversification suggests at least moderate results in most years.

Portfolio Manager: John J. Tauer, Jr.
Since: 1987

Minimum:
Initial: $250
Subsequent: $100
Telephone Exchange: No
Distributions:
Income: Quarterly
Capital Gain: Annually
Front-End Load: 4.00%
12b-1: 0.33%
Redemption Fee: None
Management Company: Piper Capital Management
Ticker Symbol: PJVLX

TOTAL RETURN (%)

1987	1988	1989	1990	1991	5-year	Bull Market	Bear Market
NA	12.2	39.2	1.2	47.9	NA	57.4	-21.9

INVESTMENT PORTFOLIO

Total Assets (mil.)	Current Yield	Turnover Ratio	Expense Ratio	Beta	Risk Return
$114	0.9%	37%	1.31%	1.16	0.08

PRINCOR CAPITAL ACCUMULATION FUND

Principal Financial Services
711 High Street
Des Moines, IA 50309
800-247-4123

Investment Objective: This fund seeks capital appreciation primarily by investing in common stocks selected on the basis of fundamental analysis. Management invests in a mix of stock types, including classic growth stocks, asset plays and turnarounds. Although it typically maintains exposure to most major industry groups, it tends to overweight unpopular, cheap sectors. Out-of-favor financial and technology stocks have been particularly prominent in recent years, largely explaining the fund's disappointing 1990 results. However, during the past year, the fund delivered a solid return as both financial and technology stocks returned to investor favor.

Portfolio Manager: Mike Hamilton
Since: 1987

Minimum:
Initial: $300
Subsequent: $50
Telephone Exchange: Yes
Distributions:
Income: Semiannually
Capital Gain: Annually
Front-End Load: 5.00%
12b-1: 0.14%
Redemption Fee: None
Management Company: Principal Management
Ticker Symbol: PCACX

TOTAL RETURN (%)

1987	1988	1989	1990	1991	5-year	Bull Market	Bear Market
6.2	13.9	14.7	-10.6	37.2	70.1	40.6	-21.2

INVESTMENT PORTFOLIO

Total Assets (mil.)	Current Yield	Turnover Ratio	Expense Ratio	Beta	Risk Return
$149	2.1%	28%	1.10%	0.99	0.07

PROVIDENT MUTUAL GROWTH FUND

Provident Mutual Financial Services
P.O. Box 15627
Wilmington, DE 19850
800-441-9490

Investment Objective: This fund aims for long-term growth of capital by investing in a wide range of companies. In selecting stocks, management seeks firms with sound balance sheets, an industry niche, strong management and earnings-growth prospects. The fund has demonstrated a bias toward small to midsized companies that helps to explain its 1991 return of 50%. Despite that showing, its 5-year average falls well short of the growth-fund average. This fund will be more volatile than a typical growth selection, but it also should offer superior long-run returns.

Portfolio Manager: Jim McCall
Since: 1990

Minimum:
Initial: None
Subsequent: None
Telephone Exchange: Yes
Distributions:
Income: Annually
Capital Gain: Annually
Front-End Load: 6.00%
12b-1: 0.25%
Redemption Fee: None
Management Company: Provident Mutual Management
Ticker Symbol: SGCPX

TOTAL RETURN (%)

1987	1988	1989	1990	1991	5-year	Bull Market	Bear Market
-1.8	11.1	11.6	-8.7	49.9	66.6	43.7	-25.8

INVESTMENT PORTFOLIO

Total Assets (mil.)	Current Yield	Turnover Ratio	Expense Ratio	Beta	Risk Return
$140	0.0%	36%	1.79%	1.16	0.10

PROVIDENT MUTUAL INVESTMENT SHARES

Provident Mutual Financial Services
P.O. Box 15627
Wilmington, DE 19850
800-441-9490

Investment Objective: This fund seeks long-term capital appreciation with income being a secondary consideration. Primarily, the fund purchases larger, established companies. These companies tend to be dividend payers with proven earnings records. This fund has returned half of what the average growth fund returned over the past 5 years. Much of this lackluster performance can be attributed to dismal 1990 and 1991 returns. During the past year, the fund returned just over 15%, while the S&P 500 was up 30%. Investors face a high beta, a 6.00% front-end load and 12b-1 fees with this offering.

Portfolio Manager: Robert Borkowski
Since: 1989

Minimum:
Initial: None
Subsequent: None
Telephone Exchange: Yes
Distributions:
Income: Quarterly
Capital Gain: Annually
Front-End Load: 6.00%
12b-1: 0.25%
Redemption Fee: None
Management Company: Provident Mutual Management
Ticker Symbol: SGIVX

TOTAL RETURN (%)

1987	1988	1989	1990	1991	5-year	Bull Market	Bear Market
3.2	11.6	28.8	-15.9	15.4	44.0	38.7	-24.2

INVESTMENT PORTFOLIO

Total Assets (mil.)	Current Yield	Turnover Ratio	Expense Ratio	Beta	Risk Return
$190	1.1%	62%	1.37%	1.15	0.08

PUTNAM VISTA FUND

Putnam Financial Services
One Post Office Square, 12th Floor
Boston, MA 02109
800-634-1590

Investment Objective: As its name suggests, this fund pursues its capital-appreciation objective by investing in companies that management believes are undervalued. Manager Gerald Zukowski adheres to the same strategy that is responsible for the long-term success of Boston Company Capital Appreciation Fund, which he formerly ran. He stresses companies that he believes sell at a discount to their underlying growth rates and/or asset values. Like most value players, the fund got caught with too many financial and industrial stocks during 1990. Still, Zukowski's excellent record suggests long-term shareholders will be amply rewarded for their patience.

Portfolio Manager: Gerald Zukowski
Since: 1989

Minimum:
Initial: $500
Subsequent: $50
Telephone Exchange: Yes
Distributions:
Income: Semiannually
Capital Gain: Annually
Front-End Load: 5.75%
12b-1: 0.16%
Redemption Fee: None
Management Company: Putnam Management Company
Ticker Symbol: PVISX

TOTAL RETURN (%)

1987	1988	1989	1990	1991	5-year	Bull Market	Bear Market
4.9	14.8	25.7	-7.0	37.2	93.0	46.7	-21.3

INVESTMENT PORTFOLIO

Total Assets (mil.)	Current Yield	Turnover Ratio	Expense Ratio	Beta	Risk Return
$279	2.3%	76%	0.99%	0.95	0.07

QUEST FOR VALUE FUND

Quest for Value Distributor
World Financial Center
New York, NY 10281
800-232-3863

Investment Objective: This fund seeks capital appreciation through investments in equity securities of companies that it believes are undervalued in relation to their underlying assets and/or potential earnings. Management favors strong niche companies with good managements and with strong balance sheets. The fund's value parameters typically cause it to overweight relatively few cheap sectors, including capital goods and finance. Like many value players, the fund suffered during 1990 and rebounded smartly during the past year.

Portfolio Manager: Eileen Rominger
Since: 1989

Minimum:
Initial: $1,000
Subsequent: $250
Telephone Exchange: No
Distributions:
Income: Annually
Capital Gain: Annually
Front-End Load: 5.50%
12b-1: 0.50%
Redemption Fee: None
Management Company: Quest for Value Advisers
Ticker Symbol: QFVFX

TOTAL RETURN (%)

1987	1988	1989	1990	1991	5-year	Bull Market	Bear Market
-2.1	17.6	20.0	-6.9	32.8	70.9	39.2	-21.2

INVESTMENT PORTFOLIO

Total Assets (mil.)	Current Yield	Turnover Ratio	Expense Ratio	Beta	Risk Return
$102	0.6%	51%	1.82%	0.93	0.06

RAINBOW FUND

Furman Anderson & Company
19 Rector Street
New York, NY 10006
212-509-8532

Investment Objective: Rainbow Fund features a highly concentrated portfolio consisting of as few as 15 stocks, with top holdings claiming as much as 7% of its assets each. Trading rapidly, management invests in an eclectic mix of large capitalization growth companies, takeover/restructuring candidates and turnarounds. Unfortunately (with the exception of the past year), this eclectic approach hasn't rewarded investors well during the past 10 years as the fund's return was bested by more than 90% of the funds in existence over that period.

Portfolio Manager: Robert Furman
Since: 1974

Minimum:
Initial: $300
Subsequent: $50
Telephone Exchange: No
Distributions:
Income: Annually
Capital Gain: Annually
Front-End Load: None
12b-1: None
Redemption Fee: None
Management Company: Furman Anderson & Company
Ticker Symbol: RBOWX

TOTAL RETURN (%)

1987	1988	1989	1990	1991	5-year	Bull Market	Bear Market
-3.8	18.1	9.3	-9.7	38.0	54.7	41.0	-21.2

INVESTMENT PORTFOLIO

Total Assets (mil.)	Current Yield	Turnover Ratio	Expense Ratio	Beta	Risk Return
$2	0.9%	212%	3.41%	0.96	0.06

REICH & TANG EQUITY FUND

Reich & Tang
100 Park Avenue
New York, NY 10017
800-221-3079

Investment Objective: Reich & Tang Equity Fund is actually more of a growth and income vehicle than a pure growth fund. With a yield approaching that of the market, its portfolio of large capitalization value stocks is highly suitable for conservative equity investors. The fund's relatively low beta and competitive long-term returns attest to its attractive risk/reward characteristics. A no-load format, reasonable expenses and an exceptionally low portfolio turnover ratio are characteristics that might appeal to conservative, long-term investors.

Minimum:
Initial: $5,000
Subsequent: None
Telephone Exchange: Yes
Distributions:
Income: Quarterly
Capital Gain: Annually
Front-End Load: None
12b-1: None
Redemption Fee: None
Management Company: Reich & Tang
Ticker Symbol: RCHTX

Portfolio Manager: Robert F. Hoerle
Since: 1985

TOTAL RETURN (%)

1987	1988	1989	1990	1991	5-year	Bull Market	Bear Market
5.1	22.9	17.9	-5.8	21.5	74.3	30.5	-18.8

INVESTMENT PORTFOLIO

Total Assets (mil.)	Current Yield	Turnover Ratio	Expense Ratio	Beta	Risk Return
$76	2.3%	27%	1.12%	0.88	0.04

RETIREMENT PLAN FUNDS OF AMERICA EQUITY

Venture Advisers
P.O. Box 1688
Santa Fe, NM 87501
800-279-0279

Investment Objective: This retirement planning equity fund seeks capital appreciation by investing primarily in common stocks. Management maintains a fairly compact portfolio of some 30-odd stocks—mostly medium caps—that sell at relatively low price/earnings ratios and, in management's view, have the potential for earnings surprise. Ideally, the fund's stocks are poised to benefit simultaneously from an acceleration in earnings growth and a price/earnings multiple expansion. Given the fund's preference for relatively cheap stocks, its results in the earnings-driven market of the past 3 years have been surprisingly strong.

Minimum:
Initial: $1,000
Subsequent: $250
Telephone Exchange: Yes
Distributions:
Income: Semiannually
Capital Gain: Annually
Front-End Load: None
12b-1: 1.25%
Redemption Fee: 5.00%
Management Company: Venture Advisers
Ticker Symbol: RPFEX

Portfolio Manager: Graham Tanaka
Since: 1987

TOTAL RETURN (%)

1987	1988	1989	1990	1991	5-year	Bull Market	Bear Market
4.6	10.5	40.1	-4.7	40.9	117.4	55.5	-27.0

INVESTMENT PORTFOLIO

Total Assets (mil.)	Current Yield	Turnover Ratio	Expense Ratio	Beta	Risk Return
$38	0.8%	41%	2.62%	1.08	0.06

RIGHTIME BLUE CHIP FUND

Rightime Family of Funds
218 Glenside Avenue, Suite 3000
Wyncote, PA 19095
800-242-1421

Investment Objective: This fund seeks growth of capital while assuming reasonable risks by investing primarily in blue chip stocks. Its investments generally have capitalizations greater than $100 million, histories of positive earnings and cash dividend payments and high degrees of liquidity. It maintains a highly flexible investment policy and will assume an aggressive posture during bull markets and a defensive posture during bear markets. The fund periodically invests in stock options and futures. Thus, its shares tend to be more volatile than the typical blue chip equity fund. Its tendency to trade aggressively and a higher-than-average expense ratio have hampered returns since its inception 4 years ago.

Portfolio Manager: David J. Rights
Since: 1987

Minimum:
Initial: $2,000
Subsequent: $100
Telephone Exchange: Yes
Distributions:
Income: Annually
Capital Gain: Annually
Front-End Load: 4.75%
12b-1: 0.90%
Redemption Fee: None
Management Company: Rightime Econometrics
Ticker Symbol: RTBCX

TOTAL RETURN (%)

1987	1988	1989	1990	1991	5-year	Bull Market	Bear Market
NA	2.6	19.6	1.3	23.1	NA	23.1	-8.2

INVESTMENT PORTFOLIO

Total Assets (mil.)	Current Yield	Turnover Ratio	Expense Ratio	Beta	Risk Return
$180	1.0%	258%	2.35%	0.57	0.05

RODNEY SQUARE MULTI-MANAGER GROWTH FUND

Scudder Stevens & Clark
160 Federal Street
Boston, MA 02110
800-225-5084

Investment Objective: Led by 3 separate management teams, this fund seeks long-term capital growth. In a somewhat unique fashion, this fund's assets are divided among 3 advisers to help diversify across management styles. This strategy has been a mixed bag as the fund beat the S&P 500 in 1988 and 1991 but trailed the benchmark in 1989 and 1990. The past year, the fund outperformed the growth average by more than 9%. The fund has exhibited a buy-and-hold philosophy as its turnover is at the low end of the group.

Portfolio Manager: Management team
Since: 1987

Minimum:
Initial: $1,000
Subsequent: None
Telephone Exchange: Yes
Distributions:
Income: Quarterly
Capital Gain: Annually
Front-End Load: 5.75%
12b-1: 0.25%
Redemption Fee: None
Management Company: Rodney Square Management
Ticker Symbol: RMGPX

TOTAL RETURN (%)

1987	1988	1989	1990	1991	5-year	Bull Market	Bear Market
NA	20.9	27.2	-7.1	41.4	NA	28.4	-17.2

INVESTMENT PORTFOLIO

Total Assets (mil.)	Current Yield	Turnover Ratio	Expense Ratio	Beta	Risk Return
$50	0.4%	26%	1.50%	1.03	0.06

ROYCE VALUE FUND

Quest Distributors
1414 Avenue of the Americas
New York, NY 10019
800-221-4268

Investment Objective: This fund seeks long-term growth of capital primarily through investments in securities of small and medium-sized companies. Without deviating from its policy of looking for undervalued situations, the fund has created a respectable long-term record. Although it has recently felt the impact of the market's distaste for value stocks, the fund rose a strong 23.6% in the value-led market of 1988. In 1991, the fund produced a below-average, but highly respectable return of 30.7%. This fund has several good characteristics, but investors should be aware of the 2.50% front-end load, 2.00% redemption fee and an ongoing 12b-1 plan.

Portfolio Manager: Charles M. Royce
Since: 1982

Minimum:
Initial: $2,000
Subsequent: $50
Telephone Exchange: Yes
Distributions:
Income: Annually
Capital Gain: Annually
Front-End Load: 2.50%
12b-1: 0.60%
Redemption Fee: 2.00%
Management Company: Quest Advisory
Ticker Symbol: RYVFX

TOTAL RETURN (%)

1987	1988	1989	1990	1991	5-year	Bull Market	Bear Market
0.6	23.6	15.9	-13.6	30.7	62.8	35.4	-20.7

INVESTMENT PORTFOLIO

Total Assets (mil.)	Current Yield	Turnover Ratio	Expense Ratio	Beta	Risk Return
$160	1.0%	18%	1.88%	0.71	0.06

RUSHMORE OVER-THE-COUNTER INDEX PLUS FUND

Rushmore Funds
4922 Fairmont Avenue
Bethesda, MD 20814
800-621-7874

Investment Objective: This fund seeks to provide results that correlate to the performance of the NASDAQ 100 Index. Stocks included in the portfolio are chosen solely on the statistical basis of their weighting in the NASDAQ Index. The fund does not utilize traditional securities analysis. Market timers should keep in mind that the fund permits just 5 switches per year. However, because of the ebbs and flows of cash, the fund's portfolio turnover rate the past year was an astronomical 1,000+%.

Portfolio Manager: Dan Ryczek
Since: 1985

Minimum:
Initial: $2,500
Subsequent: $500
Telephone Exchange: Yes
Distributions:
Income: Annually
Capital Gain: Annually
Front-End Load: None
12b-1: None
Redemption Fee: None
Management Company: Money Management Associates
Ticker Symbol: RSOIX

TOTAL RETURN (%)

1987	1988	1989	1990	1991	5-year	Bull Market	Bear Market
6.2	9.2	15.3	-17.6	50.5	65.7	62.1	-33.6

INVESTMENT PORTFOLIO

Total Assets (mil.)	Current Yield	Turnover Ratio	Expense Ratio	Beta	Risk Return
$22	0.0%	1,398%	1.00%	1.35	0.06

RUSHMORE STOCK MARKET INDEX PLUS FUND

Rushmore Funds
4922 Fairmont Avenue
Bethesda, MD 20814
800-621-7874

Investment Objective: Essentially an S&P 100 Index surrogate, the fund's portfolio is rebalanced regularly to reflect that index and a collection of S&P 100 Index options. In theory, this approach should enable the fund to achieve market-level returns at significantly lower risk. In practice, however, it has succeeded only at reducing risk. The fund underperformed the broad market in 1986, 1988, 1989 and 1991. Its somewhat better-than-market 1990 results represent its first bright spot since 1987. Its disappointing results underscores how difficult it is to improve investment results through the use of options.

Portfolio Manager: Dan Ryczek
Since: 1985

Minimum:
Initial: $2,500
Subsequent: $500
Telephone Exchange: Yes
Distributions:
Income: Semiannually
Capital Gain: Annually
Front-End Load: None
12b-1: None
Redemption Fee: None
Management Company: Money Management Associates
Ticker Symbol: RSSIX

TOTAL RETURN (%)

1987	1988	1989	1990	1991	5-year	Bull Market	Bear Market
8.9	8.9	23.2	-3.1	26.6	79.4	34.8	-19.8

INVESTMENT PORTFOLIO

Total Assets (mil.)	Current Yield	Turnover Ratio	Expense Ratio	Beta	Risk Return
$26	3.4%	576%	0.94%	0.97	0.05

SAFECO EQUITY FUND

SAFECO Securities
4333 Brooklyn Avenue N.E.
Seattle, WA 98185
800-426-6730

Investment Objective: This fund pursues its capital-appreciation objective by investing primarily in small capitalization common stocks that show above-average growth in earnings but sell at modest valuations. As a general rule, the fund normally remains fully invested in both up and down markets, leaving the responsibility of cash allocation to the investor. Thus, the fund's share price can be expected to decline along with the stock market during bear markets. However, during the past 5 years, the fund has outperformed more than 80% of the funds in existence over that period.

Portfolio Manager: Doug Johnson
Since: 1984

Minimum:
Initial: $1,000
Subsequent: $25
Telephone Exchange: Yes
Distributions:
Income: Quarterly
Capital Gain: Annually
Front-End Load: None
12b-1: None
Redemption Fee: None
Management Company: SAFECO Asset Management
Ticker Symbol: SAFQX

TOTAL RETURN (%)

1987	1988	1989	1990	1991	5-year	Bull Market	Bear Market
-4.8	25.3	35.8	-8.6	27.9	89.4	40.1	-22.6

INVESTMENT PORTFOLIO

Total Assets (mil.)	Current Yield	Turnover Ratio	Expense Ratio	Beta	Risk Return
$67	1.6%	51%	0.97%	1.04	0.04

SAFECO GROWTH FUND

SAFECO Securities
4333 Brooklyn Avenue N.E.
Seattle, WA 98185
800-426-6730

Investment Objective: This fund pursues its capital-appreciation objective by investing primarily in small capitalization stocks that show above-average earnings growth but sell at modest valuations. During recent years, the fund has been hit by a double whammy: Small cap stocks have performed poorly as have value stocks. However, during the past year, the fund returned a whopping 60+% as small cap stocks surged to the fore. The fund is among the most parsimonious on Wall Street in terms of the cost of investing. It has a no-load format, a low expense ratio and an average portfolio turnover ratio. Its shares appear to be ideal for the patient, long-term-oriented growth investor.

Portfolio Manager: Tom Maguire
Since: 1989

Minimum:
Initial: $1,000
Subsequent: $25
Telephone Exchange: Yes
Distributions:
Income: Semiannually
Capital Gain: Annually
Front-End Load: None
12b-1: None
Redemption Fee: None
Management Company: SAFECO Asset Management
Ticker Symbol: SAFGX

TOTAL RETURN (%)

1987	1988	1989	1990	1991	5-year	Bull Market	Bear Market
7.0	22.1	19.2	-15.0	62.6	115.4	84.9	-35.7

INVESTMENT PORTFOLIO

Total Assets (mil.)	Current Yield	Turnover Ratio	Expense Ratio	Beta	Risk Return
$155	0.2%	90%	1.01%	1.25	0.08

SALEM VALUE PORTFOLIO B

Federated Securities
Federated Investors Tower
Pittsburgh, PA 15222
800-356-2805

Investment Objective: This no-load fund invests primarily in large capitalization common stocks that meet management's definition of growth at discount. Most of the fund's blue chip growth stocks sell at modest valuations but show good earnings growth. Coupled with its large cap bias and broad industry diversification, the fund's dual emphasis on growth and value has enabled it to produce consistent above-average results in most years since its 1985 inception.

Portfolio Manager: Ed Outen
Since: 1990

Minimum:
Initial: $1,000
Subsequent: None
Telephone Exchange: Yes
Distributions:
Income: Quarterly
Capital Gain: Annually
Front-End Load: 4.00%
12b-1: 0.25%
Redemption Fee: 2.00%
Management Company: First Union National Bank
Ticker Symbol: SALGX

TOTAL RETURN (%)

1987	1988	1989	1990	1991	5-year	Bull Market	Bear Market
1.7	20.2	26.9	-3.4	25.1	87.4	30.9	-16.3

INVESTMENT PORTFOLIO

Total Assets (mil.)	Current Yield	Turnover Ratio	Expense Ratio	Beta	Risk Return
$123	2.3%	11%	1.55%	0.82	0.05

SALOMON BROTHERS OPPORTUNITY FUND

Salomon Brothers
7 World Trade Center
New York, NY 10048
800-725-6666

Investment Objective: This fund sticks to its knitting. Best described as a contrarian investor, manager Irving Brilliant avoids stocks with high expectations built into their prices. Instead, he favors temporarily troubled companies that sell at substantial discounts to their underlying earnings power, cash flows and/or asset values. His patient, long-term horizon allows him to wait for his companies to show fundamental improvement and for value to be realized in the market. Although the fund suffered a sharp loss during 1990, in a market that was particularly hostile to value stocks, it has produced highly competitive long-term returns with moderate risk.

Portfolio Manager: Irving Brilliant
Since: 1979

Minimum:
Initial: $1,000
Subsequent: $100
Telephone Exchange: No
Distributions:
Income: Annually
Capital Gain: Annually
Front-End Load: None
12b-1: None
Redemption Fee: None
Management Company: Salomon Brothers Asset Management
Ticker Symbol: SAOPX

TOTAL RETURN (%)

1987	1988	1989	1990	1991	5-year	Bull Market	Bear Market
4.4	23.3	21.0	-16.0	30.6	70.9	41.7	-22.7

INVESTMENT PORTFOLIO

Total Assets (mil.)	Current Yield	Turnover Ratio	Expense Ratio	Beta	Risk Return
$99	1.9%	13%	1.26%	0.91	0.05

SCHIELD VALUE FUND

Schield Securities
390 Union Boulevard, Suite 410
Denver, CO 80228
800-275-2382

Investment Objective: If ever one needs an argument against market timing, look no further than this fund. Over a period in which the S&P 500 returned 104% and the average growth fund returned 89%, this fund chalked up a 10% 5-year return. When it is invested, the fund focuses on large cap stocks. Returns have been hampered by poor timing and a high turnover ratio. Furthermore, the fund's tiny asset base helps explain the excessive 2.50% expense ratio. And to get all of this, investors must ante up 4.00% on the front end.

Portfolio Manager: Marshall L. Schield
Since: 1985

Minimum:
Initial: $1,000
Subsequent: $100
Telephone Exchange: Yes
Distributions:
Income: Annually
Capital Gain: Annually
Front-End Load: 4.00%
12b-1: 1.00%
Redemption Fee: None
Management Company: Schield Management
Ticker Symbol: SVALX

TOTAL RETURN (%)

1987	1988	1989	1990	1991	5-year	Bull Market	Bear Market
7.5	-7.6	8.9	-4.5	6.4	9.9	39.2	-17.0

INVESTMENT PORTFOLIO

Total Assets (mil.)	Current Yield	Turnover Ratio	Expense Ratio	Beta	Risk Return
$1	0.0%	194%	2.50%	0.83	0.03

SCHRODER U.S. EQUITY FUND

Schroder Capital Funds
787 Seventh Avenue
New York, NY 10019
800-344-8332

Investment Objective: The primary investment objective of this fund is growth of capital with income as a secondary consideration. The portfolio may be invested in either small or large capitalization stocks and convertible securities. The fund's 5-year return is slightly above the group average primarily because of its 39.9% return in 1991. The fund's increased allocation toward midsized caps helped boost the past year's showing. Investors should note management's commitment to stability. With this fund you'll probably never lead the pack, but rarely will you trail the field.

Portfolio Manager: Fareba Talebi
Since: 1991

Minimum:
Initial: $500
Subsequent: $100
Telephone Exchange: No
Distributions:
Income: Annually
Capital Gain: Annually
Front-End Load: None
12b-1: None
Redemption Fee: None
Management Company: Schroder Capital Management
Ticker Symbol: SUSEX

TOTAL RETURN (%)

1987	1988	1989	1990	1991	5-year	Bull Market	Bear Market
0.5	12.0	25.4	-3.5	39.9	90.6	22.9	-12.8

INVESTMENT PORTFOLIO

Total Assets (mil.)	Current Yield	Turnover Ratio	Expense Ratio	Beta	Risk Return
$20	1.2%	28%	1.34%	0.97	0.05

SCUDDER CAPITAL GROWTH FUND

Scudder Stevens & Clark
175 Federal Street, 12th Floor
Boston, MA 02110
800-225-2470

Investment Objective: This fund seeks to maximize long-term capital growth through a broad and flexible investment program. The fund may pursue companies that generate or apply new technologies, companies that own or develop natural resources and companies that benefit from changing consumer demands. Overall, management uses an aggressive value strategy when selecting securities. Management's strategy has obviously paid off as the fund's return is 104.5% over the past 5 years. In addition to being an above-average performer, the fund is sold without a sales charge and is free of any ongoing 12b-1 fees.

Portfolio Manager: Steve Aronoff
Since: 1989

Minimum:
Initial: $1,000
Subsequent: None
Telephone Exchange: Yes
Distributions:
Income: Annually
Capital Gain: Annually
Front-End Load: None
12b-1: None
Redemption Fee: None
Management Company: Scudder Stevens & Clark
Ticker Symbol: SCDUX

TOTAL RETURN (%)

1987	1988	1989	1990	1991	5-year	Bull Market	Bear Market
-0.7	29.7	33.8	-17.0	43.0	104.5	53.8	-27.2

INVESTMENT PORTFOLIO

Total Assets (mil.)	Current Yield	Turnover Ratio	Expense Ratio	Beta	Risk Return
$995	1.1%	88%	0.94%	1.30	0.06

SELECTED AMERICAN SHARES

Kemper Financial Services
333 West Wacker Drive
Chicago, IL 60606
800-553-5533

Investment Objective: This fund has built an enviable track record under the management of Donald Yachtman. Its investments have consisted of profitable, strong-franchise companies that were believed to sell at a discount to their true worth based on both earnings and asset values. The fund's performance ranks among the top 10% of all funds in terms of 3-, 5- and 10-year returns. However, Yachtman left the helm of this fund shortly after it was acquired by Kemper Financial Services. Thus, past performance may not be indicative of future potential. New Portfolio Manager James Moeller definitely has large shoes to fill.

Portfolio Manager: James Moeller
Since: 1992

Minimum:
Initial: $1,000
Subsequent: $50
Telephone Exchange: Yes
Distributions:
Income: Quarterly
Capital Gain: Annually
Front-End Load: None
12b-1: 0.59%
Redemption Fee: None
Management Company: Selected Financial Services
Ticker Symbol: SLASX

TOTAL RETURN (%)

1987	1988	1989	1990	1991	5-year	Bull Market	Bear Market
0.2	22.0	20.1	-3.9	46.3	106.4	51.0	-20.0

INVESTMENT PORTFOLIO

Total Assets (mil.)	Current Yield	Turnover Ratio	Expense Ratio	Beta	Risk Return
$587	1.3%	48%	1.35%	1.09	0.07

SELECTED SPECIAL SHARES

Kemper Financial Services
333 West Wacker Drive
Chicago, IL 60606
800-553-5533

Investment Objective: This no-load fund seeks growth of capital primarily by investing in common stocks that meet management's standards of both growth and value. Its portfolio manager has demonstrated an affinity for strong-franchise companies with low leverage and high profitability ratios. Coupled with management's value parameters, these growth criteria cause the fund to concentrate assets in relatively few companies and industries. Overweighting cheap but above-average-growth consumer durables, business services and media, the fund's 30-odd stock portfolio omits slow-growth utilities and expensive consumer nondurables.

Portfolio Manager: Ronald W. Ball
Since: 1986

Minimum:
Initial: $1,000
Subsequent: $50
Telephone Exchange: Yes
Distributions:
Income: Annually
Capital Gain: Annually
Front-End Load: None
12b-1: 0.39%
Redemption Fee: None
Management Company: Selected Financial Services
Ticker Symbol: SLSSX

TOTAL RETURN (%)

1987	1988	1989	1990	1991	5-year	Bull Market	Bear Market
0.5	19.6	28.9	-6.9	25.5	81.1	31.2	-22.4

INVESTMENT PORTFOLIO

Total Assets (mil.)	Current Yield	Turnover Ratio	Expense Ratio	Beta	Risk Return
$54	4.6%	87%	1.41%	0.92	0.04

SENTINEL GROWTH FUND

Equity Securities
National Life Drive
Montpelier, VT 05604
800-282-3863

Investment Objective: Sentinel Growth Fund offers a classic growth portfolio. Management keeps the fund near fully invested at all times, stressing established growth companies, most of which are included in the S&P 500. For the most part, the fund's companies show above-average growth in earnings, financial strength and industry leadership. Although it generally avoids high-expectation growth stocks in favor of mature companies with demonstrated stable growth characteristics, the fund usually keeps market-level representation in all major industries.

Portfolio Manager: William Hedberg
Since: 1987

Minimum:
Initial: $250
Subsequent: $25
Telephone Exchange: Yes
Distributions:
Income: Semiannually
Capital Gain: Annually
Front-End Load: 5.25%
12b-1: None
Redemption Fee: None
Management Company: Sentinel Advisers
Ticker Symbol: SNTNX

TOTAL RETURN (%)

1987	1988	1989	1990	1991	5-year	Bull Market	Bear Market
6.3	3.5	26.9	0.5	26.2	77.2	28.9	-22.2

INVESTMENT PORTFOLIO

Total Assets (mil.)	Current Yield	Turnover Ratio	Expense Ratio	Beta	Risk Return
$56	1.0%	15%	1.20%	1.00	0.04

SENTRY FUND

Sentry Equity Services
1800 North Point Drive
Stevens Point, WI 54481
800-533-7827

Investment Objective: Sentry Fund offers a classic growth portfolio. As seen in the fund's low turnover rate, management follows a buy-and-hold strategy. Its affinity for established companies with stable, above-average growth characteristics, financial strength and industry leadership leads it to mature S&P 500 names. Brand-name growth stocks from stable growth sectors dominate the portfolio, which neglects most economically sensitive sectors. Since implemented in 1983, the fund's current approach has produced better-than-average results in most markets.

Portfolio Manager: Keith Ringberg
Since: 1977

Minimum:
Initial: $200
Subsequent: $50
Telephone Exchange: No
Distributions:
Income: Semiannually
Capital Gain: Annually
Front-End Load: None
12b-1: None
Redemption Fee: None
Management Company: Sentry Investment Management
Ticker Symbol: SNTRX

TOTAL RETURN (%)

1987	1988	1989	1990	1991	5-year	Bull Market	Bear Market
-5.5	16.9	24.0	5.2	28.9	85.9	41.4	-18.0

INVESTMENT PORTFOLIO

Total Assets (mil.)	Current Yield	Turnover Ratio	Expense Ratio	Beta	Risk Return
$59	2.4%	30%	0.69%	0.84	0.06

SEQUOIA FUND

Ruane Cunniff & Company
1370 Avenue of the Americas, 29th Floor
New York, NY 10019
212-245-4500

Investment Objective: Closed to new accounts, this quintessential value player offers highly competitive long-term total returns with a low risk profile. Management's refusal to pay high multiples doesn't cause it to compromise quality. Management concentrates moneys in relatively few, well-managed, strong-franchise companies with low leverage and high profitability ratios. A proclivity for raising cash when stocks meeting its value parameters are scarce enhances the fund's defensive capabilities. It has resisted decline in 3 of this decade's 4 bear markets. While not able to completely sidestep 1990's debacle, it declined far less than most rivals and followed up with a solid return the past year.

Portfolio Manager: William J. Ruane
Since: 1970

Minimum:
Initial: Closed
Subsequent: $50
Telephone Exchange: No
Distributions:
Income: Semiannually
Capital Gain: Semiannually
Front-End Load: Closed
12b-1: None
Redemption Fee: None
Management Company: Ruane Cunniff & Company
Ticker Symbol: SEQUX

TOTAL RETURN (%)

1987	1988	1989	1990	1991	5-year	Bull Market	Bear Market
7.4	11.0	27.9	-3.8	40.0	105.5	38.9	-19.1

INVESTMENT PORTFOLIO

Total Assets (mil.)	Current Yield	Turnover Ratio	Expense Ratio	Beta	Risk Return
$1,106	2.4%	43%	1.00%	0.79	0.08

SHEARSON APPRECIATION FUND

Shearson Lehman Brothers
Two World Trade Center
New York, NY 10048
800-451-2010

Investment Objective: This growth fund seeks capital appreciation primarily by investing in large capitalization common stocks that meet its dual standards of growth and value. Most of the fund's blue chip companies show above-average earnings growth but sell at modest price/earnings ratios. Although the fund modestly overweights inexpensive growth sectors such as energy and industrial products, it keeps representation in all major industry groups. Its broad sector diversification, blue chip orientation and dual emphasis on growth and value enables this fund to keep returns in sight of the S&P 500 in most years. It is among the most dependable of growth funds.

Portfolio Manager: Harold Williamson
Since: 1981

Minimum:
Initial: $500
Subsequent: $50
Telephone Exchange: No
Distributions:
Income: Annually
Capital Gain: Annually
Front-End Load: 5.00%
12b-1: None
Redemption Fee: None
Management Company: Shearson Asset Management
Ticker Symbol: SHAPX

TOTAL RETURN (%)

1987	1988	1989	1990	1991	5-year	Bull Market	Bear Market
7.0	13.5	29.6	-0.3	26.9	99.0	32.1	-16.3

INVESTMENT PORTFOLIO

Total Assets (mil.)	Current Yield	Turnover Ratio	Expense Ratio	Beta	Risk Return
$1,577	1.9%	30%	0.80%	0.88	0.05

SHEARSON FUNDAMENTAL VALUE

Shearson Lehman Brothers
Two World Trade Center
New York, NY 10048
800-451-2010

Investment Objective: This fund seeks long-term capital appreciation and secondarily current income by investing primarily in large and medium-sized common stocks. Management pursues a moderate value discipline, stressing companies with strong earnings growth that sell at reasonable valuations. Classic, stable growth stocks are featured along with cheaper, high-growth technology, capital goods and financials. Like most value players, this fund should rebound on a return to traditional measures of value. Given its modest risk, it has delivered better-than-average returns during the past 5 years.

Portfolio Manager: John Goode
Since: 1990

Minimum:
Initial: $500
Subsequent: $200
Telephone Exchange: No
Distributions:
Income: Annually
Capital Gain: Annually
Front-End Load: 5.00%
12b-1: None
Redemption Fee: None
Management Company: Shearson Asset Management
Ticker Symbol: SHFVX

TOTAL RETURN (%)

1987	1988	1989	1990	1991	5-year	Bull Market	Bear Market
2.5	21.1	18.5	-8.4	31.4	77.1	44.5	-24.1

INVESTMENT PORTFOLIO

Total Assets (mil.)	Current Yield	Turnover Ratio	Expense Ratio	Beta	Risk Return
$57	2.0%	94%	1.20%	0.92	0.06

SMITH BARNEY EQUITY FUND

Smith Barney Harris Upham & Company
1345 Avenue of the Americas, 22nd Floor
New York, NY 10105
800-544-7835

Investment Objective: This fund seeks long-term capital appreciation and secondarily current income through investments in large capitalization common stocks. Management utilizes both top-down and bottom-up analysis to identify companies likely to exhibit earnings surprise. Reasonably priced high-momentum sectors such as industrial products and energy are prominent along with predictable growth drug stocks. As seen in 1989 and 1991, this fund figures to do best when growth stocks lead the market.

Portfolio Manager: Ed Keeley
Since: 1985

Minimum:
Initial: $3,000
Subsequent: $50
Telephone Exchange: No
Distributions:
Income: Quarterly
Capital Gain: Annually
Front-End Load: 4.50%
12b-1: 0.25%
Redemption Fee: None
Management Company: Smith Barney Advisers
Ticker Symbol: SBCEX

TOTAL RETURN (%)

1987	1988	1989	1990	1991	5-year	Bull Market	Bear Market
12.4	0.9	31.1	-3.2	26.5	82.1	31.3	-19.6

INVESTMENT PORTFOLIO

Total Assets (mil.)	Current Yield	Turnover Ratio	Expense Ratio	Beta	Risk Return
$79	2.0%	60%	0.77%	0.99	0.04

SOUND SHORE FUND

Sound Shore Fund
61 Broadway, Suite 2770
New York, NY 10006
203-629-1980

Investment Objective: This blue chip value player seeks capital appreciation. Stock selection is based on individual issues surviving various stock screens based on absolute and relative valuation criteria. The fund beat the S&P 500 the past year for the first time in 3 years, but still sports a below-average 5-year return figure. Part of the underperformance may be attributed to its out-of-favor value orientation. The fund is pure no-load and carries an average expense ratio. When value investing becomes the market's favorite son again, this fund has the potential to shine.

Portfolio Manager: Kane/Burn
Since: 1985

Minimum:
Initial: $20,000
Subsequent: None
Telephone Exchange: Yes
Distributions:
Income: Semiannually
Capital Gain: Annually
Front-End Load: None
12b-1: None
Redemption Fee: None
Management Company: Sound Shore Management
Ticker Symbol: SSHFX

TOTAL RETURN (%)

1987	1988	1989	1990	1991	5-year	Bull Market	Bear Market
-3.7	21.1	22.5	-10.6	32.2	68.8	19.8	-14.3

INVESTMENT PORTFOLIO

Total Assets (mil.)	Current Yield	Turnover Ratio	Expense Ratio	Beta	Risk Return
$32	1.9%	105%	1.33%	0.91	0.05

STAGECOACH CORPORATE STOCK FUND

Wells Fargo Investment Advisors
525 Market Street, 12th Floor
San Francisco, CA 94163
800-222-8222

Investment Objective: This index fund attempts to approximate the total rate of return of the S&P 500 Index. Like most index funds, management attempts to replicate its benchmark by using a sample of the stocks in the index. Over the past 5 years, the fund has trailed the S&P 500 each year. Its 5-year return falls more than 13% short of the S&P 500's 104% total return. As far as funds that seek to match the S&P 500 Index, there are others that have approximated the index to a closer degree.

Portfolio Manager: Geraldine Hom
Since: 1984

Minimum:
Initial: $1,000
Subsequent: $100
Telephone Exchange: Yes
Distributions:
Income: Annually
Capital Gain: Annually
Front-End Load: None
12b-1: 0.05%
Redemption Fee: None
Management Company: Wells Fargo Investment Management
Ticker Symbol: WCSTX

TOTAL RETURN (%)

1987	1988	1989	1990	1991	5-year	Bull Market	Bear Market
3.3	15.1	29.8	-3.9	28.7	90.8	35.5	-19.2

INVESTMENT PORTFOLIO

Total Assets (mil.)	Current Yield	Turnover Ratio	Expense Ratio	Beta	Risk Return
$188	0.0%	4%	0.97%	0.99	0.05

STEIN ROE PRIME EQUITIES

Stein Roe & Farnham
P.O. Box 1162
Chicago, IL 60690
800-338-2550

Investment Objective: Stein Roe Prime Equities seeks growth of capital primarily through investments in common stocks of larger well-established companies. Management stresses quality growth companies that sustain above-average earnings growth, high rates of return on investment and long histories of dividend increases. Although the fund maintains a broadly diversified portfolio with representation in most major industries, high-growth sectors, including consumer nondurables, services and retail, are overweighted. The fund figures to do best when growth stocks lead the market.

Portfolio Manager: Ralph Segall
Since: 1987

Minimum:
Initial: $1,000
Subsequent: $100
Telephone Exchange: Yes
Distributions:
Income: Quarterly
Capital Gain: Annually
Front-End Load: None
12b-1: None
Redemption Fee: None
Management Company: Stein Roe & Farnham
Ticker Symbol: SRPEX

TOTAL RETURN (%)

1987	1988	1989	1990	1991	5-year	Bull Market	Bear Market
NA	9.0	31.0	-1.7	32.4	NA	29.8	-17.6

INVESTMENT PORTFOLIO

Total Assets (mil.)	Current Yield	Turnover Ratio	Expense Ratio	Beta	Risk Return
$55	1.7%	51%	1.08%	0.90	0.06

STEIN ROE SPECIAL FUND

Stein Roe & Farnham
P.O. Box 1162
Chicago, IL 60690
800-338-2550

Investment Objective: Stein Roe Special Fund seeks maximum capital appreciation primarily by investing in common stocks. Management pursues a flexible strategy and invests in a mix of stock sizes and types. The portfolio features large capitalization growth stocks, strong franchise telephone and cable TV issues and an occasional asset play. Superb trailing 5-year total returns underscore this fund's excellent risk/reward characteristics. A pure no-load format, low expenses and a modest portfolio turnover ratio make it a fine choice for patient, growth-oriented investors.

Portfolio Manager: B. Dunn/D. Peterson
Since: 1991

Minimum:
Initial: $1,000
Subsequent: $100
Telephone Exchange: Yes
Distributions:
Income: Annually
Capital Gain: Annually
Front-End Load: None
12b-1: None
Redemption Fee: None
Management Company: Stein Roe & Farnham
Ticker Symbol: SRSPX

TOTAL RETURN (%)

1987	1988	1989	1990	1991	5-year	Bull Market	Bear Market
4.3	20.2	37.8	-5.8	34.0	118.2	38.0	-21.3

INVESTMENT PORTFOLIO

Total Assets (mil.)	Current Yield	Turnover Ratio	Expense Ratio	Beta	Risk Return
$534	1.8%	70%	1.02%	0.98	0.06

STEIN ROE STOCK FUND

Stein Roe & Farnham
P.O. Box 1162
Chicago, IL 60690
800-338-2550

Investment Objective: Stein Roe & Farnham Stock Fund seeks long-term capital appreciation primarily through investment in common stocks. Management pursues an earnings-oriented strategy, stressing above-average growth stocks with good earnings momentum, high returns on assets and financial strength. The fund's affinity for companies that show rapid-earnings growth leads it into emerging-growth industries such as pollution control, cable TV and telecommunications. Given the tone of the market during the past 5 years, the fund's growth-intensive approach has rewarded investors well.

Portfolio Manager: Capital Management Group
Since: 1991

Minimum:
Initial: $1,000
Subsequent: $100
Telephone Exchange: Yes
Distributions:
Income: Quarterly
Capital Gain: Annually
Front-End Load: None
12b-1: None
Redemption Fee: None
Management Company: Stein Roe & Farnham
Ticker Symbol: SRFSX

TOTAL RETURN (%)

1987	1988	1989	1990	1991	5-year	Bull Market	Bear Market
5.6	0.7	35.5	0.9	46.0	112.2	41.7	-21.5

INVESTMENT PORTFOLIO

Total Assets (mil.)	Current Yield	Turnover Ratio	Expense Ratio	Beta	Risk Return
$294	1.1%	40%	0.73%	1.03	0.08

STRATTON GROWTH FUND

Stratton Management
610 West Germantown Pike, Suite 361
Plymouth Meeting, PA 19462
800-634-5726

Investment Objective: Stratton Growth Fund pursues its objective of capital growth and secondly current income through a conservative discipline that stresses both value and yield. Management invests the bulk of the fund's assets in common stocks that sell at low price/earnings ratios and pay above-market yields and high-yielding convertible bonds. Traditional yield sectors such as energy, utilities and financials typically claim the bulk of its assets. As a result, the fund is highly sensitive to interest-rate movements. Although it is vulnerable to price declines during periods of rising interest rates, it has produced competitive long-term results with moderate risk.

Portfolio Manager: James Stratton
Since: 1972

Minimum:
Initial: $1,000
Subsequent: $100
Telephone Exchange: Yes
Distributions:
Income: Annually
Capital Gain: Annually
Front-End Load: None
12b-1: None
Redemption Fee: None
Management Company: Stratton Management
Ticker Symbol: STRGX

TOTAL RETURN (%)

1987	1988	1989	1990	1991	5-year	Bull Market	Bear Market
-3.9	22.6	23.8	-6.7	22.2	66.3	25.0	-13.2

INVESTMENT PORTFOLIO

Total Assets (mil.)	Current Yield	Turnover Ratio	Expense Ratio	Beta	Risk Return
$25	3.5%	57%	1.41%	0.74	0.04

STRONG COMMON STOCK

Strong/Corneliuson Capital
100 Heritage Reserve
Menomonee Falls, WI 53051
800-368-3863

Investment Objective: This relatively new offering has had a strong start. The past year the fund gained almost 57%, which followed 1990's 10% gain. Like many growth funds that achieved such stellar returns, this fund was positioned in small to midsized companies this past year. As Strong funds go, this sibling has shown the same rapid-trading techniques seen in other members of this family. If earnings falter or valuations become too excessive, issues are sold quickly.

Portfolio Manager: Weiss/Murphy
Since: 1991

Minimum:
Initial: $1,000
Subsequent: $50
Telephone Exchange: Yes
Distributions:
Income: Quarterly
Capital Gain: Annually
Front-End Load: 2.00%
12b-1: None
Redemption Fee: None
Management Company: Strong/Corneliuson Capital Management
Ticker Symbol: STCSX

TOTAL RETURN (%)

1987	1988	1989	1990	1991	5-year	Bull Market	Bear Market
NA	NA	NA	10.0	56.9	NA	NA	NA

INVESTMENT PORTFOLIO

Total Assets (mil.)	Current Yield	Turnover Ratio	Expense Ratio	Beta	Risk Return
$30	5.7%	291%	2.00%	NA	NA

STRONG OPPORTUNITY FUND

Strong/Corneliuson Capital
100 Heritage Reserve
Menomonee Falls, WI 53051
800-368-3863

Investment Objective: This fund seeks capital appreciation by investing in common stocks that appear undervalued. As is true of other Strong-managed vehicles, the fund has historically produced a very high annual turnover ratio. In part, its high turnover reflects the Strong/Corneliuson management team's willingness to shift assets into bonds and/or cash when they believe the stock market is vulnerable to a possible correction. It also reflects the tendency to trade stocks rapidly in response to market conditions. The fund's 5-year total return figure largely reflects its handsome return during 1987.

Portfolio Manager: William D. Corneliuson
Since: 1985

Minimum:
Initial: $1,000
Subsequent: $500
Telephone Exchange: Yes
Distributions:
Income: Quarterly
Capital Gain: Annually
Front-End Load: 2.00%
12b-1: None
Redemption Fee: None
Management Company: Strong/Corneliuson Capital Management
Ticker Symbol: SOPFX

TOTAL RETURN (%)

1987	1988	1989	1990	1991	5-year	Bull Market	Bear Market
11.9	16.5	18.5	-11.3	31.7	80.3	33.9	-18.4

INVESTMENT PORTFOLIO

Total Assets (mil.)	Current Yield	Turnover Ratio	Expense Ratio	Beta	Risk Return
$143	0.9%	275%	1.70%	0.80	0.06

SUN AMERICA CAPITAL APPRECIATION FUND

Sun America Capital Services
10 Union Square East, 2nd Floor
New York, NY 10003
800-821-5100

Investment Objective: This fund seeks capital appreciation by investing in the common stocks of underfollowed small and medium-sized companies that it believes are undervalued relative to their underlying earnings power, asset values and/or private market value. The fund's portfolio features a mix of out-of-favor growth stocks, distressed financials and restructuring candidates. Although its small-company focus, strict value orientation and resulting large stakes in out-of-favor industries such as finance and technology caused it to suffer a big loss during 1990, the fund stands to rebound sharply on a return to traditional measures of value. As already seen in 1991, a shift in leadership to small stocks can give it a big boost.

Portfolio Manager: Harvey Eisen
Since: 1985

Minimum:
Initial: $500
Subsequent: $100
Telephone Exchange: Yes
Distributions:
Income: Annually
Capital Gain: Annually
Front-End Load: None
12b-1: 1.25%
Redemption Fee: 5.00%
Management Company: Sun America
Ticker Symbol: SACAX

TOTAL RETURN (%)

1987	1988	1989	1990	1991	5-year	Bull Market	Bear Market
-7.7	29.3	12.8	-25.2	30.0	30.9	35.6	-29.7

INVESTMENT PORTFOLIO

Total Assets (mil.)	Current Yield	Turnover Ratio	Expense Ratio	Beta	Risk Return
$91	0.0%	90%	2.51%	0.94	0.05

SUN AMERICA GROWTH PORTFOLIO

Sun America Capital Services
10 Union Square East, 2nd Floor
New York, NY 10003
800-821-5100

Investment Objective: This fund seeks growth at a discount. The fund features a fairly compact portfolio of relatively cheap stocks with demonstrated above-average earnings growth. The fund's strict criteria cause it to concentrate assets in relatively few out-of-favor industries. Cheap but high-growth industrial products, retail and financials claim a large portion of the fund's assets, largely explaining its sharp 1990 decline. As is true of sibling Sun America Capital Appreciation, the fund should rebound sharply once the market abandons its recently narrow focus and returns to traditional measures of value.

Portfolio Manager: Elaine Goldberg-Harris
Since: 1991

Minimum:
Initial: $500
Subsequent: $100
Telephone Exchange: Yes
Distributions:
Income: Semiannually
Capital Gain: Annually
Front-End Load: 5.75%
12b-1: 0.35%
Redemption Fee: None
Management Company: Sun America
Ticker Symbol: SEGRX

TOTAL RETURN (%)

1987	1988	1989	1990	1991	5-year	Bull Market	Bear Market
NA	23.3	28.8	-14.9	42.6	NA	48.3	-28.1

INVESTMENT PORTFOLIO

Total Assets (mil.)	Current Yield	Turnover Ratio	Expense Ratio	Beta	Risk Return
$18	0.8%	65%	1.84%	1.02	0.07

T. ROWE PRICE CAPITAL APPRECIATION FUND

T. Rowe Price Investor Services
100 East Pratt Street
Baltimore, MD 21202
800-638-5660

Investment Objective: This fund, which commenced operations in June of 1986, seeks capital appreciation through investment primarily in common stocks. Management attempts to achieve its objective by investing in securities of companies that are undervalued in relation to their underlying assets, earnings and/or breakup value. Management also seeks to identify securities that have been overdiscounted because of adverse operating results, deteriorating economic and/or industry conditions or unfavorable publicity. Excellent stock selection and a practice of retreating to cash when stocks seem overvalued have given this fund a superb risk/reward profile.

Portfolio Manager: Richard P. Howard
Since: 1989

Minimum:
Initial: $2,500
Subsequent: $100
Telephone Exchange: Yes
Distributions:
Income: Annually
Capital Gain: Annually
Front-End Load: None
12b-1: None
Redemption Fee: None
Management Company: T. Rowe Price Associates
Ticker Symbol: PRWCX

TOTAL RETURN (%)

1987	1988	1989	1990	1991	5-year	Bull Market	Bear Market
5.8	21.2	21.4	-1.2	21.6	87.0	31.9	-14.3

INVESTMENT PORTFOLIO

Total Assets (mil.)	Current Yield	Turnover Ratio	Expense Ratio	Beta	Risk Return
$200	3.7%	50%	1.25%	0.59	0.05

T. ROWE PRICE GROWTH STOCK FUND

T. Rowe Price Investor Services
100 East Pratt Street
Baltimore, MD 21202
800-638-5660

Investment Objective: This fund seeks long-term growth of capital, primarily through investment in large capitalization common stocks. Management bases investments on the belief that when a company's earnings outpace inflation and the general economy, eventually the market will reward success with higher prices for the stock. Most of the fund's companies show average growth in earnings and high profitability ratios. Management's desire to keep risk moderate, however, prevents it from paying high multiples. Consequently, the fund tends to overweight out-of-favor growth industries.

Portfolio Manager: M. David Testa
Since: 1984

Minimum:
Initial: $2,500
Subsequent: $50
Telephone Exchange: Yes
Distributions:
Income: Annually
Capital Gain: Annually
Front-End Load: None
12b-1: None
Redemption Fee: None
Management Company: T. Rowe Price Associates
Ticker Symbol: PRGFX

TOTAL RETURN (%)

1987	1988	1989	1990	1991	5-year	Bull Market	Bear Market
3.7	6.1	25.4	-4.3	33.8	76.6	36.2	-22.0

INVESTMENT PORTFOLIO

Total Assets (mil.)	Current Yield	Turnover Ratio	Expense Ratio	Beta	Risk Return
$1,633	1.3%	30%	0.76%	1.05	0.06

T. ROWE PRICE NEW AMERICA GROWTH FUND

T. Rowe Price Investor Services
100 East Pratt Street
Baltimore, MD 21202
800-638-5660

Investment Objective: This fund invests primarily in common stocks of service companies. It is designed for investors seeking aggressive long-term growth of capital and, secondarily, current income. The fund's investment program is based on the belief that growth in the service sector of the economy will outpace overall economic growth. Generally, at least 75% of the fund's assets will be in common stocks of companies deriving a majority of their revenues directly from service-related activities such as financial services and media and information processing. Investments range from small, rapidly growing companies to larger blue chip firms.

Portfolio Manager: John H. Laporte
Since: 1985

Minimum:
Initial: $2,500
Subsequent: $100
Telephone Exchange: Yes
Distributions:
Income: Annually
Capital Gain: Annually
Front-End Load: None
12b-1: None
Redemption Fee: None
Management Company: T. Rowe Price Associates
Ticker Symbol: PRWAX

TOTAL RETURN (%)

1987	1988	1989	1990	1991	5-year	Bull Market	Bear Market
-9.4	18.5	38.4	-12.2	61.9	111.1	74.4	-31.1

INVESTMENT PORTFOLIO

Total Assets (mil.)	Current Yield	Turnover Ratio	Expense Ratio	Beta	Risk Return
$191	0.0%	42%	1.25%	1.23	0.09

T. ROWE PRICE NEW ERA FUND

T. Rowe Price Investor Services
100 East Pratt Street
Baltimore, MD 21202
800-638-5660

Investment Objective: The investment objective of this no-load fund is long-term growth of capital by investing in common stocks of companies expected to exhibit earnings growth at a rate greater than the inflation rate over the long run. The fund normally invests the bulk of its assets in companies that own or develop natural resources. At 30% of its assets, energy stocks dominate the portfolio. Precious metals and basic industry stocks also are prominent. Given its emphasis on tangible assets, this fund can be expected to exhibit its best relative performance during periods of rising inflation. As could be expected, the fund has delivered only modest returns in recent years as the growth in consumer prices moderated.

Portfolio Manager: George A. Roche
Since: 1979

Minimum:
Initial: $2,500
Subsequent: $100
Telephone Exchange: Yes
Distributions:
Income: Annually
Capital Gain: Annually
Front-End Load: None
12b-1: None
Redemption Fee: None
Management Company: T. Rowe Price Associates
Ticker Symbol: PRNEX

TOTAL RETURN (%)

1987	1988	1989	1990	1991	5-year	Bull Market	Bear Market
17.8	10.3	24.3	-8.8	14.7	69.1	22.6	-15.7

INVESTMENT PORTFOLIO

Total Assets (mil.)	Current Yield	Turnover Ratio	Expense Ratio	Beta	Risk Return
$717	2.7%	9%	0.83%	0.72	0.02

T. ROWE PRICE SPECTRUM GROWTH

T. Rowe Price Investor Services
100 East Pratt Street
Baltimore, MD 21202
800-638-5660

Investment Objective: A recent addition to the Price family of funds, Spectrum Growth invests in other Price funds to achieve long-term growth. Income is a secondary consideration. This all-weather vehicle invests in domestic and international stock funds plus a money market. The past year this fund returned almost 30%. This fund offers wide diversification for the equity portion of one's portfolio and utilizes the superior management of T. Rowe Price. Although new to Price, this fund of funds should offer a fine risk/return profile.

Portfolio Manager: Peter Van Dyke
Since: 1990

Minimum:
Initial: $2,500
Subsequent: $100
Telephone Exchange: Yes
Distributions:
Income: Annually
Capital Gain: Annually
Front-End Load: None
12b-1: None
Redemption Fee: None
Management Company: T. Rowe Price Associates
Ticker Symbol: PRSGX

TOTAL RETURN (%)

1987	1988	1989	1990	1991	5-year	Bull Market	Bear Market
NA	NA	NA	NA	29.9	NA	NA	NA

INVESTMENT PORTFOLIO

Total Assets (mil.)	Current Yield	Turnover Ratio	Expense Ratio	Beta	Risk Return
$111	1.8%	NA	NA	NA	NA

THOMSON GROWTH FUND B

Thomson Securities
1 Station Place
Stamford, CT 06902
800-628-1237

Investment Objective: One of the 9 portfolios in the Thomson Investment Trust, this fund seeks long-term growth of capital primarily through investments in large capitalization common stocks. Management favors above-average growth companies that it believes are likely to exhibit earnings surprise. Its focus on big cap, high-momentum growth stocks caused the fund to underperform a market led by value stocks in 1988, but has made it a top performer in the earnings-driven market of the past 3 years.

Portfolio Manager: Irwin Smith
Since: 1986

Minimum:
Initial: $1,000
Subsequent: $100
Telephone Exchange: Yes
Distributions:
Income: Semiannually
Capital Gain: Annually
Front-End Load: None
12b-1: 1.00%
Redemption Fee: 1.00%
Management Company: Thomson Asset Management
Ticker Symbol: TGWBX

TOTAL RETURN (%)

1987	1988	1989	1990	1991	5-year	Bull Market	Bear Market
7.6	9.4	37.5	0.3	41.9	130.2	44.7	-19.1

INVESTMENT PORTFOLIO

Total Assets (mil.)	Current Yield	Turnover Ratio	Expense Ratio	Beta	Risk Return
$580	0.3%	45%	1.70%	1.01	0.07

TRANSAMERICA SPECIAL BLUE CHIP FUND

TransAmerica Distributors
1000 Louisiana, Suite 6000
Houston, TX 77002
800-343-6840

Investment Objective: Formerly a member of the Criterion fund family, this fund seeks to earn a high level of total return through investments in securities of well-known and established blue chip companies. The fund's common stock selections must meet 5 criteria: earn a return on shareholders' equity greater than the average rate of return of companies in the S&P 500 Index; have a ratio of debt to total capital of less than 40%; have an historical earnings growth rate over the past 10 years greater than that of the S&P 500; have paid a dividend in each of the past 5 years; and have a market capitalization greater than $1 billion. It has delivered average returns during the past 5 years.

Portfolio Manager: Ed Larson
Since: 1989

Minimum:
Initial: $1,000
Subsequent: $50
Telephone Exchange: Yes
Distributions:
Income: Annually
Capital Gain: Annually
Front-End Load: None
12b-1: 1.19%
Redemption Fee: 6.00%
Management Company: TransAmerica Fund Management
Ticker Symbol: TSBCX

TOTAL RETURN (%)

1987	1988	1989	1990	1991	5-year	Bull Market	Bear Market
16.0	0.2	22.3	0.2	32.0	88.1	37.5	-18.9

INVESTMENT PORTFOLIO

Total Assets (mil.)	Current Yield	Turnover Ratio	Expense Ratio	Beta	Risk Return
$26	0.0%	51%	1.68%	0.85	0.06

TRINITY EQUITY

Trinity Capital Management
183 East Main Street
Rochester, NY 14604
800-456-7780

Investment Objective: This fund seeks long-term growth of capital by primarily investing in a diversified portfolio of well-known established companies. Under normal conditions, at least 65% of its assets will be invested in companies with market capitalizations above $200 million and that are in the S&P 500 Index or the Dow Jones Industrial Average. This new offering practically duplicated the S&P 500 in 1991 with its 30.3% return. As with any recent offering, investors have no track record to reference, but 1991 was a nice beginning for this industry newcomer.

Portfolio Manager: David Khalil
Since: 1990

Minimum:
Initial: $1,000
Subsequent: $100
Telephone Exchange: Yes
Distributions:
Income: Quarterly
Capital Gain: Annually
Front-End Load: None
12b-1: 0.25%
Redemption Fee: None
Management Company: Chase Lincoln First Bank
Ticker Symbol: TREQX

TOTAL RETURN (%)

1987	1988	1989	1990	1991	5-year	Bull Market	Bear Market
NA	NA	NA	NA	30.3	NA	NA	NA

INVESTMENT PORTFOLIO

Total Assets (mil.)	Current Yield	Turnover Ratio	Expense Ratio	Beta	Risk Return
$98	1.2%	NA	0.55%	NA	NA

UNIFIED GROWTH FUND

Unified Management
429 North Pennsylvania Street
Indianapolis, IN 46204
800-862-7283

Investment Objective: Unified Growth Fund has historically pursued its capital-appreciation objectives by investing in medium- and small-sized stocks. Consequently, it has mirrored the performance of the small stocks indices over the past 10 years, severely underperforming its large cap oriented rivals. The past year, however, the fund changed portfolio managers and adopted a new strategy. It now features a mix of large and small stocks that appear undervalued. While this approach has allowed recent results to improve, the fund's long-term track record remains subpar.

Portfolio Manager: Moran Asset Management
Since: 1990

Minimum:
Initial: $1,000
Subsequent: $50
Telephone Exchange: Yes
Distributions:
Income: Annually
Capital Gain: Annually
Front-End Load: 4.50%
12b-1: None
Redemption Fee: None
Management Company: Unified Management
Ticker Symbol: UNGFX

TOTAL RETURN (%)

1987	1988	1989	1990	1991	5-year	Bull Market	Bear Market
-11.6	18.2	18.3	-5.2	24.8	46.2	60.0	-32.7

INVESTMENT PORTFOLIO

Total Assets (mil.)	Current Yield	Turnover Ratio	Expense Ratio	Beta	Risk Return
$12	0.1%	115%	0.76%	1.16	0.03

UNITED ACCUMULATIVE FUND

Waddell & Reed
6300 Lamar Avenue, P.O. Box 29217
Shawnee Mission, KS 66201
800-366-5465

Investment Objective: This fund seeks capital appreciation primarily by investing in common stocks of large capitalization companies. Manager Anthony Intagliata is a top-down investor/sector rotator who trades rapidly in response to macroeconomic/industry trends. The fund's portfolio is typically comprised of above-average-yielding blue chips from industries that reflect his perception of the business cycle's current phase. Although his tactics backfired during the past 2 years, they have historically produced a winning combination of top-notch returns and moderate risk. Long-term shareholders can expect to be well rewarded for their patience.

Portfolio Manager: Anthony Intagliata
Since: 1979

Minimum:
Initial: $500
Subsequent: None
Telephone Exchange: No
Distributions:
Income: Semiannually
Capital Gain: Annually
Front-End Load: 8.50%
12b-1: None
Redemption Fee: None
Management Company: Waddell & Reed Investments
Ticker Symbol: UNACX

TOTAL RETURN (%)

1987	1988	1989	1990	1991	5-year	Bull Market	Bear Market
4.7	17.1	27.6	-10.2	23.7	73.8	31.2	-18.7

INVESTMENT PORTFOLIO

Total Assets (mil.)	Current Yield	Turnover Ratio	Expense Ratio	Beta	Risk Return
$831	2.5%	289%	0.64%	0.94	0.04

UNITED SERVICE FUNDS ALL AMERICAN EQUITY FUND

United Services Advisers
P.O. Box 29467
San Antonio, TX 78229
800-873-8637

Investment Objective: This fund seeks to provide investment results that correspond as closely as possible to the performance of the S&P 500 Index through a "passive" or "indexing" approach. Management uses a selection technique known as "stratified optimization" to select a representative sample of the stocks that make up the S&P 500. In theory, this approach should allow the fund to construct a portfolio with the same overall characteristics as the S&P 500. Unfortunately, this hasn't been the case in practice. The fund has severely trailed the S&P 500 in every year out of the past 5.

Minimum:
Initial: $1,000
Subsequent: $50
Telephone Exchange: Yes
Distributions:
Income: Annually
Capital Gain: Annually
Front-End Load: None
12b-1: None
Redemption Fee: None
Management Company: United Services Advisers
Ticker Symbol: GBTFX

Portfolio Manager: J. David Edwards
Since: 1987

TOTAL RETURN (%)

1987	1988	1989	1990	1991	5-year	Bull Market	Bear Market
0.6	-3.1	16.8	-11.3	26.6	27.9	28.7	-15.0

INVESTMENT PORTFOLIO

Total Assets (mil.)	Current Yield	Turnover Ratio	Expense Ratio	Beta	Risk Return
$11	0.6%	209%	2.80%	0.90	0.05

UNITED SERVICE FUNDS GROWTH

United Services Advisers
P.O. Box 29467
San Antonio, TX 78229
800-873-8637

Investment Objective: This fund seeks capital appreciation by investing in medium-sized companies that show above-average earnings growth. Management's growth-intensive strategy causes it to concentrate its assets in relatively few high-growth industries that recently have included technology, telecommunications and cable TV. While this focused approach gives the fund enormous upside potential, it also makes it vulnerable to sharp declines when its major industries fall out of favor, as was the case in 1990. Its 5-year performance has been subpar.

Minimum:
Initial: $1,000
Subsequent: $50
Telephone Exchange: Yes
Distributions:
Income: Annually
Capital Gain: Annually
Front-End Load: None
12b-1: None
Redemption Fee: None
Management Company: United Services Advisers
Ticker Symbol: GRTHX

Portfolio Manager: J. David Edwards
Since: 1987

TOTAL RETURN (%)

1987	1988	1989	1990	1991	5-year	Bull Market	Bear Market
-11.2	10.5	20.5	-13.3	27.0	30.1	38.0	-23.1

INVESTMENT PORTFOLIO

Total Assets (mil.)	Current Yield	Turnover Ratio	Expense Ratio	Beta	Risk Return
$5	1.6%	109%	2.75%	1.09	0.03

UNITED VANGUARD FUND

Waddell & Reed
6300 Lamar Avenue, P.O. Box 29217
Shawnee Mission, KS 66201
800-366-5465

Investment Objective: United Vanguard Fund has achieved a competitive risk-reward profile through a strategy that emphasizes relatively cheap blue chips with the potential for earnings surprise. Trading rapidly, managements favors industries that it believes are likely to benefit from macroeconomic and/or industry trends. Still, its price consciousness prevents it from investing heavily in high-expectation sectors. Major areas of emphasis include relatively unpopular industrial products and consumer durables and a host of potential restructuring/deal stocks.

Portfolio Manager: Chuck Hooper
Since: 1987

Minimum:
Initial: $500
Subsequent: None
Telephone Exchange: No
Distributions:
Income: Semiannually
Capital Gain: Annually
Front-End Load: 8.50%
12b-1: None
Redemption Fee: None
Management Company: Waddell & Reed Investments
Ticker Symbol: UNVGX

TOTAL RETURN (%)

1987	1988	1989	1990	1991	5-year	Bull Market	Bear Market
8.9	13.3	18.7	-3.6	27.4	79.9	39.1	-22.5

INVESTMENT PORTFOLIO

Total Assets (mil.)	Current Yield	Turnover Ratio	Expense Ratio	Beta	Risk Return
$846	1.6%	162%	0.98%	0.95	0.05

USAA GROWTH FUND

USAA Investment Management
USAA Building
San Antonio, TX 78288
800-531-8181

Investment Objective: This fund seeks growth of capital primarily by investing in common stocks of large established companies. Secondary goals include the pursuit of current income and conservation of capital. Portfolio Manager William Fries stresses large established companies that sell at modest valuations and that also fit with his perception of macroeconomic/market trends. The fund's good resistance to decline during 1990 underscores his ability to quickly adjust the portfolio in response to market conditions. Moreover, Fries' good results since his 1989 arrival suggests this fund now can be expected to produce competitive returns in most markets.

Portfolio Manager: William V. Fries
Since: 1989

Minimum:
Initial: $1,000
Subsequent: $25
Telephone Exchange: Yes
Distributions:
Income: Semiannually
Capital Gain: Annually
Front-End Load: None
12b-1: None
Redemption Fee: None
Management Company: USAA Investment Management
Ticker Symbol: USAAX

TOTAL RETURN (%)

1987	1988	1989	1990	1991	5-year	Bull Market	Bear Market
5.3	6.6	27.3	-0.1	27.8	82.6	33.8	-16.4

INVESTMENT PORTFOLIO

Total Assets (mil.)	Current Yield	Turnover Ratio	Expense Ratio	Beta	Risk Return
$324	2.4%	56%	1.18%	0.90	0.05

VANGUARD INDEX TRUST EXTENDED MARKET

Vanguard Group
Vanguard Financial Center
Valley Forge, PA 19482
800-662-7447

Investment Objective: The Extended Market portfolio seeks to replicate the aggregate price and yield performance of the Wilshire 4500 Index, an index comprised of more than 5,000 regularly traded medium- and small-sized U.S. stocks that are not in the S&P 500. Because the fund is unable to hold all of the issues that make up the Wilshire 4500, it utilizes a statistical technique known as "stratified sampling" to select a representative sample. With this technique, each stock is selected and weighted in an effort to duplicate the market capitalization, industry characteristics and other fundamental characteristics (i.e., dividend yield, price-earnings multiple) of the Wilshire 4500.

Portfolio Manager: George Sauter
Since: 1987

Minimum:
Initial: $3,000
Subsequent: $100
Telephone Exchange: No
Distributions:
Income: Annually
Capital Gain: Annually
Front-End Load: None
12b-1: None
Redemption Fee: None
Management Company: Vanguard Group
Ticker Symbol: VEXMX

TOTAL RETURN (%)

1987	1988	1989	1990	1991	5-year	Bull Market	Bear Market
NA	19.7	24.1	-14.0	41.8	NA	48.7	-24.0

INVESTMENT PORTFOLIO

Total Assets (mil.)	Current Yield	Turnover Ratio	Expense Ratio	Beta	Risk Return
$326	1.6%	9%	0.23%	0.99	0.07

VANGUARD INDEX TRUST 500

Vanguard Group
Vanguard Financial Center
Valley Forge, PA 19482
800-662-7447

Investment Objective: Vanguard Index Trust 500 portfolio seeks to duplicate the aggregate price and yield performance of the Standard & Poor's 500 Composite Stock Price Index. Utilizing an indexing technique known as "complete replication," the fund invests in all of the index's 500 stocks in approximately the same proportions as they are represented in the index. This method, coupled with Vanguard's traditional no-load format and well-contained operating expenses, allow the fund to closely track the S&P 500 year in and year out. Investors seeking a pure S&P 500 Index vehicle won't find a more suitable choice.

Portfolio Manager: George Sauter
Since: 1987

Minimum:
Initial: $3,000
Subsequent: $100
Telephone Exchange: No
Distributions:
Income: Quarterly
Capital Gain: Annually
Front-End Load: None
12b-1: None
Redemption Fee: None
Management Company: Vanguard Group
Ticker Symbol: VFINX

TOTAL RETURN (%)

1987	1988	1989	1990	1991	5-year	Bull Market	Bear Market
4.7	16.2	31.4	-3.3	30.2	101.2	37.1	-19.2

INVESTMENT PORTFOLIO

Total Assets (mil.)	Current Yield	Turnover Ratio	Expense Ratio	Beta	Risk Return
$3,769	2.9%	23%	0.22%	1.00	0.05

VANGUARD MORGAN GROWTH FUND

Vanguard Group
Vanguard Financial Center
Valley Forge, PA 19482
800-662-7447

Investment Objective: This fund is run by 3 separate investment advisers. Wellington Management, responsible for roughly two-thirds of the fund's equity investments, utilizes traditional methods of security selection, including fundamental company research and relative valuation techniques. In contrast, Franklin Portfolio Associates Trust and Rol and Ross Asset Management, each responsible for roughly one-sixth of the fund's equity assets, employ quantitative techniques designed to at least track the composite performance of the common stock holdings of the 50 largest growth mutual funds. This strategy has produced stellar returns during the past 5 years.

Portfolio Manager: Frank Wisneski
Since: 1979

Minimum:
Initial: $3,000
Subsequent: $100
Telephone Exchange: Yes
Distributions:
Income: Annually
Capital Gain: Annually
Front-End Load: None
12b-1: None
Redemption Fee: None
Management Company: Wellington Management
Ticker Symbol: VMRGX

TOTAL RETURN (%)

1987	1988	1989	1990	1991	5-year	Bull Market	Bear Market
5.0	22.3	22.7	-1.5	29.3	100.7	38.8	-21.0

INVESTMENT PORTFOLIO

Total Assets (mil.)	Current Yield	Turnover Ratio	Expense Ratio	Beta	Risk Return
$859	2.2%	73%	0.55%	1.00	0.05

VANGUARD PRIMECAP FUND

Vanguard Group
Vanguard Financial Center
Valley Forge, PA 19482
800-662-7447

Investment Objective: Vanguard Primecap seeks long-term capital appreciation primarily by investing in large and medium capitalization common stocks that offer favorable prospects for capital growth but little current income. Common stocks are selected on the basis of several fundamental factors, including above-average growth in corporate earnings, consistency of earnings growth and earnings quality. These criteria have led the fund to concentrate assets in relatively few growth sectors that meet its standards of value, including health care, whose relatively strong performance during 1990 help to offset losses on the fund's also sizable stake in financial stocks.

Portfolio Manager: Howard Schow
Since: 1984

Minimum:
Initial: $10,000
Subsequent: $1,000
Telephone Exchange: Yes
Distributions:
Income: Annually
Capital Gain: Annually
Front-End Load: None
12b-1: None
Redemption Fee: None
Management Company: Primecap Management
Ticker Symbol: VPMCX

TOTAL RETURN (%)

1987	1988	1989	1990	1991	5-year	Bull Market	Bear Market
-2.3	14.7	21.6	-2.8	33.1	76.3	49.3	-25.4

INVESTMENT PORTFOLIO

Total Assets (mil.)	Current Yield	Turnover Ratio	Expense Ratio	Beta	Risk Return
$438	0.9%	11%	0.75%	1.11	0.05

VANGUARD WORLD U.S. GROWTH FUND

Vanguard Group
Vanguard Financial Center
Valley Forge, PA 19482
800-662-7447

Investment Objective: Vanguard World U.S. Growth Fund invests primarily in equity securities of seasoned U.S. companies with above-average prospects for growth. Lincoln Capital Management, adviser to the portfolio since 1987, emphasizes attractively valued stocks of companies with exceptional growth records, strong market positions, financial strength and relatively low sensitivity to changing economic conditions. Since its 1987 implementation, the fund's pure-growth approach has produced superior returns.

Portfolio Manager: J. Parker Hall III
Since: 1987

Minimum:
Initial: $3,000
Subsequent: $100
Telephone Exchange: Yes
Distributions:
Income: Annually
Capital Gain: Annually
Front-End Load: None
12b-1: None
Redemption Fee: None
Management Company: Lincoln Capital Management
Ticker Symbol: VWUSX

TOTAL RETURN (%)

1987	1988	1989	1990	1991	5-year	Bull Market	Bear Market
-6.1	8.8	38.2	4.2	46.8	115.9	49.3	-23.8

INVESTMENT PORTFOLIO

Total Assets (mil.)	Current Yield	Turnover Ratio	Expense Ratio	Beta	Risk Return
$795	1.3%	30%	0.56%	1.12	0.08

WAYNE HUMMER GROWTH FUND

Wayne Hummer & Company
175 West Jackson Boulevard
Chicago, IL 60604
800-621-4477

Investment Objective: This fund seeks capital appreciation by investing in a diversified portfolio of equity securities. Management selects stocks strictly from the bottom up, stressing reasonably priced companies with growth rates that exceed that of the overall economy. It also likes to see a strong market niche, a high return on earnings, consistent dividend growth and a high degree of insider ownership. Coupled with its price discipline, these quality parameters have enabled it to build a solid trailing 5-year record with modest risk. Its mix of stock sizes makes it a good choice for conservative investors seeking some exposure to small caps. It is the only broker-sponsored equity fund to offer a no-load format.

Portfolio Manager: Alan Bird
Since: 1983

Minimum:
Initial: $1,000
Subsequent: $500
Telephone Exchange: Yes
Distributions:
Income: Quarterly
Capital Gain: Annually
Front-End Load: None
12b-1: None
Redemption Fee: None
Management Company: Wayne Hummer Management
Ticker Symbol: WHGRX

TOTAL RETURN (%)

1987	1988	1989	1990	1991	5-year	Bull Market	Bear Market
9.3	7.0	24.0	5.0	28.9	96.3	39.3	-15.7

INVESTMENT PORTFOLIO

Total Assets (mil.)	Current Yield	Turnover Ratio	Expense Ratio	Beta	Risk Return
$45	1.9%	13%	1.36%	0.79	0.06

WILLIAM BLAIR GROWTH SHARES

William Blair & Company
135 South LaSalle Street
Chicago, IL 60603
800-635-2886

Investment Objective: Achieving long-term capital appreciation by investing in well-managed companies in growing industries is this fund's investment objective. Most of the fund's companies show consistent above-average growth in earnings, high profitability ratios and low leverage. Along with being a pure no-load vehicle, the fund also has below-average turnover and expense ratios, which both contribute to an investor's total return. A total return of 113.2% over the past 5 years makes this fund all the more appealing.

Minimum:
Initial: $1,000
Subsequent: $250
Telephone Exchange: Yes
Distributions:
Income: Semiannually
Capital Gain: Annually
Front-End Load: None
12b-1: None
Redemption Fee: None
Management Company: William Blair & Company
Ticker Symbol: WBGSX

Portfolio Manager: Neal L. Seltzer
Since: 1985

TOTAL RETURN (%)

1987	1988	1989	1990	1991	5-year	Bull Market	Bear Market
8.0	7.2	30.5	-2.0	44.1	113.2	45.0	-21.2

INVESTMENT PORTFOLIO

Total Assets (mil.)	Current Yield	Turnover Ratio	Expense Ratio	Beta	Risk Return
$80	0.7%	34%	0.87%	1.04	0.08

WPG GROWTH FUND

Weiss Peck & Greer
One New York Plaza
New York, NY 10004
800-223-3332

Investment Objective: This no-load fund seeks maximum capital appreciation by investing in common stocks of growth companies. The fund owns a few big cap stocks; however, most of its assets are invested in medium and small capitalization issues of emerging-growth companies. The fund's major industries, which include health care, media and business services, underscore its high-growth aspirations. Although the fund's taste for small-growth stocks has hurt returns in recent years, this situation reversed itself the past year and the fund became one of the industry's top performers.

Minimum:
Initial: $250,000
Subsequent: $25,000
Telephone Exchange: Yes
Distributions:
Income: Semiannually
Capital Gain: Annually
Front-End Load: None
12b-1: None
Redemption Fee: None
Management Company: Tudor Management
Ticker Symbol: WPGRX

Portfolio Manager: Melville Straus
Since: 1986

TOTAL RETURN (%)

1987	1988	1989	1990	1991	5-year	Bull Market	Bear Market
-3.2	11.7	25.0	-12.8	56.8	84.7	61.6	-28.8

INVESTMENT PORTFOLIO

Total Assets (mil.)	Current Yield	Turnover Ratio	Expense Ratio	Beta	Risk Return
$169	0.2%	82%	1.05%	1.24	0.08

ZWEIG PRIORITY SELECTION FUND

Zweig Securities
5 Hanover Square, 17th Floor
New York, NY 10004
800-272-2700

Investment Objective: The fund attempts to earn a reasonable return in advancing markets and protect capital in down markets by readjusting its stock market exposure in response to its measurement of market risk. In selecting stocks, the fund gives much consideration to momentum; it quickly weeds out issues that show poor price action. Since coming under the management of Zweig/Glaser Advisers, this former Drexel offering has been a first-rate performer. After running with the bulls in 1989, the fund lowered its equity exposure on signs of increasing risk and sidestepped much of the 1990's debacle. It then produced a market-beating return the past year.

Portfolio Manager: Joseph Kalish
Since: 1991

Minimum:
Initial: $1,000
Subsequent: $100
Telephone Exchange: Yes
Distributions:
Income: Quarterly
Capital Gain: Annually
Front-End Load: 5.50%
12b-1: 0.30%
Redemption Fee: 4.00%
Management Company: Zweig/Glaser Advisers
Ticker Symbol: ZPSLX

TOTAL RETURN (%)

1987	1988	1989	1990	1991	5-year	Bull Market	Bear Market
NA	10.3	37.4	-2.3	34.9	NA	33.9	-15.9

INVESTMENT PORTFOLIO

Total Assets (mil.)	Current Yield	Turnover Ratio	Expense Ratio	Beta	Risk Return
$53	0.8%	153%	1.77%	0.92	0.07

ZWEIG STRATEGY FUND

Zweig Securities
5 Hanover Square, 17th Floor
New York, NY 10004
800-272-2700

Investment Objective: This relatively new fund seeks capital appreciation, preservation of capital and reduced market risk through investment in blue chip common stocks. The extent of the fund's investment in stocks and the selection of individual securities are determined on the basis of proprietary market timing and stock-selection techniques. Management utilizes a computer-driven model to rank roughly 600 stocks on earnings and price. Selected stocks are weighted in an effort to give the portfolio risk characteristics similar to that of the S&P 500. The fund also uses certain specialized techniques, including short-selling and the purchase of stock index futures.

Portfolio Manager: David Katzen
Since: 1989

Minimum:
Initial: $1,000
Subsequent: $100
Telephone Exchange: Yes
Distributions:
Income: Quarterly
Capital Gain: Annually
Front-End Load: 5.50%
12b-1: 0.30%
Redemption Fee: None
Management Company: Zweig/Glaser Advisers
Ticker Symbol: ZSTFX

TOTAL RETURN (%)

1987	1988	1989	1990	1991	5-year	Bull Market	Bear Market
NA	NA	NA	-2.2	23.4	NA	25.6	-9.2

INVESTMENT PORTFOLIO

Total Assets (mil.)	Current Yield	Turnover Ratio	Expense Ratio	Beta	Risk Return
$346	1.9%	105%	1.67%	0.63	0.05

PART 6

Growth and Income Funds

Growth and income funds seek a high level of current income, some capital appreciation and preservation of capital. This category includes balanced funds, total return funds and equity-income funds.

Balanced funds (generally referred to as "total-return" funds these days) invest in a portfolio of common stocks and bonds. The allocation may be either fixed by investment policy or may vary, depending on which category of assets is expected to produce the greatest total return. Some balanced funds may invest in convertible bonds and preferred stocks. Given the split allocation between common stocks and bonds, balanced funds tend to possess relatively low betas. While they provide some protection during periods of declining stock prices, they are highly interest-rate sensitive, and their per share net asset values can decline by significant amounts during periods of rising interest rates.

Equity-income funds invest primarily in common stocks that have higher dividend yields than the dividend yield of the Standard & Poor's 500 Index (a commonly accepted proxy for the stock market as a whole). In addition to higher-than-average dividend yields, the common stocks held by these funds tend to have relatively low betas, lower-than-average price-earnings multiples and relatively low price-book-value ratios. As a consequence, the per share net asset values of these funds tend to fall less than the overall stock market in a decline. However, they also rise less during bull markets.

Growth and income funds tend to be suitable for conservative investors who are not willing to assume the full risk associated with equity investments. In addition, these funds make suitable candidates for the portfolios of income-oriented investors because of their generous dividend yields. Furthermore, because these funds include common stocks in their portfolios, they offer a degree of capital appreciation and, thus, an offset against rising consumer prices. In other words, these funds offer income investors a degree of inflation protection that is not present in a pure fixed-income fund.

On average, growth and income funds possess about three-fourths the volatility of the market as a whole (median beta of 0.74). In 1991, their current yield was about 40 basis points higher than the dividend yield of the Standard & Poor's 500 Index. And, as would be expected, these funds returned less than the S&P 500 Index over the past five years: median five-year total return of 74 percent versus 104 percent for the S&P 500.

Summary of Financial Statistics (medians)

1991 Return	5-Year Return	Current Yield	Beta	Turnover Ratio	Expense Ratio
25.9%	72.4%	3.3%	0.74	58%	1.05%

BEST GROWTH AND INCOME FUNDS FOR 1991

Fund	Percent Return 1991	3-Year	5-Year
Berger 101 Fund	61.0%	78.2%	82.3%
Kemper Diversified Income Fund	51.7	43.2	56.2
Kemper Investment Portfolios—Diversified I	50.9	36.1	41.7
Financial Industrial Income Fund	46.3	94.7	135.7
Twentieth Century Balanced Investors	46.2	87.1	NA
CIGNA Value Fund	43.5	92.3	145.7
Kemper Investment Portfolios—Total Return	42.5	71.5	94.4
Fidelity Growth & Income Portfolio	41.8	71.3	122.9
CGM Mutual Fund	40.9	73.4	103.3
Franklin Custodian Funds—Income Series	40.7	43.3	62.3
WPG Growth & Income	40.7	60.9	88.1
Legg Mason Total Return Trust	40.5	36.1	52.7
Kemper Total Return Fund	40.2	74.8	85.7
Carnegie-Cappiello Total Return Series	39.5	53.9	67.6
AIM Charter Fund	37.8	105.9	136.4
Merrill Lynch Phoenix Fund A	37.0	23.7	66.4
Mainstay Total Return Fund	36.8	65.3	NA
Oppenheimer Total Return Fund	36.3	56.1	98.9
Ivy Growth With Income Fund	36.3	60.6	97.9
General Securities	35.7	62.9	89.9
PaineWebber Dividend Growth Fund A	35.3	66.9	90.5
Security Equity Fund	35.2	68.7	109.5
Stratton Monthly Dividend Shares	35.1	54.4	50.1
Strong Total Return Fund	33.6	27.3	56.1
Lutheran Brotherhood Fund	32.8	64.9	74.2

AARP GROWTH AND INCOME FUND

Scudder Stevens & Clark
175 Federal Street, 12th Floor
Boston, MA 02110
800-253-2277

Investment Objective: This member of the AARP family seeks capital growth, current income and growth of income as its investment objective. It attempts to do so by investing in a mix of high-yielding common stocks and convertible securities. From 1987–1991, the fund performed well considering the level of risk assumed. In 1991, the fund returned 26.5%, compared to the S&P 500's return of 30.4%. This was accomplished with a risk level 28% less than the S&P 500. However, future performance may be tempered because management invests in several interest-sensitive stocks. Rising interest rates tend to be a poor environment for these type of stocks.

Portfolio Manager: Robert Harvey
Since: 1985

Minimum:
Initial: $500
Subsequent: None
Telephone Exchange: Yes
Distributions:
Income: Quarterly
Capital Gain: Annually
Front-End Load: None
12b-1: None
Redemption Fee: None
Management Company: Scudder Stevens & Clark
Ticker Symbol: AGIFX

TOTAL RETURN (%)

1987	1988	1989	1990	1991	5-year	Bull Market	Bear Market
0.9	10.9	26.7	-2.1	26.5	75.5	31.9	-12.2

INVESTMENT PORTFOLIO

Total Assets (mil.)	Current Yield	Turnover Ratio	Expense Ratio	Beta	Risk Return
$411	3.5%	54%	0.96%	0.72	0.06

ABT GROWTH & INCOME TRUST

ABT Financial Services
205 Royal Palm Way
Palm Beach, FL 33480
800-289-2281

Investment Objective: This fund's objective is to achieve both dividend income and capital appreciation. Generally, the fund invests in dividend-paying common, preferred and convertible preferred stocks. Although the fund also can invest in bonds, management has chosen not to do so in recent years. As could be expected of a growth and income fund that stresses investment in common stocks, the portfolio contains relatively large allocations to the financial services, public utilities and natural resources stocks. Investors should take note of the 4.75% front-end load.

Portfolio Manager: Harold J. Ireland
Since: 1991

Minimum:
Initial: $1,000
Subsequent: $25
Telephone Exchange: Yes
Distributions:
Income: Quarterly
Capital Gain: Annually
Front-End Load: 4.75%
12b-1: 0.25%
Redemption Fee: None
Management Company: Palm Beach Capital Management
Ticker Symbol: GRWTX

TOTAL RETURN (%)

1987	1988	1989	1990	1991	5-year	Bull Market	Bear Market
4.0	19.2	15.3	-9.3	29.5	68.0	34.0	-20.0

INVESTMENT PORTFOLIO

Total Assets (mil.)	Current Yield	Turnover Ratio	Expense Ratio	Beta	Risk Return
$87	2.1%	89%	1.29%	0.86	0.06

AFFILIATED FUND

Lord Abbett & Company
767 Fifth Avenue
New York, NY 10153
800-874-3733

Investment Objective: The Affiliated Fund is a conservatively managed growth and income vehicle that primarily invests in the stocks of large, seasoned companies (blue chips). Like others in the Lord Abbett fund family, the Affiliated Fund carries a hefty front-end load charge of 6.75%. The fund also levies a 15 basis point 12b-1 fee. Overall, the fund has been an average performer over the past 5 years at a risk level 10% to 20% below that of the S&P 500 Index. A new portfolio manager, Thomas Henderson, was installed the past year with the hopes that this fund's average performance will improve.

Portfolio Manager: Thomas S. Henderson
Since: 1991

Minimum:
Initial: $250
Subsequent: None
Telephone Exchange: Yes
Distributions:
Income: Quarterly
Capital Gain: Annually
Front-End Load: 6.75%
12b-1: 0.15%
Redemption Fee: None
Management Company: Lord Abbett
Ticker Symbol: LAFFX

TOTAL RETURN (%)

1987	1988	1989	1990	1991	5-year	Bull Market	Bear Market
2.8	12.4	23.1	-5.3	22.0	64.3	30.8	-17.4

INVESTMENT PORTFOLIO

Total Assets (mil.)	Current Yield	Turnover Ratio	Expense Ratio	Beta	Risk Return
$3,353	3.6%	56%	0.58%	0.85	0.04

AIM CHARTER FUND

AIM Distributors
11 Greenway Plaza, Suite 1919
Houston, TX 77046
800-347-1919

Investment Objective: This fund seeks capital growth and, to a lesser extent, current income. Management invests primarily in common stocks of companies believed to have potential for above-average growth in revenues and earnings. At least 90% of the fund's common stock investments are in common stocks that pay dividends. The portfolio turnover ratio and expense ratio are well above the average level for this type of fund, but Portfolio Manager Julian Lerner has made up for this by posting an impressive 5-year total return of 136.4%. In addition, this fund was one of the very few to post a double-digit return during 1987 and a positive return in 1990.

Portfolio Manager: Julian Lerner
Since: 1968

Minimum:
Initial: $1,000
Subsequent: $25
Telephone Exchange: Yes
Distributions:
Income: Annually
Capital Gain: Annually
Front-End Load: 5.50%
12b-1: 0.21%
Redemption Fee: None
Management Company: AIM Management
Ticker Symbol: CHTRX

TOTAL RETURN (%)

1987	1988	1989	1990	1991	5-year	Bull Market	Bear Market
10.4	4.0	38.1	8.2	37.8	136.4	39.9	-12.2

INVESTMENT PORTFOLIO

Total Assets (mil.)	Current Yield	Turnover Ratio	Expense Ratio	Beta	Risk Return
$476	1.8%	215%	1.40%	0.89	0.07

ALGER INCOME & GROWTH PORTFOLIO

Alger Funds
75 Maiden Lane
New York, NY 10038
800-992-3863

Investment Objective: Considering the fund's primary objective is a high level of dividend income, its current yield of 0.1% is unimpressive. One might think that income has been sacrificed for capital appreciation, but the fund's returns have been lackluster as well. This fund takes above-average risk, but it hasn't seemed to find the right groove for performance. Predictably, the fund still has attracted only $3 million in assets, and these investors pay a marketing charge, a hefty redemption fee and a well above-average expense ratio of 4.72%.

Portfolio Manager: David Alger
Since: 1986

Minimum:
Initial: $1,000
Subsequent: $100
Telephone Exchange: Yes
Distributions:
Income: Annually
Capital Gain: Annually
Front-End Load: None
12b-1: 1.00%
Redemption Fee: 5.00%
Management Company: Fred Alger Management
Ticker Symbol: AINGX

TOTAL RETURN (%)

1987	1988	1989	1990	1991	5-year	Bull Market	Bear Market
0.5	16.0	25.3	-7.8	23.3	66.1	28.1	-16.1

INVESTMENT PORTFOLIO

Total Assets (mil.)	Current Yield	Turnover Ratio	Expense Ratio	Beta	Risk Return
$3	0.1%	74%	4.72%	0.86	0.04

ALLIANCE BALANCED SHARES A

Alliance Funds Distributors
500 Plaza Drive
Secaucus, NJ 07094
800-247-4154

Investment Objective: This fund seeks a high return through a combination of current income and capital appreciation. This balanced fund attempts to maintain an approximate 60/40 mix of stocks and bonds or other fixed-income securities to cushion the portfolio from adverse effects to the NAV in market downturns. Over the past 5 years, the fund has lagged the broader markets. The S&P 500 has produced a return more than 100% over the past 5 years, while this fund has turned in only a 57.5% total return. In addition, the 5.50% sales charge has further lowered investors' net total return.

Portfolio Manager: Bruce Calvert
Since: 1990

Minimum:
Initial: $250
Subsequent: $25
Telephone Exchange: Yes
Distributions:
Income: Quarterly
Capital Gain: Annually
Front-End Load: 5.50%
12b-1: 0.24%
Redemption Fee: None
Management Company: Alliance Capital Management
Ticker Symbol: CABNX

TOTAL RETURN (%)

1987	1988	1989	1990	1991	5-year	Bull Market	Bear Market
-0.2	17.4	14.1	-2.2	20.5	57.5	29.1	-12.4

INVESTMENT PORTFOLIO

Total Assets (mil.)	Current Yield	Turnover Ratio	Expense Ratio	Beta	Risk Return
$148	3.3%	169%	1.36%	0.71	0.04

ALLIANCE GROWTH AND INCOME FUND A

Alliance Funds Distributors
500 Plaza Drive
Secaucus, NJ 07094
800-247-4154

Investment Objective: This fund seeks "reasonable" current income and capital appreciation by investing in dividend-paying common stocks of good quality. High-yielding common stocks tend to decline less than the average common stock during bear markets, and this precept proved to be true in 1990 when the fund slipped only 1.7%. However, these stocks also tend to be highly interest-rate sensitive. Thus, they can decline significantly in price during periods marked by falling stock prices and rising interest rates. On a risk-adjusted basis, this fund has been a better-than-average performer.

Portfolio Manager: Tom Perkins
Since: 1990

Minimum:
Initial: $250
Subsequent: $25
Telephone Exchange: Yes
Distributions:
Income: Quarterly
Capital Gain: Annually
Front-End Load: 5.50%
12b-1: 0.17%
Redemption Fee: None
Management Company: Alliance Capital Management
Ticker Symbol: CABDX

TOTAL RETURN (%)

1987	1988	1989	1990	1991	5-year	Bull Market	Bear Market
0.9	16.8	25.6	-1.7	27.1	84.7	32.8	-18.4

INVESTMENT PORTFOLIO

Total Assets (mil.)	Current Yield	Turnover Ratio	Expense Ratio	Beta	Risk Return
$392	2.5%	76%	1.09%	0.92	0.05

AMERICAN BALANCED FUND

American Funds Distributor
333 South Hope Street, 52nd Floor
Los Angeles, CA 90071
800-421-9900

Investment Objective: By investing in both stocks and bonds, this fund strives to meet 3 objectives: conservation of capital, current income and long-term growth of capital and income. Management does not seek short-term trading profits, and changes in the fund's investments generally are gradual, as witnessed by its modest turnover ratio. Incorporated in 1932, it is one of the oldest funds available to the public today. In 1990, the fund experienced its first loss in more than 16 years. This track record, coupled with a modest risk level, make this fund a candidate for conservative growth and income investors. However, investors should note the 5.75% front-end load and the ongoing 12b-1 fee.

Portfolio Manager: Multiple Portfolio Counselors
Since: 1991

Minimum:
Initial: $500
Subsequent: $50
Telephone Exchange: Yes
Distributions:
Income: Semiannually
Capital Gain: Annually
Front-End Load: 5.75%
12b-1: 0.16%
Redemption Fee: None
Management Company: Capital Research & Management
Ticker Symbol: ABALX

TOTAL RETURN (%)

1987	1988	1989	1990	1991	5-year	Bull Market	Bear Market
4.0	12.9	21.5	-1.6	24.7	75.1	30.0	-12.4

INVESTMENT PORTFOLIO

Total Assets (mil.)	Current Yield	Turnover Ratio	Expense Ratio	Beta	Risk Return
$588	4.8%	26%	0.84%	0.62	0.06

AMERICAN CAPITAL EQUITY INCOME FUND

American Capital Marketing
P.O. Box 3528
Houston, TX 77253
800-421-5666

Investment Objective: This load fund, 5.75% front end, seeks the highest possible income consistent with safety of principal. Long-term growth of capital is an important secondary consideration. Investments are made in common stocks, preferred stocks, bonds of any rating and convertibles. The newest addition to the fund is the portfolio manager, James Gilligan. Some of the major changes Gilligan has made to the portfolio are an increased position in convertibles and a shift of assets to larger capitalization companies, which help limit the damage from 1990's bear market.

Portfolio Manager: Jim Gilligan
Since: 1990

Minimum:
Initial: $500
Subsequent: $50
Telephone Exchange: Yes
Distributions:
Income: Quarterly
Capital Gain: Annually
Front-End Load: 5.75%
12b-1: 0.13%
Redemption Fee: None
Management Company: American Capital Asset Management
Ticker Symbol: ACEIX

TOTAL RETURN (%)

1987	1988	1989	1990	1991	5-year	Bull Market	Bear Market
1.9	12.1	21.6	-4.7	26.7	67.8	29.2	-15.6

INVESTMENT PORTFOLIO

Total Assets (mil.)	Current Yield	Turnover Ratio	Expense Ratio	Beta	Risk Return
$96	4.2%	150%	0.89%	0.72	0.06

AMERICAN CAPITAL GROWTH & INCOME FUND

American Capital Marketing
P.O. Box 3528
Houston, TX 77253
800-421-5666

Investment Objective: This growth and income vehicle seeks the highest possible income consistent with safety of principle and attention to capital growth. Investments are made in common stocks, preferred stocks, bonds of any rating and convertibles. The fund has a laudable 5-year track record, besting its peer average by almost 10%. However, the fund tends to trade its portfolio rapidly and hits investors with a 5.75% front-end load. Despite its emphasis on income, the fund's yield fell below that of most funds in its category.

Portfolio Manager: Jim Gilligan
Since: 1990

Minimum:
Initial: $500
Subsequent: $50
Telephone Exchange: Yes
Distributions:
Income: Quarterly
Capital Gain: Annually
Front-End Load: 5.75%
12b-1: 0.11%
Redemption Fee: None
Management Company: American Capital Asset Management
Ticker Symbol: ACGIX

TOTAL RETURN (%)

1987	1988	1989	1990	1991	5-year	Bull Market	Bear Market
9.4	16.3	15.6	-5.2	30.2	81.6	37.8	-20.4

INVESTMENT PORTFOLIO

Total Assets (mil.)	Current Yield	Turnover Ratio	Expense Ratio	Beta	Risk Return
$157	2.8%	111%	1.13%	0.96	0.05

AMERICAN LEADERS FUND

Federated Securities
Federated Investors Tower
Pittsburgh, PA 15222
800-356-2805

Investment Objective: The fund seeks both growth of capital and current income through investments in dividend-paying blue chip common stocks. Over the past 2 years, the fund may have turned the corner as 1990's loss was pale in comparison to many of its competitors. The past year saw the fund return an above-average 31%, and the fund's 5-year return is beginning to approach that of its growth and income counterparts, trailing by just 3%. However, investors must ante up the 4.50% front-end load charged by Federated Investors.

Portfolio Manager: Peter R. Anderson
Since: 1989

Minimum:
Initial: $500
Subsequent: $100
Telephone Exchange: Yes
Distributions:
Income: Quarterly
Capital Gain: Annually
Front-End Load: 4.50%
12b-1: None
Redemption Fee: 0.50%
Management Company: Federated Investors
Ticker Symbol: FALDX

TOTAL RETURN (%)

1987	1988	1989	1990	1991	5-year	Bull Market	Bear Market
4.7	12.1	11.7	-1.8	31.0	68.7	42.8	-21.6

INVESTMENT PORTFOLIO

Total Assets (mil.)	Current Yield	Turnover Ratio	Expense Ratio	Beta	Risk Return
$147	1.7%	57%	1.02%	0.88	0.06

AMERICAN MUTUAL FUND

American Funds Distributor
333 South Hope Street, 52nd Floor
Los Angeles, CA 90071
800-421-9900

Investment Objective: This fund, which commenced operations in 1950, strives for the balanced accomplishment of 3 investment objectives: current income, capital growth and stability of the NAV through investments primarily in blue chip common stocks. The fund's management style is somewhat unique in that it has shunned both the single manager and investment committee styles and has opted to employ 4 investment counselors who each manage between 10 and 20% of the fund's assets, with the balance being managed by a team of analysts. Although the fund has not performed so well as the market during the past 5 years, its return is enviable, given the fund's relatively low beta.

Portfolio Manager: Multiple Portfolio Counselors
Since: 1983

Minimum:
Initial: $250
Subsequent: $50
Telephone Exchange: Yes
Distributions:
Income: Quarterly
Capital Gain: Annually
Front-End Load: 5.75%
12b-1: 0.15%
Redemption Fee: None
Management Company: Capital Research & Management
Ticker Symbol: AMRMX

TOTAL RETURN (%)

1987	1988	1989	1990	1991	5-year	Bull Market	Bear Market
4.4	12.8	25.3	-1.6	21.7	76.7	25.8	-12.1

INVESTMENT PORTFOLIO

Total Assets (mil.)	Current Yield	Turnover Ratio	Expense Ratio	Beta	Risk Return
$3,996	3.8%	24%	0.63%	0.70	0.05

AMERICAN NATIONAL INCOME FUND

Securities Management & Research
Two Moody Plaza
Galveston, TX 77550
800-231-4639

Investment Objective: Though deemed more of an income fund than a growth vehicle, this fund has achieved above-average returns over the past 5 years by investing in large cap consumer and natural gas stocks. Most impressive about the fund's recent performance was its ability to earn positive returns in each of the past 5 years, including 1990's bear market. Overall, the fund is more of an excellent growth vehicle than an income vehicle. Investors should note, however, that the fund carries a hefty 8.50% front-end load.

Portfolio Manager: Ben Hock
Since: 1987

Minimum:
Initial: $100
Subsequent: $20
Telephone Exchange: No
Distributions:
Income: Quarterly
Capital Gain: Annually
Front-End Load: 8.50%
12b-1: None
Redemption Fee: None
Management Company: Securities Management & Research
Ticker Symbol: AMNIX

TOTAL RETURN (%)

1987	1988	1989	1990	1991	5-year	Bull Market	Bear Market
3.8	10.1	28.1	0.8	29.1	90.3	32.0	-10.9

INVESTMENT PORTFOLIO

Total Assets (mil.)	Current Yield	Turnover Ratio	Expense Ratio	Beta	Risk Return
$90	2.4%	38%	1.22%	0.74	0.06

ANALYTIC OPTIONED EQUITY FUND

Analytic Optioned Equity
2222 Martin Street, Suite 230
Irvine, CA 92715
714-833-0294

Investment Objective: This no-load fund seeks greater long-term return with smaller fluctuations in quarterly returns. The fund maintains a well-diversified portfolio of common stocks that are selected to correspond closely to the industry group weightings of the S&P 500. But since its inception in 1977, the fund has not accomplished its goal. However, given its beta of 0.55, the fund has not done badly, on a risk-adjusted basis.

Portfolio Manager: Chuck Dobson
Since: 1978

Minimum:
Initial: $5,000
Subsequent: $1,000
Telephone Exchange: No
Distributions:
Income: Quarterly
Capital Gain: Annually
Front-End Load: None
12b-1: None
Redemption Fee: None
Management Company: Analytic Investment Management
Ticker Symbol: ANALX

TOTAL RETURN (%)

1987	1988	1989	1990	1991	5-year	Bull Market	Bear Market
4.2	15.6	17.7	1.5	13.3	63.2	22.9	-11.4

INVESTMENT PORTFOLIO

Total Assets (mil.)	Current Yield	Turnover Ratio	Expense Ratio	Beta	Risk Return
$102	9.8%	76%	1.10%	0.55	0.03

BAIRD BLUE CHIP FUND

Robert W. Baird & Company
777 East Wisconsin Avenue
Milwaukee, WI 53202
800-792-2473

Investment Objective: This pure equity fund gives more consideration to growth than income. Most of its blue chip companies are characterized by above-average growth rates and profitability ratios, plus below-average debt. Recent industry selection has, again, favored growth over income as the fund's scant 1.1% yield would indicate. Portfolio changes come slowly as the fund chalked up one of the lowest turnover ratios in the mutual fund universe. The fund's bias toward growth has enabled it to achieve a 5-year return of almost 27% above its peer average.

Portfolio Manager: John Evans
Since: 1986

Minimum:
Initial: $1,000
Subsequent: $100
Telephone Exchange: No
Distributions:
Income: Semiannually
Capital Gain: Annually
Front-End Load: 5.75%
12b-1: 0.29%
Redemption Fee: None
Management Company: Robert W. Baird & Company
Ticker Symbol: BRBCX

TOTAL RETURN (%)

1987	1988	1989	1990	1991	5-year	Bull Market	Bear Market
8.0	7.5	27.2	3.0	30.4	98.3	30.4	-16.2

INVESTMENT PORTFOLIO

Total Assets (mil.)	Current Yield	Turnover Ratio	Expense Ratio	Beta	Risk Return
$48	1.1%	12%	1.60%	0.88	0.06

BARTLETT BASIC VALUE FUND

Bartlett Capital Trust
36 East Fourth Street, 5th Floor
Cincinnati, OH 45202
800-800-4612

Investment Objective: The objective of this fund is to seek capital appreciation; current income is of secondary importance. In attempting to meet its objective, the fund invests in securities that management believes have market appreciation potential because their basic value, including the value of the issuer's assets and earning power, is not reflected in their market price. In effect, management seeks "out of favor" stocks that possess relatively low price-earnings ratios. As expected, this value strategy paid handsome dividends in 1988 and lagged the past 3 years. However, don't count this no-load fund out as value-bent iss
ues eventually will come back into favor.

Portfolio Manager: James A. Miller
Since: 1983

Minimum:
Initial: $5,000
Subsequent: $100
Telephone Exchange: Yes
Distributions:
Income: Quarterly
Capital Gain: Annually
Front-End Load: None
12b-1: None
Redemption Fee: None
Management Company: Bartlett & Company
Ticker Symbol: MBBVX

TOTAL RETURN (%)

1987	1988	1989	1990	1991	5-year	Bull Market	Bear Market
-3.8	26.3	11.7	-9.6	26.0	54.5	36.4	-22.0

INVESTMENT PORTFOLIO

Total Assets (mil.)	Current Yield	Turnover Ratio	Expense Ratio	Beta	Risk Return
$87	2.9%	92%	1.21%	0.80	0.05

BERGER 101 FUND

Berger Associates
210 University Boulevard, Suite 900
Denver, CO 80206
800-333-1001

Investment Objective: This fund seeks capital appreciation and income by investing in the common stocks of established companies that management believes offer favorable growth prospects and at the same time provide current income. Historically, this fund has maintained an annual portfolio turnover ratio greater than 100%, indicating a willingness of management to chase short-term market trends. The fund sports an impressive 6.2% yield, well above that of most growth and income funds, and has returned about 10% more than the average for these same funds over the past 5 years.

Minimum:
Initial: $250
Subsequent: $50
Telephone Exchange: Yes
Distributions:
Income: Quarterly
Capital Gain: Annually
Front-End Load: None
12b-1: 1.00%
Redemption Fee: None
Management Company: Berger Associates
Ticker Symbol: BEOOX

Portfolio Manager: William M. Berger
Since: 1974

TOTAL RETURN (%)

1987	1988	1989	1990	1991	5-year	Bull Market	Bear Market
-2.9	5.3	20.3	-8.0	61.0	82.3	58.0	-20.9

INVESTMENT PORTFOLIO

Total Assets (mil.)	Current Yield	Turnover Ratio	Expense Ratio	Beta	Risk Return
$6	6.2%	143%	2.66%	0.92	0.11

BULL & BEAR EQUITY INCOME FUND

Bull & Bear
11 Hanover Square
New York, NY 10005
800-847-4200

Investment Objective: The fund's primary objectives are to provide shareholders with long-term growth of principal without incurring undue risk, and with current income. The fund seeks to achieve these objectives by investing primarily in a diversified portfolio of senior securities that are convertible into common stock of major corporations. The fund's 5-year record significantly trails that of its peers, and investors in this fund get hit with a huge expense ratio and a high portfolio turnover rate.

Minimum:
Initial: $1,000
Subsequent: $25
Telephone Exchange: Yes
Distributions:
Income: Quarterly
Capital Gain: Annually
Front-End Load: None
12b-1: 1.00%
Redemption Fee: None
Management Company: Bull & Bear Advisers
Ticker Symbol: BBEIX

Portfolio Manager: Robert Radsch
Since: 1982

TOTAL RETURN (%)

1987	1988	1989	1990	1991	5-year	Bull Market	Bear Market
-4.7	15.4	15.2	-6.8	23.8	46.0	30.2	-19.8

INVESTMENT PORTFOLIO

Total Assets (mil.)	Current Yield	Turnover Ratio	Expense Ratio	Beta	Risk Return
$10	2.3%	188%	2.81%	0.78	0.04

CALVERT SOCIAL INVESTMENT MANAGED GROWTH

Calvert Securities
4550 Montgomery Avenue, Suite 1000
Bethesda, MD 20814
800-368-2748

Investment Objective: This fund seeks to provide capital growth and current income through investment in companies that make a contribution to society through their products and services and manner of business. Potential investments are first screened for financial soundness and then evaluated according to the fund's social criteria that include: companies that negotiate fairly with workers, those whose products sustain the natural environment and managements with an awareness of commitment to human goals. In addition, the fund does not invest in companies that produce nuclear energy, do business with South Africa or manufacture weapons systems. The fund has been an average performer over the past 5 years.

Portfolio Manager: Domenic Colasacco
Since: 1984

Minimum:
Initial: $1,000
Subsequent: $250
Telephone Exchange: Yes
Distributions:
Income: Semiannually
Capital Gain: Annually
Front-End Load: 4.75%
12b-1: 0.22%
Redemption Fee: None
Management Company: Calvert Asset Management
Ticker Symbol: CSIFX

TOTAL RETURN (%)

1987	1988	1989	1990	1991	5-year	Bull Market	Bear Market
5.4	10.7	18.7	1.8	17.8	66.1	19.5	-7.9

INVESTMENT PORTFOLIO

Total Assets (mil.)	Current Yield	Turnover Ratio	Expense Ratio	Beta	Risk Return
$337	3.7%	25%	1.31%	0.46	0.05

CARNEGIE-CAPPIELLO TOTAL RETURN SERIES

Carnegie Fund Distributor
1331 Euclid Avenue
Cleveland, OH 44115
800-321-2322

Investment Objective: This fund, managed by "Wall Street Week" regular Frank Cappiello, seeks a combination of capital appreciation and income consistent with reasonable risk. When selecting equity securities, management seeks income-producing securities having a market price that appears undervalued relative to earnings, dividends and book value or have future earnings potential that appears greater than anticipated market norms. The fund has been a bit more volatile than most growth and income selections as demonstrated by both of its 1990 and 1991 returns.

Portfolio Manager: Frank Cappiello
Since: 1985

Minimum:
Initial: $1,000
Subsequent: $500
Telephone Exchange: Yes
Distributions:
Income: Quarterly
Capital Gain: Annually
Front-End Load: 4.50%
12b-1: 0.49%
Redemption Fee: None
Management Company: Carnegie Capital Management
Ticker Symbol: CCTRX

TOTAL RETURN (%)

1987	1988	1989	1990	1991	5-year	Bull Market	Bear Market
-10.2	21.3	34.4	-17.9	39.5	67.6	32.2	-18.7

INVESTMENT PORTFOLIO

Total Assets (mil.)	Current Yield	Turnover Ratio	Expense Ratio	Beta	Risk Return
$64	4.5%	85%	1.57%	0.78	0.08

CGM MUTUAL FUND

New England Securities
Back Bay Annex, P.O. Box 449
Boston, MA 02117
800-345-4048

Investment Objective: In seeking long-term capital appreciation and preservation of capital, this pure no-load fund shifts portions of its assets among common stocks, bonds and cash equivalents. Renowned Portfolio Manager Ken Heebner has the fund back on the winning track. In 1990, the fund posted a 1.1% gain and the past year returned a remarkable 41% return. Over the past 5 years, the fund has posted a return that is equal to that of the S&P 500 Index. The fund yields an average 3.3% and has kept expenses low for a growth and income vehicle.

Portfolio Manager: Ken Heebner
Since: 1987

Minimum:
Initial: $1,000
Subsequent: $50
Telephone Exchange: Yes
Distributions:
Income: Quarterly
Capital Gain: Annually
Front-End Load: None
12b-1: None
Redemption Fee: None
Management Company: Capital Growth Management
Ticker Symbol: LOMMX

TOTAL RETURN (%)

1987	1988	1989	1990	1991	5-year	Bull Market	Bear Market
13.7	3.2	21.7	1.1	40.9	103.3	44.9	-16.1

INVESTMENT PORTFOLIO

Total Assets (mil.)	Current Yield	Turnover Ratio	Expense Ratio	Beta	Risk Return
$353	3.3%	159%	0.97%	0.94	0.07

CIGNA VALUE FUND

CIGNA Mutual Funds
One Financial Plaza, 16th Floor
Springfield, MA 01103
800-572-4462

Investment Objective: This fund's primary objective is long-term growth, with income as a secondary objective. The fund searches out undervalued equity securities to invest in, such as out-of-favor cyclicals, low price-earnings stocks and companies whose securities are selling at prices that do not reflect the value of their assets. Since its inception, the fund has obviously found a superior strategy that has produced above-average performance. Even in 1990's bear market, the fund kept its head above water. For those willing to stomach the front-end sales charge, this fund may be a solid choice with slightly above-average risk.

Portfolio Manager: James Giblin
Since: 1986

Minimum:
Initial: $500
Subsequent: $50
Telephone Exchange: Yes
Distributions:
Income: Annually
Capital Gain: Annually
Front-End Load: 5.00%
12b-1: 0.25%
Redemption Fee: None
Management Company: CIGNA Investments
Ticker Symbol: CVLFX

TOTAL RETURN (%)

1987	1988	1989	1990	1991	5-year	Bull Market	Bear Market
6.0	20.6	31.5	1.9	43.5	145.7	58.6	-27.3

INVESTMENT PORTFOLIO

Total Assets (mil.)	Current Yield	Turnover Ratio	Expense Ratio	Beta	Risk Return
$136	0.7%	131%	1.21%	1.02	0.07

COLONIAL CORPORATE CASH TRUST I

Colonial Investment Services
One Financial Center, 14th Floor
Boston, MA 02110
800-248-2828

Investment Objective: This fund seeks a high level of income qualifying for the federal tax corporate dividends-received deduction and, secondarily, relative stability of principal. The fund tries to maintain at least three-fourths of its assets invested in equity securities and typically has a large portion of this concentrated in public utilities at any given time. If you are looking for a high level of current income, this fund's 7.6% current yield may catch your eye. Otherwise, the fund's performance generally has been below average, and investors should take note of its sales charges.

Portfolio Manager: John Lennon
Since: 1984

Minimum:
Initial: $25,000
Subsequent: $5,000
Telephone Exchange: Yes
Distributions:
Income: Monthly
Capital Gain: Annually
Front-End Load: 2.00%
12b-1: 0.25%
Redemption Fee: None
Management Company: Colonial Management Associates
Ticker Symbol: COCCX

TOTAL RETURN (%)

1987	1988	1989	1990	1991	5-year	Bull Market	Bear Market
-8.2	13.9	17.7	-5.1	25.9	47.1	22.4	-2.2

INVESTMENT PORTFOLIO

Total Assets (mil.)	Current Yield	Turnover Ratio	Expense Ratio	Beta	Risk Return
$135	7.6%	2%	1.17%	0.30	0.10

COLONIAL FUND

Colonial Investment Services
One Financial Center, 14th Floor
Boston, MA 02110
800-248-2828

Investment Objective: Organized as a Massachusetts business trust, this fund seeks capital appreciation and income primarily and preservation of capital secondarily. When making selections, management seeks companies with debt/net-worth ratios of less than 1%, earnings yields equal to the yield on long-term government bonds, dividend yields equal to about two-thirds that of long-term government bonds and share prices less than either book value or per share going-concern value. This fund's strict restrictions on portfolio flexibility have produced average returns over the past 5 years with a below-average volatility level.

Portfolio Manager: Chris Bertlesen
Since: 1986

Minimum:
Initial: $1,000
Subsequent: $25
Telephone Exchange: Yes
Distributions:
Income: Quarterly
Capital Gain: Annually
Front-End Load: 5.75%
12b-1: 0.10%
Redemption Fee: None
Management Company: Colonial Management Associates
Ticker Symbol: COLFX

TOTAL RETURN (%)

1987	1988	1989	1990	1991	5-year	Bull Market	Bear Market
-1.1	21.8	20.0	-7.5	26.1	68.6	31.4	-15.1

INVESTMENT PORTFOLIO

Total Assets (mil.)	Current Yield	Turnover Ratio	Expense Ratio	Beta	Risk Return
$349	2.7%	41%	1.00%	0.76	0.05

COLONIAL STRATEGIC INCOME FUND

Colonial Investment Services
One Financial Center, 14th Floor
Boston, MA 02110
800-248-2828

Investment Objective: This fund seeks a high level of income consistent with reasonable risk by investing in fixed-income securities and dividend-paying common stocks. Its return was hampered in 1989 by a large commitment to high-yield "junk" bonds, which were battered when a number of highly leveraged firms filed for bankruptcy protection. The fund staged a bit of a rebound in 1991, after some recent disappointing years. A 4.75% front-end load only diminishes this fund's appeal.

Portfolio Manager: Carl Ericson
Since: 1991

Minimum:
Initial: $1,000
Subsequent: $25
Telephone Exchange: Yes
Distributions:
Income: Quarterly
Capital Gain: Annually
Front-End Load: 4.75%
12b-1: None
Redemption Fee: None
Management Company: Colonial Management Associates
Ticker Symbol: COLOX

TOTAL RETURN (%)

1987	1988	1989	1990	1991	5-year	Bull Market	Bear Market
3.7	16.6	9.9	-6.9	28.2	58.7	21.6	-7.0

INVESTMENT PORTFOLIO

Total Assets (mil.)	Current Yield	Turnover Ratio	Expense Ratio	Beta	Risk Return
$426	9.2%	2%	1.12%	0.29	0.11

COMPOSITE BOND & STOCK FUND

Murphey Favre Securities
601 West Riverside, Suite 900
Spokane, WA 99201
800-543-8072

Investment Objective: This conservatively managed fund, designed to provide a balance between income and long-term growth, has operated continually since 1939. The 3 objectives of the fund include: uninterrupted income, protection of principal and long-term growth of both income and principal. The fund traditionally holds a mixture of bonds, convertible bonds, common stocks and preferred stocks. In addition, the fund has at times invested in mortgage-backed securities. Although the fund produced a modest 56% total return during the past 5 years, it did so while maintaining a level of variability about one-half that of the stock market as a whole.

Portfolio Manager: Randall Yoakum
Since: 1991

Minimum:
Initial: $1,000
Subsequent: $250
Telephone Exchange: Yes
Distributions:
Income: Quarterly
Capital Gain: Annually
Front-End Load: 4.00%
12b-1: 0.30%
Redemption Fee: None
Management Company: Composite Research & Management
Ticker Symbol: CMPBX

TOTAL RETURN (%)

1987	1988	1989	1990	1991	5-year	Bull Market	Bear Market
-0.5	14.7	12.3	0.1	21.7	56.0	27.1	-10.8

INVESTMENT PORTFOLIO

Total Assets (mil.)	Current Yield	Turnover Ratio	Expense Ratio	Beta	Risk Return
$66	4.6%	38%	1.17%	0.53	0.06

COUNTRY CAPITAL INCOME FUND

Country Capital Management
1711 G.E. Road, P.O. Box 2222
Bloomington, IL 61704
800-322-3838

Investment Objective: The objective of this fund is to earn a high level of current income consistent with conservation of capital. This is one of the more conservative growth and income funds, as evidenced by its low beta and low portfolio turnover ratio. However, the fund's current yield is impressive for investors seeking income, and, although returns are slightly below growth and income fund averages, they have hardly been sacrificed for income. The fund's conservative stance has kept the fund above water in the bear markets of both 1987 and 1990. This fund is a good choice for investors willing to pay the front-end load of 3.00%.

Portfolio Manager: John Jacobs
Since: 1987

Minimum:
Initial: $100
Subsequent: $50
Telephone Exchange: Yes
Distributions:
Income: Monthly
Capital Gain: Semiannually
Front-End Load: 3.00%
12b-1: None
Redemption Fee: None
Management Company: Country Capital Management
Ticker Symbol: None

TOTAL RETURN (%)

1987	1988	1989	1990	1991	5-year	Bull Market	Bear Market
1.1	7.4	13.4	7.9	13.0	50.1	13.4	0.7

INVESTMENT PORTFOLIO

Total Assets (mil.)	Current Yield	Turnover Ratio	Expense Ratio	Beta	Risk Return
$6	6.0%	21%	1.33%	0.16	0.05

DELAWARE FUND

Delaware Distributors
10 Penn Center Plaza
Philadelphia, PA 19103
800-523-4640

Investment Objective: This fund, which charges a front-end load of 6.75%, seeks capital appreciation and income by investing in common stocks as well as high-quality bonds. Assets of the fund are concentrated in securities of established companies that have potential for long-term capital growth. When selecting securities, the fund analyzes current market conditions using a "top-down" strategy to determine what sectors of the economy are due to benefit or decline. The fund's 5-year record meets the average of the growth and income funds in our universe, despite a below-average 1991 return.

Portfolio Manager: Stanton Feeley
Since: 1988

Minimum:
Initial: $250
Subsequent: $25
Telephone Exchange: Yes
Distributions:
Income: Quarterly
Capital Gain: Annually
Front-End Load: 6.75%
12b-1: None
Redemption Fee: None
Management Company: Delaware Management
Ticker Symbol: DELFX

TOTAL RETURN (%)

1987	1988	1989	1990	1991	5-year	Bull Market	Bear Market
-6.2	21.0	25.6	-0.5	20.8	71.5	26.2	-12.9

INVESTMENT PORTFOLIO

Total Assets (mil.)	Current Yield	Turnover Ratio	Expense Ratio	Beta	Risk Return
$432	3.4%	212%	0.71%	0.72	0.04

DELAWARE GROUP DECATUR I SERIES

Delaware Distributors
10 Penn Center Plaza
Philadelphia, PA 19103
800-523-4640

Investment Objective: This fund's objective is to achieve the highest possible current income by investing primarily in common stocks with the potential for income and capital appreciation without undue risk. The fund has a below-average 5-year performance record, given the low amount of risk assumed. Furthermore, the fund sports a low turnover ratio and a low expense ratio that both contribute to an investor's return. This growth and income fund sports a hefty 8.50% front-end load, which limits its attractiveness to no-load investors.

Portfolio Manager: Marion Dixon
Since: 1991

Minimum:
Initial: $250
Subsequent: $25
Telephone Exchange: Yes
Distributions:
Income: Quarterly
Capital Gain: Annually
Front-End Load: 8.50%
12b-1: None
Redemption Fee: None
Management Company: Delaware Management
Ticker Symbol: DELDX

TOTAL RETURN (%)

1987	1988	1989	1990	1991	5-year	Bull Market	Bear Market
3.3	19.9	21.5	-12.4	21.8	60.6	32.0	-19.1

INVESTMENT PORTFOLIO

Total Assets (mil.)	Current Yield	Turnover Ratio	Expense Ratio	Beta	Risk Return
$1,580	4.4%	44%	0.70%	0.88	0.04

DELAWARE GROUP DECATUR II SERIES

Delaware Distributors
10 Penn Center Plaza
Philadelphia, PA 19103
800-523-4640

Investment Objective: The goal of this fund, which commenced operations in August of 1986, is to achieve long-term growth by investing primarily in securities that provide potential for income and capital appreciation without undue risk to principal. The fund's yield is above average for its group, while its risk level is consistent with its conservative strategy. When making selections, Portfolio Manager Marion Dixon seeks securities that have a better dividend yield than the average of S&P's 500 Stock Index as well as capital appreciation potential. As might be expected, the fund's portfolio contains a concentration of investments in the energy, utility and financial industries, which produced below-average results in 1991.

Portfolio Manager: Marion Dixon
Since: 1988

Minimum:
Initial: $250
Subsequent: $25
Telephone Exchange: Yes
Distributions:
Income: Quarterly
Capital Gain: Annually
Front-End Load: 4.75%
12b-1: 0.30%
Redemption Fee: None
Management Company: Delaware Management
Ticker Symbol: DEDTX

TOTAL RETURN (%)

1987	1988	1989	1990	1991	5-year	Bull Market	Bear Market
-4.0	25.8	26.6	-8.3	20.4	68.6	30.8	-15.5

INVESTMENT PORTFOLIO

Total Assets (mil.)	Current Yield	Turnover Ratio	Expense Ratio	Beta	Risk Return
$394	3.7%	67%	1.23%	0.80	0.04

DODGE & COX BALANCED FUND

Dodge & Cox
One Sansome Street, 35th Floor
San Francisco, CA 94104
415-434-0311

Investment Objective: This fund seeks current income, capital appreciation and long-term growth of principal and income by investing in both stocks and bonds in a 60/40 asset mix. Its stock selections are drawn from a broad array of industry groups. Its defensive nature is evidenced by a beta of 0.70%. Over the past 5 years, the fund has demonstrated both the upside appreciation with a minimum of downside risk (i.e., 1987, 1990). The fund is best suited for conservative investors who value income more than growth, as the fund's yield of 4.5% would indicate.

Minimum:
Initial: $2,500
Subsequent: $100
Telephone Exchange: No
Distributions:
Income: Quarterly
Capital Gain: Annually
Front-End Load: None
12b-1: None
Redemption Fee: None
Management Company: Dodge & Cox
Ticker Symbol: DODBX

Portfolio Manager: Investment Policy Committee
Since: 1990

TOTAL RETURN (%)

1987	1988	1989	1990	1991	5-year	Bull Market	Bear Market
7.2	11.5	23.0	0.9	20.7	79.2	29.1	-13.4

INVESTMENT PORTFOLIO

Total Assets (mil.)	Current Yield	Turnover Ratio	Expense Ratio	Beta	Risk Return
$164	4.5%	10%	0.70%	0.70	0.04

DODGE & COX STOCK FUND

Dodge & Cox
One Sansome Street, 35th Floor
San Francisco, CA 94104
415-434-0311

Investment Objective: The primary investment objective of this no-load fund is to provide long-term growth of principal and income. Diversification in the types of common stocks that are held in the portfolio receives heavy emphasis. Individual securities are chosen based on their financial strength, underlying asset values and prospective earnings and dividend growth. Moreover, management employs a long-term, buy-and-hold strategy, reflected in the fund's incredibly low 7% turnover ratio. This long-term view has been rewarded by above-average returns over the past 5 years.

Minimum:
Initial: $2,500
Subsequent: $100
Telephone Exchange: No
Distributions:
Income: Quarterly
Capital Gain: Annually
Front-End Load: None
12b-1: None
Redemption Fee: None
Management Company: Dodge & Cox
Ticker Symbol: DODGX

Portfolio Manager: Investment Policy Committee
Since: 1990

TOTAL RETURN (%)

1987	1988	1989	1990	1991	5-year	Bull Market	Bear Market
11.9	13.8	26.9	-5.1	21.5	86.4	35.8	-21.1

INVESTMENT PORTFOLIO

Total Assets (mil.)	Current Yield	Turnover Ratio	Expense Ratio	Beta	Risk Return
$258	3.0%	7%	0.65%	1.02	0.03

DREYFUS CAPITAL VALUE FUND

Dreyfus Service
200 Park Avenue, 7th Floor
New York, NY 10166
800-782-6620

Investment Objective: The fund's goal is to maximize total return by following an asset-allocation strategy that may entail frequent shifts among a wide range of investments (stocks, bonds and cash) and market sectors. The fund is managed by Comstock Partners under Dreyfus supervision. Although the fund may at times invest a significant percentage of its assets in bonds, management insists that it will not be managed as a balanced portfolio. Instead, management will allocate assets to those sectors that it perceives will provide the greatest return potential. The fund's 5-year performance is quite impressive, but management's defensive posture in 1990 translated into a lackluster year in 1991.

Portfolio Manager: H. Stein/S. Saluigsen
Since: 1987

Minimum:
Initial: $2,500
Subsequent: $100
Telephone Exchange: Yes
Distributions:
Income: Annually
Capital Gain: Annually
Front-End Load: 4.50%
12b-1: 0.26%
Redemption Fee: None
Management Company: Comstock Partners
Ticker Symbol: DRCVX

TOTAL RETURN (%)

1987	1988	1989	1990	1991	5-year	Bull Market	Bear Market
34.4	8.1	25.2	1.3	4.1	92.0	12.5	0.6

INVESTMENT PORTFOLIO

Total Assets (mil.)	Current Yield	Turnover Ratio	Expense Ratio	Beta	Risk Return
$742	4.3%	63%	1.46%	-0.10	NA

DREYFUS FUND

Dreyfus Service
200 Park Avenue, 7th Floor
New York, NY 10166
800-782-6620

Investment Objective: The flagship fund of the Dreyfus family of funds, this blue chip portfolio prioritized income and safety without foregoing growth potential. Depending on market conditions, the fund attempts to be fully invested at all times in common stocks. However, the fund allows itself to move into bonds and other fixed-income securities. The fund invests primarily in "seasoned" companies, and very few companies with a record of fewer than 3 years would be considered appropriate for the fund. The fund has an impressive performance, as seen by its 5-year return of 80.7%. Additionally, it is free from sales charges, making it an even more attractive investment.

Portfolio Manager: H. Stein/W. Wronskj
Since: 1951

Minimum:
Initial: $2,500
Subsequent: $25
Telephone Exchange: Yes
Distributions:
Income: Quarterly
Capital Gain: Annually
Front-End Load: None
12b-1: None
Redemption Fee: None
Management Company: Dreyfus Corporation
Ticker Symbol: DREVX

TOTAL RETURN (%)

1987	1988	1989	1990	1991	5-year	Bull Market	Bear Market
8.6	8.7	23.6	-3.3	28.0	80.7	28.2	-15.7

INVESTMENT PORTFOLIO

Total Assets (mil.)	Current Yield	Turnover Ratio	Expense Ratio	Beta	Risk Return
$2,552	2.6%	99%	0.77%	0.79	0.06

EATON VANCE INVESTORS FUND

Eaton Vance
24 Federal Street, 5th Floor
Boston, MA 02110
800-225-6265

Investment Objective: In seeking current income and long-term growth of capital, this fund invests in a broadly diversified list of seasoned securities, representing a number of industries. In making selections, management looks toward companies of high or improving quality. In general, the fund has tended to maintain a portfolio with about equal allocations to common stocks and bonds. This posture has led to a beta of about half that of the S&P 500 Index. Management has kept the portfolio turnover low and has avoided losses in both 1987 and 1990. Investors should note, however, that this fund carries a 4.75% front-end load.

Minimum:
Initial: $1,000
Subsequent: $20
Telephone Exchange: Yes
Distributions:
Income: Quarterly
Capital Gain: Semiannually
Front-End Load: 4.75%
12b-1: 0.25%
Redemption Fee: None
Management Company: Eaton Vance Management
Ticker Symbol: EVIFX

Portfolio Manager: M. Dozier Gardner
Since: 1987

TOTAL RETURN (%)

1987	1988	1989	1990	1991	5-year	Bull Market	Bear Market
5.7	10.7	20.8	1.0	21.3	73.0	22.3	-7.8

INVESTMENT PORTFOLIO

Total Assets (mil.)	Current Yield	Turnover Ratio	Expense Ratio	Beta	Risk Return
$206	4.3%	66%	0.89%	0.55	0.06

EATON VANCE STOCK FUND

Eaton Vance
24 Federal Street, 5th Floor
Boston, MA 02110
800-225-6265

Investment Objective: This fund's objective is to provide growth of principal and income for its shareholders by investment in a number of securities, with an emphasis on common stocks. In some cases, however, the fund may invest in other types of securities, including bonds, preferred stocks, securities convertible into common stocks and U.S. government obligations. The fund purchases stocks for investment rather than with a view to realizing trading profits. Without taking too many chances with high price-earnings ratios or high-beta stocks, this portfolio has one of the better risk-return ratios in the growth and income universe.

Minimum:
Initial: $1,000
Subsequent: $20
Telephone Exchange: Yes
Distributions:
Income: Quarterly
Capital Gain: Annually
Front-End Load: 4.75%
12b-1: 0.25%
Redemption Fee: None
Management Company: Eaton Vance Management
Ticker Symbol: EHSTX

Portfolio Manager: A. Walker Martin
Since: 1990

TOTAL RETURN (%)

1987	1988	1989	1990	1991	5-year	Bull Market	Bear Market
1.7	14.7	28.7	0.6	21.5	83.6	23.9	-13.0

INVESTMENT PORTFOLIO

Total Assets (mil.)	Current Yield	Turnover Ratio	Expense Ratio	Beta	Risk Return
$85	2.9%	42%	0.99%	0.84	0.04

EATON VANCE TOTAL RETURN TRUST

Eaton Vance
24 Federal Street, 5th Floor
Boston, MA 02110
800-225-6265

Investment Objective: Providing decent performances in both up and down markets, this fund seeks a balance of current income and growth of capital. Investments are made primarily in common stocks of utility issues. The other portion of the portfolio is invested in banks and insurance companies. Although the fund's high allocation to utility concerns makes it interest-rate sensitive, it does provide a high dividend yield of 4.7%. Over the past 5 years, the fund has provided investors with average returns at below-average risk. Potential investors should note the fund carries a 4.75% front-end load.

Portfolio Manager: Edwin Bragdon
Since: 1981

Minimum:
Initial: $1,000
Subsequent: $20
Telephone Exchange: Yes
Distributions:
Income: Quarterly
Capital Gain: Annually
Front-End Load: 4.75%
12b-1: 0.21%
Redemption Fee: None
Management Company: Eaton Vance Management
Ticker Symbol: EVTMX

TOTAL RETURN (%)

1987	1988	1989	1990	1991	5-year	Bull Market	Bear Market
-15.7	11.9	33.5	0.2	23.6	55.8	21.3	0.6

INVESTMENT PORTFOLIO

Total Assets (mil.)	Current Yield	Turnover Ratio	Expense Ratio	Beta	Risk Return
$526	4.7%	52%	1.27%	0.41	0.06

ENTERPRISE GROWTH & INCOME PORTFOLIO

Enterprise Fund Distributor
1200 Ashwood Parkway, Suite 290
Atlanta, GA 30338
800-432-4320

Investment Objective: This growth and income fund is run by two different subadvisers with varying investment mandates. MONY Advisers of New York emphasizes energy, financial and interest-sensitive stocks and employs a decided value strategy. On the other hand, Carl Domino Associates of West Palm Beach looks for stocks with above-average dividend yields, that operate in recession-resistant industries and that sport strong balance sheets. The fund has an average yield of 3.2% and management does not trade the portfolio rapidly. However, investors are hit with a 4.75% load and a 12b-1 fee.

Portfolio Manager: J. Rock/C. Domino
Since: 1987

Minimum:
Initial: $500
Subsequent: $25
Telephone Exchange: Yes
Distributions:
Income: Semiannually
Capital Gain: Annually
Front-End Load: 4.75%
12b-1: 0.45%
Redemption Fee: None
Management Company: Enterprise Capital Management
Ticker Symbol: ENGIX

TOTAL RETURN (%)

1987	1988	1989	1990	1991	5-year	Bull Market	Bear Market
NA	13.6	17.6	-8.2	23.6	NA	33.0	-17.8

INVESTMENT PORTFOLIO

Total Assets (mil.)	Current Yield	Turnover Ratio	Expense Ratio	Beta	Risk Return
$31	3.2%	21%	1.50%	0.84	0.04

EVERGREEN TOTAL RETURN FUND

Evergreen Funds
2500 Westchester Avenue
Purchase, NY 10577
800-235-0064

Investment Objective: In seeking a balance of current income and capital growth, this fund is defensive in nature. Management allocates 20 to 30% of the fund's assets to fixed-income securities, with the balance to common stocks. A large portion of these stocks is invested in utilities, banks and insurance companies. Although this mixture makes the portfolio interest-rate sensitive, it does provide an above-average dividend yield, which currently stands at 5.6%. Since its inception in 1978, this no-load fund has provided investors with above-average returns at a below-market level of risk. For investors seeking a conservative growth and income fund with proven results, this true no-load vehicle should be looked into.

Portfolio Manager: Nola M. Falcone
Since: 1978

Minimum:
Initial: $2,000
Subsequent: None
Telephone Exchange: Yes
Distributions:
Income: Quarterly
Capital Gain: Annually
Front-End Load: None
12b-1: None
Redemption Fee: None
Management Company: Evergreen Asset Management
Ticker Symbol: EVTRX

TOTAL RETURN (%)

1987	1988	1989	1990	1991	5-year	Bull Market	Bear Market
-8.0	15.7	16.2	-6.3	23.0	42.7	30.6	-13.0

INVESTMENT PORTFOLIO

Total Assets (mil.)	Current Yield	Turnover Ratio	Expense Ratio	Beta	Risk Return
$1,060	5.6%	137%	1.23%	0.67	0.05

EVERGREEN VALUE TIMING FUND

Evergreen Funds
2500 Westchester Avenue
Purchase, NY 10577
800-235-0064

Investment Objective: This no-load, contrarian fund seeks long-term capital appreciation primarily by investing in special situations. Manager Ed Nicklin's flexible interpretation of value prevents the fund from focusing on one stock profile. Rather, it features a mix of undervalued securities, with turnarounds and asset plays most prominent. Considering the market's recent narrow earnings orientation and neglect of value stocks, the fund's performance is well above average for a growth and income vehicle. Patient shareholders can expect highly competitive long-term gains with moderate risk from this well-managed fund.

Portfolio Manager: Edmund Nicklin
Since: 1986

Minimum:
Initial: $2,000
Subsequent: None
Telephone Exchange: Yes
Distributions:
Income: Annually
Capital Gain: Annually
Front-End Load: None
12b-1: None
Redemption Fee: None
Management Company: Evergreen Asset Management
Ticker Symbol: EVVTX

TOTAL RETURN (%)

1987	1988	1989	1990	1991	5-year	Bull Market	Bear Market
-4.3	24.6	25.4	-4.5	25.8	79.6	23.2	-17.4

INVESTMENT PORTFOLIO

Total Assets (mil.)	Current Yield	Turnover Ratio	Expense Ratio	Beta	Risk Return
$44	1.4%	41%	1.50%	0.90	0.09

FIDELITY BALANCED FUND

Fidelity Distributors Corporation
82 Devonshire Street, Mail Zone L7b
Boston, MA 02109
800-544-8888

Investment Objective: The investment objectives of this no-load fund are income and preservation of capital. The fund purchases high-yielding securities, which include bonds, stocks and convertible securities; growth is certainly a secondary investment objective. The investment strategy of this fund is conservative, and the fund must maintain at least 25% of its assets invested in fixed-income securities that are rated BBB or better; stocks rarely make up more than 50% of the fund's assets. The fund's performance over the past 5 years has been above average at a risk level half that of the S&P 500 Index.

Portfolio Manager: Robert J. Haber
Since: 1988

Minimum:
Initial: $2,500
Subsequent: $250
Telephone Exchange: Yes
Distributions:
Income: Quarterly
Capital Gain: Semiannually
Front-End Load: None
12b-1: None
Redemption Fee: None
Management Company: Fidelity Management & Research
Ticker Symbol: FBALX

TOTAL RETURN (%)

1987	1988	1989	1990	1991	5-year	Bull Market	Bear Market
2.0	16.0	19.5	-0.5	26.8	78.3	31.5	-8.1

INVESTMENT PORTFOLIO

Total Assets (mil.)	Current Yield	Turnover Ratio	Expense Ratio	Beta	Risk Return
$669	4.7%	238%	0.98%	0.45	0.09

FIDELITY EQUITY-INCOME FUND

Fidelity Distributors Corporation
82 Devonshire Street, Mail Zone L7b
Boston, MA 02109
800-544-8888

Investment Objective: This fund seeks reasonable yield by investing primarily in income-producing equity securities. In choosing these securities, management looks for a yield that exceeds the composite yield of stocks composing the Standard & Poor's 500 Index and securities that offer some capital appreciation. The fund sports an above-average yield and still returned almost 30% in 1991. Its 5-year record also outpaces the average growth and income fund. However, investors must pay a 2.00% front-end load.

Portfolio Manager: Beth Terrana
Since: 1990

Minimum:
Initial: $2,500
Subsequent: $250
Telephone Exchange: Yes
Distributions:
Income: Quarterly
Capital Gain: Annually
Front-End Load: 2.00%
12b-1: None
Redemption Fee: None
Management Company: Fidelity Management & Research
Ticker Symbol: FEQIX

TOTAL RETURN (%)

1987	1988	1989	1990	1991	5-year	Bull Market	Bear Market
-1.6	22.5	18.7	-14.0	29.4	59.1	35.5	-17.5

INVESTMENT PORTFOLIO

Total Assets (mil.)	Current Yield	Turnover Ratio	Expense Ratio	Beta	Risk Return
$4,108	4.5%	107%	0.70%	0.87	0.06

FIDELITY FUND

Fidelity Distributors Corporation
82 Devonshire Street, Mail Zone L7b
Boston, MA 02109
800-544-8888

Investment Objective: This fund, under the direction of Portfolio Manager Barry Greenfield, seeks capital appreciation with reasonable current income by investing in growth-oriented common stocks. A "bottom-up" investment strategy is employed (i.e., selecting stocks based solely on their own merits rather than first drawing economic conclusions and making industry sector commitments). The fund has more than $1 billion in assets, a higher-than-average portfolio turnover and a modest expense ratio. This rapidly traded fund offers investors a bit more capital appreciation than most growth and income funds, but this comes at the expense of the fund's yield.

Portfolio Manager: Barry Greenfield
Since: 1982

Minimum:
Initial: $2,500
Subsequent: $250
Telephone Exchange: Yes
Distributions:
Income: Quarterly
Capital Gain: Annually
Front-End Load: None
12b-1: None
Redemption Fee: None
Management Company: Fidelity Management & Research
Ticker Symbol: FFIDX

TOTAL RETURN (%)

1987	1988	1989	1990	1991	5-year	Bull Market	Bear Market
3.3	17.8	28.8	-5.1	24.2	84.8	33.5	-17.1

INVESTMENT PORTFOLIO

Total Assets (mil.)	Current Yield	Turnover Ratio	Expense Ratio	Beta	Risk Return
$1,216	2.5%	259%	0.66%	0.87	0.04

FIDELITY GROWTH & INCOME PORTFOLIO

Fidelity Distributors Corporation
82 Devonshire Street, Mail Zone L7b
Boston, MA 02109
800-544-8888

Investment Objective: This fund seeks long-term capital growth, current income and growth of income, consistent with reasonable investment risk. The fund invests in securities of firms with growth potential that currently pay dividends. The fund generally will sell those stocks whose yield falls to less than the yield of the S&P 500 Index. Despite holding a large portion of assets in interest-sensitive finance and natural resource stocks, the fund has done a remarkable job over the past 5 years. The fund's above-average performance record, below-average expense ratio and below-average volatility level make this an excellent growth and income vehicle.

Portfolio Manager: Jeff Vinik
Since: 1990

Minimum:
Initial: $2,500
Subsequent: $250
Telephone Exchange: Yes
Distributions:
Income: Quarterly
Capital Gain: Annually
Front-End Load: 2.00%
12b-1: None
Redemption Fee: None
Management Company: Fidelity Management & Research
Ticker Symbol: FGRIX

TOTAL RETURN (%)

1987	1988	1989	1990	1991	5-year	Bull Market	Bear Market
5.8	23.0	29.6	-6.8	41.8	122.9	51.2	-19.1

INVESTMENT PORTFOLIO

Total Assets (mil.)	Current Yield	Turnover Ratio	Expense Ratio	Beta	Risk Return
$3,008	1.8%	215%	0.87%	0.94	0.08

FIDELITY PURITAN FUND

Fidelity Distributors Corporation
82 Devonshire Street, Mail Zone L7B
Boston, MA 02109
800-544-8888

Investment Objective: This balanced fund is ideally suited for conservative investors who seek current income and some capital appreciation. Its recent portfolio splits its attention 60/40 between stocks and bonds, with a small cash stake thrown in for good measure. Utility and finance stocks make up the largest equity portions, and only the bond stake kept the fund alive during the recent bear market. The fund sports an impressive current yield of 5.5% and is a decent holding for income-oriented investors.

Portfolio Manager: Rich Fentin
Since: 1987

Minimum:
Initial: $2,500
Subsequent: $250
Telephone Exchange: Yes
Distributions:
Income: Quarterly
Capital Gain: Annually
Front-End Load: 2.00%
12b-1: None
Redemption Fee: None
Management Company: Fidelity Management & Research
Ticker Symbol: FPURX

TOTAL RETURN (%)

1987	1988	1989	1990	1991	5-year	Bull Market	Bear Market
-1.8	18.9	19.6	-6.4	24.5	62.8	32.2	-14.2

INVESTMENT PORTFOLIO

Total Assets (mil.)	Current Yield	Turnover Ratio	Expense Ratio	Beta	Risk Return
$4,844	5.5%	108%	0.66%	0.69	0.05

FINANCIAL INDUSTRIAL INCOME FUND

INVESCO Funds Group
P.O. Box 2040
Denver, CO 80201
800-525-8085

Investment Objective: This fund's primary objective is to obtain the best possible current income, with capital growth potential as a secondary objective. During the past 5 years, this fund's performance has not only beaten the growth and income fund average, but it has beaten the S&P 500 as well. During 1991, the fund heavily emphasized financial and health-care stocks, a strategy that paid off handsomely with a year-end 46.3% return. This no-load fund also has a very low expense ratio and a below-average beta. Investors will find a lot to like about this growth and income fund.

Portfolio Manager: John Kaweske
Since: 1985

Minimum:
Initial: $250
Subsequent: $25
Telephone Exchange: Yes
Distributions:
Income: Quarterly
Capital Gain: Semiannually
Front-End Load: None
12b-1: None
Redemption Fee: None
Management Company: INVESCO Funds Group
Ticker Symbol: FIIIX

TOTAL RETURN (%)

1987	1988	1989	1990	1991	5-year	Bull Market	Bear Market
4.9	15.3	31.9	0.9	46.3	135.7	50.2	-16.9

INVESTMENT PORTFOLIO

Total Assets (mil.)	Current Yield	Turnover Ratio	Expense Ratio	Beta	Risk Return
$1,362	2.5%	104%	0.94%	0.89	0.09

FORTRESS HIGH QUALITY STOCK FUND

Federated Securities
Federated Investors Tower
Pittsburgh, PA 15222
800-245-4770

Investment Objective: This fund's objective is to provide growth of income and capital. It seeks to do so by investing in what the adviser considers to be "high-quality" companies. These generally are companies that are leaders in their industries and are characterized by sound management and sound financial condition. These companies are usually in the top 25% of their industries with regard to total revenues. Some companies may be chosen on factors that suggest that the companies may be in the top 25% of their industries within 5 years. The fund's 5-year return lags the growth and income fund average, but while the fund has not had particularly high returns, it has not experienced significant declines either.

Portfolio Manager: Peter Anderson
Since: 1986

Minimum:
Initial: $1,500
Subsequent: $100
Telephone Exchange: Yes
Distributions:
Income: Quarterly
Capital Gain: Annually
Front-End Load: 1.00%
12b-1: 0.50%
Redemption Fee: 0.75%
Management Company: Federated Investors
Ticker Symbol: FHQSX

TOTAL RETURN (%)

1987	1988	1989	1990	1991	5-year	Bull Market	Bear Market
1.8	12.5	14.2	-4.0	29.2	62.2	40.8	-21.2

INVESTMENT PORTFOLIO

Total Assets (mil.)	Current Yield	Turnover Ratio	Expense Ratio	Beta	Risk Return
$15	2.4%	54%	1.30%	0.95	0.05

FOUNDERS BLUE CHIP FUND

Founders Asset Management
2930 East Third Avenue
Denver, CO 80206
800-525-2440

Investment Objective: This fund seeks long-term growth of both capital and income. Its low current yield indicates the fund's emphasis on capital appreciation. Investments are made in large capitalization companies that have proven records of earnings and dividends and are in sound financial condition. Patience has paid off for this fund, a 28.3% return in 1991 being one of the better returns in its category. Furthermore, this return was achieved with less risk than the S&P 500 Index (beta 0.91). Finally, a positive 0.4% return in 1990's bear market further solidifies this fund's investment appeal.

Portfolio Manager: Management team
Since: 1990

Minimum:
Initial: $1,000
Subsequent: $25
Telephone Exchange: Yes
Distributions:
Income: Quarterly
Capital Gain: Annually
Front-End Load: None
12b-1: 0.25%
Redemption Fee: None
Management Company: Founders Asset Management
Ticker Symbol: FRMUX

TOTAL RETURN (%)

1987	1988	1989	1990	1991	5-year	Bull Market	Bear Market
1.9	10.1	35.6	0.4	28.3	96.0	27.0	-16.2

INVESTMENT PORTFOLIO

Total Assets (mil.)	Current Yield	Turnover Ratio	Expense Ratio	Beta	Risk Return
$262	1.4%	82%	1.07%	0.91	0.05

FOUNDERS EQUITY INCOME FUND

Founders Asset Management
2930 East Third Avenue
Denver, CO 80206
800-525-2440

Investment Objective: If yield is your game, then this fund has your name on it. On top of declining interest rates, consolidation in the banking industry and investor confidence in telephone profits have driven up stocks in these segments. Despite losing 5.0% in 1990 as telephone stocks fared poorly, the fund bounced back strongly in 1991 with a respectable 22.9% return. Additionally, the fund's 65.6% 5-year return is worth some note. The fund's returns generally have been close to growth and income funds' averages, and the fund's low beta is a perk for investors wishing to lessen risk. Investors could find this growth and income fund quite attractive.

Portfolio Manager: Management team
Since: 1990

Minimum:
Initial: $1,000
Subsequent: $25
Telephone Exchange: Yes
Distributions:
Income: Quarterly
Capital Gain: Annually
Front-End Load: None
12b-1: 0.25%
Redemption Fee: None
Management Company: Founders Asset Management
Ticker Symbol: FRINX

TOTAL RETURN (%)

1987	1988	1989	1990	1991	5-year	Bull Market	Bear Market
2.0	11.1	25.3	-5.0	22.9	65.6	22.2	-9.2

INVESTMENT PORTFOLIO

Total Assets (mil.)	Current Yield	Turnover Ratio	Expense Ratio	Beta	Risk Return
$18	3.7%	103%	1.65%	0.58	0.06

FPA PARAMOUNT

Angeles Securities
10301 West Pico Boulevard
Los Angeles, CA 90064
800-421-4374

Investment Objective: From its diversified portfolio of securities, this fund seeks high return as its investment objective. Management believes this objective can be accomplished by investing in common stocks that have an above-average ability to increase in market value. In the past, the fund has held bonds and convertible securities, and management will not hesitate to hold a substantial portion of the fund's assets in cash. Returns over the past 5 years have been extremely good, especially considering the fund's low risk level. It should be noted that the fund is open only to current investors.

Portfolio Manager: William Sams
Since: 1981

Minimum:
Initial: Closed
Subsequent: $25
Telephone Exchange: Yes
Distributions:
Income: Semiannually
Capital Gain: Annually
Front-End Load: Closed
12b-1: None
Redemption Fee: None
Management Company: First Pacific Advisors
Ticker Symbol: FPRAX

TOTAL RETURN (%)

1987	1988	1989	1990	1991	5-year	Bull Market	Bear Market
21.9	19.8	22.6	1.6	24.3	126.2	34.4	-11.1

INVESTMENT PORTFOLIO

Total Assets (mil.)	Current Yield	Turnover Ratio	Expense Ratio	Beta	Risk Return
$255	3.0%	101%	0.93%	0.56	0.06

FPA PERENNIAL FUND

Angeles Securities
10301 West Pico Boulevard
Los Angeles, CA 90064
800-421-4374

Investment Objective: This fund's primary objective is long-term growth of capital, and current income is a secondary concern. The fund tends to avoid overpaying for stocks and most likely searches out stocks with impressive records that have fallen out of favor and, therefore, have low price/earnings ratios. Though this vehicle prides itself on its value orientation, it actually has performed best in growth-led markets. Nonetheless, with a yield of 3.0%, a below-average beta and modest expenses, this is a good choice for growth investors seeking some income. Investors should be aware, however, of the fund's rather high front-end load of 6.50%.

Portfolio Manager: Christopher Linden
Since: 1984

Minimum:
Initial: $1,500
Subsequent: $100
Telephone Exchange: Yes
Distributions:
Income: Semiannually
Capital Gain: Annually
Front-End Load: 6.50%
12b-1: None
Redemption Fee: None
Management Company: First Pacific Advisors
Ticker Symbol: FPPFX

TOTAL RETURN (%)

1987	1988	1989	1990	1991	5-year	Bull Market	Bear Market
-1.1	19.9	25.8	1.0	21.7	83.4	27.9	-14.9

INVESTMENT PORTFOLIO

Total Assets (mil.)	Current Yield	Turnover Ratio	Expense Ratio	Beta	Risk Return
$60	3.0%	29%	1.14%	0.62	0.05

FRANKLIN CUSTODIAN FUNDS—INCOME SERIES

Franklin Distributors
777 Mariners Island Boulevard, 6th Floor
San Mateo, CA 94404
800-342-5236

Investment Objective: This fund's 10.0% yield is far above the average growth and income fund's yield of 3.3%. Franklin is known for its high-yield (as opposed to junk) approach to both stock and bond investing; most of its funds yield substantially more than the overall market. In this case, the fund offers shareholders more than 3 times the yield available in the S&P 500. The few stocks in the portfolio are mostly utilities and financial, and, not surprisingly, the fund sports a beta of 0.41. However, the portfolio doesn't come without risk, and its return figures tend to vary on the upside or downside from growth and income fund averages.

Portfolio Manager: Charles Johnson
Since: 1956

Minimum:
Initial: $100
Subsequent: $25
Telephone Exchange: Yes
Distributions:
Income: Quarterly
Capital Gain: Annually
Front-End Load: 4.00%
12b-1: None
Redemption Fee: None
Management Company: Franklin Advisors
Ticker Symbol: FKINX

TOTAL RETURN (%)

1987	1988	1989	1990	1991	5-year	Bull Market	Bear Market
4.5	8.4	12.2	-9.2	40.7	62.3	39.3	-12.2

INVESTMENT PORTFOLIO

Total Assets (mil.)	Current Yield	Turnover Ratio	Expense Ratio	Beta	Risk Return
$1,755	10.0%	34%	0.56%	0.41	0.11

FRANKLIN PREMIER RETURN FUND

Franklin Distributors
777 Mariners Island Boulevard, 6th Floor
San Mateo, CA 94404
800-342-5236

Investment Objective: This fund seeks a high level of current income to be derived primarily from dividends, interest and premiums from option-writing activity. The fund invests in dividend-paying stocks with capital-appreciation potential, on which options may be traded on a national securities exchange. Its strategy has produced a slightly below-average 5-year return as well as a below-average yield. Although this fund is a bit riskier than the average growth and income fund, it provides an alternative to investors seeking diversion from the traditional methods of pursuing income for much of its activity is through options.

Portfolio Manager: Martin Wiskeman
Since: 1972

Minimum:
Initial: $100
Subsequent: $25
Telephone Exchange: Yes
Distributions:
Income: Quarterly
Capital Gain: Quarterly
Front-End Load: 4.00%
12b-1: None
Redemption Fee: None
Management Company: Franklin Advisors
Ticker Symbol: FKBRX

TOTAL RETURN (%)

1987	1988	1989	1990	1991	5-year	Bull Market	Bear Market
2.1	18.8	13.6	-8.8	30.1	63.4	30.5	-18.5

INVESTMENT PORTFOLIO

Total Assets (mil.)	Current Yield	Turnover Ratio	Expense Ratio	Beta	Risk Return
$27	2.4%	73%	0.85%	0.83	0.06

FUNDAMENTAL INVESTORS

American Funds Distributor
333 South Hope Street, 52nd Floor
Los Angeles, CA 90071
800-421-9900

Investment Objective: As fundamental investors, the management of this fund favors companies with above-average growth in sales, earnings and dividends, plus low debt and uncomplicated financial structures. They also recognize the need to hold these investments for long periods of time to allow their potential to be fully realized. The fund's 12% portfolio turnover ratio is one of the lowest among equity funds. The fund's concentration on large cap, growth-oriented companies caused it to fall more than 6% in 1990's weak market. However, the fund has shown strong upside potential as it matched the performance of the S&P 500 Index.

Portfolio Manager: Multiple Portfolio Counselors
Since: 1991

Minimum:
Initial: $250
Subsequent: $50
Telephone Exchange: Yes
Distributions:
Income: Quarterly
Capital Gain: Semiannually
Front-End Load: 5.75%
12b-1: 0.10%
Redemption Fee: None
Management Company: Capital Research & Management
Ticker Symbol: ANCFX

TOTAL RETURN (%)

1987	1988	1989	1990	1991	5-year	Bull Market	Bear Market
3.8	16.0	28.6	-6.2	30.3	89.1	35.4	-21.4

INVESTMENT PORTFOLIO

Total Assets (mil.)	Current Yield	Turnover Ratio	Expense Ratio	Beta	Risk Return
$1,030	2.1%	12%	0.70%	0.98	0.05

FUND TRUST GROWTH AND INCOME FUND

Signature Broker Dealer
6 St. James Avenue, 9th Floor
Boston, MA 02116
800-638-1896

Investment Objective: This fund seeks a combination of capital appreciation and current income and it attempts to achieve this goal by investing in 10 to 15 other mutual funds. The underlying funds in which it invests consist of funds that seek income from dividends, income from interest, growth of income or any combination of these. The funds that make up the parent fund may invest in common or preferred stocks, bonds and other fixed-income securities, foreign issues, cash or cash equivalents. Because the fund uses a strategy that would imply maximum diversification, its returns have been average at best. The overlapping of expenses that goes along with investing in several funds cannot help but add to expenses.

Portfolio Manager: Michael Hirsch
Since: 1984

Minimum:
Initial: $1,000
Subsequent: $100
Telephone Exchange: Yes
Distributions:
Income: Quarterly
Capital Gain: Semiannually
Front-End Load: 1.50%
12b-1: 0.50%
Redemption Fee: None
Management Company: Republic National Bank of New York
Ticker Symbol: FTGIX

TOTAL RETURN (%)

1987	1988	1989	1990	1991	5-year	Bull Market	Bear Market
-4.3	19.2	19.4	-8.3	23.3	54.0	31.3	-17.0

INVESTMENT PORTFOLIO

Total Assets (mil.)	Current Yield	Turnover Ratio	Expense Ratio	Beta	Risk Return
$61	2.5%	48%	1.85%	0.80	0.05

GATEWAY INDEX PLUS

Gateway Investment Advisors
400 Technecenter Drive, Suite 220
Milford, OH 45150
800-354-6339

Investment Objective: A closet indexer employing options to reduce risk is seemingly a recipe for investment disappointment. However, this option-income vehicle has spent more of its time looking out for risk than trying to boost payout artificially through option premiums. Although the fund dropped precipitously in 1987, its post-crash returns have been better than expected, given the below-average risk and the surprisingly strong 1990 return of 10.3%. In 1991, the fund's performance lagged its peers, but it still sports one of the lowest betas of 0.37%.

Portfolio Manager: Peter Thayer
Since: 1977

Minimum:
Initial: $1,000
Subsequent: $100
Telephone Exchange: Yes
Distributions:
Income: Quarterly
Capital Gain: Annually
Front-End Load: None
12b-1: None
Redemption Fee: None
Management Company: Gateway Investment Advisors
Ticker Symbol: GATEX

TOTAL RETURN (%)

1987	1988	1989	1990	1991	5-year	Bull Market	Bear Market
-5.7	19.8	19.4	10.3	17.8	75.4	28.2	-8.2

INVESTMENT PORTFOLIO

Total Assets (mil.)	Current Yield	Turnover Ratio	Expense Ratio	Beta	Risk Return
$78	1.9%	79%	1.34%	0.37	0.06

GENERAL SECURITIES

General Securities
701 4th Avenue South, 10th Floor
Minneapolis, MN 55415
800-331-4923

Investment Objective: This fund seeks to select issues with long-term appreciation potential and security of principal. Though the fund typically invests most of its assets in common stocks, it does not hesitate to move into bonds, U.S. government securities or other types of securities if economic conditions make it necessary. The fund's relatively low beta implies below-average risk, and the fund achieves this by keeping a very well-diversified portfolio of issues that are most consistent with its objective. Return data, however, are impressive and above the returns of the average growth and income fund. Investors should, however, be aware of the fund's 5.00% front-end load and redemption fee of 1.50%.

Portfolio Manager: John Robinson
Since: 1951

Minimum:
Initial: $500
Subsequent: $100
Telephone Exchange: No
Distributions:
Income: Quarterly
Capital Gain: Annually
Front-End Load: 5.00%
12b-1: None
Redemption Fee: 1.50%
Management Company: Craig-Hallum
Ticker Symbol: GSECX

TOTAL RETURN (%)

1987	1988	1989	1990	1991	5-year	Bull Market	Bear Market
2.2	14.0	20.4	-0.3	35.7	89.9	43.5	-17.4

INVESTMENT PORTFOLIO

Total Assets (mil.)	Current Yield	Turnover Ratio	Expense Ratio	Beta	Risk Return
$22	3.8%	54%	1.39%	0.66	0.09

GIT EQUITY TRUST— EQUITY INCOME PORTFOLIO

GIT Investment Services
1655 Fort Myer Drive
Arlington, VA 22209
800-336-3063

Investment Objective: This portfolio seeks to earn substantial current dividend income through the selection of securities offering current income with some capital-appreciation potential. Consideration is given to each investment's potential for appreciation and factors tending to protect the investment's value. Employing a mixture of common stocks, preferred stocks and convertible bonds allowed the fund to offer a yield of 3.3% and upside potential rivaling that of an index portfolio. Though its 1991 return of 14.8% is below the average growth and income fund's return, this young no-load fund has a very low portfolio turnover and may be a little less risky than its counterparts with fancier returns.

Portfolio Manager: John Edwards
Since: 1988

Minimum:
Initial: $2,500
Subsequent: None
Telephone Exchange: Yes
Distributions:
Income: Quarterly
Capital Gain: Annually
Front-End Load: None
12b-1: None
Redemption Fee: None
Management Company: Bankers Finance Investment Management
Ticker Symbol: None

TOTAL RETURN (%)

1987	1988	1989	1990	1991	5-year	Bull Market	Bear Market
-4.9	13.3	26.3	0.5	14.8	57.2	14.5	-4.2

INVESTMENT PORTFOLIO

Total Assets (mil.)	Current Yield	Turnover Ratio	Expense Ratio	Beta	Risk Return
$3	3.3%	9%	2.25%	0.45	0.03

IAI STOCK FUND

Investment Advisers
1100 Dain Tower, P.O. Box 357
Minneapolis, MN 55440
800-945-3863

Investment Objective: The primary objective of this fund is capital appreciation, with income being its secondary objective. When selecting investments, this fund considers a number of factors, including product development and demand, operating ratios, utilization of earnings for expansion, management abilities, analysis of intrinsic values, market action and the condition of the economy. The fund's 5-year return supports that capital appreciation is its primary objective, but its current yield of only 0.9% does little to imply that current income is even secondary. Investors willing to back off on their pursuit of income in exchange for capital appreciation will find this fund attractive.

Portfolio Manager: Bing Carlin
Since: 1991

Minimum:
Initial: $5,000
Subsequent: $100
Telephone Exchange: No
Distributions:
Income: Semiannually
Capital Gain: Semiannually
Front-End Load: None
12b-1: 0.20%
Redemption Fee: None
Management Company: Investment Advisers
Ticker Symbol: IASKX

TOTAL RETURN (%)

1987	1988	1989	1990	1991	5-year	Bull Market	Bear Market
15.5	8.5	29.8	-6.7	26.7	92.3	28.6	-19.3

INVESTMENT PORTFOLIO

Total Assets (mil.)	Current Yield	Turnover Ratio	Expense Ratio	Beta	Risk Return
$104	0.9%	69%	1.05%	0.89	0.05

IDS EQUITY PLUS FUND

IDS Financial Services
1000 Roanoke Building
Minneapolis, MN 55402
800-328-8300

Investment Objective: This fund seeks capital appreciation through investments in a diversified portfolio of high-yielding equity securities. This midwestern-managed fund favors using midwestern companies. The past year the fund posted an above-average 32% return. This enabled the fund to maintain its superior 5-year return relative to other growth and income funds. For the past 5 years, the portfolio has returned a respectable 96.4%. However, potential investors should note that the fund levies a 5.00% front-end sales charge.

Portfolio Manager: Joseph Barsky
Since: 1983

Minimum:
Initial: $2,000
Subsequent: $25
Telephone Exchange: Yes
Distributions:
Income: Quarterly
Capital Gain: Annually
Front-End Load: 5.00%
12b-1: 0.05%
Redemption Fee: None
Management Company: IDS Financial
Ticker Symbol: INVPX

TOTAL RETURN (%)

1987	1988	1989	1990	1991	5-year	Bull Market	Bear Market
9.5	8.5	29.0	-3.2	32.4	96.4	37.1	-20.0

INVESTMENT PORTFOLIO

Total Assets (mil.)	Current Yield	Turnover Ratio	Expense Ratio	Beta	Risk Return
$400	1.5%	55%	0.63%	0.95	0.06

IDS MUTUAL

IDS Financial Services
1000 Roanoke Building
Minneapolis, MN 55402
800-328-8300

Investment Objective: Unlike most of its IDS peers, this fund isn't invested aggressively. With a current yield of 4.8%, because of a one-third allocation to bonds, the fund offers cautious, income-oriented investors a safe haven. By staying almost fully invested in either the stock market and/or the bond market, the fund is geared for interest-rate-related rallies. If rates rise, however, investors could be in store for rough sailing. The fund's returns have generally been slightly above average and may be a good investment for those willing to pay the sales charges.

Minimum:
Initial: $2,000
Subsequent: $25
Telephone Exchange: Yes
Distributions:
Income: Quarterly
Capital Gain: Annually
Front-End Load: 5.00%
12b-1: 0.06%
Redemption Fee: None
Management Company: IDS Financial
Ticker Symbol: INMUX

Portfolio Manager: Thomas Medcalf
Since: 1983

TOTAL RETURN (%)

1987	1988	1989	1990	1991	5-year	Bull Market	Bear Market
7.4	12.7	18.6	-3.0	23.7	72.1	29.1	-11.7

INVESTMENT PORTFOLIO

Total Assets (mil.)	Current Yield	Turnover Ratio	Expense Ratio	Beta	Risk Return
$1,862	4.8%	37%	0.69%	0.66	0.06

IDS STOCK FUND

IDS Financial Services
1000 Roanoke Building
Minneapolis, MN 55402
800-328-8300

Investment Objective: If you're scared off by the high price/earnings ratios, high-risk strategies of IDS's other stock funds, this moderate-risk vehicle may be to your liking. And if you desire decent returns and a below-market beta, you'll like this fund even better. This fund concentrates its investments in large cap stocks that offer both growth and modest income. The fund's low turnover ratio, low expense ratio and below-average volatility are just a few of the reasons why management has turned in one of the best 5-year records. Investors should note, however, that the fund levies a 5.00% front-end load.

Minimum:
Initial: $2,000
Subsequent: $25
Telephone Exchange: Yes
Distributions:
Income: Quarterly
Capital Gain: Annually
Front-End Load: 5.00%
12b-1: 0.04%
Redemption Fee: None
Management Company: IDS Financial
Ticker Symbol: INSTX

Portfolio Manager: Robert Healy
Since: 1991

TOTAL RETURN (%)

1987	1988	1989	1990	1991	5-year	Bull Market	Bear Market
9.2	10.4	29.7	1.7	27.6	102.9	30.6	-13.7

INVESTMENT PORTFOLIO

Total Assets (mil.)	Current Yield	Turnover Ratio	Expense Ratio	Beta	Risk Return
$1,457	3.0%	58%	0.65%	0.85	0.05

IDS STRATEGY EQUITY FUND

IDS Financial Services
1000 Roanoke Building
Minneapolis, MN 55402
800-328-8300

Investment Objective: In seeking a combination of long-term capital appreciation and income, the fund invests mostly in dividend-paying common stocks, with a secondary bond position for added income. The fund has done well with this strategy, returning more than 89% for the past 5 years. This was achieved with a risk level less than that of the S&P 500 Index. The secondary investment objective of income also has been achieved, with a current dividend yield of 2.6%. Potential investors should note that the fund levies a 5.00% redemption fee.

Portfolio Manager: Thomas Medcalf
Since: 1989

Minimum:
Initial: $2,000
Subsequent: $100
Telephone Exchange: Yes
Distributions:
Income: Quarterly
Capital Gain: Annually
Front-End Load: None
12b-1: 0.82%
Redemption Fee: 5.00%
Management Company: IDS Financial
Ticker Symbol: INEGX

TOTAL RETURN (%)

1987	1988	1989	1990	1991	5-year	Bull Market	Bear Market
3.6	24.5	21.4	-5.9	28.4	89.3	37.7	-19.3

INVESTMENT PORTFOLIO

Total Assets (mil.)	Current Yield	Turnover Ratio	Expense Ratio	Beta	Risk Return
$422	2.6%	65%	1.66%	0.90	0.05

INCOME FUND OF AMERICA

American Funds Distributor
333 South Hope Street, 52nd Floor
Los Angeles, CA 90071
800-421-9900

Investment Objective: This fund emphasizes current income while secondarily striving to attain capital growth. Its portfolio typically consists of common stocks, bonds and preferred stocks. Because it has maintained a relatively high allocation to fixed-income securities, the fund's volatility level is one of the lowest in the growth and income category. Until 1990's fateful market, the fund had risen 15 straight years. Though the fund's long-term performance probably will trail the popular average, investors who seek high income with proven growth potential should like this fund. Investors should, however, be aware of the 5.75% front-end load.

Portfolio Manager: Multiple Portfolio Counselors
Since: 1991

Minimum:
Initial: $1,000
Subsequent: $50
Telephone Exchange: Yes
Distributions:
Income: Quarterly
Capital Gain: Annually
Front-End Load: 5.75%
12b-1: 0.15%
Redemption Fee: None
Management Company: Capital Research & Management
Ticker Symbol: AMECX

TOTAL RETURN (%)

1987	1988	1989	1990	1991	5-year	Bull Market	Bear Market
0.7	14.8	23.0	-3.0	23.8	70.7	28.3	-10.2

INVESTMENT PORTFOLIO

Total Assets (mil.)	Current Yield	Turnover Ratio	Expense Ratio	Beta	Risk Return
$3,242	6.0%	23%	0.73%	0.50	0.07

INVESTMENT COMPANY OF AMERICA

American Funds Distributor
333 South Hope Street, 52nd Floor
Los Angeles, CA 90071
800-421-9900

Investment Objective: This fund, which carries a 5.75% front-end load, seeks long-term growth of both capital and income. Management believes these objectives can be achieved through maintaining a broadly diversified portfolio of common stocks of well-established companies that regularly pay dividends. Though providing an average dividend yield, the portfolio is more aggressive than other funds in the growth and income category. The fund's performance record has been above average, given the amount of risk assumed, returning almost 15% annualized over the long haul.

Portfolio Manager: Multiple Portfolio Counselors
Since: 1991

Minimum:
Initial: $250
Subsequent: $50
Telephone Exchange: Yes
Distributions:
Income: Quarterly
Capital Gain: Semiannually
Front-End Load: 5.75%
12b-1: 0.13%
Redemption Fee: None
Management Company: Capital Research & Management
Ticker Symbol: AIVSX

TOTAL RETURN (%)

1987	1988	1989	1990	1991	5-year	Bull Market	Bear Market
5.4	13.3	29.4	0.7	26.5	97.0	32.2	-15.2

INVESTMENT PORTFOLIO

Total Assets (mil.)	Current Yield	Turnover Ratio	Expense Ratio	Beta	Risk Return
$9,341	2.3%	11%	0.55%	0.83	0.05

IVY GROWTH WITH INCOME FUND

Mackenzie Investment Management
P.O. Box 5007
Boca Raton, FL 33431
800-235-3322

Investment Objective: This fund and its family, the Ivy funds, were acquired in 1991 by Mackenzie Investment Management. Although the fund's objective has remained the same under the new parent company, the fund is not so attractive as it used to be, for it was formerly sold without sales charges. That aside, after running rings around the market in the mid-1980s, the fund has slowly matured in recent years. Yet though it rose strongly in 1988, with a 22% return, performances in 1986, 1987 and 1989 weren't storied successes. Though its stocks pay handsome dividends, these stock prices are highly sensitive to interest rates.

Portfolio Manager: Michael Peers
Since: 1989

Minimum:
Initial: $1,000
Subsequent: None
Telephone Exchange: Yes
Distributions:
Income: Annually
Capital Gain: Annually
Front-End Load: 5.75%
12b-1: 0.25%
Redemption Fee: None
Management Company: Ivy Management
Ticker Symbol: IVYIX

TOTAL RETURN (%)

1987	1988	1989	1990	1991	5-year	Bull Market	Bear Market
1.0	22.0	18.1	-0.2	36.3	97.9	24.2	-19.5

INVESTMENT PORTFOLIO

Total Assets (mil.)	Current Yield	Turnover Ratio	Expense Ratio	Beta	Risk Return
$13	1.9%	80%	1.51%	0.96	0.10

KEMPER DIVERSIFIED INCOME FUND

Kemper Financial Services
120 South LaSalle Street, 20th Floor
Chicago, IL 60603
800-621-1048

Investment Objective: Patience may finally be paying off for shareholders of Kemper Diversified Income. The fund is more of an income fund than growth and income, because less than 5% of the fund's assets are invested in stocks. The past year the fund returned an astounding 52% as this portfolio of junk bonds performed remarkably well. Investors should be aware that the switch to a junk-bond portfolio occurred in 1989, and, thus, past performance does not reflect possible future results. If junk bonds are your thing, this may be the portfolio for you.

Portfolio Manager: Mike McNamara
Since: 1989

Minimum:
Initial: $1,000
Subsequent: $100
Telephone Exchange: Yes
Distributions:
Income: Monthly
Capital Gain: Annually
Front-End Load: 4.50%
12b-1: None
Redemption Fee: None
Management Company: Kemper Financial Services
Ticker Symbol: KDIFX

TOTAL RETURN (%)

1987	1988	1989	1990	1991	5-year	Bull Market	Bear Market
-7.2	17.6	8.0	-12.6	51.7	56.2	49.1	-18.2

INVESTMENT PORTFOLIO

Total Assets (mil.)	Current Yield	Turnover Ratio	Expense Ratio	Beta	Risk Return
$226	12.0%	45%	1.15%	0.45	0.12

KEMPER INVESTMENT PORTFOLIOS—DIVERSIFIED INCOME

Kemper Financial Services
120 South LaSalle Street, 20th Floor
Chicago, IL 60603
800-621-1048

Investment Objective: This fund seeks high current returns by investing primarily in fixed-income securities and dividend-paying stocks, and by writing options. The percentages of these portions vary depending on economic conditions, such as interest rates. Investors seeking high current income as their primary objective will be impressed by this fund's current dividend yield of 11.3%. Suffering somewhat, however, have been returns, and this fund's 5-year return is well below that of the average growth and income fund. Additionally, this fund has sales and marketing expenses and a relatively high expense ratio.

Portfolio Manager: Mike McNamara
Since: 1989

Minimum:
Initial: $250
Subsequent: $50
Telephone Exchange: Yes
Distributions:
Income: Monthly
Capital Gain: Annually
Front-End Load: None
12b-1: 1.25%
Redemption Fee: 3.00%
Management Company: Kemper Financial Services
Ticker Symbol: INPDX

TOTAL RETURN (%)

1987	1988	1989	1990	1991	5-year	Bull Market	Bear Market
-9.4	15.0	7.1	-15.8	50.9	41.7	47.3	-19.7

INVESTMENT PORTFOLIO

Total Assets (mil.)	Current Yield	Turnover Ratio	Expense Ratio	Beta	Risk Return
$247	11.3%	51%	2.20%	0.47	0.11

KEMPER INVESTMENT PORTFOLIOS—TOTAL RETURN

Kemper Financial Services
120 South LaSalle Street, 20th Floor
Chicago, IL 60603
800-621-1048

Investment Objective: This fund seek a combination of income and capital appreciation consistent with reasonable risk, and emphasizes liberal current income in seeking its objective. The fund invests in a combination of fixed-income and equity securities, percentages of which will vary according to market conditions, such as interest rates. Indeed, the fund's 2.7% current yield and impressive 5-year return of 94.4% is attractive to investors seeking the ideal combination of growth and income. A high expense ratio and marketing charges lessen the attractiveness of this fund.

Portfolio Manager: Beth Cotner
Since: 1986

Minimum:
Initial: $250
Subsequent: $50
Telephone Exchange: Yes
Distributions:
Income: Semiannually
Capital Gain: Annually
Front-End Load: None
12b-1: 1.25%
Redemption Fee: 3.00%
Management Company: Kemper Financial Services
Ticker Symbol: INPTX

TOTAL RETURN (%)

1987	1988	1989	1990	1991	5-year	Bull Market	Bear Market
1.3	11.9	20.0	0.3	42.5	94.4	37.8	-15.8

INVESTMENT PORTFOLIO

Total Assets (mil.)	Current Yield	Turnover Ratio	Expense Ratio	Beta	Risk Return
$656	2.7%	70%	2.18%	0.78	0.09

KEMPER TOTAL RETURN FUND

Kemper Financial Services
120 South LaSalle Street, 20th Floor
Chicago, IL 60603
800-621-1048

Investment Objective: By investing in a combination of debt securities and common stocks, this fund attempts to provide investors the highest return (dividends plus capital appreciation) consistent with a reasonable amount of risk. In both cases, the fund has lived up to its billing. In addition, the fund can engage in options and financial futures transactions, which adds a degree of risk. The fund has a good long-term performance record, with a 5-year total return of 85.7%. Potential investors should note that the fund carries a 5.75% front-end load.

Portfolio Manager: Gordon Wilson
Since: 1971

Minimum:
Initial: $1,000
Subsequent: $100
Telephone Exchange: Yes
Distributions:
Income: Semiannually
Capital Gain: Annually
Front-End Load: 5.75%
12b-1: None
Redemption Fee: None
Management Company: Kemper Financial Services
Ticker Symbol: KMRTX

TOTAL RETURN (%)

1987	1988	1989	1990	1991	5-year	Bull Market	Bear Market
-2.4	8.8	19.8	4.1	40.2	85.7	40.0	-14.9

INVESTMENT PORTFOLIO

Total Assets (mil.)	Current Yield	Turnover Ratio	Expense Ratio	Beta	Risk Return
$990	3.1%	157%	0.87%	0.75	0.09

KEYSTONE AMERICA EQUITY INCOME FUND

Keystone Distributors
99 High Street, 29th Floor
Boston, MA 02110
800-633-4900

Investment Objective: With modest expenses, a yield of 3.0% and returns that nearly match those of the market in each of the past 4 years, this fund is off to an auspicious start. The fund's equity portion is basically a mixed bag of consumer growth, industrial and utility stocks, helping the portfolio weather any particular sector's decline through each market cycle. The fund also may invest up to 25% of its assets in foreign stocks. Note, however, that initial purchases are subject to a 4.75% load, and the fund does have a 12b-1 plan.

Portfolio Manager: Walter McCormick
Since: 1987

Minimum:
Initial: $1,000
Subsequent: None
Telephone Exchange: Yes
Distributions:
Income: Quarterly
Capital Gain: Annually
Front-End Load: 4.75%
12b-1: 0.29%
Redemption Fee: None
Management Company: Keystone Custodian Funds
Ticker Symbol: KAEIX

TOTAL RETURN (%)

1987	1988	1989	1990	1991	5-year	Bull Market	Bear Market
NA	12.1	26.7	-2.3	25.2	NA	32.9	-12.3

INVESTMENT PORTFOLIO

Total Assets (mil.)	Current Yield	Turnover Ratio	Expense Ratio	Beta	Risk Return
$24	3.0%	51%	2.00%	0.75	0.05

KEYSTONE CUSTODIAN FUNDS K1

Keystone Distributors
99 High Street, 29th Floor
Boston, MA 02110
800-633-4900

Investment Objective: Having a large allocation of bonds and being an equity portfolio weighted toward interest-sensitive utilities and industrial stocks, this fund is highly dependent on the ebb and flow of interest rates. As its current yield of 4.8% suggests, the fund is no miser when it comes to dividends—making it attractive to income-oriented investors. However, if such conservative shareholders expect to see a perfectly stable NAV, they'll have to think again; the fund can tumble when rates rise. Yet with a beta of 0.65, the fund comes with 35% less risk than the broader market. Investors also should note that the fund carries a 4.00% redemption fee and a 12b-1 fee.

Portfolio Manager: Walter McCormick
Since: 1984

Minimum:
Initial: $1,000
Subsequent: None
Telephone Exchange: Yes
Distributions:
Income: Quarterly
Capital Gain: Annually
Front-End Load: None
12b-1: 0.98%
Redemption Fee: 4.00%
Management Company: Keystone Custodian Funds
Ticker Symbol: KKONX

TOTAL RETURN (%)

1987	1988	1989	1990	1991	5-year	Bull Market	Bear Market
3.7	11.5	19.8	-1.8	24.0	68.8	26.8	-10.5

INVESTMENT PORTFOLIO

Total Assets (mil.)	Current Yield	Turnover Ratio	Expense Ratio	Beta	Risk Return
$968	4.8%	60%	1.88%	0.65	0.06

KEYSTONE CUSTODIAN FUNDS S1

Keystone Distributors
99 High Street, 29th Floor
Boston, MA 02110
800-633-4900

Investment Objective: Though it's easy to criticize a fund that blindly adopts an indexlike strategy and still carries above-average expenses, it's hard not to respect above-average returns for much of the past 5 years. For although we might have a beef with 2% expenses for a fund with more than $150 million in assets and a straightforward portfolio strategy, the fund still offers investors a reasonable though below-average 1.5% yield. Its stocks are of the pedestrian, large cap variety. Investors won't get burned too badly in such an investment vehicle, nor will they see sky-high returns. A 4.00% redemption fee will further dampen an investor's total return.

Portfolio Manager: Maureen Cullinane
Since: 1989

Minimum:
Initial: $1,000
Subsequent: None
Telephone Exchange: Yes
Distributions:
Income: Quarterly
Capital Gain: Annually
Front-End Load: None
12b-1: 1.10%
Redemption Fee: 4.00%
Management Company: Keystone Custodian Funds
Ticker Symbol: KSONX

TOTAL RETURN (%)

1987	1988	1989	1990	1991	5-year	Bull Market	Bear Market
3.7	8.5	29.3	-5.2	28.8	77.5	33.3	-18.0

INVESTMENT PORTFOLIO

Total Assets (mil.)	Current Yield	Turnover Ratio	Expense Ratio	Beta	Risk Return
$168	1.5%	64%	2.33%	1.02	0.05

LEGG MASON TOTAL RETURN TRUST

Legg Mason Distributors
7 East Redwood Street
Baltimore, MD 21202
800-822-5544

Investment Objective: This fund seeks capital growth and income by using a value discipline. As can be expected from Baltimore-based Legg Mason, this fund tore up the track in 1988, as its value picks stormed higher after the crash. Performance in previous and ensuing periods hasn't been up to snuff, partly because of above-average cash levels and partly because of a preference for cyclical companies. However, the cyclical-type companies have come back into favor as the fund rose by more than 40% the past year. This fund's performance is a good example of why an investor must be there for the long haul.

Portfolio Manager: William Miller III
Since: 1990

Minimum:
Initial: $1,000
Subsequent: $500
Telephone Exchange: Yes
Distributions:
Income: Quarterly
Capital Gain: Annually
Front-End Load: None
12b-1: 0.97%
Redemption Fee: None
Management Company: Legg Mason Fund Advisor
Ticker Symbol: LMTRX

TOTAL RETURN (%)

1987	1988	1989	1990	1991	5-year	Bull Market	Bear Market
-7.8	21.8	16.4	-16.8	40.5	52.7	44.4	-22.4

INVESTMENT PORTFOLIO

Total Assets (mil.)	Current Yield	Turnover Ratio	Expense Ratio	Beta	Risk Return
$33	1.5%	62%	2.50%	0.86	0.08

LEPERCQ-ISTEL FUND

Lepercq-Istel de Neuflize Securities
1675 Broadway, 16th Floor
New York, NY 10019
800-338-1579

Investment Objective: This no-load fund seeks long-term growth of capital and reasonable current income. Management stresses safety of capital and a buy-and-hold strategy. The portfolio is typically composed of near-equal weightings of stocks and bonds. Founded in 1954, this fund has used its wisdom to become an expert in the balanced approach to investing. The fund has a risk level about 35% below that of the S&P 500 Index. Performance has been below average compared to other funds in its category, however, and investors must be willing to give up returns for reduced risk exposure in this portfolio.

Portfolio Manager: Bruno Desforges
Since: 1974

Minimum:
Initial: $500
Subsequent: None
Telephone Exchange: No
Distributions:
Income: Semiannually
Capital Gain: Annually
Front-End Load: None
12b-1: None
Redemption Fee: None
Management Company: Lepercq de Neuflize
Ticker Symbol: ISTLX

TOTAL RETURN (%)

1987	1988	1989	1990	1991	5-year	Bull Market	Bear Market
2.2	7.0	21.7	-6.6	17.3	45.9	18.5	-11.9

INVESTMENT PORTFOLIO

Total Assets (mil.)	Current Yield	Turnover Ratio	Expense Ratio	Beta	Risk Return
$16	3.8%	24%	1.50%	0.65	0.03

LEXINGTON CORPORATE LEADERS TRUST FUND

Lexington Funds Distributors
P.O. Box 1515
Saddle Brook, NJ 07662
800-526-0056

Investment Objective: This fund's objective is long-term capital growth and income through investment in an equal number of shares of a fixed list of American blue chip companies. Accordingly, the performance of this fund is more closely like the performance of the broader markets than that of the average growth and income fund. Investors looking for high current income may be attracted to this fund's dividend yield of 8.3%, along with the fact that the fund is sold with no sales charges, which makes it even more attractive. Investing in blue chip companies has helped this fund to lower risk without stifling returns.

Portfolio Manager: Lexington Management
Since: 1988

Minimum:
Initial: $1,000
Subsequent: $50
Telephone Exchange: Yes
Distributions:
Income: Semiannually
Capital Gain: Annually
Front-End Load: None
12b-1: None
Redemption Fee: None
Management Company: Lexington Management Corporation
Ticker Symbol: LEXCX

TOTAL RETURN (%)

1987	1988	1989	1990	1991	5-year	Bull Market	Bear Market
1.7	19.9	30.3	-4.2	19.4	81.9	26.4	-15.1

INVESTMENT PORTFOLIO

Total Assets (mil.)	Current Yield	Turnover Ratio	Expense Ratio	Beta	Risk Return
$92	8.3%	0%	0.67%	0.82	0.03

LEXINGTON GROWTH AND INCOME FUND

Lexington Funds Distributors
P.O. Box 1515
Saddle Brook, NJ 07662
800-526-0056

Investment Objective: This fund, formerly Lexington Research Fund, takes home trophies because of its format more than its stock picks. Employing a fully no-load structure and keeping expenses down below 1.1% per annum makes this fund a winner. Its stocks are nothing exciting, mainly large cap consumer growth and industrial picks, but the fund picks up some of its yield through a 5 to 10% cash position and a 5% bonds stake. Returns have been about average over the past 5 years, but don't count this high-quality growth and income fund out of the game. The capability of management eventually will bring this fund back into the limelight.

Portfolio Manager: William S. Stack
Since: 1991

Minimum:
Initial: $1,000
Subsequent: $50
Telephone Exchange: Yes
Distributions:
Income: Quarterly
Capital Gain: Annually
Front-End Load: None
12b-1: None
Redemption Fee: None
Management Company: Lexington Management Corporation
Ticker Symbol: LEXRX

TOTAL RETURN (%)

1987	1988	1989	1990	1991	5-year	Bull Market	Bear Market
0.1	9.5	27.6	-10.3	24.9	56.6	29.4	-18.1

INVESTMENT PORTFOLIO

Total Assets (mil.)	Current Yield	Turnover Ratio	Expense Ratio	Beta	Risk Return
$110	2.0%	67%	1.04%	0.95	0.04

LINDNER DIVIDEND FUND

Lindner Group
P.O. Box 11208
St. Louis, MO 63105
314-727-5305

Investment Objective: This growth and income fund stresses a high level of current income. Thus, the portfolio generally contains only a few common stocks. Instead, it contains convertible preferred stocks, convertible bonds and straight debt instruments such as corporate bonds, government bonds and preferred stocks. As a result, the fund's share price is considerably more stable than that of the typical growth and income fund (a beta of 0.28). During the declining interest-rate environment of the 1980s, the fund delivered a better-than-average 20.5% compound annual rate of return. If you're looking for a high-quality growth and income fund, look no further.

Portfolio Manager: Eric Ryback
Since: 1982

Minimum:
Initial: $2,000
Subsequent: $100
Telephone Exchange: No
Distributions:
Income: Quarterly
Capital Gain: Annually
Front-End Load: None
12b-1: None
Redemption Fee: None
Management Company: Lindner Management
Ticker Symbol: LDDVX

TOTAL RETURN (%)

1987	1988	1989	1990	1991	5-year	Bull Market	Bear Market
-4.1	24.2	11.9	-6.5	27.4	58.8	20.3	-3.7

INVESTMENT PORTFOLIO

Total Assets (mil.)	Current Yield	Turnover Ratio	Expense Ratio	Beta	Risk Return
$223	8.6%	3%	0.87%	0.28	0.11

LINDNER FUND

Lindner Group
P.O. Box 11208
St. Louis, MO 63105
314-727-5305

Investment Objective: This growth and income fund, managed by Robert Lange, has consistently maintained a highly conservative bent. While conservatism usually is equated with modest returns, the fund provided its shareholders with a 21% compound annual return during the 1980s. Its success had not been solely generated by above-average returns during bull markets but by not giving back a significant percentage of gains during bear markets. For example, the fund returned 8.8% during 1987. However, like most funds with a high-yield bent, the portfolio fell 11.3% in 1990 as interest rates rose and finance stocks plummeted. The fund got back on track in 1991 with a 23.4% return.

Portfolio Manager: Robert Lange
Since: 1977

Minimum:
Initial: $2,000
Subsequent: $100
Telephone Exchange: Yes
Distributions:
Income: Semiannually
Capital Gain: Annually
Front-End Load: None
12b-1: None
Redemption Fee: None
Management Company: Lindner Management
Ticker Symbol: LDNRX

TOTAL RETURN (%)

1987	1988	1989	1990	1991	5-year	Bull Market	Bear Market
8.8	20.4	21.2	-11.3	23.4	73.8	23.2	-14.2

INVESTMENT PORTFOLIO

Total Assets (mil.)	Current Yield	Turnover Ratio	Expense Ratio	Beta	Risk Return
$818	3.6%	13%	0.83%	0.60	0.05

LMH FUND

LMH Fund
P.O. Box 5006, 253 Post Road West
Westport, CT 06881
203-226-4768

Investment Objective: This fund seeks a total rate of return composed of capital appreciation and current income, although current income is of lesser importance. Large bets and intermittent forays into cash have made this fund's returns mildly inconsistent. For a fund with limited resources, investing in a few stocks that management knows well can be an excellent strategy. However, if one or more of the fund's large positions takes a dive, the results can send tremors throughout the portfolio. Management has been fond of keeping about 20% of its assets in cash, crippling its upside potential in bullish markets. However, with a 0.88 beta and a respectable 2.6% yield, the fund may be attractive for cautious investors.

Portfolio Manager: Leonard M. Heine, Jr.
Since: 1983

Minimum:
Initial: $2,500
Subsequent: $2,000
Telephone Exchange: Yes
Distributions:
Income: Annually
Capital Gain: Annually
Front-End Load: None
12b-1: None
Redemption Fee: None
Management Company: Heine Management
Ticker Symbol: LMHFX

TOTAL RETURN (%)

1987	1988	1989	1990	1991	5-year	Bull Market	Bear Market
-6.3	18.0	12.1	-18.6	18.5	19.6	17.4	-23.7

INVESTMENT PORTFOLIO

Total Assets (mil.)	Current Yield	Turnover Ratio	Expense Ratio	Beta	Risk Return
$8	2.6%	133%	2.39%	0.88	0.07

LUTHERAN BROTHERHOOD FUND

Lutheran Brotherhood Securities
625 Fourth Avenue South
Minneapolis, MN 55415
800-328-4552

Investment Objective: The Lutheran Brotherhood Fund has done quite well since current management, Lutheran Brotherhood Resources, took over as adviser. Until May of 1988, the fund was contracted out to Federated Research Corporation for advisory services. Under in-house management, the fund took on a concerted growth strategy. As the fund's yield would indicate, management has significantly downplayed the income aspect of the fund. The past year's return of almost 33% is a testament to the fund's growth concentration.

Portfolio Manager: Don Nelson
Since: 1987

Minimum:
Initial: $500
Subsequent: $50
Telephone Exchange: Yes
Distributions:
Income: Quarterly
Capital Gain: Annually
Front-End Load: 5.00%
12b-1: None
Redemption Fee: None
Management Company: Lutheran Brotherhood Resources
Ticker Symbol: LUBRX

TOTAL RETURN (%)

1987	1988	1989	1990	1991	5-year	Bull Market	Bear Market
-3.3	9.2	26.6	-1.9	32.8	74.2	36.9	-19.9

INVESTMENT PORTFOLIO

Total Assets (mil.)	Current Yield	Turnover Ratio	Expense Ratio	Beta	Risk Return
$340	1.4%	148%	1.05%	1.02	0.05

MACKENZIE NORTH AMERICAN TOTAL RETURN FUND

Mackenzie Investment Management
P.O. Box 5007
Boca Raton, FL 33431
800-456-5111

Investment Objective: If anything, this fund's future returns should mirror that of natural resource prices. Though not one of the better performers over the past 5 years, some explaining is in order. This fund only recently abdicated its use of options to boost current income, a strategy that has fallen on hard times of late. Today, the portfolio is basically committed to cyclical industrial stocks and natural resource plays. Thus, an expansionary, if not inflationary, environment would treat it best. Though inflation may not be the problem it was in the 1970s or early 1980s, investors fearing a rebirth of this monster may want to take shelter here.

Portfolio Manager: Investment Committee
Since: 1989

Minimum:
Initial: $250
Subsequent: $50
Telephone Exchange: Yes
Distributions:
Income: Quarterly
Capital Gain: Semiannually
Front-End Load: 5.75%
12b-1: 0.02%
Redemption Fee: None
Management Company: Rampart Institutional Investors
Ticker Symbol: INOPX

TOTAL RETURN (%)

1987	1988	1989	1990	1991	5-year	Bull Market	Bear Market
-1.1	4.2	10.8	-9.5	16.4	20.3	22.9	-16.4

INVESTMENT PORTFOLIO

Total Assets (mil.)	Current Yield	Turnover Ratio	Expense Ratio	Beta	Risk Return
$52	5.4%	83%	2.12%	0.64	0.03

MAINSTAY TOTAL RETURN FUND

NYLIFE Securities
51 Madison Avenue, Room 117
New York, NY 10010
800-522-4202

Investment Objective: The primary objective of this fund is current income consistent with reasonable opportunity for future growth of capital and income. The fund has a diversified approach to investing, choosing from a variety of companies and industries. The fund looks for companies with growth in revenues and earnings per share superior to that of the average index-held stock. In its rather short history, this fund has performed quite well, outperforming the growth and income average in 1991 and providing even a small return in 1990's bear market. Investors should be aware of the fund's 5.00% redemption fee.

Portfolio Manager: Ravi Akhoury
Since: 1987

Minimum:
Initial: $500
Subsequent: $50
Telephone Exchange: Yes
Distributions:
Income: Quarterly
Capital Gain: Annually
Front-End Load: None
12b-1: 1.00%
Redemption Fee: 5.00%
Management Company: MacKay-Shields Financial
Ticker Symbol: MKTRX

TOTAL RETURN (%)

1987	1988	1989	1990	1991	5-year	Bull Market	Bear Market
NA	7.6	15.0	5.1	36.8	NA	38.4	-12.2

INVESTMENT PORTFOLIO

Total Assets (mil.)	Current Yield	Turnover Ratio	Expense Ratio	Beta	Risk Return
$138	1.3%	213%	2.40%	0.70	0.09

MASSACHUSETTS FINANCIAL TOTAL RETURN

Massachusetts Financial Services
500 Boylston Street
Boston, MA 02116
800-225-2606

Investment Objective: This fund uses a balanced investment approach to reach its investment objective. By varying the percentages invested in common stocks, bonds and cash, the fund strives to achieve both income and capital growth without stomaching much market-related risk. Its beta is well below that of the market, indicating that the fund has accomplished its one objective. Returns, too, have been strong and rank in the top third of all growth and income funds over the past 5 years. Investors should be aware of the fund's 4.75% sales charge.

Portfolio Manager: Richard Dalberg
Since: 1984

Minimum:
Initial: $1,000
Subsequent: $50
Telephone Exchange: Yes
Distributions:
Income: Quarterly
Capital Gain: Annually
Front-End Load: 4.75%
12b-1: 0.25%
Redemption Fee: None
Management Company: Massachusetts Financial Services
Ticker Symbol: MSFRX

TOTAL RETURN (%)

1987	1988	1989	1990	1991	5-year	Bull Market	Bear Market
3.5	15.0	23.1	-2.3	21.6	74.1	15.8	-8.8

INVESTMENT PORTFOLIO

Total Assets (mil.)	Current Yield	Turnover Ratio	Expense Ratio	Beta	Risk Return
$980	5.5%	50%	0.85%	0.60	0.02

MASSACHUSETTS INVESTORS TRUST

Massachusetts Financial Services
500 Boylston Street
Boston, MA 02116
800-225-2606

Investment Objective: As the first open-end mutual fund, founded in 1924, Massachusetts Investors Trust was created with the idea that small investors could share the wealth, too. Prior to the 1920s, closed-end funds dominated the fledgling industry. Massachusetts Investors Trust, in fact, could attract only 200 investors in its first year. But by the 1929 crash, it had 5,000 shareholders. Nevertheless, the fund survived that era and many others. The fund concentrates its investments in large cap stocks that provide above-average dividend income. Over the past 5 years, the fund has had an impressive track record at a below-average risk level.

Portfolio Manager: Laurence Leonard
Since: 1985

Minimum:
Initial: $1,000
Subsequent: $50
Telephone Exchange: Yes
Distributions:
Income: Quarterly
Capital Gain: Annually
Front-End Load: 5.75%
12b-1: 0.25%
Redemption Fee: None
Management Company: Massachusetts Financial Services
Ticker Symbol: MITTX

TOTAL RETURN (%)

1987	1988	1989	1990	1991	5-year	Bull Market	Bear Market
7.5	10.4	36.1	-0.1	27.7	105.9	31.6	-16.9

INVESTMENT PORTFOLIO

Total Assets (mil.)	Current Yield	Turnover Ratio	Expense Ratio	Beta	Risk Return
$1,424	2.4%	26%	0.47%	0.94	0.05

MERRILL LYNCH BALANCED FUND FOR INVEST/RETIRE—B

Merrill Lynch Funds Distributor
P.O. Box 9011
Princeton, NJ 08543
800-637-3863

Investment Objective: This fund invests in high-quality, large cap stocks, fixed-income securities and convertible securities to achieve its objective. Typically, the fund will avoid those companies that are sensitive to economic pressures and choose, rather, recession-resistant issues. Accordingly, the fund does not have a large position in cyclical companies, although those companies that do not expend cash to reduce costs may be held. This fund has lagged its more aggressively positioned growth and income rivals. However, its attraction to strong companies that resist varying economic climates may help reduce risk.

Portfolio Manager: Denis Cummings
Since: 1992

Minimum:
Initial: $1,000
Subsequent: $250
Telephone Exchange: No
Distributions:
Income: Semiannually
Capital Gain: Annually
Front-End Load: None
12b-1: 0.10%
Redemption Fee: 4.00%
Management Company: Merrill Lynch Asset Management
Ticker Symbol: MRYRX

TOTAL RETURN (%)

1987	1988	1989	1990	1991	5-year	Bull Market	Bear Market
1.7	8.1	17.0	-3.3	25.2	55.8	25.2	-12.2

INVESTMENT PORTFOLIO

Total Assets (mil.)	Current Yield	Turnover Ratio	Expense Ratio	Beta	Risk Return
$945	2.5%	174%	1.90%	0.70	0.06

MERRILL LYNCH CORPORATE DIVIDEND FUND

Merrill Lynch Funds Distributor
P.O. Box 9011
Princeton, NJ 08543
800-637-3863

Investment Objective: This fund invests mainly in preferred stocks to capture the dividends-received deduction for corporate investors. Thus, the fund is both highly interest sensitive and not for the average investor, who must pay the full-boat tax liability incurred from the generous stream of dividend distributions that this fund generates. Even the minimum initial investment, $10,000, and subsequent investments, $5,000, should be enough to scare away even the largest individual investor. For corporate investors, though, this fund offers an incredibly high current yield of 8.4% on top of low expenses of 0.59%.

Portfolio Manager: Brian Ison
Since: 1984

Minimum:
Initial: $10,000
Subsequent: $5,000
Telephone Exchange: No
Distributions:
Income: Monthly
Capital Gain: Annually
Front-End Load: 2.00%
12b-1: None
Redemption Fee: None
Management Company: Merrill Lynch Asset Management
Ticker Symbol: MLQDX

TOTAL RETURN (%)

1987	1988	1989	1990	1991	5-year	Bull Market	Bear Market
4.9	3.7	6.7	-6.9	22.5	32.4	19.6	-5.0

INVESTMENT PORTFOLIO

Total Assets (mil.)	Current Yield	Turnover Ratio	Expense Ratio	Beta	Risk Return
$42	8.4%	17%	0.59%	0.21	0.09

MERRILL LYNCH PHOENIX FUND A

Merrill Lynch Funds Distributor
P.O. Box 9011
Princeton, NJ 08543
800-637-3863

Investment Objective: This fund seeks capital appreciation through investments in equity and fixed-income securities of companies that are in weak financial condition or are experiencing poor operating results. If these negative conditions improve, investors can expect large increases in value. As a result of this higher risk exposure, the fund reserves the right to not sell shares to investors who do not have adequate income to weather the fluctuation in value of the fund's shares. The performance of the fund had been above average in each year since 1987 except 1990 when poor economic conditions hammered many of the fund's holdings. Investors should note the fund's hefty 6.50% front-end load.

Portfolio Manager: Robert Martorelli
Since: 1986

Minimum:
Initial: $1,000
Subsequent: $50
Telephone Exchange: No
Distributions:
Income: Semiannually
Capital Gain: Semiannually
Front-End Load: 6.50%
12b-1: None
Redemption Fee: None
Management Company: Merrill Lynch Asset Management
Ticker Symbol: MLPNX

TOTAL RETURN (%)

1987	1988	1989	1990	1991	5-year	Bull Market	Bear Market
1.0	33.2	13.9	-20.7	37.0	66.4	42.5	-25.9

INVESTMENT PORTFOLIO

Total Assets (mil.)	Current Yield	Turnover Ratio	Expense Ratio	Beta	Risk Return
$117	7.5%	72%	1.42%	0.92	0.06

MFS LIFETIME TOTAL RETURN FUND

Massachusetts Financial Services
500 Boylston Street
Boston, MA 02116
800-225-2606

Investment Objective: The objective of this fund is to provide investors with a mixture of growth and income with a heavy emphasis on capital preservation. The fund usually is 45% invested in stocks and 45% invested in bonds, with the remainder in cash equivalents. Portfolio Manager John Laupheimer favors strong blue chip stocks that are committed to paying regular dividends. Unfortunately, Laupheimer has not been able to provide investors with superior returns. Part of the reason why the fund's performance has been so poor is its expenses. The fund's hefty 2.37% expense ratio, which includes a 1.00% 12b-1 fee, consistently hampers investors' total return. In addition, the fund carries a stiff redemption fee.

Portfolio Manager: John Laupheimer
Since: 1987

Minimum:
Initial: $1,000
Subsequent: $50
Telephone Exchange: Yes
Distributions:
Income: Quarterly
Capital Gain: Annually
Front-End Load: None
12b-1: 1.00%
Redemption Fee: 6.00%
Management Company: Lifetime Advisers
Ticker Symbol: LTRTX

TOTAL RETURN (%)

1987	1988	1989	1990	1991	5-year	Bull Market	Bear Market
-6.8	10.8	16.4	2.3	19.4	46.7	21.1	-6.3

INVESTMENT PORTFOLIO

Total Assets (mil.)	Current Yield	Turnover Ratio	Expense Ratio	Beta	Risk Return
$268	2.7%	119%	2.37%	0.47	0.06

MUTUAL QUALIFIED FUND

Heine Securities
51 John F. Kennedy Parkway
Short Hills, NJ 07078
800-553-3014

Investment Objective: This fund's primary investment objective is capital appreciation, with income a secondary consideration. Investments are made in common stocks, preferred stocks and bonds that management believes are undervalued by the market relative to assets, takeover potential, etc. The fund's value and special situation stance put a damper on performance in 1991 as the fund managed a return of 21%. However, this fund's long-term track record of continual success should continue to serve shareholders well.

Portfolio Manager: Michael F. Price
Since: 1980

Minimum:
Initial: $1,000
Subsequent: $100
Telephone Exchange: No
Distributions:
Income: Semiannually
Capital Gain: Annually
Front-End Load: None
12b-1: None
Redemption Fee: None
Management Company: Heine Securities
Ticker Symbol: MQIFX

TOTAL RETURN (%)

1987	1988	1989	1990	1991	5-year	Bull Market	Bear Market
7.7	30.4	14.4	-10.1	21.1	74.9	26.6	-14.4

INVESTMENT PORTFOLIO

Total Assets (mil.)	Current Yield	Turnover Ratio	Expense Ratio	Beta	Risk Return
$1,098	3.1%	52%	0.87%	0.58	0.05

MUTUAL SHARES FUND

Heine Securities
51 John F. Kennedy Parkway
Short Hills, NJ 07078
800-553-3014

Investment Objective: Another value-oriented growth and income vehicle run by Michael Price, this fund did not have one of its better years in 1991. However, management stuck to its guns and continued utilizing its proven value-driven philosophy in equity and bond selection. The fund has returned an annualized 11.8% over the past 5 years despite some recent lackluster performance. However, as investor sentiment shifts to the value plays represented in this fund, this offering should regain some of its lost limelight.

Portfolio Manager: Michael F. Price
Since: 1975

Minimum:
Initial: $5,000
Subsequent: $100
Telephone Exchange: No
Distributions:
Income: Semiannually
Capital Gain: Annually
Front-End Load: None
12b-1: None
Redemption Fee: None
Management Company: Heine Securities
Ticker Symbol: MUTHX

TOTAL RETURN (%)

1987	1988	1989	1990	1991	5-year	Bull Market	Bear Market
6.4	30.7	14.9	-9.8	21.0	74.4	27.3	-14.8

INVESTMENT PORTFOLIO

Total Assets (mil.)	Current Yield	Turnover Ratio	Expense Ratio	Beta	Risk Return
$2,592	3.0%	48%	0.82%	0.59	0.05

NEW ENGLAND BALANCED

TNE Investment Services
399 Boylston Street
Boston, MA 02116
800-343-7104

Investment Objective: Expect to see more value and less growth in the years ahead for this fund. Former manager, Ken Heebner, known for his aggressive tendencies and high-growth selections, recently yielded the tiller to Don Shepard, who, in turn, placed it in the hands of Doug Ramos. Ramos wants to add more consistency to the fund's returns and thus is taking a new tack. Large cap stocks with modest price-earnings and price-book ratios, reasonable Wall Street expectations for earnings growth and above-average yields will become more commonplace. This may be good news to the fund's shareholders, but new investors seeking a more aggressive growth and income vehicle will have to look elsewhere.

Portfolio Manager: Beck/Ramos
Since: 1990

Minimum:
Initial: $1,000
Subsequent: $25
Telephone Exchange: Yes
Distributions:
Income: Quarterly
Capital Gain: Annually
Front-End Load: 6.50%
12b-1: 0.25%
Redemption Fee: None
Management Company: Loomis Sayles
Ticker Symbol: NELEX

TOTAL RETURN (%)

1987	1988	1989	1990	1991	5-year	Bull Market	Bear Market
0.8	10.0	10.3	-10.6	29.2	41.3	30.2	-15.9

INVESTMENT PORTFOLIO

Total Assets (mil.)	Current Yield	Turnover Ratio	Expense Ratio	Beta	Risk Return
$65	2.9%	54%	1.57%	0.90	0.08

OPPENHEIMER BLUE CHIP FUND

Oppenheimer Investor Services
P.O. Box 300
Denver, CO 80201
800-255-2755

Investment Objective: By investing in the common stocks of large, well-known companies, this fund seeks to achieve capital growth for its shareholders. These blue chip companies usually have long operating histories and a reputation of paying dividends. The fund's 3.1% yield is average for growth and income funds, but its 1-year and 5-year returns trail those of its peers. The fund also charges a steep 5.75% front-end load.

Portfolio Manager: Susan Wilder
Since: 1987

Minimum:
Initial: $1,000
Subsequent: $25
Telephone Exchange: Yes
Distributions:
Income: Quarterly
Capital Gain: Annually
Front-End Load: 5.75%
12b-1: 0.24%
Redemption Fee: None
Management Company: Oppenheimer Management
Ticker Symbol: OPBLX

TOTAL RETURN (%)

1987	1988	1989	1990	1991	5-year	Bull Market	Bear Market
-11.9	11.8	26.0	-2.9	17.7	41.8	21.1	-11.1

INVESTMENT PORTFOLIO

Total Assets (mil.)	Current Yield	Turnover Ratio	Expense Ratio	Beta	Risk Return
$20	3.1%	62%	1.64%	0.69	0.03

OPPENHEIMER EQUITY INCOME FUND

Oppenheimer Investor Services
P.O. Box 300
Denver, CO 80201
800-255-2755

Investment Objective: Though investors face the daunting task of paying a full-load entrance fee into this fund, its historical returns indicate that they won't be disappointed. A beta of about one-half that of the market, an above-average yield of 4.9% and below-average expenses of 0.79% position this fund for success. Indeed, the fund has demonstrated respectable performance over the past 5 years—especially in 1987—though its risk is significantly less than that of the market. Investing in higher-yielding cyclical, utility and consumer stocks has been the fund's pathway to high returns, and we expect more of the same to continue in the future. Note that a 5.75% front-end load is imposed on investors' purchases.

Portfolio Manager: Susan Wilder
Since: 1990

Minimum:
Initial: $1,000
Subsequent: $50
Telephone Exchange: Yes
Distributions:
Income: Quarterly
Capital Gain: Annually
Front-End Load: 5.75%
12b-1: 0.02%
Redemption Fee: None
Management Company: Oppenheimer Management
Ticker Symbol: OPPEX

TOTAL RETURN (%)

1987	1988	1989	1990	1991	5-year	Bull Market	Bear Market
9.3	14.0	18.6	-1.4	17.3	70.9	21.7	-10.3

INVESTMENT PORTFOLIO

Total Assets (mil.)	Current Yield	Turnover Ratio	Expense Ratio	Beta	Risk Return
$1,509	4.9%	64%	0.79%	0.59	0.04

OPPENHEIMER TOTAL RETURN FUND

Oppenheimer Investor Services
P.O. Box 300
Denver, CO 80201
800-255-2755

Investment Objective: In uncharacteristic fashion, this Oppenheimer vehicle is actually looking toward smaller capitalization stocks to help on its next leg upward. The fund's median equity cap is far below that of most growth and income funds. To reduce risk, however, the fund invests in bonds and utilities as well. This fund, along with having decent returns over the past several years, has a good yield as well, particularly for a fund that has income as a secondary objective. Though this fund may be a bit riskier than its counterparts, based on its tendency to invest in small companies, the risk has paid off and the fund may be worth looking into.

Portfolio Manager: John Wallace
Since: 1990

Minimum:
Initial: $1,000
Subsequent: $20
Telephone Exchange: Yes
Distributions:
Income: Quarterly
Capital Gain: Annually
Front-End Load: 5.75%
12b-1: 0.05%
Redemption Fee: None
Management Company: Oppenheimer Management
Ticker Symbol: OPTRX

TOTAL RETURN (%)

1987	1988	1989	1990	1991	5-year	Bull Market	Bear Market
12.3	13.3	19.2	-3.9	36.3	98.9	44.6	-18.0

INVESTMENT PORTFOLIO

Total Assets (mil.)	Current Yield	Turnover Ratio	Expense Ratio	Beta	Risk Return
$504	2.7%	114%	0.98%	0.89	0.07

PAINEWEBBER DIVIDEND GROWTH FUND A

PaineWebber
1285 Avenue of the Americas, 18th Floor
New York, NY 10019
800-647-1568

Investment Objective: This fund seeks capital growth and current income as its investment objective. Despite declines of 3.2% and 1.0% in 1987 and 1990, the fund has managed an above-average 90.5% total return over the past 5 years. In effect, the portfolio is more of a bull-market performer than a bear-market shelter. The fund invests in a fairly typical array of large cap, consumer-growth and cyclical industrial stocks, and it offers a below-average 1.1% current yield. In sum, investors who can weather this vehicle's bumpy ride may like the final destination. However, investors should note that the fund carries a 4.50% front-end load as well as an ongoing 12b-1 fee.

Portfolio Manager: Whitney Merrill
Since: 1988

Minimum:
Initial: $1,000
Subsequent: $100
Telephone Exchange: No
Distributions:
Income: Semiannually
Capital Gain: Annually
Front-End Load: 4.50%
12b-1: 0.17%
Redemption Fee: None
Management Company: Mitchell Hutchins Asset Management
Ticker Symbol: PDGAX

TOTAL RETURN (%)

1987	1988	1989	1990	1991	5-year	Bull Market	Bear Market
-3.2	17.8	24.6	-1.0	35.3	90.5	30.8	-16.3

INVESTMENT PORTFOLIO

Total Assets (mil.)	Current Yield	Turnover Ratio	Expense Ratio	Beta	Risk Return
$257	1.1%	52%	1.42%	0.74	0.08

PAX WORLD FUND

Pax World Fund
224 State Street
Portsmouth, NH 03801
800-767-1729

Investment Objective: This fund, one of the so-called socially conscious funds, uses a balanced investment approach by investing in both stocks and bonds. It invests in the securities of companies engaged in life-supportive goods and services, while excluding companies engaged in military/defense industries and those involved in the gambling, liquor and tobacco industries. Given the risk exposure, investors who share the fund's philosophy have been well served, especially in 1990, when its health-care stocks and lack of defense stocks helped generate strong returns. However, the fund's narrow investment selection produced a below-par performance the past year. Nevertheless, its long-run results are very respectable.

Portfolio Manager: Anthony S. Brown
Since: 1971

Minimum:
Initial: $250
Subsequent: $50
Telephone Exchange: No
Distributions:
Income: Semiannually
Capital Gain: Annually
Front-End Load: None
12b-1: 0.23%
Redemption Fee: None
Management Company: Pax World Management
Ticker Symbol: PAXWX

TOTAL RETURN (%)

1987	1988	1989	1990	1991	5-year	Bull Market	Bear Market
2.5	11.7	24.8	10.5	20.7	90.6	30.2	-7.5

INVESTMENT PORTFOLIO

Total Assets (mil.)	Current Yield	Turnover Ratio	Expense Ratio	Beta	Risk Return
$249	4.8%	39%	1.20%	0.44	0.07

PENN SQUARE MUTUAL FUND

Penn Square Management
2650 Westview Drive
Wyomissing, PA 19610
800-523-8440

Investment Objective: Seeking long-term capital growth and current income, the fund invests in large, well-established, blue chip companies that pay dividends. Although the yield is lower than the average growth and income fund, the growth aspect of the portfolio has more than compensated for the lack of current income. Given its level of risk assumed, the fund has performed adequately in both up and down markets. The fund has on average returned more than 12% per year over the past 5 years, with a risk level less than the S&P 500's (beta 0.88). Potential investors should note that the fund carries a 4.75% front-end load and a 12b-1 fee.

Portfolio Manager: James Jordon
Since: 1986

Minimum:
Initial: $500
Subsequent: $100
Telephone Exchange: Yes
Distributions:
Income: Quarterly
Capital Gain: Annually
Front-End Load: 4.75%
12b-1: 0.08%
Redemption Fee: None
Management Company: Penn Square Management
Ticker Symbol: PESQX

TOTAL RETURN (%)

1987	1988	1989	1990	1991	5-year	Bull Market	Bear Market
5.0	14.2	25.6	-5.2	27.1	81.6	33.3	-17.8

INVESTMENT PORTFOLIO

Total Assets (mil.)	Current Yield	Turnover Ratio	Expense Ratio	Beta	Risk Return
$212	2.6%	23%	0.95%	0.88	0.05

PHOENIX BALANCED FUND SERIES

Phoenix Equity Planning
100 Bright Meadow Boulevard
Enfield, CT 06082
800-243-4361

Investment Objective: This load fund seeks current income, long-term capital growth and conservation of capital. Investments in equity securities usually are maintained at a level of 60% of the portfolio, while senior debt securities make up the remaining 40%. Following a more conservative approach, a large portion of the debt securities usually consist of U.S. Treasury notes and bonds. This additional safety has come at the expense of returns in some periods. However, the strategy provided for handsome rewards in 1990 as the fund rose 7.3%, bucking the market's downward trend. Investors should note that the fund carries a 4.75% front-end load and a 12b-1 fee.

Portfolio Manager: Patricia Bannan
Since: 1986

Minimum:
Initial: $500
Subsequent: $25
Telephone Exchange: Yes
Distributions:
Income: Quarterly
Capital Gain: Annually
Front-End Load: 4.75%
12b-1: 0.25%
Redemption Fee: None
Management Company: Phoenix Investment Counsel
Ticker Symbol: PHBLX

TOTAL RETURN (%)

1987	1988	1989	1990	1991	5-year	Bull Market	Bear Market
9.7	2.9	24.9	7.3	25.9	90.6	28.2	-8.0

INVESTMENT PORTFOLIO

Total Assets (mil.)	Current Yield	Turnover Ratio	Expense Ratio	Beta	Risk Return
$975	3.3%	196%	0.98%	0.58	0.07

PHOENIX TOTAL RETURN FUND

Phoenix Equity Planning
100 Bright Meadow Boulevard
Enfield, CT 06082
800-243-4361

Investment Objective: We have few complaints about this risk-averse growth and income vehicle. Its beta is well below average at 0.60; it possesses a modest current yield of 2.1%; finally, its expense ratio of 1.58% isn't bad, considering the fund's modest asset base. However, turnover that has averaged nearly 350% a year goes against every adage of buy-and-hold investing. As the fund attempts to time the market by rushing into cash when the market appears overvalued, it periodically dumps stocks only to buy them back a short time later. This adds "hidden" costs that don't show up in the annual report. In addition, investors have to fork up 4.75% up front for new purchases.

Portfolio Manager: Robert Milnamow
Since: 1990

Minimum:
Initial: $500
Subsequent: $25
Telephone Exchange: Yes
Distributions:
Income: Semiannually
Capital Gain: Annually
Front-End Load: 4.75%
12b-1: 0.25%
Redemption Fee: None
Management Company: Phoenix Investment Counsel
Ticker Symbol: PTRFX

TOTAL RETURN (%)

1987	1988	1989	1990	1991	5-year	Bull Market	Bear Market
11.0	3.3	18.4	4.4	28.6	82.5	28.6	-8.8

INVESTMENT PORTFOLIO

Total Assets (mil.)	Current Yield	Turnover Ratio	Expense Ratio	Beta	Risk Return
$35	2.1%	279%	1.58%	0.60	0.07

PILGRIM SHORT TERM MULTI-MARKET INCOME FUND

Pilgrim Distributors
10100 Santa Monica Boulevard, 21st Floor
Los Angeles, CA 90067
800-336-3436

Investment Objective: This fund's objective is to provide investors with high current income with capital preservation as a secondary objective. Though investors may be tantalized by the fund's 10.6% yield, its returns have been nothing short of awful over the past 4 years. Part of the problem is the fund's core strategy of selecting nonconvertible preferred stocks that are currently in financial straits. In many cases, the preferred stocks were initially bought at 12 to 14% yields, but their prices have subsequently dropped. Unfortunately, shareholders who have invested over $100 million in this vehicle have seen the NAV of their investment drop precipitously over the past 5 years.

Portfolio Manager: Greg Barnett
Since: 1991

Minimum:
Initial: $5,000
Subsequent: $250
Telephone Exchange: Yes
Distributions:
Income: Monthly
Capital Gain: Annually
Front-End Load: 3.50%
12b-1: 0.30%
Redemption Fee: None
Management Company: Pilgrim Management Corporation
Ticker Symbol: PSTFX

TOTAL RETURN (%)

1987	1988	1989	1990	1991	5-year	Bull Market	Bear Market
-9.3	10.0	-14.2	-14.6	1.4	-25.9	7.9	3.4

INVESTMENT PORTFOLIO

Total Assets (mil.)	Current Yield	Turnover Ratio	Expense Ratio	Beta	Risk Return
$177	10.6%	247%	1.65%	0.04	NA

PIONEER FUND

Pioneer Funds Distributor
60 State Street
Boston, MA 02109
800-225-6292

Investment Objective: This growth and income fund has seen the advantages and pitfalls of taking a more aggressive position than most of its peers. Typically, the fund's beta is higher and yield lower than the market, though this has changed recently as management has more conservatively positioned the fund. In the late 1980s, the fund enjoyed above-average returns for its group. However, 1990's 10.5% loss shows the risk of the fund's aggressiveness. In retrospect, we can't fault the fund for staying nearly fully invested and pinning its hopes on large cap industrial, retail and finance companies. In the long run, this strategy should produce above-average returns.

Portfolio Manager: John Carey
Since: 1985

Minimum:
Initial: $50
Subsequent: $25
Telephone Exchange: Yes
Distributions:
Income: Quarterly
Capital Gain: Annually
Front-End Load: 5.75%
12b-1: 0.25%
Redemption Fee: None
Management Company: Pioneer Management
Ticker Symbol: PIODX

TOTAL RETURN (%)

1987	1988	1989	1990	1991	5-year	Bull Market	Bear Market
5.4	18.3	23.4	-10.5	22.8	69.1	31.7	-18.3

INVESTMENT PORTFOLIO

Total Assets (mil.)	Current Yield	Turnover Ratio	Expense Ratio	Beta	Risk Return
$1,522	2.6%	22%	0.84%	0.88	0.04

PIPER JAFFRAY INVEST TRUST—BALANCED FUND

Piper Jaffray Hopwood
222 South 9th Street
Minneapolis, MN 55402
800-333-6000

Investment Objective: This fund pursues the objectives of both current income and long-term capital appreciation consistent with conservation of capital. The fund may invest in any type or class of securities, and at least 35% of the fund's assets must be invested in fixed-income securities. This fund has an impressive, albeit short, history. Its hyper turnover ratio has done the job in producing returns, and its current yield is also attractive at an above-average 3.5%. Though saddled with sales charges and an above-average expense ratio, this fund's performance has treated investors fairly well otherwise.

Portfolio Manager: Benjamin S. Rinkey
Since: 1987

Minimum:
Initial: $250
Subsequent: $100
Telephone Exchange: No
Distributions:
Income: Quarterly
Capital Gain: Annually
Front-End Load: 4.00%
12b-1: 0.33%
Redemption Fee: None
Management Company: Piper Capital Management
Ticker Symbol: PBALX

TOTAL RETURN (%)

1987	1988	1989	1990	1991	5-year	Bull Market	Bear Market
NA	7.5	16.9	-2.7	27.4	NA	30.4	-12.6

INVESTMENT PORTFOLIO

Total Assets (mil.)	Current Yield	Turnover Ratio	Expense Ratio	Beta	Risk Return
$15	3.5%	105%	1.31%	0.67	0.07

PRIMARY TREND FUND

Primary Trend Funds
First Financial Centre, 700 North Water St.
Milwaukee, WI 53202
800-443-6544

Investment Objective: In seeking a combination of capital growth and current income, this no-load fund invests in mostly large capitalization, high-yielding common stocks. The fund's philosophy is very conservative, providing a modest return during up markets and some downside protection in the form of steady dividends. Management focuses on value situations, refusing to pay up for the high-growth companies that led during the 1980s. However, as market focus shifts from earnings momentum to value stocks, this fund may have the potential to perform quite well.

Portfolio Manager: David R. Aushwitz
Since: 1989

Minimum:
Initial: $5,000
Subsequent: $100
Telephone Exchange: No
Distributions:
Income: Semiannually
Capital Gain: Semiannually
Front-End Load: None
12b-1: None
Redemption Fee: None
Management Company: Arnold Investment Council
Ticker Symbol: PTFDX

TOTAL RETURN (%)

1987	1988	1989	1990	1991	5-year	Bull Market	Bear Market
3.6	18.4	8.9	-1.7	19.5	57.0	30.7	-10.7

INVESTMENT PORTFOLIO

Total Assets (mil.)	Current Yield	Turnover Ratio	Expense Ratio	Beta	Risk Return
$34	4.3%	77%	1.20%	0.64	0.04

PUTNAM CORPORATE ASSET TRUST

Putnam Financial Services
One Post Office Square, 12th Floor
Boston, MA 02109
800-634-1590

Investment Objective: The objective of this fund is to achieve high after-tax income for corporate shareholders and current income for all investors with minimum fluctuations in principal. As one of the few funds still catering to companies searching for tax-advantaged investments, this fund has had more success than its brethren. Though a 37% return over the past 5 years may seem miserly, the fund isn't managed for growth but for income, as witnessed by its very low 0.17 beta. By investing in preferred stocks and high-yield equities, the dividends are partially tax-free to corporations (although the tax law of 1986 scaled down this shelter's benefits). Thus, its effective after-tax returns are much higher.

Portfolio Manager: John C. Talanian
Since: 1987

Minimum:
Initial: $25,000
Subsequent: $5,000
Telephone Exchange: Yes
Distributions:
Income: Monthly
Capital Gain: Annually
Front-End Load: 2.50%
12b-1: None
Redemption Fee: None
Management Company: Putnam Management
Ticker Symbol: PCPAX

TOTAL RETURN (%)

1987	1988	1989	1990	1991	5-year	Bull Market	Bear Market
-4.7	6.1	11.3	-0.1	21.6	36.8	17.6	0.3

INVESTMENT PORTFOLIO

Total Assets (mil.)	Current Yield	Turnover Ratio	Expense Ratio	Beta	Risk Return
$129	8.2%	209%	0.95%	0.17	0.13

PUTNAM FUND FOR GROWTH AND INCOME

Putnam Financial Services
One Post Office Square, 12th Floor
Boston, MA 02109
800-634-1590

Investment Objective: This fund is for investors seeking a diversified portfolio offering opportunity for capital growth while also providing current income. Its investments will vary from time to time depending on interest rates, economic conditions and other factors. For example, this fund kept its head above water in 1990 because of a 15 to 20% cash stake and a small allocation to bonds. In other years, its returns have been impressive as well, and its 5-year return of 82.1% is above average. Also attractive is its current dividend yield of 4.4%, respectable for a fund seeking income as its secondary objective. Its returns and yield have not let investors down, but its sales and marketing charges are a bit hard to stomach.

Portfolio Manager: John Maurice
Since: 1968

Minimum:
Initial: $500
Subsequent: $50
Telephone Exchange: Yes
Distributions:
Income: Quarterly
Capital Gain: Annually
Front-End Load: 5.75%
12b-1: 0.25%
Redemption Fee: None
Management Company: Putnam Management
Ticker Symbol: PGRWX

TOTAL RETURN (%)

1987	1988	1989	1990	1991	5-year	Bull Market	Bear Market
2.4	20.7	20.7	2.4	19.2	82.1	31.4	-14.5

INVESTMENT PORTFOLIO

Total Assets (mil.)	Current Yield	Turnover Ratio	Expense Ratio	Beta	Risk Return
$2,620	4.4%	81%	0.89%	0.68	0.04

PUTNAM, GEORGE FUND OF BOSTON

Putnam Financial Services
One Post Office Square, 12th Floor
Boston, MA 02109
800-634-1590

Investment Objective: This growth and income fund, founded in 1937, has found that experience pays off in the investment world. Over the past 5 and 10 years, the fund has maintained a below-average level of risk exposure while providing investors with strong returns. The 5-year return for the fund is 74.9%, which was achieved with a risk level that equals 68% of the level for the S&P 500 Index. However, investors should note that the fund levies a 5.75% front-end load, which reduces returns.

Minimum:
Initial: $500
Subsequent: $50
Telephone Exchange: Yes
Distributions:
Income: Quarterly
Capital Gain: Annually
Front-End Load: 5.75%
12b-1: 0.15%
Redemption Fee: None
Management Company: Putnam Management
Ticker Symbol: PGEOX

Portfolio Manager: Thomas V. Reilly
Since: 1987

TOTAL RETURN (%)

1987	1988	1989	1990	1991	5-year	Bull Market	Bear Market
3.7	12.1	23.6	-0.9	22.8	74.9	29.0	-12.9

INVESTMENT PORTFOLIO

Total Assets (mil.)	Current Yield	Turnover Ratio	Expense Ratio	Beta	Risk Return
$487	4.6%	65%	0.94%	0.68	0.05

PUTNAM INVESTORS FUND

Putnam Financial Services
One Post Office Square, 12th Floor
Boston, MA 02109
800-634-1590

Investment Objective: Cyclical and noncyclical growth stocks are the primary investments for this fairly aggressive growth and income portfolio. Though classed by some analysts as a pure growth vehicle, we beg to disagree. For one thing, this fund's yield occasionally rises above that of the market, as management attempts to add more dividend payers. Secondly, cash levels of 10% aren't uncommon for the fund, helping to keep a lid on its market-level beta. Finally, the fund's stocks trade at average price-earnings and price-book ratios, which helped prevent a catastrophe in 1987's and 1990's perilous markets. Investors with an eye for growth but a desire for income may like what they receive with this fund.

Minimum:
Initial: $500
Subsequent: $50
Telephone Exchange: Yes
Distributions:
Income: Quarterly
Capital Gain: Annually
Front-End Load: 5.75%
12b-1: 0.25%
Redemption Fee: None
Management Company: Putnam Management
Ticker Symbol: PINVX

Portfolio Manager: Brooke Cobb
Since: 1986

TOTAL RETURN (%)

1987	1988	1989	1990	1991	5-year	Bull Market	Bear Market
4.0	7.5	33.9	-2.8	28.6	87.1	41.5	-23.9

INVESTMENT PORTFOLIO

Total Assets (mil.)	Current Yield	Turnover Ratio	Expense Ratio	Beta	Risk Return
$684	1.5%	58%	0.89%	1.09	0.04

PUTNAM OPTION INCOME TRUST II

Putnam Financial Services
One Post Office Square, 12th Floor
Boston, MA 02109
800-634-1590

Investment Objective: The fund seeks high current returns by investing in dividend-paying common stocks. The fund utilizes options and futures contracts to hedge against changes in the market prices of the portfolio's stocks. This strategy benefits the objective of stability of principal, but tends to limit the capital-appreciation potential of the overall portfolio. The fund's 5-year record falls well short of the average growth and income vehicle, although it has a beta slightly above that group's average. Investors also should be aware of the hefty 5.75% front-end load and 12b-1 fees.

Portfolio Manager: Douglas S. Foreman
Since: 1991

Minimum:
Initial: $500
Subsequent: $50
Telephone Exchange: Yes
Distributions:
Income: Quarterly
Capital Gain: Quarterly
Front-End Load: 5.75%
12b-1: 0.25%
Redemption Fee: None
Management Company: Putnam Management
Ticker Symbol: POITX

TOTAL RETURN (%)

1987	1988	1989	1990	1991	5-year	Bull Market	Bear Market
-5.5	18.2	19.0	-3.0	24.1	60.1	31.7	-13.9

INVESTMENT PORTFOLIO

Total Assets (mil.)	Current Yield	Turnover Ratio	Expense Ratio	Beta	Risk Return
$650	1.6%	152%	1.03%	0.77	0.05

PUTNAM STRATEGIC INCOME TRUST

Putnam Financial Services
One Post Office Square, 12th Floor
Boston, MA 02109
800-634-1590

Investment Objective: This fund seeks a high level of current income by investing primarily in dividend-paying common stocks. This fund's portfolio turnover ratio is unusually high and has worked to saddle the fund with returns slightly below the average growth and income fund. Investors may be attracted to its current yield of 3.7%, which is just slightly above average. The fund's sales and marketing charges are something to note, especially considering the fund's below-average return performance and slightly above-average yield.

Portfolio Manager: Robert Stephenson
Since: 1984

Minimum:
Initial: $500
Subsequent: $25
Telephone Exchange: Yes
Distributions:
Income: Quarterly
Capital Gain: Annually
Front-End Load: 5.75%
12b-1: 0.25%
Redemption Fee: None
Management Company: Putnam Management
Ticker Symbol: PSITX

TOTAL RETURN (%)

1987	1988	1989	1990	1991	5-year	Bull Market	Bear Market
-6.5	22.5	15.4	-7.1	24.7	53.1	NA	NA

INVESTMENT PORTFOLIO

Total Assets (mil.)	Current Yield	Turnover Ratio	Expense Ratio	Beta	Risk Return
$421	3.7%	223%	1.09%	0.81	0.04

REA-GRAHAM BALANCED FUND

Rea-Graham
10966 Chalon Road
Los Angeles, CA 90077
800-433-1998

Investment Objective: Don't look at this fund's recent returns as indicative of its quality. Though the portfolio has lagged the broader averages for much of the past 5 years, it has an eye-popping beta 70% less than that of the market, making it 70% less risky than the overall market. It also offers investors a current yield of 4.8%—at the high end for growth and income funds. In addition, the fund survived the bear market better than the bulk of its peer group, making it a comfortable fund for conservative, income-oriented investors. All this apart, investors' investments are still punished by a 4.75% front-end load and a 12b-1 fee.

Minimum:
Initial: $1,000
Subsequent: $200
Telephone Exchange: No
Distributions:
Income: Annually
Capital Gain: Annually
Front-End Load: 4.75%
12b-1: 0.35%
Redemption Fee: None
Management Company: James Buchanan Rea
Ticker Symbol: REAGX

Portfolio Manager: James B. Rea
Since: 1976

TOTAL RETURN (%)

1987	1988	1989	1990	1991	5-year	Bull Market	Bear Market
-0.3	11.0	7.9	-5.9	14.9	29.2	NA	NA

INVESTMENT PORTFOLIO

Total Assets (mil.)	Current Yield	Turnover Ratio	Expense Ratio	Beta	Risk Return
$30	4.8%	100%	2.04%	0.31	0.05

ROYCE EQUITY INCOME FUND

Quest Distributors
1414 Avenue of the Americas
New York, NY 10019
800-221-4268

Investment Objective: This fund has done a good job of achieving its primary objective of reasonable income, as evidenced by its 4.4% current yield. The fund primarily invests in dividend-paying common stocks and securities convertible into common stocks of small- and medium-sized companies, making this one of the more aggressive growth and income funds. Its short history already looks volatile, with an above-average 1991 return and a sorry 1990 bear market return. This fund has potential for investors willing to take on the risks associated with the small and medium cap markets. Be aware also of the myriad of charges.

Minimum:
Initial: $2,000
Subsequent: $50
Telephone Exchange: No
Distributions:
Income: Quarterly
Capital Gain: Annually
Front-End Load: 2.50%
12b-1: 0.01%
Redemption Fee: 2.00%
Management Company: Quest Advisory
Ticker Symbol: RYEQX

Portfolio Manager: Charles Royce
Since: 1989

TOTAL RETURN (%)

1987	1988	1989	1990	1991	5-year	Bull Market	Bear Market
NA	NA	NA	-15.3	30.3	NA	NA	NA

INVESTMENT PORTFOLIO

Total Assets (mil.)	Current Yield	Turnover Ratio	Expense Ratio	Beta	Risk Return
$40	4.4%	28%	1.00%	NA	NA

SAFECO INCOME FUND

SAFECO Securities
4333 Brooklyn Avenue N.E.
Seattle, WA 98185
800-426-6730

Investment Objective: This fund seeks to provide a combination of current income and capital growth by investing in common stocks with above-average yields and in bonds. The fund strives to provide a current yield at least 50% greater than that of the S&P 500 Index. The equity portion of the portfolio tends to have a value bent and, thus, recent results have been a bit sluggish. With a beta of 0.72, the fund offers a degree of downside protection in bear markets. However, that protection would largely disappear if falling stock prices were accompanied by rising interest rates, as it did in 1990 when the fund plunged 10.8%.

Portfolio Manager: Arley Hudson
Since: 1978

Minimum:
Initial: $1,000
Subsequent: $25
Telephone Exchange: Yes
Distributions:
Income: Quarterly
Capital Gain: Annually
Front-End Load: None
12b-1: None
Redemption Fee: None
Management Company: SAFECO Asset Management
Ticker Symbol: SAFIX

TOTAL RETURN (%)

1987	1988	1989	1990	1991	5-year	Bull Market	Bear Market
-6.0	19.0	19.2	-10.8	23.3	46.7	31.7	-16.2

INVESTMENT PORTFOLIO

Total Assets (mil.)	Current Yield	Turnover Ratio	Expense Ratio	Beta	Risk Return
$172	5.1%	22%	0.93%	0.72	0.05

SALOMON BROTHERS INVESTORS FUND

Salomon Brothers
7 World Trade Center
New York, NY 10048
800-725-6666

Investment Objective: This fund's primary objective is long-term growth of capital, and current income is its secondary objective. The fund may invest in any type of securities in any proportions, but common stocks with growth potential are typically chosen. The fund's returns have been closely aligned with growth and income fund averages, and its current yield is respectable, despite its secondary rank of importance. The fund's beta is just a little high for a growth and income fund, and its turnover ratio is low, implying that the fund tends to invest in above-average risk stocks and hold them for their potential. This fund is a solid choice for investors willing to pay the sales fee.

Portfolio Manager: John Weed
Since: 1989

Minimum:
Initial: $500
Subsequent: $50
Telephone Exchange: No
Distributions:
Income: Quarterly
Capital Gain: Annually
Front-End Load: 5.00%
12b-1: None
Redemption Fee: None
Management Company: Salomon Brothers Asset Management
Ticker Symbol: SAIFX

TOTAL RETURN (%)

1987	1988	1989	1990	1991	5-year	Bull Market	Bear Market
0.2	16.7	21.9	-6.4	29.3	72.6	35.8	-19.3

INVESTMENT PORTFOLIO

Total Assets (mil.)	Current Yield	Turnover Ratio	Expense Ratio	Beta	Risk Return
$348	2.4%	22%	0.68%	0.94	0.05

SBSF GROWTH FUND

Spears Benzak Salomon & Farrell
45 Rockefeller Plaza, 33rd Floor
New York, NY 10020
800-422-7273

Investment Objective: This fund seeks current income along with capital appreciation by investing in common and preferred stock and convertible securities. The fund had enjoyed respectable returns in 1989 and 1990, but failed to capture the limelight in 1991. The past year the fund returned just 19%, a full 7% below the average return for growth and income funds. However, the fund still has an attractive 5-year record, a 3.3% yield, moderate expenses and a consistently low portfolio turnover rate. Long-term investors have been well rewarded despite the lagging 1991 return.

Portfolio Manager: Louis Benzak
Since: 1983

Minimum:
Initial: $5,000
Subsequent: $100
Telephone Exchange: Yes
Distributions:
Income: Semiannually
Capital Gain: Annually
Front-End Load: None
12b-1: None
Redemption Fee: None
Management Company: SBSF, Inc.
Ticker Symbol: SBFFX

TOTAL RETURN (%)

1987	1988	1989	1990	1991	5-year	Bull Market	Bear Market
-0.5	17.2	34.0	-2.7	19.0	81.2	21.7	-10.9

INVESTMENT PORTFOLIO

Total Assets (mil.)	Current Yield	Turnover Ratio	Expense Ratio	Beta	Risk Return
$103	3.3%	42%	1.15%	0.64	0.04

SCUDDER GROWTH & INCOME FUND

Scudder Stevens & Clark
175 Federal Street, 12th Floor
Boston, MA 02110
800-225-2470

Investment Objective: Designed as a conservative fund, this no-load vehicle seeks a combination of current income and capital growth through a balanced portfolio of investments. The majority of the assets are in blue chip, dividend-paying common stocks, with the remainder invested in convertibles. Given its conservative posture, the fund tries to maintain a moderate level of volatility, usually much lower than that of the S&P 500. Currently, the fund has a risk level about three-fourths that of the S&P 500. The fund's performance has been above average compared to other funds in its category. These factors, combined with its low turnover ratio and low expense ratio, make this fund an excellent growth and income vehicle.

Portfolio Manager: Robert Harvey
Since: 1991

Minimum:
Initial: $1,000
Subsequent: $500
Telephone Exchange: Yes
Distributions:
Income: Quarterly
Capital Gain: Annually
Front-End Load: None
12b-1: None
Redemption Fee: None
Management Company: Scudder Stevens & Clark
Ticker Symbol: SCDGX

TOTAL RETURN (%)

1987	1988	1989	1990	1991	5-year	Bull Market	Bear Market
3.5	11.9	26.5	-2.3	28.2	83.4	33.0	-13.1

INVESTMENT PORTFOLIO

Total Assets (mil.)	Current Yield	Turnover Ratio	Expense Ratio	Beta	Risk Return
$661	3.5%	65%	0.95%	0.76	0.06

SECURITY EQUITY FUND

Security Distributors
700 Harrison
Topeka, KS 66636
800-888-2461

Investment Objective: As interest-sensitive portfolios go, this is one of the best. Typically 40% of its assets are invested in utilities and financial stocks and it wouldn't be surprising to see this fund rise and fall with the ebb and flow of interest rates. However, when rates started rising in 1987 and again in late 1988, this vehicle continued its upward march. In 1990, manager Terry Milberger restructured the portfolio to reduce exposure to weak bank and utility stocks, saving it from disaster. Because management structures the fund with a number of consumer growth stocks to counterbalance its interest sensitivity, the fund has the best of both worlds: current income and capital-appreciation potential.

Portfolio Manager: Terry Milberger
Since: 1981

Minimum:
Initial: $100
Subsequent: $100
Telephone Exchange: Yes
Distributions:
Income: Annually
Capital Gain: Annually
Front-End Load: 5.75%
12b-1: None
Redemption Fee: None
Management Company: Security Management Company
Ticker Symbol: SECEX

TOTAL RETURN (%)

1987	1988	1989	1990	1991	5-year	Bull Market	Bear Market
4.2	19.2	30.8	-4.6	35.2	109.5	41.5	-21.7

INVESTMENT PORTFOLIO

Total Assets (mil.)	Current Yield	Turnover Ratio	Expense Ratio	Beta	Risk Return
$292	2.2%	97%	1.08%	1.10	0.05

SECURITY INVESTMENT FUND

Security Distributors
700 Harrison
Topeka, KS 66636
800-888-2461

Investment Objective: A highly concentrated portfolio makes this fund more risky than one would expect. With only 10 to 15 stocks in the entire fund, a hit in 1 or 2 securities could send this fund reeling. Such was the case in 1987, when the fund dropped 17% in the fourth quarter. Upside return potential also is limited by a heavy commitment to bonds. Together, the stocks and bonds in the portfolio tend to be highly interest sensitive, making the fund vulnerable to higher rates (e.g., early 1990). The entrance fee for this type of risk is 5.75%.

Portfolio Manager: John D. Cleland
Since: 1965

Minimum:
Initial: $100
Subsequent: $100
Telephone Exchange: Yes
Distributions:
Income: Quarterly
Capital Gain: Annually
Front-End Load: 5.75%
12b-1: None
Redemption Fee: None
Management Company: Security Management Company
Ticker Symbol: SECIX

TOTAL RETURN (%)

1987	1988	1989	1990	1991	5-year	Bull Market	Bear Market
0.9	10.7	20.4	-3.0	21.9	59.0	27.6	-7.4

INVESTMENT PORTFOLIO

Total Assets (mil.)	Current Yield	Turnover Ratio	Expense Ratio	Beta	Risk Return
$77	5.3%	66%	1.28%	0.56	0.06

SELIGMAN COMMON STOCK FUND

Seligman Financial Services
130 Liberty Street, 22nd Floor
New York, NY 10006
800-221-2450

Investment Objective: By not straying too far off the path beaten by the S&P 500, this fund's returns are fairly comparable to that large cap index. The fund strives to produce favorable, but not the highest, current income and long-term growth of both capital and income. Even though the fund does not take unusual measures for current income, its current yield of 2.9% is not far below the growth and income average. The fund's strategy of staying close to the S&P 500 Index has produced decent returns, notwithstanding its 1990 bear market return of -3.9%. Although the fund is sold with a 4.75% front-end load, its expense ratio of only 0.66% is below average.

Portfolio Manager: Paul Rodriquez
Since: 1981

Minimum:
Initial: $1,000
Subsequent: $50
Telephone Exchange: Yes
Distributions:
Income: Quarterly
Capital Gain: Annually
Front-End Load: 4.75%
12b-1: None
Redemption Fee: None
Management Company: J. W. Seligman
Ticker Symbol: SCSFX

TOTAL RETURN (%)

1987	1988	1989	1990	1991	5-year	Bull Market	Bear Market
0.2	10.1	26.8	-3.9	29.9	74.5	42.7	-22.5

INVESTMENT PORTFOLIO

Total Assets (mil.)	Current Yield	Turnover Ratio	Expense Ratio	Beta	Risk Return
$474	2.9%	45%	0.66%	0.98	0.05

SENTINEL BALANCED FUND

Equity Services
National Life Drive
Montpelier, VT 05604
800-282-3863

Investment Objective: As with the rest of its Sentinel siblings, this income-oriented fund can pride itself with consistently modest turnover rates. Though such an accolade doesn't seem to amount to much, the reduced brokerage and bid-ask spread costs associated with a buy-and-hold approach can add up to many investment dollars over the long run. Couple that with a below-1% expense ratio, a current yield of 4.8% and a beta half that of the market's, and you have a strong contender for your portfolio. However, the price of admission is a high 8.50%, making the fund unpalatable for some no-load investors.

Portfolio Manager: Rodney Buck
Since: 1982

Minimum:
Initial: $250
Subsequent: $25
Telephone Exchange: Yes
Distributions:
Income: Quarterly
Capital Gain: Annually
Front-End Load: 8.50%
12b-1: None
Redemption Fee: None
Management Company: Sentinel Advisers
Ticker Symbol: SEBLX

TOTAL RETURN (%)

1987	1988	1989	1990	1991	5-year	Bull Market	Bear Market
0.6	9.9	19.3	1.9	23.3	65.8	25.8	-9.1

INVESTMENT PORTFOLIO

Total Assets (mil.)	Current Yield	Turnover Ratio	Expense Ratio	Beta	Risk Return
$91	4.8%	40%	0.91%	0.52	0.07

SENTINEL COMMON STOCK FUND

Equity Services
National Life Drive
Montpelier, VT 05604
800-282-3863

Investment Objective: With one of the lowest average turnover rates of any fund in the equity universe, management proves it's good on its word to pursue a buy-and-hold strategy. Simply put, the fund holds large cap companies with established histories of growing faster than the average S&P 500 stock. The fund yields 2.7%, average for a conservative growth and income fund, but its returns have been relatively strong over the past 5 years. Its market-like returns in 1986, 1989, 1990 and 1991 indicate that the fund falls in line with growth stocks more than value names.

Portfolio Manager: Chris Martin
Since: 1977

Minimum:
Initial: $250
Subsequent: $25
Telephone Exchange: Yes
Distributions:
Income: Quarterly
Capital Gain: Annually
Front-End Load: 8.50%
12b-1: None
Redemption Fee: None
Management Company: Sentinel Advisers
Ticker Symbol: SENCX

TOTAL RETURN (%)

1987	1988	1989	1990	1991	5-year	Bull Market	Bear Market
0.2	13.4	27.6	-2.7	30.8	84.1	36.0	-16.4

INVESTMENT PORTFOLIO

Total Assets (mil.)	Current Yield	Turnover Ratio	Expense Ratio	Beta	Risk Return
$620	2.7%	6%	0.76%	0.91	0.06

SHEARSON EQUITY PORTFOLIO STRATEGIC INVESTORS

Shearson Lehman Brothers
Two World Trade Center
New York, NY 10048
800-451-2010

Investment Objective: This fund splits its objective between capital appreciation and current income. It invests in a combination of equity, fixed-income and money market instruments and gold securities. During the fund's 4-year history, it has produced impressive returns and maintained a decent current yield. The fund's attraction to small and medium cap stocks makes it an offering with above-average risk, but its returns will likely be above-average as well when these smaller issues are in favor in the markets. This fund promises some excitement for investors who can tolerate some risk as well as some fees.

Portfolio Manager: William Carter
Since: 1987

Minimum:
Initial: $500
Subsequent: $200
Telephone Exchange: No
Distributions:
Income: Quarterly
Capital Gain: Annually
Front-End Load: None
12b-1: 1.00%
Redemption Fee: 5.00%
Management Company: Shearson Lehman Advisors
Ticker Symbol: SESIX

TOTAL RETURN (%)

1987	1988	1989	1990	1991	5-year	Bull Market	Bear Market
NA	16.9	21.2	-2.2	26.5	NA	34.9	-15.7

INVESTMENT PORTFOLIO

Total Assets (mil.)	Current Yield	Turnover Ratio	Expense Ratio	Beta	Risk Return
$215	3.0%	56%	2.09%	0.74	0.06

SHEARSON INCOME PORTFOLIO OPTION

Shearson Lehman Brothers
Two World Trade Center
New York, NY 10048
800-451-2010

Investment Objective: With lots of assets under its belt, a fairly decent record over the past 2 years and a yield that could make many a retiree a happy camper, this fund seems to have it all. But not so fast: Options are part of this fund's game, and the risks are higher than first meets the eye. For one, the fund can be whipsawed in fast-rising or declining markets, as witnessed by a negative 9% return in 1987. For another, the high distributions this fund is known for are partially a payback of principal because the options allow management to earn high dividends, occasionally earn premiums, while some of the underlying stocks decline in value.

Portfolio Manager: John Fullerton
Since: 1985

Minimum:
Initial: $500
Subsequent: $200
Telephone Exchange: No
Distributions:
Income: Monthly
Capital Gain: Annually
Front-End Load: None
12b-1: 0.75%
Redemption Fee: 5.00%
Management Company: Boston Company Advisers
Ticker Symbol: SOPTX

TOTAL RETURN (%)

1987	1988	1989	1990	1991	5-year	Bull Market	Bear Market
-9.2	25.8	17.4	2.1	28.9	76.3	41.9	-19.1

INVESTMENT PORTFOLIO

Total Assets (mil.)	Current Yield	Turnover Ratio	Expense Ratio	Beta	Risk Return
$465	8.1%	43%	1.75%	0.71	0.06

SIT NEW BEGINNING INCOME/GROWTH FUND

Sit Investment Associates
4600 Norwest Center, 90 South 7th Street
Minneapolis, MN 55402
800-332-5580

Investment Objective: This pure no-load fund has been known to split its attention between large cap industrial and consumer stocks and fixed-income securities. This strategy, as can be expected, works best in falling-interest-rate environments. On the flip side, returns can slide when rates rise. Unlike many growth and income funds, this portfolio doesn't hold many financial or utility stocks, relying instead on bonds and cash to boost yield (which isn't particularly high, in part because of the 1.50% expense ratio). The stock portfolio is mainly a hodgepodge of consumer growth names and industrial stocks, both of which usually perform best in low-rate environments.

Portfolio Manager: Peter Mitchelson
Since: 1982

Minimum:
Initial: $2,000
Subsequent: $100
Telephone Exchange: Yes
Distributions:
Income: Quarterly
Capital Gain: Semiannually
Front-End Load: None
12b-1: None
Redemption Fee: None
Management Company: Sit Investment Management
Ticker Symbol: SNIGX

TOTAL RETURN (%)

1987	1988	1989	1990	1991	5-year	Bull Market	Bear Market
5.3	5.3	32.1	-2.4	32.7	89.8	30.8	-16.7

INVESTMENT PORTFOLIO

Total Assets (mil.)	Current Yield	Turnover Ratio	Expense Ratio	Beta	Risk Return
$27	2.0%	70%	1.50%	0.86	0.06

STEIN ROE TOTAL RETURN FUND

Stein Roe & Farnham
P.O. Box 1162
Chicago, IL 60690
800-338-2550

Investment Objective: This no-load fund seeks to provide current income and capital appreciation. However, the fund invests a greater percentage of its assets in convertible and fixed-income securities and is considered a balanced fund. The fund, originally named Stein Roe & Farnham Fund, dates back to 1949 and is Stein Roe's oldest offering. The fund has returned a below par 66.5% over the past 5 years, but outperformed a number of its peers in 1991 by returning almost 30%.

Portfolio Manager: Bob Christensen
Since: 1981

Minimum:
Initial: $1,000
Subsequent: $100
Telephone Exchange: Yes
Distributions:
Income: Quarterly
Capital Gain: Annually
Front-End Load: None
12b-1: None
Redemption Fee: None
Management Company: Stein Roe & Farnham
Ticker Symbol: SRFBX

TOTAL RETURN (%)

1987	1988	1989	1990	1991	5-year	Bull Market	Bear Market
0.7	7.9	20.3	-1.7	29.6	66.5	33.9	-14.3

INVESTMENT PORTFOLIO

Total Assets (mil.)	Current Yield	Turnover Ratio	Expense Ratio	Beta	Risk Return
$144	4.8%	75%	0.88%	0.69	0.07

STRATTON MONTHLY DIVIDEND SHARES

Stratton Management
610 West Germantown Pike, Suite 361
Plymouth Meeting, PA 19462
800-634-5726

Investment Objective: The twin objectives of this fund are income and capital growth. However, as its name suggests, the fund pays regular monthly income dividends to shareholders. It derives its above-average income by investing a portion of its assets in convertible bonds and convertible preferred stocks. In addition, the equity portion of its portfolio is heavily concentrated in utility stocks. Although its average return during the past 5 years is well below average for an equity fund, its beta is also quite low for an equity fund. Thus, its return has amply rewarded investors for the modest risk it has assumed.

Portfolio Manager: James Stratton
Since: 1980

Minimum:
Initial: $2,000
Subsequent: $100
Telephone Exchange: Yes
Distributions:
Income: Monthly
Capital Gain: Annually
Front-End Load: None
12b-1: None
Redemption Fee: None
Management Company: Stratton Management Company
Ticker Symbol: STMDX

TOTAL RETURN (%)

1987	1988	1989	1990	1991	5-year	Bull Market	Bear Market
-11.4	9.8	18.8	-3.8	35.1	50.1	32.8	-7.9

INVESTMENT PORTFOLIO

Total Assets (mil.)	Current Yield	Turnover Ratio	Expense Ratio	Beta	Risk Return
$39	6.9%	14%	1.27%	0.48	0.10

STRONG INVESTMENT FUND

Strong/Corneliuson Capital
100 Heritage Reserve
Menomonee Falls, WI 53051
800-368-3863

Investment Objective: This fund seeks a combination of income and capital appreciation for the highest possible return, assuming reasonable risks. The most conservative of the Strong equity funds, it invests in a diversified portfolio of common stocks, other equity-type securities and debt securities. Investments in common stocks, preferred stocks and convertibles may not exceed 65% of its assets. Though its returns have been below average, the fund was able to hold its own during 1990's bear market. Its current yield of 4.8% emphasizes its primary objective. A low beta also underscores the risk-averse nature of the fund, and those investors confident in lower interest rates may want to take the plunge.

Portfolio Manager: William Corneliuson
Since: 1981

Minimum:
Initial: $250
Subsequent: $200
Telephone Exchange: Yes
Distributions:
Income: Quarterly
Capital Gain: Annually
Front-End Load: 1.00%
12b-1: None
Redemption Fee: None
Management Company: Strong/Corneliuson Management
Ticker Symbol: STIFX

TOTAL RETURN (%)

1987	1988	1989	1990	1991	5-year	Bull Market	Bear Market
-0.3	9.2	11.2	2.8	19.6	48.9	15.9	-2.1

INVESTMENT PORTFOLIO

Total Assets (mil.)	Current Yield	Turnover Ratio	Expense Ratio	Beta	Risk Return
$204	4.8%	320%	1.30%	0.36	0.06

STRONG TOTAL RETURN FUND

Strong/Corneliuson Capital
100 Heritage Reserve
Menomonee Falls, WI 53051
800-368-3863

Investment Objective: The fund seeks a combination of income and capital appreciation that will produce the highest total return while assuming reasonable risks. The adviser judges reasonable risk on an ongoing basis, in light of current and anticipated future financial conditions, and the fund's high portfolio turnover may imply some risk of its own. The fund had a decent year in 1991, but even its 5-year performance is well below average for funds of its kind. Likewise, its yield is not impressive for a growth and income fund.

Portfolio Manager: R. Strong/W. Corneliuson
Since: 1981

Minimum:
Initial: $250
Subsequent: $200
Telephone Exchange: Yes
Distributions:
Income: Semiannually
Capital Gain: Annually
Front-End Load: 1.00%
12b-1: None
Redemption Fee: None
Management Company: Strong/Corneliuson Management
Ticker Symbol: STRFX

TOTAL RETURN (%)

1987	1988	1989	1990	1991	5-year	Bull Market	Bear Market
6.0	15.6	2.6	-7.1	33.6	56.1	28.6	-11.5

INVESTMENT PORTFOLIO

Total Assets (mil.)	Current Yield	Turnover Ratio	Expense Ratio	Beta	Risk Return
$619	1.1%	312%	1.40%	0.73	0.07

SUN AMERICA BALANCED ASSETS FUND

Sun America Capital Services
10 Union Square East, 2nd Floor
New York, NY 10003
800-821-5100

Investment Objective: The stated objective of this fund is to realize the combination of income and capital appreciation that will produce the highest return consistent with reasonable risk. When selecting stocks, management seeks companies of medium to large capitalizations (generally $200 million or more) that it believes are undervalued using traditional "value" measures (price-earnings, price-book ratios, etc.). When selecting bonds, which make up around 90% of its assets, the selections are limited to higher-quality issues (those rated A or above). Although the fund was able to dodge an array of bullets during 1987, the fund's performance has been below average.

Portfolio Manager: Harvey Eisen
Since: 1991

Minimum:
Initial: $2,500
Subsequent: None
Telephone Exchange: Yes
Distributions:
Income: Quarterly
Capital Gain: Annually
Front-End Load: None
12b-1: 0.81%
Redemption Fee: 5.00%
Management Company: Sun America Asset Management
Ticker Symbol: ESTRX

TOTAL RETURN (%)

1987	1988	1989	1990	1991	5-year	Bull Market	Bear Market
2.8	6.5	18.4	-2.3	26.7	60.5	35.4	-18.1

INVESTMENT PORTFOLIO

Total Assets (mil.)	Current Yield	Turnover Ratio	Expense Ratio	Beta	Risk Return
$87	1.5%	56%	1.94%	0.70	0.06

SUN AMERICA MULTI ASSET TOTAL RETURN

Sun America Capital Services
10 Union Square East, 2nd Floor
New York, NY 10003
800-821-5100

Investment Objective: This fund seeks to provide investors with a long-term total investment return with moderate risk. It invests in a diversified group of securities among growth equity securities, aggressive growth securities, convertible securities, foreign securities, investment-grade fixed-income securities and money market instruments. Considering that current income is not an overt objective of the fund, its current yield of 2.6% is noteworthy. Still, its performance has swung from good to average to poor, depending on the conditions that accompanied a given year. Its sales and marketing charges, along with an above-average expense ratio, make this fund a bit expensive for investors.

Portfolio Manager: Harvey Eisen
Since: 1987

Minimum:
Initial: $500
Subsequent: $100
Telephone Exchange: Yes
Distributions:
Income: Semiannually
Capital Gain: Annually
Front-End Load: 5.75%
12b-1: 0.35%
Redemption Fee: None
Management Company: Sun America Asset Management
Ticker Symbol: SMTRX

TOTAL RETURN (%)

1987	1988	1989	1990	1991	5-year	Bull Market	Bear Market
NA	17.7	17.7	-11.0	22.5	NA	26.6	-18.3

INVESTMENT PORTFOLIO

Total Assets (mil.)	Current Yield	Turnover Ratio	Expense Ratio	Beta	Risk Return
$27	2.6%	20%	2.05%	0.73	0.04

T. ROWE PRICE EQUITY INCOME FUND

T. Rowe Price Investor Services
100 East Pratt Street
Baltimore, MD 21202
800-638-5660

Investment Objective: Although similar to most growth and income funds' objectives of current income and capital appreciation, this fund leans toward the conservative in stressing a higher dividend yield rather than growth of capital. The fund primarily invests in established companies that have favorable prospects for increasing dividend income. In doing so, the fund strives to achieve a steadier return with less volatility. In addition, the fund sports an above-average dividend yield of 4.1%. This no-load fund is well suited for conservative, growth and income-oriented investors.

Portfolio Manager: Brian Rogers
Since: 1989

Minimum:
Initial: $2,500
Subsequent: $100
Telephone Exchange: Yes
Distributions:
Income: Quarterly
Capital Gain: Annually
Front-End Load: None
12b-1: None
Redemption Fee: None
Management Company: T. Rowe Price Associates
Ticker Symbol: PRFDX

TOTAL RETURN (%)

1987	1988	1989	1990	1991	5-year	Bull Market	Bear Market
3.5	27.7	13.7	-6.8	25.3	75.5	35.9	-17.1

INVESTMENT PORTFOLIO

Total Assets (mil.)	Current Yield	Turnover Ratio	Expense Ratio	Beta	Risk Return
$1,241	4.1%	34%	1.05%	0.73	0.05

T. ROWE PRICE GROWTH INCOME FUND

T. Rowe Price Investor Services
100 East Pratt Street
Baltimore, MD 21202
800-638-5660

Investment Objective: As its name implies, the fund seeks to provide both growth of capital and current income. Investments include dividend-paying common stocks, preferred stocks and convertible bonds. Although the fund has maintained an above-average current yield and lower-than-average risk, its 5-year return is below the average of its growth and income counterparts. However, one benefit this fund does provide is low expenses, and it's a true no-load fund.

Portfolio Manager: Stephen W. Boesel
Since: 1987

Minimum:
Initial: $2,500
Subsequent: $100
Telephone Exchange: Yes
Distributions:
Income: Quarterly
Capital Gain: Annually
Front-End Load: None
12b-1: None
Redemption Fee: None
Management Company: T. Rowe Price Associates
Ticker Symbol: PRGIX

TOTAL RETURN (%)

1987	1988	1989	1990	1991	5-year	Bull Market	Bear Market
-4.2	25.1	19.3	-11.1	31.5	67.0	44.9	-22.0

INVESTMENT PORTFOLIO

Total Assets (mil.)	Current Yield	Turnover Ratio	Expense Ratio	Beta	Risk Return
$603	4.0%	48%	0.93%	0.88	0.06

TRANSAMERICA GROWTH AND INCOME FUND A

TransAmerica Distributors
1000 Louisiana, Suite 6000
Houston, TX 77002
800-343-6840

Investment Objective: Before a recent transformation to its current form as a growth and income fund, this vehicle was called Commerce Income Shares. The portfolio invested in U.S. government treasuries and agencies and was highly reliant on prevailing interest rates for its success. The fund seeks to obtain a combination of capital appreciation and current income by investing in a combination of common stocks, fixed-income securities and money market instruments. The fund has had above-average returns, but also carries slightly higher risk than most growth and income funds; thus, aggressive growth and income investors may want to consider this offering.

Portfolio Manager: Management team
Since: 1949

Minimum:
Initial: $100
Subsequent: $50
Telephone Exchange: Yes
Distributions:
Income: Quarterly
Capital Gain: Annually
Front-End Load: 4.75%
12b-1: 0.25%
Redemption Fee: None
Management Company: TransAmerica Fund Management
Ticker Symbol: TAGRX

TOTAL RETURN (%)

1987	1988	1989	1990	1991	5-year	Bull Market	Bear Market
7.9	6.5	22.5	-0.4	32.3	85.4	34.1	-17.6

INVESTMENT PORTFOLIO

Total Assets (mil.)	Current Yield	Turnover Ratio	Expense Ratio	Beta	Risk Return
$73	1.5%	70%	1.38%	0.88	0.06

TRIFLEX FUND

Securities Management & Research
Two Moody Plaza
Galveston, TX 77550
800-231-4639

Investment Objective: This fund's 3 objectives are conservation of principal, current income and long-term growth. The fund invests in a balanced portfolio of fixed-income securities such as bonds, commercial paper, preferred stock and short-term obligations, combined with common stocks and securities convertible into common stocks. Allocations will fluctuate, depending on management's appraisal of market conditions. Given its risk level, the fund has produced a satisfactory 5-year return of 62%. Also slightly above average is its yield, attractive for investors seeking income. The fund has, remarkably, held its own during the 1987 and 1990 bear markets.

Portfolio Manager: Ben Hock
Since: 1987

Minimum:
Initial: $100
Subsequent: $20
Telephone Exchange: No
Distributions:
Income: Quarterly
Capital Gain: Annually
Front-End Load: 7.50%
12b-1: None
Redemption Fee: None
Management Company: Securities Management & Research
Ticker Symbol: ANTRX

TOTAL RETURN (%)

1987	1988	1989	1990	1991	5-year	Bull Market	Bear Market
2.3	10.4	13.7	1.4	24.5	62.1	26.1	-10.1

INVESTMENT PORTFOLIO

Total Assets (mil.)	Current Yield	Turnover Ratio	Expense Ratio	Beta	Risk Return
$20	3.4%	185%	1.31%	0.58	0.06

TWENTIETH CENTURY BALANCED INVESTORS

Twentieth Century Investors
4500 Main Street, P.O. Box 418210
Kansas City, MO 64111
800-345-2021

Investment Objective: A far cry from the typical balanced vehicle, this fund bears all the earmarks of the potent, earning-momentum style that characterizes most Twentieth Century offerings. Rapid, high-growth stocks dominate the portfolio, with the balance being held in bonds and other fixed-income securities. Although a generally sizable bond position tempers some of its volatility, the fund isn't for the risk wary. Moreover, investors who attempt to buy and sell shares at key intervals are likely to get badly whipsawed. Risk tolerant investors with the discipline to buy and hold, however, can expect excellent long-term results.

Portfolio Manager: Team System
Since: 1988

Minimum:
Initial: None
Subsequent: None
Telephone Exchange: Yes
Distributions:
Income: Quarterly
Capital Gain: Annually
Front-End Load: None
12b-1: None
Redemption Fee: None
Management Company: Investors Research
Ticker Symbol: TWBIX

TOTAL RETURN (%)

1987	1988	1989	1990	1991	5-year	Bull Market	Bear Market
NA	NA	25.7	1.8	46.2	NA	44.0	-16.2

INVESTMENT PORTFOLIO

Total Assets (mil.)	Current Yield	Turnover Ratio	Expense Ratio	Beta	Risk Return
$280	1.7%	116%	1.00%	0.81	0.10

UNIFIED INCOME FUND

Unified Management
429 North Pennsylvania Street
Indianapolis, IN 46204
800-862-7283

Investment Objective: This fund's objectives are current income and preservation of capital and are pursued by investing in income-producing securities such as corporate and government bonds, notes, preferred stocks and dividend-paying stocks. This tiny fund has had less than impressive returns, but its current yield of 3.6% may be attractive for those investors seeking current income. Additionally, its low portfolio turnover ratio implies that the fund is not a market timer, thus reducing risk somewhat.

Portfolio Manager: Bottoms/Bune
Since: 1990

Minimum:
Initial: $1,000
Subsequent: $50
Telephone Exchange: Yes
Distributions:
Income: Quarterly
Capital Gain: Annually
Front-End Load: 4.50%
12b-1: None
Redemption Fee: None
Management Company: Unified Advisers
Ticker Symbol: UNIIX

TOTAL RETURN (%)

1987	1988	1989	1990	1991	5-year	Bull Market	Bear Market
-11.5	12.7	11.3	6.6	11.1	31.6	12.0	0

INVESTMENT PORTFOLIO

Total Assets (mil.)	Current Yield	Turnover Ratio	Expense Ratio	Beta	Risk Return
$5	3.6%	25%	1.58%	0.26	0.03

UNIFIED MUTUAL SHARES

Unified Management
429 North Pennsylvania Street
Indianapolis, IN 46204
800-862-7283

Investment Objective: The primary objectives of this fund are capital growth and current income, and the fund seeks to obtain these objectives by investing in high-quality income-producing securities. Investments suitable for life insurance companies under the Code of the District of Columbia are considered high-quality securities. A very low portfolio turnover rate of 6% implies that this fund is not a market timer and may be somewhat less risky than its other growth and income counterparts. Both its returns and current yield are conservative compared to growth and income averages. Although the fund is saddled with a 4.50% front-end load, its expense ratio of only 0.43% is low for a fund with only $14 million in assets.

Portfolio Manager: Fiduciary Counsel
Since: 1990

Minimum:
Initial: $1,000
Subsequent: $50
Telephone Exchange: Yes
Distributions:
Income: Semiannually
Capital Gain: Annually
Front-End Load: 4.50%
12b-1: None
Redemption Fee: None
Management Company: Unified Advisers
Ticker Symbol: UNFMX

TOTAL RETURN (%)

1987	1988	1989	1990	1991	5-year	Bull Market	Bear Market
-2.2	14.2	20.0	-3.3	29.5	67.7	31.5	-14.3

INVESTMENT PORTFOLIO

Total Assets (mil.)	Current Yield	Turnover Ratio	Expense Ratio	Beta	Risk Return
$14	2.0%	6%	0.43%	0.79	0.06

UNITED CONTINENTAL INCOME FUND

Waddell & Reed
6300 Lamar Avenue, P.O. Box 29217
Shawnee Mission, KS 66201
800-366-5465

Investment Objective: This fund's primary objective is current income, with a secondary objective of capital appreciation. It seeks to achieve this objective by investing in a balanced portfolio of debt securities and common stock. If its deems necessary or prudent, this fund does not hesitate to move into cash reserves as a means of taking profits and/or defending itself against market conditions. This fund has an unusually active portfolio turnover ratio, which may bring a little extra risk. A 3.6% current yield is a bit weak for a fund seeking income as its primary objective, and its returns have not been much to celebrate either, making this fund hardly worth its hefty sales charge.

Portfolio Manager: Tony Intagliata
Since: 1979

Minimum:
Initial: $500
Subsequent: $25
Telephone Exchange: No
Distributions:
Income: Quarterly
Capital Gain: Annually
Front-End Load: 8.50%
12b-1: None
Redemption Fee: None
Management Company: Waddell & Reed Investments
Ticker Symbol: UNCIX

TOTAL RETURN (%)

1987	1988	1989	1990	1991	5-year	Bull Market	Bear Market
-7.8	11.7	23.8	-6.1	25.9	50.8	28.5	-13.2

INVESTMENT PORTFOLIO

Total Assets (mil.)	Current Yield	Turnover Ratio	Expense Ratio	Beta	Risk Return
$313	3.6%	208%	0.85%	0.72	0.06

UNITED INCOME FUND

Waddell & Reed
6300 Lamar Avenue, P.O. Box 29217
Shawnee Mission, KS 66201
800-366-5465

Investment Objective: Investors may not be sure what to make of this hybrid animal. With consistent allocations to bonds and cash, you could make a case for investing heavily in this portfolio. The cash and bonds should help smooth out the ride shareholders take with the fund. However, as the 5.4% tumble it took in 1990 tells us, the fund is anything but rock solid. The problem, of course, is that higher interest rates hurt both stocks and bonds, and stocks usually rise faster when rates fall. In 1990, when rates jumped and the market plunged, this fund suffered on both fronts. Overall, the fund is still a good holding despite its heavy 8.50% front-end load.

Portfolio Manager: Russell Thompson
Since: 1979

Minimum:
Initial: $500
Subsequent: $25
Telephone Exchange: No
Distributions:
Income: Quarterly
Capital Gain: Annually
Front-End Load: 8.50%
12b-1: None
Redemption Fee: None
Management Company: Waddell & Reed Investments
Ticker Symbol: UNCMX

TOTAL RETURN (%)

1987	1988	1989	1990	1991	5-year	Bull Market	Bear Market
7.3	19.8	27.5	-5.4	29.6	100.9	39.2	-22.9

INVESTMENT PORTFOLIO

Total Assets (mil.)	Current Yield	Turnover Ratio	Expense Ratio	Beta	Risk Return
$1,918	2.4%	25%	0.66%	1.05	0.05

UNITED SERVICES INCOME

United Services Advisers
P.O. Box 29467
San Antonio, TX 78229
800-873-8637

Investment Objective: The objective of this fund is preservation of capital and production of current income. The fund invests in a variety of domestic securities, as well as some foreign issues listed on domestic exchanges. By prospectus, at least 80% of the fund's assets must be invested in income-producing securities. Since its impressive gain in 1989, the fund has performed below average, damaging its 5-year return. Also below average is its current yield. The fund's no-load feature makes it attractive, but its expense ratio is unusually high.

Portfolio Manager: J. David Edwards
Since: 1987

Minimum:
Initial: $1,000
Subsequent: $50
Telephone Exchange: Yes
Distributions:
Income: Quarterly
Capital Gain: Annually
Front-End Load: None
12b-1: None
Redemption Fee: None
Management Company: United Services Advisers
Ticker Symbol: USINX

TOTAL RETURN (%)

1987	1988	1989	1990	1991	5-year	Bull Market	Bear Market
-4.3	16.9	37.7	-8.7	14.3	60.8	12.8	-7.2

INVESTMENT PORTFOLIO

Total Assets (mil.)	Current Yield	Turnover Ratio	Expense Ratio	Beta	Risk Return
$9	2.8%	110%	2.22%	0.52	0.02

USAA BALANCED PORTFOLIO FUND

USAA Investment Management
USAA Building
San Antonio, TX 78288
800-531-8181

Investment Objective: This fund's objective is to seek a conservative balance between income, the majority of which is exempt from federal income tax, and the potential for long-term growth of capital. The fund attempts to maintain prescribed allocations among short-term and long-term tax-exempt securities, basic value stocks and gold stocks. In its brief history, it has done an above-average job producing income and a mediocre job producing returns, although it did produce a small return during 1990. The fund has a rather low beta and a high turnover ratio, implying that it invests in high-quality securities but quickly trades them when the tides turn. Investors seeking income may want to look twice at this young no-load fund.

Portfolio Manager: John W. Saunders
Since: 1989

Minimum:
Initial: $1,000
Subsequent: $50
Telephone Exchange: Yes
Distributions:
Income: Quarterly
Capital Gain: Annually
Front-End Load: None
12b-1: None
Redemption Fee: None
Management Company: USAA Investment Management
Ticker Symbol: USBLX

TOTAL RETURN (%)

1987	1988	1989	1990	1991	5-year	Bull Market	Bear Market
NA	NA	NA	1.4	14.5	NA	NA	NA

INVESTMENT PORTFOLIO

Total Assets (mil.)	Current Yield	Turnover Ratio	Expense Ratio	Beta	Risk Return
$57	4.3%	106%	1.00%	0.37	0.04

USF&G AXE-HOUGHTON FUND B

USF&G Investment Services
275 Commerce Drive, Suite 228
Fort Washington, PA 19034
800-323-8734

Investment Objective: The objectives of this fund are threefold: conservation of capital, reasonable income and long-term capital growth. It attempts to achieve these objectives by using a balanced investment approach. Common stocks are limited to a maximum of 75% of its assets; bonds are at least 25% of its assets. This investment approach has suited conservative growth and income investors well over the past 5 years. The fund has one of the better performance records given its below-average risk level. This fact is punctuated by its positive 7.2% return in 1990.

Portfolio Manager: Porter Sutro
Since: 1987

Minimum:
Initial: $1,000
Subsequent: $50
Telephone Exchange: Yes
Distributions:
Income: Quarterly
Capital Gain: Annually
Front-End Load: 5.75%
12b-1: 0.25%
Redemption Fee: None
Management Company: USF&G Review Management
Ticker Symbol: AXEBX

TOTAL RETURN (%)

1987	1988	1989	1990	1991	5-year	Bull Market	Bear Market
-3.4	9.0	20.7	7.2	22.0	66.1	24.3	-4.5

INVESTMENT PORTFOLIO

Total Assets (mil.)	Current Yield	Turnover Ratio	Expense Ratio	Beta	Risk Return
$172	4.8%	298%	1.18%	0.44	0.07

VALLEY FORGE FUND

Valley Forge Fund
P.O. Box 262
Valley Forge, PA 19481
800-548-1942

Investment Objective: The fund's investment objective is listed as capital appreciation, but it tends to follow a very defensive strategy and is, therefore, classified as a growth and income fund. Preservation of capital is more the norm, as the fund is often 50% or more in cash and short-term securities. The fund has had a very low degree of risk over the past 5 years and, consequently, had a below-average return for its stated objective. Nevertheless, this no-load offering is well suited for conservative growth and income investors.

Minimum:
Initial: $1,000
Subsequent: $100
Telephone Exchange: No
Distributions:
Income: Annually
Capital Gain: Annually
Front-End Load: None
12b-1: None
Redemption Fee: None
Management Company: Valley Forge Management
Ticker Symbol: VAFGX

Portfolio Manager: Bernard B. Klawans
Since: 1971

TOTAL RETURN (%)

1987	1988	1989	1990	1991	5-year	Bull Market	Bear Market
4.9	7.0	13.0	-5.4	7.9	29.4	9.7	-8.4

INVESTMENT PORTFOLIO

Total Assets (mil.)	Current Yield	Turnover Ratio	Expense Ratio	Beta	Risk Return
$7	4.3%	17%	1.40%	0.20	0.01

VALUE LINE INCOME FUND

Value Line Securities
711 Third Avenue
New York, NY 10017
800-223-0818

Investment Objective: As the name implies, the fund's primary investment objective is a high level of income. Capital appreciation is a secondary objective. Management hopes to achieve its objective by investing in common stocks, preferred stocks and bonds. There is no limitation on the proportions of the fund's assets that may be invested in each asset class. In seeking securities for purchase, management relies on the Value Line Ranking System. With an above-average 5-year performance record, it is obvious that the Value Line system has worked for this fund. In addition, its low expense ratio and low turnover rate make this no-load fund an excellent growth and income vehicle.

Minimum:
Initial: $1,000
Subsequent: $100
Telephone Exchange: Yes
Distributions:
Income: Quarterly
Capital Gain: Annually
Front-End Load: None
12b-1: None
Redemption Fee: None
Management Company: Value Line
Ticker Symbol: VALIX

Portfolio Manager: Managemen team
Since: 1990

TOTAL RETURN (%)

1987	1988	1989	1990	1991	5-year	Bull Market	Bear Market
-2.4	12.2	22.5	2.0	28.5	75.9	29.1	-8.5

INVESTMENT PORTFOLIO

Total Assets (mil.)	Current Yield	Turnover Ratio	Expense Ratio	Beta	Risk Return
$157	3.9%	57%	0.77%	0.62	0.07

VANGUARD EQUITY INCOME FUND

Vanguard Group
Vanguard Financial Center
Valley Forge, PA 19482
800-662-7447

Investment Objective: This pure no-load fund seeks a high level of income by investing in a broad array of dividend-paying equity securities. Capital appreciation is a secondary investment objective. Management hopes to maintain an income yield at least 50% greater than that of the S&P 500 Index. This relatively new fund has been managed well in its short history. With the fund's current yield of 5.2%, Portfolio Manager Roger Newell has done an excellent job of following the guidelines set by the fund's investment objective. A low turnover ratio and a low expense ratio make this fund extremely appealing to growth and income investors.

Portfolio Manager: Roger Newell
Since: 1988

Minimum:
Initial: $3,000
Subsequent: $100
Telephone Exchange: Yes
Distributions:
Income: Quarterly
Capital Gain: Annually
Front-End Load: None
12b-1: None
Redemption Fee: None
Management Company: Newell Associates
Ticker Symbol: VEIPX

TOTAL RETURN (%)

1987	1988	1989	1990	1991	5-year	Bull Market	Bear Market
NA	NA	26.5	-11.9	25.4	NA	33.8	-19.1

INVESTMENT PORTFOLIO

Total Assets (mil.)	Current Yield	Turnover Ratio	Expense Ratio	Beta	Risk Return
$517	5.2%	9%	0.46%	0.85	0.04

VANGUARD PREFERRED STOCK FUND

Vanguard Group
Vanguard Financial Center
Valley Forge, PA 19482
800-662-7447

Investment Objective: This pure no-load fund's investment objective is to provide investors with current income by investing in medium- and high-grade preferred stocks. These types of funds were designed to offer higher yields than money market funds and less risk than long-term bond funds. Most of the risks associated with these funds can be attributed to interest rates rather than stock market factors. Given the fund's risk level, performance has been well above average. Also, like many Vanguard offerings, the expense ratio is a low 0.63%. Furthermore, the fund's low portfolio turnover exhibits management's long-term outlook.

Portfolio Manager: Earl McEvoy
Since: 1982

Minimum:
Initial: $3,000
Subsequent: $50
Telephone Exchange: Yes
Distributions:
Income: Semiannually
Capital Gain: Annually
Front-End Load: None
12b-1: None
Redemption Fee: None
Management Company: Wellington Management
Ticker Symbol: VQIIX

TOTAL RETURN (%)

1987	1988	1989	1990	1991	5-year	Bull Market	Bear Market
-7.7	8.0	18.7	6.4	21.0	52.3	22.9	-1.5

INVESTMENT PORTFOLIO

Total Assets (mil.)	Current Yield	Turnover Ratio	Expense Ratio	Beta	Risk Return
$93	7.9%	18%	0.63%	0.25	0.08

VANGUARD QUANTITATIVE PORTFOLIOS

Vanguard Group
Vanguard Financial Center
Valley Forge, PA 19482
800-662-7447

Investment Objective: In seeking a return greater than that of the S&P 500 Index, this no-load fund invests in approximately 200 stocks that closely mirror the performance of the S&P 500 Index. Management uses a strategy it calls "portfolio optimization," which refers to the fund's quantitative attempts to enhance the returns of an Index portfolio. Since its inception in 1986, the portfolio has outperformed the S&P 500 by about 1% per year. This return was achieved at a market risk level. Thus, the fund has managed to beat the S&P 500 while maintaining a risk level equal to that of the market.

Portfolio Manager: John Nagorniak
Since: 1986

Minimum:
Initial: $3,000
Subsequent: $100
Telephone Exchange: No
Distributions:
Income: Semiannually
Capital Gain: Annually
Front-End Load: None
12b-1: None
Redemption Fee: None
Management Company: Franklin Advisers
Ticker Symbol: VQNPX

TOTAL RETURN (%)

1987	1988	1989	1990	1991	5-year	Bull Market	Bear Market
4.0	16.8	32.0	-2.4	30.3	103.8	37.3	-18.9

INVESTMENT PORTFOLIO

Total Assets (mil.)	Current Yield	Turnover Ratio	Expense Ratio	Beta	Risk Return
$302	2.8%	81%	0.48%	1.01	0.05

VANGUARD STAR FUND

Vanguard Group
Vanguard Financial Center
Valley Forge, PA 19482
800-662-7447

Investment Objective: To say this fund epitomizes balanced investing is an understatement. The fund buys shares in some of the best mutual funds in Vanguard's portfolio. The concept behind the fund is risk reduction through diversification, and it's surprising that other fund families have not followed Vanguard's lead. The fund is run at no cost to shareholders, for Vanguard receives its fees with the funds included within the Star portfolio. With a beta about two-thirds that of the market, a yield of 4.9% and returns that have been fairly strong over the past 5 years, this fund is both an innovator and a winner.

Portfolio Manager: Vanguard Group
Since: 1985

Minimum:
Initial: $500
Subsequent: $100
Telephone Exchange: Yes
Distributions:
Income: Semiannually
Capital Gain: Semiannually
Front-End Load: None
12b-1: None
Redemption Fee: None
Management Company: Vanguard Group
Ticker Symbol: VGSTX

TOTAL RETURN (%)

1987	1988	1989	1990	1991	5-year	Bull Market	Bear Market
1.7	19.0	18.8	-3.6	24.1	71.9	30.6	-13.6

INVESTMENT PORTFOLIO

Total Assets (mil.)	Current Yield	Turnover Ratio	Expense Ratio	Beta	Risk Return
$1,445	4.9%	11%	0.00%	0.65	0.06

VANGUARD TRUSTEES COMMINGLED UNITED STATES

Vanguard Group
Vanguard Financial Center
Valley Forge, PA 19482
800-662-7447

Investment Objective: Capital appreciation and income are the objectives for this Vanguard fund. This fund selects income-producing equities based on fundamental factors such as relative growth rates, price/earnings ratios and yields. In the fund's search for common stocks, the fund also tries to identify undervalued or out-of-favor companies. Given the fund's below-average risk exposure, its performance over the past 5 years has been in the middle of the pack for growth and income funds. Potential investors also should note the minimum initial investment of $10,000, which is higher than most funds.

Portfolio Manager: Jarrod Wilcox
Since: 1991

Minimum:
Initial: $10,000
Subsequent: $1,000
Telephone Exchange: Yes
Distributions:
Income: Quarterly
Capital Gain: Annually
Front-End Load: None
12b-1: None
Redemption Fee: None
Management Company: Batterymarch Financial Management
Ticker Symbol: VTRSX

TOTAL RETURN (%)

1987	1988	1989	1990	1991	5-year	Bull Market	Bear Market
1.7	24.6	17.2	-8.3	26.6	72.4	32.2	-20.3

INVESTMENT PORTFOLIO

Total Assets (mil.)	Current Yield	Turnover Ratio	Expense Ratio	Beta	Risk Return
$105	2.5%	81%	0.52%	0.96	0.04

VANGUARD WELLESLEY INCOME FUND

Vanguard Group
Vanguard Financial Center
Valley Forge, PA 19482
800-662-7447

Investment Objective: By investing in a balanced portfolio of corporate bonds and high-yielding common stocks, this no-load fund seeks to achieve current income with moderate capital growth. When picking corporate bonds, management prefers AAA-rated instruments. The portfolio has done an excellent job of achieving its objective. Over the past 5 years, the fund has returned 69.9%, with a risk level significantly lower than that of the average growth and income portfolio. Furthermore, the fund sports one of the better current yields, 7.0%. This fund has all the makings of an excellent growth and income vehicle.

Portfolio Manager: E. McEvoy/J. Ryan
Since: 1982

Minimum:
Initial: $3,000
Subsequent: $100
Telephone Exchange: Yes
Distributions:
Income: Quarterly
Capital Gain: Annually
Front-End Load: None
12b-1: None
Redemption Fee: None
Management Company: Wellington Management
Ticker Symbol: VWINX

TOTAL RETURN (%)

1987	1988	1989	1990	1991	5-year	Bull Market	Bear Market
-1.9	13.6	20.9	3.8	21.5	69.9	23.5	-4.8

INVESTMENT PORTFOLIO

Total Assets (mil.)	Current Yield	Turnover Ratio	Expense Ratio	Beta	Risk Return
$1,762	7.0%	12%	0.45%	0.39	0.07

VANGUARD WELLINGTON FUND

Vanguard Group
Vanguard Financial Center
Valley Forge, PA 19482
800-662-7447

Investment Objective: This fund's objective is to provide investors with conservation of principal, reasonable income and capital growth without assuming undue risk. The fund has performed well during the 1980s (a 10-year compound annual return of 16.6%) and, considering its low beta, has more than accomplished its multiple objectives. In 1990, the fund's interest sensitivity caused the portfolio to sink slightly. The fund rebounded the past year with an average return of 23.6%. With a low expense ratio, low turnover ratio and a solid performance history, this fund is an excellent choice for growth and income investors.

Minimum:
Initial: $3,000
Subsequent: $100
Telephone Exchange: Yes
Distributions:
Income: Semiannually
Capital Gain: Annually
Front-End Load: None
12b-1: None
Redemption Fee: None
Management Company: Wellington Management
Ticker Symbol: VWELX

Portfolio Manager: Vincent Bajakian
Since: 1972

TOTAL RETURN (%)

1987	1988	1989	1990	1991	5-year	Bull Market	Bear Market
2.3	16.1	21.6	-2.8	23.6	73.5	29.7	-13.1

INVESTMENT PORTFOLIO

Total Assets (mil.)	Current Yield	Turnover Ratio	Expense Ratio	Beta	Risk Return
$3,473	5.0%	35%	0.35%	0.73	0.05

VANGUARD WINDSOR FUND

Vanguard Group
Vanguard Financial Center
Valley Forge, PA 19482
800-662-7447

Investment Objective: This famed, John Neff–managed vehicle has become one of the most popular mutual funds in the industry. The fund emphasizes a value approach toward investing that usually includes several cyclical issues, as their price/earnings and price/book ratios are typically lower than those of consumer growth stocks. Unfortunately, cyclical stocks have been out of favor over the past 5 years, and therefore, this fund's performance has suffered. However, performance should improve as these issues usually do exceptionally well in the early stages of an economic recovery. The only drawback to the fund is that it is closed to new investors.

Minimum:
Initial: Closed
Subsequent: $100
Telephone Exchange: Yes
Distributions:
Income: Semiannually
Capital Gain: Annually
Front-End Load: Closed
12b-1: None
Redemption Fee: None
Management Company: Wellington Management
Ticker Symbol: VWNDX

Portfolio Manager: John Neff
Since: 1964

TOTAL RETURN (%)

1987	1988	1989	1990	1991	5-year	Bull Market	Bear Market
1.2	28.7	15.0	-15.5	28.6	62.8	43.9	-25.8

INVESTMENT PORTFOLIO

Total Assets (mil.)	Current Yield	Turnover Ratio	Expense Ratio	Beta	Risk Return
$7,374	4.5%	36%	0.30%	1.00	0.04

VANGUARD WINDSOR II

Vanguard Group
Vanguard Financial Center
Valley Forge, PA 19482
800-662-7447

Investment Objective: This no-load fund was created to cash in on the success of the highly popular Windsor Fund, which is currently closed to new investors. Windsor II, like its predecessor, is a growth and income fund. The fund emphasizes income-producing common stocks that are largely characterized by above-average income yields and below-average price/earnings ratios. Although this fund was created to duplicate the Windsor Fund, investors should keep in mind that the management of the two funds is different. Windsor is managed by Wellington Management Company, while Windsor II is managed by Barrow, Hanely, Mewhinney & Strauss Invesco Capital.

Portfolio Manager: Barrow/Starke
Since: 1985

Minimum:
Initial: $3,000
Subsequent: $100
Telephone Exchange: Yes
Distributions:
Income: Semiannually
Capital Gain: Annually
Front-End Load: None
12b-1: None
Redemption Fee: None
Management Company: BHMS/Invesco Capital
Ticker Symbol: VWNFX

TOTAL RETURN (%)

1987	1988	1989	1990	1991	5-year	Bull Market	Bear Market
-2.1	24.7	27.8	-10.0	28.7	80.7	37.8	-18.1

INVESTMENT PORTFOLIO

Total Assets (mil.)	Current Yield	Turnover Ratio	Expense Ratio	Beta	Risk Return
$3,256	4.0%	41%	0.48%	0.93	0.05

VAN KAMPEN MERRITT GROWTH & INCOME FUND

Van Kampen Merritt
17W110 22nd Street
Oakbrook Terrace, IL 60181
800-225-2222

Investment Objective: This fund seeks to provide long-term growth of both capital and income. Management will purchase dividend-paying common stocks to achieve the fund's investment objective. The performance for this relatively young fund has been well above average for its category. Over the past 4 years, the fund has provided investors with a 65.6% return and maintained a risk level less than that of the S&P 500 Index. By staying fully invested through thick and thin and keeping about one-third of its assets in financials and utilities, the fund has provided both above-average income and high exposure to the stock market. Potential investors should note that the fund carries a 4.90% front-end load and a 12b-1 fee.

Portfolio Manager: Susan Saltus
Since: 1986

Minimum:
Initial: $1,500
Subsequent: $100
Telephone Exchange: Yes
Distributions:
Income: Semiannually
Capital Gain: Annually
Front-End Load: 4.90%
12b-1: 0.17%
Redemption Fee: None
Management Company: Van Kampen Merritt Investment
Ticker Symbol: VKGIX

TOTAL RETURN (%)

1987	1988	1989	1990	1991	5-year	Bull Market	Bear Market
NA	16.6	19.0	-7.9	29.6	NA	39.7	-18.7

INVESTMENT PORTFOLIO

Total Assets (mil.)	Current Yield	Turnover Ratio	Expense Ratio	Beta	Risk Return
$26	1.7%	48%	1.84%	0.92	0.05

WASHINGTON MUTUAL INVESTORS FUND

American Funds Distributor
333 South Hope Street, 52nd Floor
Los Angeles, CA 90071
800-421-9900

Investment Objective: This fund, incorporated in 1952, seeks to produce income and growth of principal by investing exclusively in common stocks and/or convertible securities that are legal for investment of trust funds in the District of Columbia. The fund was founded to provide fiduciaries, organizations and institutions with a convenient and "prudent" medium of investment in high-quality equity securities. The District of Columbia's "eligible list" consists of approximately 400 stocks that meet criteria established according to the historic Prudent Man Rule. With almost $7.4 billion in assets, this is one of the largest equity funds in the industry. Investors should note the fund carries a 5.75% front-end load and a 12b-1 fee.

Portfolio Manager: Multiple Portfolio Counselors
Since: 1991

Minimum:
Initial: $250
Subsequent: $50
Telephone Exchange: Yes
Distributions:
Income: Quarterly
Capital Gain: Annually
Front-End Load: 5.75%
12b-1: 0.17%
Redemption Fee: None
Management Company: Capital Research & Management
Ticker Symbol: AWSHX

TOTAL RETURN (%)

1987	1988	1989	1990	1991	5-year	Bull Market	Bear Market
1.4	17.7	29.0	-3.9	23.5	82.7	34.8	-17.0

INVESTMENT PORTFOLIO

Total Assets (mil.)	Current Yield	Turnover Ratio	Expense Ratio	Beta	Risk Return
$7,363	3.3%	11%	0.77%	0.92	0.04

WPG GROWTH & INCOME

Weiss Peck Greer
One New York Plaza
New York, NY 10004
800-223-3332

Investment Objective: As one of the more aggressive growth and income vehicles, this fund seeks long-term growth of capital, a reasonable level of current income and an increase in future income through investments in primarily income-producing equity securities. The fund invests in common stocks, convertible securities of companies believed to have better-than-average growth prospects and investment-grade fixed-income securities. Management has racked up one of the best 5-year returns around, a high 88.2%. This pure no-load fund is ideally suited for growth and income investors who can handle management's aggressive touch.

Portfolio Manager: Gerald Levine
Since: 1985

Minimum:
Initial: $2,500
Subsequent: $100
Telephone Exchange: Yes
Distributions:
Income: Quarterly
Capital Gain: Annually
Front-End Load: None
12b-1: None
Redemption Fee: None
Management Company: WPG Advisers
Ticker Symbol: WPGFX

TOTAL RETURN (%)

1987	1988	1989	1990	1991	5-year	Bull Market	Bear Market
6.8	9.5	27.6	-10.4	40.7	88.2	49.4	-27.1

INVESTMENT PORTFOLIO

Total Assets (mil.)	Current Yield	Turnover Ratio	Expense Ratio	Beta	Risk Return
$47	1.4%	93%	1.50%	1.18	0.05

PART 7

International Funds

The following pages contain descriptions of 72 funds that invest in equity securities of companies domiciled outside the United States. These "foreign" funds can be divided into four groups: global funds, which invest in both U.S. and foreign securities; international funds that restrict their security holdings to companies domiciled outside the United States; regional funds that invest in countries in a specific geographic region such as Europe or the Pacific Basin; and country-specific funds that limit their investments to issuers of a single country.

Investment risk tends to parallel a fund's degree of diversification, with the most diversified (global funds) possessing the least risk and the most concentrated (single-country funds) possessing the most risk. Returns from foreign securities tend to have relatively low correlations with returns from U.S. securities. Thus, a portfolio consisting of investment in both U.S. and comparable foreign securities tends to possess less variability (risk) than a portfolio whose assets are concentrated in a single country. Some academic studies indicate that the optimally balanced portfolio is one that contains 67 percent of its assets allocated to stocks of U.S. domiciled companies and 33 percent allocated to foreign stocks. This mix delivers the greatest equity return for the least amount of volatility, or risk.

The median (middle) financial statistics of this group of funds are outlined below. On average, international and global funds possess greater expense ratios than do funds that specialize in U.S. equities. Funds justify this on the grounds that information on foreign securities is more difficult to obtain and analyze than for U.S. stocks. As a result, the international funds tend to possess higher management fees. In addition, international and global funds tend to pay relatively scant income distributions (median 1.4 percent versus about 3 percent for funds that invest in U.S. equities exclusively).

During most of the 1980s, international equity returns were above average as a result of both a runaway stock market in Japan and the falling value of the U.S. dollar. Thus, it is not surprising to find that, on average, funds that invested internationally have posted enviable track records over the past ten years. However, beginning in 1990, the value of the U.S. dollar began to stabilize against most international currencies and in some cases showed considerable strength. In addition, stock prices on most international exchanges hit the skids. Declines in foreign stock exchange indices in excess of 15 percent were commonplace during 1990. As a result, international funds, on average, returned –11.5 percent that year versus –3.1 percent for the Standard & Poor's 500 Index. Furthermore, international funds rebounded only marginally during 1991, a median return of 13 percent versus a return for approximately 30 percent for the typical domestic equity fund. The median beta of these funds is 0.70 versus a beta of 1.00 for the Standard & Poor's 500 Index (a proxy for the U.S. stock market). While a beta less than 1.00 suggests that these funds possess lower risk than the U.S. stock market, the beta is somewhat misleading in that it results from the relatively low correlation of returns between U.S. and foreign securities and not from a relatively low level of volatility of international equities. In fact, the returns of foreign stocks tend to be more volatile than those of U.S. stocks because of changing rates of exchange among the U.S. dollar and major foreign currencies. When the value of the dollar is rising, returns from international securities (restated in dollar terms) tend to fall. On the other hand, when the value of the dollar is falling, returns of international securities are enhanced. Finally, investors should be aware of the fact that investing internationally entails the assumption of political risk. Thus, international investments suffer the compound effects of economic, foreign exchange and political risks.

Summary of Financial Statistics (medians)

1991 Return	Five-Year Return	Current Yield	Beta	Turnover Ratio	Expense Ratio
13.0%	54.9%	1.4%	0.70	52%	1.59%

BEST INTERNATIONAL FUNDS FOR 1991

Fund	Percent Return 1991	3-Year	5-Year
G. T. Global Health Care Fund	57.9%	78.6%	NA
Templeton Smaller Companies Growth Fund	39.5	38.6	57.9%
Founders Worldwide Growth Fund	34.8	43.8	NA
Templeton Global Opportunities Trust	33.2	33.2	NA
Templeton Value Fund	32.9	26.9	NA
Templeton World Fund	29.8	33.8	65.6
Oppenheimer Global Fund	27.4	70.8	102.8
Alliance Global Small Cap Fund A	25.3	17.2	45.3
National Worldwide Opportunity	24.4	5.0	12.7
Lexington Worldwide Emerging Markets	24.2	36.2	50.8
New Perspective Fund	22.6	51.1	89.4
G. T. Worldwide Growth Fund	20.3	44.8	NA
Thomson Global Fund B	19.9	30.2	52.5

ALLIANCE CANADIAN FUND

Alliance Funds Distributor
500 Plaza Drive
Secaucus, NJ 07094
800-247-4154

Investment Objective: This fund seeks long-term capital growth by investing in companies that may be expected to benefit by any growth or development in Canada. The fund invests in securities of companies doing business or having interest in Canada whether directly or through ownership of securities of other companies doing business in the country. In recent years, both the Canadian economy and financial markets have experienced difficulties. The economy remained in recession, which was aggravated by high real-interest rates. As a result, performance has been lackluster in recent years. However, an improving Canadian economy could boost returns in the years ahead.

Portfolio Manager: Glenn Wellman
Since: 1986

Minimum:
Initial: $250
Subsequent: $25
Telephone Exchange: Yes
Distributions:
Income: Annually
Capital Gain: Annually
Front-End Load: 5.50%
12b-1: 0.19%
Redemption Fee: None
Management Company: Alliance Capital Management
Ticker Symbol: CABCX

TOTAL RETURN (%)

1987	1988	1989	1990	1991	5-year	Bull Market	Bear Market
11.7	31.0	21.8	-19.9	0.5	43.4	4.1	-15.7

INVESTMENT PORTFOLIO

Total Assets (mil.)	Current Yield	Turnover Ratio	Expense Ratio	Beta	Risk Return
$19	0.0%	40%	2.59%	0.78	NA

ALLIANCE GLOBAL SMALL CAP FUND A

Alliance Funds Distributor
500 Plaza Drive
Secaucus, NJ 07094
800-247-4154

Investment Objective: This fund, which changed its name from the Surveyor Fund in late 1990, aggressively seeks capital growth by investing in a global portfolio of the equity securities of relatively small companies with individual market capitalizations of between $50 million and $1 billion. Normally, it will invest at least 65% of its assets in equity securities of such smaller capitalization issues located in at least 3 countries, one of which may be the United States. Up to 35% of its assets may be invested in large cap stocks. As a small cap fund, its per share net asset value may be more volatile than that of global funds that invest in the stocks of larger companies. That has been the case in recent years.

Portfolio Manager: Jenkel/Burr
Since: 1984

Minimum:
Initial: $250
Subsequent: $500
Telephone Exchange: Yes
Distributions:
Income: Annually
Capital Gain: Annually
Front-End Load: 5.50%
12b-1: 0.30%
Redemption Fee: None
Management Company: Alliance Capital Management
Ticker Symbol: GSCAX

TOTAL RETURN (%)

1987	1988	1989	1990	1991	5-year	Bull Market	Bear Market
-3.8	28.8	24.6	-24.9	25.3	45.3	36.8	-32.2

INVESTMENT PORTFOLIO

Total Assets (mil.)	Current Yield	Turnover Ratio	Expense Ratio	Beta	Risk Return
$78	0.0%	89%	1.73%	1.21	0.03

ALLIANCE INTERNATIONAL FUND A

Alliance Funds Distributor
500 Plaza Drive
Secaucus, NJ 07094
800-247-4154

Investment Objective: This fund seeks a high total return from a diversified portfolio of marketable securities of established non-U.S. companies. Recently, it has made a heavy commitment to stable growth companies in industries such as health care and consumer-growth staples. Its largest country allocations include: Japan, United Kingdom, Netherlands and Canada. While the fund has historically allocated the vast majority of its assets to equities, it can invest in fixed-income securities when management believes the total return on debt will exceed that of common stocks. Performance has suffered in recent years because of the collapse of stock prices in Japan and a widening economic recession in Europe.

Portfolio Manager: Glenn Wellman
Since: 1981

Minimum:
Initial: $250
Subsequent: $1,000
Telephone Exchange: Yes
Distributions:
Income: Annually
Capital Gain: Annually
Front-End Load: 5.50%
12b-1: 0.16%
Redemption Fee: None
Management Company: Alliance Capital Management
Ticker Symbol: ALIFX

TOTAL RETURN (%)

1987	1988	1989	1990	1991	5-year	Bull Market	Bear Market
-5.4	32.7	29.6	-21.0	7.7	38.6	4.3	-21.5

INVESTMENT PORTFOLIO

Total Assets (mil.)	Current Yield	Turnover Ratio	Expense Ratio	Beta	Risk Return
$205	0.4%	71%	1.73%	0.77	0.01

COLONIAL INTERNATIONAL EQUITY INDEX TRUST

Colonial Investment Services
One Financial Center, 14th Floor
Boston, MA 02110
800-248-2828

Investment Objective: This index fund seeks to duplicate the capital performance and dividend income of the Morgan Stanley Capital International Europe, Australia and the Far East Gross Domestic Product Index (EAFE). The EAFE is representative of the performance of common stocks traded outside the United States. Stocks included in the EAFE are selected based on national and industry representation and are weighted according to their market values. The relative market value of each country is further weighted with reference to the country's relative gross domestic product. As an index fund, its goal is to improve returns by minimizing transaction costs.

Portfolio Manager: Betsy Palmer
Since: 1990

Minimum:
Initial: $1,000
Subsequent: $25
Telephone Exchange: Yes
Distributions:
Income: Annually
Capital Gain: Annually
Front-End Load: 5.75%
12b-1: 0.25%
Redemption Fee: None
Management Company: Colonial Management Associates
Ticker Symbol: COIEX

TOTAL RETURN (%)

1987	1988	1989	1990	1991	5-year	Bull Market	Bear Market
16.4	21.2	12.5	-19.0	7.8	38.7	3.9	-17.0

INVESTMENT PORTFOLIO

Total Assets (mil.)	Current Yield	Turnover Ratio	Expense Ratio	Beta	Risk Return
$9	0.7%	11%	1.88%	0.68	0.01

DFA CONTINENTAL SMALL COMPANY PORTFOLIO

Dimensional Fund Advisers
1299 Ocean Avenue, Suite 650
Santa Monica, CA 90401
213-395-8005

Investment Objective: The fund invests in readily marketable stocks of companies domiciled in France, Germany, Italy, the Netherlands, Sweden, Belgium, Norway, Spain, Austria, Finland and Denmark. The fund is a quasi-index fund that attempts to capture the so-called "European market small cap effect" by investing in the existing universe of small-firm European stocks. Small is defined as companies with equity capitalizations below that of the largest company in the smallest 20% of companies listed in the Financial Times Actuaries World Index. The fund attempts to deliver superior returns by reducing investment costs.

Portfolio Manager: Rex Singuefield
Since: 1988

Minimum:
Initial: $50,000
Subsequent: None
Telephone Exchange: No
Distributions:
Income: Annually
Capital Gain: Annually
Front-End Load: None
12b-1: None
Redemption Fee: None
Management Company: Dimensional Fund Advisers
Ticker Symbol: DFCSX

TOTAL RETURN (%)

1987	1988	1989	1990	1991	5-year	Bull Market	Bear Market
NA	NA	44.7	-4.1	-4.2	NA	-9.5	-14.6

INVESTMENT PORTFOLIO

Total Assets (mil.)	Current Yield	Turnover Ratio	Expense Ratio	Beta	Risk Return
$214	1.8%	6%	0.89%	0.50	NA

DFA JAPANESE SMALL COMPANY PORTFOLIO

Dimensional Fund Advisers
1299 Ocean Avenue, Suite 650
Santa Monica, CA 90401
213-395-8005

Investment Objective: This institutional offering restricts purchases to the smallest stocks listed in the Tokyo Stock Exchange. Propelled by a buoyant domestic economy, small Japanese stocks rallied sharply from 1987 to 1989, allowing the fund to whip most international fund rivals. In 1990, the fund faced its first unfavorable climate and the loss the past year illustrates the risk inherent in its single-country, small cap focus. That said, the fund offers considerable benefits (low costs and no sales charge) to investors seeking exposure to small Japanese stocks.

Portfolio Manager: Rex Singuefield
Since: 1986

Minimum:
Initial: $50,000
Subsequent: None
Telephone Exchange: No
Distributions:
Income: Annually
Capital Gain: Annually
Front-End Load: None
12b-1: None
Redemption Fee: None
Management Company: Dimensional Fund Advisers
Ticker Symbol: DFJSX

TOTAL RETURN (%)

1987	1988	1989	1990	1991	5-year	Bull Market	Bear Market
87.5	32.4	38.5	-33.4	7.1	145.5	3.9	-23.0

INVESTMENT PORTFOLIO

Total Assets (mil.)	Current Yield	Turnover Ratio	Expense Ratio	Beta	Risk Return
$159	0.0%	10%	0.83%	0.81	0.00

DFA UNITED KINGDOM SMALL COMPANY PORTFOLIO

Dimensional Fund Advisers
1299 Ocean Avenue, Suite 650
Santa Monica, CA 90401
213-395-8005

Investment Objective: The fund seeks capital appreciation by investing in small-company stocks that are readily marketable and traded on the International Stock Exchange (ISE) of the United Kingdom and the Republic of Ireland. Small companies are defined as those with shares listed on the ISE whose market cap is not larger than the largest of those in the smaller one-half of companies included in the Financial Times Actuaries All Shares Index. Currently, about 900 small U.K. companies are eligible. The fund seeks to invest in each company by making allocations on the basis of the relative market cap. This is a quasi-index fund that attempts to deliver superior returns by minimizing the cost of investing.

Portfolio Manager: Rex Singuefield
Since: 1986

Minimum:
Initial: $50,000
Subsequent: None
Telephone Exchange: No
Distributions:
Income: Annually
Capital Gain: Annually
Front-End Load: None
12b-1: None
Redemption Fee: None
Management Company: Dimensional Fund Advisers
Ticker Symbol: DFUKX

TOTAL RETURN (%)

1987	1988	1989	1990	1991	5-year	Bull Market	Bear Market
51.4	6.7	-6.3	-6.7	14.8	62.1	8.1	-10.6

INVESTMENT PORTFOLIO

Total Assets (mil.)	Current Yield	Turnover Ratio	Expense Ratio	Beta	Risk Return
$147	3.1%	11%	0.83%	0.56	0.01

EUROPACIFIC GROWTH FUND

American Funds Distributor
333 South Hope Street, 52nd Floor
Los Angeles, CA 90071
800-421-9900

Investment Objective: EuroPacific Growth Fund epitomizes dependability. Run by Capital Research & Management, this pure international fund takes a patient, disciplined approach to achieving superior long-term returns. For the most part, the fund buys its companies before the market has recognized their underlying fundamentals; it then waits patiently for value to be realized. Management's extensive industry/company research, its value discipline, its emphasis on quality companies and its judicious use of cash have enabled the fund to produce highly competitive results in each of the past 5 years. International investors who prioritize all-weather performance will be hard pressed to find a more suitable fund.

Portfolio Manager: Multiple Portfolio Counselors
Since: 1990

Minimum:
Initial: $250
Subsequent: $50
Telephone Exchange: Yes
Distributions:
Income: Annually
Capital Gain: Annually
Front-End Load: 5.75%
12b-1: 0.16%
Redemption Fee: None
Management Company: Capital Research & Management
Ticker Symbol: AEPGX

TOTAL RETURN (%)

1987	1988	1989	1990	1991	5-year	Bull Market	Bear Market
7.5	21.0	24.2	-0.1	18.6	91.3	16.3	-13.1

INVESTMENT PORTFOLIO

Total Assets (mil.)	Current Yield	Turnover Ratio	Expense Ratio	Beta	Risk Return
$1,577	1.7%	9%	1.28%	0.63	0.03

FIDELITY CANADA FUND

Fidelity Distributors Corporation
82 Devonshire Street, Mail Zone L7B
Boston, MA 02109
800-544-8888

Investment Objective: As its name implies, this fund invests in securities of companies that have their principle business activities in Canada. The fund tends to stay fully invested at all times. During its brief existence, the fund has managed to post a double-digit return despite the fact that the Canadian economy and financial markets have operated under the twin evils of recession and high real-interest rates. Given management's success in a difficult financial environment, the fund should be a stellar performer once the Canadian economy begins to improve. Investors are charged a modest 3.00% entrance fee and the fund limits exchanges from this fund to other Fidelity funds to 2 per year.

Portfolio Manager: George Domolky
Since: 1987

Minimum:
Initial: $2,500
Subsequent: $250
Telephone Exchange: Yes
Distributions:
Income: Annually
Capital Gain: Annually
Front-End Load: 3.00%
12b-1: None
Redemption Fee: None
Management Company: First Investors Management
Ticker Symbol: FICDX

TOTAL RETURN (%)

1987	1988	1989	1990	1991	5-year	Bull Market	Bear Market
NA	19.5	27.0	-5.5	17.7	NA	23.9	-9.2

INVESTMENT PORTFOLIO

Total Assets (mil.)	Current Yield	Turnover Ratio	Expense Ratio	Beta	Risk Return
$22	0.0%	164%	2.05%	0.63	0.02

FIDELITY EUROPE FUND

Fidelity Distributors Corporation
82 Devonshire Street, Mail Zone L7B
Boston, MA 02109
800-544-8888

Investment Objective: By investing in the securities of companies whose principal business activities are in western Europe, the fund strives to obtain capital growth. The fund appears to be strategically positioned to participate in expanding economic growth in the "new" Europe. Investing internationally diversifies investment portfolios, though currency exchange risks as well as the economic and political risks specific to individual countries make all international funds risky stand-alone investments. With stock prices on most European stock exchanges plummeting more than 20% during 1990, fund management dodged a bullet as its loss was less than 5%.

Portfolio Manager: John R. Hickling
Since: 1991

Minimum:
Initial: $2,500
Subsequent: $250
Telephone Exchange: Yes
Distributions:
Income: Annually
Capital Gain: Annually
Front-End Load: 3.00%
12b-1: None
Redemption Fee: None
Management Company: Fidelity Management & Research
Ticker Symbol: FIEUX

TOTAL RETURN (%)

1987	1988	1989	1990	1991	5-year	Bull Market	Bear Market
14.9	5.8	32.3	-4.6	4.2	59.9	-0.4	-14.3

INVESTMENT PORTFOLIO

Total Assets (mil.)	Current Yield	Turnover Ratio	Expense Ratio	Beta	Risk Return
$280	3.1%	148%	1.45%	0.70	NA

FIDELITY INTERNATIONAL GROWTH & INCOME FUND

Fidelity Distributors Corporation
82 Devonshire Street, Mail Zone L7B
Boston, MA 02109
800-544-8888

Investment Objective: This relatively tame international offering seeks capital growth, current income and growth of income by investing in a combination of equity and fixed-income securities. Although the fund's conservative asset mix (fixed-income securities make up about one-third of its assets) slowed 1987-to-1988 returns, this mix enabled the fund to resist decline better than most rivals in bear markets. The fund lost 3.2% in 1990, while the average international fund lost more than 10%. Such good defensive abilities suggest highly competitive long-term results with less risk than the average international fund.

Portfolio Manager: John R. Hickling
Since: 1987

Minimum:
Initial: $2,500
Subsequent: $250
Telephone Exchange: Yes
Distributions:
Income: Annually
Capital Gain: Annually
Front-End Load: 2.00%
12b-1: None
Redemption Fee: None
Management Company: Fidelity Management & Research
Ticker Symbol: FIGRX

TOTAL RETURN (%)

1987	1988	1989	1990	1991	5-year	Bull Market	Bear Market
8.3	11.6	19.1	-3.2	8.0	50.5	7.7	-10.3

INVESTMENT PORTFOLIO

Total Assets (mil.)	Current Yield	Turnover Ratio	Expense Ratio	Beta	Risk Return
$51	1.2%	102%	1.98%	0.54	0.00

FIDELITY OVERSEAS FUND

Fidelity Distributors Corporation
82 Devonshire Street, Mail Zone L7B
Boston, MA 02109
800-544-8888

Investment Objective: This fund has performed very well since its inception in late 1984, despite a subpar 1991. During that time, a majority of its assets were invested in Japanese common stocks. Although the fund has provided investors with above-average returns, a falling dollar and a booming Japanese stock market (now the world's largest) during this period virtually ensured success. However, during 1990, stock prices around the world took a tumble with losses ranging from 12% in Germany to nearly 40% in Tokyo. As a result, this fund experienced its first down year ever.

Portfolio Manager: Penelope Dobkin
Since: 1991

Minimum:
Initial: $2,500
Subsequent: $250
Telephone Exchange: Yes
Distributions:
Income: Annually
Capital Gain: Annually
Front-End Load: 3.00%
12b-1: None
Redemption Fee: None
Management Company: Fidelity Management & Research
Ticker Symbol: FOSFX

TOTAL RETURN (%)

1987	1988	1989	1990	1991	5-year	Bull Market	Bear Market
18.4	8.3	16.9	-6.6	8.6	52.0	5.3	-12.9

INVESTMENT PORTFOLIO

Total Assets (mil.)	Current Yield	Turnover Ratio	Expense Ratio	Beta	Risk Return
$928	1.6%	96%	1.26%	0.60	0.01

FIDELITY PACIFIC BASIN

Fidelity Distributors Corporation
82 Devonshire Street, Mail Zone L7B
Boston, MA 02109
800-544-8888

Investment Objective: This fund primarily invests in the securities of companies that operate in the Pacific Basin (i.e., firms operating in Australia, Hong Kong, India, Japan, Korea, Malaysia, New Zealand, People's Republic of China, Philippines, Singapore, Taiwan and Thailand). A booming Japanese stock market aided the fund in obtaining its respectable performance during the first year of its existence (1987). However, with most Pacific Rim stock markets taking a beating during 1990, the fund's total return plummeted more than 27% in 1990. Given the fund's relatively large allocation to Japanese stocks, future performance will be closely tied to trends in the Japanese economy.

Portfolio Manager: John R. Hickling
Since: 1990

Minimum:
Initial: $2,500
Subsequent: $250
Telephone Exchange: Yes
Distributions:
Income: Annually
Capital Gain: Annually
Front-End Load: 3.00%
12b-1: None
Redemption Fee: None
Management Company: Fidelity Management & Research
Ticker Symbol: FPBFX

TOTAL RETURN (%)

1987	1988	1989	1990	1991	5-year	Bull Market	Bear Market
25.0	10.4	11.4	-27.2	12.5	26.0	7.8	-21.8

INVESTMENT PORTFOLIO

Total Assets (mil.)	Current Yield	Turnover Ratio	Expense Ratio	Beta	Risk Return
$81	0.0%	118%	1.59%	0.62	0.01

FINANCIAL STRATEGIC EUROPEAN

INVESCO Funds Group
P.O. Box 2040
Denver, CO 80201
800-525-8085

Investment Objective: The assets of this fund are invested primarily in securities of companies domiciled in Europe. The fund's securities usually will be listed on a major stock exchange in those countries. The fund also is biased toward large cap, more established issues, which have fared better than the typical international stock over the past 4 years. There are no restrictions on how much can or cannot be invested in a specific country or specific industry, so management can exercise a great deal of flexibility. This relatively new fund is strategically positioned to take advantage of economic developments in the "new" Europe.

Portfolio Manager: Jerry Mill
Since: 1988

Minimum:
Initial: $250
Subsequent: $50
Telephone Exchange: Yes
Distributions:
Income: Annually
Capital Gain: Annually
Front-End Load: None
12b-1: None
Redemption Fee: None
Management Company: INVESCO Funds Group
Ticker Symbol: FEURX

TOTAL RETURN (%)

1987	1988	1989	1990	1991	5-year	Bull Market	Bear Market
-4.6	10.6	24.2	0.7	7.9	42.5	4.2	-10.6

INVESTMENT PORTFOLIO

Total Assets (mil.)	Current Yield	Turnover Ratio	Expense Ratio	Beta	Risk Return
$71	3.2%	20%	1.29%	0.66	0.00

FINANCIAL STRATEGIC PACIFIC BASIN

INVESCO Funds Group
P.O. Box 2040
Denver, CO 80201
800-525-8085

Investment Objective: One of 10 series portfolios, this fund seeks capital appreciation by investing in the common stocks of companies domiciled in the following Far Eastern or Far Western Pacific countries: Japan, Australia, Hong Kong, Malaysia, Singapore and the Philippines. The fund also may invest in the securities issued by U.S. companies. While there are no limitations on the percentage of portfolio assets that may be invested in any one country, in recent years, the largest proportion of assets have been invested in companies domiciled in Japan. As a result, performance in recent years has skidded along with the Japanese stock market.

Portfolio Manager: William Keithler
Since: 1986

Minimum:
Initial: $250
Subsequent: $50
Telephone Exchange: Yes
Distributions:
Income: Annually
Capital Gain: Annually
Front-End Load: None
12b-1: None
Redemption Fee: None
Management Company: INVESCO Funds Group
Ticker Symbol: FPBSX

TOTAL RETURN (%)

1987	1988	1989	1990	1991	5-year	Bull Market	Bear Market
9.8	23.2	20.2	-24.4	13.2	39.0	16.3	-25.8

INVESTMENT PORTFOLIO

Total Assets (mil.)	Current Yield	Turnover Ratio	Expense Ratio	Beta	Risk Return
$18	0.8%	93%	1.79%	0.81	0.01

FIRST INVESTORS GLOBAL FUND

First Investors Management
10 Woodbridge Center Drive
Woodbridge, NJ 07095
800-423-4026

Investment Objective: This fund, which began operations in 1981, seeks capital growth primarily by investing in both U.S. and foreign securities. However, no more than 35% of the fund's assets will be allocated to U.S. securities. In making allocations to individual countries, management tends to go where it believes the most undervalued securities are traded. In addition, management tends to concentrate its investments in those countries in which the local currencies are strong. Management's view is toward the longer run and it does not attempt to actively time either short-term market trends or short-term currency trends.

Portfolio Manager: Jerrold Mitchell
Since: 1991

Minimum:
Initial: $200
Subsequent: $50
Telephone Exchange: Yes
Distributions:
Income: Annually
Capital Gain: Annually
Front-End Load: 6.90%
12b-1: 0.30%
Redemption Fee: None
Management Company: Fidelity Management & Research
Ticker Symbol: FIISX

TOTAL RETURN (%)

1987	1988	1989	1990	1991	5-year	Bull Market	Bear Market
28.8	15.8	38.0	-12.2	16.8	111.0	12.1	-21.1

INVESTMENT PORTFOLIO

Total Assets (mil.)	Current Yield	Turnover Ratio	Expense Ratio	Beta	Risk Return
$212	0.0%	116%	1.88%	0.88	0.01

FLAG INVESTORS INTERNATIONAL TRUST

Alex Brown & Sons
135 East Baltimore Street
Baltimore, MD 21202
800-767-3524

Investment Objective: This fund seeks long-term growth of capital primarily through investment in a diversified portfolio of marketable equity securities of issuers domiciled outside of the United States. In making asset selections, management takes a top-down approach, which consists of an evaluation of economic prospects for a geographical region, then the relative economic prospects of industries in those regions and, finally, the characteristics of particular issuers within those industries. Securities of any one issuer are evaluated on the basis of such measures as price-earnings ratios, price-book ratios, cash flow and, incidentally, dividends and interest income.

Portfolio Manager: Chick Hastings
Since: 1991

Minimum:
Initial: $2,000
Subsequent: $500
Telephone Exchange: Yes
Distributions:
Income: Annually
Capital Gain: Annually
Front-End Load: 4.50%
12b-1: 0.25%
Redemption Fee: None
Management Company: Bessemer Trust Company
Ticker Symbol: FLITX

TOTAL RETURN (%)

1987	1988	1989	1990	1991	5-year	Bull Market	Bear Market
11.1	14.4	24.4	-20.0	4.2	31.8	-3.0	-18.0

INVESTMENT PORTFOLIO

Total Assets (mil.)	Current Yield	Turnover Ratio	Expense Ratio	Beta	Risk Return
$36	0.6%	62%	1.50%	0.73	NA

FOUNDERS WORLDWIDE GROWTH FUND

Founders Asset Management
Founders Financial Center
Denver, CO 80206
800-525-2440

Investment Objective: This relatively new fund pursues its capital-appreciation objective through a portfolio of established growth companies. Its major industries, which include business services, food, pharmaceutical, pollution control and telecommunications underscore its growth aspirations. Besides operating in growing markets, most of the fund's companies also boast industry leadership, quality products and good management. Major markets include the United States, the United Kingdom, Switzerland, Germany, France and Norway. Although currently above average, the fund's expense ratio should decline as its asset base grows.

Portfolio Manager: Management team
Since: 1989

Minimum:
Initial: $1,000
Subsequent: $100
Telephone Exchange: Yes
Distributions:
Income: Annually
Capital Gain: Annually
Front-End Load: None
12b-1: 0.20%
Redemption Fee: None
Management Company: Founders Asset Management
Ticker Symbol: FWWGX

TOTAL RETURN (%)

1987	1988	1989	1990	1991	5-year	Bull Market	Bear Market
NA	NA	NA	6.7	34.8	NA	29.1	-8.8

INVESTMENT PORTFOLIO

Total Assets (mil.)	Current Yield	Turnover Ratio	Expense Ratio	Beta	Risk Return
$17	0.2%	170%	2.10%	0.70	0.07

F.T. INTERNATIONAL EQUITY FUND

Federated Securities
Federated Investors Tower
Pittsburgh, PA 15222
800-245-2423

Investment Objective: This fund, established in 1984, seeks to obtain a total return on its assets from a combination of long-term capital growth and income through a balanced portfolio of equity and fixed-income securities of established companies in economically developed countries. The fund seeks to reduce volatility by diversifying broadly among foreign countries with a minimum of 3 different countries being represented. The past year, the fund's portfolio contained investments in 15 countries. Most prominent were investments in Pacific Rim countries, which management believes will benefit from an improving U.S. acumen.

Portfolio Manager: Christopher Wiles
Since: 1990

Minimum:
Initial: $500
Subsequent: $100
Telephone Exchange: Yes
Distributions:
Income: Annually
Capital Gain: Annually
Front-End Load: 4.50%
12b-1: None
Redemption Fee: 0.50%
Management Company: Fiduciary International
Ticker Symbol: FTITX

TOTAL RETURN (%)

1987	1988	1989	1990	1991	5-year	Bull Market	Bear Market
1.4	16.2	18.3	-11.6	7.5	32.5	8.3	-16.9

INVESTMENT PORTFOLIO

Total Assets (mil.)	Current Yield	Turnover Ratio	Expense Ratio	Beta	Risk Return
$103	0.4%	114%	1.32%	0.70	0.01

G.T. EUROPE GROWTH FUND

G.T. Global Financial Services
50 California Street, 27th Floor
San Francisco, CA 94111
800-824-1580

Investment Objective: By concentrating investments in the equity securities of companies domiciled in western Europe, this fund strives to provide long-term capital appreciation to investors. The fund began operations in mid-1985 and has benefited from a weaker dollar during most of its existence. Because of the relatively low correlation of returns of international equities with U.S. stocks, coupling these stocks with U.S. equities can lower portfolio variability. This fund has been one of the best-performing European-oriented portfolios. Although the economies of western Europe stumbled in recent years, the 1990s should be kind to investors who concentrate their international investments in European markets.

Portfolio Manager: John Legat
Since: 1985

Minimum:
Initial: $500
Subsequent: $100
Telephone Exchange: Yes
Distributions:
Income: Annually
Capital Gain: Annually
Front-End Load: 4.75%
12b-1: 0.35%
Redemption Fee: None
Management Company: G.T. Capital Management
Ticker Symbol: GTGEX

TOTAL RETURN (%)

1987	1988	1989	1990	1991	5-year	Bull Market	Bear Market
6.6	11.1	40.7	-14.7	4.3	48.3	-3.0	-19.0

INVESTMENT PORTFOLIO

Total Assets (mil.)	Current Yield	Turnover Ratio	Expense Ratio	Beta	Risk Return
$1,164	1.3%	34%	1.90%	0.79	NA

G.T. GLOBAL GROWTH & INCOME FUND

G.T. Global Financial Services
50 California Street, 27th Floor
San Francisco, CA 94111
800-824-1580

Investment Objective: This new fund offers investors the opportunity to follow the traditional approach of blue chip stocks and bond investing, while choosing securities from all world markets. The fund invests primarily in a blend of global blue chip stocks and government bonds. Fund management is quite risk conscious and seeks to reduce portfolio volatility by diversifying across both markets and industries. Its fixed-income investments consist solely of government guaranteed bonds. In addition, the fund is one of the few that applies a systematic and disciplined approach to currency hedging.

Minimum:
Initial: $500
Subsequent: $100
Telephone Exchange: Yes
Distributions:
Income: Quarterly
Capital Gain: Annually
Front-End Load: 4.75%
12b-1: 0.35%
Redemption Fee: None
Management Company: G.T. Capital Management
Ticker Symbol: GTGIX

Portfolio Manager: Nick Train
Since: 1990

TOTAL RETURN (%)

1987	1988	1989	1990	1991	5-year	Bull Market	Bear Market
NA	NA	NA	NA	19.1	NA	16.3	NA

INVESTMENT PORTFOLIO

Total Assets (mil.)	Current Yield	Turnover Ratio	Expense Ratio	Beta	Risk Return
$75	4.9%	0%	0.54%	0.50	0.04

G.T. GLOBAL HEALTH CARE FUND

G.T. Global Financial Services
50 California Street, 27th Floor
San Francisco, CA 94111
800-824-1580

Investment Objective: G.T. Capital Management, known for its international expertise, created this industry-specific global fund in response to high customer demand. In fact, the fund has already attracted more than half a billion dollars in assets in little more than 2 years. Management searches the world over for promising growth issues in 4 categories: pharmaceutical, health-care service, biotechnology and medical. And although it's still early, the fund offers plenty of potential for aggressive investors as its returns during the past 2 years attest.

Minimum:
Initial: $500
Subsequent: $100
Telephone Exchange: Yes
Distributions:
Income: Annually
Capital Gain: Annually
Front-End Load: 4.75%
12b-1: 0.50%
Redemption Fee: None
Management Company: G.T. Capital Management
Ticker Symbol: GGHCX

Portfolio Manager: Ted Gomoll
Since: 1989

TOTAL RETURN (%)

1987	1988	1989	1990	1991	5-year	Bull Market	Bear Market
NA	NA	NA	13.1	57.9	NA	54.2	-13.0

INVESTMENT PORTFOLIO

Total Assets (mil.)	Current Yield	Turnover Ratio	Expense Ratio	Beta	Risk Return
$558	0.0%	34%	2.39%	1.02	0.10

G.T. INTERNATIONAL GROWTH FUND

G.T. Global Financial Services
50 California Street, 27th Floor
San Francisco, CA 94111
800-824-1580

Investment Objective: This fund seeks capital appreciation by investing in common and preferred stocks of companies domiciled outside the United States. The fund can invest in up to 22 markets around the world, which include the Pacific and European regions and exclude the United States and Canada. Its equity investments in recent years have been concentrated among large cap, blue chip companies. The fund presents an opportunity for equity investors to reduce the volatility of their portfolios by combining a diversified portfolio of foreign stocks with their investments in U.S.-domiciled companies. Currency hedging coupled with disciplined asset selection have produced a steady performance in recent years.

Portfolio Manager: Christian Wignall
Since: 1987

Minimum:
Initial: $500
Subsequent: $100
Telephone Exchange: Yes
Distributions:
Income: Annually
Capital Gain: Annually
Front-End Load: 4.75%
12b-1: 0.35%
Redemption Fee: None
Management Company: G.T. Capital Management
Ticker Symbol: GINGX

TOTAL RETURN (%)

1987	1988	1989	1990	1991	5-year	Bull Market	Bear Market
6.2	19.4	38.6	-14.3	13.2	70.4	11.5	-14.9

INVESTMENT PORTFOLIO

Total Assets (mil.)	Current Yield	Turnover Ratio	Expense Ratio	Beta	Risk Return
$437	1.2%	58%	1.90%	0.62	0.02

G.T. JAPAN GROWTH FUND

G.T. Global Financial Services
50 California Street, 27th Floor
San Francisco, CA 94111
800-824-1580

Investment Objective: This fund aggressively seeks capital appreciation by investing in the stocks of companies domiciled in Japan. As goes the Nikkei Index, so goes the performance of this fund. Its performance in the late 1980s was nothing short of phenomenal. However, a strengthening of the dollar against the yen and a scandal-plagued Tokyo stock market have taken their toll on Japanese stocks in recent years. The Nikkei, for example, has declined by more than 50% during the past 2 years. However, G.T.'s on-site presence in Tokyo provides its managers with economic and political insight that gives the fund an edge over some of its competitors.

Portfolio Manager: Marshall Auerback
Since: 1990

Minimum:
Initial: $500
Subsequent: $100
Telephone Exchange: Yes
Distributions:
Income: Annually
Capital Gain: Annually
Front-End Load: 4.75%
12b-1: 0.35%
Redemption Fee: None
Management Company: G.T. Capital Management
Ticker Symbol: GJGRX

TOTAL RETURN (%)

1987	1988	1989	1990	1991	5-year	Bull Market	Bear Market
52.1	21.9	60.7	-28.7	-2.8	106.4	5.8	-26.0

INVESTMENT PORTFOLIO

Total Assets (mil.)	Current Yield	Turnover Ratio	Expense Ratio	Beta	Risk Return
$63	0.0%	138%	2.20%	0.76	NA

G.T. PACIFIC GROWTH FUND

G.T. Global Services
50 California Street, 27th Floor
San Francisco, CA 94111
800-824-1580

Investment Objective: Through investments in equity securities of companies domiciled in Japan, Southeast Asia and Australia, the fund strives to provide investors with long-term capital growth. Management uses a top-down approach to investing, whereby they first attempt to identify trends and changes in economic factors and then locate specific companies that will be affected by these trends. A major factor that boosted returns from this fund during the late 1980s was the falling value of the dollar. However, tumbling stock prices in the Pacific Rim during 1990 nipped a 5-year string of superior performance. Although the fund possesses a modest beta, its NAV can be highly volatile.

Portfolio Manager: Christian Wignall
Since: 1987

Minimum:
Initial: $500
Subsequent: $100
Telephone Exchange: Yes
Distributions:
Income: Annually
Capital Gain: Annually
Front-End Load: 4.75%
12b-1: 0.35%
Redemption Fee: None
Management Company: G.T. Capital Management
Ticker Symbol: GTPAX

TOTAL RETURN (%)

1987	1988	1989	1990	1991	5-year	Bull Market	Bear Market
5.7	23.2	48.1	-11.0	13.0	94.1	17.1	-16.6

INVESTMENT PORTFOLIO

Total Assets (mil.)	Current Yield	Turnover Ratio	Expense Ratio	Beta	Risk Return
$331	3.4%	75%	2.10%	0.64	0.01

G.T. WORLDWIDE GROWTH FUND

G.T. Global Financial Services
50 California Street, 27th Floor
San Francisco, CA 94111
800-824-1580

Investment Objective: The most broadly defined of G.T. global growth funds, this fund attempts to capitalize on worldwide structural changes. While the world's largest markets—the United States and Japan—are most heavily represented, the fund makes plenty of room for emerging-growth, secondary markets such as Singapore and Mexico as well as European markets such as Germany and France—obvious beneficiaries of German reunification. Unsurprisingly, this relatively bold fund felt the full blow of 1990's bear market, illustrating that it's not for the faint of heart. Patient risk-tolerant investors, however, can expect to be rewarded with above-average returns over time.

Portfolio Manager: Christian Wignall
Since: 1987

Minimum:
Initial: $500
Subsequent: $100
Telephone Exchange: Yes
Distributions:
Income: Annually
Capital Gain: Annually
Front-End Load: 4.75%
12b-1: 0.35%
Redemption Fee: None
Management Company: G.T. Capital Management
Ticker Symbol: GTWGX

TOTAL RETURN (%)

1987	1988	1989	1990	1991	5-year	Bull Market	Bear Market
NA	16.3	37.6	-12.5	20.3	NA	21.6	-19.1

INVESTMENT PORTFOLIO

Total Assets (mil.)	Current Yield	Turnover Ratio	Expense Ratio	Beta	Risk Return
$118	1.0%	107%	2.10%	0.81	0.03

IAI INTERNATIONAL FUND

Investment Advisers
1100 Dain Tower, P.O. Box 357
Minneapolis, MN 55440
800-945-3863

Investment Objective: Like its domestic siblings, this fund is guided by a value orientation. Its country exposures are a residual of its strength and potential earnings growth, not a reflection of its top-down views. Compared to the average international fund, it is likely to have greater exposure to unpopular bourses at the expense of high-expectation markets. For example, it emphasizes the troubled markets of the United Kingdom and Australia. Such contrarian tactics may prevent it from leading the charts in a speculative bull market, but they should allow the fund to build a solid track record over time with less volatility than more conventional rivals.

Portfolio Manager: Roy Gillson
Since: 1990

Minimum:
Initial: $5,000
Subsequent: $100
Telephone Exchange: No
Distributions:
Income: Semiannually
Capital Gain: Annually
Front-End Load: None
12b-1: 0.28%
Redemption Fee: None
Management Company: Investment Advisers
Ticker Symbol: IAINX

TOTAL RETURN (%)

1987	1988	1989	1990	1991	5-year	Bull Market	Bear Market
NA	18.0	18.2	-13.1	16.6	NA	13.4	-12.7

INVESTMENT PORTFOLIO

Total Assets (mil.)	Current Yield	Turnover Ratio	Expense Ratio	Beta	Risk Return
$35	1.9%	41%	1.73%	0.63	0.02

IDS INTERNATIONAL FUND

IDS Financial Services
1000 Roanoke Building
Minneapolis, MN 55402
800-328-8300

Investment Objective: This fund seeks capital appreciation primarily by investing in the common stocks of foreign issuers. The goal is to produce returns that exceed that of the EAFE Index. Management may invest up to 20% of its assets in U.S. securities. Management also may invest in bonds issued or guaranteed by countries that are members of the Organization for Economic Cooperation and Development. Ordinarily, the fund will invest in companies domiciled in at least 3 foreign countries. In recent years, the majority of its assets have been allocated to investments in developed countries. The management team, based in London, has been together since the fund began operations in 1984.

Portfolio Manager: Peter L. Lamaison
Since: 1984

Minimum:
Initial: $2,000
Subsequent: $100
Telephone Exchange: Yes
Distributions:
Income: Annually
Capital Gain: Annually
Front-End Load: 5.00%
12b-1: 0.12%
Redemption Fee: None
Management Company: IDS Financial Services
Ticker Symbol: INIFX

TOTAL RETURN (%)

1987	1988	1989	1990	1991	5-year	Bull Market	Bear Market
0.0	12.8	18.2	-6.2	11.8	39.8	8.5	-16.1

INVESTMENT PORTFOLIO

Total Assets (mil.)	Current Yield	Turnover Ratio	Expense Ratio	Beta	Risk Return
$225	0.5%	98%	1.35%	0.67	0.01

IDS STRATEGY WORLDWIDE GROWTH FUND

IDS Financial Services
1000 Roanoke Building
Minneapolis, MN 55402
800-328-8300

Investment Objective: This relatively new fund invests at least 50% of its assets in the equity securities of firms located in Pacific Basin countries. The fund also can invest in foreign or domestic corporate or government bonds. To hedge against uncertainty in future exchange rates, the fund engages in foreign-exchange transactions, such as forward contracts. However, no more than 15% of the fund's assets may be used for this hedging technique. Since its inception, the fund has been a lackluster performer as a combination of higher interest rates and volatile dollars have siphoned off potential returns.

Minimum:
Initial: $2,000
Subsequent: $100
Telephone Exchange: Yes
Distributions:
Income: Annually
Capital Gain: Annually
Front-End Load: None
12b-1: 0.97%
Redemption Fee: 5.00%
Management Company: IDS Financial Services
Ticker Symbol: IWWGX

Portfolio Manager: Peter L. Lamaison
Since: 1991

TOTAL RETURN (%)

1987	1988	1989	1990	1991	5-year	Bull Market	Bear Market
NA	11.6	12.3	-13.5	9.6	NA	9.4	-23.1

INVESTMENT PORTFOLIO

Total Assets (mil.)	Current Yield	Turnover Ratio	Expense Ratio	Beta	Risk Return
$40	0.5%	91%	2.47%	0.83	0.01

IVY INTERNATIONAL FUND

Mackenzie Investment Management
P.O. Box 5007
Boca Raton, FL 33431
800-235-3322

Investment Objective: Ivy International Fund proves that slow and steady wins the race. The fund, which selects investments from the bottom up, takes a patient, long-term approach to investing. Its search for stocks that sell at a discount to their underlying fundamentals prevents it from chasing hot markets and sectors. Since its 1986 inception, the fund has greatly underweighted Japan, while overweighting cheaper bourses, including the United Kingdom, France and Spain. So far, its contrarian tactics have produced highly competitive results. The fund was sold to Mackenzie Investment Management the past year and a front-end load sales charge was adopted.

Minimum:
Initial: $1,000
Subsequent: $100
Telephone Exchange: Yes
Distributions:
Income: Annually
Capital Gain: Annually
Front-End Load: 5.75%
12b-1: 0.25%
Redemption Fee: None
Management Company: Ivy Management
Ticker Symbol: IVINX

Portfolio Manager: Hakan Castegren
Since: 1986

TOTAL RETURN (%)

1987	1988	1989	1990	1991	5-year	Bull Market	Bear Market
19.6	29.7	28.2	-12.9	16.9	102.5	13.6	-17.6

INVESTMENT PORTFOLIO

Total Assets (mil.)	Current Yield	Turnover Ratio	Expense Ratio	Beta	Risk Return
$94	1.3%	29%	1.66%	0.73	0.02

JAPAN FUND

Scudder Stevens & Clark
175 Federal Street, 12th Floor
Boston, MA 02110
800-225-5084

Investment Objective: This fund, which operated as a closed-end fund prior to August of 1987, seeks capital appreciation by investing in securities of companies that have either 50% or more of their assets in Japan or derive 50% or more of their revenues from Japan. As expected, a plunging Nikkei has taken its toll on recent fund performance. However, the fund's defensive cash position and heavy investment in small to medium cap issues have shielded its share price from the full brunt of the collapse in speculative Japanese stocks. With the Nikkei recently trading more than 50% below its all-time high, Tokyo stocks are more reasonably valued. That should bode well for this well-managed single-country fund.

Portfolio Manager: O. Robert Theurkauf
Since: 1990

Minimum:
Initial: $1,000
Subsequent: $100
Telephone Exchange: Yes
Distributions:
Income: Annually
Capital Gain: Annually
Front-End Load: None
12b-1: None
Redemption Fee: None
Management Company: Asia Management
Ticker Symbol: SJPNX

TOTAL RETURN (%)

1987	1988	1989	1990	1991	5-year	Bull Market	Bear Market
33.0	19.5	11.6	-16.4	3.1	52.9	3.9	-14.8

INVESTMENT PORTFOLIO

Total Assets (mil.)	Current Yield	Turnover Ratio	Expense Ratio	Beta	Risk Return
$331	0.0%	53%	1.05%	0.47	NA

KEMPER INTERNATIONAL FUND

Kemper Financial Services
120 South LaSalle Street
Chicago, IL 60603
800-621-1048

Investment Objective: The objective of this fund is total return through investments in stocks of foreign companies. The fund does, however, also have the option of investing in U.S. companies. Although the fund cushioned 1990's international blow by losing just 7%, it fell below the average of the past year's international offerings with its low 9.1% return. Potential investors also should take note that this Kemper fund carries a 5.75% front-end load.

Portfolio Manager: Gordon Wilson
Since: 1989

Minimum:
Initial: $1,000
Subsequent: $100
Telephone Exchange: Yes
Distributions:
Income: Annually
Capital Gain: Annually
Front-End Load: 5.75%
12b-1: None
Redemption Fee: None
Management Company: Kemper Financial Services
Ticker Symbol: KMIFX

TOTAL RETURN (%)

1987	1988	1989	1990	1991	5-year	Bull Market	Bear Market
6.5	17.3	18.6	-7.5	9.1	49.4	8.5	-16.1

INVESTMENT PORTFOLIO

Total Assets (mil.)	Current Yield	Turnover Ratio	Expense Ratio	Beta	Risk Return
$172	0.6%	191%	1.20%	0.64	0.01

KEYSTONE INTERNATIONAL FUND

Keystone Distributors
99 High Street
Boston, MA 02110
800-633-4900

Investment Objective: Through investment in the securities of companies located in both the United States and foreign nations, the fund seeks long-term growth of capital for its investors. While the fund turned in solid performance numbers during 1986, it has been a below-par performer through 1990. Its overexposure to the Japanese market caused the fund to tumble more than 24%, making it one of the worst in the group. However, the fund staged a bit of a rebound by returning more than 14% in 1991. In addition to a maximum redemption charge of 4.00%, the fund possesses a relatively high 12b-1 charge that could impair long-term returns.

Portfolio Manager: Gilman Gunn
Since: 1991

Minimum:
Initial: $1,000
Subsequent: None
Telephone Exchange: Yes
Distributions:
Income: Annually
Capital Gain: Annually
Front-End Load: None
12b-1: 1.03%
Redemption Fee: 4.00%
Management Company: Keystone Advisers
Ticker Symbol: KESTX

TOTAL RETURN (%)

1987	1988	1989	1990	1991	5-year	Bull Market	Bear Market
9.0	16.8	4.3	-24.0	14.2	15.2	8.3	-15.2

INVESTMENT PORTFOLIO

Total Assets (mil.)	Current Yield	Turnover Ratio	Expense Ratio	Beta	Risk Return
$65	3.9%	42%	2.92%	0.70	0.01

KLEINWORTH BENSON INTERNATIONAL EQUITY FUND

Kleinworth Benson International Investment
200 Park Avenue, 24th Floor
New York, NY 10166
800-233-9164

Investment Objective: Using a top-down approach and investing completely outside of the U.S. market, the fund has enjoyed decent returns for much of the past 5 years. A hefty concentration in industrial goods—seemingly at odds with the consumer-growth-led U.S. market—has powered the fund higher. Aided, of course, by a falling dollar in 1986, the fund continued streaking forward in 1987 and 1988, as foreign machinery, construction and capital-goods stocks marched higher. The fund was hurt more than most in 1990 because of its many cyclical stocks, but 1991 saw it regain some momentum with a slightly subpar 12% return. The fund does offer an attractive yield to investors.

Portfolio Manager: John Trott
Since: 1987

Minimum:
Initial: $1,000
Subsequent: $100
Telephone Exchange: Yes
Distributions:
Income: Annually
Capital Gain: Semiannually
Front-End Load: None
12b-1: 0.10%
Redemption Fee: None
Management Company: Kleinworth Benson International
Ticker Symbol: KBIEX

TOTAL RETURN (%)

1987	1988	1989	1990	1991	5-year	Bull Market	Bear Market
9.3	21.0	23.0	-14.8	11.8	55.0	13.4	-19.2

INVESTMENT PORTFOLIO

Total Assets (mil.)	Current Yield	Turnover Ratio	Expense Ratio	Beta	Risk Return
$68	4.1%	52%	1.82%	0.78	0.01

LEXINGTON GLOBAL FUND

Lexington Funds Distributor
P.O. Box 1515
Saddle Brook, NJ 07662
800-526-0056

Investment Objective: This fund offers a fairly traditional global portfolio. Stressing blue chip companies, the fund concentrates on identifying global trends and their potential benefits. Although the fund may invest in developing countries, it can place no more than 65% of its assets in any one country. Also, at least 4 countries must be represented in the portfolio. Major markets currently include the United States, Japan, the United Kingdom, France and Germany. Long-term returns shouldn't stray too far from international-fund averages.

Minimum:
Initial: $1,000
Subsequent: $50
Telephone Exchange: Yes
Distributions:
Income: Annually
Capital Gain: Annually
Front-End Load: None
12b-1: None
Redemption Fee: None
Management Company: Lexington Management
Ticker Symbol: LXGLX

Portfolio Manager: Caesar Bryan
Since: 1987

TOTAL RETURN (%)

1987	1988	1989	1990	1991	5-year	Bull Market	Bear Market
NA	16.3	25.1	-16.7	15.5	NA	16.0	-16.7

INVESTMENT PORTFOLIO

Total Assets (mil.)	Current Yield	Turnover Ratio	Expense Ratio	Beta	Risk Return
$51	2.4%	82%	1.59%	0.80	0.02

LEXINGTON WORLDWIDE EMERGING MARKETS

Lexington Funds Distributor
P.O. Box 1515
Saddle Brook, NJ 07662
800-526-0056

Investment Objective: This fund seeks long-term growth of capital by investing in what management considers emerging countries. By the adviser's definition, an emerging country is one in which the gross national product per capita is less than $6,000. The fund also invests in emerging markets that it defines as those security markets not currently being one of the largest 4. This fund is the former Lexington Growth Fund and offers ample growth opportunity, but with significant risk. The past year the fund returned an above-average 24.2%

Minimum:
Initial: $1,000
Subsequent: $50
Telephone Exchange: Yes
Distributions:
Income: Annually
Capital Gain: Annually
Front-End Load: None
12b-1: None
Redemption Fee: None
Management Company: Lexington Management
Ticker Symbol: LEXGX

Portfolio Manager: William Stack
Since: 1991

TOTAL RETURN (%)

1987	1988	1989	1990	1991	5-year	Bull Market	Bear Market
0.2	10.5	28.1	-14.4	24.2	50.8	34.9	-24.3

INVESTMENT PORTFOLIO

Total Assets (mil.)	Current Yield	Turnover Ratio	Expense Ratio	Beta	Risk Return
$24	1.0%	52%	1.42%	0.98	0.04

MACKENZIE CANADA FUND

Mackenzie Investment Management
P.O. Box 5007
Boca Raton, FL 33431
800-456-5111

Investment Objective: As one of the premier investment houses in Canada, Mackenzie Investment Management is in a good position to manage this Canadian portfolio successfully. However, the road has been a bit rocky. Despite using a value strategy of selecting low-price/earnings and low-price/book stocks, the fund failed to live up to expectations in 1988's value-driven market: It rose only 6%. Again in 1989, the fund lagged not only the U.S. market by a wide margin but also its international peers. The past 2 years also have been tough as the fund lost 21% in 1990 and 8% in 1991. The past year's results placed it second to last on our international-fund list.

Portfolio Manager: Investment Committee
Since: 1987

Minimum:
Initial: $250
Subsequent: $50
Telephone Exchange: Yes
Distributions:
Income: Annually
Capital Gain: Annually
Front-End Load: 5.75%
12b-1: 0.40%
Redemption Fee: None
Management Company: Mackenzie Investment Management
Ticker Symbol: MCCNX

TOTAL RETURN (%)

1987	1988	1989	1990	1991	5-year	Bull Market	Bear Market
NA	NA	10.0	-21.1	-8.0	NA	-6.6	-9.0

INVESTMENT PORTFOLIO

Total Assets (mil.)	Current Yield	Turnover Ratio	Expense Ratio	Beta	Risk Return
$13	0.0%	4%	2.78%	0.32	NA

MAINSTAY GLOBAL FUND

NYLIFE Securities
51 Madison Avenue
New York, NY 10010
800-522-4202

Investment Objective: Up until 1991, this fund has been a disappointment. However, a new adviser has come on the scene and helped salvage a 12.5% gain for the year. The fund has many investment options, including a low required foreign allocation (only 25%). The fund's commitment to U.S. stocks enabled it to offset some of the international turmoil many funds were exposed to in 1991. High expenses and a redemption fee, however, may cause investors to look elsewhere.

Portfolio Manager: L. Debenham/D. Finning
Since: 1987

Minimum:
Initial: $500
Subsequent: $50
Telephone Exchange: Yes
Distributions:
Income: Annually
Capital Gain: Annually
Front-End Load: None
12b-1: 1.00%
Redemption Fee: 5.00%
Management Company: Quorum Capital Management
Ticker Symbol: MKGLX

TOTAL RETURN (%)

1987	1988	1989	1990	1991	5-year	Bull Market	Bear Market
NA	7.1	8.6	-12.0	12.5	NA	11.1	-17.0

INVESTMENT PORTFOLIO

Total Assets (mil.)	Current Yield	Turnover Ratio	Expense Ratio	Beta	Risk Return
$20	0.0%	201%	3.40%	0.74	0.01

MERRILL LYNCH INTERNATIONAL HOLDINGS A

Merrill Lynch Funds Distributor
P.O. Box 9011
Princeton, NJ 08543
800-637-3863

Investment Objective: This fund, with a 6.50% sales charge, invests in well-established, large cap growth stocks in the United States and abroad. The fund performed reasonably well over the years, propelled mostly by a declining dollar and investors' preference for larger firms. In 1989, for example, the fund mirrored the international indexes with a 23% return. However, as 1990's mediocre 9.2% loss attests, a falling dollar cannot always protect the fund from investment losses. The fund did bounce back with an above-average 1991 return of 17% and its 5-year return remains above that of the crowd.

Portfolio Manager: Frederick Ives
Since: 1985

Minimum:
Initial: $1,000
Subsequent: $50
Telephone Exchange: No
Distributions:
Income: Semiannually
Capital Gain: Annually
Front-End Load: 6.50%
12b-1: None
Redemption Fee: None
Management Company: Merrill Lynch Asset Management
Ticker Symbol: MLHDX

TOTAL RETURN (%)

1987	1988	1989	1990	1991	5-year	Bull Market	Bear Market
6.5	10.0	23.5	-9.2	17.1	54.0	12.6	-14.4

INVESTMENT PORTFOLIO

Total Assets (mil.)	Current Yield	Turnover Ratio	Expense Ratio	Beta	Risk Return
$166	1.0%	34%	1.59%	0.79	0.02

MERRILL LYNCH PACIFIC FUND A

Merrill Lynch Funds Distributor
P.O. Box 9011
Princeton, NJ 08543
800-637-3863

Investment Objective: This fund invests in stocks of companies domiciled in Japan, Australia, Hong Kong and Singapore. It possesses a concentrated geographic portfolio and, thus, is more risky than international funds with wider geographic diversification. The fund has performed exceptionally well during the past 5 years, even when including the portfolio's 7.9% drop in 1990. Heavy allocation to the Hong Kong market and cash helped plug the potential losses seen on the Tokyo exchange. Pacific market returns may be moderate in coming years as growth slows; however, the fund shows no signs of letting up in 1991 as it returned 17%.

Portfolio Manager: Stephen Silverman
Since: 1983

Minimum:
Initial: $250
Subsequent: $50
Telephone Exchange: No
Distributions:
Income: Annually
Capital Gain: Annually
Front-End Load: 6.50%
12b-1: None
Redemption Fee: None
Management Company: Merrill Lynch Asset Management
Ticker Symbol: MLPAX

TOTAL RETURN (%)

1987	1988	1989	1990	1991	5-year	Bull Market	Bear Market
10.7	34.5	14.5	-7.9	17.0	83.7	16.4	-3.3

INVESTMENT PORTFOLIO

Total Assets (mil.)	Current Yield	Turnover Ratio	Expense Ratio	Beta	Risk Return
$295	2.1%	31%	1.07%	0.32	0.02

MFS LIFETIME GLOBAL EQUITY TRUST

Massachusetts Financial Services
500 Boylston
Boston, MA 02116
800-225-2606

Investment Objective: This international vehicle invests with a value orientation, contrasting with the growth bias of many of its peers. Stocks with reasonable price/earnings and price/book ratios abound in the portfolio. The fund gears itself to modestly priced industrial, conglomerate and capital-goods stocks from the United States and Europe. In 1987, this strategy worked like a charm, as the fund soared 32.4% in the face of the October market plunge. Lately, the fund has been unpredictable, with 1988— a value year—a disappointment and 1989 a surprise. In 1990, the fund held on better than its peers, but it had a subpar 1991. As a defensive move, the fund may invest 100% of its assets in the United States or Canada.

Portfolio Manager: Nancy Langwiser
Since: 1987

Minimum:
Initial: $1,000
Subsequent: $50
Telephone Exchange: Yes
Distributions:
Income: Annually
Capital Gain: Annually
Front-End Load: None
12b-1: 1.00%
Redemption Fee: 6.00%
Management Company: Lifetime Advisors
Ticker Symbol: LGETX

TOTAL RETURN (%)

1987	1988	1989	1990	1991	5-year	Bull Market	Bear Market
32.4	0.8	27.5	-4.7	7.3	74.1	5.5	-11.0

INVESTMENT PORTFOLIO

Total Assets (mil.)	Current Yield	Turnover Ratio	Expense Ratio	Beta	Risk Return
$83	0.0%	173%	3.14%	0.63	0.00

NATIONAL WORLDWIDE OPPORTUNITY

NSR Distributors
2 Pickwick Plaza
Greenwich, CT 06830
800-356-5535

Investment Objective: This fund, which previously operated as an aggressive growth domestic vehicle, changed its investment objectives during 1990. In keeping with its new global orientation, the fund now relies on a moderate value discipline to invest in a mix of large and small stocks of both foreign and domestic issuers. Although the fund has yet to prove itself as a global vehicle, its subpar 1986 and 1990 results owe to its once significant exposure to small capitalization stocks, which underperformed blue chips for most of the past decade. However, this strategy paid off handsomely in 1991, as the fund returned an excellent 24%.

Portfolio Manager: J. Dorey/R. Rawe
Since: 1990

Minimum:
Initial: $1,500
Subsequent: $50
Telephone Exchange: Yes
Distributions:
Income: Annually
Capital Gain: Annually
Front-End Load: 5.75%
12b-1: 0.30%
Redemption Fee: None
Management Company: National Securities & Research
Ticker Symbol: NWWOX

TOTAL RETURN (%)

1987	1988	1989	1990	1991	5-year	Bull Market	Bear Market
-3.4	11.1	9.1	-22.6	24.4	12.7	26.1	-19.8

INVESTMENT PORTFOLIO

Total Assets (mil.)	Current Yield	Turnover Ratio	Expense Ratio	Beta	Risk Return
$65	0.1%	119%	1.33%	0.94	0.05

NEW PERSPECTIVE FUND

American Funds Distributor
333 South Hope Street, 52nd Floor
Los Angeles, CA 90071
800-421-9900

Investment Objective: This fund relies on a patient value discipline to ensure competitive results in most markets. Typically, it purchases its quality companies when they are misunderstood by the market and selling cheaply. It then waits patiently for the market to recognize their true worth. Like most price-conscious global investors, the fund has greatly underweighted Japan in recent years in favor of the smaller Far Eastern markets, the United States and continental Europe. That the fund's patient, often-contrarian approach results in minimal risk relative to other global funds is seen in its good resistance to decline in the past year's bear market and in its above-average returns in 1991.

Portfolio Manager: Multiple Portfolio Counselors
Since: 1990

Minimum:
Initial: $250
Subsequent: $50
Telephone Exchange: Yes
Distributions:
Income: Semiannually
Capital Gain: Annually
Front-End Load: 5.75%
12b-1: 0.15%
Redemption Fee: None
Management Company: Capital Research & Management
Ticker Symbol: ANWPX

TOTAL RETURN (%)

1987	1988	1989	1990	1991	5-year	Bull Market	Bear Market
13.5	10.4	25.9	-2.1	22.6	89.4	22.6	-15.9

INVESTMENT PORTFOLIO

Total Assets (mil.)	Current Yield	Turnover Ratio	Expense Ratio	Beta	Risk Return
$2,257	2.0%	14%	0.82%	0.79	0.04

NOMURA PACIFIC BASIN FUND

Nomura Securities
180 Maiden Lane
New York, NY 10038
800-833-0018

Investment Objective: Until recently, it paid big dividends to invest in Japan. This fund aptly demonstrates this point; in its first 4 years, it achieved double-digit annual returns, including a phenomenal 75% gain in 1986. Nonetheless, this fund is not for lightweights, as 1990's negative 15.3% pounding attests. Investors must ante up $10,000 to enter the portfolio, thus limiting its appeal to smaller investors, though its no-load design is attractive. Investors who believe that the Pacific Rim will again lead the international markets should consider this fund.

Portfolio Manager: Takeo Nakamura
Since: 1985

Minimum:
Initial: $10,000
Subsequent: $5,000
Telephone Exchange: No
Distributions:
Income: Semianually
Capital Gain: Semiannually
Front-End Load: None
12b-1: None
Redemption Fee: None
Management Company: Nomura Capital Management
Ticker Symbol: NPBFX

TOTAL RETURN (%)

1987	1988	1989	1990	1991	5-year	Bull Market	Bear Market
33.4	16.4	22.7	-15.3	11.7	80.3	15.0	-1.04

INVESTMENT PORTFOLIO

Total Assets (mil.)	Current Yield	Turnover Ratio	Expense Ratio	Beta	Risk Return
$50	3.5%	76%	1.42%	0.58	0.01

OPPENHEIMER GLOBAL FUND

Oppenheimer Fund Management
P.O. Box 300
Denver, CO 80201
800-255-2755

Investment Objective: This fund seeks capital appreciation by investing in worldwide growth companies. The fund has been riding a prolonged hot streak as it ranks in the top 10 for 1-year, 3-year and 5-year performance. Returns have been consistently above average, with 1991's 27.4% return being no exception. Even during 1990's international free-fall, this fund barely lost any ground. The only drawback is the hefty front-end load charged by Oppenheimer. Otherwise, this offering is first-rate.

Portfolio Manager: Kenneth Oberman
Since: 1981

Minimum:
Initial: $1,000
Subsequent: $25
Telephone Exchange: Yes
Distributions:
Income: Annually
Capital Gain: Annually
Front-End Load: 5.75%
12b-1: 0.25%
Redemption Fee: None
Management Company: Oppenheimer Management
Ticker Symbol: OPPAX

TOTAL RETURN (%)

1987	1988	1989	1990	1991	5-year	Bull Market	Bear Market
-3.5	23.0	35.0	-0.7	27.4	102.8	21.2	-17.4

INVESTMENT PORTFOLIO

Total Assets (mil.)	Current Yield	Turnover Ratio	Expense Ratio	Beta	Risk Return
$1,062	0.3%	27%	1.68%	0.75	0.04

PAINEWEBBER ATLAS GLOBAL GROWTH FUND A

PaineWebber
1285 Avenue of the Americas
New York, NY 10019
800-647-1568

Investment Objective: Among the most innovative of international funds, PaineWebber Atlas stresses pure growth. Most of its companies operate in rapidly growing industries and/or markets, show good earnings momentum and are poised to benefit from macroeconomic, political and/or industry trends. Some also represent undervalued assets. Further distinguishing the fund from most rivals is its willingness to diverge from conventional, world-index country weightings. Both its long-term returns and risks have been quite competitive.

Portfolio Manager: Nimrod Fachler
Since: 1986

Minimum:
Initial: $1,000
Subsequent: $100
Telephone Exchange: No
Distributions:
Income: Annually
Capital Gain: Annually
Front-End Load: 4.50%
12b-1: 0.18%
Redemption Fee: None
Management Company: Mitchell Hutchins Asset Management
Ticker Symbol: PAGAX

TOTAL RETURN (%)

1987	1988	1989	1990	1991	5-year	Bull Market	Bear Market
6.6	19.9	20.0	-7.6	9.4	54.9	9.4	-14.2

INVESTMENT PORTFOLIO

Total Assets (mil.)	Current Yield	Turnover Ratio	Expense Ratio	Beta	Risk Return
$197	1.4%	65%	1.49%	0.65	0.01

PRINCOR WORLD FUND

Princor Financial Services
711 High Street
Des Moines, IA 50309
800-247-4123

Investment Objective: This fund seeks capital appreciation by investing in a portfolio of equities of companies domiciled anywhere in the world. The fund intends to have at least 65% of its assets invested in 3 countries (the United States included) at all times. The fund has an unenviable 5-year record that mainly reflects 1987–1989. In the past 2 years, returns have been slightly above average. Whether this is a trend or not will have to be seen. Investors must pay a 5.00% load and are subjected to a 12b-1 fee.

Minimum:
Initial: $300
Subsequent: $25
Telephone Exchange: Yes
Distributions:
Income: Annually
Capital Gain: Annually
Front-End Load: 5.00%
12b-1: 0.20%
Redemption Fee: None
Management Company: Principal Management
Ticker Symbol: PRWLX

Portfolio Manager: Dan Jaworski
Since: 1989

TOTAL RETURN (%)

1987	1988	1989	1990	1991	5-year	Bull Market	Bear Market
-18.9	20.3	14.7	-9.5	15.2	16.6	15.3	-18.1

INVESTMENT PORTFOLIO

Total Assets (mil.)	Current Yield	Turnover Ratio	Expense Ratio	Beta	Risk Return
$27	1.2%	38%	1.79%	0.71	0.02

PUTNAM GLOBAL GROWTH FUND

Putnam Financial Services
One Post Office Square
Boston, MA 02109
800-634-1590

Investment Objective: This fund searches the world over for growth-oriented common stocks, including the United States. With more than $600 million in total assets, it possesses a relatively high portfolio turnover rate as it shifts into and out of various markets. However, it has been a respectable performer during the past 5 years. This fund's relatively large asset base and proclivity for high turnover necessitates a large cap bias; it must avoid low-liquidity small cap issues. The fund's modest beta of 0.77 is due more to the low correlation between international investment returns and the U.S. market than its large cap holdings.

Minimum:
Initial: $500
Subsequent: $50
Telephone Exchange: Yes
Distributions:
Income: Annually
Capital Gain: Annually
Front-End Load: 5.75%
12b-1: 0.25%
Redemption Fee: None
Management Company: Putnam Management
Ticker Symbol: PEQUX

Portfolio Manager: Tony Regan
Since: 1988

TOTAL RETURN (%)

1987	1988	1989	1990	1991	5-year	Bull Market	Bear Market
7.2	9.0	24.6	-9.2	18.0	56.0	19.4	-18.2

INVESTMENT PORTFOLIO

Total Assets (mil.)	Current Yield	Turnover Ratio	Expense Ratio	Beta	Risk Return
$603	1.4%	95%	1.44%	0.77	0.03

SCUDDER GLOBAL

Scudder Stevens & Clark
175 Federal Street, 12th Floor
Boston, MA 02110
800-225-2470

Investment Objective: This international fund seeks long-term growth by investing primarily in the equity securities of both domestic and foreign firms. While the fund generally invests in established companies whose stocks are listed on major stock exchanges, it also may invest in over-the-counter securities. The fund is relatively new (it began operations in 1986), but it has performed reasonably well during the past 5 years. Although most overseas stock markets tanked in 1990, this fund posted a modest 6.4% loss thanks to significant investments in U.S. stocks. The past year the fund returned an above-average 17%.

Portfolio Manager: W. Holzer/C. Franklin
Since: 1986

Minimum:
Initial: $1,000
Subsequent: $500
Telephone Exchange: Yes
Distributions:
Income: Annually
Capital Gain: Annually
Front-End Load: None
12b-1: None
Redemption Fee: None
Management Company: Scudder Stevens & Clark
Ticker Symbol: SCOBX

TOTAL RETURN (%)

1987	1988	1989	1990	1991	5-year	Bull Market	Bear Market
-0.3	23.3	37.4	-6.4	17.0	85.0	13.9	-12.6

INVESTMENT PORTFOLIO

Total Assets (mil.)	Current Yield	Turnover Ratio	Expense Ratio	Beta	Risk Return
$290	1.6%	38%	1.81%	0.75	0.02

SCUDDER INTERNATIONAL FUND

Scudder Stevens & Clark
175 Federal Street, 12th Floor
Boston, MA 02110
800-225-2470

Investment Objective: This no-load fund seeks long-term capital growth by investing in foreign securities. The fund has provided better-than-average investment returns during the past 5 years. Like many international funds, a great deal of its success can be attributed to the plummeting U.S. dollar. Given that the world economy will continue to grow at a sluggish pace and that the value of the U.S. dollar has begun to stabilize, future investment returns may not mirror those of the recent past. However, this fund plans on a rebound in the Pacific Rim and a pickup in the European economy.

Portfolio Manager: Nicholas Bratt
Since: 1986

Minimum:
Initial: $1,000
Subsequent: $500
Telephone Exchange: Yes
Distributions:
Income: Annually
Capital Gain: Annually
Front-End Load: None
12b-1: None
Redemption Fee: None
Management Company: Scudder Stevens & Clark
Ticker Symbol: SCINX

TOTAL RETURN (%)

1987	1988	1989	1990	1991	5-year	Bull Market	Bear Market
0.9	18.8	27.0	-8.9	11.8	55.0	7.5	-15.7

INVESTMENT PORTFOLIO

Total Assets (mil.)	Current Yield	Turnover Ratio	Expense Ratio	Beta	Risk Return
$927	0.0%	70%	1.24%	0.68	0.01

SHEARSON GLOBAL OPPORTUNITIES

Shearson Lehman Brothers
Two World Trade Center
New York, NY 10048
800-451-2010

Investment Objective: This fund's growth-oriented investment style has been alternately blessed and betrayed. After storming into the mid-1980s with a 30% return in 1986, the fund has since struggled. It plunged 9.5% in 1987, followed by a sluggish gain of 8.6% in 1988. The fund's growth bias was mostly to blame, as such stocks fared poorly during the October, 1987, crash and rebounded only modestly the following year. After slogging through 1989 with a below-average return, the fund was whipsawed by 1990's difficult market. Five-year returns fall well short of the average international fund despite 1991's middle-of-the-pack performance.

Portfolio Manager: Nittin Mehta
Since: 1990

Minimum:
Initial: $500
Subsequent: $200
Telephone Exchange: No
Distributions:
Income: Annually
Capital Gain: Annually
Front-End Load: 5.00%
12b-1: None
Redemption Fee: None
Management Company: S. L. Global Asset Management
Ticker Symbol: SHRGX

TOTAL RETURN (%)

1987	1988	1989	1990	1991	5-year	Bull Market	Bear Market
-9.5	8.6	18.4	-11.3	12.6	16.3	13.8	-15.6

INVESTMENT PORTFOLIO

Total Assets (mil.)	Current Yield	Turnover Ratio	Expense Ratio	Beta	Risk Return
$53	0.0%	54%	1.51%	0.71	0.01

SHEARSON INTERNATIONAL EQUITY PORTFOLIO

Shearson Lehman Brothers
Two World Trade Center
New York, NY 10048
800-451-2010

Investment Objective: In its short life, this fund hasn't yet struck gold. Panning foreign markets for growth-oriented stocks hasn't been the boon the fund first anticipated. After taking it on the chin in 1987, when the fund dropped more than 6%, returns have been stuck in low gear. A 30+% weighting in Japan hurt in both 1989 and 1990, as the market rose only marginally in 1989 and plunged nearly 37% in 1990 (on a dollar-adjusted basis). A high expense ratio of 2.78% hasn't helped either, and investors also must note the redemption charge of 5.00%. This fund will need a few years of respectable performance before we jump on its bandwagon.

Portfolio Manager: N. Mehta/E. Stock
Since: 1990

Minimum:
Initial: $500
Subsequent: $200
Telephone Exchange: No
Distributions:
Income: Annually
Capital Gain: Annually
Front-End Load: None
12b-1: 1.00%
Redemption Fee: 5.00%
Management Company: S. L. Global Asset Management
Ticker Symbol: SHIEX

TOTAL RETURN (%)

1987	1988	1989	1990	1991	5-year	Bull Market	Bear Market
-6.3	10.9	17.1	-10.6	7.8	17.3	12.9	-14.2

INVESTMENT PORTFOLIO

Total Assets (mil.)	Current Yield	Turnover Ratio	Expense Ratio	Beta	Risk Return
$34	0.0%	92%	2.78%	0.64	0.00

SOGEN INTERNATIONAL FUND

SoGen Securities
50 Rockefeller Plaza, 2nd Floor
New York, NY 10020
800-334-2143

Investment Objective: SoGen International Fund is first-rate. This quintessential value player barely resembles the prototypical international portfolio. Its emphasis on low price/earnings and price/book stocks leads it away from hot markets. The fund's 1.3% 1990 decline (versus the average international fund's 10.4% loss) underscores the superior defensive characteristics inherent in its price consciousness. Furthermore, it produced a strong near-18% gain in 1991. A low load and below-average expense ratio make the fund an excellent choice for a wide range of investors, particularly those who prioritize safety.

Portfolio Manager: Jean-Marie Eveillard
Since: 1979

Minimum:
Initial: $1,000
Subsequent: $50
Telephone Exchange: No
Distributions:
Income: Annually
Capital Gain: Annually
Front-End Load: 3.75%
12b-1: 0.18%
Redemption Fee: None
Management Company: SoGen Securities
Ticker Symbol: SGENX

TOTAL RETURN (%)

1987	1988	1989	1990	1991	5-year	Bull Market	Bear Market
13.8	14.1	17.2	-1.3	17.9	77.2	16.6	-7.4

INVESTMENT PORTFOLIO

Total Assets (mil.)	Current Yield	Turnover Ratio	Expense Ratio	Beta	Risk Return
$298	4.4%	24%	1.30%	0.35	0.06

STEIN ROE INTERNATIONAL GROWTH FUND

Stein Roe & Farnham
P.O. Box 1162
Chicago, IL 60690
800-338-2550

Investment Objective: Better known for its fixed-income department, Stein Roe has taken a shot at an international vehicle with this offering. Knowing full well its strengths and weaknesses, management farmed out the stock-selection responsibilities to Touche Remnant Investment Management, which has performed adequately thus far. While worldwide stock markets have been buoyant during the past decade, nearly all suffered a sharp reversal during 1990. Most international funds tumbled and this fund was no exception, losing 11.5% during 1990. The past year the fund posted a subpar 9.3% return.

Portfolio Manager: William D. Bryant
Since: 1987

Minimum:
Initial: $1,000
Subsequent: $100
Telephone Exchange: Yes
Distributions:
Income: Annually
Capital Gain: Annually
Front-End Load: None
12b-1: None
Redemption Fee: None
Management Company: Touche Remnant Investment Management
Ticker Symbol: None

TOTAL RETURN (%)

1987	1988	1989	1990	1991	5-year	Bull Market	Bear Market
NA	11.0	15.0	-11.5	9.3	NA	7.0	-17.3

INVESTMENT PORTFOLIO

Total Assets (mil.)	Current Yield	Turnover Ratio	Expense Ratio	Beta	Risk Return
$18	0.9%	113%	2.23%	0.69	0.01

T. ROWE PRICE EUROPEAN STOCK FUND

T. Rowe Price Investor Services
100 East Pratt Street
Baltimore, MD 21202
800-638-5660

Investment Objective: This fund seeks long-term capital growth with income considered a secondary objective. The fund will be invested in a minimum of 5 countries and will maintain at least 65% of its assets in either eastern or western European equities. Companies will be larger, more established firms. This is a relatively new offering with 1991 being the fund's first full year. Europe had a difficult time in 1991, as can be seen in the fund's minimal gain of 7%. In time, however, long-term shareholders should be well rewarded by this fund.

Portfolio Manager: Martin G. Wade
Since: 1990

Minimum:
Initial: $2,500
Subsequent: $100
Telephone Exchange: Yes
Distributions:
Income: Annually
Capital Gain: Annually
Front-End Load: None
12b-1: None
Redemption Fee: None
Management Company: Rowe-Price Fleming International
Ticker Symbol: PRESX

TOTAL RETURN (%)

1987	1988	1989	1990	1991	5-year	Bull Market	Bear Market
NA	NA	NA	NA	7.3	NA	2.3	-12.2

INVESTMENT PORTFOLIO

Total Assets (mil.)	Current Yield	Turnover Ratio	Expense Ratio	Beta	Risk Return
$99	0.8%	35%	1.75%	0.75	0.00

T. ROWE PRICE INTERNATIONAL DISCOVERY

T. Rowe Price Investor Services
100 East Pratt Street
Baltimore, MD 21202
800-638-5660

Investment Objective: This fund seeks long-term capital appreciation by investing in small to midsized companies in foreign countries. The fund would prefer to invest in more than 10 countries at all times. The companies may be found in both developing or established countries with no parameters dictating what percentage of assets may be invested where. After a spectacular return in 1989, the fund has had average returns in 1990 and 1991. However, if the small-firm effect is truly international, this may be the fund to utilize.

Portfolio Manager: Testa/Wade
Since: 1988

Minimum:
Initial: $2,500
Subsequent: $100
Telephone Exchange: Yes
Distributions:
Income: Annually
Capital Gain: Annually
Front-End Load: None
12b-1: None
Redemption Fee: None
Management Company: Rowe Price-Fleming International
Ticker Symbol: PRIDX

TOTAL RETURN (%)

1987	1988	1989	1990	1991	5-year	Bull Market	Bear Market
NA	NA	41.8	-12.8	11.8	NA	3.0	-5.3

INVESTMENT PORTFOLIO

Total Assets (mil.)	Current Yield	Turnover Ratio	Expense Ratio	Beta	Risk Return
$173	1.0%	44%	1.50%	0.65	0.03

T. ROWE PRICE INTERNATIONAL STOCK FUND

T. Rowe Price Investor Services
100 East Pratt Street
Baltimore, MD 21202
800-638-5660

Investment Objective: This pure international fund invests exclusively in foreign securities; it holds no U.S. stocks. Like most international funds, it stresses macroeconomic themes and above-average growth markets. Management's price consciousness, however, prevents the fund from having significant exposure to what it considers speculative markets/sectors. Despite its pure foreign exposure, which makes the fund more sensitive to exchange-rate fluctuations than its global-fund rivals, the fund hasn't shown excessive volatility and has outperformed most international funds over the past 1-, 3- and 5-year periods.

Portfolio Manager: Martin G. Wade
Since: 1980

Minimum:
Initial: $2,500
Subsequent: $100
Telephone Exchange: Yes
Distributions:
Income: Annually
Capital Gain: Annually
Front-End Load: None
12b-1: None
Redemption Fee: None
Management Company: Rowe Price-Fleming International
Ticker Symbol: PRITX

TOTAL RETURN (%)

1987	1988	1989	1990	1991	5-year	Bull Market	Bear Market
8.0	17.9	23.7	-8.9	15.9	66.3	12.3	-15.1

INVESTMENT PORTFOLIO

Total Assets (mil.)	Current Yield	Turnover Ratio	Expense Ratio	Beta	Risk Return
$1,386	1.5%	47%	1.09%	0.70	0.02

TEMPLETON FOREIGN FUND

Templeton Funds Distributor
700 Central Avenue
St. Petersburg, FL 33701
800-237-0738

Investment Objective: This front-end load fund seeks long-term capital growth by investing in companies domiciled outside the United States. The fund, which follows a philosophy established by the legendary John Templeton, who has always espoused international diversification, sports an impressive track record, returning more than 20% during 3 of the past 5 years. In addition, the fund sidestepped the widespread bear market of 1990. The past year the fund again outperformed most others by returning more than 18% and its 5-year record is second in our international-fund universe.

Portfolio Manager: John M. Templeton
Since: 1982

Minimum:
Initial: $500
Subsequent: $25
Telephone Exchange: Yes
Distributions:
Income: Annually
Capital Gain: Annually
Front-End Load: 8.50%
12b-1: None
Redemption Fee: None
Management Company: Templeton Galbraith & Hansberger
Ticker Symbol: TEMFX

TOTAL RETURN (%)

1987	1988	1989	1990	1991	5-year	Bull Market	Bear Market
24.7	22.0	30.5	-3.0	18.3	127.8	12.8	-12.7

INVESTMENT PORTFOLIO

Total Assets (mil.)	Current Yield	Turnover Ratio	Expense Ratio	Beta	Risk Return
$1,241	2.6%	12%	0.77%	0.62	0.03

TEMPLETON GLOBAL OPPORTUNITIES TRUST

Templeton Funds Distributors
700 Central Avenue
St. Petersburg, FL 33701
800-237-0738

Investment Objective: By Templeton's standards, this 6.25% load is a "cheap" way to jump on the adviser's bandwagon. The past year was the first full year this fund was in business and it immediately paid big dividends with a return of more than 33%. This return placed it 4th on the international list. The fund may invest in the United States, which helps explain 1991's stellar performance. However, many of the fund's international plays also paid off handsomely the past year.

Portfolio Manager: John M. Templeton
Since: 1990

Minimum:
Initial: $500
Subsequent: $25
Telephone Exchange: Yes
Distributions:
Income: Annually
Capital Gain: Annually
Front-End Load: 6.25%
12b-1: 0.25%
Redemption Fee: None
Management Company: Templeton Galbraith & Hansberger
Ticker Symbol: TEGOX

TOTAL RETURN (%)

1987	1988	1989	1990	1991	5-year	Bull Market	Bear Market
NA	NA	NA	NA	33.2	NA	35.9	-19.9

INVESTMENT PORTFOLIO

Total Assets (mil.)	Current Yield	Turnover Ratio	Expense Ratio	Beta	Risk Return
$191	1.5%	0%	1.96%	0.89	0.05

TEMPLETON SMALLER COMPANIES GROWTH FUND

Templeton Funds Distributors
700 Central Avenue
St. Petersburg, FL 33701
800-237-0738

Investment Objective: This global fund invests primarily in small companies with market values between $8 million and $200 million (as measured in 1980 U.S. dollar terms). Like all Templeton-managed funds, it selects investments strictly from the bottom up, adhering to a patient value discipline. Inevitably, its refusal to pay high multiples leads it into low-momentum markets. This fund's disciplined, patient approach promises highly competitive long-term returns with moderate risk, although 1990's 15% loss might raise a few eyebrows. However, in 1991, the fund posted the second highest return of all the international funds we track.

Portfolio Manager: John M. Templeton
Since: 1981

Minimum:
Initial: $500
Subsequent: $25
Telephone Exchange: Yes
Distributions:
Income: Annually
Capital Gain: Annually
Front-End Load: 8.50%
12b-1: None
Redemption Fee: None
Management Company: Templeton Galbraith & Hansberger
Ticker Symbol: TEMGX

TOTAL RETURN (%)

1987	1988	1989	1990	1991	5-year	Bull Market	Bear Market
-11.6	28.8	17.9	-15.7	39.5	57.9	43.5	-25.2

INVESTMENT PORTFOLIO

Total Assets (mil.)	Current Yield	Turnover Ratio	Expense Ratio	Beta	Risk Return
$868	1.7%	27%	0.96%	0.89	0.07

TEMPLETON VALUE FUND

Templeton Funds Distributor
700 Central Avenue
St. Petersburg, FL 33701
800-237-0738

Investment Objective: This former closed-end fund became open-ended in February of 1991. It seeks long-term capital appreciation by investing in emerging growth companies worldwide. Management searches for undervalued companies with market capitalizations below $500 million. The fund returned a strong 32.9% in 1991 as the small-stock bull market ran wild. Much of the gain can be attributed to the fund's position in smaller U.S. equities. Investors will have one of the finest worldwide managers in John Templeton, but it will cost them 8.50% in the form of a hefty front-end load.

Portfolio Manager: John M. Templeton
Since: 1988

Minimum:
Initial: $500
Subsequent: $25
Telephone Exchange: Yes
Distributions:
Income: Annually
Capital Gain: Annually
Front-End Load: 8.50%
12b-1: None
Redemption Fee: 1.00%
Management Company: Templeton Galbraith & Hansberger
Ticker Symbol: TEMVX

TOTAL RETURN (%)

1987	1988	1989	1990	1991	5-year	Bull Market	Bear Market
NA	NA	11.4	-14.3	32.9	NA	NA	NA

INVESTMENT PORTFOLIO

Total Assets (mil.)	Current Yield	Turnover Ratio	Expense Ratio	Beta	Risk Return
$128	0.8%	33%	1.23%	0.95	0.05

TEMPLETON WORLD FUND

Templeton Funds Distributor
700 Central Avenue
St. Petersburg, FL 33701
800-237-0738

Investment Objective: This member of the Templeton family of funds is one of the largest of all international funds, with assets of nearly $4 billion. It can invest in both equity and debt securities of any company around the world. Primarily, it is invested in equity securities, and U.S. securities tend to make up a significant portion of its assets. According to John Templeton, U.S. stocks are very reasonably priced and accordingly should deliver better-than-average returns during the decade of the 1990s. With a U.S. bias, the fund returned almost 30% in 1991. Like many Templeton funds, it charges a hefty 8.50% front-end load.

Portfolio Manager: John M. Templeton
Since: 1978

Minimum:
Initial: $500
Subsequent: $25
Telephone Exchange: Yes
Distributions:
Income: Annually
Capital Gain: Annually
Front-End Load: 8.50%
12b-1: None
Redemption Fee: None
Management Company: Templeton Galbraith & Hansberger
Ticker Symbol: TEMWX

TOTAL RETURN (%)

1987	1988	1989	1990	1991	5-year	Bull Market	Bear Market
3.4	19.7	22.6	-15.9	29.8	65.6	29.0	-21.7

INVESTMENT PORTFOLIO

Total Assets (mil.)	Current Yield	Turnover Ratio	Expense Ratio	Beta	Risk Return
$3,976	2.5%	20%	0.69%	0.94	0.05

THOMSON GLOBAL FUND B

Thomson Investor Services
One Station Place
Stamford, CT 06902
800-628-1237

Investment Objective: The objective of this fund is to maximize total return by using stocks, convertible securities and fixed-income instruments in domestic or foreign markets. Like many of the global offerings, this fund benefited from its U.S. stock position, and it posted a 1991 gain of almost 20%. Its 5-year return is average by international-fund standards. However, the fund has a high expense ratio of 2.80%, a 12b-1 fee and a redemption fee of 1.00%.

Portfolio Manager: I. Smith/B. Michaelson
Since: 1986

Minimum:
Initial: $1,000
Subsequent: $100
Telephone Exchange: Yes
Distributions:
Income: Annually
Capital Gain: Annually
Front-End Load: None
12b-1: 1.00%
Redemption Fee: 1.00%
Management Company: Thomson Advisory Group
Ticker Symbol: TGOBX

TOTAL RETURN (%)

1987	1988	1989	1990	1991	5-year	Bull Market	Bear Market
5.9	10.6	28.5	-15.5	19.9	52.5	14.1	-18.2

INVESTMENT PORTFOLIO

Total Assets (mil.)	Current Yield	Turnover Ratio	Expense Ratio	Beta	Risk Return
$31	0.0%	43%	2.80%	0.90	0.03

UNITED INTERNATIONAL GROWTH FUND

Waddell & Reed
6300 Lamar Avenue, P.O. Box 29217
Shawnee Mission, KS 66201
800-366-5465

Investment Objective: It looks like the somewhat recent portfolio manager change has been paying off. Mark Yockey came aboard in February of 1990 and weathered the fund's 14% loss that year. However, in 1991, his first full year at the helm, the fund scored an impressive 19% return. The latest 5-year total return, however, still trails that of the pack, but a fresh face may have turned the fund around. Investors must note, though, that the fund carries a hefty 8.50% front-end load.

Portfolio Manager: Mark Yockey
Since: 1990

Minimum:
Initial: $500
Subsequent: $25
Telephone Exchange: No
Distributions:
Income: Semiannually
Capital Gain: Annually
Front-End Load: 8.50%
12b-1: None
Redemption Fee: None
Management Company: Waddell & Reed Investments
Ticker Symbol: UNCGX

TOTAL RETURN (%)

1987	1988	1989	1990	1991	5-year	Bull Market	Bear Market
17.1	10.0	13.4	-13.7	19.1	50.2	15.5	-16.8

INVESTMENT PORTFOLIO

Total Assets (mil.)	Current Yield	Turnover Ratio	Expense Ratio	Beta	Risk Return
$280	1.2%	193%	1.13%	0.71	0.03

UNITED SERVICE EUROPEAN EQUITY FUND

United Services Advisors
P.O. Box 29467
San Antonio, TX 78229
800-873-8637

Investment Objective: This fund seeks to approximate the investment results of the European portion of the Morgan Stanley Capital International Index. By investing in various issues of the Index, the fund is intending to give the individual investor large diversification in the European market. This fund was formerly known as the U.S. LoCap Fund, which had a completely different investment objective. Investors may want to wait and see if this fund proves worthy. One thing that may put a damper on possible future returns is the excessively high expense ratio the fund currently carries.

Portfolio Manager: Bankers Trust Company
Since: 1990

Minimum:
Initial: $1,000
Subsequent: $50
Telephone Exchange: Yes
Distributions:
Income: Annually
Capital Gain: Annually
Front-End Load: None
12b-1: None
Redemption Fee: None
Management Company: United Services Advisors
Ticker Symbol: LOCFX

TOTAL RETURN (%)

1987	1988	1989	1990	1991	5-year	Bull Market	Bear Market
-13.2	3.4	-1.6	-26.2	5.8	-31.0	-0.9	-29.5

INVESTMENT PORTFOLIO

Total Assets (mil.)	Current Yield	Turnover Ratio	Expense Ratio	Beta	Risk Return
$1	0.0%	200%	3.64%	0.80	NA

USAA INTERNATIONAL FUND

USAA Investment Management
USAA Building
San Antonio, TX 78288
800-531-8181

Investment Objective: The fund's objective is capital appreciation with income as a secondary consideration. Normally, at least 80% of its assets will be invested in foreign securities. Management will consider a company as "foreign" if at least 50% of the company's revenues are derived from activities outside of the United States. Primarily, companies chosen will be of the larger capitalization variety. In its brief existence, the fund has been an average performer, but it should be noted that it carries a high expense ratio of more than 2.00%.

Portfolio Manager: David G. Peebles
Since: 1988

Minimum:
Initial: $1,000
Subsequent: $50
Telephone Exchange: Yes
Distributions:
Income: Annually
Capital Gain: Annually
Front-End Load: None
12b-1: None
Redemption Fee: None
Management Company: USAA Investment Management
Ticker Symbol: USIFX

TOTAL RETURN (%)

1987	1988	1989	1990	1991	5-year	Bull Market	Bear Market
NA	NA	17.4	-9.3	13.4	NA	10.3	-16.5

INVESTMENT PORTFOLIO

Total Assets (mil.)	Current Yield	Turnover Ratio	Expense Ratio	Beta	Risk Return
$29	0.8%	70%	2.09%	0.65	0.01

USF&G EUROPEAN EMERGING COMPANIES

USF&G Investment Services
275 Commerce Drive
Fort Washington, PA 19034
800-323-8734

Investment Objective: This fund seeks long-term capital appreciation by investing at least 80% of its assets in western European equities. Management looks to invest the bulk of its assets in companies with market capitalizations below $350 million. The fund will diversify across European borders as well as across a broad range of companies. The fund had a difficult 1991 when it lost more than 9%. This loss placed it at the bottom of the 1-year returns of the international funds tracked on our list. Also, expenses still are more than 2.00% and the fund charges a 5.75% front-end load.

Portfolio Manager: Bridges/Horn
Since: 1990

Minimum:
Initial: $1,000
Subsequent: $50
Telephone Exchange: No
Distributions:
Income: Annually
Capital Gain: Annually
Front-End Load: 5.75%
12b-1: 0.25%
Redemption Fee: None
Management Company: USF&G Review Management
Ticker Symbol: EECFX

TOTAL RETURN (%)

1987	1988	1989	1990	1991	5-year	Bull Market	Bear Market
NA	NA	26.6	-7.6	-9.2	NA	-9.4	-14.8

INVESTMENT PORTFOLIO

Total Assets (mil.)	Current Yield	Turnover Ratio	Expense Ratio	Beta	Risk Return
$25	0.6%	10%	2.25%	0.43	NA

VAN ECK WORLD TRENDS FUND

Van Eck Securities
122 East 42nd Street
New York, NY 10168
800-221-2220

Investment Objective: This fund seeks long-term capital growth with income as a secondary objective. The fund will invest in companies in Europe, the Pacific Rim and North America. However, its fairly liberal charter allows it to invest in emerging-growth companies as well. The fund returned an average 13% the past year, while posting an 8% loss in 1990. Its 5-year record falls short of most international funds, but recent results have been on the upswing. Unfortunately, investors must weigh the effect of the 5.75% load before deciding to invest in this offering.

Portfolio Manager: Klaus Buescher
Since: 1985

Minimum:
Initial: $1,000
Subsequent: $100
Telephone Exchange: Yes
Distributions:
Income: Annually
Capital Gain: Annually
Front-End Load: 5.75%
12b-1: 0.25%
Redemption Fee: None
Management Company: Van Eck Associates
Ticker Symbol: WTFDX

TOTAL RETURN (%)

1987	1988	1989	1990	1991	5-year	Bull Market	Bear Market
7.9	6.1	13.3	-7.9	12.5	34.5	12.5	-13.8

INVESTMENT PORTFOLIO

Total Assets (mil.)	Current Yield	Turnover Ratio	Expense Ratio	Beta	Risk Return
$43	0.4%	21%	1.56%	0.62	0.01

VANGUARD INTERNATIONAL EQUITY INDEX EUROPEAN

Vanguard Group
Vanguard Financial Center
Valley Forge, PA 19487
800-662-7447

Investment Objective: This relatively new Vanguard offering seeks to mirror the MSCI Europe Index, a European index comprised of more than 600 companies. Management believes that a sampling of the index should provide investors with a close approximation of the index's return. Investors seeking a no-load index of Europe should consider this fund as expenses will be minimal. However, one may want to wait and see if this young fund has the ability to replicate its benchmark.

Minimum:
Initial: $3,000
Subsequent: $100
Telephone Exchange: Yes
Distributions:
Income: Annually
Capital Gain: Annually
Front-End Load: None
12b-1: None
Redemption Fee: None
Management Company: Vanguard Group
Ticker Symbol: VEURX

Portfolio Manager: George Sauter
Since: 1990

TOTAL RETURN (%)

1987	1988	1989	1990	1991	5-year	Bull Market	Bear Market
NA	NA	NA	NA	12.4	NA	NA	NA

INVESTMENT PORTFOLIO

Total Assets (mil.)	Current Yield	Turnover Ratio	Expense Ratio	Beta	Risk Return
$165	2.6%	0%	0.40%	NA	NA

VANGUARD INTERNATIONAL EQUITY INDEX PACIFIC

Vanguard Group
Vanguard Financial Center
Valley Forge, PA 19482
800-662-7447

Investment Objective: This Vanguard Index offering looks to replicate the MSCI Pacific Index, a 400-company stock index that covers Australia, Japan, Hong Kong, New Zealand and Singapore. As with many of the Vanguard Index offerings, management believes that a sampling of the stocks within the index will provide a sufficient approximation of the benchmark. The fund will have a bias toward Japan, as the index is heavily weighted with stocks of this country. Like Vanguard's European Index Fund, this fund is just over 1 year old and does not have a track record. Thus, it cannot be compared to the index it seeks to replicate.

Minimum:
Initial: $3,000
Subsequent: $100
Telephone Exchange: No
Distributions:
Income: Annually
Capital Gain: Annually
Front-End Load: None
12b-1: None
Redemption Fee: None
Management Company: Vanguard Group
Ticker Symbol: VPACX

Portfolio Manager: George Sauter
Since: 1990

TOTAL RETURN (%)

1987	1988	1989	1990	1991	5-year	Bull Market	Bear Market
NA	NA	NA	NA	10.7	NA	17.4	-18.7

INVESTMENT PORTFOLIO

Total Assets (mil.)	Current Yield	Turnover Ratio	Expense Ratio	Beta	Risk Return
$78	0.5%	2%	0.35%	0.60	0.01

VANGUARD TRUSTEES COMMINGLED INTERNATIONAL

Vanguard Group
Vanguard Financial Center
Valley Forge, PA 19482
800-662-7447

Investment Objective: This fund seeks long-term capital growth and income return by investing primarily in foreign securities. Investment adviser, Batterymarch Financial Management, relies on quantitative methods to screen for stocks that sell at a discount to their true worth. The fund's methods have historically proven successful at identifying companies with significant restructuring potential. This fund offers value investors broad diversification by investing in a large number of companies across many borders. The minimum investment, however, is $10,000.

Portfolio Manager: Jarrod Wilcox
Since: 1991

Minimum:
Initial: $10,000
Subsequent: $100
Telephone Exchange: Yes
Distributions:
Income: Quarterly
Capital Gain: Annually
Front-End Load: None
12b-1: None
Redemption Fee: None
Management Company: Batterymarch Financial Management
Ticker Symbol: VTRIX

TOTAL RETURN (%)

1987	1988	1989	1990	1991	5-year	Bull Market	Bear Market
24.0	18.8	26.0	-12.3	10.0	79.0	4.2	-15.1

INVESTMENT PORTFOLIO

Total Assets (mil.)	Current Yield	Turnover Ratio	Expense Ratio	Beta	Risk Return
$856	2.7%	18%	0.44%	0.65	0.01

VANGUARD WORLD INTERNATIONAL

Vanguard Group
Vanguard Financial Center
Valley Forge, PA 19482
800-662-7447

Investment Objective: This fund seeks long-term capital growth by investing in non-U.S. securities. The fund attempts to diversify its portfolio by investing in a large number of companies in various countries. The fund had a difficult 1991 when it gained just more than 4%. This performance came on the heels of an average 1990 when the fund lost 12%. The past 2 years have dropped the fund's 5-year return below the group's mean.

Portfolio Manager: Richard Foulkes
Since: 1981

Minimum:
Initial: $3,000
Subsequent: $100
Telephone Exchange: Yes
Distributions:
Income: Annually
Capital Gain: Annually
Front-End Load: None
12b-1: None
Redemption Fee: None
Management Company: Schroder Capital Management
Ticker Symbol: VWIGX

TOTAL RETURN (%)

1987	1988	1989	1990	1991	5-year	Bull Market	Bear Market
16.6	11.6	24.8	-12.0	4.7	49.6	0.3	-5.7

INVESTMENT PORTFOLIO

Total Assets (mil.)	Current Yield	Turnover Ratio	Expense Ratio	Beta	Risk Return
$875	1.8%	49%	0.67%	0.65	0.01

PART 8

Precious Metals Funds

The following pages contain the descriptions of 27 mutual funds that invest in precious metals. Some of the funds invest in gold bullion and the shares of gold mining companies only; others expand their portfolios to include investments in silver and platinum. A few funds restrict their investments to specific geographic areas such as South Africa or North America.

On average, the net asset values of precious metals funds tend to be more volatile than the underlying prices of gold or silver bullion. That is because most funds invest heavily in mining stocks whose earnings and share prices possess high volatility as a result of doing business in a high-fixed-cost industry. For example, suppose that it costs a mining company $200 million to mine 600,000 ounces of gold annually. When the price of gold is $360 an ounce, revenues total $216 million and operating profits are $16 million. Now suppose the price of gold rises 20 percent to $432 an ounce. Revenues rise to $259 million and, since operating costs are unaffected, operating profits rise by 270 percent to $59 million.

The price of gold is driven by one basic force: fear (or the lack of it). Political instability, the prospect of higher inflation and a falling value of the U.S. dollar tend to drive the price of gold higher. Thus, the return from investing in a precious metals fund tends to fluctuate inversely with the returns of most financial assets. As a result, investment in gold tends to lower portfolio variability (i.e., investment risk) when coupled with investment in stocks and bonds. However, to the extent that many precious metals funds invest in gold mining shares of companies doing business outside of the United States, there are also elements of political and foreign exchange risk inherent in these investments.

The price of gold bullion rose nearly every year during the inflation years of the 1970s, rising from $32 per ounce in 1972, when U.S. citizens were again allowed to speculate in this precious metal, to nearly $800 an ounce for a brief instant in 1980. During the double-digit inflation years (1978–1980), the price of gold bullion nearly quadrupled. However, after rising by nearly 92 percent during 1980, the price of gold bullion fell by 33 percent over the next ten years. Thus, gold bullion during the decade of the 1980s returned investors less than 4 percent compounded annually, or less than the total return on short-term treasury bills.

Given the depressed conditions that have existed in the gold and silver bullion markets in recent years, it is not surprising to find that precious metals funds as a group have been among the industry's poorest performers. During the past five years, the median precious metals fund returned a total of slightly less than 1 percent per year.

Although precious metals funds sport relatively low average betas, their net asset values are extremely volatile. The low beta results from a very low correlation with returns from equities. On average, these funds pay very little current income (with the exception of funds specializing in South African gold mining shares) and have average portfolio turnover ratios equal to about one-half those of diversified equity funds. The median (middle) financial statistics for this group are outlined below.

Summary of Financial Statistics (medians)

1991 Return	5-Year Return	Current Yield	Beta	Turnover Ratio	Expense Ratio
–3.9%	3.6%	0.8%	0.01	45%	1.59%

BEST PRECIOUS METALS FUNDS FOR 1991

Fund	Percent Return 1991	3-Year	5-Year
Sherman Dean	12.2%	-7.6%	16.2%
Keystone Precious Metals	8.2	-0.6	19.9
Franklin Gold	5.8	20.6	62.8
United Services Global Resources	5.0	7.8	17.0
Vanguard Specialized Gold & Precious Metals	4.4	9.0	29.8
Mainstay Gold & Precious Metals	3.5	-4.9	NA
Van Eck International Investors	2.6	13.3	19.0
Fidelity Select Precious Metals & Minerals	1.5	5.9	10.9
Oppenheimer Gold Investors	0.3	-1.2	83.9
Bull & Bear Gold Investors	-1.1	-8.1	3.6
Enterprise Precious Metals	-1.8	5.6	NA
Blanchard Precious Metals	-2.3	-18.6	NA
United Services World Gold	-3.4	-18.9	-13.5
IDS Precious Metals	-3.7	-13.4	13.4
Shearson Precious Metals & Minerals	-3.9	-10.9	-4.4
Van Eck Gold Resources	-4.1	-16.1	-2.7
USAA Gold	-4.4	-17.1	-20.2
Lexington Goldfund	-6.1	-7.9	-14.4
Fidelity Select American Gold	-6.1	-5.1	-16.7
Scudder Gold	-6.9	-14.1	NA

BENHAM GOLD EQUITIES INDEX FUND

Benham Group
1665 Charleston Road
Mountain View, CA 94043
800-472-3389

Investment Objective: This fund strives to duplicate the total returns of an index of North American gold stocks by investing at least 85% of its assets in companies included in the index. For inclusion in the index, a company must derive at least 50% of its revenues from gold operations, have a market capitalization of at least $50 million, have a liquid trading market, be headquartered in North America and have no operations in South Africa. In addition, the value of a company's North American gold production must equal or exceed 50% of the value of its total gold production. The fund may invest up to 10% of its assets in gold, certificates of ownership in gold or gold futures.

Portfolio Manager: Steve Colton
Since: 1989

Minimum:
Initial: $1,000
Subsequent: $100
Telephone Exchange: Yes
Distributions:
Income: Annually
Capital Gain: Annually
Front-End Load: None
12b-1: None
Redemption Fee: None
Management Company: Benham Management
Ticker Symbol: BGEIX

TOTAL RETURN (%)

1987	1988	1989	1990	1991	5-year	Bull Market	Bear Market
NA	NA	30.4	-19.7	-11.2	NA	-7.1	-11.0

INVESTMENT PORTFOLIO

Total Assets (mil.)	Current Yield	Turnover Ratio	Expense Ratio	Beta	Risk Return
$134	0.2%	21%	0.96%	-0.07	NA

BLANCHARD PRECIOUS METALS FUND

Sheffield Investments
41 Madison Avenue, 24th Floor
New York, NY 10010
800-922-7771

Investment Objective: Started in 1989, this relative newcomer attempts to reduce the high volatility usually associated with gold investing by adjusting its asset mix in response to market conditions. So far, however, its risk reduction tactic shave only backfired. While the fund severely lagged 1989's bull market for gold, it failed to exhibit superior resistance to decline during the bear market of the past 2 years. Results to date also have been slowed by the fund's above-average operating expenses, which owe to its relatively small asset base.

Portfolio Manager: Peter Cavelti
Since: 1988

Minimum:
Initial: $3,000
Subsequent: $200
Telephone Exchange: Yes
Distributions:
Income: Annually
Capital Gain: Annually
Front-End Load: None
12b-1: 0.78%
Redemption Fee: None
Management Company: Cavelti Capital Management
Ticker Symbol: BLPMX

TOTAL RETURN (%)

1987	1988	1989	1990	1991	5-year	Bull Market	Bear Market
NA	NA	8.0	-22.9	-2.3	NA	-2.6	-3.8

INVESTMENT PORTFOLIO

Total Assets (mil.)	Current Yield	Turnover Ratio	Expense Ratio	Beta	Risk Return
$27	0.0%	57%	3.05%	-0.09	NA

BULL & BEAR GOLD INVESTORS LIMITED

Bull & Bear
11 Hanover Square
New York, NY 10005
800-847-4200

Investment Objective: This fund attempts to temper the risk inherent in gold investing by shifting assets among gold equities, bullion and cash in response to relative valuations and the outlook for gold. Investments in gold equities are generally geographically diversified across each of the free world's major gold mining regions, with North American gold stocks claiming the bulk of assets. South African investments have generally claimed less than 10% of the fund's assets in recent years. While large stocks predominate, the fund owns some secondary gold stocks.

Portfolio Manager: Robert Radsch
Since: 1982

Minimum:
Initial: $1,000
Subsequent: $25
Telephone Exchange: Yes
Distributions:
Income: Annually
Capital Gain: Annually
Front-End Load: None
12b-1: 1.00%
Redemption Fee: None
Management Company: Bull & Bear International Advisers
Ticker Symbol: BBGIX

TOTAL RETURN (%)

1987	1988	1989	1990	1991	5-year	Bull Market	Bear Market
30.4	-13.5	19.3	-22.1	-1.1	3.6	-1.4	-8.7

INVESTMENT PORTFOLIO

Total Assets (mil.)	Current Yield	Turnover Ratio	Expense Ratio	Beta	Risk Return
$29	0.4%	95%	2.59%	0.06	NA

ENTERPRISE PRECIOUS METALS PORTFOLIO

Enterprise Fund Distributor
1200 Ashwood Parkway, Suite 290
Atlanta, GA 30338
800-432-4320

Investment Objective: This relatively new entrant into the precious metals arena has so far proven one of its category's tamer offerings. A willingness to hold as much as 30% of its assets in gold bullion, which is much less sensitive to gold price movements than gold equities, enabled it to exhibit superior defensive characteristics during the 2-year bear market for gold. The fund's 2-year 15% decline is considerably smaller than the average precious metals fund. With a minor South African stake, the bulk of the fund's investments consist of North American and Australian gold equities.

Portfolio Manager: Harry Bingham
Since: 1990

Minimum:
Initial: $500
Subsequent: $25
Telephone Exchange: Yes
Distributions:
Income: Annually
Capital Gain: Annually
Front-End Load: 4.75%
12b-1: 0.45%
Redemption Fee: None
Management Company: Enterprise Capital Management
Ticker Symbol: ENPMX

TOTAL RETURN (%)

1987	1988	1989	1990	1991	5-year	Bull Market	Bear Market
NA	-3.9	23.3	-12.8	-1.8	NA	-2.6	-2.0

INVESTMENT PORTFOLIO

Total Assets (mil.)	Current Yield	Turnover Ratio	Expense Ratio	Beta	Risk Return
$6	0.3%	45%	2.50%	-0.12	NA

FIDELITY SELECT AMERICAN GOLD

Fidelity Distributors Corporation
82 Devonshire Street, Mail Zone L7B
Boston, MA 02109
800-544-6666

Investment Objective: Investors seeking a tame version of a precious metals fund will be hard pressed to find a more suitable alternative than Fidelity Select American Gold. Although the fund stays fully invested at all times, its exclusive focus on top-quality North American gold stocks, which are significantly less volatile than South African and Australian gold stocks, enables it to offer a fairly smooth ride, at least by precious metals standards. Risk is further mitigated by a smattering of gold bullion and diversified metals stocks and the fund's neglect of highly leveraged secondary gold stocks.

Portfolio Manager: Malcolm MacNaught
Since: 1985

Minimum:
Initial: $1,000
Subsequent: $250
Telephone Exchange: Yes
Distributions:
Income: Annually
Capital Gain: Annually
Front-End Load: 3.00%
12b-1: None
Redemption Fee: 0.75%
Management Company: Fidelity Management & Research
Ticker Symbol: FSAGX

TOTAL RETURN (%)

1987	1988	1989	1990	1991	5-year	Bull Market	Bear Market
40.5	-12.5	22.0	-17.2	-6.1	16.7	-3.6	-9.7

INVESTMENT PORTFOLIO

Total Assets (mil.)	Current Yield	Turnover Ratio	Expense Ratio	Beta	Risk Return
$181	0.0%	38%	1.75%	0.08	NA

FIDELITY SELECT PRECIOUS METALS AND MINERALS

Fidelity Distributors Corporation
82 Devonshire Street, Mail Zone L7B
Boston, MA 02109
800-544-6666

Investment Objective: This fund's geographic diversification makes it a much riskier investment than sibling Fidelity Select American Gold. Specifically, a 40% stake in South African gold stocks makes the fund vulnerable to that country's volatile politics. This risk is partially offset by the fund's equal stake in North American gold stocks and its quality orientation. In all parts of the world, it stresses top-quality, major gold producers and neglects leveraged, secondary gold stocks and exploration and development plays. Considering its South African and Australian (20% of assets) exposures, returns have been relatively steady. Like all gold funds, however, the fund isn't for risk-intolerant investors.

Portfolio Manager: Malcolm MacNaught
Since: 1984

Minimum:
Initial: $1,000
Subsequent: $250
Telephone Exchange: Yes
Distributions:
Income: Annually
Capital Gain: Annually
Front-End Load: 3.00%
12b-1: None
Redemption Fee: 0.75%
Management Company: Fidelity Management & Research
Ticker Symbol: FDPMX

TOTAL RETURN (%)

1987	1988	1989	1990	1991	5-year	Bull Market	Bear Market
37.5	-23.9	32.2	-21.1	1.5	10.9	2.2	-6.2

INVESTMENT PORTFOLIO

Total Assets (mil.)	Current Yield	Turnover Ratio	Expense Ratio	Beta	Risk Return
$180	0.9%	41%	1.79%	-0.09	NA

FINANCIAL STRATEGIC GOLD

INVESCO Funds Group
P. O. Box 2040
Denver, CO 80201
800-525-8085

Investment Objective: This pure gold fund invests primarily in North American gold mining stocks. Besides stinting risky South African and Australian gold stocks, it employs few other risk reduction tactics. It doesn't purchase gold bullion or diversified metals stocks, nor will it raise much cash when the prospects for gold are unfavorable. This, coupled with its willingness to invest up to 10% of its assets in leveraged, secondary gold stocks, makes the fund highly sensitive to gold price movements. It promises significant upside in the face of a rising gold price, but also should be expected to underperform its tamer rivals in bear gold markets such as the one that has persisted during the past 2 years.

Portfolio Manager: Dan Leonard
Since: 1989

Minimum:
Initial: $250
Subsequent: $50
Telephone Exchange: Yes
Distributions:
Income: Annually
Capital Gain: Annually
Front-End Load: None
12b-1: None
Redemption Fee: None
Management Company: INVESCO Funds Group
Ticker Symbol: FGLDX

TOTAL RETURN (%)

1987	1988	1989	1990	1991	5-year	Bull Market	Bear Market
16.0	-20.0	21.3	-23.0	-7.2	-19.6	-4.1	-12.3

INVESTMENT PORTFOLIO

Total Assets (mil.)	Current Yield	Turnover Ratio	Expense Ratio	Beta	Risk Return
$43	0.0%	43%	1.47%	0.04	NA

FRANKLIN GOLD

Franklin Distributors
777 Mariners Island Boulevard, 6th Floor
San Mateo, CA 94404
800-342-5236

Investment Objective: This relatively pure gold fund has traditionally offered the best of both worlds, outperforming most precious metals rivals in both bull and bear markets. Its success owes primarily to its quality orientation. Investing in each of the free world's major gold mining regions (South Africa, North America and Australia), it invests exclusively in medium- and long-life gold mines. In addition, about 20% of the portfolio is invested in companies that mine other metals and minerals, including silver, platinum and diamonds. As the fund's relatively low turnover rate shows, it doesn't time the market; cash rarely exceeds 15% of its assets.

Portfolio Manager: Martin Wiskemann
Since: 1972

Minimum:
Initial: $100
Subsequent: $25
Telephone Exchange: Yes
Distributions:
Income: Semiannually
Capital Gain: Annually
Front-End Load: 4.00%
12b-1: None
Redemption Fee: None
Management Company: Franklin Advisers
Ticker Symbol: FKRCX

TOTAL RETURN (%)

1987	1988	1989	1990	1991	5-year	Bull Market	Bear Market
51.2	-10.7	41.8	-19.6	5.8	62.8	9.6	-10.2

INVESTMENT PORTFOLIO

Total Assets (mil.)	Current Yield	Turnover Ratio	Expense Ratio	Beta	Risk Return
$288	2.3%	53%	0.75%	0.04	NA

IDS PRECIOUS METALS

IDS Financial Services
IDS Tower 10
Minneapolis, MN 55440
800-328-8300

Investment Objective: A series of managerial changes makes this precious metals vehicle somewhat of an unknown quantity. Its portfolio has changed considerably since 1986 and 1987, when a fairly aggressive stake in leveraged, sec-ondary gold stocks, including Australian issues, allowed it to whip most rivals as gold rallied. Less favorable gold market conditions and more conservative management have given the fund a more moderate cast in recent years. Consequently, its more recent results (about average in comparison to other precious funds) seem a better indication of its future potential than its superb gains attained during the mid-1980s.

Portfolio Manager: Richard Warden
Since: 1991

Minimum:
Initial: $2,000
Subsequent: $100
Telephone Exchange: Yes
Distributions:
Income: Annually
Capital Gain: Annually
Front-End Load: 5.00%
12b-1: 0.18%
Redemption Fee: None
Management Company: IDS Financial Services
Ticker Symbol: INPMX

TOTAL RETURN (%)

1987	1988	1989	1990	1991	5-year	Bull Market	Bear Market
52.6	-14.1	17.8	-23.7	-3.7	13.4	0.3	-10.2

INVESTMENT PORTFOLIO

Total Assets (mil.)	Current Yield	Turnover Ratio	Expense Ratio	Beta	Risk Return
$63	1.3%	54%	1.48%	0.08	NA

KEYSTONE PRECIOUS METALS

Keystone Distributors
99 High Street, 29th Floor
Boston, MA 02110
800-633-4900

Investment Objective: This precious metals fund is neither the most aggressive nor the tamest in its category. Although it maintains a fairly large gold equities position at most times, its affinity for large, quality gold stocks and neglect of highly volatile secondary gold issues allows it to hug the middle of the road in most markets. With roughly two-thirds of its assets invested in North America and most remaining monies spread across South Africa and Australia, it offers a fairly moderate, geographically diversified gold play. Regardless of gold market conditions, the fund tends not to increase either its cash or gold bullion allocations.

Portfolio Manager: F. Thorne/ M. Pirmie
Since: 1979

Minimum:
Initial: $1,000
Subsequent: None
Telephone Exchange: Yes
Distributions:
Income: Semiannually
Capital Gain: Annually
Front-End Load: None
12b-1: 0.98%
Redemption Fee: 4.00%
Management Company: Keystone Advisers
Ticker Symbol: KSPMX

TOTAL RETURN (%)

1987	1988	1989	1990	1991	5-year	Bull Market	Bear Market
42.6	-15.4	24.6	-26.3	8.2	19.9	7.9	-8.7

INVESTMENT PORTFOLIO

Total Assets (mil.)	Current Yield	Turnover Ratio	Expense Ratio	Beta	Risk Return
$146	0.8%	68%	2.76%	0.06	NA

LEXINGTON GOLDFUND

Lexington Funds Distributor
P. O. Box 1515
Saddle Brook, NJ 07662
800-526-0056

Investment Objective: Among the more tame of precious metals vehicles, this no-load fund successfully tempers the volatility associated with gold investing by adjusting its asset mix in response to market conditions. Besides raising cash and bullion when the prospects for gold seem unfavorable, it reduces risk by stressing top-quality gold stocks and neglecting leveraged junior mines. Modest stakes in platinum and diversified metals stocks also help keep risk moderate relative to other precious metals funds. While the bulk of its holdings consist of North American gold equities, the fund typically has some exposure to South African and Australian gold mines.

Minimum:
Initial: $1,000
Subsequent: $50
Telephone Exchange: Yes
Distributions:
Income: Annually
Capital Gain: Annually
Front-End Load: None
12b-1: None
Redemption Fee: None
Management Company: Lexington Management
Ticker Symbol: LEXMX

Portfolio Manager: Caesar Bryan
Since: 1987

TOTAL RETURN (%)

1987	1988	1989	1990	1991	5-year	Bull Market	Bear Market
46.3	-15.0	23.8	-20.8	-6.1	14.4	-3.1	-6.3

INVESTMENT PORTFOLIO

Total Assets (mil.)	Current Yield	Turnover Ratio	Expense Ratio	Beta	Risk Return
$106	0.9%	12%	1.36%	-0.10	NA

MAINSTAY GOLD AND PRECIOUS METALS

NYLIFE Securities
51 Madison Avenue, Room 117
New York, NY 10010
800-522-4202

Investment Objective: Mainstay Gold offers a moderately aggressive gold play. Although the fund currently owns no South African gold stocks or highly leveraged secondary issues, its inability to invest more than 5% of its assets in gold bullion,which is much less volatile than gold equities, prevents it from ranking among its category's tamer vehicles. Its pure equity focus enabled the fund to perform well when gold rallied in 1989 (its 20% 1989 gain is competitive considering the fund's neglect of South African gold stocks that whipped both their North American and Australian counterparts that year), but also caused the fund to take a 23% hit during 1990's gold market sell-off. It was one of the few gold funds to post a gain the past year.

Minimum:
Initial: $500
Subsequent: $50
Telephone Exchange: Yes
Distributions:
Income: Annually
Capital Gain: Annually
Front-End Load: None
12b-1: 1.00%
Redemption Fee: 5.00%
Management Company: MacKay-Shields Financial
Ticker Symbol: MKGPX

Portfolio Manager: Lisa Debenham/Dennis Finning
Since: 1987

TOTAL RETURN (%)

1987	1988	1989	1990	1991	5-year	Bull Market	Bear Market
NA	-9.6	20.1	-23.5	3.5	NA	-2.0	-10.3

INVESTMENT PORTFOLIO

Total Assets (mil.)	Current Yield	Turnover Ratio	Expense Ratio	Beta	Risk Return
$8	0.0%	49%	3.30%	0.06	NA

OPPENHEIMER GOLD & SPECIAL MINERALS

Oppenheimer Fund Management
P. O. Box 300
Denver, CO 80201
800-255-2755

Investment Objective: A liberal charter makes this fund one of the precious metals category's most dependable. Typically, it invests the bulk of its assets in gold equities. But when its leading indicator—the value of the U.S. dollar—suggests the prospects for gold are unfavorable, it may boost nonprecious metals stocks as high as 70% of its assets. This practice isn't foolproof, but it generally allows the fund to ride gold rallies and to sidestep bear markets. While it shouldn't be expected to repeat its 1987 heroics (its current manager is a lot more moderate than the manager responsible for those results), the fund promises competitive long-term returns with considerably less risk than the average precious metals fund.

Portfolio Manager: Kenneth Oberman
Since: 1988

Minimum:
Initial: $1,000
Subsequent: $25
Telephone Exchange: Yes
Distributions:
Income: Annually
Capital Gain: Annually
Front-End Load: 5.75%
12b-1: 0.03%
Redemption Fee: None
Management Company: Oppenheimer Management
Ticker Symbol: OPGSX

TOTAL RETURN (%)

1987	1988	1989	1990	1991	5-year	Bull Market	Bear Market
71.6	8.4	34.6	-26.8	0.3	83.9	2.0	-15.0

INVESTMENT PORTFOLIO

Total Assets (mil.)	Current Yield	Turnover Ratio	Expense Ratio	Beta	Risk Return
$143	1.7%	113%	1.43%	0.32	NA

SCUDDER GOLD

Scudder Stevens & Clark
175 Federal Street, 12th Floor
Boston, MA 02110
800-225-2470

Investment Objective: By precious metals funds' standards, Scudder Gold Fund is awfully tame. The fund's relatively low volatility owes primarily to its fairly constant 25% bullion stake. Cash reserves, which may rise as high as 15% of its assets, also have helped minimize losses in recent years, as has the fund's neglect of South African gold stocks and relatively low exposure to Australian shares. Although the fund does invest a portion of its assets in secondary gold stocks and exploration/development plays, these highly leveraged shares rarely claim more than 15% of its assets. Most of its stocks are large liquid shares of quality gold producers with low to medium production costs.

Portfolio Manager: D. Donald/D. Loudon
Since: 1988

Minimum:
Initial: $1,000
Subsequent: $100
Telephone Exchange: Yes
Distributions:
Income: Annually
Capital Gain: Annually
Front-End Load: None
12b-1: None
Redemption Fee: None
Management Company: Scudder Stevens & Clark
Ticker Symbol: SCGDX

TOTAL RETURN (%)

1987	1988	1989	1990	1991	5-year	Bull Market	Bear Market
NA	NA	10.7	-16.7	-6.9	NA	-5.5	-3.9

INVESTMENT PORTFOLIO

Total Assets (mil.)	Current Yield	Turnover Ratio	Expense Ratio	Beta	Risk Return
$25	0.0%	71%	2.54%	-0.04	NA

SHEARSON PRECIOUS METALS & MINERALS

Shearson Lehman Brothers
Two World Trade Center
New York, NY 10048
800-451-2010

Investment Objective: While hardly the most aggressive of precious metals funds, this fund is still the bolder of Shearson's two precious metals vehicles. Its increased volatility stems primarily from its practice of holding less cash and bullion than its sibling. In keeping with adviser Shearson Lehman Global Asset Management policy, the fund doesn't invest in South Africa. North American and Australian gold producers claim about 65% and 20% of its assets, respectively. Emphasis is on large liquid shares of senior gold producers at the neglect of secondary issues.

Portfolio Manager: Erich Stock
Since: 1990

Minimum:
Initial: $500
Subsequent: $200
Telephone Exchange: Yes
Distributions:
Income: Annually
Capital Gain: Annually
Front-End Load: 5.00%
12b-1: None
Redemption Fee: None
Management Company: S. L. Global Asset Management
Ticker Symbol: SPMMX

TOTAL RETURN (%)

1987	1988	1989	1990	1991	5-year	Bull Market	Bear Market
36.3	-21.3	15.5	-19.7	-3.9	-4.4	-3.3	-8.9

INVESTMENT PORTFOLIO

Total Assets (mil.)	Current Yield	Turnover Ratio	Expense Ratio	Beta	Risk Return
$17	0.6%	61%	2.44%	0.03	NA

SHEARSON PRECIOUS METALS PORTFOLIO

Shearson Lehman Brothers
Two World Trade Center
New York, NY 10048
800-451-2010

Investment Objective: This moderate gold fund offers a relatively low risk profile in comparison to other precious metals funds, thanks to its willingness to raise cash upon signs of a decline in the gold price. In 1988, for example, the fund's cash position rose as high as 50% of its assets, allowing the fund to protect capital better than its average rivals. The fund's efforts to minimize risk also prevent it from investing in leveraged shares of junior mines. Most monies are concentrated in financially strong, major North American gold mines with low production costs. The fund typically allocates a small portion of its assets to top-quality South African and Australian shares.

Portfolio Manager: Marc Loew
Since: 1990

Minimum:
Initial: $500
Subsequent: $250
Telephone Exchange: Yes
Distributions:
Income: Annually
Capital Gain: Annually
Front-End Load: None
12b-1: 1.00%
Redemption Fee: 5.00%
Management Company: S. L. Global Asset Management
Ticker Symbol: EFPMX

TOTAL RETURN (%)

1987	1988	1989	1990	1991	5-year	Bull Market	Bear Market
45.1	-14.7	17.4	-23.6	-9.7	0.1	-4.8	-9.2

INVESTMENT PORTFOLIO

Total Assets (mil.)	Current Yield	Turnover Ratio	Expense Ratio	Beta	Risk Return
$42	0.2%	168%	2.54%	-0.02	NA

SHERMAN DEAN

Sherman Dean
6061 N.W. Expressway, Suite 465
San Antonio, TX 78201
800-247-6375

Investment Objective: Although the fund is classified as a precious metals fund, the fund's adviser is inclined to march to a different drummer. This very small fund tends to hold a very concentrated portfolio and thus its returns may be hit or miss. It missed during 1990 as its net asset value tumbled nearly 45%. Although it failed to hit a home run the past year, its 12% return topped all others in the group. Given the fund's investment strategy, its shares are suited for only highly risk-tolerant investors.

Portfolio Manager: J. Walter Sherman
Since: 1967

Minimum:
Initial: $1,000
Subsequent: $100
Telephone Exchange: No
Distributions:
Income: Annually
Capital Gain: Annually
Front-End Load: None
12b-1: None
Redemption Fee: None
Management Company: Sherman Dean Management & Research
Ticker Symbol: SHDNX

TOTAL RETURN (%)

1987	1988	1989	1990	1991	5-year	Bull Market	Bear Market
0.2	25.7	47.3	-44.1	12.2	16.2	11.1	-31.2

INVESTMENT PORTFOLIO

Total Assets (mil.)	Current Yield	Turnover Ratio	Expense Ratio	Beta	Risk Return
$2	0.0%	9%	2.75%	1.06	0.01

STRATEGIC GOLD & MINERALS

Lexington Funds Distributor
P.O. Box 1515
Saddle Brook, NJ 07662
800-526-0056

Investment Objective: At press time the directors of this fund decided not to renew the fund's advisory contract with Strategic Management. Instead, it appointed Lexington Management Corporation, the manager of the Lexington Goldfund, as the fund's investment adviser, subject to shareholder approval. The directors also appointed Lexington to serve as the fund's distributor. Although unusual, the change came as no surprise, considering the fact that previous management has amassed the poorest track record in the group during the past 5 years.

Portfolio Manager: Caesar Bryan
Since: 1991

Minimum:
Initial: $1,000
Subsequent: $100
Telephone Exchange: Yes
Distributions:
Income: Annually
Capital Gain: Annually
Front-End Load: 8.50%
12b-1: None
Redemption Fee: None
Management Company: Lexington Management
Ticker Symbol: STAUX

TOTAL RETURN (%)

1987	1988	1989	1990	1991	5-year	Bull Market	Bear Market
-33.0	5.5	-17.7	-12.5	-28.0	-63.4	-18.8	-12.1

INVESTMENT PORTFOLIO

Total Assets (mil.)	Current Yield	Turnover Ratio	Expense Ratio	Beta	Risk Return
$1	0.0%	45%	1.63%	-0.20	NA

STRATEGIC INVESTMENTS

Lexington Funds Distributor
P.O. Box 1515
Saddle Brook, NJ 07662
800-526-0056

Investment Objective: At press time, the directors of this fund decided not to renew the fund's advisory contract with Strategic Management. Instead, it appointed Lexington Management Corporation, the manager of the Lexington Goldfund, as the fund's investment adviser, subject to shareholder approval. The directors also appointed Lexington to serve as the fund's distributor. Although unusual, the change came as no surprise, considering the fact that previous management had amassed the poorest track record in the group during the past 5 years.

Portfolio Manager: Caesar Bryan
Since: 1991

Minimum:
Initial: $1,000
Subsequent: $100
Telephone Exchange: Yes
Distributions:
Income: Annually
Capital Gain: Annually
Front-End Load: 8.50%
12b-1: None
Redemption Fee: None
Management Company: Lexington Management
Ticker Symbol: STIVX

TOTAL RETURN (%)

1987	1988	1989	1990	1991	5-year	Bull Market	Bear Market
23.6	-43.0	61.2	-42.4	-18.9	-46.9	-20.1	-1.6

INVESTMENT PORTFOLIO

Total Assets (mil.)	Current Yield	Turnover Ratio	Expense Ratio	Beta	Risk Return
$27	0.5%	73%	1.59%	-0.43	NA

STRATEGIC SILVER

Lexington Funds Distributor
P. O. Box 1515
Saddle Brook, NJ 07662
800-526-0056

Investment Objective: At press time, the directors of this fund decided not to renew the fund's advisory contract with Strategic Management. Instead, it appointed Lexington Management Corporation, the manager of the Lexington Goldfund, as the fund's investment adviser, subject to shareholder approval. The directors also appointed Lexington to serve as the fund's distributor. Although unusual, the change came as no surprise, considering the fact that previous management had amassed the poorest track record in the group during the past 5 years.

Portfolio Manager: Caesar Bryan
Since: 1991

Minimum:
Initial: $1,000
Subsequent: $100
Telephone Exchange: Yes
Distributions:
Income: Annually
Capital Gain: Annually
Front-End Load: 8.50%
12b-1: None
Redemption Fee: None
Management Company: Lexington Management
Ticker Symbol: STSLX

TOTAL RETURN (%)

1987	1988	1989	1990	1991	5-year	Bull Market	Bear Market
16.2	-15.9	16.1	-32.1	-14.5	-34.2	-10.1	-28.8

INVESTMENT PORTFOLIO

Total Assets (mil.)	Current Yield	Turnover Ratio	Expense Ratio	Beta	Risk Return
$12	0.0%	11%	1.53%	0.11	NA

UNITED SERVICES WORLD GOLD

United Services Advisors
P. O. Box 29467
San Antonio, TX 78229
800-873-8637

Investment Objective: Previously known as U.S. New Prospector Fund, this fund is among the precious metals category's most volatile offerings. Its volatility stems from its pure gold equity focus, its practice of staying fully invested at all times and its relatively large exposure to intermediate gold stocks. Although the fund does not invest in South Africa, its exposure to smaller mining companies gives it enormous leverage to a rising gold price. But, as seen last year, the fund is equally vulnerable to sharp price corrections when the gold price declines. It is best suited to the most aggressive goldbugs who wish to sidestep South African gold mining stocks.

Minimum:
Initial: $1,000
Subsequent: $50
Telephone Exchange: Yes
Distributions:
Income: Annually
Capital Gain: Annually
Front-End Load: None
12b-1: None
Redemption Fee: None
Management Company: United Services Advisors
Ticker Symbol: UNWPX

Portfolio Manager: Victor Flores
Since: 1990

TOTAL RETURN (%)

1987	1988	1989	1990	1991	5-year	Bull Market	Bear Market
31.1	-18.8	16.5	-27.9	-3.4	-13.5	-0.2	-10.1

INVESTMENT PORTFOLIO

Total Assets (mil.)	Current Yield	Turnover Ratio	Expense Ratio	Beta	Risk Return
$66	0.0%	44%	2.22%	0.06	NA

UNITED SERVICES GLOBAL RESOURCES

United Services Advisors
P. O. Box 29467
San Antonio, TX 78229
800-873-8637

Investment Objective: Formerly the Prospector Fund, this fund closed in 1985 pending the resolution of certain legal/regulatory matters. Since reopening in 1990, the previously pure gold fund amended its charter. It now invests in securities of companies engaged in all types of natural resources activities, adjusting its asset mix in response to economic conditions. Major sectors are currently gold and energy. The fund also has some exposure to diversified, nonprecious metals stocks. It does not invest in South African gold mining stocks.

Minimum:
Initial: $1,000
Subsequent: $50
Telephone Exchange: No
Distributions:
Income: Annually
Capital Gain: Annually
Front-End Load: None
12b-1: None
Redemption Fee: None
Management Company: United Services Advisors
Ticker Symbol: PSPFX

Portfolio Manager: Victor Flores
Since: 1990

TOTAL RETURN (%)

1987	1988	1989	1990	1991	5-year	Bull Market	Bear Market
23.6	-12.2	22.1	-15.9	5.0	17.0	6.9	-6.9

INVESTMENT PORTFOLIO

Total Assets (mil.)	Current Yield	Turnover Ratio	Expense Ratio	Beta	Risk Return
$28	1.2%	82%	2.43%	0.46	NA

UNITED SERVICES GOLD SHARES

United Services Advisors
P. O. Box 29467
San Antonio, TX 78229
800-873-8637

Investment Objective: Investing exclusively in South African gold stocks, this fund is among the category's most volatile. Although these stocks pay very high dividends, they're prone to sharp price swings in response to both gold price movements and changes in South Africa's political climate. As evidenced by the fund's 65% 1989 gain, South African gold shares offer enormous upside in the face of a rising gold price and signs of improving politics. But they're also vulnerable to sharp downward price swings when conditions reverse, as has been the case during the past 2 years. Only investors who understand and are willing to assume the South African equities' significant political and investment risks should consider this fund.

Portfolio Manager: Edmond Serfaty
Since: 1987

Minimum:
Initial: $1,000
Subsequent: $50
Telephone Exchange: Yes
Distributions:
Income: Semiannually
Capital Gain: Annually
Front-End Load: None
12b-1: None
Redemption Fee: None
Management Company: United Services Advisors
Ticker Symbol: USERX

TOTAL RETURN (%)

1987	1988	1989	1990	1991	5-year	Bull Market	Bear Market
31.6	-35.7	64.7	-34.2	-15.6	-22.7	-8.3	-9.2

INVESTMENT PORTFOLIO

Total Assets (mil.)	Current Yield	Turnover Ratio	Expense Ratio	Beta	Risk Return
$332	2.9%	49%	1.54%	-0.33	NA

USAA GOLD

USAA Investment Management
USAA Building
San Antonio, TX 78288
800-531-8181

Investment Objective: Holding neither gold bullion nor significant amounts of cash, this fund maintains a fairly pure gold equity portfolio. North American gold stocks predominate, but the fund also keeps some exposure to major South African and Australian gold producers. While far from the tamest entrants in the precious metals group, management has been upgrading the quality of the fund's holdings in recent years. On balance, the fund's return should parallel that of the average gold mining stock.

Portfolio Manager: David G. Peebles
Since: 1990

Minimum:
Initial: $1,000
Subsequent: $50
Telephone Exchange: Yes
Distributions:
Income: Annually
Capital Gain: Annually
Front-End Load: None
12b-1: None
Redemption Fee: None
Management Company: USAA Investment Management
Ticker Symbol: USAGX

TOTAL RETURN (%)

1987	1988	1989	1990	1991	5-year	Bull Market	Bear Market
16.2	-17.1	18.1	-26.6	-4.4	-20.2	-4.7	-7.4

INVESTMENT PORTFOLIO

Total Assets (mil.)	Current Yield	Turnover Ratio	Expense Ratio	Beta	Risk Return
$127	1.2%	42%	1.43%	0.01	NA

VAN ECK GOLD RESOURCES

Van Eck Securities
122 East 42nd Street
New York, NY 10168
800-221-2220

Investment Objective: Among the least actively traded precious metals funds, this fund has traditionally been one of the category's riskier offerings. Management keeps the fund fully invested in North American and Australian gold mining shares, with cash rarely exceeding 5% of assets. By charter, the fund doesn't invest in South African equities, nor does it purchase gold bullion. Although top-quality gold stocks predominate, the fund also has a sizable stake in more leveraged, secondary gold stocks. Consequently, it has shown above-average upside potential in gold rallies and a corresponding degree of downside volatility when the price of gold is declining.

Portfolio Manager: Henry J. Bingham
Since: 1986

Minimum:
Initial: $1,000
Subsequent: $100
Telephone Exchange: Yes
Distributions:
Income: Annually
Capital Gain: Annually
Front-End Load: 6.75%
12b-1: 0.25%
Redemption Fee: None
Management Company: Van Eck Associates
Ticker Symbol: GRFRX

TOTAL RETURN (%)

1987	1988	1989	1990	1991	5-year	Bull Market	Bear Market
47.2	-21.3	18.9	-26.4	-4.1	-2.7	-5.3	-7.9

INVESTMENT PORTFOLIO

Total Assets (mil.)	Current Yield	Turnover Ratio	Expense Ratio	Beta	Risk Return
$145	0.3%	12%	1.44%	0.05	NA

VAN ECK INTERNATIONAL INVESTORS

Van Eck Securities
122 East 42nd Street
New York, NY 10168
800-221-2220

Investment Objective: This geographically diversified gold fund allocates its assets across each of the free world's major gold mining regions, with South African gold stocks claiming the largest portion of assets. Consequently, the fund responds to both gold price movements as well as developments in South Africa's political climate. The fund was a top performer in 1989 when gold rallied and South Africa's political situation seemed to be improving. But when these factors reversed in 1990, the fund showed relatively poor resistance to decline, underperforming about three-quarters of its gold-fund rivals.

Portfolio Manager: J. Van Eck/H. Bingham
Since: 1986

Minimum:
Initial: $1,000
Subsequent: $100
Telephone Exchange: Yes
Distributions:
Income: Quarterly
Capital Gain: Annually
Front-End Load: 8.50%
12b-1: None
Redemption Fee: None
Management Company: Van Eck Associates
Ticker Symbol: INIVX

TOTAL RETURN (%)

1987	1988	1989	1990	1991	5-year	Bull Market	Bear Market
34.8	-22.0	51.3	-27.0	2.6	19.0	4.4	-8.7

INVESTMENT PORTFOLIO

Total Assets (mil.)	Current Yield	Turnover Ratio	Expense Ratio	Beta	Risk Return
$628	1.4%	2%	0.97%	-0.09	NA

VANGUARD SPECIALIZED GOLD & PRECIOUS METALS

Vanguard Group
Vanguard Financial Center
Valley Forge, PA 19482
800-662-7447

Investment Objective: Typically, Vanguard's entrant in the precious metals arena is among the best of its kind. Sporting 5 straight years of above-average returns, the fund is among the category's most consistent performers. Its ability to outpace its average rival in most markets owes in part to Vanguard's usual low expenses. Also responsible is the fund's quality focus and neglect of highly volatile secondary gold stocks. Some exposure to diversified metals/minerals producers and bullion also helps mitigate risk. For investors seeking exposure to each of the free world's major gold mining regions, this no-load fund is an excellent choice.

Portfolio Manager: David Hutchins
Since: 1987

Minimum:
Initial: $3,000
Subsequent: $100
Telephone Exchange: Yes
Distributions:
Income: Annually
Capital Gain: Annually
Front-End Load: None
12b-1: None
Redemption Fee: 1.00%
Management Company: M&G Investment Management
Ticker Symbol: VGPMX

TOTAL RETURN (%)

1987	1988	1989	1990	1991	5-year	Bull Market	Bear Market
38.7	-14.2	30.4	-19.9	4.4	29.8	6.6	-6.5

INVESTMENT PORTFOLIO

Total Assets (mil.)	Current Yield	Turnover Ratio	Expense Ratio	Beta	Risk Return
$187	2.7%	10%	0.42%	-0.02	NA

PART 9

Sector Funds

Sector funds invest in very concentrated portfolios of common stocks, usually drawing their selections from a single industry. Although most sector funds got their start during the past decade, this investment strategy is not new to the mutual fund industry. For example, Century Shares Trust, which invests the vast majority of its assets in insurance stocks, began operations in 1931. In 1981, Fidelity Management and Research opened the floodgates to sector investing with the initiation of the Fidelity Select Portfolios Fund, which gave investors the opportunity to concentrate in, and switch between, one or more of the following industries: technology, utilities, health care, energy, precious metals and financial services. Financial Programs and Vanguard shortly followed suit, establishing funds with similar group portfolios. Except for popular industries such as technology, health care, utilities and energy, fund distributors have had a difficult time attracting large numbers of investors to industry-concentrated funds in recent years. Thus, growth in the number of sector funds has been virtually nonexistent during the past 2 years. In fact, a number of sector funds merged with other funds during the past few years.

One of the benefits of investing in mutual funds is the risk reduction that investors receive by holding a highly diversified portfolio of common stocks. On average, the typical diversified common stock fund contains one-third the risk contained in a portfolio consisting of a single stock. Industry-concentrated portfolios, on the other hand, contain significantly more risk than the typical equity fund.

That's because the factors that affect one stock in an industry-concentrated portfolio tend to affect all stocks in the industry. Thus, industry-concentrated funds can be highly variable.

Sector funds appeal to three types of investors. First, investors who seek above-average current yields from their equity portfolios might seek investment in funds that concentrate their investments in utility, bank or insurance stocks. Second, aggressive-growth investors may wish to include investments in rapid-growth industries such as health care biotechnology or technology in their portfolios. Finally, investors who attempt to time the economic cycle by practicing "sector rotation" will find these funds of interest. Sector rotation is an attempt to continually allocate assets among industries that are affected differently by changes in the business cycle, for example, investing in interest-rate-sensitive industries during an economic downturn, cyclical stocks during the early stages of an economic turnaround and consumer stocks during a period of robust economic growth.

Because of the high degree of concentration of assets and the extreme volatility contained in their shares, investment in sector funds is not for the faint of heart. Although some of the best performing funds in recent years concentrate their investments in a single industry, a much larger number tend to reside at the bottom of the performance charts. Thus, investors should approach this category of mutual funds with a high degree of caution.

Summary of Financial Statistics (medians)

1991 Return	5-Year Return	Current Yield	Beta	Turnover Ratio	Expense Ratio
35.5%	78.7%	0.6%	1.09	110%	1.79%

BEST SECTOR FUNDS FOR 1991

Fund	PercentReturn 1991	3-Year	5-Year
Oppenheimer Global Bio-Tech	121.1%	207.2%	NA
Fidelity Select Biotechnology	99.0	313.2	316.1
Financial Strategic Health Science	91.8	284.8	378.0
Fidelity Select Health Care	83.7	225.4	251.9
Fidelity Select Brokerage & Investment	82.3	74.3	30.5
Fidelity Select Medical Delivery	77.8	226.7	232.5
Financial Strategic Technology	76.9	133.2	152.3
Financial Strategic Financial Services	74.0	121.1	130.5
Fidelity Select Retailing	68.1	106.8	165.8
Fidelity Select Regional Banks	65.8	66.5	103.0
Fidelity Select Savings & Loan	64.6	52.7	66.7
Fidelity Select Financial Services	61.6	45.9	36.5
Fidelity Select Developing Communication	61.4	NA	NA
T. Rowe Price Science & Technology	60.2	122.5	NA
United Science & Energy	59.3	95.8	140.4
Fidelity Select Technology	59.0	105.6	76.4
Seligman Communications & Information	54.9	79.4	121.5
Alliance Technology Fund	54.2	58.4	90.0
Fidelity Select Transportation	54.1	55.2	77.4
Financial Strategic Leisure	52.7	88.0	143.4
Putnam Health Sciences Trust	49.1	144.5	184.0
Vanguard Specialized Technology	47.3	57.8	52.2
Vanguard Specialized Health Care	46.3	127.3	190.3

ABT UTILITY INCOME FUND

ABT Financial Services
205 Royal Palm Way
Palm Beach, FL 33480
800-289-2281

Investment Objective: This fund seeks high dividend income and some capital appreciation through investing at least 65% of its assets in the securities of public utilities, which includes companies engaged in providing electric, gas, energy and communications services. While public utility stocks are considered "widow and orphan" securities because of their low risk and modest returns, these stocks can produce handsome returns during periods of declining interest rates as witnessed by the double-digit total returns this fund delivered during 1988, 1989 and 1991.

Portfolio Manager: Ted Wolff
Since: 1992

Minimum:
Initial: $1,000
Subsequent: $50
Telephone Exchange: Yes
Distributions:
Income: Quarterly
Capital Gain: Quarterly
Front-End Load: 4.75%
12b-1: 0.25%
Redemption Fee: None
Management Company: Palm Beach Capital Management
Ticker Symbol: ABUIX

TOTAL RETURN (%)

1987	1988	1989	1990	1991	5-year	Bull Market	Bear Market
-4.0	15.6	34.1	-6.1	17.9	64.7	16.6	-5.2

INVESTMENT PORTFOLIO

Total Assets (mil.)	Current Yield	Turnover Ratio	Expense Ratio	Beta	Risk Return
$146	4.7%	33%	1.25%	0.50	0.04

ALLIANCE TECHNOLOGY FUND

Alliance Funds Distributor
500 Plaza Drive
Secaucus, NJ 07094
800-247-4154

Investment Objective: This fund seeks to achieve its objective of capital growth by investing primarily in equity securities of companies that are expected to benefit from technological advances and improvements (i.e., companies that use technology extensively in the development of new or improved products or processes). When selecting individual securities, the adviser considers such factors as the economic and political outlook, the value of individual securities relative to other investment alternatives, trends in the determinants of corporate profits and management capability and practices. In general, the philosophy of management is to identify innovators, anticipate trends and invest aggressively.

Portfolio Manager: Roger Honour
Since: 1990

Minimum:
Initial: $250
Subsequent: $250
Telephone Exchange: Yes
Distributions:
Income: Annually
Capital Gain: Annually
Front-End Load: 5.50%
12b-1: 0.30%
Redemption Fee: None
Management Company: Alliance Capital Management
Ticker Symbol: ALTFX

TOTAL RETURN (%)

1987	1988	1989	1990	1991	5-year	Bull Market	Bear Market
19.2	0.6	6.0	-3.1	54.2	90.0	69.4	-39.9

INVESTMENT PORTFOLIO

Total Assets (mil.)	Current Yield	Turnover Ratio	Expense Ratio	Beta	Risk Return
$167	0.0%	147%	1.77%	1.37	0.06

AMERICAN GAS INDEX

Rushmore Family of Funds
4922 Fairmont Avenue
Bethesda, MD 20814
800-343-3355

Investment Objective: American Gas Index has the unfortunate luck of being concentrated in an industry that has not been performing well, as its unimpressive returns indicate. The fund tries to duplicate the returns of an index made up of stocks of natural gas distribution and transmission company members of the American Gas Association. The main thing this fund has going for it is probable potential for the long term, because gas is the environmentally sound choice, and it is abundant in the states. A combination of these factors eventually may improve the performance of this fund.

Portfolio Manager: Daniel Ryczek
Since: 1984

Minimum:
Initial: $2,500
Subsequent: None
Telephone Exchange: Yes
Distributions:
Income: Quarterly
Capital Gain: Annually
Front-End Load: None
12b-1: None
Redemption Fee: None
Management Company: Money Management Associates
Ticker Symbol: GASFX

TOTAL RETURN (%)

1987	1988	1989	1990	1991	5-year	Bull Market	Bear Market
NA	NA	NA	-10.5	3.2	NA	NA	NA

INVESTMENT PORTFOLIO

Total Assets (mil.)	Current Yield	Turnover Ratio	Expense Ratio	Beta	Risk Return
$140	4.6%	30%	0.79%	NA	NA

CENTURY SHARES TRUST

Century Shares Trust
One Liberty Square
Boston, MA 02109
800-321-1928

Investment Objective: This fund seeks capital appreciation by investing primarily in insurance stocks. Although sector funds are more risky than diversified funds, insurance stocks tend to have below-average volatility. Rising interest rates tend to affect insurance stocks more than the typical industrial stock. Because insurance companies hold large portfolios of bonds, rising interest rates cause insurance company assets (and book values) to decline. However, the reverse is true during a period of declining interest rates. In addition, this fund provides a better-than-average current yield for a fund that seeks capital appreciation.

Portfolio Manager: Allan W. Fulkerson
Since: 1976

Minimum:
Initial: $500
Subsequent: $25
Telephone Exchange: No
Distributions:
Income: Semiannually
Capital Gain: Annually
Front-End Load: None
12b-1: None
Redemption Fee: None
Management Company: Century Shares Trustees
Ticker Symbol: CENSX

TOTAL RETURN (%)

1987	1988	1989	1990	1991	5-year	Bull Market	Bear Market
-8.0	15.7	41.6	-7.8	31.5	82.7	49.5	-26.6

INVESTMENT PORTFOLIO

Total Assets (mil.)	Current Yield	Turnover Ratio	Expense Ratio	Beta	Risk Return
$145	2.2%	3%	1.03%	1.03	0.05

CIGNA UTILITIES FUND

CIGNA Mutual Funds
One Financial Plaza, 16th Floor
Springfield, MA 01103
800-572-4462

Investment Objective: The fund, which invests exclusively in common stocks of electric, telephone and gas utilities, strives to achieve a high level of current income coupled with capital appreciation. Electric utility stocks tend to be the most prominent. However, an allocation to telephone stocks gives the fund a higher-than-average appreciation potential. Like other utility funds, share price is highly sensitive to change in interest rates. With better-than-average income for an equity fund, this fund is appropriate for conservative income investors who also seek capital appreciation to offset the impact of inflation.

Portfolio Manager: Bo Bohannon
Since: 1991

Minimum:
Initial: $500
Subsequent: $50
Telephone Exchange: Yes
Distributions:
Income: Annually
Capital Gain: Monthly
Front-End Load: 5.00%
12b-1: 0.25%
Redemption Fee: None
Management Company: CIGNA Investments
Ticker Symbol: CGUTX

TOTAL RETURN (%)

1987	1988	1989	1990	1991	5-year	Bull Market	Bear Market
NA	NA	36.1	-3.0	23.9	NA	24.6	-8.0

INVESTMENT PORTFOLIO

Total Assets (mil.)	Current Yield	Turnover Ratio	Expense Ratio	Beta	Risk Return
$86	4.3%	123%	1.21%	0.6	0.05

FIDELITY REAL ESTATE INVESTMENTS

Fidelity Distributors Corporation
82 Devonshire Street, Mail Zone L7B
Boston, MA 02109
800-544-8888

Investment Objective: This fund, which began in late 1986, seeks income and capital growth by investing in equity securities of companies in the real estate industry. This is a sector fund and as such is subject to additional risks specific to the real estate industry. The fund can invest in real estate and mortgage investment trusts and companies engaged in related businesses. However, the fund also can invest up to one-third of its assets in unrelated industries and also can use options and futures as portfolio insurance. The fund's performance has been mediocre at best since its inception. However, the volatility level (beta 0.57) is lower than that of the average fund.

Portfolio Manager: Barry Greenfield
Since: 1986

Minimum:
Initial: $2,500
Subsequent: $250
Telephone Exchange: Yes
Distributions:
Income: Quarterly
Capital Gain: Annually
Front-End Load: None
12b-1: None
Redemption Fee: None
Management Company: Fidelity Management & Research
Ticker Symbol: FRESX

TOTAL RETURN (%)

1987	1988	1989	1990	1991	5-year	Bull Market	Bear Market
-7.7	10.4	13.8	-8.7	39.2	47.3	38.4	-13.3

INVESTMENT PORTFOLIO

Total Assets (mil.)	Current Yield	Turnover Ratio	Expense Ratio	Beta	Risk Return
$55	4.5%	86%	1.34%	0.57	0.09

FIDELITY SELECT AIR TRANSPORTATION

Fidelity Distributors Corporation
82 Devonshire Street, Mail Zone L7B
Boston, MA 02109
800-544-8888

Investment Objective: Fidelity Select Air Transportation Fund invests in a specialized portfolio of equity securities of companies engaged in the air transportation of passengers, mail and air freight. Although the fund invests in aviation service and manufacturing firms, airlines claim the bulk of its assets. As such, its returns are highly correlated to the airline industry's fortunes, which have suffered in recent years as mounting costs and sluggish air traffic put pressure on earnings. However, the airline industry is highly sensitive to the economic cycle. An economic rebound could thus catapult airline stocks and this fund's shares to new heights.

Portfolio Manager: Karen Firestone
Since: 1987

Minimum:
Initial: $2,500
Subsequent: $250
Telephone Exchange: Yes
Distributions:
Income: Semiannually
Capital Gain: Annually
Front-End Load: 3.00%
12b-1: None
Redemption Fee: 0.75%
Management Company: Fidelity Management & Research
Ticker Symbol: FSAIZ

TOTAL RETURN (%)

1987	1988	1989	1990	1991	5-year	Bull Market	Bear Market
-20.7	29.1	26.3	-18.2	37.1	45.0	50.1	-28.5

INVESTMENT PORTFOLIO

Total Assets (mil.)	Current Yield	Turnover Ratio	Expense Ratio	Beta	Risk Return
$5	0.0%	41%	2.51%	1.14	0.08

FIDELITY SELECT AUTOMOTIVE

Fidelity Distributors Corporation
82 Devonshire Street, Mail Zone L7B
Boston, MA 02109
800-544-8888

Investment Objective: As the name implies, the fund invests in the automotive industry. Specifically, these companies are engaged in the manufacturing, marketing and selling of automobiles, trucks, specialty vehicles, parts, tires and related services. In addition, the portfolio may invest in companies that provide automotive-related services to manufacturers, distributors or consumers. This particular industry is highly sensitive to business cycles. While the shares of companies in the industry perform worst during the early stages of an economic recession, they tend to be excellent performers during the early stages of a recovery.

Portfolio Manager: Steve Wymer
Since: 1990

Minimum:
Initial: $1,000
Subsequent: $250
Telephone Exchange: Yes
Distributions:
Income: Annually
Capital Gain: Annually
Front-End Load: 3.00%
12b-1: None
Redemption Fee: 0.75%
Management Company: Fidelity Management & Research
Ticker Symbol: FSAVX

TOTAL RETURN (%)

1987	1988	1989	1990	1991	5-year	Bull Market	Bear Market
6.5	20.1	4.1	-6.7	37.4	70.6	49.1	-29.9

INVESTMENT PORTFOLIO

Total Assets (mil.)	Current Yield	Turnover Ratio	Expense Ratio	Beta	Risk Return
$2	0.0%	219%	2.25%	0.92	0.06

FIDELITY SELECT BIOTECHNOLOGY

Fidelity Distributors Corporation
82 Devonshire Street, Mail Zone L7B
Boston, MA 02109
800-544-8888

Investment Objective: This fund seeks capital appreciation by investing in a relatively concentrated portfolio of biotechnology stocks. The fund's holdings generally include stocks in such industries as drugs and pharmaceuticals, medical equipment and supplies and medical facilities management. Although funds with concentrated portfolios are capable of producing large returns in the short run, their shares tend to be much more volatile than those of diversified equity funds. The fund has participated fully in the bull market in biotech stocks and was among the past year's top performing funds. Of course, share price could suffer during a severe correction that generally follows overdone bull markets.

Portfolio Manager: Michael Gordon
Since: 1990

Minimum:
Initial: $1,000
Subsequent: $250
Telephone Exchange: Yes
Distributions:
Income: Annually
Capital Gain: Semiannually
Front-End Load: 3.00%
12b-1: None
Redemption Fee: 0.75%
Management Company: Fidelity Management & Research
Ticker Symbol: FBIOX

TOTAL RETURN (%)

1987	1988	1989	1990	1991	5-year	Bull Market	Bear Market
-3.4	4.1	43.9	44.3	99.0	316.1	108.8	-11.6

INVESTMENT PORTFOLIO

Total Assets (mil.)	Current Yield	Turnover Ratio	Expense Ratio	Beta	Risk Return
$903	0.1%	166%	1.63%	1.10	0.15

FIDELITY SELECT BROADCAST & MEDIA

Fidelity Distributors Corporation
82 Devonshire Street, Mail Zone L7B
Boston, MA 02109
800-544-8888

Investment Objective: Fidelity Select Broadcast & Media Portfolio invests in a specialized portfolio of equity securities of companies engaged in the development, production, sale and distribution of goods and services used in the broadcasting and media industries. Areas of concentration include cable TV, cellular communications, newspapers and motion pictures. The fund's emphasis on these strong franchise, high-growth industries gives it significant appreciation potential. However, 1990's results show that it also is vulnerable to big setbacks in the face of actual and/or anticipated earnings disappointments. It is suitable only for risk-tolerant investors.

Portfolio Manager: David Calabro
Since: 1991

Minimum:
Initial: $1,000
Subsequent: $250
Telephone Exchange: Yes
Distributions:
Income: Annually
Capital Gain: Annually
Front-End Load: 3.00%
12b-1: None
Redemption Fee: 0.75%
Management Company: Fidelity Management & Research
Ticker Symbol: FBMPX

TOTAL RETURN (%)

1987	1988	1989	1990	1991	5-year	Bull Market	Bear Market
19.9	26.8	32.5	-26.2	37.8	105.1	55.0	-28.3

INVESTMENT PORTFOLIO

Total Assets (mil.)	Current Yield	Turnover Ratio	Expense Ratio	Beta	Risk Return
$6	0.0%	150%	2.53%	1.27	0.05

FIDELITY SELECT BROKERAGE & INVESTMENT

Fidelity Distributors Corporation
82 Devonshire Street, Mail Zone L7B
Boston, MA 02109
800-544-8888

Investment Objective: In many ways, this is a good way to place bets on the strength or weakness of the overall stock market. As brokerage firms are "leveraged" to the market, meaning their profits jump as trading increases in a rising market and fall when the market slumps, investors bullish on the market's prospects could find the shares of brokerage firms—and the shares of this fund—a good bet. Conversely, getting caught in the fund when the market tanks can be painful, as the fund's nearly 37% plunge in 1987 attests.

Portfolio Manager: Scott Offen
Since: 1990

Minimum:
Initial: $1,000
Subsequent: $250
Telephone Exchange: Yes
Distributions:
Income: Annually
Capital Gain: Annually
Front-End Load: 3.00%
12b-1: None
Redemption Fee: 0.75%
Management Company: Fidelity Management & Research
Ticker Symbol: FSLBX

TOTAL RETURN (%)

1987	1988	1989	1990	1991	5-year	Bull Market	Bear Market
-36.8	18.5	14.1	-16.2	82.3	30.5	74.6	-28.4

INVESTMENT PORTFOLIO

Total Assets (mil.)	Current Yield	Turnover Ratio	Expense Ratio	Beta	Risk Return
$20	0.1%	62%	2.50%	1.39	0.11

FIDELITY SELECT CHEMICALS

Fidelity Distributors Corporation
82 Devonshire Street, Mail Zone L7B
Boston, MA 02109
800-544-8888

Investment Objective: This fund seeks capital appreciation by investing in a relatively concentrated portfolio of common stocks of companies in all aspects of the chemical industry, including agricultural chemicals, industrial gases, inorganic chemicals, plastics, synthetic resins and specialty chemicals. Although mutual funds with concentrated portfolios are capable of producing large returns in the short run, their share prices tend to be much more volatile than those of diversified equity funds.

Portfolio Manager: Steve Pesek
Since: 1988

Minimum:
Initial: $1,000
Subsequent: $250
Telephone Exchange: Yes
Distributions:
Income: Semiannually
Capital Gain: Annually
Front-End Load: 3.00%
12b-1: None
Redemption Fee: 0.75%
Management Company: Fidelity Management & Research
Ticker Symbol: FSCHX

TOTAL RETURN (%)

1987	1988	1989	1990	1991	5-year	Bull Market	Bear Market
14.8	21.0	17.3	-4.2	38.7	116.5	52.1	-21.7

INVESTMENT PORTFOLIO

Total Assets (mil.)	Current Yield	Turnover Ratio	Expense Ratio	Beta	Risk Return
$22	0.6%	87%	2.50%	1.05	0.06

FIDELITY SELECT COMPUTERS

Fidelity Distributors Corporation
82 Devonshire Street, Mail Zone L7B
Boston, MA 02109
800-544-8888

Investment Objective: This fund invests in common stocks of companies engaged in the research, design, development, manufacture or distribution of products, processes and services used in the computer industry, including computer services, peripherals and software. Management has attempted to negotiate a difficult market for technology stocks in recent years by avoiding hardware manufacturers in favor of companies involved in workstations, personal computers, networking systems and software companies with relatively strong earnings momentum. A lack of industry diversification implied by this fund's sector mandate and the volatile nature of technology stocks suggest significant share-price fluctuations.

Portfolio Manager: Bob Chow
Since: 1991

Minimum:
Initial: $1,000
Subsequent: $250
Telephone Exchange: Yes
Distributions:
Income: Annually
Capital Gain: Annually
Front-End Load: 3.0%
12b-1: None
Redemption Fee: 0.75%
Management Company: Fidelity Management & Research
Ticker Symbol: FDCPX

TOTAL RETURN (%)

1987	1988	1989	1990	1991	5-year	Bull Market	Bear Market
-6.4	-5.0	6.8	18.4	30.7	47.1	76.1	-35.1

INVESTMENT PORTFOLIO

Total Assets (mil.)	Current Yield	Turnover Ratio	Expense Ratio	Beta	Risk Return
$16	1.5%	695%	2.26%	1.37	0.03

FIDELITY SELECT CONSTRUCTION & HOUSING

Fidelity Distributors Corporation
82 Devonshire Street, Mail Zone L7B
Boston, MA 02109
800-544-8888

Investment Objective: This fund seeks capital appreciation by investing in companies engaged in the design and construction of residential, commercial, industrial and public-works facilities. It also invests in companies engaged in the manufacture, supply, distribution or sale of products or services to these construction companies. Examples include those that provide engineering and contracting services and companies that produce basic building materials such as cement, aggregates, gypsum, timber, wall coverings and coatings. The fund is highly sensitive to the economic cycle. Its shares tend to perform exceptionally well during the initial stages of an economic rebound.

Portfolio Manager: Michael Kagan
Since: 1989

Minimum:
Initial: $1,000
Subsequent: $250
Telephone Exchange: Yes
Distributions:
Income: Annually
Capital Gain: Annually
Front-End Load: 3.00%
12b-1: None
Redemption Fee: 0.75%
Management Company: Fidelity Management & Research
Ticker Symbol: FSHOX

TOTAL RETURN (%)

1987	1988	1989	1990	1991	5-year	Bull Market	Bear Market
-12.4	29.2	16.6	-9.6	41.3	68.5	60.5	-30.2

INVESTMENT PORTFOLIO

Total Assets (mil.)	Current Yield	Turnover Ratio	Expense Ratio	Beta	Risk Return
$2	0.0%	137%	2.48%	1.16	0.06

FIDELITY SELECT CONSUMER PRODUCTS

Fidelity Distributors Corporation
82 Devonshire Street, Mail Zone L7B
Boston, MA 02109
800-544-8888

Investment Objective: Among the newer additions to the Fidelity Select Funds, Fidelity Select Consumer Products Portfolio seeks capital appreciation through investments in equity securities of companies engaged in the manufacture and distribution of consumer products. Major industries include food, beverages, pharmaceuticals, soaps, detergents and tobacco. Although the fund owns a few young companies, most of the fund's companies are mature S&P 500 names such as Philip Morris, Coca-Cola and Bristol-Myers Squibb. While the fund's nondiversified character suggests additional risk, the stable growth characteristics of most consumer-products companies figure to temper some of this added volatility.

Portfolio Manager: Fedgus Shiel
Since: 1991

Minimum:
Initial: $2,500
Subsequent: $250
Telephone Exchange: Yes
Distributions:
Income: Annually
Capital Gain: Annually
Front-End Load: 3.00%
12b-1: None
Redemption Fee: 0.75%
Management Company: Fidelity Management & Research
Ticker Symbol: FSCPX

TOTAL RETURN (%)

1987	1988	1989	1990	1991	5-year	Bull Market	Bear Market
NA	NA	NA	-1.1	38.5	NA	50.1	-20.9

INVESTMENT PORTFOLIO

Total Assets (mil.)	Current Yield	Turnover Ratio	Expense Ratio	Beta	Risk Return
$5	0.0%	137%	2.51%	NA	NA

FIDELITY SELECT DEFENSE & AEROSPACE

Fidelity Distributors Corporation
82 Devonshire Street, Mail Zone L7B
Boston, MA 02109
800-544-8888

Investment Objective: As the Cold War ends, this fund could freeze over. As one of the oldest Select funds in Fidelity's portfolio, it has seen the rise and fall of the military-industrial complex during the Reagan and post-Reagan era. In 1985, for example, the fund rose a strong 26% on the back of an increasing military budget and fat profits for companies such as Raytheon and Northrop. However, with the end of the Cold War, Congress could be pressured into drastically cutting the defense budget. In other words, this industry could experience rough sledding during the 1990s.

Portfolio Manager: Jeffery Ubben
Since: 1990

Minimum:
Initial: $1,000
Subsequent: $250
Telephone Exchange: Yes
Distributions:
Income: Annually
Capital Gain: Annually
Front-End Load: 3.00%
12b-1: None
Redemption Fee: 0.75%
Management Company: Fidelity Management & Research
Ticker Symbol: FSDAX

TOTAL RETURN (%)

1987	1988	1989	1990	1991	5-year	Bull Market	Bear Market
-23.2	4.3	8.8	-4.6	26.9	5.6	35.8	-18.9

INVESTMENT PORTFOLIO

Total Assets (mil.)	Current Yield	Turnover Ratio	Expense Ratio	Beta	Risk Return
$2	0.4%	162%	2.49%	0.85	0.05

FIDELITY SELECT DEVELOPING COMMUNICATIONS

Fidelity Distributors Corporation
82 Devonshire Street, Mail Zone L7B
Boston, MA 02109
800-544-8888

Investment Objective: Hailed as one of the promising growth industries of the 1990s, this newly organized Select portfolio seeks to capitalize on expanding technology in the communications industry and the expansion of global telecommunications networks. Since inception, its investments have been concentrated in 3 industry sectors: cellular communications, cable systems and international telephone systems such as Telefonos de Mexico. Its short-term return potential is explosive, as witnessed by its 61% return the past year.

Portfolio Manager: Abigail Johnson
Since: 1991

Minimum:
Initial: $2,500
Subsequent: $250
Telephone Exchange: Yes
Distributions:
Income: Annually
Capital Gain: Annually
Front-End Load: 3.00%
12b-1: None
Redemption Fee: 0.75%
Management Company: Fidelity Management & Research
Ticker Symbol: FSDCP

TOTAL RETURN (%)

1987	1988	1989	1990	1991	5-year	Bull Market	Bear Market
NA	NA	NA	-9.7	61.4	NA	58.5	-36.4

INVESTMENT PORTFOLIO

Total Assets (mil.)	Current Yield	Turnover Ratio	Expense Ratio	Beta	Risk Return
$20	0.0%	83%	2.50%	NA	NA

FIDELITY SELECT ELECTRIC UTILITIES

Fidelity Distributors Corporation
82 Devonshire Street, Mail Zone L7B
Boston, MA 02109
800-544-8888

Investment Objective: As the name suggests, this low-load fund invests in electric utility concerns. The securities in the portfolio are of companies that may engage in activities related to electric utilities, including fuel, construction, pollution control and waste disposal. Although this fund does not provide a hefty yield like other utility funds, its future performance still is closely tied to interest rates. Should interest rates head upward, the fund should perform poorly and vice versa.

Portfolio Manager: Jeffery Ubben
Since: 1991

Minimum:
Initial: $1,000
Subsequent: $250
Telephone Exchange: Yes
Distributions:
Income: Semiannually
Capital Gain: Semiannually
Front-End Load: 3.00%
12b-1: None
Redemption Fee: 0.75%
Management Company: Fidelity Management & Research
Ticker Symbol: FSEUX

TOTAL RETURN (%)

1987	1988	1989	1990	1991	5-year	Bull Market	Bear Market
-17.2	20.1	28.2	-1.8	26.3	58.2	28.1	-6.8

INVESTMENT PORTFOLIO

Total Assets (mil.)	Current Yield	Turnover Ratio	Expense Ratio	Beta	Risk Return
$39	3.6%	50%	2.27%	0.43	0.07

FIDELITY SELECT ELECTRONICS

Fidelity Distributors Corporation
82 Devonshire Street, Mail Zone L7B
Boston, MA 02109
800-544-8888

Investment Objective: This fund seeks capital appreciation primarily through investments in companies engaged in the design, manufacture or sale of electronic components, including electronic component manufacturers, equipment vendors and electronic component distributors. Started in 1986, the fund was launched at a difficult time. A fiercely competitive pricing environment and, more recently, a weak economy have lead to severe earnings disappointment in the electronic industry, causing the fund to lose capital in 4 out of its first 5 years of operations. However, a rebound in the technology sector of the market helped the fund produce its best annual return since its inception during 1991.

Portfolio Manager: Tom Sprague
Since: 1990

Minimum:
Initial: $1,000
Subsequent: $250
Telephone Exchange: Yes
Distributions:
Income: Annually
Capital Gain: Annually
Front-End Load: 3.00%
12b-1: None
Redemption Fee: 0.75%
Management Company: Fidelity Management & Research
Ticker Symbol: FSELX

TOTAL RETURN (%)

1987	1988	1989	1990	1991	5-year	Bull Market	Bear Market
-13.5	-8.5	15.7	5.8	35.3	31.1	51.6	-38.1

INVESTMENT PORTFOLIO

Total Assets (mil.)	Current Yield	Turnover Ratio	Expense Ratio	Beta	Risk Return
$9	0.0%	268%	2.26%	1.28	0.04

FIDELITY SELECT ENERGY

Fidelity Distributors Corporation
82 Devonshire Street, Mail Zone L7B
Boston, MA 02109
800-544-8888

Investment Objective: If you think this fund invests only in high-yield oil stocks, think again. It has "diversified" into geothermal production, exploration for coal, oil and gas and, most important in terms of recent performance, pollution control. Though this expanded definition of energy doesn't seem to make much sense, its near-43% total return in 1989 was worth a lot of pennies. Its disappointing 1991 return resulted from tumbling oil prices and an economic slump that surprisingly exacted a heavy toll on waste collection and environmental cleanup stocks.

Portfolio Manager: Brian Posner
Since: 1991

Minimum:
Initial: $1,000
Subsequent: $250
Telephone Exchange: Yes
Distributions:
Income: Semiannually
Capital Gain: Annually
Front-End Load: 3.00%
12b-1: None
Redemption Fee: 0.75%
Management Company: Fidelity Management & Research
Ticker Symbol: FSENX

TOTAL RETURN (%)

1987	1988	1989	1990	1991	5-year	Bull Market	Bear Market
-1.8	15.9	42.8	-4.5	0.0	55.4	-0.3	-0.2

INVESTMENT PORTFOLIO

Total Assets (mil.)	Current Yield	Turnover Ratio	Expense Ratio	Beta	Risk Return
$74	1.0%	61%	1.79%	0.42	NA

FIDELITY SELECT ENERGY SERVICES

Fidelity Distributors Corporation
82 Devonshire Street, Mail Zone L7B
Boston, MA 02109
800-544-8888

Investment Objective: The investment objective of this fund is capital appreciation. The fund invests in more than just "oil patch" industries such as drilling, exploration and pipelines; the specialized portfolio looks at all types of energy services and equipment companies, including geothermal shale, coal and nuclear services. The Energy Services Fund was among the best in 1989, returning 59.4%. However, its near-24% decline during the past year was a major disappointment for investors, who withdrew more than $30 million from the fund.

Portfolio Manager: Bill Monkivsky
Since: 1991

Minimum:
Initial: $1,000
Subsequent: $250
Telephone Exchange: Yes
Distributions:
Income: Annually
Capital Gain: Annually
Front-End Load: 3.00%
12b-1: None
Redemption Fee: 0.75%
Management Company: Fidelity Management & Research
Ticker Symbol: FSESX

TOTAL RETURN (%)

1987	1988	1989	1990	1991	5-year	Bull Market	Bear Market
-11.8	-0.4	59.4	1.8	-23.5	9.1	-14.2	-8.6

INVESTMENT PORTFOLIO

Total Assets (mil.)	Current Yield	Turnover Ratio	Expense Ratio	Beta	Risk Return
$31	0.0%	62%	1.82%	0.87	NA

FIDELITY SELECT ENVIRONMENTAL SERVICES

Fidelity Distributors Corporation
82 Devonshire Street, Mail Zone L7B
Boston, MA 02109
800-544-8888

Investment Objective: Designed to capitalize on the rapid-growth prospects of the environmental services industry, the fund invests primarily in equity securities of companies engaged in the research, development, manufacture and distribution of products, processes and/or services related to waste management and pollution control. Although this is a high-growth-rate industry, the profits of waste collection and environmental cleanup companies have suffered during the 1989–1990 economic recession. This was a surprise to most analysts who believed that this industry was recession resistant. However, investors should fare well over the long term.

Portfolio Manager: Tom Sprague
Since: 1991

Minimum:
Initial: $1,000
Subsequent: $250
Telephone Exchange: Yes
Distributions:
Income: Annually
Capital Gain: Annually
Front-End Load: 3.00%
12b-1: None
Redemption Fee: 0.75%
Management Company: Fidelity Management & Research
Ticker Symbol: FSLEX

TOTAL RETURN (%)

1987	1988	1989	1990	1991	5-year	Bull Market	Bear Market
NA	NA	NA	-2.5	7.7	NA	22.8	-26.1

INVESTMENT PORTFOLIO

Total Assets (mil.)	Current Yield	Turnover Ratio	Expense Ratio	Beta	Risk Return
$68	0.0%	122%	2.03%	1.03	NA

FIDELITY SELECT FINANCIAL SERVICES

Fidelity Distributors Corporation
82 Devonshire Street, Mail Zone L7B
Boston, MA 02109
800-544-8888

Investment Objective: In the vein of Fidelity Select Brokerage, this fund invests in the 1980s version of a growth industry: financial services. Banks, S&Ls, finance companies, brokerage firms and money management companies are included in its holdings. This makes the fund a bit less sensitive to the gyrations of the market, though 1987's performance didn't earn the fund any bragging rights. For investors with a continuing interest in this field, the fund offers some diversification (relative to other Select funds). Its dismal performance during the late 1980s is directly related to a beleaguered banking industry. However, it was a stellar performer during the past year as investors bid up depressed bank and S&L stocks.

Portfolio Manager: Bruce Herring
Since: 1991

Minimum:
Initial: $1,000
Subsequent: $250
Telephone Exchange: Yes
Distributions:
Income: Annually
Capital Gain: Annually
Front-End Load: 3.00%
12b-1: None
Redemption Fee: 0.75%
Management Company: Fidelity Management & Research
Ticker Symbol: FIDSX

TOTAL RETURN (%)

1987	1988	1989	1990	1991	5-year	Bull Market	Bear Market
-16.5	12.0	19.3	-24.3	61.6	36.5	77.8	-3.03

INVESTMENT PORTFOLIO

Total Assets (mil.)	Current Yield	Turnover Ratio	Expense Ratio	Beta	Risk Return
$35	0.9%	237%	2.49%	1.40	0.07

FIDELITY SELECT FOOD & AGRICULTURE

Fidelity Distributors Corporation
82 Devonshire Street, Mail Zone L7B
Boston, MA 02109
800-544-8888

Investment Objective: Capital appreciation is this fund's investment objective. As the name implies, the fund invests in food and agriculture-related products. Management also may look for opportunities anywhere from food-processing companies, farm equipment and forest product companies, to restaurants, vitamin pill makers and beverage companies. Management uses a value-based approach to investing and emphasizes companies whose price-earnings multiples lag those of the market. The fund sports an enviable 5-year track record, and is only one of two funds to beat the market during each of the past 6 years.

Portfolio Manager: Deborah Wheeler
Since: 1991

Minimum:
Initial: $1,000
Subsequent: $250
Telephone Exchange: Yes
Distributions:
Income: Annually
Capital Gain: Semiannually
Front-End Load: 3.00%
12b-1: None
Redemption Fee: 0.75%
Management Company: Fidelity Management & Research
Ticker Symbol: FDFAX

TOTAL RETURN (%)

1987	1988	1989	1990	1991	5-year	Bull Market	Bear Market
7.5	26.8	38.9	9.3	34.1	177.5	33.8	-12.4

INVESTMENT PORTFOLIO

Total Assets (mil.)	Current Yield	Turnover Ratio	Expense Ratio	Beta	Risk Return
$88	0.3%	124%	2.22%	0.86	0.07

FIDELITY SELECT HEALTH CARE

Fidelity Distributors Corporation
82 Devonshire Street, Mail Zone L7B
Boston, MA 02109
800-544-8888

Investment Objective: This fund seeks capital appreciation by investing in a relatively concentrated portfolio of common stocks of companies in the health-care industry, including drug stores, pharmaceuticals, medical equipment and supplies and medical facilities management. The graying of America could cause this industry to become one of the great growth industries of the 1990s and beyond. However, mutual funds that hold concentrated portfolios experience more price volatility in general than diversified equities funds. This fund was a stellar performer during both the past year and the past 5 years.

Portfolio Manager: Andrew Offit
Since: 1990

Minimum:
Initial: $1,000
Subsequent: $250
Telephone Exchange: Yes
Distributions:
Income: Annually
Capital Gain: Semiannually
Front-End Load: 3.00%
12b-1: None
Redemption Fee: 0.75%
Management Company: Fidelity Management & Research
Ticker Symbol: FSPHX

TOTAL RETURN (%)

1987	1988	1989	1990	1991	5-year	Bull Market	Bear Market
-0.6	8.8	42.5	24.3	83.7	251.9	89.0	-11.6

INVESTMENT PORTFOLIO

Total Assets (mil.)	Current Yield	Turnover Ratio	Expense Ratio	Beta	Risk Return
$917	0.3%	159%	1.53%	1.15	0.13

FIDELITY SELECT INDUSTRIAL MATERIALS

Fidelity Distributors Corporation
82 Devonshire Street, Mail Zone L7B
Boston, MA 02109
800-544-8888

Investment Objective: This fund normally invests at least 80% of its assets in companies engaged in the mining, processing or distribution of raw materials and intermediate goods used in the industrial sector. Some examples of raw materials that its companies are engaged in are cement, timber, chemicals, steel and iron ore. Recently, management has been focusing on the paper/forest product, chemicals and steel segments. As could be expected, a slumping economy negatively impacted cyclical stocks during 1990. However, the fund should perform well during the early stages of an economic recovery as evidenced by its better-than-average return the past year.

Portfolio Manager: Steve Pesek
Since: 1990

Minimum:
Initial: $1,000
Subsequent: $250
Telephone Exchange: Yes
Distributions:
Income: Annually
Capital Gain: Annually
Front-End Load: 3.00%
12b-1: None
Redemption Fee: 0.75%
Management Company: Fidelity Management & Research
Ticker Symbol: FSDPX

TOTAL RETURN (%)

1987	1988	1989	1990	1991	5-year	Bull Market	Bear Market
15.6	10.8	4.4	-17.2	35.8	50.6	47.9	-23.5

INVESTMENT PORTFOLIO

Total Assets (mil.)	Current Yield	Turnover Ratio	Expense Ratio	Beta	Risk Return
$4	0.4%	148%	2.49%	1.10	0.05

FIDELITY SELECT INDUSTRIAL TECHNOLOGY

Fidelity Distributors Corporation
82 Devonshire Street, Mail Zone L7B
Boston, MA 02109
800-544-8888

Investment Objective: This fund seeks capital appreciation through investments in companies engaged in the manufacture, distribution or service of products and equipment for the industrial sector, including integrated producers of capital equipment (such as general industry machinery, farm equipment and computers), parts suppliers and subcontractors. This portfolio also may invest in companies that manufacture products or service equipment for the food, clothing or sporting goods industries. Recently, the fund absorbed two smaller Select portfolios, Select Automation and Select Capital Goods.

Portfolio Manager: Albert Roback
Since: 1991

Minimum:
Initial: $2,500
Subsequent: $250
Telephone Exchange: Yes
Distributions:
Income: Annually
Capital Gain: Annually
Front-End Load: 3.00%
12b-1: None
Redemption Fee: 0.75%
Management Company: Fidelity Management & Research
Ticker Symbol: FSCGX

TOTAL RETURN (%)

1987	1988	1989	1990	1991	5-year	Bull Market	Bear Market
-9.3	4.9	18.0	-15.5	26.8	20.3	34.4	-19.9

INVESTMENT PORTFOLIO

Total Assets (mil.)	Current Yield	Turnover Ratio	Expense Ratio	Beta	Risk Return
$2	0.9%	180%	2.49%	1.09	0.07

FIDELITY SELECT INSURANCE

Fidelity Distributors Corporation
82 Devonshire Street, Mail Zone L7B
Boston, MA 02109
800-544-8888

Investment Objective: If a life insurance salesperson giving a talk on mortality tables isn't your idea of a good time, you're not alone. Obviously, Fidelity didn't pick the best topic for this Select vehicle, and it shows in the fund's tiny $4 million asset base. Then again, performance, which has been a roller coaster ride in recent years, doesn't help either; few investors are willing to stomach return volatility of this nature. Overall, this fund invests in accident, life and medical insurers, and its share price should generally rise and fall with the ebb and flow of interest rates.

Portfolio Manager: Steve Pesek
Since: 1990

Minimum:
Initial: $1,000
Subsequent: $250
Telephone Exchange: Yes
Distributions:
Income: Semiannually
Capital Gain: Annually
Front-End Load: 3.00%
12b-1: None
Redemption Fee: 0.75%
Management Company: Fidelity Management & Research
Ticker Symbol: FSPCX

TOTAL RETURN (%)

1987	1988	1989	1990	1991	5-year	Bull Market	Bear Market
-12.2	17.4	37.8	-9.8	36.7	75.2	50.9	-25.3

INVESTMENT PORTFOLIO

Total Assets (mil.)	Current Yield	Turnover Ratio	Expense Ratio	Beta	Risk Return
$4	1.4%	98%	2.49%	1.00	0.06

FIDELITY SELECT LEISURE & ENTERTAINMENT

Fidelity Distributors Corporation
82 Devonshire Street, Mail Zone L7B
Boston, MA 02109
800-544-8888

Investment Objective: This fund seeks capital appreciation by investing in a relatively concentrated portfolio of common stocks in all aspects of the leisure and entertainment industry. Although the fund has been a stellar performer during 4 of the past 5 years, funds that hold concentrated portfolios are much more volatile than funds that hold diversified portfolios of common stocks. During 1990, for example, the fund's return plummeted along with consumer confidence and consumer willingness to spend for all but essentials. However, its share price should rebound along with the overall economy.

Portfolio Manager: Karen Firestone
Since: 1989

Minimum:
Initial: $1,000
Subsequent: $250
Telephone Exchange: Yes
Distributions:
Income: Annually
Capital Gain: Annually
Front-End Load: 3.00%
12b-1: None
Redemption Fee: 0.75%
Management Company: Fidelity Management & Research
Ticker Symbol: FDLSX

TOTAL RETURN (%)

1987	1988	1989	1990	1991	5-year	Bull Market	Bear Market
5.7	26.0	31.2	-22.3	32.9	80.5	45.0	-25.5

INVESTMENT PORTFOLIO

Total Assets (mil.)	Current Yield	Turnover Ratio	Expense Ratio	Beta	Risk Return
$35	0.0%	75%	2.27%	1.16	0.05

FIDELITY SELECT MEDICAL DELIVERY

Fidelity Distributors Corporation
82 Devonshire Street, Mail Zone L7B
Boston, MA 02109
800-544-8888

Investment Objective: As one would expect, this sector fund primarily invests in stocks of firms in the medical delivery field. The explosion in new forms of health-care delivery creates many new businesses and investment alternatives. This specialized fund can target not only for-profit hospitals, nursing homes and HMOs but also acute-care, psychiatric and specialized hospitals. The fund had an excellent showing during the past 4 years. The health-care industry has been one of the hottest on Wall Street in recent years and this fund's 278% 4-year return rates among the best of all funds.

Portfolio Manager: Charles Mangum
Since: 1991

Minimum:
Initial: $1,000
Subsequent: $250
Telephone Exchange: Yes
Distributions:
Income: Annually
Capital Gain: Semiannually
Front-End Load: 3.00%
12b-1: None
Redemption Fee: 0.75%
Management Company: Fidelity Management & Research
Ticker Symbol: FSHCX

TOTAL RETURN (%)

1987	1988	1989	1990	1991	5-year	Bull Market	Bear Market
-12.1	15.8	58.0	16.3	77.8	232.5	98.6	-22.7

INVESTMENT PORTFOLIO

Total Assets (mil.)	Current Yield	Turnover Ratio	Expense Ratio	Beta	Risk Return
$137	0.0%	165%	1.94%	1.36	0.10

FIDELITY SELECT PAPER & FOREST PRODUCTS

Fidelity Distributors Corporation
82 Devonshire Street, Mail Zone L7B
Boston, MA 02109
800-544-8888

Investment Objective: Fidelity Select Paper & Forest Products seeks capital appreciation by investing in a specialized portfolio of equity securities of companies engaged in the manufacture, research, sale or distribution of paper products, packaging products, building materials and other products related to the paper and forest products industry. Management tends to maintain a fairly compact portfolio, with an emphasis on companies that produce commodity-grade paper and show good long-term earnings momentum. As is true of all sector funds, this fund is suitable only for investors who are willing to assume the additional risk inherent in its lack of industry diversification.

Portfolio Manager: Bob Chow
Since: 1990

Minimum:
Initial: $1,000
Subsequent: $250
Telephone Exchange: Yes
Distributions:
Income: Annually
Capital Gain: Annually
Front-End Load: 3.00%
12b-1: None
Redemption Fee: 0.75%
Management Company: Fidelity Management & Research
Ticker Symbol: FSPFX

TOTAL RETURN (%)

1987	1988	1989	1990	1991	5-year	Bull Market	Bear Market
3.9	6.8	4.1	-15.1	34.8	32.1	55.0	-23.5

INVESTMENT PORTFOLIO

Total Assets (mil.)	Current Yield	Turnover Ratio	Expense Ratio	Beta	Risk Return
$9	2.1%	171%	2.49%	1.12	0.05

FIDELITY SELECT REGIONAL BANKS

Fidelity Distributors Corporation
82 Devonshire Street, Mail Zone L7B
Boston, MA 02109
800-544-8888

Investment Objective: At last count, there were more than 10,000 banks in the United States. Though this makes for hearty competition, most small and medium-sized banks are finding it difficult to compete in the globalized financial market. Thus, growing numbers of mergers and acquisitions are to be expected in the 1990s, and this fund is well poised to benefit. Widespread and highly publicized banking problems led to its dismal performance during 1990. However, its fortunes improved dramatically the past year as investors bid up the depressed prices of bank stocks on the belief that the industry's worst has been left behind.

Portfolio Manager: Steve Binder
Since: 1990

Minimum:
Initial: $1,000
Subsequent: $200
Telephone Exchange: Yes
Distributions:
Income: Annually
Capital Gain: Annually
Front-End Load: 3.00%
12b-1: None
Redemption Fee: 0.75%
Management Company: Fidelity Management & Research
Ticker Symbol: FSRBX

TOTAL RETURN (%)

1987	1988	1989	1990	1991	5-year	Bull Market	Bear Market
-3.0	25.7	26.6	-20.7	65.8	103.0	81.3	-24.7

INVESTMENT PORTFOLIO

Total Assets (mil.)	Current Yield	Turnover Ratio	Expense Ratio	Beta	Risk Return
$30	1.0%	110%	2.51%	1.23	0.09

FIDELITY SELECT RETAILING

Fidelity Distributors Corporation
82 Devonshire Street, Mail Zone L7B
Boston, MA 02109
800-544-8888

Investment Objective: This fund seeks capital appreciation from a specialized portfolio of equity securities of companies that are engaged in merchandising finished goods and services to the individual customer. Management maintains a broadly diversified portfolio, spreading the fund's $37-million asset base across numerous large- and small-capitalization retail stocks. Like most sector funds, the fund's nondiversified industry exposure implies above-average risk. This, coupled with the added volatility associated with the market's often high earnings expectations for retail stocks (which leaves plenty of room for big disappointments), suggests that this fund is suitable only for risk-tolerant investors.

Portfolio Manager: Jennifer Uhrig
Since: 1991

Minimum:
Initial: $1,000
Subsequent: $250
Telephone Exchange: Yes
Distributions:
Income: Annually
Capital Gain: Annually
Front-End Load: 3.00%
12b-1: None
Redemption Fee: 0.75%
Management Company: Fidelity Management & Research
Ticker Symbol: FSRPX

TOTAL RETURN (%)

1987	1988	1989	1990	1991	5-year	Bull Market	Bear Market
-7.4	38.7	29.5	-5.0	68.1	165.8	88.8	-34.7

INVESTMENT PORTFOLIO

Total Assets (mil.)	Current Yield	Turnover Ratio	Expense Ratio	Beta	Risk Return
$37	0.0%	115%	2.54%	1.30	0.09

FIDELITY SELECT SAVINGS & LOAN

Fidelity Distributors Corporation
82 Devonshire Street, Mail Zone L7B
Boston, MA 02109
800-544-8888

Investment Objective: As the name implies, this sector fund concentrates its holdings in companies engaged in accepting public deposits and making mortgages. These companies also may be engaged in discount brokerage service, various insurance products, leasing services or joint ventures in financing. Because it is a sector fund, its performance is very dependent on economic factors in that industry. Interest rates play a big part in determining the value of the fund, which explains its volatility and the below-market returns that the fund has produced in the late 1980s. However, share price ballooned the past year as S&L stocks returned to investor favor.

Portfolio Manager: David Ellison
Since: 1985

Minimum:
Initial: $1,000
Subsequent: $250
Telephone Exchange: Yes
Distributions:
Income: Annually
Capital Gain: Annually
Front-End Load: 3.00%
12b-1: None
Redemption Fee: 0.75%
Management Company: Fidelity Management & Research
Ticker Symbol: FSVLX

TOTAL RETURN (%)

1987	1988	1989	1990	1991	5-year	Bull Market	Bear Market
-7.9	18.5	9.3	-15.1	64.6	66.7	78.1	-28.6

INVESTMENT PORTFOLIO

Total Assets (mil.)	Current Yield	Turnover Ratio	Expense Ratio	Beta	Risk Return
$5	1.0%	159%	2.50%	1.25	0.08

FIDELITY SELECT SOFTWARE & COMPUTER

Fidelity Distributors Corporation
82 Devonshire Street, Mail Zone L7B
Boston, MA 02109
800-544-8888

Investment Objective: Even as investors were crooning the death knell of technology-related stocks, this fund continued to show relative strength. Investing in both large and small computer-application companies, the fund has been able to keep results positive for each of its 6 years of existence. This is no small feat, considering how weakly the computer industry performed in 1989 and 1990, and how many growth funds plummeted in 1987. For investors willing to bet on continued expansion in the software industry and on technology in general, this is a suitable investment.

Portfolio Manager: Arieh Coll
Since: 1991

Minimum:
Initial: $1,000
Subsequent: $250
Telephone Exchange: Yes
Distributions:
Income: Annually
Capital Gain: Semiannually
Front-End Load: 3.00%
12b-1: None
Redemption Fee: 0.75%
Management Company: Fidelity Management & Research
Ticker Symbol: FSCSX

TOTAL RETURN (%)

1987	1988	1989	1990	1991	5-year	Bull Market	Bear Market
9.4	9.0	12.0	0.9	45.8	96.7	84.1	-35.9

INVESTMENT PORTFOLIO

Total Assets (mil.)	Current Yield	Turnover Ratio	Expense Ratio	Beta	Risk Return
$16	0.0%	326%	2.50%	1.26	0.05

FIDELITY SELECT TECHNOLOGY

Fidelity Distributors Corporation
82 Devonshire Street, Mail Zone L7B
Boston, MA 02109
800-544-8888

Investment Objective: This fund, one of the original Select portfolios, began operations in 1981. It seeks capital appreciation by investing in a relatively concentrated portfolio of common stocks of companies operating in the technology sector, including aerospace and defense, cellular communications equipment, computer services and software, electronics, electronic instruments and medical equipment and supplies. Depressed conditions in the technology sector have greatly impaired returns during the late 1980s. However, this industry is capable of generating explosive short-term returns, as witnessed by this fund's stellar performance the past year.

Portfolio Manager: Larry Bowman
Since: 1990

Minimum:
Initial: $1,000
Subsequent: $250
Telephone Exchange: Yes
Distributions:
Income: Semiannually
Capital Gain: Annually
Front-End Load: 3.00%
12b-1: None
Redemption Fee: 0.75%
Management Company: Fidelity Management & Research
Ticker Symbol: FSPTX

TOTAL RETURN (%)

1987	1988	1989	1990	1991	5-year	Bull Market	Bear Market
-11.8	-2.7	17.0	10.5	59.0	76.4	96.3	-33.4

INVESTMENT PORTFOLIO

Total Assets (mil.)	Current Yield	Turnover Ratio	Expense Ratio	Beta	Risk Return
$94	0.5%	442%	1.83%	1.26	0.07

FIDELITY SELECT TELECOMMUNICATIONS

Fidelity Distributors Corporation
82 Devonshire Street, Mail Zone L7B
Boston, MA 02109
800-544-8888

Investment Objective: This fund seeks capital appreciation by investing in a relatively concentrated portfolio of common stocks in the telecommunications sector, including broadcasting, cellular communications equipment, computers and office equipment, electrical equipment and telephone services. Although funds with concentrated portfolios are capable of producing above-average returns during short-run periods, they tend to be more volatile than the typical diversified equity fund. During the first 5 years of its existence, the fund has produced handsome double-digit annual returns, topped by the whopping 50.9% in 1989. It should continue to perform well over the long run given its investment concentration in a high-growth industry.

Portfolio Manager: Abigail Johnson
Since: 1991

Minimum:
Initial: $1,000
Subsequent: $250
Telephone Exchange: Yes
Distributions:
Income: Annually
Capital Gain: Annually
Front-End Load: 3.00%
12b-1: None
Redemption Fee: 0.75%
Management Company: Fidelity Management & Research
Ticker Symbol: FSTCX

TOTAL RETURN (%)

1987	1988	1989	1990	1991	5-year	Bull Market	Bear Market
15.2	27.8	50.9	-16.4	30.9	143.0	38.0	-20.8

INVESTMENT PORTFOLIO

Total Assets (mil.)	Current Yield	Turnover Ratio	Expense Ratio	Beta	Risk Return
$58	0.9%	262%	1.97%	1.04	0.05

FIDELITY SELECT TRANSPORTATION

Fidelity Distributors Corporation
82 Devonshire Street, Mail Zone L7B
Boston, MA 02109
800-544-8888

Investment Objective: As the name suggests, the fund invests in companies that are related to the transportation field. This field includes the movement of freight or passengers by airlines, railroads, ships and bus companies. As is the case with most cyclical industries, investors either feast or famine. Thus, this tiny fund is best suited for shorter-term-oriented investors who are adept at business cycle timing. Note that the fund has produced either double-digit gains or losses during each of the past 5 years.

Portfolio Manager: Rick Mace
Since: 1989

Minimum:
Initial: $1,000
Subsequent: $250
Telephone Exchange: Yes
Distributions:
Income: Annually
Capital Gain: Annually
Front-End Load: 3.00%
12b-1: None
Redemption Fee: 0.75%
Management Company: Fidelity Management & Research
Ticker Symbol: FSRFX

TOTAL RETURN (%)

1987	1988	1989	1990	1991	5-year	Bull Market	Bear Market
-17.5	38.5	28.5	-21.6	54.1	77.4	58.7	-30.0

INVESTMENT PORTFOLIO

Total Assets (mil.)	Current Yield	Turnover Ratio	Expense Ratio	Beta	Risk Return
$1	0.3%	187%	2.39%	1.15	0.08

FIDELITY SELECT UTILITIES

Fidelity Distributors Corporation
82 Devonshire Street, Mail Zone L7B
Boston, MA 02109
800-544-8888

Investment Objective: Unlike most utility funds that stress a combination of current yield and growth, Select Utilities primarily seeks capital appreciation when making its utility stock selections. Thus, its current yield tends to be lower and its portfolio turnover ratio is higher than that of the "typical" utilities fund. However, this strategy is capable of producing handsome returns as witnessed by its 39% return in 1989 and its 21% return the past year. With nearly $25 billion in assets, it is one of the more popular Select portfolios.

Portfolio Manager: Jeffery Ubben
Since: 1991

Minimum:
Initial: $1,000
Subsequent: $250
Telephone Exchange: Yes
Distributions:
Income: Semiannually
Capital Gain: Semiannually
Front-End Load: 3.00%
12b-1: None
Redemption Fee: 0.75%
Management Company: Fidelity Management & Research
Ticker Symbol: FSUTX

TOTAL RETURN (%)

1987	1988	1989	1990	1991	5-year	Bull Market	Bear Market
-9.3	16.5	39.0	0.6	21.0	78.8	21.1	-3.2

INVESTMENT PORTFOLIO

Total Assets (mil.)	Current Yield	Turnover Ratio	Expense Ratio	Beta	Risk Return
$244	4.2%	45%	1.65%	0.46	0.05

FINANCIAL STRATEGIC ENERGY

INVESCO Funds Group
P. O. Box 2040
Denver, CO 80201
800-525-8085

Investment Objective: One of Financial Programs' 9 sector funds, Strategic Energy invests in energy-related companies, although fund management has stretched this definition fairly broadly to include firms involved in energy conservation and pollution control as well as the more commonly thought of areas such as coal mining and oil and gas exploration and development. Like the Strategic sector funds in general, this fund sports an extremely high portfolio turnover ratio. In addition, like all sector funds, it possesses a higher-than-average level of risk because of the concentration of its assets. With its concentration in a cyclical industry, the fund's fortunes rise and fall with the U.S. economy.

Portfolio Manager: Jerry Mill
Since: 1990

Minimum:
Initial: $250
Subsequent: $50
Telephone Exchange: Yes
Distributions:
Income: Annually
Capital Gain: Annually
Front-End Load: None
12b-1: None
Redemption Fee: None
Management Company: INVESCO Funds Group
Ticker Symbol: FSTEX

TOTAL RETURN (%)

1987	1988	1989	1990	1991	5-year	Bull Market	Bear Market
4.9	15.0	43.5	-16.5	-3.5	39.5	-5.7	-5.2

INVESTMENT PORTFOLIO

Total Assets (mil.)	Current Yield	Turnover Ratio	Expense Ratio	Beta	Risk Return
$10	1.1%	321%	1.42%	0.61	NA

FINANCIAL STRATEGIC FINANCIAL SERVICES

INVESCO Funds Group
P. O. Box 2040
Denver, CO 80201
800-525-8085

Investment Objective: Financial Strategic Financial Services Portfolio invests primarily in equity securities of companies engaged in such financial services as banking, leasing, brokerage and insurance. Management trades rapidly in an effort to weed out stocks with deteriorating fundamentals and/or earnings momentum. Unlike most specialized financial-services vehicles, the fund has stinted money-center banks in recent years in favor of less troubled, relatively small regional and service-oriented firms. This stance largely explains the fund's good resistance to decline in 1990, when the average financial stocks declined by approximately 40%. Its rebound during the past year was nothing short of phenomenal.

Portfolio Manager: Phil Dubuque
Since: 1990

Minimum:
Initial: $250
Subsequent: $50
Telephone Exchange: Yes
Distributions:
Income: Annually
Capital Gain: Annually
Front-End Load: None
12b-1: None
Redemption Fee: None
Management Company: INVESCO Funds Group
Ticker Symbol: FSFSX

TOTAL RETURN (%)

1987	1988	1989	1990	1991	5-year	Bull Market	Bear Market
-11.0	17.1	36.9	-7.2	74.0	130.5	102.8	-24.2

INVESTMENT PORTFOLIO

Total Assets (mil.)	Current Yield	Turnover Ratio	Expense Ratio	Beta	Risk Return
$84	0.8%	528%	2.50%	1.12	0.11

FINANCIAL STRATEGIC HEALTH SCIENCES

INVESCO Funds Group
P. O. Box 2040
Denver, CO 80201
800-525-8085

Investment Objective: As the name implies, the assets of this fund are largely invested in the stocks of firms engaged in some facet of the health field. Like the health field itself, the fund's investments span a wide variety of firms, ranging from pharmaceutical giants such as Eli Lilly and Schering-Plough to exotic biotechnology concerns. The fund is capable of producing spectacular short-term returns, as witnessed by the almost 92% total return provided the past year. As a result of a bull market in health-care stocks that has lasted more than 5 years, this fund's 5-year return has beaten the market averages by nearly 4 to 1.

Portfolio Manager: John Kaweske
Since: 1985

Minimum:
Initial: $250
Subsequent: $50
Telephone Exchange: Yes
Distributions:
Income: Annually
Capital Gain: Annually
Front-End Load: None
12b-1: None
Redemption Fee: None
Management Company: INVESCO Funds Group
Ticker Symbol: FHLSX

TOTAL RETURN (%)

1987	1988	1989	1990	1991	5-year	Bull Market	Bear Market
7.1	16.0	59.5	25.8	91.8	378.0	112.5	-20.3

INVESTMENT PORTFOLIO

Total Assets (mil.)	Current Yield	Turnover Ratio	Expense Ratio	Beta	Risk Return
$760	0.2%	242%	1.12%	1.29	0.13

FINANCIAL STRATEGIC LEISURE

INVESCO Funds Group
P. O. Box 2040
Denver, CO 80201
800-525-8085

Investment Objective: This fund normally invests 80% of its assets in companies in so-called leisure-time industries. While classified as a sector fund, it maintains a diverse portfolio that may include stocks of companies that supply travel services and lodging, operate amusement parks, produce tobacco and food products, manufacture toys and games, operate restaurants and print and distribute newspapers. Portfolio Manager Roger Maurer has loaded the portfolio with high-growth companies, both large and small, in recent years. As a result, the performance has been exceptional during the past 5 years during which the fund ranks in the top 5% of all funds.

Portfolio Manager: Roger Maurer
Since: 1989

Minimum:
Initial: $250
Subsequent: $50
Telephone Exchange: Yes
Distributions:
Income: Annually
Capital Gain: Annually
Front-End Load: None
12b-1: None
Redemption Fee: None
Management Company: INVESCO Funds Group
Ticker Symbol: FLISX

TOTAL RETURN (%)

1987	1988	1989	1990	1991	5-year	Bull Market	Bear Market
0.7	28.5	38.3	-11.0	52.7	143.4	67.4	-30.7

INVESTMENT PORTFOLIO

Total Assets (mil.)	Current Yield	Turnover Ratio	Expense Ratio	Beta	Risk Return
$14	0.0%	89%	1.84%	1.21	0.08

FINANCIAL STRATEGIC TECHNOLOGY

INVESCO Funds Group
P. O. Box 2040
Denver, CO 80201
800-525-8085

Investment Objective: As its name suggests, this fund invests in the equity securities of companies principally engaged in the field of technology including computers, communications, video, electronics, oceanography, office and factory automation and robotics. Traditionally, the fund's portfolio reflects broad diversification across a number of areas. Favored segments of recent years include software, computer peripherals and biotechnology stocks. During the past 5 years, the fund has performed better than the overall market. However, portfolio turnover is exceptionally high and the fund sports one of the highest betas in the industry, indicating a significant degree of share-price volatility.

Portfolio Manager: Dan Leonard
Since: 1984

Minimum:
Initial: $250
Subsequent: $50
Telephone Exchange: Yes
Distributions:
Income: Annually
Capital Gain: Annually
Front-End Load: None
12b-1: None
Redemption Fee: None
Management Company: INVESCO Funds Group
Ticker Symbol: FTCHX

TOTAL RETURN (%)

1987	1988	1989	1990	1991	5-year	Bull Market	Bear Market
-5.3	14.2	21.4	8.6	76.9	152.3	106.0	-36.8

INVESTMENT PORTFOLIO

Total Assets (mil.)	Current Yield	Turnover Ratio	Expense Ratio	Beta	Risk Return
$74	0.0%	345%	1.25%	1.31	0.10

FINANCIAL STRATEGIC UTILITIES

INVESCO Funds Group
P. O. Box 2040
Denver, CO 80201
800-525-8085

Investment Objective: This fund is one of the few no-load funds that specializes in the utility sector. Because utility stocks possess lower-than-average price volatility because of their stability of earnings and higher-than-average yields, this fund possesses a defensive quality. However, the fund's share price is slightly more volatile and its current yield is slightly below that of the typical utility portfolio because it held a significant investment in telephone utility stocks in recent years. Like utility stocks themselves, this fund's performance is highly sensitive to interest-rate changes. It can be expected to perform best during a period of declining interest rates.

Portfolio Manager: Phil Dubuque
Since: 1990

Minimum:
Initial: $250
Subsequent: $50
Telephone Exchange: Yes
Distributions:
Income: Quarterly
Capital Gain: Annually
Front-End Load: None
12b-1: None
Redemption Fee: None
Management Company: INVESCO Funds Group
Ticker Symbol: FSTUX

TOTAL RETURN (%)

1987	1988	1989	1990	1991	5-year	Bull Market	Bear Market
-4.9	14.2	31.5	-10.0	28.0	64.5	28.6	-12.1

INVESTMENT PORTFOLIO

Total Assets (mil.)	Current Yield	Turnover Ratio	Expense Ratio	Beta	Risk Return
$79	3.2%	264%	1.26%	0.65	0.06

FLAG TELEPHONE INCOME

Alex Brown & Sons
135 East Baltimore Street
Baltimore, MD 21202
800-767-3524

Investment Objective: The fund seeks high current income and long-term growth of capital without undue risk by investing at least 65% of its assets in companies in the telephone industry. In light of the small number of telephone companies, the fund's assets are highly concentrated, and the fund is classified as nondiversified, according to the Investment Company Act of 1940. The fund was created at the time of the 1984 reorganization of AT&T. The fund initially was designed as an investment vehicle that would provide both convenience and professional management for common shareholders of AT&T. In recent years, however, the fund has broadened its portfolio and has become a bit more diversified.

Portfolio Manager: B. Behrens/H. Buppert
Since: 1984

Minimum:
Initial: $2,000
Subsequent: $500
Telephone Exchange: No
Distributions:
Income: Quarterly
Capital Gain: Annually
Front-End Load: 4.50%
12b-1: 0.25%
Redemption Fee: None
Management Company: Flag Investors Management
Ticker Symbol: TISHX

TOTAL RETURN (%)

1987	1988	1989	1990	1991	5-year	Bull Market	Bear Market
1.6	19.9	48.8	-7.6	23.4	106.5	20.0	-7.2

INVESTMENT PORTFOLIO

Total Assets (mil.)	Current Yield	Turnover Ratio	Expense Ratio	Beta	Risk Return
$219	3.9%	151%	0.92%	0.72	0.04

FRANKLIN DYNATECH

Franklin Distributors
777 Mariners Island Boulevard
San Mateo, CA 94404
800-342-5236

Investment Objective: This fund seeks to invest in smaller, rapidly growing companies that have a leadership position in their field or have a competitive advantage because of special marketing expertise or proprietary technology. The fund is designed for investors willing to accept the risks involved in aggressively seeking capital appreciation. Although the fund's investments all have a "technology" bent, individual selections have been drawn from such diverse industries as computers, environmental cleanup, health sciences, precision instruments, retail, semiconductors and telecommunications.

Portfolio Manager: R. Johnson/L. Costa
Since: 1980

Minimum:
Initial: $100
Subsequent: $25
Telephone Exchange: Yes
Distributions:
Income: Annually
Capital Gain: Annually
Front-End Load: 4.00%
12b-1: None
Redemption Fee: None
Management Company: Franklin Advisers
Ticker Symbol: FKDNX

TOTAL RETURN (%)

1987	1988	1989	1990	1991	5-year	Bull Market	Bear Market
13.7	6.5	29.7	3.1	35.5	119.1	60.2	-32.4

INVESTMENT PORTFOLIO

Total Assets (mil.)	Current Yield	Turnover Ratio	Expense Ratio	Beta	Risk Return
$49	1.2%	NA	0.81%	0.97	0.06

FRANKLIN UTILITIES

Franklin Distributors
777 Mariners Island Boulevard
San Mateo, CA 94404
800-342-5236

Investment Objective: If ever there was a utility fund that lived up to the industry's high-yield, slow-growth reputation, this one takes the prize. Electric utilities tend to dominate the portfolio. As one of the highest-yielding growth and income funds (and one of the highest yields in the entire equity-fund universe), this vehicle is suitable for conservative, income-oriented investors. However, don't be surprised if the fund's return lags that of the more aggressively situated utility funds and many other growth and income funds, for most of them have at least a smattering of growth names.

Portfolio Manager: Charles Johnson
Since: 1957

Minimum:
Initial: $100
Subsequent: $25
Telephone Exchange: Yes
Distributions:
Income: Quarterly
Capital Gain: Annually
Front-End Load: 4.00%
12b-1: None
Redemption Fee: None
Management Company: Franklin Advisers
Ticker Symbol: FKUTX

TOTAL RETURN (%)

1987	1988	1989	1990	1991	5-year	Bull Market	Bear Market
-5.8	11.3	25.5	0.1	23.8	63.1	23.2	-3.0

INVESTMENT PORTFOLIO

Total Assets (mil.)	Current Yield	Turnover Ratio	Expense Ratio	Beta	Risk Return
$1,355	6.0%	2%	0.60%	0.41	0.06

IDS UTILITIES INCOME

IDS Financial Services
IDS Tower 10
Minneapolis, MN 55440
800-328-8300

Investment Objective: Investing primarily in the stocks of public utilities, the fund's main objective is a high level of current income. The fund will typically invest at least 65% of its assets in companies that supply electric power, natural gas, water, sanitary services and telecommunications, with the balance in other high-yielding common stocks, foreign issues and/or cash. Up to 25% of its total assets may be invested in the securities of a single company, while the other 75% must be invested so that no more than 5% is invested in any one company. The resulting impact of that company's performance, therefore, can greatly influence the returns of this fund on the upside or the downside. So far, the strategy has worked.

Portfolio Manager: Richard Lazarchic
Since: 1989

Minimum:
Initial: $2,000
Subsequent: $100
Telephone Exchange: Yes
Distributions:
Income: Quarterly
Capital Gain: Annually
Front-End Load: 5.00%
12b-1: None
Redemption Fee: None
Management Company: IDS Financial
Ticker Symbol: INUTX

TOTAL RETURN (%)

1987	1988	1989	1990	1991	5-year	Bull Market	Bear Market
NA	NA	28.9	-1.8	22.0	NA	25.4	-10.8

INVESTMENT PORTFOLIO

Total Assets (mil.)	Current Yield	Turnover Ratio	Expense Ratio	Beta	Risk Return
$280	5.3%	57%	0.90%	0.45	0.06

JOHN HANCOCK GLOBAL TECHNOLOGY FUND

John Hancock Distributors
101 Huntington Avenue, 6th Floor
Boston, MA 02199
800-225-5291

Investment Objective: Under normal market conditions, at least 65% of the fund's total assets are invested in securities of companies that rely extensively on technology in the product development or operations. Such companies may be expected to benefit from scientific developments and the application of technical advances resulting from improving technology in many different fields such as computer software or hardware, semiconductors, telecommunications, biotechnology, defense and commercial electronics and data storage and retrieval. As its name suggests, the fund invests in U.S. and foreign securities.

Portfolio Manager: Barry J. Gordon
Since: 1983

Minimum:
Initial: $1,000
Subsequent: $100
Telephone Exchange: Yes
Distributions:
Income: Annually
Capital Gain: Annually
Front-End Load: 5.00%
12b-1: 0.25%
Redemption Fee: None
Management Company: John Hancock Advisers
Ticker Symbol: NTTFX

TOTAL RETURN (%)

1987	1988	1989	1990	1991	5-year	Bull Market	Bear Market
2.8	10.5	16.7	-18.5	33.5	44.2	47.3	-32.5

INVESTMENT PORTFOLIO

Total Assets (mil.)	Current Yield	Turnover Ratio	Expense Ratio	Beta	Risk Return
$31	0.2%	38%	2.36%	1.26	0.04

JOHN HANCOCK NATIONAL AVIATION & TECHNOLOGY

John Hancock Distributors
101 Huntington Avenue, 6th Floor
Boston, MA 02199
800-225-5291

Investment Objective: Organized in the 1930s for the purpose of investing in stocks in the aviation industry, this fund now concentrates its investments in 3 areas: airlines, aerospace and technology. Because of its portfolio concentration, it is registered as a nondiversified fund under the Investment Company Act of 1940. After soaring in 1989, the fund's share price fell back to earth the past year as rocketing oil prices took their toll on airline profits. Adding to the airline industry's woes was reduced passenger traffic resulting from a general economic slowdown. However, shareholders should benefit from industry consolidation and a long-awaited economic recovery.

Portfolio Manager: Barry J. Gordon
Since: 1973

Minimum:
Initial: $1,000
Subsequent: $25
Telephone Exchange: Yes
Distributions:
Income: Semiannually
Capital Gain: Annually
Front-End Load: 5.00%
12b-1: 0.25%
Redemption Fee: None
Management Company: John Hancock Advisers
Ticker Symbol: NAVTX

TOTAL RETURN (%)

1987	1988	1989	1990	1991	5-year	Bull Market	Bear Market
-12.3	24.9	39.5	-19.3	31.2	61.9	31.4	-30.4

INVESTMENT PORTFOLIO

Total Assets (mil.)	Current Yield	Turnover Ratio	Expense Ratio	Beta	Risk Return
$69	0.3%	29%	1.67%	1.27	0.04

KEMPER ENVIRONMENTAL SERVICES

Kemper Financial Services
120 South LaSalle Street
Chicago, IL 60603
800-621-1048

Investment Objective: This fund had an impressive inaugural full year. Its 1991 return of 24.2% may have made investors as well as competing funds look twice and try to figure out the fund's secret to success. It typically invests up to 65% of its assets in companies related to environmental research, consultation, investigation, development, design, engineering, etc. It also leaves some room for the purchase of foreign issues and cash or cash equivalents. Looking at this fund's list of major holdings, it is easy to see why the fund enjoyed a high return the past year, for many of the holdings are small companies in lieu of blue chip issues. The past year's returns enjoyed the small stock rally, which many analysts predict will continue for several years.

Portfolio Manager: Frank Korth
Since: 1990

Minimum:
Initial: $1,000
Subsequent: $100
Telephone Exchange: Yes
Distributions:
Income: Annually
Capital Gain: Annually
Front-End Load: 5.75%
12b-1: None
Redemption Fee: None
Management Company: Kemper Financial Services
Ticker Symbol: KESFX

TOTAL RETURN (%)

1987	1988	1989	1990	1991	5-year	Bull Market	Bear Market
NA	NA	NA	NA	24.2	NA	NA	NA

INVESTMENT PORTFOLIO

Total Assets (mil.)	Current Yield	Turnover Ratio	Expense Ratio	Beta	Risk Return
$70	0.0%	101%	1.54%	NA	NA

KEMPER TECHNOLOGY

Kemper Financial Services
120 South LaSalle Street
Chicago, IL 60603
800-621-1048

Investment Objective: The objective of this fund is growth of capital by investing in securities that are expected to benefit from technology advancements. Examples are companies whose processes or services will be improved by scientific developments in aerospace, chemistry, electronics and engineering. Despite some diversification into different fields, the technology orientation of the fund means that there is more risk and a higher degree of volatility than in a well-diversified fund. Recently, the fund reduced its front-end sales charge from a full 8.50% to 5.75%. Despite its higher-than-average beta, the fund has managed to post gains during each of the past 5 years.

Portfolio Manager: Richard Goers
Since: 1991

Minimum:
Initial: $1,000
Subsequent: $100
Telephone Exchange: Yes
Distributions:
Income: Semiannually
Capital Gain: Annually
Front-End Load: 5.75%
12b-1: None
Redemption Fee: None
Management Company: Kemper Financial Services
Ticker Symbol: SPTCX

TOTAL RETURN (%)

1987	1988	1989	1990	1991	5-year	Bull Market	Bear Market
6.9	3.1	24.8	0.4	44.4	99.4	40.2	-24.3

INVESTMENT PORTFOLIO

Total Assets (mil.)	Current Yield	Turnover Ratio	Expense Ratio	Beta	Risk Return
$590	1.0%	25%	0.71%	1.09	0.07

MERRILL LYNCH NATURAL RESOURCES TRUST B

Merrill Lynch Funds Distributor
P. O. Box 9011
Princeton, NJ 08543
800-637-3863

Investment Objective: As one would expect based on its name, this fund primarily invests in the common stocks of firms with substantial natural resources assets. The fund also may invest in so-called "asset-based securities" — securities with market values related to the price of some natural resource. In addition, during periods of significant political or economic pressures, the fund may invest a majority of its assets in gold-related firms and asset-based securities indexed to the value of gold. Investors should note that the fund's class B shares carry a 4% redemption fee.

Portfolio Manager: Richard Price
Since: 1985

Minimum:
Initial: $500
Subsequent: $50
Telephone Exchange: No
Distributions:
Income: Semiannually
Capital Gain: Annually
Front-End Load: None
12b-1: 1.00%
Redemption Fee: 4.00%
Management Company: Merrill Lynch Asset Management
Ticker Symbol: MRNTX

TOTAL RETURN (%)

1987	1988	1989	1990	1991	5-year	Bull Market	Bear Market
21.2	-7.9	26.1	-1.7	4.8	45.1	5.2	-1.5

INVESTMENT PORTFOLIO

Total Assets (mil.)	Current Yield	Turnover Ratio	Expense Ratio	Beta	Risk Return
$281	7.8%	57%	0.96%	0.38	NA

MERRILL LYNCH SCI/TECH HOLDINGS A

Merrill Lynch Funds Distributor
P.O. Box 9011
Princeton, NJ 08543
800-637-3863

Investment Objective: This fund holds the philosophy that advances in science and technology throughout the world are providing new opportunities for global companies. Thus, investing in these technology-related firms and companies benefiting from technological advances offers the potential for solid, long-term capital appreciation, which is the fund's basic objective. The fund also invests in smaller companies that can benefit most from rapid growth. However, small-cap stocks underperformed large-cap stocks during the late 1980s. However, as smaller-cap stocks surged to the fore during the past year, so did the fund's performance.

Portfolio Manager: J. Schreiben/J. Renck
Since: 1986

Minimum:
Initial: $1,000
Subsequent: $50
Telephone Exchange: No
Distributions:
Income: Semiannually
Capital Gain: Annually
Front-End Load: 6.50%
12b-1: None
Redemption Fee: None
Management Company: Merrill Lynch Asset Management
Ticker Symbol: MLSTX

TOTAL RETURN (%)

1987	1988	1989	1990	1991	5-year	Bull Market	Bear Market
10.2	6.4	11.5	-6.2	45.7	78.7	46.4	-26.6

INVESTMENT PORTFOLIO

Total Assets (mil.)	Current Yield	Turnover Ratio	Expense Ratio	Beta	Risk Return
$126	13.5%	159%	1.77%	1.06	0.07

NEUBERGER BERMAN SELECTED SECTORS

Neuberger & Berman
605 Third Avenue, 2nd Floor
New York, NY 10158
800-877-9700

Investment Objective: This fund is designed for investors seeking long-term capital appreciation. It is unique among sector funds because it invests in common stocks selected from among 13 economic sectors rather than from one single industry. Instead, each of the sectors in which the fund selects investments consists of several related industries. Its portfolio manager identifies and focuses the fund's investments in a limited number of these sectors by using a value-oriented approach to the selection of individual stocks. Through this approach, 90% or more of the fund's investments are normally focused in not more than 6 sectors, including the energy sector. The fund normally maintains at least 25% of its investments in energy stocks.

Portfolio Manager: Mark Baskir/Larry Marx
Since: 1970

Minimum:
Initial: $1,000
Subsequent: $100
Telephone Exchange: Yes
Distributions:
Income: Semiannually
Capital Gain: Semiannually
Front-End Load: None
12b-1: None
Redemption Fee: None
Management Company: Neuberger & Berman Management
Ticker Symbol: NBSSX

TOTAL RETURN (%)

1987	1988	1989	1990	1991	5-year	Bull Market	Bear Market
0.6	16.5	29.8	-5.9	24.7	78.4	28.5	-16.0

INVESTMENT PORTFOLIO

Total Assets (mil.)	Current Yield	Turnover Ratio	Expense Ratio	Beta	Risk Return
$380	1.7%	60%	0.93%	0.97	0.04

OPPENHEIMER GLOBAL BIO-TECH

Oppenheimer Fund Management
P.O. Box 300
Denver, CO 80201
800-525-7048

Investment Objective: Temporarily closed to new investors since October of 1991, this fund opened the eyes of many investors during the past year, and no wonder. Its 121.1% 1991 return was no less than stunning, and hopeful investors were eager to invest in this fund whose principal objective is capital appreciation. It invests 65% of its assets in biotechnology concerns in the United States and in at least 3 foreign countries. The industry enjoyed tremendous investor recognition the past year, and this fund was forced to close its doors once total assets neared an amount that threatened the fund's objective. This fund's fortunes hang strictly on the performance of biotechs, making it much riskier than a diversified fund.

Portfolio Manager: Kenneth Oberman
Since: 1988

Minimum:
Initial: Closed
Subsequent: $25
Telephone Exchange: Yes
Distributions:
Income: Annually
Capital Gain: Annually
Front-End Load: Closed
12b-1: 0.25%
Redemption Fee: None
Management Company: Oppenheimer Management
Ticker Symbol: OPBTX

TOTAL RETURN (%)

1987	1988	1989	1990	1991	5-year	Bull Market	Bear Market
NA	1.3	23.4	12.6	121.1	NA	119.7	-25.4

INVESTMENT PORTFOLIO

Total Assets (mil.)	Current Yield	Turnover Ratio	Expense Ratio	Beta	Risk Return
$105	0.0%	11%	1.50%	1.07	0.10

PUTNAM ENERGY RESOURCES

Putnam Financial Services
One Post Office Square
Boston, MA 02109
800-634-1590

Investment Objective: Putnam Energy Resources seeks capital appreciation primarily through investments in common stocks of companies engaged in activities related to the energy and natural resources industries. Management follows a value discipline, increasing the fund's investments in energy stocks when they appear cheap and shifting up to 20% of its assets into other areas when it believes energy stocks are expensive. Blue chip integrated oil companies claim most assets, but the fund also has exposure to energy service stocks and chemicals. Nonenergy related investments, which may total up to 20% of its assets, typically stress inexpensive out-of-favor sectors.

Portfolio Manager: Edward T. Shadek
Since: 1990

Minimum:
Initial: $500
Subsequent: $50
Telephone Exchange: Yes
Distributions:
Income: Quarterly
Capital Gain: Annually
Front-End Load: 5.75%
12b-1: 0.25%
Redemption Fee: None
Management Company: Putnam Management
Ticker Symbol: EBERX

TOTAL RETURN (%)

1987	1988	1989	1990	1991	5-year	Bull Market	Bear Market
8.7	20.2	34.8	-4.9	7.2	79.7	17.8	-10.7

INVESTMENT PORTFOLIO

Total Assets (mil.)	Current Yield	Turnover Ratio	Expense Ratio	Beta	Risk Return
$105	2.4%	48%	1.50%	0.67	0.02

PUTNAM HEALTH SCIENCES TRUST

Putnam Financial Services
One Post Office Square
Boston, MA 02109
800-634-1590

Investment Objective: Organized in 1982, this fund seeks capital appreciation by investing at least 80% of its total assets in the health-sciences industries. This includes companies engaged in the development, production or distribution of products or services related to the treatment of diseases, disorders or other medical conditions. Examples of such industries include pharmaceuticals, hospitals and rehabilitation centers, home health care, research and development such as biotechnology, and medical equipment or supplies. The fund tends to invest in stocks of large, blue chip companies rather than smaller firms. The fund may, from time to time, invest up to 20% of its assets in foreign securities.

Portfolio Manager: Cheryl Alexander
Since: 1986

Minimum:
Initial: $500
Subsequent: $500
Telephone Exchange: Yes
Distributions:
Income: Annually
Capital Gain: Annually
Front-End Load: 5.75%
12b-1: 0.25%
Redemption Fee: None
Management Company: Putnam Management
Ticker Symbol: PHSTX

TOTAL RETURN (%)

1987	1988	1989	1990	1991	5-year	Bull Market	Bear Market
5.1	10.6	42.0	15.5	49.1	184.0	51.7	-14.5

INVESTMENT PORTFOLIO

Total Assets (mil.)	Current Yield	Turnover Ratio	Expense Ratio	Beta	Risk Return
$760	0.7%	37%	1.18%	1.09	0.08

PUTNAM INFORMATION SCIENCES

Putnam Financial Services
One Post Office Square
Boston, MA 02109
800-634-1590

Investment Objective: This fund invests primarily in equity securities of companies engaged in the development, production or distribution of products or services related to the storage, processing or transmission of information, including statistical data, voice communications and printed media. The fund's major areas of emphasis have traditionally included computer hardware, computer service, software, cable TV, cellular telephones and publishing. Its relatively broad industry diversification—by sector-fund standards—suggests it will show less share-price volatility than most specialized technology vehicles. Still, it offers substantial exposure to technology stocks.

Portfolio Manager: Richard Frucci
Since: 1986

Minimum:
Initial: Closed
Subsequent: $50
Telephone Exchange: Yes
Distributions:
Income: Annually
Capital Gain: Annually
Front-End Load: Closed
12b-1: 0.25%
Redemption Fee: None
Management Company: Putnam Management
Ticker Symbol: PISTX

TOTAL RETURN (%)

1987	1988	1989	1990	1991	5-year	Bull Market	Bear Market
12.2	5.9	37.9	-6.2	34.8	107.4	55.9	-31.1

INVESTMENT PORTFOLIO

Total Assets (mil.)	Current Yield	Turnover Ratio	Expense Ratio	Beta	Risk Return
$87	0.1%	109%	1.69%	1.37	0.04

SELIGMAN COMMUNICATIONS & INFORMATION

Seligman Financial Services
130 Liberty Street
New York, NY 10006
800-221-2450

Investment Objective: Organized 9 years ago, the fund seeks capital appreciation by investing primarily in securities of companies in the communications, information and related industries. Companies engaged in the production of methods for using electronic technology to communicate information have made up a large portion of the fund's portfolio in recent years. Although the fund does not focus on company size when making its selections, the rapidly changing technologies and the expansion of the communications, information and related industries has provided a favorable environment for small-growth companies. Thus, a large portion of the fund's assets tend to be invested in small and medium-sized companies.

Portfolio Manager: Paul Wick
Since: 1990

Minimum:
Initial: $1,000
Subsequent: $50
Telephone Exchange: Yes
Distributions:
Income: Annually
Capital Gain: Annually
Front-End Load: 4.75%
12b-1: None
Redemption Fee: None
Management Company: J. & W. Seligman
Ticker Symbol: SLMCX

TOTAL RETURN (%)

1987	1988	1989	1990	1991	5-year	Bull Market	Bear Market
15.0	7.3	30.1	-11.0	54.9	121.5	83.8	-40.6

INVESTMENT PORTFOLIO

Total Assets (mil.)	Current Yield	Turnover Ratio	Expense Ratio	Beta	Risk Return
$45	0.0%	86%	1.67%	1.45	0.06

T. ROWE PRICE SCIENCE & TECHNOLOGY

T. Rowe Price Investor Services
100 East Pratt Street
Baltimore, MD 21202
800-638-5660

Investment Objective: This fund seeks aggressive growth of capital through investments in common stocks of companies that are expected to benefit from the development, advancement and utilization of science and technology. Although the fund may invest in stocks of all sizes, it has substantial exposure to very small capitalization companies that are experiencing very rapid growth in earnings. The fund's affinity for emerging-growth companies gives it enormous potential, as demonstrated the past year, but also makes it very vulnerable to sharp price corrections if and when market sentiment turns against secondary stocks and technology. Bold investors will like its enormous potential.

Portfolio Manager: Chip Morris
Since: 1991

Minimum:
Initial: $2,500
Subsequent: $100
Telephone Exchange: Yes
Distributions:
Income: Annually
Capital Gain: Annually
Front-End Load: None
12b-1: None
Redemption Fee: None
Management Company: T. Rowe Price Associates
Ticker Symbol: PRSCX

TOTAL RETURN (%)

1987	1988	1989	1990	1991	5-year	Bull Market	Bear Market
NA	13.3	40.7	-1.3	60.2	NA	79.4	-34.5

INVESTMENT PORTFOLIO

Total Assets (mil.)	Current Yield	Turnover Ratio	Expense Ratio	Beta	Risk Return
$143	0.0%	183%	1.25%	1.47	0.07

TRANSAMERICA SPECIAL NATURAL RESOURCES

TransAmerica Distributors
1000 Louisiana, Suite 6000
Houston, TX 77002
800-343-6840

Investment Objective: As a sector fund, specializing in oil, natural gas, paper and primary metals, this fund's fortunes rise and fall with the ebb and flow of commodity prices. And in the fund's short history, commodity prices have been on an upward spiral. So from 1987–1989, the fund has been a pronounced winner, rising 15, 14 and 31% in respective years. However, falling oil prices and an economic recession have exacted a toll on performance during the past 2 years. The fund is appropriate only for investors seeking natural resources exposure—specifically, oil and gas. The fund also has a diversified portfolio of funds.

Portfolio Manager: Management team
Since: 1987

Minimum:
Initial: $1,000
Subsequent: $50
Telephone Exchange: Yes
Distributions:
Income: Annually
Capital Gain: Annually
Front-End Load: None
12b-1: 1.18%
Redemption Fee: 6.00%
Management Company: TransAmerica Fund Management
Ticker Symbol: TSNRX

TOTAL RETURN (%)

1987	1988	1989	1990	1991	5-year	Bull Market	Bear Market
15.7	14.0	31.1	-15.1	14.1	67.6	7.9	-12.6

INVESTMENT PORTFOLIO

Total Assets (mil.)	Current Yield	Turnover Ratio	Expense Ratio	Beta	Risk Return
$10	0.0%	47%	1.74%	0.63	0.02

UNITED SCIENCE & ENERGY

Waddell & Reed
6300 Lamar Avenue, P.O. Box 29217
Shawnee Mission, KS 66201
800-366-5465

Investment Objective: This fund seeks long-term capital growth by investing in science and energy securities. Science securities include those of companies that, in the opinion of management, are expected to benefit significantly by the utilization of commercial applications of scientific discoveries or developments in any field of science. Energy companies include those that develop sources of energy, such as solar power, or use various forms of transformed energy, such as electricity and gasoline. The dichotomous nature of its portfolio allows management to become aggressive (emphasize science) during bull markets and defensive (emphasize higher-yielding energy stocks) during bear markets.

Portfolio Manager: Abel Garcia
Since: 1984

Minimum:
Initial: $500
Subsequent: $25
Telephone Exchange: No
Distributions:
Income: Semiannually
Capital Gain: Annually
Front-End Load: 8.50%
12b-1: None
Redemption Fee: None
Management Company: Waddell & Reed
Ticker Symbol: UNSCX

TOTAL RETURN (%)

1987	1988	1989	1990	1991	5-year	Bull Market	Bear Market
12.6	9.1	27.4	-3.5	59.3	140.4	57.7	-20.7

INVESTMENT PORTFOLIO

Total Assets (mil.)	Current Yield	Turnover Ratio	Expense Ratio	Beta	Risk Return
$350	0.5%	64%	0.90%	1.05	0.10

VANGUARD SPECIALIZED ENERGY

Vanguard Group
Vanguard Financial Center
Valley Forge, PA 19482
800-662-7447

Investment Objective: This fund seeks growth of capital by investing in the securities of companies whose activities are related directly to the field of energy. These companies may engage in the production, transmission, marketing and control or measurement of energy or energy fuels. As with all concentrated portfolios, the fund can experience wide fluctuations in net asset value, which are not directly related to the market. In addition, earnings and dividends of companies in the energy industry are greatly affected by changes in the prices and supplies of oil and other fuels, which can fluctuate significantly over a short period of time.

Portfolio Manager: Ernst von Metzsh
Since: 1984

Minimum:
Initial: $3,000
Subsequent: $100
Telephone Exchange: Yes
Distributions:
Income: Annually
Capital Gain: Annually
Front-End Load: None
12b-1: None
Redemption Fee: 1.00%
Management Company: Wellington Management
Ticker Symbol: VGENX

TOTAL RETURN (%)

1987	1988	1989	1990	1991	5-year	Bull Market	Bear Market
6.1	21.4	43.5	-1.4	0.3	82.8	7.7	-4.1

INVESTMENT PORTFOLIO

Total Assets (mil.)	Current Yield	Turnover Ratio	Expense Ratio	Beta	Risk Return
$113	3.1%	40%	0.35%	0.59	NA

VANGUARD SPECIALIZED HEALTH CARE

Vanguard Group
Vanguard Financial Center
Valley Forge, PA 19482
800-662-7447

Investment Objective: This fund seeks capital appreciation by investing in securities of companies in the health-care industry. Companies include pharmaceutical firms, companies that design, manufacture or sell medical supplies, equipment and support services and companies that operate hospitals and health-care facilities. At times, the portfolio contains stocks of companies engaged in medical, diagnostic, biochemical and biotechnological research and development. During the past 5 years, this fund (which is a tad more conservatively managed than most health-care funds) has delivered the goods, returning 190% during that period.

Portfolio Manager: Edward Owens
Since: 1984

Minimum:
Initial: $3,000
Subsequent: $100
Telephone Exchange: Yes
Distributions:
Income: Annually
Capital Gain: Annually
Front-End Load: None
12b-1: None
Redemption Fee: 1.00%
Management Company: Wellington Management
Ticker Symbol: VGHCX

TOTAL RETURN (%)

1987	1988	1989	1990	1991	5-year	Bull Market	Bear Market
-0.5	28.4	33.0	16.8	46.3	190.3	55.7	-13.3

INVESTMENT PORTFOLIO

Total Assets (mil.)	Current Yield	Turnover Ratio	Expense Ratio	Beta	Risk Return
$465	1.4%	17%	0.36%	0.97	0.09

VANGUARD SPECIALIZED SERVICE ECONOMY

Vanguard Group
Vanguard Financial Center
Valley Forge, PA 19482
800-662-7447

Investment Objective: The fund seeks to capitalize on the shift in the U.S. economy away from companies that produce capital goods to firms that provide services by investing in service industries, including financial services, information and media services, business services and consumer services. Most of the fund's companies are growing earnings at well above average rates, suggesting both significant appreciation potential and high price volatility, which is usually associated with growth stocks. The fund's 15% 1990 loss occurred mainly because of its big stake in financial stocks, which experienced sharp declines as asset-quality problems surfaced. However, fund shares rebounded smartly the past year.

Portfolio Manager: Matthew E. Megargel
Since: 1984

Minimum:
Initial: $3,000
Subsequent: $100
Telephone Exchange: Yes
Distributions:
Income: Annually
Capital Gain: Annually
Front-End Load: None
12b-1: None
Redemption Fee: 1.00%
Management Company: Wellington Management
Ticker Symbol: VGSEX

TOTAL RETURN (%)

1987	1988	1989	1990	1991	5-year	Bull Market	Bear Market
-13.0	19.1	31.5	-15.4	34.3	54.9	39.4	-27.1

INVESTMENT PORTFOLIO

Total Assets (mil.)	Current Yield	Turnover Ratio	Expense Ratio	Beta	Risk Return
$19	1.4%	34%	0.59%	1.15	0.05

VANGUARD SPECIALIZED TECHNOLOGY

Vanguard Group
Vanguard Financial Center
Valley Forge, PA 19482
800-662-7447

Investment Objective: Vanguard Specialized Technology Portfolio invests primarily in equity securities of companies related to advances in technology. Management invests with a view to the longer term, keeping portfolio turnover significantly below that of most specialized technology funds. Its strict interpretation of the fund's charter keeps the fund a technology play, with most of its assets concentrated in software, data processing, computers, communications, electronics and aerospace. For those who can tolerate substantial volatility, this fund will be a full participant in the next bull market for technology stocks.

Portfolio Manager: Perry Traquina
Since: 1984

Minimum:
Initial: $3,000
Subsequent: $100
Telephone Exchange: Yes
Distributions:
Income: Annually
Capital Gain: Annually
Front-End Load: None
12b-1: None
Redemption Fee: 1.00%
Management Company: Wellington Management
Ticker Symbol: VGTCX

TOTAL RETURN (%)

1987	1988	1989	1990	1991	5-year	Bull Market	Bear Market
-11.9	9.5	14.6	-6.5	47.3	52.2	63.6	-32.4

INVESTMENT PORTFOLIO

Total Assets (mil.)	Current Yield	Turnover Ratio	Expense Ratio	Beta	Risk Return
$21	1.2%	55%	0.48%	1.21	0.06

PART 10

Convertible Bond Funds

A convertible bond is a debenture, issued by a corporation, that, at the option of the holder, can be exchanged for shares of the company's common stock. When the price of the company's common stock rises above the conversion price, the price of the bond tends to move in tandem with the price of the underlying stock. On the other hand, because these instruments also pay interest and have limited lives, their prices tend to behave like bond prices when the common stock price falls below the conversion price. Thus, a well-diversified portfolio of convertible bonds allows investors to participate in rising stock markets while giving them a considerable degree of protection during severe bear markets.

While investment in convertible bonds, at first glance, appears to be the ideal investment strategy for risk-averse, growth-oriented investors, implementation of a convertible bond strategy does not come without its pitfalls. The convertible bond market tends to be a rather thinly traded market. Thus, bid and ask prices can widen substantially when a large block of bonds is purchased or sold. In addition, the price of convertible bonds can sink when a bear stock market results from rising interest rates. First, the bonds lose value because their underlying stocks are losing value. Second, the value of the instrument as a bond also decreases along with other bonds in a rising-interest-rate environment.

The following pages contain descriptions of 15 convertible bond funds. These funds differ significantly from each other with respect to the degree to which they stress convertibles' fixed-income and equity characteristics. In varying degrees, most convertible bond funds blend the pursuit of growth and income. But some funds go to extremes, greatly prioritizing one over the other. A fund's potential risks are directly proportionate to the degree to which it stresses growth over income.

Much insight into a convertible bond fund's objectives can be gained by looking at its income stream. Generally, the higher a fund's yield, the more it stresses income and price stability at the expense of potential capital gains. At the opposite end of the spectrum are bolder vehicles that aggressively pursue growth. These types of funds tend to invest heavily in securities of emerging-growth companies and stress high-growth industries such as technology, health care and pollution control. The majority of convertible bond funds, however, falls somewhere in between these two extremes.

As can be seen from the financial summary below, convertible bond funds tend to possess far less volatility than the stock market as a whole (median beta, 0.63). In addition, while their yields are less than comparable-risk straight-debt securities, their current yields are greater than those available in the stock market. Note, however, that these lower-risk funds have returned significantly less than general equity funds during the past five years.

Summary of Financial Statistics (medians)

1991 Return	5-Year Return	Current Yield	Beta	Turnover Ratio	Expense Ratio
29.4%	49.5%	4.6%	0.63	71%	1.14%

BEST CONVERTIBLE BOND FUNDS FOR 1991

Fund	Percent Return 1991	3-Year	5-Year
Mainstay Convertible Fund	48.5%	47.8%	48.5%
AIM Convertible Securities	42.9	57.5	52.8
Fidelity Convertible Securities Fund	38.7	70.1	NA
Lord Abbett Bond-Debenture Fund	38.5	34.5	55.9
Calamos Convertible Income Fund	36.8	52.7	55.0
Vanguard Convertible Securities Fund	34.3	42.8	47.8
Dreyfus Convertible Securities Fund	33.1	27.2	53.3
Seligman Income Fund	30.1	37.3	45.9
Putnam Convertible Income-Growth Trust	29.4	35.7	43.7
Value Line Convertible Fund	28.7	37.2	49.5
Rochester Convertible Fund	28.6	27.4	29.5
Sun America Income Portfolio Convertible	25.4	20.6	NA
Thomson Convertible Securities B	23.4	16.1	NA
American Capital Harbor Fund	23.1	46.7	64.7
Phoenix Convertible Fund	12.8	41.0	62.9

AIM CONVERTIBLE SECURITIES

AIM Distributors
11 Greenway Plaza, Suite 1919
Houston, TX 77046
800-347-1919

Investment Objective: This fund stresses convertible bonds with underlying common stocks that show good earnings momentum. It also invests about a third of its assets in high-momentum common stocks. Most of its securities overlap with siblings AIM Weingarten and AIM Constellation. The fund's relatively low current yield reveals its willingness to sacrifice some income in return for potentially higher capital gains and quality; most of its convertible bonds are rated BB or higher. Thanks to its earnings orientation and sizable exposure to blue chip companies, the fund posted an enviable total return during the 1991 bull market.

Portfolio Manager: J. Schoolar/L. Sachowitz
Since: 1989

Minimum:
Initial: $1,000
Subsequent: $100
Telephone Exchange: Yes
Distributions:
Income: Quarterly
Capital Gain: Annually
Front-End Load: 4.75%
12b-1: 0.14%
Redemption Fee: None
Management Company: AIM Advisers
Ticker Symbol: CONVX

TOTAL RETURN (%)

1987	1988	1989	1990	1991	5-year	Bull Market	Bear Market
-12.1	10.3	14.8	-4.0	42.9	52.8	41.7	-22.6

INVESTMENT PORTFOLIO

Total Assets (mil.)	Current Yield	Turnover Ratio	Expense Ratio	Beta	Risk Return
$11	2.2%	307%	2.15%	0.92	0.08

AMERICAN CAPITAL HARBOR FUND

American Capital Marketing
P.O. Box 3528
Houston, TX 77253
800-421-5666

Investment Objective: This fund pursues its dual objective of capital growth and current income by investing in common stocks, convertible bonds and straight debt. In recent years, management has opted to gradually reduce the fund's allocation to common stocks. With more than two-thirds of its assets in bonds, the fund has a decidedly conservative bent. Its ample income stream, relatively good credit quality, emphasis on established—rather than emerging-growth—companies and broad industry diversification have enabled it to produce highly competitive results over the past 5 years.

Portfolio Manager: James Behrmann
Since: 1984

Minimum:
Initial: $500
Subsequent: $50
Telephone Exchange: Yes
Distributions:
Income: Quarterly
Capital Gain: Annually
Front-End Load: 5.75%
12b-1: None
Redemption Fee: None
Management Company: American Capital Asset Management
Ticker Symbol: ACHBX

TOTAL RETURN (%)

1987	1988	1989	1990	1991	5-year	Bull Market	Bear Market
-3.8	16.8	20.6	-1.2	23.1	64.7	25.1	-12.0

INVESTMENT PORTFOLIO

Total Assets (mil.)	Current Yield	Turnover Ratio	Expense Ratio	Beta	Risk Return
$366	5.8%	71%	0.89%	0.56	0.06

CALAMOS CONVERTIBLE INCOME FUND

Calamos Financial Services
2001 Spring Road, Suite 750
Oak Brook, IL 60521
800-323-9943

Investment Objective: A quality, large-company orientation distinguishes this fund from the average convertible bond fund. Unlike most rivals, which invest heavily in below-investment-grade, small-company securities, the fund stresses established, quality names. Its largest positions include well-known blue chips such as American Brands, IBM and Baxter. This practice doesn't make for the highest income stream, nor will it permit the fund to ride small-cap rallies as much as its bolder rivals. On the bright side, the fund participates in blue chip advances and offers considerably better-than-average resistance to decline in turbulence as witnessed in 1987 and 1990.

Portfolio Manager: John P. Calamos
Since: 1985

Minimum:
Initial: $5,000
Subsequent: $500
Telephone Exchange: No
Distributions:
Income: Quarterly
Capital Gain: Quarterly
Front-End Load: None
12b-1: None
Redemption Fee: None
Management Company: Calamos Asset Management
Ticker Symbol: CCVIX

TOTAL RETURN (%)

1987	1988	1989	1990	1991	5-year	Bull Market	Bear Market
-4.5	6.2	15.8	-3.6	36.8	55.0	39.0	-17.4

INVESTMENT PORTFOLIO

Total Assets (mil.)	Current Yield	Turnover Ratio	Expense Ratio	Beta	Risk Return
$15	3.5%	63%	1.20%	0.77	0.08

DREYFUS CONVERTIBLE SECURITIES FUND

Dreyfus Service
200 Park Avenue, 7th Floor
New York, NY 10166
800-782-6620

Investment Objective: A relatively new portfolio manager makes this convertible bond fund somewhat of an unknown quantity at this juncture. Replacing longtime manager Jeffrey Friedman, new manager Catherine Jacobson made substantial portfolio revisions during her first year at the helm. Her taste for small, emerging-growth stocks saw the fund plunge 17% in 1990, versus a 22% average decline in small-firm stock prices. However, the situation reversed itself the past year when small-firm stocks returned 44%. Accordingly, the fund provided a better-than-average return as Jacobson's bet paid off during 1991.

Portfolio Manager: Catherine Jacobson
Since: 1990

Minimum:
Initial: $2,500
Subsequent: $50
Telephone Exchange: Yes
Distributions:
Income: Monthly
Capital Gain: Annually
Front-End Load: None
12b-1: None
Redemption Fee: None
Management Company: Dreyfus Corporation
Ticker Symbol: DRCSX

TOTAL RETURN (%)

1987	1988	1989	1990	1991	5-year	Bull Market	Bear Market
-2.1	23.0	14.9	-16.8	33.1	53.3	23.4	-23.1

INVESTMENT PORTFOLIO

Total Assets (mil.)	Current Yield	Turnover Ratio	Expense Ratio	Beta	Risk Return
$218	3.6%	169%	1.07%	0.68	0.07

FIDELITY CONVERTIBLE SECURITIES FUND

Fidelity Distributors Corporation
82 Devonshire Street, Mail Zone L7B
Boston, MA 02109
800-544-8888

Investment Objective: More than most convertible bond funds, this fund offers a fine risk/reward profile. Its ample, after-expense income stream provides a solid cushion during market declines, as seen in its decent 1990 results. Still, the fund offers significant stock market participation. Its bull-market gains are among the convertible bond category's highest. In selecting securities, the fund doesn't focus on one particular profile. Both its convertibles and its common stocks consist of a mix of high-growth companies, special situations and value plays. Its major sectors the past year included technology, health care and basic industry.

Portfolio Manager: Harris Leviton
Since: 1990

Minimum:
Initial: $2,500
Subsequent: $250
Telephone Exchange: Yes
Distributions:
Income: Quarterly
Capital Gain: Annually
Front-End Load: None
12b-1: None
Redemption Fee: None
Management Company: Fidelity Management & Research
Ticker Symbol: FCVSX

TOTAL RETURN (%)

1987	1988	1989	1990	1991	5-year	Bull Market	Bear Market
NA	15.9	26.3	-2.9	38.7	NA	46.1	-15.0

INVESTMENT PORTFOLIO

Total Assets (mil.)	Current Yield	Turnover Ratio	Expense Ratio	Beta	Risk Return
$126	4.6%	223%	1.31%	0.63	0.10

LORD ABBETT BOND-DEBENTURE FUND

Lord Abbett & Company
767 Fifth Avenue
New York, NY 10153
800-874-3733

Investment Objective: The goal of this fund is to provide high current income and the opportunity for capital appreciation to produce a high total return from a portfolio consisting primarily of convertible and discount debt securities, many of which are lower rated. Unlike most convertible bond funds, this fund tends to allocate a high percentage of assets to straight debt instruments, especially so-called junk bonds. Because of its historically high proportion of straight debt securities, it has the lowest beta of the group. Consequently, its returns tend to be lower than more aggressive convertible bond funds. However, falling interest rates and a rejuvenation of the junk bond market led to an impressive return the past year.

Portfolio Manager: Robert Dow
Since: 1982

Minimum:
Initial: $1,000
Subsequent: None
Telephone Exchange: Yes
Distributions:
Income: Quarterly
Capital Gain: Annually
Front-End Load: 4.75%
12b-1: 0.16%
Redemption Fee: None
Management Company: Lord Abbett
Ticker Symbol: LBNDX

TOTAL RETURN (%)

1987	1988	1989	1990	1991	5-year	Bull Market	Bear Market
1.9	13.8	5.1	-7.6	38.5	55.9	36.8	-13.0

INVESTMENT PORTFOLIO

Total Assets (mil.)	Current Yield	Turnover Ratio	Expense Ratio	Beta	Risk Return
$583	10.4%	145%	0.80%	0.37	0.12

MAINSTAY CONVERTIBLE FUND

NYLIFE Securities
51 Madison Avenue, Room 117
New York, NY 10010
800-522-4202

Investment Objective: This fund's relatively low 2.2% yield reveals its quality orientation. Unlike most rivals, which mirror the convertible universe's average BB credit rating, this fund is restricted to investment-grade securities. Both its convertibles and its common stocks, which may make up a maximum 25% of its assets, consist of large and medium-sized issues from industries, such as health care, energy and technology, with above-average growth prospects because of economic/demographic trends. Although the fund's quality bias has caused it to underperform higher-yielding rivals in years past, its strategy paid off the past year with a category-leading 48.5% total return.

Portfolio Manager: Ronald J. Worobel
Since: 1990

Minimum:
Initial: $500
Subsequent: $50
Telephone Exchange: Yes
Distributions:
Income: Quarterly
Capital Gain: Annually
Front-End Load: None
12b-1: 1.00%
Redemption Fee: 5.00%
Management Company: MacKay-Shields Financial
Ticker Symbol: MCSVX

TOTAL RETURN (%)

1987	1988	1989	1990	1991	5-year	Bull Market	Bear Market
-8.6	9.8	6.7	-6.7	48.5	48.5	43.1	-15.2

INVESTMENT PORTFOLIO

Total Assets (mil.)	Current Yield	Turnover Ratio	Expense Ratio	Beta	Risk Return
$21	2.2%	283%	2.70%	0.65	0.12

PHOENIX CONVERTIBLE FUND

Phoenix Equity Planning
100 Bright Meadow Boulevard
Enfield, CT 06082
800-243-4361

Investment Objective: This fund seeks both income and the potential for capital appreciation, which are to be considered as relatively equal objectives. The fund normally invests at least 65% of its assets in convertible preferred stocks. Rather than stress diversification, management stresses the selection of securities believed to have good potential for capital appreciation. Although the fund has amassed an impressive track record during the past 10 years, it stubbed its toe the past year as it increased its exposure to cyclical industries. However, because of its conservative nature, the fund has posted gains in each of the past 5 years.

Portfolio Manager: Jack Martin
Since: 1982

Minimum:
Initial: $500
Subsequent: $25
Telephone Exchange: Yes
Distributions:
Income: Quarterly
Capital Gain: Annually
Front-End Load: 4.75%
12b-1: None
Redemption Fee: None
Management Company: Phoenix Investment Counsel
Ticker Symbol: PHCVX

TOTAL RETURN (%)

1987	1988	1989	1990	1991	5-year	Bull Market	Bear Market
10.5	4.5	20.1	4.1	12.8	62.9	18.5	-8.7

INVESTMENT PORTFOLIO

Total Assets (mil.)	Current Yield	Turnover Ratio	Expense Ratio	Beta	Risk Return
$168	4.0%	284%	1.14%	0.44	0.03

PUTNAM CONVERTIBLE INCOME-GROWTH TRUST

Putnam Financial Services
One Post Office Square, 12th Floor
Boston, MA 02109
800-634-1590

Investment Objective: This fund features a broadly diversified portfolio consisting of roughly two-thirds convertible bonds and convertible preferred stocks and one-third common stocks. Although the fund owns some blue chips, most of its convertibles are small-company issues. Consequently, the fund has suffered from small stocks' unpopularity since 1983. Its value orientation also has dampened returns, for it has led it to numerous cyclicals, which have been neglected by a recession-wary market. While recent results have been disappointing, an inevitable return to traditional measures of value could give the fund's small stocks and value plays a big boost during an economic recovery.

Portfolio Manager: Anthony Kreisel
Since: 1989

Minimum:
Initial: $500
Subsequent: $50
Telephone Exchange: Yes
Distributions:
Income: Quarterly
Capital Gain: Annually
Front-End Load: 5.75%
12b-1: 0.25%
Redemption Fee: None
Management Company: Putnam Management
Ticker Symbol: PCONX

TOTAL RETURN (%)

1987	1988	1989	1990	1991	5-year	Bull Market	Bear Market
-5.5	12.1	16.5	-10.0	29.4	43.7	36.0	-18.7

INVESTMENT PORTFOLIO

Total Assets (mil.)	Current Yield	Turnover Ratio	Expense Ratio	Beta	Risk Return
$548	5.7%	60%	1.12%	0.70	0.06

ROCHESTER CONVERTIBLE FUND

Rochester Funds Distributor
70 Linden Oaks
Rochester, NY 14625
716-383-1300

Investment Objective: The convertible bond fund stresses capital appreciation over current income. Like other convertible bond funds, it normally invests 65% of its assets in convertible fixed-income securities. In addition, the fund writes covered call options to boost its current yield, which is among the highest in the group. The fund also may invest up to 15% of its assets in warrants to purchase the common stock. Because of its somewhat aggressive investment strategy, the fund tends to perform well during bull markets but its share price can tumble during bear markets as witnessed by its two annual declines during 1987 and 1990.

Portfolio Manager: Michael S. Rosen
Since: 1986

Minimum:
Initial: $2,000
Subsequent: $100
Telephone Exchange: Yes
Distributions:
Income: Quarterly
Capital Gain: Annually
Front-End Load: 3.25%
12b-1: 0.75%
Redemption Fee: None
Management Company: Fielding Management
Ticker Symbol: RCVGX

TOTAL RETURN (%)

1987	1988	1989	1990	1991	5-year	Bull Market	Bear Market
-9.3	12.2	7.9	-8.2	28.6	29.5	28.7	-14.4

INVESTMENT PORTFOLIO

Total Assets (mil.)	Current Yield	Turnover Ratio	Expense Ratio	Beta	Risk Return
$6	7.3%	33%	2.92%	0.46	0.08

SELIGMAN INCOME FUND

Seligman Financial Services
130 Liberty Street, 22nd Floor
New York, NY 10006
800-221-2450

Investment Objective: The Seligman Income Fund is primarily concerned with income, and, although it is not ignored, capital appreciation is secondary. At least 80% of the fund is invested in income-producing securities at any given time, with the balance being invested in bonds and preferred stocks and cash or cash equivalents. New Portfolio Manager Charles Smith isn't likely to make many changes, and he is attracted to the growth potential of convertibles. This fairly low-risk fund is perfect for the investor looking for a high yield as well as potential for capital appreciation.

Portfolio Manager: Charles Smith
Since: 1984

Minimum:
Initial: $1,000
Subsequent: $50
Telephone Exchange: Yes
Distributions:
Income: Quarterly
Capital Gain: Annually
Front-End Load: 4.75%
12b-1: None
Redemption Fee: None
Management Company: J. W. Seligman
Ticker Symbol: SINFX

TOTAL RETURN (%)

1987	1988	1989	1990	1991	5-year	Bull Market	Bear Market
-4.0	10.6	15.1	-8.3	30.1	45.9	31.8	-13.0

INVESTMENT PORTFOLIO

Total Assets (mil.)	Current Yield	Turnover Ratio	Expense Ratio	Beta	Risk Return
$150	7.4%	53%	0.76%	0.45	0.09

SUN AMERICA INCOME PORTFOLIO CONVERTIBLE SECURITIES

Sun America Capital Services
10 Union Square East, 2nd Floor
New York, NY 10003
800-821-5100

Investment Objective: This fund is one of several series of a Massachusetts business trust organized in 1986. The fund seeks to produce high current income together with appreciation of capital by investing 65% of its assets in convertible securities. The fund also engages in activities designed to boost current income including: writing covered call options, lending portfolio securities, selling securities on a forward-commitment basis and entering into repurchase agreements. Because of the fund's modest size, its portfolio tends to be somewhat compact and its expense ratio is a bit higher than the average of funds in the group.

Portfolio Manager: Harvey Eisen
Since: 1989

Minimum:
Initial: $500
Subsequent: $100
Telephone Exchange: Yes
Distributions:
Income: Monthly
Capital Gain: Annually
Front-End Load: 4.75%
12b-1: 0.35%
Redemption Fee: None
Management Company: Sun America Asset Management
Ticker Symbol: SICVX

TOTAL RETURN (%)

1987	1988	1989	1990	1991	5-year	Bull Market	Bear Market
NA	12.1	6.7	-9.9	25.4	NA	32.9	-17.8

INVESTMENT PORTFOLIO

Total Assets (mil.)	Current Yield	Turnover Ratio	Expense Ratio	Beta	Risk Return
$8	6.4%	2%	1.94%	0.48	0.06

THOMSON CONVERTIBLE SECURITIES B

Thomson Investor Services
One Station Place
Stamford, CT 06902
800-628-6237

Investment Objective: This fund seeks total return primarily through investment in convertible bonds and convertible preferred stocks. At least 65% of the fund's assets normally are invested in convertible securities. Up to 15% of its assets may be invested in foreign securities, and non-convertible debt must be at least single-B quality rated at the time of purchase. In addition, the fund may invest in common stock, preferred stock, U.S. government bonds, options, corporate bonds and synthetic convertibles. During its brief existence, the fund has been a subpar performer. In addition, it possesses an above-average expense ratio.

Minimum:
Initial: $1,000
Subsequent: $100
Telephone Exchange: Yes
Distributions:
Income: Quarterly
Capital Gain: Annually
Front-End Load: None
12b-1: 1.00%
Redemption Fee: 1.00%
Management Company: Thomson Advisory Group
Ticker Symbol: TCVBX

Portfolio Manager: Irwin Smith
Since: 1990

TOTAL RETURN (%)

1987	1988	1989	1990	1991	5-year	Bull Market	Bear Market
NA	NA	11.2	-15.4	23.4	NA	23.1	-21.0

INVESTMENT PORTFOLIO

Total Assets (mil.)	Current Yield	Turnover Ratio	Expense Ratio	Beta	Risk Return
$21	3.4%	76%	2.10%	0.69	0.07

VALUE LINE CONVERTIBLE FUND

Value Line Securities
711 Third Avenue
New York, NY 10017
800-223-0818

Investment Objective: Like Value Line's pure equity vehicles, this convertible bond fund is distinguished by its earnings orientation. Most of its better-than-average quality convertibles have underlying common stocks of a high-growth nature. Rapid-growth industries, such as technology, health care and retail issues, are particularly prominent. While the fund's securities pay decent yields, their main attraction is their potential to participate in stock market advances. The fund should continue to perform relatively well as long as growth stocks lead the market.

Minimum:
Initial: $1,000
Subsequent: $250
Telephone Exchange: Yes
Distributions:
Income: Quarterly
Capital Gain: Annually
Front-End Load: None
12b-1: None
Redemption Fee: None
Management Company: Value Line
Ticker Symbol: VALCX

Portfolio Manager: Management team
Since: 1990

TOTAL RETURN (%)

1987	1988	1989	1990	1991	5-year	Bull Market	Bear Market
-6.1	16.0	10.7	-3.7	28.7	49.5	32.8	-16.1

INVESTMENT PORTFOLIO

Total Assets (mil.)	Current Yield	Turnover Ratio	Expense Ratio	Beta	Risk Return
$36	5.0%	216%	1.19%	0.64	0.07

VANGUARD CONVERTIBLE SECURITIES FUND

Vanguard Group
Vanguard Financial Center
Valley Forge, PA 19482
800-662-7447

Investment Objective: In seeking to meet its objective of current income and long-term growth of capital, the fund, under normal circumstances, invests at least 80% of its assets in convertible securities. When making investment selections, the adviser emphasizes the securities of companies with above-average growth potential whose convertibles offer attractive yields. In addition, the adviser seeks convertibles that are priced at a "reasonable" premium to their conversion values. The fund's relatively large commitment to equity securities has made it one of the more volatile funds in the group. However, it tends to perform exceptionally well during bull stock markets.

Portfolio Manager: Rohit Desai
Since: 1986

Minimum:
Initial: $3,000
Subsequent: $100
Telephone Exchange: Yes
Distributions:
Income: Quarterly
Capital Gain: Annually
Front-End Load: None
12b-1: None
Redemption Fee: None
Management Company: Desai Capital Management
Ticker Symbol: VCVSX

TOTAL RETURN (%)

1987	1988	1989	1990	1991	5-year	Bull Market	Bear Market
-10.6	15.7	15.8	-8.2	34.3	47.8	41.8	-20.9

INVESTMENT PORTFOLIO

Total Assets (mil.)	Current Yield	Turnover Ratio	Expense Ratio	Beta	Risk Return
$55	5.2%	55%	0.88%	0.76	0.07

PART 11

Taxable Bond Funds

At the onset of the decade of the 1980s, there were fewer than 120 bond funds of all types in existence. By the decade's end, that number had swelled to more than 1,700. During the ten-year period of hectic growth, several categories of specialized bond funds were created, including: Ginnie Mae funds, government income funds, international bond funds and municipal bond funds that concentrate their investments in the issues of a single state. In addition, a growing number of funds "target" their maturities by investing in zero-coupon bonds with a specific target maturity. More recently, investors have been offered the opportunity to invest in renegotiable-rate home mortgages, which dominate the portfolios of so-called ARM funds. Thus, today's income-oriented investor can find bond funds that assume a wide spectrum of risks in the pursuit of current income.

U.S. government income funds invest in a variety of government securities. These include: U.S. Treasury bonds, federally guaranteed mortgage-backed securities and issues of government agencies such as the Federal Home Loan Bank, Federal Farm Credit, Student Loan Marketing, TVA, etc. These bonds pay interest that is taxable at the federal level but free of state and local taxes. U.S. government bond fund shareholders receive a pass-through of the exemption from state and local taxes on interest income earned.

GNMA (Government National Mortgage Association), or Ginnie Mae, funds invest in government-backed mortgage securities. To qualify for this category, the majority of the fund's portfolio must always be invested in mortgage-backed securities. ARM funds, for the most part, are short-term GNMA funds.

Corporate bond funds seek a high level of income. They do so by buying bonds of corporations for the majority of the fund's portfolio. The balance of the portfolio may be invested in U.S. Treasury bonds and bonds of other government entities.

High-yield bond funds invest in lower-quality corporate issues. In recent years, these bonds, which possess a very high degree of risk, have become known as "junk bonds." After the near collapse of the junk bond market two years ago, a number of junk bond funds upgraded the quality of their holdings. Many of these funds now also invest in investment-grade obligations.

As their name implies, international bond funds invest in public and private debt of governments and corporations domiciled outside the United States. In addition to credit risks, international bond fund investors face the risk that returns will be impaired by political events or by changing values of international currencies relative to the U.S. dollar.

While individuals have the option of investing directly in government securities, bond funds provide several advantages. First, bond funds make investment in government securities possible for investors with limited resources. Instead of buying bonds in large denominations, income investors can purchase a diversified portfolio by initially investing $2,500 or less in an appropriate government bond fund. Second, by investing in a bond fund, individuals obtain needed risk reduction since they own a pro rata share of a highly diversified portfolio rather than a small handful of issues. Third, small lots of bonds traded in the open market possess relatively large bid-ask spreads. In some instances, the difference can amount to an entire year's yield. Finally, bond fund investors obtain a high degree of liquidity. Since the fund must purchase shares tendered at the end of a business day, investors with changing investment needs can easily adjust their bond fund holdings.

Summary Financial Statistics (medians)

Number of Funds	1991 Return	Five-Year Return	Turnover Ratio	Expense Ratio
Corporate Bond Funds				
71	16.8%	51.2%	82%	0.91%
High-Yield Bond Funds				
49	35.4%	41.1%	59%	1.15%
International Bond Funds				
19	15.0%	67.4%	154%	1.65%
GNMA Funds				
26	15.2%	56.2%	72%	0.90%
Government Bond Funds				
84	14.2%	52.2%	116%	1.00%

BEST TAXABLE BOND FUNDS FOR 1991

Fund	Percent Return 1991	3-Year	5-Year
Liberty High Income Bond	60.5%	39.4%	60.6%
Federated High Yield Trust	52.5	31.7	55.0
MFS Lifetime High Income Trust	50.0	22.0	34.2
National Bond Fund	49.8	11.3	12.7
Massachusetts Financial High Income Trust I	48.6	18.8	31.2
Age High Income Fund	47.4	20.0	37.3
PaineWebber High Income A	47.0	32.1	41.2
Kemper High Yield Fund	46.8	26.3	57.6
Kemper Investment Portfolios High Yield	45.8	18.6	41.3
Putnam High Yield Trust II	45.7	28.1	56.4
Keystone America High Yield Bond Fund	44.1	7.8	NA
Delaware Group Delchester I High Yield Bond	43.9	28.2	53.6
Colonial High Yield Securities Fund	43.6	22.6	44.5

Corporate Bond Funds

AARP HIGH QUALITY BOND FUND

Scudder Stevens & Clark
175 Federal Street, 12th Floor
Boston, MA 02110
800-532-7700

Minimum: $500
Front-End Load: None
12b-1: None
Redemption Fee: None
Ticker Symbol: AGBFX

TOTAL RETURNS (%)

1987	1988	1989	1990	1991	5-year
1.8	8.1	12.3	7.6	15.4	53.4

INVESTMENT PORTFOLIO

Total Assets (mil.)	Expense Ratio	Turnover Ratio
$219	1.14%	47%

ALLIANCE BOND FUND MONTHLY INCOME PORTFOLIO

Alliance Funds Distributor
500 Plaza Drive
Secaucus, NJ 07094
800-474-5400

Minimum: $250
Front-End Load: 4.75%
12b-1: 0.30%
Redemption Fee: None
Ticker Symbol: CABMX

TOTAL RETURNS (%)

1987	1988	1989	1990	1991	5-year
3.0	8.2	13.1	5.5	18.1	57.1

INVESTMENT PORTFOLIO

Total Assets (mil.)	Expense Ratio	Turnover Ratio
$61	1.44%	357%

AMERICAN CAPITAL CORPORATE BOND FUND

American Capital Marketing
P.O. Box 3528
Houston, TX 77253
800-215-6600

Minimum: $500
Front-End Load: 4.75%
12b-1: 0.15%
Redemption Fee: None
Ticker Symbol: ACCBX

TOTAL RETURNS (%)

1987	1988	1989	1990	1991	5-year
6.2	12.9	4.0	7.0	16.7	55.8

INVESTMENT PORTFOLIO

Total Assets (mil.)	Expense Ratio	Turnover Ratio
$186	0.94%	54%

BABSON BOND TRUST PORTFOLIO-LONG TERM

Jones & Babson
3 Crown Center, 2440 Pershing Road
Kansas City, MO 64108
800-222-6600

Minimum: $500
Front-End Load: None
12b-1: None
Redemption Fee: None
Ticker Symbol: BABIX

TOTAL RETURNS (%)

1987	1988	1989	1990	1991	5-year
1.9	7.2	13.1	7.8	15.0	53.2

INVESTMENT PORTFOLIO

Total Assets (mil.)	Expense Ratio	Turnover Ratio
$114	0.97%	51%

BARTLETT CAPITAL FIXED INCOME FUND

Bartlett & Company
36 East Fourth Street, 5th Floor
Cincinnati, OH 45202
800-004-1200

Minimum: $5,000
Front-End Load: None
12b-1: None
Redemption Fee: None
Ticker Symbol: BFXFX

TOTAL RETURNS (%)

1987	1988	1989	1990	1991	5-year
2.7	7.7	12.6	6.0	14.4	51.2

INVESTMENT PORTFOLIO

Total Assets (mil.)	Expense Ratio	Turnover Ratio
$156	1.00%	96%

BOND FUND OF AMERICA FUND

American Funds Distributor
333 South Hope Street, 52nd Floor
Los Angeles, CA 90071
800-219-0000

Minimum: $1,000
Front-End Load: 4.75%
12b-1: 0.17%
Redemption Fee: None
Ticker Symbol: ABNDX

TOTAL RETURNS (%)

1987	1988	1989	1990	1991	5-year
2.0	10.7	10.1	3.3	21.0	55.4

INVESTMENT PORTFOLIO

Total Assets (mil.)	Expense Ratio	Turnover Ratio
$2,859	0.76%	60%

BOSTON COMPANY MANAGED INCOME

Boston Company Advisors
53 State St., Exchange Place, 4th Floor-B
Boston, MA 02114
800-255-6700

Minimum: $1,000
Front-End Load: None
12b-1: 0.07%
Redemption Fee: None
Ticker Symbol: BOSGX

TOTAL RETURNS (%)

1987	1988	1989	1990	1991	5-year
5.7	10.0	5.6	4.5	16.9	50.0

INVESTMENT PORTFOLIO

Total Assets (mil.)	Expense Ratio	Turnover Ratio
$81	1.19%	183%

CALVERT INCOME FUND

Calvert Securities
4550 Montgomery Avenue, Suite 1000 N.
Bethesda, MD 20814
800-682-4800

Minimum: $2,000
Front-End Load: 4.75%
12b-1: None
Redemption Fee: None
Ticker Symbol: CFICX

TOTAL RETURNS (%)

1987	1988	1989	1990	1991	5-year
2.2	10.3	15.1	4.2	18.2	59.7

INVESTMENT PORTFOLIO

Total Assets (mil.)	Expense Ratio	Turnover Ratio
$37	1.05%	5%

CIGNA INCOME FUND

CIGNA Mutual Funds
One Financial Plaza, 16th Floor
Springfield, MA 01103
800-724-6200

Minimum: $500
Front-End Load: 5.00%
12b-1: 0.25%
Redemption Fee: None
Ticker Symbol: CGIFX

TOTAL RETURNS (%)

1987	1988	1989	1990	1991	5-year
0.6	9.0	13.6	3.6	18.0	52.3

INVESTMENT PORTFOLIO

Total Assets (mil.)	Expense Ratio	Turnover Ratio
$225	1.00%	106%

COLONIAL INCOME TRUST

Colonial Investment Services
One Financial Center, 14th Floor
Boston, MA 02110
800-482-2800

Minimum: $1,000
Front-End Load: 4.75%
12b-1: 0.25%
Redemption Fee: None
Ticker Symbol: COLIX

TOTAL RETURNS (%)

1987	1988	1989	1990	1991	5-year
0.6	12.4	7.6	2.6	19.0	48.7

INVESTMENT PORTFOLIO

Total Assets (mil.)	Expense Ratio	Turnover Ratio
$143	1.23%	29%

COLUMBIA FIXED INCOME SECURITIES FUND

Columbia Funds Management
1301 S.W. 5th Avenue, P.O. Box 1350
Portland, OR 97207
800-471-0700

Minimum: $1,000
Front-End Load: None
12b-1: None
Redemption Fee: None
Ticker Symbol: CFISX

TOTAL RETURNS (%)

1987	1988	1989	1990	1991	5-year
1.4	7.7	14.4	8.3	16.8	58.0

INVESTMENT PORTFOLIO

Total Assets (mil.)	Expense Ratio	Turnover Ratio
$207	0.73%	132%

COMPOSITE INCOME FUND

Murphy Favre Securities
W. 601 Riverside, Suite 900
Spokane, WA 99201
800-438-7200

Minimum: $1,000
Front-End Load: 4.00%
12b-1: 0.15%
Redemption Fee: None
Ticker Symbol: CMPIX

TOTAL RETURNS (%)

1987	1988	1989	1990	1991	5-year
6.0	7.1	6.8	8.2	17.3	53.8

INVESTMENT PORTFOLIO

Total Assets (mil.)	Expense Ratio	Turnover Ratio
$76	1.04%	64%

DFA ONE YEAR FIXED INCOME

Dimensional Fund Advisors
1299 Ocean Avenue, Suite 650
Santa Monica, CA 90401
213-395-8005

Minimum: $50,000
Front-End Load: None
12b-1: None
Redemption Fee: None
Ticker Symbol: DFIHX

TOTAL RETURNS (%)

1987	1988	1989	1990	1991	5-year
6.5	7.4	9.6	9.1	8.7	48.7

INVESTMENT PORTFOLIO

Total Assets (mil.)	Expense Ratio	Turnover Ratio
$477	0.21%	96%

DREYFUS A BONDS PLUS

Dreyfus Service
200 Park Avenue, 7th Floor
New York, NY 10166
800-826-2000

Minimum: $2,500
Front-End Load: None
12b-1: None
Redemption Fee: None
Ticker Symbol: DRBDX

TOTAL RETURNS (%)

1987	1988	1989	1990	1991	5-year
-0.3	9.0	14.2	4.8	18.8	54.4

INVESTMENT PORTFOLIO

Total Assets (mil.)	Expense Ratio	Turnover Ratio
$438	0.85%	26%

DREYFUS STRATEGIC INCOME

Dreyfus Service
200 Park Avenue, 7th Floor
New York, NY 10166
800-826-2000

Minimum: $2,500
Front-End Load: 4.50%
12b-1: None
Redemption Fee: None
Ticker Symbol: DSINX

TOTAL RETURNS (%)

1987	1988	1989	1990	1991	5-year
5.6	11.1	13.9	5.5	19.1	67.9

INVESTMENT PORTFOLIO

Total Assets (mil.)	Expense Ratio	Turnover Ratio
$60	0.82%	16%

FIDELITY FLEXIBLE BOND FUND

Fidelity Distributors Corporation
82 Devonshire Street, Mail Zone L7b
Boston, MA 02109
800-448-8800

Minimum: $2,500
Front-End Load: None
12b-1: None
Redemption Fee: None
Ticker Symbol: FBNDX

TOTAL RETURNS (%)

1987	1988	1989	1990	1991	5-year
0.1	7.9	13.0	6.1	18.9	54.0

INVESTMENT PORTFOLIO

Total Assets (mil.)	Expense Ratio	Turnover Ratio
$617	0.67%	101%

FIDELITY INTERMEDIATE BOND FUND

Fidelity Distributors Corporation
82 Devonshire Street, Mail Zone L7b
Boston, MA 02109
800-448-8800

Minimum: $2,500
Front-End Load: None
12b-1: None
Redemption Fee: None
Ticker Symbol: FTHRX

TOTAL RETURNS (%)

1987	1988	1989	1990	1991	5-year
2.0	7.2	11.8	7.5	14.5	50.6

INVESTMENT PORTFOLIO

Total Assets (mil.)	Expense Ratio	Turnover Ratio
$1,119	0.66%	73%

FIDELITY SHORT-TERM BOND PORTFOLIO

Fidelity Distributors Corporation
82 Devonshire Street, Mail Zone L7b
Boston, MA 02109
800-448-8800

Minimum: $2,500
Front-End Load: None
12b-1: None
Redemption Fee: None
Ticker Symbol: FSHBX

TOTAL RETURNS (%)

1987	1988	1989	1990	1991	5-year
4.0	5.7	10.5	5.8	14.0	46.5

INVESTMENT PORTFOLIO

Total Assets (mil.)	Expense Ratio	Turnover Ratio
$512	0.83%	164%

FINANCIAL BOND SHARES—SELECT INCOME

INVESCO Funds Group
P. O. Box 2040
Denver, CO 80201
800-258-8500

Minimum: $250
Front-End Load: None
12b-1: 0.25%
Redemption Fee: None
Ticker Symbol: FBDSX

TOTAL RETURNS (%)

1987	1988	1989	1990	1991	5-year
-1.5	10.4	8.2	4.9	18.6	46.4

INVESTMENT PORTFOLIO

Total Assets (mil.)	Expense Ratio	Turnover Ratio
$84	1.01%	38%

FLEX BOND FUND

R. Meeder & Associates
6000 Memorial Drive
Dublin, OH 43017
800-253-3900

Minimum: $2,500
Front-End Load: None
12b-1: 0.15%
Redemption Fee: None
Ticker Symbol: FLXBX

TOTAL RETURNS (%)

1987	1988	1989	1990	1991	5-year
-0.6	2.7	8.7	8.3	15.3	38.7

INVESTMENT PORTFOLIO

Total Assets (mil.)	Expense Ratio	Turnover Ratio
$8	0.99%	500%

FPA NEW INCOME FUND

First Pacific Advisors
10301 W. Pico Boulevard
Los Angeles, CA 90064
800-214-7400

Minimum: $1,500
Front-End Load: 4.50%
12b-1: None
Redemption Fee: None
Ticker Symbol: FPNIX

TOTAL RETURNS (%)

1987	1988	1989	1990	1991	5-year
7.7	8.5	12.2	8.4	18.7	68.7

INVESTMENT PORTFOLIO

Total Assets (mil.)	Expense Ratio	Turnover Ratio
$52	0.94%	29%

FUND TRUST INCOME FUND

Signature Financial Group
6 St. James Avenue, 9th Floor
Boston, MA 02116
800-381-9600

Minimum: $1,000
Front-End Load: 1.50%
12b-1: 0.50%
Redemption Fee: None
Ticker Symbol: FTINX

TOTAL RETURNS (%)

1987	1988	1989	1990	1991	5-year
0.4	9.1	8.0	4.8	14.8	42.4

INVESTMENT PORTFOLIO

Total Assets (mil.)	Expense Ratio	Turnover Ratio
$34	1.75%	48%

IAI BOND FUND

Investment Advisers
1100 Dain Tower, P. O. Box 357
Minneapolis, MN 55440
800-453-6300

Minimum: $5,000
Front-End Load: None
12b-1: 0.23%
Redemption Fee: None
Ticker Symbol: IAIBX

TOTAL RETURNS (%)

1987	1988	1989	1990	1991	5-year
2.0	6.4	15.9	7.1	17.3	58.1

INVESTMENT PORTFOLIO

Total Assets (mil.)	Expense Ratio	Turnover Ratio
$124	0.88%	43%

IAI RESERVE FUND

Investment Advisers
1100 Dain Tower, P. O. Box 357
Minneapolis, MN 55440
800-453-6300

Minimum: $5,000
Front-End Load: None
12b-1: None
Redemption Fee: None
Ticker Symbol: IARVX

TOTAL RETURNS (%)

1987	1988	1989	1990	1991	5-year
5.9	6.8	8.8	8.4	8.0	43.9

INVESTMENT PORTFOLIO

Total Assets (mil.)	Expense Ratio	Turnover Ratio
$89	0.85%	87%

IDEX TOTAL INCOME TRUST

Idex Management
201 Highland Avenue
Largo, FL 34640
800-244-3900

Minimum: $500
Front-End Load: 7.00%
12b-1: None
Redemption Fee: None
Ticker Symbol: ITITX

TOTAL RETURNS (%)

1987	1988	1989	1990	1991	5-year
NA	10.7	3.7	-5.3	25.2	NA

INVESTMENT PORTFOLIO

Total Assets (mil.)	Expense Ratio	Turnover Ratio
$19	1.50%	72%

IDS BOND FUND

IDS Financial Services
1000 Roanoke Building
Minneapolis, MN 55402
800-328-8300

Minimum: $2,000
Front-End Load: 5.00%
12b-1: 0.04%
Redemption Fee: None
Ticker Symbol: INBNX

TOTAL RETURNS (%)

1987	1988	1989	1990	1991	5-year
-0.4	10.1	10.6	4.7	20.7	53.2

INVESTMENT PORTFOLIO

Total Assets (mil.)	Expense Ratio	Turnover Ratio
$1,971	0.77%	81%

IDS SELECTIVE FUND

IDS Financial Services
1000 Roanoke Building
Minneapolis, MN 55402
800-328-8300

Minimum: $2,000
Front-End Load: 5.00%
12b-1: 0.04%
Redemption Fee: None
Ticker Symbol: INSEX

TOTAL RETURNS (%)

1987	1988	1989	1990	1991	5-year
1.2	9.6	12.2	6.6	17.0	55.2

INVESTMENT PORTFOLIO

Total Assets (mil.)	Expense Ratio	Turnover Ratio
$1,403	0.76%	54%

IDS STRATEGY INCOME FUND

IDS Financial Services
1000 Roanoke Building
Minneapolis, MN 55402
800-328-8300

Minimum: $2,000
Front-End Load: None
12b-1: 0.86%
Redemption Fee: 5.00%
Ticker Symbol: ININX

TOTAL RETURNS (%)

1987	1988	1989	1990	1991	5-year
0.1	8.9	9.8	5.6	16.6	47.4

INVESTMENT PORTFOLIO

Total Assets (mil.)	Expense Ratio	Turnover Ratio
$310	1.67%	62%

INVESTORS PREFERENCE FUND FOR INCOME

Dollar Dry Dock
50 Main Street
White Plains, NY 10606
800-446-9300

Minimum: $1,000
Front-End Load: 4.00%
12b-1: 0.20%
Redemption Fee: None
Ticker Symbol: IPFIX

TOTAL RETURNS (%)

1987	1988	1989	1990	1991	5-year
NA	9.5	14.4	10.6	15.3	NA

INVESTMENT PORTFOLIO

Total Assets (mil.)	Expense Ratio	Turnover Ratio
$57	0.50%	5%

JP INCOME FUND

Jefferson-Pilot Equity Sales
101 North Elm Street
Greensboro, NC 27401
800-584-9800

Minimum: $300
Front-End Load: 5.50%
12b-1: None
Redemption Fee: None
Ticker Symbol: JPINX

TOTAL RETURNS (%)

1987	1988	1989	1990	1991	5-year
2.2	7.9	12.6	6.5	13.8	50.5

INVESTMENT PORTFOLIO

Total Assets (mil.)	Expense Ratio	Turnover Ratio
$19	0.91%	0%

KEMPER INCOME & CAPITAL PRESERVATION FUND

Kemper Financial Services
120 South LaSalle Street, 20th Floor
Chicago, IL 60603
800-211-4800

Minimum: $1,000
Front-End Load: 4.50%
12b-1: None
Redemption Fee: None
Ticker Symbol: KMICX

TOTAL RETURNS (%)

1987	1988	1989	1990	1991	5-year
3.1	10.4	8.6	6.5	17.9	55.2

INVESTMENT PORTFOLIO

Total Assets (mil.)	Expense Ratio	Turnover Ratio
$436	0.73%	189%

KEYSTONE AMERICA INVESTMENT GRADE BOND FUND

Keystone Distributors
99 High Street, 29th Floor
Boston, MA 02110
800-334-0000

Minimum: $1,000
Front-End Load: 4.75%
12b-1: 0.24%
Redemption Fee: None
Ticker Symbol: KAIGX

TOTAL RETURNS (%)

1987	1988	1989	1990	1991	5-year
NA	4.5	6.4	5.9	16.8	NA

INVESTMENT PORTFOLIO

Total Assets (mil.)	Expense Ratio	Turnover Ratio
$21	2.00%	107%

KEYSTONE CUSTODIAN SERIES-B1

Keystone Distributors
99 High Street, 29th Floor
Boston, MA 02110
800-334-0000

Minimum: $1,000
Front-End Load: None
12b-1: 1.05%
Redemption Fee: 4.00%
Ticker Symbol: KBONX

TOTAL RETURNS (%)

1987	1988	1989	1990	1991	5-year
-2.6	6.3	12.0	6.7	14.9	42.1

INVESTMENT PORTFOLIO

Total Assets (mil.)	Expense Ratio	Turnover Ratio
$453	1.95%	117%

KEYSTONE CUSTODIAN SERIES-B2

Keystone Distributors
99 High Street, 29th Floor
Boston, MA 02110
800-334-0000

Minimum: $1,000
Front-End Load: None
12b-1: 1.06%
Redemption Fee: 4.00%
Ticker Symbol: KBTWX

TOTAL RETURNS (%)

1987	1988	1989	1990	1991	5-year
0.3	11.0	5.2	-2.1	18.7	36.0

INVESTMENT PORTFOLIO

Total Assets (mil.)	Expense Ratio	Turnover Ratio
$819	1.89%	43%

LUTHERAN BROTHERHOOD INCOME FUND

Lutheran Brotherhood Securities
625 Fourth Avenue South
Minneapolis, MN 55415
800-284-5200

Minimum: $500
Front-End Load: 5.00%
12b-1: None
Redemption Fee: None
Ticker Symbol: LBUIX

TOTAL RETURNS (%)

1987	1988	1989	1990	1991	5-year
2.7	10.8	12.6	5.7	17.2	58.7

INVESTMENT PORTFOLIO

Total Assets (mil.)	Expense Ratio	Turnover Ratio
$797	1.02%	118%

MACKENZIE FIXED INCOME TRUST

Mackenzie Investment Management
P. O. Box 5007
Boca Raton, FL 33431
800-565-1100

Minimum: $250
Front-End Load: 4.75%
12b-1: 0.25%
Redemption Fee: None
Ticker Symbol: MCFIX

TOTAL RETURNS (%)

1987	1988	1989	1990	1991	5-year
9.7	11.6	15.1	4.3	14.4	68.2

INVESTMENT PORTFOLIO

Total Assets (mil.)	Expense Ratio	Turnover Ratio
$98	1.50%	118%

MASSACHUSETTS FINANCIAL BOND FUND

Massachusetts Financial Services
500 Boylston Street
Boston, MA 02116
800-252-0600

Minimum: $1,000
Front-End Load: 4.75%
12b-1: None
Redemption Fee: None
Ticker Symbol: MFBFX

TOTAL RETURNS (%)

1987	1988	1989	1990	1991	5-year
-0.6	8.3	13.5	7.2	18.0	54.7

INVESTMENT PORTFOLIO

Total Assets (mil.)	Expense Ratio	Turnover Ratio
$346	0.79%	189%

MERRILL LYNCH CORPORATE BOND HIGH QUALITY A

Merrill Lynch Funds Distributor
P. O. Box 9011
Princeton, NJ 08543
800-373-6300

Minimum: $1,000
Front-End Load: 4.00%
12b-1: None
Redemption Fee: None
Ticker Symbol: MLHQX

TOTAL RETURNS (%)

1987	1988	1989	1990	1991	5-year
0.4	8.3	13.6	7.0	17.1	54.8

INVESTMENT PORTFOLIO

Total Assets (mil.)	Expense Ratio	Turnover Ratio
$331	0.64%	126%

MERRILL LYNCH CORPORATE BOND INTERMEDIATE

Merrill Lynch Funds Distributor
P. O. Box 9011
Princeton, NJ 08543
800-373-6300

Minimum: $1,000
Front-End Load: 2.00%
12b-1: None
Redemption Fee: None
Ticker Symbol: MLITX

TOTAL RETURNS (%)

1987	1988	1989	1990	1991	5-year
0.6	7.5	12.3	8.4	15.5	52.3

INVESTMENT PORTFOLIO

Total Assets (mil.)	Expense Ratio	Turnover Ratio
$111	0.71%	103%

NATIONAL BOND FUND

National Securities & Research
2 Pickwick Plaza
Greenwich, CT 06830
800-356-5535

Minimum: $2,500
Front-End Load: 4.75%
12b-1: None
Redemption Fee: None
Ticker Symbol: NABDX

TOTAL RETURNS (%)

1987	1988	1989	1990	1991	5-year
-5.6	7.3	-12.8	-14.8	49.8	12.7

INVESTMENT PORTFOLIO

Total Assets (mil.)	Expense Ratio	Turnover Ratio
$399	1.15%	97%

NATIONWIDE BOND

Nationwide Financial Services
One Nationwide Plaza, P.O. Box 1492
Columbus, OH 43216
800-848-0920

Minimum: $250
Front-End Load: 7.50%
12b-1: None
Redemption Fee: None
Ticker Symbol: MUIBX

TOTAL RETURNS (%)

1987	1988	1989	1990	1991	5-year
0.2	8.2	10.7	8.2	16.9	51.8

INVESTMENT PORTFOLIO

Total Assets (mil.)	Expense Ratio	Turnover Ratio
$52	0.68%	82%

NEUBERGER & BERMAN LIMITED MATURITY BOND FUND

Neuberger & Berman
605 Third Avenue, 2nd Floor
New York, NY 10158
800-779-0000

Minimum: $5,000
Front-End Load: None
12b-1: None
Redemption Fee: None
Ticker Symbol: NLMBX

TOTAL RETURNS (%)

1987	1988	1989	1990	1991	5-year
3.6	6.7	11.2	8.7	11.8	49.4

INVESTMENT PORTFOLIO

Total Assets (mil.)	Expense Ratio	Turnover Ratio
$159	0.65%	88%

NEUBERGER & BERMAN ULTRA SHORT BOND FUND

Neuberger & Berman
605 Third Avenue, 2nd Floor
New York, NY 10158
800-877-9700

Minimum: $2,000
Front-End Load: None
12b-1: None
Redemption Fee: None
Ticker Symbol: NBMMX

TOTAL RETURNS (%)

1987	1988	1989	1990	1991	5-year
5.5	6.8	9.4	8.4	7.4	43.6

INVESTMENT PORTFOLIO

Total Assets (mil.)	Expense Ratio	Turnover Ratio
$94	0.65%	120%

NEW ENGLAND BOND INCOME FUND

TNE Investment Services
399 Boylston Street, 8th Floor
Boston, MA 02116
800-437-0400

Minimum: $1,000
Front-End Load: 4.50%
12b-1: 0.25%
Redemption Fee: None
Ticker Symbol: NELIX

TOTAL RETURNS (%)

1987	1988	1989	1990	1991	5-year
2.1	7.4	11.9	7.5	18.1	55.7

INVESTMENT PORTFOLIO

Total Assets (mil.)	Expense Ratio	Turnover Ratio
$108	1.18%	126%

NEWTON INCOME FUND

M&I Investment Management
411 East Wisconsin Avenue
Milwaukee, WI 53202
800-427-2900

Minimum: $1,000
Front-End Load: None
12b-1: None
Redemption Fee: None
Ticker Symbol: NWTNX

TOTAL RETURNS (%)

1987	1988	1989	1990	1991	5-year
2.4	6.4	11.7	8.2	14.1	50.2

INVESTMENT PORTFOLIO

Total Assets (mil.)	Expense Ratio	Turnover Ratio
$21	0.85%	75%

NORTHEAST INVESTORS TRUST

Northeast Management & Research
50 Congress Street, Suite 1000
Boston, MA 02109
800-256-0400

Minimum: $1,000
Front-End Load: None
12b-1: None
Redemption Fee: None
Ticker Symbol: NTHEX

TOTAL RETURNS (%)

1987	1988	1989	1990	1991	5-year
0.2	14.1	0.0	-9.2	26.4	31.2

INVESTMENT PORTFOLIO

Total Assets (mil.)	Expense Ratio	Turnover Ratio
$316	1.47%	21%

PAINEWEBBER INVESTMENT GRADE INCOME A

PaineWebber
1285 Avenue of the Americas, 18th Floor
New York, NY 10019
800-647-1568

Minimum: $1,000
Front-End Load: 4.00%
12b-1: None
Redemption Fee: None
Ticker Symbol: PIGAX

TOTAL RETURNS (%)

1987	1988	1989	1990	1991	5-year
-1.5	8.9	12.0	6.5	18.6	51.6

INVESTMENT PORTFOLIO

Total Assets (mil.)	Expense Ratio	Turnover Ratio
$220	0.65%	47%

PHOENIX HIGH QUALITY BOND FUND

Phoenix Equity Planning
100 Bright Meadow Boulevard
Enfield, CT 06082
800-434-6100

Minimum: $500
Front-End Load: 4.75%
12b-1: None
Redemption Fee: None
Ticker Symbol: PHHQX

TOTAL RETURNS (%)

1987	1988	1989	1990	1991	5-year
-1.6	7.7	12.2	4.6	16.1	44.4

INVESTMENT PORTFOLIO

Total Assets (mil.)	Expense Ratio	Turnover Ratio
$25	1.00%	489%

PIONEER BOND FUND

Pioneer Funds Distributor
60 State Street
Boston, MA 02109
800-256-9200

Minimum: $1,000
Front-End Load: 4.50%
12b-1: 0.25%
Redemption Fee: None
Ticker Symbol: PIOBX

TOTAL RETURNS (%)

1987	1988	1989	1990	1991	5-year
2.7	7.7	11.6	7.3	15.5	53.0

INVESTMENT PORTFOLIO

Total Assets (mil.)	Expense Ratio	Turnover Ratio
$85	0.88%	34%

PUTNAM INCOME FUND

Putnam Financial Services
One Post Office Square, 12th Floor
Boston, MA 02109
800-341-9000

Minimum: $500
Front-End Load: 4.75%
12b-1: 0.25%
Redemption Fee: None
Ticker Symbol: PINCX

TOTAL RETURNS (%)

1987	1988	1989	1990	1991	5-year
1.9	10.4	12.2	4.4	18.4	55.8

INVESTMENT PORTFOLIO

Total Assets (mil.)	Expense Ratio	Turnover Ratio
$511	0.80%	68%

SCUDDER INCOME FUND

Scudder Stevens & Clark
175 Federal Street, 12th Floor
Boston, MA 02110
800-252-7000

Minimum: $1,000
Front-End Load: None
12b-1: None
Redemption Fee: None
Ticker Symbol: SCSBX

TOTAL RETURNS (%)

1987	1988	1989	1990	1991	5-year
0.7	8.9	12.7	8.3	17.3	57.2

INVESTMENT PORTFOLIO

Total Assets (mil.)	Expense Ratio	Turnover Ratio
$385	0.95%	48%

SCUDDER SHORT TERM BOND

Scudder Stevens & Clark
175 Federal Street, 12th Floor
Boston, MA 02110
800-225-2470

Minimum: $1,000
Front-End Load: None
12b-1: None
Redemption Fee: None
Ticker Symbol: SCSTX

TOTAL RETURNS (%)

1987	1988	1989	1990	1991	5-year
1.3	6.3	13.3	9.9	14.5	53.5

INVESTMENT PORTFOLIO

Total Assets (mil.)	Expense Ratio	Turnover Ratio
$1,495	0.25%	107%

SECURITY INCOME FUND CORPORATE BOND SERIES

Security Distributors
700 Harrison
Topeka, KS 66636
800-882-6100

Minimum: $100
Front-End Load: 4.75%
12b-1: 0.25%
Redemption Fee: None
Ticker Symbol: SBDFX

TOTAL RETURNS (%)

1987	1988	1989	1990	1991	5-year
4.0	6.5	9.9	6.6	16.1	50.6

INVESTMENT PORTFOLIO

Total Assets (mil.)	Expense Ratio	Turnover Ratio
$84	1.10%	87%

SENTINEL BOND FUND

Equity Securities
National Life Drive
Montpelier, VT 05604
800-823-6300

Minimum: $250
Front-End Load: 5.25%
12b-1: None
Redemption Fee: None
Ticker Symbol: SNBDX

TOTAL RETURNS (%)

1987	1988	1989	1990	1991	5-year
0.7	8.6	12.5	7.2	18.0	55.6

INVESTMENT PORTFOLIO

Total Assets (mil.)	Expense Ratio	Turnover Ratio
$43	0.83%	108%

SHEARSON INVESTMENT GRADE BOND

Shearson Lehman Brothers
388 Greenwich, 37th Floor
New York, NY 10013
800-451-2010

Minimum: $500
Front-End Load: None
12b-1: 0.75%
Redemption Fee: 5.00%
Ticker Symbol: HBDIX

TOTAL RETURNS (%)

1987	1988	1989	1990	1991	5-year
-3.0	8.4	15.8	3.0	22.7	53.9

INVESTMENT PORTFOLIO

Total Assets (mil.)	Expense Ratio	Turnover Ratio
$401	1.52%	59%

SIT NEW BEGINNING INVESTMENT RESERVE

Sit Investment Associates
4600 Norwest Center, 90 S. 7th Street
Minneapolis, MN 55402
800-332-5580

Minimum: $2,000
Front-End Load: None
12b-1: None
Redemption Fee: None
Ticker Symbol: NA

TOTAL RETURNS (%)

1987	1988	1989	1990	1991	5-year
6.5	6.7	8.5	7.6	6.1	40.7

INVESTMENT PORTFOLIO

Total Assets (mil.)	Expense Ratio	Turnover Ratio
$10	0.86%	7%

STEIN ROE INTERMEDIATE BOND FUND

Stein Roe & Farnham
P. O. Box 1162
Chicago, IL 60690
800-382-5000

Minimum: $1,000
Front-End Load: None
12b-1: None
Redemption Fee: None
Ticker Symbol: SRBFX

TOTAL RETURNS (%)

1987	1988	1989	1990	1991	5-year
2.5	7.2	12.6	7.1	15.1	52.6

INVESTMENT PORTFOLIO

Total Assets (mil.)	Expense Ratio	Turnover Ratio
$212	0.74%	296%

STRONG ADVANTAGE FUND

Strong/Corneliuson Capital Management
100 Heritage Reserve
Menomonee Falls, WI 53051
800-683-6300

Minimum: $1,000
Front-End Load: None
12b-1: None
Redemption Fee: None
Ticker Symbol: STADX

TOTAL RETURNS (%)

1987	1988	1989	1990	1991	5-year
NA	NA	9.4	6.6	10.6	NA

INVESTMENT PORTFOLIO

Total Assets (mil.)	Expense Ratio	Turnover Ratio
$133	1.20%	274%

STRONG INCOME FUND

Strong/Corneliuson Capital Management
100 Heritage Reserve
Menomonee Falls, WI 53051
800-683-6300

Minimum: $1,000
Front-End Load: None
12b-1: None
Redemption Fee: None
Ticker Symbol: SRNCX

TOTAL RETURNS (%)

1987	1988	1989	1990	1991	5-year
4.5	12.5	0.4	-6.2	14.8	27.0

INVESTMENT PORTFOLIO

Total Assets (mil.)	Expense Ratio	Turnover Ratio
$92	1.40%	294%

STRONG SHORT-TERM BOND FUND

Strong/Corneliuson Capital Management
100 Heritage Reserve
Menomonee Falls, WI 53051
800-683-6300

Minimum: $1,000
Front-End Load: None
12b-1: None
Redemption Fee: None
Ticker Symbol: SSTBX

TOTAL RETURNS (%)

1987	1988	1989	1990	1991	5-year
NA	10.1	8.2	5.3	14.6	NA

INVESTMENT PORTFOLIO

Total Assets (mil.)	Expense Ratio	Turnover Ratio
$132	1.30%	314%

SUN AMERICA INCOME PLUS FUND

Sun America Capital Services
10 Union Square East, 2nd Floor
New York, NY 10003
800-215-0000

Minimum: $500
Front-End Load: None
12b-1: 1.25%
Redemption Fee: 5.00%
Ticker Symbol: SAIPX

TOTAL RETURNS (%)

1987	1988	1989	1990	1991	5-year
0.6	14.9	-6.9	-9.9	36.6	32.5

INVESTMENT PORTFOLIO

Total Assets (mil.)	Expense Ratio	Turnover Ratio
$21	3.13%	59%

T. ROWE PRICE NEW INCOME FUND

T. Rowe Price Investor Services
100 East Pratt Street
Baltimore, MD 21202
800-385-6000

Minimum: $2,500
Front-End Load: None
12b-1: None
Redemption Fee: None
Ticker Symbol: PRCIX

TOTAL RETURNS (%)

1987	1988	1989	1990	1991	5-year
2.1	7.6	12.2	8.8	15.5	54.8

INVESTMENT PORTFOLIO

Total Assets (mil.)	Expense Ratio	Turnover Ratio
$1,365	0.88%	21%

T. ROWE PRICE SHORT TERM BOND FUND

T. Rowe Price Investor Services
100 East Pratt Street
Baltimore, MD 21202
800-385-6000

Minimum: $2,500
Front-End Load: None
12b-1: None
Redemption Fee: None
Ticker Symbol: PRWBX

TOTAL RETURNS (%)

1987	1988	1989	1990	1991	5-year
5.2	5.5	9.9	8.6	11.2	47.4

INVESTMENT PORTFOLIO

Total Assets (mil.)	Expense Ratio	Turnover Ratio
$389	0.93%	980%

THOMSON INCOME FUND B

Thomson Securities
1 Station Place
Stamford, CT 06902
800-281-3700

Minimum: $1,000
Front-End Load: None
12b-1: 1.00%
Redemption Fee: 1.00%
Ticker Symbol: TINBX

TOTAL RETURNS (%)

1987	1988	1989	1990	1991	5-year
4.5	10.1	5.5	2.1	12.0	38.7

INVESTMENT PORTFOLIO

Total Assets (mil.)	Expense Ratio	Turnover Ratio
$261	1.80%	51%

TRANSAMERICA INVESTMENT QUALITY BOND FUND

TransAmerica Distributors
1000 Louisiana, Suite 6000
Houston, TX 77002
800-436-4000

Minimum: $100
Front-End Load: 4.75%
12b-1: 0.25%
Redemption Fee: None
Ticker Symbol: TABFX

TOTAL RETURNS (%)

1987	1988	1989	1990	1991	5-year
1.0	6.4	11.6	7.8	18.0	52.5

INVESTMENT PORTFOLIO

Total Assets (mil.)	Expense Ratio	Turnover Ratio
$93	1.25%	134%

TWENTIETH CENTURY LONG-TERM BOND

Twentieth Century Investors
4500 Main Street, P. O. Box 418210
Kansas City, MO 64111
800-452-2100

Minimum: None
Front-End Load: None
12b-1: None
Redemption Fee: None
Ticker Symbol: TWLBX

TOTAL RETURNS (%)

1987	1988	1989	1990	1991	5-year
NA	8.3	14.0	6.0	17.5	NA

INVESTMENT PORTFOLIO

Total Assets (mil.)	Expense Ratio	Turnover Ratio
$116	1.00%	98%

UNITED BOND FUND

Waddell & Reed
6300 Lamar Avenue, P. O. Box 29217
Shawnee Mission, KS 66201
913-362-0000

Minimum: $500
Front-End Load: 8.50%
12b-1: None
Redemption Fee: None
Ticker Symbol: UNBDX

TOTAL RETURNS (%)

1987	1988	1989	1990	1991	5-year
4.5	9.0	10.6	4.2	18.8	56.0

INVESTMENT PORTFOLIO

Total Assets (mil.)	Expense Ratio	Turnover Ratio
$496	0.67%	295%

USF&G AXE HOUGHTON INCOME FUND

USF&G Review Management
275 Commerce Drive, Suite 228
Fort Washington, PA 19034
800-238-3400

Minimum: $1,000
Front-End Load: 4.75%
12b-1: 0.25%
Redemption Fee: None
Ticker Symbol: AXEAX

TOTAL RETURNS (%)

1987	1988	1989	1990	1991	5-year
1.8	8.7	10.2	4.2	15.9	47.3

INVESTMENT PORTFOLIO

Total Assets (mil.)	Expense Ratio	Turnover Ratio
$60	1.20%	79%

VANGUARD BOND MARKET FUND

Vanguard Group
Vanguard Financial Center
Valley Forge, PA 19482
800-627-4700

Minimum: $3,000
Front-End Load: None
12b-1: None
Redemption Fee: None
Ticker Symbol: VBMFX

TOTAL RETURNS (%)

1987	1988	1989	1990	1991	5-year
1.5	7.4	13.6	8.6	15.2	55.1

INVESTMENT PORTFOLIO

Total Assets (mil.)	Expense Ratio	Turnover Ratio
$797	0.21%	29%

VANGUARD FIXED INCOME INVESTMENT GRADE BOND

Vanguard Group
Vanguard Financial Center
Valley Forge, PA 19482
800-627-4700

Minimum: $3,000
Front-End Load: None
12b-1: None
Redemption Fee: None
Ticker Symbol: VWESX

TOTAL RETURNS (%)

1987	1988	1989	1990	1991	5-year
0.2	9.7	15.2	6.2	20.9	62.6

INVESTMENT PORTFOLIO

Total Assets (mil.)	Expense Ratio	Turnover Ratio
$1,863	0.37%	62%

VANGUARD FIXED INCOME SHORT TERM BOND

Vanguard Group
Vanguard Financial Center
Valley Forge, PA 19482
800-662-7447

Minimum: $3,000
Front-End Load: None
12b-1: None
Redemption Fee: None
Ticker Symbol: VFSTX

TOTAL RETURNS (%)

1987	1988	1989	1990	1991	5-year
4.4	7.0	11.5	9.2	13.1	53.8

INVESTMENT PORTFOLIO

Total Assets (mil.)	Expense Ratio	Turnover Ratio
$1,789	0.31%	107%

High-Yield Bond Funds

AEGON USA HIGH YIELD

MidAmerica Management
4333 Edgewood Road N.E.
Cedar Rapids, IA 52499
800-538-5111

Minimum: $1,000
Front-End Load: 4.75%
12b-1: None
Redemption Fee: None
Ticker Symbol: AEGHX

TOTAL RETURNS (%)

1987	1988	1989	1990	1991	5-year
1.8	11.0	12.3	2.8	21.8	59.0

INVESTMENT PORTFOLIO

Total Assets (mil.)	Expense Ratio	Turnover Ratio
$47	0.70%	58%

AGE HIGH INCOME FUND

Franklin Distributors
777 Mariners Island Blvd., 6th Floor
San Mateo, CA 94404
800-342-5236

Minimum: $100
Front-End Load: 4.00%
12b-1: None
Redemption Fee: None
Ticker Symbol: AGEFX

TOTAL RETURNS (%)

1987	1988	1989	1990	1991	5-year
0.7	13.5	-4.2	-15.0	47.4	37.3

INVESTMENT PORTFOLIO

Total Assets (mil.)	Expense Ratio	Turnover Ratio
$1,764	0.59%	29%

AIM HIGH YIELD SECURITIES

AIM Distributors
11 Greenway Plaza, Suite 1919
Houston, TX 77046
800-347-1919

Minimum: $1,000
Front-End Load: 4.75%
12b-1: 0.11%
Redemption Fee: None
Ticker Symbol: HGSIX

TOTAL RETURNS (%)

1987	1988	1989	1990	1991	5-year
2.0	7.5	-4.0	-17.3	19.8	4.1

INVESTMENT PORTFOLIO

Total Assets (mil.)	Expense Ratio	Turnover Ratio
$32	1.63%	68%

ALLIANCE BOND FUND—HIGH YIELD PORTFOLIO

Alliance Funds Distributor
500 Plaza Drive
Secaucus, NJ 07094
800-247-4154

Minimum: $250
Front-End Load: 4.75%
12b-1: 0.30%
Redemption Fee: None
Ticker Symbol: ALBYX

TOTAL RETURNS (%)

1987	1988	1989	1990	1991	5-year
-1.9	10.2	-12.9	-15.0	33.0	6.4

INVESTMENT PORTFOLIO

Total Assets (mil.)	Expense Ratio	Turnover Ratio
$104	1.66%	88%

AMERICAN CAPITAL HIGH YIELD INVESTMENTS

American Capital Marketing
P.O. Box 3528
Houston, TX 77253
800-421-5666

Minimum: $500
Front-End Load: 4.75%
12b-1: 0.15%
Redemption Fee: None
Ticker Symbol: ACHYX

TOTAL RETURNS (%)

1987	1988	1989	1990	1991	5-year
3.2	13.2	-12.0	-15.8	41.3	22.3

INVESTMENT PORTFOLIO

Total Assets (mil.)	Expense Ratio	Turnover Ratio
$362	1.02%	59%

AMERICAN INVESTORS INCOME FUND

American Investors Funds
P.O. Box 2500, 777 W. Putnam Avenue
Greenwich, CT 06836
800-243-5353

Minimum: $1,000
Front-End Load: 4.50%
12b-1: None
Redemption Fee: None
Ticker Symbol: AMINX

TOTAL RETURNS (%)

1987	1988	1989	1990	1991	5-year
5.8	9.0	-12.3	-13.3	19.9	5.1

INVESTMENT PORTFOLIO

Total Assets (mil.)	Expense Ratio	Turnover Ratio
$9	1.63%	74%

BULL & BEAR HIGH YIELD FUND

Bull & Bear Group
11 Hanover Square
New York, NY 10005
800-847-4200

Minimum: $1,000
Front-End Load: None
12b-1: 0.50%
Redemption Fee: None
Ticker Symbol: BBHYX

TOTAL RETURNS (%)

1987	1988	1989	1990	1991	5-year
-6.5	5.0	-3.0	-3.0	18.0	8.9

INVESTMENT PORTFOLIO

Total Assets (mil.)	Expense Ratio	Turnover Ratio
$45	1.95%	555%

CIGNA FUNDS GROUP HIGH YIELD FUND

CIGNA Mutual Funds
One Financial Plaza, 16th Floor
Springfield, MA 01103
800-572-4462

Minimum: $500
Front-End Load: 5.00%
12b-1: 0.25%
Redemption Fee: None
Ticker Symbol: INAHX

TOTAL RETURNS (%)

1987	1988	1989	1990	1991	5-year
3.1	16.4	1.2	-9.0	42.5	57.4

INVESTMENT PORTFOLIO

Total Assets (mil.)	Expense Ratio	Turnover Ratio
$261	1.21%	27%

COLONIAL HIGH YIELD SECURITIES FUND

Colonial Investment Services
One Financial Center, 14th Floor
Boston, MA 02110
800-248-2828

Minimum: $1,000
Front-End Load: 4.75%
12b-1: 0.25%
Redemption Fee: None
Ticker Symbol: COLHX

TOTAL RETURNS (%)

1987	1988	1989	1990	1991	5-year
4.3	13.0	0.1	-14.7	43.6	44.5

INVESTMENT PORTFOLIO

Total Assets (mil.)	Expense Ratio	Turnover Ratio
$303	1.33%	9%

DELAWARE GROUP DELCHESTER I HIGH YIELD BOND

Delaware Distributors
10 Penn Center Plaza
Philadelphia, PA 19103
800-523-4640

Minimum: $250
Front-End Load: 6.75%
12b-1: None
Redemption Fee: None
Ticker Symbol: DELCX

TOTAL RETURNS (%)

1987	1988	1989	1990	1991	5-year
5.2	14.0	1.1	-11.9	43.9	53.6

INVESTMENT PORTFOLIO

Total Assets (mil.)	Expense Ratio	Turnover Ratio
$536	0.90%	38%

DELAWARE GROUP DELCHESTER II HIGH YIELD BOND

Delaware Distributors
10 Penn Center Plaza
Philadelphia, PA 19103
800-523-4640

Minimum: $250
Front-End Load: 4.75%
12b-1: 0.30%
Redemption Fee: None
Ticker Symbol: DETWX

TOTAL RETURNS (%)

1987	1988	1989	1990	1991	5-year
NA	13.7	0.7	-12.2	43.5	NA

INVESTMENT PORTFOLIO

Total Assets (mil.)	Expense Ratio	Turnover Ratio
$129	1.20%	38%

EATON VANCE HIGH INCOME TRUST

Eaton Vance
24 Federal Street, 5th Floor
Boston, MA 02110
800-225-6265

Minimum: $1,000
Front-End Load: None
12b-1: 1.19%
Redemption Fee: 6.00%
Ticker Symbol: EVHIX

TOTAL RETURNS (%)

1987	1988	1989	1990	1991	5-year
2.5	16.3	1.1	-18.5	38.3	36.0

INVESTMENT PORTFOLIO

Total Assets (mil.)	Expense Ratio	Turnover Ratio
$224	2.37%	57%

EATON VANCE INCOME FUND OF BOSTON

Eaton Vance
24 Federal Street, 5th Floor
Boston, MA 02110
800-225-6265

Minimum: $1,000
Front-End Load: 4.75%
12b-1: 0.25%
Redemption Fee: None
Ticker Symbol: EVIBX

TOTAL RETURNS (%)

1987	1988	1989	1990	1991	5-year
3.4	15.2	4.2	-15.5	42.8	49.8

INVESTMENT PORTFOLIO

Total Assets (mil.)	Expense Ratio	Turnover Ratio
$74	1.15%	80%

EXECUTIVE INVESTORS HIGH YIELD FUND

First Investors Management
10 Woodbridge Center Drive
Woodbridge, NJ 07095
800-423-4026

Minimum: $1,000
Front-End Load: 4.75%
12b-1: None
Redemption Fee : None
Ticker Symbol: None

TOTAL RETURNS (%)

1987	1988	1989	1990	1991	5-year
NA	21.1	-1.1	-12.5	35.4	NA

INVESTMENT PORTFOLIO

Total Assets (mil.)	Expense Ratio	Turnover Ratio
$11	0.31%	44%

FEDERATED HIGH YIELD TRUST

Federated Securities
1001 Liberty Avenue
Pittsburgh, PA 15222
800-245-2423

Minimum: $25,000
Front-End Load: None
12b-1: None
Redemption Fee: None
Ticker Symbol: FHYTX

TOTAL RETURNS (%)

1987	1988	1989	1990	1991	5-year
1.2	16.2	-1.2	-12.6	52.5	55.0

INVESTMENT PORTFOLIO

Total Assets (mil.)	Expense Ratio	Turnover Ratio
$165	0.78%	31%

FIDELITY CAPITAL & INCOME FUND

Fidelity Distributors Corporation
82 Devonshire Street, Mail Zone L7b
Boston, MA 02109
800-544-8888

Minimum: $2,500
Front-End Load: None
12b-1: None
Redemption Fee: None
Ticker Symbol: FAGIX

TOTAL RETURNS (%)

1987	1988	1989	1990	1991	5-year
1.3	12.6	-3.1	-4.0	29.8	37.8

INVESTMENT PORTFOLIO

Total Assets (mil.)	Expense Ratio	Turnover Ratio
$1,162	0.81%	108%

FINANCIAL BOND SHARES HIGH YIELD PORTFOLIO

INVESCO Funds Group
P. O. Box 2040
Denver, CO 80201
800-525-8085

Minimum: $250
Front-End Load: None
12b-1: 0.25%
Redemption Fee: None
Ticker Symbol: FHYPX

TOTAL RETURNS (%)

1987	1988	1989	1990	1991	5-year
3.6	13.4	3.7	-4.6	23.5	43.7

INVESTMENT PORTFOLIO

Total Assets (mil.)	Expense Ratio	Turnover Ratio
$110	0.94%	28%

FIRST INVESTORS FUND FOR INCOME

First Investors Management
10 Woodbridge Center Drive
Woodbridge, NJ 07095
800-423-4026

Minimum: $200
Front-End Load: 6.90%
12b-1: 0.30%
Redemption Fee: None
Ticker Symbol: FIFIX

TOTAL RETURNS (%)

1987	1988	1989	1990	1991	5-year
-1.5	14.0	-8.1	-17.2	42.8	22.1

INVESTMENT PORTFOLIO

Total Assets (mil.)	Expense Ratio	Turnover Ratio
$435	1.02%	44%

FIRST INVESTORS HIGH YIELD FUND

First Investors Management
10 Woodbridge Center Drive
Woodbridge, NJ 07095
800-423-4026

Minimum: $1,000
Front-End Load: 6.90%
12b-1: 0.30%
Redemption Fee: None
Ticker Symbol: FIHYX

TOTAL RETURNS (%)

1987	1988	1989	1990	1991	5-year
-2.1	11.8	-9.0	-18.0	35.4	10.6

INVESTMENT PORTFOLIO

Total Assets (mil.)	Expense Ratio	Turnover Ratio
$214	1.23%	45%

GIT INCOME TRUST—MAXIMUM INCOME PORTFOLIO

Bankers Finance Investment Management
1655 Fort Myer Drive
Arlington, VA 22209
800-336-3063

Minimum: $2,500
Front-End Load: None
12b-1: None
Redemption Fee: None
Ticker Symbol: GITMX

TOTAL RETURNS (%)

1987	1988	1989	1990	1991	5-year
-2.9	10.2	2.8	-7.5	25.6	27.9

INVESTMENT PORTFOLIO

Total Assets (mil.)	Expense Ratio	Turnover Ratio
$6	1.66%	54%

IDS BOND FUND

IDS Financial Services
1000 Roanoke Building
Minneapolis, MN 55420
800-328-8300

Minimum: $2,000
Front-End Load: 5.00%
12b-1: 0.04%
Redemption Fee: None
Ticker Symbol: INBNX

TOTAL RETURNS (%)

1987	1988	1989	1990	1991	5-year
-0.4	10.1	10.6	4.7	20.7	53.2

INVESTMENT PORTFOLIO

Total Assets (mil.)	Expense Ratio	Turnover Ratio
$1,971	0.81%	77%

IDS EXTRA INCOME

IDS Financial Services
1000 Roanoke Building
Minneapolis, MN 55402
800-328-8300

Minimum: $2,000
Front-End Load: 5.00%
12b-1: 0.06%
Redemption Fee: None
Ticker Symbol: INEAX

TOTAL RETURNS (%)

1987	1988	1989	1990	1991	5-year
0.7	13.1	-3.8	-10.6	38.1	35.2

INVESTMENT PORTFOLIO

Total Assets (mil.)	Expense Ratio	Turnover Ratio
$1,056	0.84%	88%

JANUS FLEXIBLE INCOME FUND

Janus Capital Corporation
100 Fillmore Street, Suite 300
Denver, CO 80206
800-525-8983

Minimum: $1,000
Front-End Load: None
12b-1: None
Redemption Fee: None
Ticker Symbol: JAFIX

TOTAL RETURNS (%)

1987	1988	1989	1990	1991	5-year
NA	10.7	4.1	-4.6	26.0	NA

INVESTMENT PORTFOLIO

Total Assets (mil.)	Expense Ratio	Turnover Ratio
$64	1.00%	96%

KEMPER HIGH YIELD FUND

Kemper Financial Services
120 South LaSalle Street, 20th Floor
Chicago, IL 60603
800-621-1048

Minimum: $1,000
Front-End Load: 4.50%
12b-1: None
Redemption Fee: None
Ticker Symbol: KMHYX

TOTAL RETURNS (%)

1987	1988	1989	1990	1991	5-year
9.0	14.4	-1.1	-13.0	46.8	57.6

INVESTMENT PORTFOLIO

Total Assets (mil.)	Expense Ratio	Turnover Ratio
$1,721	0.73%	37%

KEMPER INVESTMENT PORTFOLIOS HIGH YIELD

Kemper Financial Services
120 South LaSalle Street, 20th Floor
Chicago, IL 60603
800-621-1048

Minimum: $250
Front-End Load: None
12b-1: 1.25%
Redemption Fee: 3.00%
Ticker Symbol: IPHYX

TOTAL RETURNS (%)

1987	1988	1989	1990	1991	5-year
5.9	12.5	-3.5	-15.7	45.8	41.3

INVESTMENT PORTFOLIO

Total Assets (mil.)	Expense Ratio	Turnover Ratio
$811	2.09%	33%

KEYSTONE AMERICA HIGH YIELD BOND FUND

Keystone Distributors
99 High Street, 29th Floor
Boston, MA 02110
800-633-4900

Minimum: $1,000
Front-End Load: 2.00%
12b-1: 0.70%
Redemption Fee: 2.00%
Ticker Symbol: KAHBX

TOTAL RETURNS (%)

1987	1988	1989	1990	1991	5-year
NA	10.6	0.3	-25.4	44.1	NA

INVESTMENT PORTFOLIO

Total Assets (mil.)	Expense Ratio	Turnover Ratio
$66	2.00%	82%

KEYSTONE CUSTODIAN FUNDS—B4

Keystone Distributors
99 High Street, 29th Floor
Boston, MA 02110
800-633-4900

Minimum: $1,000
Front-End Load: None
12b-1: 1.11%
Redemption Fee: 4.00%
Ticker Symbol: KBFOX

TOTAL RETURNS (%)

1987	1988	1989	1990	1991	5-year
-3.9	11.8	-5.2	-21.8	41.8	12.9

INVESTMENT PORTFOLIO

Total Assets (mil.)	Expense Ratio	Turnover Ratio
$782	2.34%	78%

LIBERTY HIGH INCOME BOND

Federated Securities
1001 Liberty Avenue
Pittsburgh, PA 15222
800-356-2805

Minimum: $500
Front-End Load: 4.50%
12b-1: None
Redemption Fee: 0.50%
Ticker Symbol: FHIIX

TOTAL RETURNS (%)

1987	1988	1989	1990	1991	5-year
0.0	15.1	-0.4	-12.8	60.5	60.6

INVESTMENT PORTFOLIO

Total Assets (mil.)	Expense Ratio	Turnover Ratio
$303	1.03%	32%

LUTHERAN BROTHERHOOD HIGH YIELD FUND

Lutheran Brotherhood Securities
625 Fourth Avenue South
Minneapolis, MN 55415
800-328-4552

Minimum: $500
Front-End Load: 5.00%
12b-1: None
Redemption Fee: None
Ticker Symbol: LBHYX

TOTAL RETURNS (%)

1987	1988	1989	1990	1991	5-year
NA	12.3	-2.7	-7.4	36.1	NA

INVESTMENT PORTFOLIO

Total Assets (mil.)	Expense Ratio	Turnover Ratio
$198	1.23%	120%

MAINSTAY HIGH YIELD CORPORATE BOND

NYLIFE Securities
51 Madison Avenue, Room 117
New York, NY 10010
800-522-4202

Minimum: $500
Front-End Load: None
12b-1: 1.00%
Redemption Fee: 5.00%
Ticker Symbol: MKHCX

TOTAL RETURNS (%)

1987	1988	1989	1990	1991	5-year
0.2	16.9	-5.0	-7.8	32.3	35.6

INVESTMENT PORTFOLIO

Total Assets (mil.)	Expense Ratio	Turnover Ratio
$296	2.10%	305%

MASSACHUSETTS FINANCIAL HIGH INCOME TRUST I

Massachusetts Financial Services
500 Boylston Street
Boston, MA 02116
800-225-2606

Minimum: $1,000
Front-End Load: 4.75%
12b-1: 0.25%
Redemption Fee: None
Ticker Symbol: MHITX

TOTAL RETURNS (%)

1987	1988	1989	1990	1991	5-year
-0.7	11.4	-2.9	-17.7	48.6	31.2

INVESTMENT PORTFOLIO

Total Assets (mil.)	Expense Ratio	Turnover Ratio
$541	1.05%	24%

MERRILL LYNCH CORPORATE BOND FUND HIGH INCOME A

Merrill Lynch Funds Distributor
P. O. Box 9011
Princeton, NJ 08543
800-637-3863

Minimum: $1,000
Front-End Load: 4.00%
12b-1: None
Redemption Fee: None
Ticker Symbol: MLHIX

TOTAL RETURNS (%)

1987	1988	1989	1990	1991	5-year
4.9	12.7	4.3	-4.6	39.8	64.5

INVESTMENT PORTFOLIO

Total Assets (mil.)	Expense Ratio	Turnover Ratio
$538	0.68%	48%

MFS LIFETIME HIGH INCOME TRUST

Massachusetts Financial Services
500 Boylston Street
Boston, MA 02116
800-225-2606

Minimum: $1,000
Front-End Load: None
12b-1: 1.00%
Redemption Fee: 6.00%
Ticker Symbol: LTHIX

TOTAL RETURNS (%)

1987	1988	1989	1990	1991	5-year
-2.1	12.2	-5.1	-14.2	50.0	34.2

INVESTMENT PORTFOLIO

Total Assets (mil.)	Expense Ratio	Turnover Ratio
$196	2.60%	34%

NICHOLAS INCOME

Nicholas
700 W. Water Street, Suite 1010
Milwaukee, WI 53202
800-275-8700

Minimum: $500
Front-End Load: None
12b-1: None
Redemption Fee: None
Ticker Symbol: NCINX

TOTAL RETURNS (%)

1987	1988	1989	1990	1991	5-year
2.5	11.5	3.9	-1.0	23.1	44.8

INVESTMENT PORTFOLIO

Total Assets (mil.)	Expense Ratio	Turnover Ratio
$78	0.77%	40%

OPPENHEIMER HIGH YIELD FUND

Oppenheimer Fund Management
P. O. Box 300
Denver, CO 80201
800-255-2755

Minimum: $1,000
Front-End Load: 4.75%
12b-1: 0.02%
Redemption Fee: None
Ticker Symbol: OPPHX

TOTAL RETURNS (%)

1987	1988	1989	1990	1991	5-year
7.2	11.9	3.9	-3.2	28.6	55.2

INVESTMENT PORTFOLIO

Total Assets (mil.)	Expense Ratio	Turnover Ratio
$737	0.96%	90%

PAINEWEBBER HIGH INCOME A

PaineWebber
1285 Avenue of the Americas, 18th Floor
New York, NY 10019
800-647-1568

Minimum: $1,000
Front-End Load: 4.00%
12b-1: None
Redemption Fee: None
Ticker Symbol: PHIAX

TOTAL RETURNS (%)

1987	1988	1989	1990	1991	5-year
-2.0	9.1	-1.8	-8.5	47.0	41.2

INVESTMENT PORTFOLIO

Total Assets (mil.)	Expense Ratio	Turnover Ratio
$243	0.71%	132%

PHOENIX HIGH YIELD FUND

Phoenix Equity Planning
100 Bright Meadow Boulevard
Enfield, CT 06082
800-243-4361

Minimum: $500
Front-End Load: 4.75%
12b-1: None
Redemption Fee: None
Ticker Symbol: PHCHX

TOTAL RETURNS (%)

1987	1988	1989	1990	1991	5-year
1.6	13.6	-0.9	-1.1	24.7	41.1

INVESTMENT PORTFOLIO

Total Assets (mil.)	Expense Ratio	Turnover Ratio
$94	0.89%	321%

PUTNAM HIGH YIELD TRUST

Putnam Financial Services
One Post Office Square, 12th Floor
Boston, MA 02109
800-634-1590

Minimum: $500
Front-End Load: 4.75%
12b-1: 0.07%
Redemption Fee: None
Ticker Symbol: PHIGX

TOTAL RETURNS (%)

1987	1988	1989	1990	1991	5-year
4.6	14.0	-3.1	-5.9	39.2	51.4

INVESTMENT PORTFOLIO

Total Assets (mil.)	Expense Ratio	Turnover Ratio
$1,936	0.95%	48%

PUTNAM HIGH YIELD TRUST II

Putnam Financial Services
One Post Office Square, 12th Floor
Boston, MA 02109
800-634-1590

Minimum: $500
Front-End Load: 4.75%
12b-1: 0.25%
Redemption Fee: None
Ticker Symbol: PHYIX

TOTAL RETURNS (%)

1987	1988	1989	1990	1991	5-year
6.1	15.1	-4.3	-8.1	45.7	56.4

INVESTMENT PORTFOLIO

Total Assets (mil.)	Expense Ratio	Turnover Ratio
$369	1.37%	63%

SELIGMAN HIGH INCOME FUND HIGH YIELD BOND

Financial Services
130 Liberty Street, 22nd Floor
New York, NY 10006
800-221-2450

Minimum: $1,000
Front-End Load: 4.75%
12b-1: 0.11%
Redemption Fee: None
Ticker Symbol: SHYBX

TOTAL RETURNS (%)

1987	1988	1989	1990	1991	5-year
3.1	11.4	3.8	-7.3	30.7	44.5

INVESTMENT PORTFOLIO

Total Assets (mil.)	Expense Ratio	Turnover Ratio
$32	1.21%	118%

SHEARSON INCOME PORTFOLIO HIGH INCOME

Shearson Lehman Brothers
Two World Trade Center
New York, NY 10048
212-464-8068

Minimum: $500
Front-End Load: None
12b-1: 0.75%
Redemption Fee: 5.00%
Ticker Symbol: SHIBX

TOTAL RETURNS (%)

1987	1988	1989	1990	1991	5-year
6.9	12.4	-4.6	-13.2	34.8	34.1

INVESTMENT PORTFOLIO

Total Assets (mil.)	Expense Ratio	Turnover Ratio
$249	1.68%	43%

SUN AMERICA HIGH INCOME

Sun America Capital Services
10 Union Square East, 2nd Floor
New York, NY 10003
800-821-5100

Minimum: $2,500
Front-End Load: None
12b-1: 0.84%
Redemption Fee: 5.00%
Ticker Symbol: SAHCX

TOTAL RETURNS (%)

1987	1988	1989	1990	1991	5-year
2.1	8.7	4.5	-13.2	30.9	31.7

INVESTMENT PORTFOLIO

Total Assets (mil.)	Expense Ratio	Turnover Ratio
$18	2.11%	109%

SUN AMERICA INCOME PORTFOLIO HIGH YIELD

Sun America Capital Services
10 Union Square East, 2nd Floor
New York, NY 10003
800-821-5100

Minimum: $500
Front-End Load: 4.75%
12b-1: 0.35%
Redemption Fee: None
Ticker Symbol: SAHYX

TOTAL RETURNS (%)

1987	1988	1989	1990	1991	5-year
0.4	17.2	-4.4	-7.1	36.6	42.8

INVESTMENT PORTFOLIO

Total Assets (mil.)	Expense Ratio	Turnover Ratio
$21	1.90%	95%

T. ROWE PRICE HIGH YIELD FUND

T. Rowe Price Investor Services
100 East Pratt Street
Baltimore, MD 21202
800-638-5660

Minimum: $2,500
Front-End Load: None
12b-1: None
Redemption Fee: None
Ticker Symbol: PRHYX

TOTAL RETURNS (%)

1987	1988	1989	1990	1991	5-year
3.0	17.9	-1.5	-11.0	30.9	39.5

INVESTMENT PORTFOLIO

Total Assets (mil.)	Expense Ratio	Turnover Ratio
$981	1.03%	83%

TRANSAMERICA SPECIAL HIGH YIELD BOND FUND

TransAmerica Distributors
1000 Louisiana, Suite 6000
Houston, TX 77002
800-343-6840

Minimum: $1,000
Front-End Load: None
12b-1: 1.05%
Redemption Fee: 6.00%
Ticker Symbol: TSHYX

TOTAL RETURNS (%)

1987	1988	1989	1990	1991	5-year
NA	6.9	-5.1	-6.6	33.8	NA

INVESTMENT PORTFOLIO

Total Assets (mil.)	Expense Ratio	Turnover Ratio
$77	1.12%	51%

VALUE LINE AGGRESSIVE INCOME TRUST

Value Line Securities
711 Third Avenue
New York, NY 10017
800-223-0818

Minimum: $1,000
Front-End Load: None
12b-1: None
Redemption Fee: None
Ticker Symbol: VAGIX

TOTAL RETURNS (%)

1987	1988	1989	1990	1991	5-year
-2.0	6.3	2.4	-3.7	26.6	30.0

INVESTMENT PORTFOLIO

Total Assets (mil.)	Expense Ratio	Turnover Ratio
$30	1.43%	36%

VANGUARD FIXED INCOME HIGH YIELD CORPORATE

Vanguard Group
Vanguard Financial Center
Valley Forge, PA 19482
800-662-7447

Minimum: $3,000
Front-End Load: None
12b-1: None
Redemption Fee: None
Ticker Symbol: VWEHX

TOTAL RETURNS (%)

1987	1988	1989	1990	1991	5-year
2.7	13.6	1.9	-5.8	29.0	44.3

INVESTMENT PORTFOLIO

Total Assets (mil.)	Expense Ratio	Turnover Ratio
$1,409	0.40%	61%

VAN KAMPEN MERRITT HIGH YIELD FUND

Van Kampen Merritt
Parkview Plaza, 17W110 22nd Street
Oakbrook Terrace, IL 60181
800-225-2222

Minimum: $1,500
Front-End Load: 4.90%
12b-1: 0.25%
Redemption Fee: None
Ticker Symbol: VKHYX

TOTAL RETURNS (%)

1987	1988	1989	1990	1991	5-year
7.0	13.6	-8.6	-11.6	35.1	32.8

INVESTMENT PORTFOLIO

Total Assets (mil.)	Expense Ratio	Turnover Ratio
$207	1.28%	67%

VENTURE INCOME PLUS

Venture Advisers
P. O. Box 1688
Santa Fe, NM 87501
800-279-0279

Minimum: $1,000
Front-End Load: 4.75%
12b-1: 0.20%
Redemption Fee: None
Ticker Symbol: VIPIX

TOTAL RETURNS (%)

1987	1988	1989	1990	1991	5-year
1.6	6.9	-5.1	-16.1	20.6	4.4

INVESTMENT PORTFOLIO

Total Assets (mil.)	Expense Ratio	Turnover Ratio
$21	2.09%	77%

International Bond Funds

ALLIANCE SHORT TERM MULTIPLE MARKET A

Alliance Funds Distributor
500 Plaza Drive
Secaucus, NJ 07096
800-227-4618

Minimum: $250
Front-End Load: 3.00%
12b-1: 0.30%
Redemption Fee: None
Ticker Symbol: ASTTX

TOTAL RETURNS (%)

1987	1988	1989	1990	1991	5-year
NA	NA	NA	12.2	9.5	NA

INVESTMENT PORTFOLIO

Total Assets (mil.)	Expense Ratio	Turnover Ratio
$2,126	1.09%	152%

CAPITAL WORLD BOND

American Funds Distributor
333 South Hope Street
Los Angeles, CA 90071
800-421-0180

Minimum: $1,000
Front-End Load: 4.80%
12b-1: 0.30%
Redemption Fee: None
Ticker Symbol: CWBFX

TOTAL RETURNS (%)

1987	1988	1989	1990	1991	5-year
NA	2.7	4.6	11.7	15.0	NA

INVESTMENT PORTFOLIO

Total Assets (mil.)	Expense Ratio	Turnover Ratio
$76	1.52%	76%

DEAN WITTER WORLD WIDE INCOME TRUST

Dean Witter Reynolds
Two World Trade Center, 72nd Floor
New York, NY 10048
800-869-3863

Minimum: $1,000
Front-End Load: None
12b-1: 0.84%
Redemption Fee: 5.00%
Ticker Symbol: DWITX

TOTAL RETURNS (%)

1987	1988	1989	1990	1991	5-year
NA	NA	NA	16.6	1.1	NA

INVESTMENT PORTFOLIO

Total Assets (mil.)	Expense Ratio	Turnover Ratio
$407	1.82%	109%

FIDELITY GLOBAL BOND FUND

Fidelity Distributors Corporation
82 Devonshire Street, Mail Zone L7b
Boston, MA 02109
800-544-8888

Minimum: $2,500
Front-End Load: None
12b-1: None
Redemption Fee: None
Ticker Symbol: FGBDX

TOTAL RETURNS (%)

1987	1988	1989	1990	1991	5-year
19.2	3.7	7.9	12.3	12.8	68.8

INVESTMENT PORTFOLIO

Total Assets (mil.)	Expense Ratio	Turnover Ratio
$166	1.45%	154%

GT GLOBAL BOND FUND

GT Global Financial Services
50 California Street, 27th Floor
San Francisco, CA 94111
800-824-1580

Minimum: $500
Front-End Load: 4.75%
12b-1: 0.35%
Redemption Fee: None
Ticker Symbol: GGLBX

TOTAL RETURNS (%)

1987	1988	1989	1990	1991	5-year
NA	NA	10.2	8.4	15.8	NA

INVESTMENT PORTFOLIO

Total Assets (mil.)	Expense Ratio	Turnover Ratio
$60	1.86%	501%

GT GLOBAL GOVERNMENT INCOME FUND

GT Global Financial Services
50 California Street, 27th Floor
San Francisco, CA 94111
800-824-1580

Minimum: $500
Front-End Load: 4.75%
12b-1: 0.35%
Redemption Fee: None
Ticker Symbol: GGINX

TOTAL RETURNS (%)

1987	1988	1989	1990	1991	5-year
NA	NA	11.1	8.8	13.7	NA

INVESTMENT PORTFOLIO

Total Assets (mil.)	Expense Ratio	Turnover Ratio
$410	1.75%	334%

HUNTINGTON INTERNATIONAL GLOBAL CURRENCY

Huntington Advisers
251 South Lake Avenue, Suite 600
Pasadena, CA 91101
800-354-4111

Minimum: $2,500
Front-End Load: 2.25%
12b-1: 0.45%
Redemption Fee: None
Ticker Symbol: ICPGX

TOTAL RETURNS (%)

1987	1988	1989	1990	1991	5-year
22.6	2.2	4.2	14.4	7.6	60.8

INVESTMENT PORTFOLIO

Total Assets (mil.)	Expense Ratio	Turnover Ratio
$70	1.82%	0%

IDS GLOBAL BOND

IDS Financial Services
1000 Roanoke Building
Minneapolis, MN 55402
800-328-8300

Minimum: $2,000
Front-End Load: 5.00%
12b-1: 0.11%
Redemption Fee: None
Ticker Symbol: IGBFX

TOTAL RETURNS (%)

1987	1988	1989	1990	1991	5-year
NA	NA	NA	13.0	15.3	NA

INVESTMENT PORTFOLIO

Total Assets (mil.)	Expense Ratio	Turnover Ratio
$51	1.73%	130%

KEMPER GLOBAL INCOME FUND

Kemper Financial Services
120 South LaSalle Street, 20th Floor
Chicago, IL 60603
800-621-1048

Minimum: $1,000
Front-End Load: 4.50%
12b-1: None
Redemption Fee: None
Ticker Symbol: KGIFX

TOTAL RETURNS (%)

1987	1988	1989	1990	1991	5-year
NA	NA	NA	22.7	11.1	NA

INVESTMENT PORTFOLIO

Total Assets (mil.)	Expense Ratio	Turnover Ratio
$81	1.65%	346%

KEYSTONE AMERICA WORLD BOND FUND

Keystone Distributors
99 High Street, 29th Floor
Boston, MA 02110
800-633-4900

Minimum: $1,000
Front-End Load: 4.75%
12b-1: 0.23%
Redemption Fee: None
Ticker Symbol: KAWBX

TOTAL RETURNS (%)

1987	1988	1989	1990	1991	5-year
NA	-3.4	3.1	10.2	17.4	NA

INVESTMENT PORTFOLIO

Total Assets (mil.)	Expense Ratio	Turnover Ratio
$11	2.50%	154%

MERRILL LYNCH GLOBAL BOND FOR INVEST/RETIRE—B

Merrill Lynch Funds Distributor
P. O. Box 9011
Princeton, NJ 08543
800-637-3863

Minimum: $1,000
Front-End Load: None
12b-1: 0.75%
Redemption Fee: 4.00%
Ticker Symbol: MRRGX

TOTAL RETURNS (%)

1987	1988	1989	1990	1991	5-year
23.2	3.8	6.5	14.7	15.2	80.1

INVESTMENT PORTFOLIO

Total Assets (mil.)	Expense Ratio	Turnover Ratio
$345	1.84%	160%

MFS WORLDWIDE GOVERNMENTS TRUST

Massachusetts Financial Services
500 Boylston Street
Boston, MA 02116
800-225-2606

Minimum: $1,000
Front-End Load: 4.75%
12b-1: 0.13%
Redemption Fee: 1.00%
Ticker Symbol: MWGTX

TOTAL RETURNS (%)

1987	1988	1989	1990	1991	5-year
24.5	4.4	7.4	17.9	13.4	86.6

INVESTMENT PORTFOLIO

Total Assets (mil.)	Expense Ratio	Turnover Ratio
$269	1.44%	220%

PAINEWEBBER GLOBAL INCOME

PaineWebber
1285 Avenue of the Americas, 18th Floor
New York, NY 10019
800-647-1568

Minimum: $1,000
Front-End Load: None
12b-1: 1.00%
Redemption Fee: 5.00%
Ticker Symbol: PGBBX

TOTAL RETURNS (%)

1987	1988	1989	1990	1991	5-year
NA	12.2	5.4	17.7	5.1	NA

INVESTMENT PORTFOLIO

Total Assets (mil.)	Expense Ratio	Turnover Ratio
$1,470	1.90%	125%

PUTNAM GLOBAL GOVERNMENT INCOME

Putnam Financial Services
One Post Office Square
Boston, MA 02109
800-225-1581

Minimum: $500
Front-End Load: 4.80%
12b-1: None
Redemption Fee: None
Ticker Symbol: PGGIX

TOTAL RETURNS (%)

1987	1988	1989	1990	1991	5-year
NA	14.9	7.6	16.3	15.1	NA

INVESTMENT PORTFOLIO

Total Assets (mil.)	Expense Ratio	Turnover Ratio
$330	1.58%	498%

SCUDDER INTERNATIONAL BOND FUND

Scudder Stevens & Clark
175 Federal Street, 12th Floor
Boston, MA 02110
800-225-2470

Minimum: $1,000
Front-End Load: None
12b-1: None
Redemption Fee: None
Ticker Symbol: SCIBX

TOTAL RETURNS (%)

1987	1988	1989	1990	1991	5-year
NA	NA	7.2	21.1	22.2	NA

INVESTMENT PORTFOLIO

Total Assets (mil.)	Expense Ratio	Turnover Ratio
$231	1.25%	260%

SHEARSON GLOBAL BOND

Shearson Lehman Brothers
Two World Trade Center
New York, NY 10048
212-464-8068

Minimum: $500
Front-End Load: None
12b-1: 0.75%
Redemption Fee: 5.00%
Ticker Symbol: SSGLX

TOTAL RETURNS (%)

1987	1988	1989	1990	1991	5-year
20.2	1.5	6.6	9.1	15.9	64.4

INVESTMENT PORTFOLIO

Total Assets (mil.)	Expense Ratio	Turnover Ratio
$48	2.05%	309%

T. ROWE PRICE INTERNATIONAL BOND

T. Rowe Price Investor Services
100 East Pratt Street
Baltimore, MD 21202
800-638-5660

Minimum: $2,500
Front-End Load: None
12b-1: None
Redemption Fee: None
Ticker Symbol: RPIBX

TOTAL RETURNS (%)

1987	1988	1989	1990	1991	5-year
28.1	-1.3	-3.2	16.1	17.7	67.4

INVESTMENT PORTFOLIO

Total Assets (mil.)	Expense Ratio	Turnover Ratio
$365	1.15%	211%

TEMPLETON INCOME FUND

Templeton Funds
700 Central Avenue
St. Petersburg, FL 33701
800-237-0738

Minimum: $500
Front-End Load: 4.50%
12b-1: None
Redemption Fee: None
Ticker Symbol: TPINX

TOTAL RETURNS (%)

1987	1988	1989	1990	1991	5-year
8.4	7.1	8.5	9.9	14.9	59.1

INVESTMENT PORTFOLIO

Total Assets (mil.)	Expense Ratio	Turnover Ratio
$139	1.05%	86%

VAN ECK WORLD INCOME FUND

Van Eck Associates Corporation
122 East 42nd Street
New York, NY 10168
800-221-2220

Minimum: $1,000
Front-End Load: 4.75%
12b-1: 0.25%
Redemption Fee: None
Ticker Symbol: WIFRX

TOTAL RETURNS (%)

1987	1988	1989	1990	1991	5-year
NA	11.2	12.4	16.7	19.6	NA

INVESTMENT PORTFOLIO

Total Assets (mil.)	Expense Ratio	Turnover Ratio
$131	1.43%	289%

GNMA Bond Funds

AARP GNMA AND U.S. TREASURY FUND

Scudder Stevens & Clark
175 Federal Street, 12th Floor
Boston, MA 02110
800-253-2277

Minimum: $500
Front-End Load: None
12b-1: None
Redemption Fee: None
Ticker Symbol: AGNMX

TOTAL RETURNS (%)

1987	1988	1989	1990	1991	5-year
2.7	7.1	11.7	9.7	14.4	54.2

INVESTMENT PORTFOLIO

Total Assets (mil.)	Expense Ratio	Turnover Ratio
$3,861	0.80%	60%

ALLIANCE MORTGAGE SECURITIES INCOME FUND

Alliance Funds Distributor
500 Plaza Drive
Secaucus, NJ 07094
800-247-4154

Minimum: $250
Front-End Load: 4.75%
12b-1: 0.30%
Redemption Fee: None
Ticker Symbol: ALMSX

TOTAL RETURNS (%)

1987	1988	1989	1990	1991	5-year
3.5	8.6	11.0	11.0	15.4	59.9

INVESTMENT PORTFOLIO

Total Assets (mil.)	Expense Ratio	Turnover Ratio
$527	1.13%	393%

AMERICAN CAPITAL FEDERAL MORTGAGE TRUST A

American Capital Marketing
P.O. Box 3528
Houston, TX 77253
800-421-5666

Minimum: $500
Front-End Load: 4.00%
12b-1: 0.23%
Redemption Fee: None
Ticker Symbol: ACFMX

TOTAL RETURNS (%)

1987	1988	1989	1990	1991	5-year
-1.1	5.1	13.7	9.5	9.8	42.1

INVESTMENT PORTFOLIO

Total Assets (mil.)	Expense Ratio	Turnover Ratio
$95	1.39%	341%

BENHAM GNMA INCOME FUND

Benham Group
1665 Charleston Road
Mountain View, CA 94043
800-472-3389

Minimum: $1,000
Front-End Load: None
12b-1: None
Redemption Fee: None
Ticker Symbol: BGNMX

TOTAL RETURNS (%)

1987	1988	1989	1990	1991	5-year
2.8	8.5	13.9	10.2	15.6	61.7

INVESTMENT PORTFOLIO

Total Assets (mil.)	Expense Ratio	Turnover Ratio
$661	0.73%	207%

DREYFUS GNMA FUND

Dreyfus Service
200 Park Avenue, 7th Floor
New York, NY 10166
800-782-6620

Minimum: $2,500
Front-End Load: None
12b-1: 0.20%
Redemption Fee: None
Ticker Symbol: DRGMX

TOTAL RETURNS (%)

1987	1988	1989	1990	1991	5-year
2.6	6.4	11.6	9.7	14.5	53.0

INVESTMENT PORTFOLIO

Total Assets (mil.)	Expense Ratio	Turnover Ratio
$1,755	0.98%	26%

FEDERATED GNMA TRUST

Federated Securities
1001 Liberty Avenue
Pittsburgh, PA 15222
800-245-2423

Minimum: $25,000
Front-End Load: None
12b-1: None
Redemption Fee: None
Ticker Symbol: FGMAX

TOTAL RETURNS (%)

1987	1988	1989	1990	1991	5-year
3.5	8.2	15.1	10.4	15.3	64.1

INVESTMENT PORTFOLIO

Total Assets (mil.)	Expense Ratio	Turnover Ratio
$1,292	0.53%	48%

FEDERATED INCOME TRUST

Federated Securities
1001 Liberty Avenue
Pittsburgh, PA 15222
800-245-2423

Minimum: $25,000
Front-End Load: None
12b-1: None
Redemption Fee: None
Ticker Symbol: FICMX

TOTAL RETURNS (%)

1987	1988	1989	1990	1991	5-year
4.6	7.6	12.5	10.4	13.9	59.3

INVESTMENT PORTFOLIO

Total Assets (mil.)	Expense Ratio	Turnover Ratio
$1,193	0.55%	36%

FIDELITY GNMA PORTFOLIO

Fidelity Distributors Corporation
82 Devonshire Street, Mail Zone L7b
Boston, MA 02109
800-544-8888

Minimum: $2,500
Front-End Load: None
12b-1: None
Redemption Fee: None
Ticker Symbol: FGMNX

TOTAL RETURNS (%)

1987	1988	1989	1990	1991	5-year
1.2	7.2	13.8	10.5	13.6	54.9

INVESTMENT PORTFOLIO

Total Assets (mil.)	Expense Ratio	Turnover Ratio
$872	0.84%	125%

FIDELITY MORTGAGE SECURITIES FUND

Fidelity Distributors Corporation
82 Devonshire Street, Mail Zone L7b
Boston, MA 02109
800-544-8888

Minimum: $2,500
Front-End Load: None
12b-1: None
Redemption Fee: None
Ticker Symbol: FMSFX

TOTAL RETURNS (%)

1987	1988	1989	1990	1991	5-year
2.7	6.7	13.6	10.4	13.6	56.2

INVESTMENT PORTFOLIO

Total Assets (mil.)	Expense Ratio	Turnover Ratio
$431	0.83%	209%

FIRST TRUST FUND U.S. GOVERNMENT SERIES

Clayton Brown & Associates
500 West Madison Street, Suite 3000
Chicago, IL 60606
800-848-8222

Minimum: $1,000
Front-End Load: 4.50%
12b-1: 0.25%
Redemption Fee: None
Ticker Symbol: FTUSX

TOTAL RETURNS (%)

1987	1988	1989	1990	1991	5-year
2.3	5.0	13.5	10.4	15.6	55.6

INVESTMENT PORTFOLIO

Total Assets (mil.)	Expense Ratio	Turnover Ratio
$164	0.90%	60%

HOME INVESTORS GOVERNMENT INCOME FUND

Sun America Capital Services
10 Union Square East, 2nd Floor
New York, NY 10003
800-821-5100

Minimum: $500
Front-End Load: None
12b-1: 0.95%
Redemption Fee: 5.00%
Ticker Symbol: HIVFX

TOTAL RETURNS (%)

1987	1988	1989	1990	1991	5-year
1.3	7.5	12.0	9.5	14.3	52.7

INVESTMENT PORTFOLIO

Total Assets (mil.)	Expense Ratio	Turnover Ratio
$126	1.94%	23%

KEMPER U.S. GOVERNMENT SECURITIES

Kemper Financial Services
120 South LaSalle Street, 20th Floor
Chicago, IL 60603
800-621-1048

Minimum: $1,000
Front-End Load: 4.50%
12b-1: None
Redemption Fee: None
Ticker Symbol: KPGVX

TOTAL RETURNS (%)

1987	1988	1989	1990	1991	5-year
2.7	6.3	14.0	9.7	17.3	60.1

INVESTMENT PORTFOLIO

Total Assets (mil.)	Expense Ratio	Turnover Ratio
$5,634	0.53%	497%

LEXINGTON GNMA INCOME FUND

Lexington Funds Distributor
P.O. Box 1515
Saddle Brook, NJ 07662
800-526-0056

Minimum: $1,000
Front-End Load: None
12b-1: None
Redemption Fee: None
Ticker Symbol: LEXNX

TOTAL RETURNS (%)

1987	1988	1989	1990	1991	5-year
1.6	6.9	15.6	9.2	15.7	58.8

INVESTMENT PORTFOLIO

Total Assets (mil.)	Expense Ratio	Turnover Ratio
$117	1.05%	113%

LORD ABBETT U.S. GOVERNMENT SECURITIES

Lord Abbett & Company
767 Fifth Avenue
New York, NY 10153
800-874-3733

Minimum: $500
Front-End Load: 4.75%
12b-1: 0.25%
Redemption Fee: None
Ticker Symbol: LAGVX

TOTAL RETURNS (%)

1987	1988	1989	1990	1991	5-year
2.1	7.8	12.7	9.3	16.9	58.5

INVESTMENT PORTFOLIO

Total Assets (mil.)	Expense Ratio	Turnover Ratio
$2,293	0.89%	503%

OPPENHEIMER GNMA FUND

Oppenheimer Fund Management
P. O. Box 300
Denver, CO 80201
800-255-2755

Minimum: $1,000
Front-End Load: 4.75%
12b-1: 0.22%
Redemption Fee: None
Ticker Symbol: OPGNX

TOTAL RETURNS (%)

1987	1988	1989	1990	1991	5-year
4.1	6.6	12.1	10.1	14.3	56.5

INVESTMENT PORTFOLIO

Total Assets (mil.)	Expense Ratio	Turnover Ratio
$94	1.23%	48%

PAINEWEBBER U.S. GOVERNMENT

PaineWebber
1285 Avenue of the Americas, 18th Floor
New York, NY 10019
800-647-1568

Minimum: $1,000
Front-End Load: 4.00%
12b-1: 0.25%
Redemption Fee: None
Ticker Symbol: PUGAX

TOTAL RETURNS (%)

1987	1988	1989	1990	1991	5-year
0.6	7.4	13.1	9.7	15.0	54.2

INVESTMENT PORTFOLIO

Total Assets (mil.)	Expense Ratio	Turnover Ratio
$754	0.66%	34%

PILGRIM GNMA FUND

Pilgrim Management
10100 Santa Monica Boulevard, 21st Floor
Los Angeles, CA 90067
800-336-3436

Minimum: $1,000
Front-End Load: 4.75%
12b-1: 0.25%
Redemption Fee: None
Ticker Symbol: PGMAX

TOTAL RETURNS (%)

1987	1988	1989	1990	1991	5-year
0.8	7.4	12.7	8.0	11.9	47.6

INVESTMENT PORTFOLIO

Total Assets (mil.)	Expense Ratio	Turnover Ratio
$105	1.15%	448%

PRINCOR GOVERNMENT SECURITIES INCOME

Principal Financial Group
Mutual Fund Accounting, 711 High Street
Des Moines, IA 50309
800-247-4123

Minimum: $1,000
Front-End Load: 5.00%
12b-1: 0.16%
Redemption Fee: None
Ticker Symbol: PRGVX

TOTAL RETURNS (%)

1987	1988	1989	1990	1991	5-year
0.9	8.8	15.0	9.5	16.8	61.5

INVESTMENT PORTFOLIO

Total Assets (mil.)	Expense Ratio	Turnover Ratio
$100	1.07%	22%

PUTNAM FEDERAL INCOME TRUST

Putnam Financial Services
One Post Office Square, 12th Floor
Boston, MA 02109
800-634-1590

Minimum: $500
Front-End Load: 4.75%
12b-1: 0.24%
Redemption Fee: None
Ticker Symbol: PGPTX

TOTAL RETURNS (%)

1987	1988	1989	1990	1991	5-year
-1.2	5.8	14.4	8.2	15.2	49.1

INVESTMENT PORTFOLIO

Total Assets (mil.)	Expense Ratio	Turnover Ratio
$725	1.14%	269%

RETIREMENT PLAN FUNDS OF AMERICA BOND

Venture Advisers
P. O. Box 1688
Santa Fe, NM 87501
800-279-0279

Minimum: $1,000
Front-End Load: None
12b-1: 1.25%
Redemption Fee: 5.00%
Ticker Symbol: VRPFX

TOTAL RETURNS (%)

1987	1988	1989	1990	1991	5-year
1.2	5.7	9.5	6.1	12.4	39.7

INVESTMENT PORTFOLIO

Total Assets (mil.)	Expense Ratio	Turnover Ratio
$59	2.55%	72%

SCUDDER GNMA FUND

Scudder Stevens & Clark
175 Federal Street, 12th Floor
Boston, MA 02110
800-225-2470

Minimum: $1,000
Front-End Load: None
12b-1: None
Redemption Fee: None
Ticker Symbol: SGMSX

TOTAL RETURNS (%)

1987	1988	1989	1990	1991	5-year
2.2	6.8	12.8	10.1	15.0	56.0

INVESTMENT PORTFOLIO

Total Assets (mil.)	Expense Ratio	Turnover Ratio
$316	1.05%	52%

SHEARSON INCOME PORTFOLIO MORTGAGE

Shearson Lehman Brothers
Two World Trade Center
New York, NY 10048
212-464-8068

Minimum: $500
Front-End Load: None
12b-1: 0.75%
Redemption Fee: 5.00%
Ticker Symbol: SLIMX

TOTAL RETURNS (%)

1987	1988	1989	1990	1991	5-year
-0.3	5.8	10.8	9.2	17.0	49.3

INVESTMENT PORTFOLIO

Total Assets (mil.)	Expense Ratio	Turnover Ratio
$529	1.67%	134%

T. ROWE PRICE GNMA FUND

T. Rowe Price Investor Services
100 East Pratt Street
Baltimore, MD 21202
800-638-5660

Minimum: $2,500
Front-End Load: None
12b-1: None
Redemption Fee: None
Ticker Symbol: PRGMX

TOTAL RETURNS (%)

1987	1988	1989	1990	1991	5-year
0.9	5.9	14.0	10.0	15.0	54.2

INVESTMENT PORTFOLIO

Total Assets (mil.)	Expense Ratio	Turnover Ratio
$693	0.86%	92%

USAA MUTUAL INCOME

USAA Investment Management
USAA Building
San Antonio, TX 78288
800-531-8181

Minimum: $1,000
Front-End Load: None
12b-1: None
Redemption Fee: None
Ticker Symbol: USAIX

TOTAL RETURNS (%)

1987	1988	1989	1990	1991	5-year
3.4	10.0	16.3	7.7	20.0	71.0

INVESTMENT PORTFOLIO

Total Assets (mil.)	Expense Ratio	Turnover Ratio
$826	0.51%	12%

VANGUARD FIXED INCOME GNMA

Vanguard Group
Vanguard Financial Center
Valley Forge, PA 19482
800-662-7447

Minimum: $3,000
Front-End Load: None
12b-1: None
Redemption Fee: None
Ticker Symbol: VFIIX

TOTAL RETURNS (%)

1987	1988	1989	1990	1991	5-year
2.1	8.8	14.8	10.3	16.8	64.3

INVESTMENT PORTFOLIO

Total Assets (mil.)	Expense Ratio	Turnover Ratio
$4,974	0.35%	1%

VAN KAMPEN MERRITT U.S. GOVERNMENT

Van Kampen Merritt
Parkview Plaza, 17W110 22nd Street
Oakbrook Terrace, IL 60181
800-225-2222

Minimum: $1,500
Front-End Load: 4.90%
12b-1: 0.11%
Redemption Fee: None
Ticker Symbol: VKMGX

TOTAL RETURNS (%)

1987	1988	1989	1990	1991	5-year
1.4	7.5	13.9	9.6	15.8	57.6

INVESTMENT PORTFOLIO

Total Assets (mil.)	Expense Ratio	Turnover Ratio
$3,431	0.72%	56%

Government Bond Funds

AIM LIMITED MATURITY TREASURY SHARES

AIM Distributors
11 Greenway Plaza, Suite 1919
Houston, TX 77046
800-347-1919

Minimum: $1,000
Front-End Load: 1.75%
12b-1: 0.15%
Redemption Fee: None
Ticker Symbol: SHTIX

TOTAL RETURNS (%)

1987	1988	1989	1990	1991	5-year
NA	5.9	9.6	9.0	10.4	NA

INVESTMENT PORTFOLIO

Total Assets (mil.)	Expense Ratio	Turnover Ratio
$150	0.50%	192%

ALLIANCE BOND—U.S. GOVERNMENT PORTFOLIO

Alliance Funds Distributor
500 Plaza Drive
Secaucus, NJ 07094
800-247-4154

Minimum: $250
Front-End Load: 4.75%
12b-1: 0.30%
Redemption Fee: None
Ticker Symbol: ABUSX

TOTAL RETURNS (%)

1987	1988	1989	1990	1991	5-year
3.7	6.5	12.5	7.9	15.7	55.1

INVESTMENT PORTFOLIO

Total Assets (mil.)	Expense Ratio	Turnover Ratio
$498	1.09%	455%

AMERICAN CAPITAL GOVERNMENT SECURITIES A

American Capital Marketing
P.O. Box 3528
Houston, TX 77253
800-421-5666

Minimum: $500
Front-End Load: 4.75%
12b-1: 0.25%
Redemption Fee: None
Ticker Symbol: ACGVX

TOTAL RETURNS (%)

1987	1988	1989	1990	1991	5-year
-1.5	6.9	14.9	8.7	16.3	52.9

INVESTMENT PORTFOLIO

Total Assets (mil.)	Expense Ratio	Turnover Ratio
$3,803	0.93%	177%

AMERICAN U.S. GOVERNMENT SECURITIES

American Funds Distributor
333 South Hope Street, 52nd Floor
Los Angeles, CA 90071
800-421-9900

Minimum: $1,000
Front-End Load: 4.75%
12b-1: 0.30%
Redemption Fee: None
Ticker Symbol: AMUSX

TOTAL RETURNS (%)

1987	1988	1989	1990	1991	5-year
1.0	6.9	11.7	9.8	14.2	51.2

INVESTMENT PORTFOLIO

Total Assets (mil.)	Expense Ratio	Turnover Ratio
$1,107	0.95%	53%

AMEV U.S. GOVERNMENT SECURITIES FUND

AMEV Investors
P. O. Box 64284
St. Paul, MN 55164
800-872-2638

Minimum: $500
Front-End Load: 4.50%
12b-1: None
Redemption Fee: None
Ticker Symbol: AMUGX

TOTAL RETURNS (%)

1987	1988	1989	1990	1991	5-year
3.7	7.3	12.5	10.4	13.9	57.4

INVESTMENT PORTFOLIO

Total Assets (mil.)	Expense Ratio	Turnover Ratio
$433	0.81%	118%

BENHAM TARGET MATURITIES TRUST SERIES 1995

Benham Group
1665 Charleston Road
Mountain View, CA 94043
800-472-3389

Minimum: $1,000
Front-End Load: None
12b-1: None
Redemption Fee: None
Ticker Symbol: BTMFX

TOTAL RETURNS (%)

1987	1988	1989	1990	1991	5-year
-3.9	7.9	15.3	9.2	15.6	50.9

INVESTMENT PORTFOLIO

Total Assets (mil.)	Expense Ratio	Turnover Ratio
$96	0.70%	121%

BENHAM TARGET MATURITIES TRUST SERIES 2000

Benham Group
1665 Charleston Road
Mountain View, CA 94043
800-472-3389

Minimum: $1,000
Front-End Load: None
12b-1: None
Redemption Fee: None
Ticker Symbol: BTMTX

TOTAL RETURNS (%)

1987	1988	1989	1990	1991	5-year
-5.9	11.5	19.8	6.3	20.3	60.7

INVESTMENT PORTFOLIO

Total Assets (mil.)	Expense Ratio	Turnover Ratio
$89	0.70%	79%

BENHAM TARGET MATURITIES TRUST SERIES 2005

Benham Group
1665 Charleston Road
Mountain View, CA 94043
800-472-3389

Minimum: $1,000
Front-End Load: None
12b-1: None
Redemption Fee: None
Ticker Symbol: BTFIX

TOTAL RETURNS (%)

1987	1988	1989	1990	1991	5-year
-10.3	14.5	23.9	3.6	21.5	60.0

INVESTMENT PORTFOLIO

Total Assets (mil.)	Expense Ratio	Turnover Ratio
$173	0.70%	186%

BENHAM TARGET MATURITIES TRUST SERIES 2010

Benham Group
1665 Charleston Road
Mountain View, CA 94043
800-472-3389

Minimum: $1,000
Front-End Load: None
12b-1: None
Redemption Fee: None
Ticker Symbol: BTTNX

TOTAL RETURNS (%)

1987	1988	1989	1990	1991	5-year
-15.2	15.7	28.0	0.3	21.1	52.4

INVESTMENT PORTFOLIO

Total Assets (mil.)	Expense Ratio	Turnover Ratio
$49	0.70%	191%

BENHAM TARGET MATURITIES TRUST SERIES 2015

Benham Group
1665 Charleston Road
Mountain View, CA 94043
800-472-3389

Minimum: $1,000
Front-End Load: None
12b-1: None
Redemption Fee: None
Ticker Symbol: BTFTX

TOTAL RETURNS (%)

1987	1988	1989	1990	1991	5-year
-20.2	11.1	33.5	-3.4	22.5	40.1

INVESTMENT PORTFOLIO

Total Assets (mil.)	Expense Ratio	Turnover Ratio
$203	0.70%	81%

BENHAM TARGET MATURITIES TRUST SERIES 2020

Benham Group
1665 Charleston Road
Mountain View, CA 94043
800-472-3389

Minimum: $1,000
Front-End Load: None
12b-1: None
Redemption Fee: None
Ticker Symbol: BTTTX

TOTAL RETURNS (%)

1987	1988	1989	1990	1991	5-year
NA	NA	NA	-4.5	17.4	NA

INVESTMENT PORTFOLIO

Total Assets (mil.)	Expense Ratio	Turnover Ratio
$82	0.70%	189%

BENHAM TREASURY NOTE FUND

Benham Group
1665 Charleston Road
Mountain View, CA 94043
800-472-3389

Minimum: $1,000
Front-End Load: None
12b-1: None
Redemption Fee: None
Ticker Symbol: CPTNX

TOTAL RETURNS (%)

1987	1988	1989	1990	1991	5-year
-1.0	5.2	11.9	9.2	13.7	44.8

INVESTMENT PORTFOLIO

Total Assets (mil.)	Expense Ratio	Turnover Ratio
$279	0.73%	217%

BOSTON COMPANY INTERMEDIATE TERM GOVERNMENT

Boston Company Advisors
53 State Street Exchange Place, 4th Floor - B
Boston, MA 02114
800-225-5267

Minimum: $1,000
Front-End Load: None
12b-1: None
Redemption Fee: None
Ticker Symbol: BGMFX

TOTAL RETURNS (%)

1987	1988	1989	1990	1991	5-year
0.8	6.5	10.9	7.3	13.5	45.0

INVESTMENT PORTFOLIO

Total Assets (mil.)	Expense Ratio	Turnover Ratio
$16	1.92%	300%

BULL & BEAR U.S. GOVERNMENT SECURITIES

Bull & Bear Group
11 Hanover Square
New York, NY 10005
800-847-4200

Minimum: $1,000
Front-End Load: None
12b-1: 0.50%
Redemption Fee: None
Ticker Symbol: BBUSX

TOTAL RETURNS (%)

1987	1988	1989	1990	1991	5-year
5.4	4.5	10.4	7.8	15.3	51.2

INVESTMENT PORTFOLIO

Total Assets (mil.)	Expense Ratio	Turnover Ratio
$26	1.86%	486%

CALVERT U.S. GOVERNMENT FUND

Calvert Securities
4550 Montgomery Avenue, Suite 1000 N.
Bethesda, MD 20814
800-368-2748

Minimum: $2,000
Front-End Load: 4.75%
12b-1: None
Redemption Fee: None
Ticker Symbol: CGUSX

TOTAL RETURNS (%)

1987	1988	1989	1990	1991	5-year
1.7	8.1	13.8	7.9	12.8	52.2

INVESTMENT PORTFOLIO

Total Assets (mil.)	Expense Ratio	Turnover Ratio
$12	0.75%	0%

CARNEGIE GOVERNMENT SECURITIES TRUST

Carnegie Capital Management
1331 Euclid Avenue
Cleveland, OH 44115
800-321-2322

Minimum: $1,000
Front-End Load: 4.50%
12b-1: 0.33%
Redemption Fee: None
Ticker Symbol: CGITX

TOTAL RETURNS (%)

1987	1988	1989	1990	1991	5-year
2.9	5.8	12.0	8.3	13.8	50.2

INVESTMENT PORTFOLIO

Total Assets (mil.)	Expense Ratio	Turnover Ratio
$45	1.30%	12%

CIGNA GOVERNMENT SECURITIES

CIGNA Mutual Funds
One Financial Plaza, 16th Floor
Springfield, MA 01103
800-572-4462

Minimum: $500
Front-End Load: 5.00%
12b-1: 0.12%
Redemption Fee: None
Ticker Symbol: CGOSX

TOTAL RETURNS (%)

1987	1988	1989	1990	1991	5-year
NA	6.4	11.3	9.4	13.0	NA

INVESTMENT PORTFOLIO

Total Assets (mil.)	Expense Ratio	Turnover Ratio
$96	1.00%	16%

COLONIAL GOVERNMENT SECURITIES PLUS TRUST

Colonial Management Associates
One Financial Center, 14th Floor
Boston, MA 02110
800-248-2828

Minimum: $1,000
Front-End Load: 4.75%
12b-1: 0.25%
Redemption Fee: None
Ticker Symbol: COGVX

TOTAL RETURNS (%)

1987	1988	1989	1990	1991	5-year
0.1	8.7	13.4	6.7	15.2	51.7

INVESTMENT PORTFOLIO

Total Assets (mil.)	Expense Ratio	Turnover Ratio
$2,010	1.16%	6%

COLONIAL U.S. GOVERNMENT TRUST

Colonial Investment Services
One Financial Center, 14th Floor
Boston, MA 02110
800-248-2828

Minimum: $1,000
Front-End Load: 4.75%
12b-1: 0.25%
Redemption Fee: None
Ticker Symbol: CUSGX

TOTAL RETURNS (%)

1987	1988	1989	1990	1991	5-year
NA	7.1	10.6	9.7	11.1	NA

INVESTMENT PORTFOLIO

Total Assets (mil.)	Expense Ratio	Turnover Ratio
$629	1.25%	82%

COLUMBIA U.S. GOVERNMENT SECURITIES

Columbia Funds Management
1301 S.W. 5th Avenue, P. O. Box 1350
Portland, OR 97207
800-547-1707

Minimum: $1,000
Front-End Load: None
12b-1: None
Redemption Fee: None
Ticker Symbol: CUGGX

TOTAL RETURNS (%)

1987	1988	1989	1990	1991	5-year
4.1	5.3	9.6	9.3	12.7	48.2

INVESTMENT PORTFOLIO

Total Assets (mil.)	Expense Ratio	Turnover Ratio
$36	0.85%	222%

COMPOSITE U.S. GOVERNMENT SECURITIES

Murphy Favre Securities
W. 601 Riverside, Suite 900
Spokane, WA 99201
800-543-8072

Minimum: $1,000
Front-End Load: 4.00%
12b-1: 0.15%
Redemption Fee: None
Ticker Symbol: CMPGX

TOTAL RETURNS (%)

1987	1988	1989	1990	1991	5-year
2.0	7.6	13.3	9.5	14.7	56.1

INVESTMENT PORTFOLIO

Total Assets (mil.)	Expense Ratio	Turnover Ratio
$125	1.03%	65%

DELAWARE GROUP GOVERNMENT INCOME SERIES II

Delaware Distributors
10 Penn Center Plaza
Philadelphia, PA 19103
800-523-4640

Minimum: $1,000
Front-End Load: 4.75%
12b-1: 0.25%
Redemption Fee: None
Ticker Symbol: DEGGX

TOTAL RETURNS (%)

1987	1988	1989	1990	1991	5-year
3.8	6.6	11.4	8.8	15.1	54.5

INVESTMENT PORTFOLIO

Total Assets (mil.)	Expense Ratio	Turnover Ratio
$160	1.14%	127%

DELAWARE TREASURY RESERVES—INVESTORS SERIES 2

Delaware Distributors
10 Penn Center Plaza
Philadelphia, PA 19103
800-523-4640

Minimum: $1,000
Front-End Load: None
12b-1: 0.15%
Redemption Fee: None
Ticker Symbol: DTRIX

TOTAL RETURNS (%)

1987	1988	1989	1990	1991	5-year
5.3	6.9	9.1	9.2	13.0	51.6

INVESTMENT PORTFOLIO

Total Assets (mil.)	Expense Ratio	Turnover Ratio
$135	0.99%	175%

DFA FIVE-YEAR GOVERNMENT PORTFOLIO

Dimensional Fund Advisors
1299 Ocean Avenue, Suite 650
Santa Monica, CA 90401
213-395-8005

Minimum: $50,000
Front-End Load: None
12b-1: None
Redemption Fee: None
Ticker Symbol: DFFGX

TOTAL RETURNS (%)

1987	1988	1989	1990	1991	5-year
NA	6.3	9.5	10.8	14.6	NA

INVESTMENT PORTFOLIO

Total Assets (mil.)	Expense Ratio	Turnover Ratio
$57	0.30%	166%

DODGE & COX INCOME

Dodge & Cox
One Sansome Street, 35th Floor
San Francisco, CA 94104
415-434-0311

Minimum: $2,500
Front-End Load: None
12b-1: None
Redemption Fee: None
Ticker Symbol: DODIX

TOTAL RETURNS (%)

1987	1988	1989	1990	1991	5-year
NA	NA	NA	7.4	17.9	NA

INVESTMENT PORTFOLIO

Total Assets (mil.)	Expense Ratio	Turnover Ratio
$90	0.69%	13%

DREYFUS SHORT INTERMEDIATE GOVERNMENT FUND

Dreyfus Service
200 Park Avenue, 7th Floor
New York, NY 10166
800-782-6620

Minimum: $2,500
Front-End Load: None
12b-1: None
Redemption Fee: None
Ticker Symbol: DSIGX

TOTAL RETURNS (%)

1987	1988	1989	1990	1991	5-year
NA	5.6	11.3	10.0	13.5	NA

INVESTMENT PORTFOLIO

Total Assets (mil.)	Expense Ratio	Turnover Ratio
$143	0.00%	25%

EATON VANCE GOVERNMENT OBLIGATIONS TRUST

Eaton Vance
24 Federal Street, 5th Floor
Boston, MA 02110
800-225-6265

Minimum: $1,000
Front-End Load: 4.75%
12b-1: 0.21%
Redemption Fee: None
Ticker Symbol: EVGOX

TOTAL RETURNS (%)

1987	1988	1989	1990	1991	5-year
4.2	7.4	13.3	9.0	14.4	58.0

INVESTMENT PORTFOLIO

Total Assets (mil.)	Expense Ratio	Turnover Ratio
$335	2.41%	22%

ENTERPRISE GOVERNMENT SECURITIES PORTFOLIO

Enterprise Capital Management
1200 Ashwood Parkway, Suite 290
Atlanta, GA 30338
800-432-4320

Minimum: $500
Front-End Load: 4.75%
12b-1: 0.45%
Redemption Fee: None
Ticker Symbol: ENGVX

TOTAL RETURNS (%)

1987	1988	1989	1990	1991	5-year
NA	4.5	10.0	9.2	12.7	NA

INVESTMENT PORTFOLIO

Total Assets (mil.)	Expense Ratio	Turnover Ratio
$45	1.00%	70%

FEDERATED FLOATING RATE TRUST

Federated Securities
1001 Liberty Avenue
Pittsburgh, PA 15222
800-245-2423

Minimum: $25,000
Front-End Load: None
12b-1: None
Redemption Fee: None
Ticker Symbol: FFLRX

TOTAL RETURNS (%)

1987	1988	1989	1990	1991	5-year
4.8	8.6	9.4	2.0	13.9	44.6

INVESTMENT PORTFOLIO

Total Assets (mil.)	Expense Ratio	Turnover Ratio
$40	0.52%	23%

FEDERATED INTERMEDIATE GOVERNMENT TRUST

Federated Securities
1001 Liberty Avenue
Pittsburgh, PA 15222
800-245-2423

Minimum: $25,000
Front-End Load: None
12b-1: None
Redemption Fee: None
Ticker Symbol: FIGTX

TOTAL RETURNS (%)

1987	1988	1989	1990	1991	5-year
3.9	5.3	12.1	9.4	13.5	52.1

INVESTMENT PORTFOLIO

Total Assets (mil.)	Expense Ratio	Turnover Ratio
$771	0.51%	60%

FEDERATED SHORT INTERMEDIATE GOVERNMENT TRUST

Federated Securities
1001 Liberty Avenue
Pittsburgh, PA 15222
800-245-2423

Minimum: $25,000
Front-End Load: None
12b-1: None
Redemption Fee: None
Ticker Symbol: FSGVX

TOTAL RETURNS (%)

1987	1988	1989	1990	1991	5-year
5.3	5.7	10.3	9.3	10.4	48.1

INVESTMENT PORTFOLIO

Total Assets (mil.)	Expense Ratio	Turnover Ratio
$1,172	0.48%	96%

FEDERATED U.S. GOVERNMENT

Federated Securities
1001 Liberty Avenue
Pittsburgh, PA 15222
800-245-2423

Minimum: $25,000
Front-End Load: None
12b-1: None
Redemption Fee: None
Ticker Symbol: FEUGX

TOTAL RETURNS (%)

1987	1988	1989	1990	1991	5-year
-1.8	7.3	15.9	6.6	15.7	50.5

INVESTMENT PORTFOLIO

Total Assets (mil.)	Expense Ratio	Turnover Ratio
$30	0.78%	170%

FIDELITY CORPORATE TRUST ADJUSTABLE RATE PREFERRED

Fidelity Distributors Corporation
82 Devonshire Street, Mail Zone L7b
Boston, MA 02109
800-544-6666

Minimum: $50,000
Front-End Load: None
12b-1: None
Redemption Fee: None
Ticker Symbol: FCPTX

TOTAL RETURNS (%)

1987	1988	1989	1990	1991	5-year
6.8	-0.7	4.4	-5.3	29.7	35.9

INVESTMENT PORTFOLIO

Total Assets (mil.)	Expense Ratio	Turnover Ratio
$18	1.10%	14%

FIDELITY GOVERNMENT SECURITIES

Fidelity Distributors Corporation
82 Devonshire Street, Mail Zone L7b
Boston, MA 02109
800-544-8888

Minimum: $2,500
Front-End Load: None
12b-1: None
Redemption Fee: None
Ticker Symbol: FGOVX

TOTAL RETURNS (%)

1987	1988	1989	1990	1991	5-year
1.1	6.4	12.6	9.5	16.0	53.8

INVESTMENT PORTFOLIO

Total Assets (mil.)	Expense Ratio	Turnover Ratio
$507	0.66%	302%

FINANCIAL BOND SHARES U.S. GOVERNMENT PORTFOLIO

INVESCO Funds Group
P.O. Box 2040
Denver, CO 80201
800-525-8085

Minimum: $250
Front-End Load: None
12b-1: 0.25%
Redemption Fee: None
Ticker Symbol: FBDGX

TOTAL RETURNS (%)

1987	1988	1989	1990	1991	5-year
-5.1	6.3	12.4	7.3	15.5	40.6

INVESTMENT PORTFOLIO

Total Assets (mil.)	Expense Ratio	Turnover Ratio
$26	1.07%	38%

FIRST INVESTORS GOVERNMENT

First Investors Management
10 Woodbridge Center Drive
Woodbridge, NJ 07095
800-423-4026

Minimum: $1,000
Front-End Load: 6.90%
12b-1: 0.30%
Redemption Fee: None
Ticker Symbol: FIGVX

TOTAL RETURNS (%)

1987	1988	1989	1990	1991	5-year
-0.9%	8.7	12.0	9.3	15.7	52.7

INVESTMENT PORTFOLIO

Total Assets (mil.)	Expense Ratio	Turnover Ratio
$308	1.28%	94%

FOUNDERS GOVERNMENT SECURITIES

Founders Asset Management
2930 East Third Avenue
Denver, CO 80206
800-525-2440

Minimum: $1,000
Front-End Load: None
12b-1: None
Redemption Fee: None
Ticker Symbol: FGVSX

TOTAL RETURNS (%)

1987	1988	1989	1990	1991	5-year
NA	NA	13.3	4.4	14.9	NA

INVESTMENT PORTFOLIO

Total Assets (mil.)	Expense Ratio	Turnover Ratio
$17	1.03%	103%

FRANKLIN ADJUSTABLE U.S. GOVERNMENT SECURITIES

Franklin Distributors
777 Mariners Island Blvd., 6th Floor
San Mateo, CA 94404
800-342-5236

Minimum: $100
Front-End Load: 4.00%
12b-1: 0.25%
Redemption Fee: None
Ticker Symbol: FISAX

TOTAL RETURNS (%)

1987	1988	1989	1990	1991	5-year
NA	6.4	10.3	9.5	8.7	NA

INVESTMENT PORTFOLIO

Total Assets (mil.)	Expense Ratio	Turnover Ratio
$3,556	0.30%	97%

FUND FOR U.S. GOVERNMENT SECURITIES

Federated Securities
1001 Liberty Avenue
Pittsburgh, PA 15222
800-356-2805

Minimum: $500
Front-End Load: 4.50%
12b-1: None
Redemption Fee: 0.50%
Ticker Symbol: FUSGX

TOTAL RETURNS (%)

1987	1988	1989	1990	1991	5-year
5.4	7.4	13.5	9.7	13.4	59.8

INVESTMENT PORTFOLIO

Total Assets (mil.)	Expense Ratio	Turnover Ratio
$1,308	0.97%	27%

GIT INCOME TRUST GOVERNMENT PORTFOLIO

Bankers Finance Investment Management
1655 Fort Myer Drive
Arlington, VA 22209
800-336-3063

Minimum: $2,500
Front-End Load: None
12b-1: None
Redemption Fee: None
Ticker Symbol: GTTAX

TOTAL RETURNS (%)

1987	1988	1989	1990	1991	5-year
-1.0	7.1	11.1	7.1	13.9	43.7

INVESTMENT PORTFOLIO

Total Assets (mil.)	Expense Ratio	Turnover Ratio
$7	1.65%	116%

GOVERNMENT INCOME SECURITIES

Federated Securities
1001 Liberty Avenue
Pittsburgh, PA 15222
800-245-4770

Minimum: $1,500
Front-End Load: None
12b-1: None
Redemption Fee: 0.75%
Ticker Symbol: FGOIX

TOTAL RETURNS (%)

1987	1988	1989	1990	1991	5-year
4.1	7.3	13.6	9.5	13.1	57.2

INVESTMENT PORTFOLIO

Total Assets (mil.)	Expense Ratio	Turnover Ratio
$1,910	0.90%	37%

GRADISON GOVERNMENT INCOME

Gradison and Company
580 Walnut Street
Cincinnati, OH 45202
800-869-5999

Minimum: $1,000
Front-End Load: 2.00%
12b-1: 0.25%
Redemption Fee: None
Ticker Symbol: GGIFX

TOTAL RETURNS (%)

1987	1988	1989	1990	1991	5-year
NA	7.1	12.7	8.8	14.2	NA

INVESTMENT PORTFOLIO

Total Assets (mil.)	Expense Ratio	Turnover Ratio
$143	1.25%	90%

HEARTLAND U.S. GOVERNMENT FUND

Heartland Group
790 N. Milwaukee Street
Milwaukee, WI 53202
800-432-7856

Minimum: $1,000
Front-End Load: 4.50%
12b-1: 0.30%
Redemption Fee: None
Ticker Symbol: HRUSX

TOTAL RETURNS (%)

1987	1988	1989	1990	1991	5-year
NA	6.4	11.3	10.0	17.0	NA

INVESTMENT PORTFOLIO

Total Assets (mil.)	Expense Ratio	Turnover Ratio
$28	1.50%	127%

IDS FEDERAL INCOME

IDS Financial Services
1000 Roanoke Building
Minneapolis, MN 55402
800-328-8300

Minimum: $2,000
Front-End Load: 5.00%
12b-1: 0.05%
Redemption Fee: None
Ticker Symbol: IFINX

TOTAL RETURNS (%)

1987	1988	1989	1990	1991	5-year
2.4	8.9	10.6	10.0	11.0	50.6

INVESTMENT PORTFOLIO

Total Assets (mil.)	Expense Ratio	Turnover Ratio
$507	0.82%	104%

KEMPER INVESTMENT PORTFOLIOS GOVERNMENT PORTFOLIO

Kemper Financial Services
120 South LaSalle Street, 20th Floor
Chicago, IL 60603
800-621-1048

Minimum: $250
Front-End Load: None
12b-1: 1.25%
Redemption Fee: 3.00%
Ticker Symbol: INPGX

TOTAL RETURNS (%)

1987	1988	1989	1990	1991	5-year
1.8	4.5	11.4	7.1	17.0	48.5

INVESTMENT PORTFOLIO

Total Assets (mil.)	Expense Ratio	Turnover Ratio
$5,190	1.99%	206%

KEYSTONE AMERICA GOVERNMENT SECURITIES

Keystone Distributors
99 High Street, 29th Floor
Boston, MA 02110
800-633-4900

Minimum: $1,000
Front-End Load: 2.00%
12b-1: 0.71%
Redemption Fee: 2.00%
Ticker Symbol: KAGSX

TOTAL RETURNS (%)

1987	1988	1989	1990	1991	5-year
NA	4.2	12.4	8.4	14.7	NA

INVESTMENT PORTFOLIO

Total Assets (mil.)	Expense Ratio	Turnover Ratio
$58	1.91%	58%

MAINSTAY GOVERNMENT PLUS

NYLIFE Securities
51 Madison Avenue, Room 117
New York, NY 10010
800-522-4202

Minimum: $500
Front-End Load: None
12b-1: 1.00%
Redemption Fee: 5.00%
Ticker Symbol: MCSGX

TOTAL RETURNS (%)

1987	1988	1989	1990	1991	5-year
2.6	6.4	12.2	6.9	13.4	48.5

INVESTMENT PORTFOLIO

Total Assets (mil.)	Expense Ratio	Turnover Ratio
$683	1.80%	228%

MERRILL LYNCH FEDERAL SECURITIES TRUST A

Merrill Lynch Funds Distributor
P.O. Box 9011
Princeton, NJ 08543
800-637-3863

Minimum: $1,000
Front-End Load: 4.00%
12b-1: 0.18%
Redemption Fee: None
Ticker Symbol: MLFSX

TOTAL RETURNS (%)

1987	1988	1989	1990	1991	5-year
2.6	7.7	13.6	10.4	13.6	57.5

INVESTMENT PORTFOLIO

Total Assets (mil.)	Expense Ratio	Turnover Ratio
$2,234	0.77%	325%

MERRIMAN GOVERNMENT FUND

Merriman Investment Management
1200 Westlake Avenue North, #507
Seattle, WA 98109
800-423-4893

Minimum: $1,000
Front-End Load: None
12b-1: None
Redemption Fee: None
Ticker Symbol: MTGVX

TOTAL RETURNS (%)

1987	1988	1989	1990	1991	5-year
NA	NA	8.5	6.1	13.3	NA

INVESTMENT PORTFOLIO

Total Assets (mil.)	Expense Ratio	Turnover Ratio
$11	1.73%	234%

MFS GOVERNMENT SECURITIES TRUST

Massachusetts Financial Services
500 Boylston Street
Boston, MA 02116
800-225-2606

Minimum: $1,000
Front-End Load: 4.75%
12b-1: 0.35%
Redemption Fee: None
Ticker Symbol: MFGSX

TOTAL RETURNS (%)

1987	1988	1989	1990	1991	5-year
0.9	6.4	12.0	7.8	14.2	48.1

INVESTMENT PORTFOLIO

Total Assets (mil.)	Expense Ratio	Turnover Ratio
$350	1.28%	95%

MFS LIFETIME GOVERNMENT INCOME PLUS TRUST

Massachusetts Financial Services
500 Boylston Street
Boston, MA 02116
800-225-2606

Minimum: $1,000
Front-End Load: None
12b-1: 1.00%
Redemption Fee: 6.00%
Ticker Symbol: LGIPX

TOTAL RETURNS (%)

1987	1988	1989	1990	1991	5-year
-5.2	5.7	11.7	4.4	11.8	30.6

INVESTMENT PORTFOLIO

Total Assets (mil.)	Expense Ratio	Turnover Ratio
$2,868	1.92%	446%

MIDWEST INCOME TRUST—INTERMEDIATE TERM GOVERNMENT

Midwest Group of Funds
312 Walnut Street, 21st Floor
Cincinnati, OH 45202
800-543-8721

Minimum: $1,000
Front-End Load: 1.00%
12b-1: 0.16%
Redemption Fee: None
Ticker Symbol: MDITX

TOTAL RETURNS (%)

1987	1988	1989	1990	1991	5-year
2.2	5.0	10.6	7.0	15.1	46.1

INVESTMENT PORTFOLIO

Total Assets (mil.)	Expense Ratio	Turnover Ratio
$38	1.02%	92%

MUTUAL OF OMAHA AMERICA

Mutual of Omaha Fund Management
10235 Regency Circle
Omaha, NE 68114
800-228-9596

Minimum: $1,000
Front-End Load: 4.75%
12b-1: 0.25%
Redemption Fee: None
Ticker Symbol: MOMAX

TOTAL RETURNS (%)

1987	1988	1989	1990	1991	5-year
0.6	8.4	14.3	7.8	15.1	54.6

INVESTMENT PORTFOLIO

Total Assets (mil.)	Expense Ratio	Turnover Ratio
$61	1.15%	52%

NEW ENGLAND GOVERNMENT SECURITIES

TNE Investment Services
399 Boylston Street, 8th Floor
Boston, MA 02116
800-343-7104

Minimum: $1,000
Front-End Load: 4.50%
12b-1: 0.25%
Redemption Fee: None
Ticker Symbol: NELSX

TOTAL RETURNS (%)

1987	1988	1989	1990	1991	5-year
0.2	6.4	12.6	5.6	14.9	45.7

INVESTMENT PORTFOLIO

Total Assets (mil.)	Expense Ratio	Turnover Ratio
$170	1.21%	737%

OPPENHEIMER U.S. GOVERNMENT TRUST

Oppenheimer Fund Management
P.O. Box 300
Denver, CO 80201
800-255-2755

Minimum: $1,000
Front-End Load: 4.75%
12b-1: 0.22%
Redemption Fee: None
Ticker Symbol: OUSGX

TOTAL RETURNS (%)

1987	1988	1989	1990	1991	5-year
3.5	6.8	11.9	7.7	15.2	53.6

INVESTMENT PORTFOLIO

Total Assets (mil.)	Expense Ratio	Turnover Ratio
$385	1.19%	134%

PIPER JAFFRAY GOVERNMENT INCOME

Piper Jaffray & Hopwood
222 South 9th Street
Minneapolis, MN 55402
800-333-6000

Minimum: $250
Front-End Load: 4.00%
12b-1: 0.33%
Redemption Fee: None
Ticker Symbol: PJGIX

TOTAL RETURNS (%)

1987	1988	1989	1990	1991	5-year
NA	7.1	9.9	8.7	18.9	NA

INVESTMENT PORTFOLIO

Total Assets (mil.)	Expense Ratio	Turnover Ratio
$78	1.13%	202%

PUTNAM ADJUSTABLE RATE U.S. GOVERNMENT

Putnam Financial Services
One Post Office Square, 12th Floor
Boston, MA 02109
800-634-1590

Minimum: $500
Front-End Load: 4.75%
12b-1: 0.25%
Redemption Fee: None
Ticker Symbol: PARUX

TOTAL RETURNS (%)

1987	1988	1989	1990	1991	5-year
NA	NA	10.1	8.6	7.0	NA

INVESTMENT PORTFOLIO

Total Assets (mil.)	Expense Ratio	Turnover Ratio
$234	1.26%	247%

PUTNAM HIGH INCOME GOVERNMENT TRUST

Putnam Financial Services
One Post Office Square, 12th Floor
Boston, MA 02109
800-634-1590

Minimum: $500
Front-End Load: 4.75%
12b-1: 0.24%
Redemption Fee: None
Ticker Symbol: PIGTX

TOTAL RETURNS (%)

1987	1988	1989	1990	1991	5-year
-1.2	5.1	13.6	7.4	9.2	38.5

INVESTMENT PORTFOLIO

Total Assets (mil.)	Expense Ratio	Turnover Ratio
$4,913	0.95%	255%

PUTNAM U.S. GOVERNMENT INCOME TRUST

Putnam Financial Services
One Post Office Square, 12th Floor
Boston, MA 02109
800-634-1590

Minimum: $500
Front-End Load: 4.75%
12b-1: 0.25%
Redemption Fee: None
Ticker Symbol: PGSIX

TOTAL RETURNS (%)

1987	1988	1989	1990	1991	5-year
4.6	7.5	12.8	9.9	11.9	56.0

INVESTMENT PORTFOLIO

Total Assets (mil.)	Expense Ratio	Turnover Ratio
$2,863	0.75%	63%

RIGHTIME GOVERNMENT SECURITIES

Rightime Family of Funds
218 Glenside Avenue, Suite 3000
Wyncote, PA 19095
800-242-1421

Minimum: $2,000
Front-End Load: 4.75%
12b-1: 0.50%
Redemption Fee: None
Ticker Symbol: RTGSX

TOTAL RETURNS (%)

1987	1988	1989	1990	1991	5-year
NA	10.1	14.3	-3.6	4.4	NA

INVESTMENT PORTFOLIO

Total Assets (mil.)	Expense Ratio	Turnover Ratio
$41	1.85%	420%

SAFECO U.S. GOVERNMENT SECURITIES

SAFECO Securities
4333 Brooklyn Avenue N.E.
Seattle, WA 98185
800-426-6730

Minimum: $1,000
Front-End Load: None
12b-1: None
Redemption Fee: None
Ticker Symbol: SFUSX

TOTAL RETURNS (%)

1987	1988	1989	1990	1991	5-year
0.9	7.8	12.9	8.7	14.8	53.3

INVESTMENT PORTFOLIO

Total Assets (mil.)	Expense Ratio	Turnover Ratio
$45	0.99%	90%

SCUDDER TARGET ZERO COUPON BOND 1995

Scudder Stevens & Clark
175 Federal Street, 12th Floor
Boston, MA 02110
800-225-2470

Minimum: $1,000
Front-End Load: None
12b-1: None
Redemption Fee: None
Ticker Symbol: SGZFX

TOTAL RETURNS (%)

1987	1988	1989	1990	1991	5-year
-3.8	7.9	19.4	7.3	16.9	55.4

INVESTMENT PORTFOLIO

Total Assets (mil.)	Expense Ratio	Turnover Ratio
$13	1.00%	52%

SCUDDER TARGET ZERO COUPON BOND 2000

Scudder Stevens & Clark
175 Federal Street, 12th Floor
Boston, MA 02110
800-225-2470

Minimum: $1,000
Front-End Load: None
12b-1: None
Redemption Fee: None
Ticker Symbol: SGZTX

TOTAL RETURNS (%)

1987	1988	1989	1990	1991	5-year
-8.0	11.7	20.4	4.6	20.0	55.3

INVESTMENT PORTFOLIO

Total Assets (mil.)	Expense Ratio	Turnover Ratio
$33	1.00%	99%

SECURITY INCOME FUND GOVERNMENT SERIES

Security Distributors
700 Harrison
Topeka, KS 66636
800-888-2461

Minimum: $100
Front-End Load: 4.75%
12b-1: 0.25%
Redemption Fee: None
Ticker Symbol: SIUSX

TOTAL RETURNS (%)

1987	1988	1989	1990	1991	5-year
3.7	6.2	11.8	9.8	13.8	53.9

INVESTMENT PORTFOLIO

Total Assets (mil.)	Expense Ratio	Turnover Ratio
$7	1.11%	22%

SELECTED U.S. GOVERNMENT INCOME

Selected Financial Services
1331 Euclid Avenue
Cleveland, OH 44115
800-553-5533

Minimum: $1,000
Front-End Load: None
12b-1: 0.50%
Redemption Fee: None
Ticker Symbol: SSGTX

TOTAL RETURNS (%)

1987	1988	1989	1990	1991	5-year
NA	3.0	9.2	8.5	13.6	NA

INVESTMENT PORTFOLIO

Total Assets (mil.)	Expense Ratio	Turnover Ratio
$22	1.44%	29%

SELIGMAN U.S. GOVERNMENT

Seligman Financial Services
130 Liberty Street, 22nd Floor
New York, NY 10006
800-221-2450

Minimum: $1,000
Front-End Load: 4.75%
12b-1: 0.25%
Redemption Fee: None
Ticker Symbol: SUSGX

TOTAL RETURNS (%)

1987	1988	1989	1990	1991	5-year
-2.8	7.8	9.3	6.4	14.1	39.0

INVESTMENT PORTFOLIO

Total Assets (mil.)	Expense Ratio	Turnover Ratio
$69	1.19%	300%

SENTINEL GOVERNMENT SECURITIES

Equity Securities
National Life Drive
Montpelier, VT 05604
800-282-3863

Minimum: $250
Front-End Load: 5.25%
12b-1: None
Redemption Fee: None
Ticker Symbol: SEGSX

TOTAL RETURNS (%)

1987	1988	1989	1990	1991	5-year
1.8	7.3	12.6	9.2	15.1	54.6

INVESTMENT PORTFOLIO

Total Assets (mil.)	Expense Ratio	Turnover Ratio
$46	0.78%	22%

SHEARSON INTERMEDIATE GOVERNMENT

Shearson Lehman Brothers
Two World Trade Center
New York, NY 10048
212-464-8068

Minimum: $500
Front-End Load: None
12b-1: 0.75%
Redemption Fee: 5.00%
Ticker Symbol: SINGX

TOTAL RETURNS (%)

1987	1988	1989	1990	1991	5-year
1.9	5.0	9.5	9.4	14.7	47.0

INVESTMENT PORTFOLIO

Total Assets (mil.)	Expense Ratio	Turnover Ratio
$37	1.81%	225%

SHEARSON MANAGED GOVERNMENTS

Shearson Lehman Brothers
Two World Trade Center
New York, NY 10048
212-464-8068

Minimum: $500
Front-End Load: 5.00%
12b-1: None
Redemption Fee: None
Ticker Symbol: SHMGX

TOTAL RETURNS (%)

1987	1988	1989	1990	1991	5-year
1.9	6.7	10.1	10.1	16.2	53.2

INVESTMENT PORTFOLIO

Total Assets (mil.)	Expense Ratio	Turnover Ratio
$483	0.81%	163%

SIT NEW BEGINNING U.S. GOVERNMENT SECURITIES

Sit Investment Associates
4600 Norwest Center, 90 S. 7th Street
Minneapolis, MN 55402
800-332-5580

Minimum: $2,000
Front-End Load: None
12b-1: None
Redemption Fee: None
Ticker Symbol: SNGVX

TOTAL RETURNS (%)

1987	1988	1989	1990	1991	5-year
NA	7.9	11.0	10.9	12.8	NA

INVESTMENT PORTFOLIO

Total Assets (mil.)	Expense Ratio	Turnover Ratio
$34	0.90%	118%

STEIN ROE GOVERNMENT INCOME

Stein Roe & Farnham
P.O. Box 1162
Chicago, IL 60690
800-338-2550

Minimum: $1,000
Front-End Load: None
12b-1: None
Redemption Fee: None
Ticker Symbol: SRGPX

TOTAL RETURNS (%)

1987	1988	1989	1990	1991	5-year
1.6	6.9	13.3	8.4	15.0	53.5

INVESTMENT PORTFOLIO

Total Assets (mil.)	Expense Ratio	Turnover Ratio
$52	1.00%	181%

STRONG GOVERNMENT SECURITIES

Strong/Corneliuson Capital Management
100 Heritage Reserve
Menomonee Falls, WI 53051
800-368-3863

Minimum: $1,000
Front-End Load: None
12b-1: None
Redemption Fee: None
Ticker Symbol: STVSX

TOTAL RETURNS (%)

1987	1988	1989	1990	1991	5-year
3.4	10.5	9.9	8.7	16.6	59.2

INVESTMENT PORTFOLIO

Total Assets (mil.)	Expense Ratio	Turnover Ratio
$49	1.30%	254%

SUN AMERICA INCOME PORTFOLIO GOVERNMENT INCOME

Sun America Capital Services
10 Union Square East, 2nd Floor
New York, NY 10003
800-821-5100

Minimum: $500
Front-End Load: 4.75%
12b-1: 0.35%
Redemption Fee: None
Ticker Symbol: SIGSX

TOTAL RETURNS (%)

1987	1988	1989	1990	1991	5-year
NA	8.3	8.0	5.5	13.6	NA

INVESTMENT PORTFOLIO

Total Assets (mil.)	Expense Ratio	Turnover Ratio
$64	1.43%	41%

SUN AMERICA U.S. GOVERNMENT SECURITIES

Sun America Capital Services
10 Union Square East, 2nd Floor
New York, NY 10003
800-821-5100

Minimum: $2,500
Front-End Load: None
12b-1: 0.96%
Redemption Fee: 5.00%
Ticker Symbol: ESUSX

TOTAL RETURNS (%)

1987	1988	1989	1990	1991	5-year
3.4	7.7	8.3	9.0	9.9	44.3

INVESTMENT PORTFOLIO

Total Assets (mil.)	Expense Ratio	Turnover Ratio
$744	1.98%	31%

THOMSON U.S. GOVERNMENT B

Thomson Securities
1 Station Place
Stamford, CT 06902
800-628-1237

Minimum: $1,000
Front-End Load: None
12b-1: 1.00%
Redemption Fee: 1.00%
Ticker Symbol: TUSBX

TOTAL RETURNS (%)

1987	1988	1989	1990	1991	5-year
-0.1	6.1	12.3	6.5	15.9	46.8

INVESTMENT PORTFOLIO

Total Assets (mil.)	Expense Ratio	Turnover Ratio
$420	1.70%	99%

TRANSAMERICA GOVERNMENT INCOME TRUST

TransAmerica Distributors
1000 Louisiana, Suite 6000
Houston, TX 77002
800-343-6840

Minimum: $250,000
Front-End Load: 2.50%
12b-1: 0.25%
Redemption Fee: None
Ticker Symbol: TAIGX

TOTAL RETURNS (%)

1987	1988	1989	1990	1991	5-year
1.2	6.7	10.8	8.2	14.4	48.1

INVESTMENT PORTFOLIO

Total Assets (mil.)	Expense Ratio	Turnover Ratio
$112	1.13%	154%

TRANSAMERICA GOVERNMENT SECURITIES TRUST

TransAmerica Distributors
1000 Louisiana, Suite 6000
Houston, TX 77002
800-343-6840

Minimum: $1,000
Front-End Load: 4.75%
12b-1: 0.23%
Redemption Fee: None
Ticker Symbol: TAGSX

TOTAL RETURNS (%)

1987	1988	1989	1990	1991	5-year
2.1	6.2	10.2	9.1	16.7	52.1

INVESTMENT PORTFOLIO

Total Assets (mil.)	Expense Ratio	Turnover Ratio
$740	1.11%	117%

TRANSAMERICA SPECIAL GOVERNMENT INCOME

TransAmerica Distributors
1000 Louisiana, Suite 6000
Houston, TX 77002
800-343-6840

Minimum: $1,000
Front-End Load: None
12b-1: 0.90%
Redemption Fee: 6.00%
Ticker Symbol: TSGIX

TOTAL RETURNS (%)

1987	1988	1989	1990	1991	5-year
NA	NA	10.6	8.5	14.1	NA

INVESTMENT PORTFOLIO

Total Assets (mil.)	Expense Ratio	Turnover Ratio
$140	0.98%	41%

TWENTIETH CENTURY U.S. GOVERNMENTS

Twentieth Century Investors
4500 Main Street, P.O. Box 418210
Kansas City, MO 64111
800-345-2021

Minimum: None
Front-End Load: None
12b-1: None
Redemption Fee: None
Ticker Symbol: TWUSX

TOTAL RETURNS (%)

1987	1988	1989	1990	1991	5-year
3.8	5.6	10.0	7.5	11.6	44.8

INVESTMENT PORTFOLIO

Total Assets (mil.)	Expense Ratio	Turnover Ratio
$544	1.00%	620%

VALUE LINE U.S. GOVERNMENT SECURITIES

Value Line Securities
711 Third Avenue
New York, NY 10017
800-223-0818

Minimum: $1,000
Front-End Load: None
12b-1: None
Redemption Fee: None
Ticker Symbol: VALBX

TOTAL RETURNS (%)

1987	1988	1989	1990	1991	5-year
3.5	7.9	12.0	10.3	16.4	60.6

INVESTMENT PORTFOLIO

Total Assets (mil.)	Expense Ratio	Turnover Ratio
$364	0.67%	59%

VANGUARD FIXED INCOME LONG TERM U.S. TREASURIES

Vanguard Group
Vanguard Financial Center
Valley Forge, PA 19482
800-662-7447

Minimum: $3,000
Front-End Load: None
12b-1: None
Redemption Fee: None
Ticker Symbol: VUSTX

TOTAL RETURNS (%)

1987	1988	1989	1990	1991	5-year
-2.9	9.2	17.9	5.8	17.4	55.3

INVESTMENT PORTFOLIO

Total Assets (mil.)	Expense Ratio	Turnover Ratio
$843	0.30%	147%

VANGUARD FIXED INCOME SHORT TERM FEDERAL

Vanguard Group
Vanguard Financial Center
Valley Forge, PA 19482
800-662-7447

Minimum: $3,000
Front-End Load: None
12b-1: None
Redemption Fee: None
Ticker Symbol: VSGBX

TOTAL RETURNS (%)

1987	1988	1989	1990	1991	5-year
NA	5.7	11.3	9.3	12.2	NA

INVESTMENT PORTFOLIO

Total Assets (mil.)	Expense Ratio	Turnover Ratio
$1,051	0.30%	141%

WPG GOVERNMENT SECURITIES

Weiss Peck & Greer
One New York Plaza
New York, NY 10004
800-223-3332

Minimum: $2,500
Front-End Load: None
12b-1: None
Redemption Fee: None
Ticker Symbol: WPGVX

TOTAL RETURNS (%)

1987	1988	1989	1990	1991	5-year
2.3	7.7	14.0	8.9	14.0	56.0

INVESTMENT PORTFOLIO

Total Assets (mil.)	Expense Ratio	Turnover Ratio
$200	0.75%	184%

ZWEIG SERIES TRUST GOVERNMENT SECURITIES

Zweig/Glaser Advisers
5 Hanover Square, 17th Floor
New York, NY 10004
800-272-2700

Minimum: $1,000
Front-End Load: 4.75%
12b-1: 0.30%
Redemption Fee: None
Ticker Symbol: ZGOVX

TOTAL RETURNS (%)

1987	1988	1989	1990	1991	5-year
-2.0	4.6	12.5	6.1	14.4	39.9

INVESTMENT PORTFOLIO

Total Assets (mil.)	Expense Ratio	Turnover Ratio
$82	1.44%	263%

PART 12

Tax-Exempt Bond Funds

Tax-exempt, or municipal, bonds are debt obligations of local and state governments. The interest on these bonds is exempt from federal taxes and from state and local taxes in the states where the bonds are issued. While called "tax-exempt," municipal bond investors generally must pay state and local taxes on interest income earned on bonds issued outside the investor's state of residence. In addition, capital gains income earned on municipal bond investments is not exempt from federal taxation.

Municipal bonds are classified as general obligation bonds (interest and principal repayments are met by the taxing power of municipalities and states) and revenue bonds (ability to pay principal and interest is a function of the income earned by facilities such as toll roads, hospitals, etc.). Single-state municipal bond funds are similar to other municipal bond funds except that their portfolios contain the issues of only one state. Residents of that state receive a so-called "triple tax advantage" since interest income is exempt from federal, state and local taxation.

The Tax Reform Act of 1976 allowed open-end funds to pass through tax-free income to shareholders. Prior to that time, only unit investment trusts were granted the tax-free pass-through. As a result, the municipal bond fund was born that year, with the organization of the Kemper Municipal Bond Fund in April. Since then, hundreds of tax-exempt bond funds have come to market. Some invest in only high-quality issues while others seek a higher current yield by investing in bonds of marginal credit quality (generally revenue bonds). In addition, investors can find municipal bond funds whose managers target their average maturities to specific periods, such as short-term, intermediate-term and long-term. With the expansion of tax rates levied by states and cities, municipal bonds issued outside an investor's state of residence have lost some of their tax-advantage appeal. As a result, a number of fund companies greatly expanded their offerings of single-state municipal bond funds. This has been one of the fastest growing areas in the bond fund category in recent years.

Like taxable bond funds, municipal bond funds offer shareholders several advantages. First, they offer a high degree of liquidity. Most municipal bonds are traded infrequently; however, municipal bond fund shareholders can purchase or sell bond fund shares daily. Second, because of the relatively low level of trading activity, municipal bonds possess very large bid-ask spreads. Thus, when purchasing and selling municipal bonds directly, investors trading in less than $100,000 lots face trading costs that can easily erode an entire year's interest income. Finally, bond fund investors can obtain a wide degree of portfolio diversification with the investment of a modest amount of money.

Summary Financial Statistics (medians)

Number of Funds	1991 Return	Five-Year Return	Turnover Ratio	Expense Ratio
180	11.4%	41.9%	31%	0.75%

BEST TAX-EXEMPT FUNDS FOR 1991

Fund	Percent Returns 1991	3-Year	5-Year
Vanguard Municipal Bond High Yield	14.8%	35.1%	51.2%
TransAmerica Tax-Free Bond	14.8	NA	NA
Dreyfus General Municipal Bond Fund	14.7	37.6	46.4
Putnam New York Tax Exempt Income Fund	14.3	29.9	47.2
Shearson Managed Municipals	14.2	32.4	47.5
SAFECO Municipal Bond Fund	13.8	33.7	52.4
Nuveen Tax-Free Bond Fund New York Portfolio	13.8	31.1	41.9
Lord Abbett Tax Free Income—New York Series	13.7	32.1	49.2
Bull & Bear Tax Free Income Fund	13.6	28.5	42.2
Vanguard Municipal Bond Long Term	13.5	35.2	50.1
Eaton Vance Municipal Bond Fund	13.5	34.3	51.7
Nuveen Insured Tax Free Bond New York Portfolio	13.4	31.1	39.4
Franklin New York Tax-Free Income Fund	13.3	29.3	41.6
CIGNA Funds Group-Municipal Bond Fund	13.3	30.9	44.2
Strong Municipal Bond	13.3	26.9	34.3
Shearson New York Municipals	13.0	29.9	43.6
Franklin Federal Tax-Free Income Fund	12.9	29.1	42.2
DMC Tax Free Income Trust Pennsylvania	12.9	29.7	44.5
Vanguard New York Insured Tax Free Fund	12.8	32.3	43.0
Nuveen Insured Tax Free Bond National Portfolio	12.8	33.1	50.9
Merrill Lynch New York Municipal Bond Fund B	12.8	28.1	39.9
MFS Managed Municipal Bond Trust	12.8	31.5	49.5
Kemper Municipal Bond Fund	12.8	34.0	49.9
Putnam Tax Exempt Income Fund	12.7	31.1	46.5
Lord Abbett California Tax-Free Income Fund	12.7	32.8	46.0

AARP INSURED TAX FREE GENERAL BOND FUND

Scudder Stevens & Clark
175 Federal Street, 12th Floor
Boston, MA 02110
800-253-2277

Minimum: $500
Front-End Load: None
12b-1: None
Redemption Fee: None
Ticker Symbol: AITGX

TOTAL RETURNS (%)

1987	1988	1989	1990	1991	5-year
-0.9	12.2	10.8	6.3	12.3	47.0

INVESTMENT PORTFOLIO

Total Assets (mil.)	Expense Ratio	Turnover Ratio
$1,111	0.85%	48%

AEGON USA TAX EXEMPT PORTFOLIO

MidAmerica Management
4333 Edgewood Road N.E.
Cedar Rapids, IA 52499
800-538-5111

Minimum: $1,000
Front-End Load: 4.75%
12b-1: None
Redemption Fee: None
Ticker Symbol: AEGTX

TOTAL RETURNS (%)

1987	1988	1989	1990	1991	5-year
-1.9	11.4	10.6	5.6	10.2	40.6

INVESTMENT PORTFOLIO

Total Assets (mil.)	Expense Ratio	Turnover Ratio
$28	0.75%	67%

ALLIANCE MUNICIPAL INCOME FUND—INSURED NATIONAL

Alliance Funds Distributor
500 Plaza Drive
Secaucus, NJ 07094
800-247-4154

Minimum: $250
Front-End Load: 4.50%
12b-1: 0.28%
Redemption Fee: None
Ticker Symbol: CABTX

TOTAL RETURNS (%)

1987	1988	1989	1990	1991	5-year
-0.6	12.8	9.8	6.9	12.2	47.6

INVESTMENT PORTFOLIO

Total Assets (mil.)	Expense Ratio	Turnover Ratio
$130	0.93%	69%

ALLIANCE MUNICIPAL INCOME NATIONAL PORTFOLIO

Alliance Funds Distributor
500 Plaza Drive
Secaucus, NJ 07094
800-247-4154

Minimum: $250
Front-End Load: 4.50%
12b-1: 0.29%
Redemption Fee: None
Ticker Symbol: ALTHX

TOTAL RETURNS (%)

1987	1988	1989	1990	1991	5-year
-0.6	14.8	10.1	7.4	12.4	51.8

INVESTMENT PORTFOLIO

Total Assets (mil.)	Expense Ratio	Turnover Ratio
$206	0.65%	105%

AMERICAN CAPITAL MUNICIPAL BOND FUND

American Capital Marketing
P.O. Box 3528
Houston, TX 77253
800-421-5666

Minimum: $500
Front-End Load: 4.75%
12b-1: 0.16%
Redemption Fee: None
Ticker Symbol: ACMBX

TOTAL RETURNS (%)

1987	1988	1989	1990	1991	5-year
-5.7	14.0	11.0	5.5	11.9	40.8

INVESTMENT PORTFOLIO

Total Assets (mil.)	Expense Ratio	Turnover Ratio
$267	0.87%	17%

BABSON TAX FREE INCOME LONG TERM

Jones & Babson
3 Crown Center, 2440 Pershing Road
Kansas City, MO 64108
800-422-2766

Minimum: $1,000
Front-End Load: None
12b-1: None
Redemption Fee: None
Ticker Symbol: BALTX

TOTAL RETURNS (%)

1987	1988	1989	1990	1991	5-year
-1.3	11.6	8.8	6.2	12.2	42.9

INVESTMENT PORTFOLIO

Total Assets (mil.)	Expense Ratio	Turnover Ratio
$29	0.98%	116%

BENHAM CALIFORNIA TAX FREE INTERMEDIATE

Benham Group
1665 Charleston Road
Mountain View, CA 94043
800-472-3389

Minimum: $1,000
Front-End Load: None
12b-1: None
Redemption Fee: None
Ticker Symbol: BCITX

TOTAL RETURNS (%)

1987	1988	1989	1990	1991	5-year
0.8	5.9	7.9	7.0	10.4	36.1

INVESTMENT PORTFOLIO

Total Assets (mil.)	Expense Ratio	Turnover Ratio
$252	0.59%	20%

BENHAM CALIFORNIA TAX FREE LONG TERM

Benham Group
1665 Charleston Road
Mountain View, CA 94043
800-472-3389

Minimum: $1,000
Front-End Load: None
12b-1: None
Redemption Fee: None
Ticker Symbol: BCLTX

TOTAL RETURNS (%)

1987	1988	1989	1990	1991	5-year
-4.6	10.4	9.8	6.7	11.8	37.9

INVESTMENT PORTFOLIO

Total Assets (mil.)	Expense Ratio	Turnover Ratio
$255	0.58%	74%

BULL & BEAR TAX FREE INCOME FUND

Bull & Bear Group
11 Hanover Square
New York, NY 10005
800-847-4200

Minimum: $1,000
Front-End Load: None
12b-1: 0.35%
Redemption Fee: None
Ticker Symbol: BBTIX

TOTAL RETURNS (%)

1987	1988	1989	1990	1991	5-year
-0.9	11.6	8.9	3.9	13.6	42.2

INVESTMENT PORTFOLIO

Total Assets (mil.)	Expense Ratio	Turnover Ratio
$20	1.55%	172%

CIGNA FUNDS GROUP—MUNICIPAL BOND FUND

CIGNA Mutual Funds
One Financial Plaza, 16th Floor
Springfield, MA 01103
800-572-4462

Minimum: $500
Front-End Load: 5.00%
12b-1: 0.25%
Redemption Fee: None
Ticker Symbol: CGMBX

TOTAL RETURNS (%)

1987	1988	1989	1990	1991	5-year
-1.9	12.3	9.7	5.3	13.3	44.2

INVESTMENT PORTFOLIO

Total Assets (mil.)	Expense Ratio	Turnover Ratio
$265	0.92%	230%

COLONIAL TAX-EXEMPT FUND

Colonial Investment Services
One Financial Center, 14th Floor
Boston, MA 02110
800-248-2828

Minimum: $1,000
Front-End Load: 4.75%
12b-1: 0.25%
Redemption Fee: 1.00%
Ticker Symbol: COLTX

TOTAL RETURNS (%)

1987	1988	1989	1990	1991	5-year
0.5	10.4	8.1	6.4	11.7	42.5

INVESTMENT PORTFOLIO

Total Assets (mil.)	Expense Ratio	Turnover Ratio
$2,485	1.03%	10%

COLUMBIA MUNICIPAL BOND FUND

Columbia Funds Management
1301 S.W. 5th Avenue, P. O. Box 1350
Portland, OR 97207
800-547-1707

Minimum: $1,000
Front-End Load: None
12b-1: None
Redemption Fee: None
Ticker Symbol: CMBFX

TOTAL RETURNS (%)

1987	1988	1989	1990	1991	5-year
1.2	10.2	9.0	6.9	11.7	45.1

INVESTMENT PORTFOLIO

Total Assets (mil.)	Expense Ratio	Turnover Ratio
$277	0.65%	7%

COMPOSITE TAX EXEMPT BOND FUND

Murphy Favre Securities
W. 601 Riverside, Suite 900
Spokane, WA 99201
800-543-8072

Minimum: $1,000
Front-End Load: 4.00%
12b-1: 0.15%
Redemption Fee: None
Ticker Symbol: CMTEX

TOTAL RETURNS (%)

1987	1988	1989	1990	1991	5-year
1.3	10.7	8.1	6.7	11.4	43.9

INVESTMENT PORTFOLIO

Total Assets (mil.)	Expense Ratio	Turnover Ratio
$135	0.78%	115%

COUNTRY CAPITAL TAX EXEMPT BOND FUND

Country Capital Management
1711 G.E. Road, P. O. Box 2222
Bloomington, IL 61704
800-322-3838

Minimum: $100
Front-End Load: 3.00%
12b-1: None
Redemption Fee: None
Ticker Symbol: None

TOTAL RETURNS (%)

1987	1988	1989	1990	1991	5-year
0.0	10.1	8.2	6.7	10.1	39.9

INVESTMENT PORTFOLIO

Total Assets (mil.)	Expense Ratio	Turnover Ratio
$17	0.83%	6%

DELAWARE GROUP TAX FREE FUND—USA SERIES

Delaware Distributors
10 Penn Center Plaza
Philadelphia, PA 19103
800-523-4640

Minimum: $1,000
Front-End Load: 4.75%
12b-1: None
Redemption Fee: None
Ticker Symbol: DMTFX

TOTAL RETURNS (%)

1987	1988	1989	1990	1991	5-year
-1.8	14.2	10.5	3.9	12.4	44.7

INVESTMENT PORTFOLIO

Total Assets (mil.)	Expense Ratio	Turnover Ratio
$676	0.76%	14%

DELAWARE GROUP TAX FREE INSURED SERIES

Delaware Distributors
10 Penn Center Plaza
Philadelphia, PA 19103
800-523-4640

Minimum: $1,000
Front-End Load: 4.75%
12b-1: None
Redemption Fee: None
Ticker Symbol: DMFIX

TOTAL RETURNS (%)

1987	1988	1989	1990	1991	5-year
0.4	10.4	9.6	6.1	11.2	43.4

INVESTMENT PORTFOLIO

Total Assets (mil.)	Expense Ratio	Turnover Ratio
$80	0.84%	13%

DMC TAX FREE INCOME TRUST PENNSYLVANIA

Delaware Distributors
10 Penn Center Plaza
Philadelphia, PA 19103
800-523-4640

Minimum: $1,000
Front-End Load: 4.75%
12b-1: None
Redemption Fee: None
Ticker Symbol: DELIX

TOTAL RETURNS (%)

1987	1988	1989	1990	1991	5-year
-0.7	12.3	9.8	4.6	12.9	44.5

INVESTMENT PORTFOLIO

Total Assets (mil.)	Expense Ratio	Turnover Ratio
$741	0.73%	31%

DREYFUS CALIFORNIA TAX EXEMPT BOND FUND

Dreyfus Service
200 Park Avenue, 7th Floor
New York, NY 10166
800-829-3733

Minimum: $2,500
Front-End Load: None
12b-1: None
Redemption Fee: None
Ticker Symbol: DRCAX

TOTAL RETURNS (%)

1987	1988	1989	1990	1991	5-year
-1.7	9.7	8.6	6.7	10.3	37.8

INVESTMENT PORTFOLIO

Total Assets (mil.)	Expense Ratio	Turnover Ratio
$1,708	0.70%	56%

DREYFUS GENERAL MUNICIPAL BOND FUND

Dreyfus Service
200 Park Avenue, 7th Floor
New York, NY 10166
800-829-3733

Minimum: $2,500
Front-End Load: None
12b-1: None
Redemption Fee: None
Ticker Symbol: GMBDX

TOTAL RETURNS (%)

1987	1988	1989	1990	1991	5-year
-5.5	12.6	11.5	7.6	14.7	46.4

INVESTMENT PORTFOLIO

Total Assets (mil.)	Expense Ratio	Turnover Ratio
$637	NA	50%

DREYFUS INSURED MUNICIPAL BOND

Dreyfus Service
200 Park Avenue, 7th Floor
New York, NY 10166
800-829-3733

Minimum: $2,500
Front-End Load: None
12b-1: 0.20%
Redemption Fee: None
Ticker Symbol: DTBDX

TOTAL RETURNS (%)

1987	1988	1989	1990	1991	5-year
-1.9	10.2	8.7	7.1	11.4	40.1

INVESTMENT PORTFOLIO

Total Assets (mil.)	Expense Ratio	Turnover Ratio
$232	0.97%	62%

DREYFUS INTERMEDIATE MUNICIPAL BOND

Dreyfus Service
200 Park Avenue, 7th Floor
New York, NY 10166
800-829-3733

Minimum: $2,500
Front-End Load: None
12b-1: None
Redemption Fee: None
Ticker Symbol: DITEX

TOTAL RETURNS (%)

1987	1988	1989	1990	1991	5-year
1.1	8.0	8.7	6.8	11.1	40.9

INVESTMENT PORTFOLIO

Total Assets (mil.)	Expense Ratio	Turnover Ratio
$1,333	0.70%	31%

DREYFUS MASSACHUSETTS TAX EXEMPT BOND FUND

Dreyfus Service
200 Park Avenue, 7th Floor
New York, NY 10166
800-829-3733

Minimum: $2,500
Front-End Load: None
12b-1: None
Redemption Fee: None
Ticker Symbol: DMEBX

TOTAL RETURNS (%)

1987	1988	1989	1990	1991	5-year
-3.4	10.5	7.7	6.1	12.7	37.4

INVESTMENT PORTFOLIO

Total Assets (mil.)	Expense Ratio	Turnover Ratio
$143	0.82%	50%

DREYFUS NEW YORK TAX EXEMPT BOND FUND

Dreyfus Service
200 Park Avenue, 7th Floor
New York, NY 10166
800-829-3733

Minimum: $2,500
Front-End Load: None
12b-1: None
Redemption Fee: None
Ticker Symbol: DRNYX

TOTAL RETURNS (%)

1987	1988	1989	1990	1991	5-year
-2.6	10.1	8.9	5.5	12.4	38.5

INVESTMENT PORTFOLIO

Total Assets (mil.)	Expense Ratio	Turnover Ratio
$1,800	0.75%	26%

DREYFUS TAX EXEMPT BOND FUND

Dreyfus Service
200 Park Avenue, 7th Floor
New York, NY 10166
800-829-3733

Minimum: $2,500
Front-End Load: None
12b-1: None
Redemption Fee: None
Ticker Symbol: DRTAX

TOTAL RETURNS (%)

1987	1988	1989	1990	1991	5-year
-1.7	11.5	9.4	6.4	12.0	42.8

INVESTMENT PORTFOLIO

Total Assets (mil.)	Expense Ratio	Turnover Ratio
$3,969	0.68%	28%

EATON VANCE CALIFORNIA MUNICIPALS TRUST

Eaton Vance
24 Federal Street, 5th Floor
Boston, MA 02110
800-225-6265

Minimum: $1,000
Front-End Load: None
12b-1: 1.15%
Redemption Fee: 6.00%
Ticker Symbol: EVCAX

TOTAL RETURNS (%)

1987	1988	1989	1990	1991	5-year
-3.1	8.9	9.0	5.0	9.4	32.1

INVESTMENT PORTFOLIO

Total Assets (mil.)	Expense Ratio	Turnover Ratio
$357	1.96%	13%

EATON VANCE MUNICIPAL BOND FUND

Eaton Vance
24 Federal Street, 5th Floor
Boston, MA 02110
800-225-6265

Minimum: $1,000
Front-End Load: 4.75%
12b-1: None
Redemption Fee: None
Ticker Symbol: EVMBX

TOTAL RETURNS (%)

1987	1988	1989	1990	1991	5-year
0.1	12.8	10.6	7.0	13.5	51.7

INVESTMENT PORTFOLIO

Total Assets (mil.)	Expense Ratio	Turnover Ratio
$90	0.86%	187%

EATON VANCE NATIONAL MUNICIPALS FUND

Eaton Vance
24 Federal Street, 5th Floor
Boston, MA 02110
800-225-6265

Minimum: $1,000
Front-End Load: None
12b-1: 1.18%
Redemption Fee: 6.00%
Ticker Symbol: EVHMX

TOTAL RETURNS (%)

1987	1988	1989	1990	1991	5-year
-2.7	10.6	8.2	3.4	11.8	34.5

INVESTMENT PORTFOLIO

Total Assets (mil.)	Expense Ratio	Turnover Ratio
$1,190	1.95%	15%

FEDERATED INTERMEDIATE MUNICIPAL TRUST

Federated Securities
1001 Liberty Avenue
Pittsburgh, PA 15222
800-245-2423

Minimum: $25,000
Front-End Load: None
12b-1: None
Redemption Fee: None
Ticker Symbol: FIMTX

TOTAL RETURNS (%)

1987	1988	1989	1990	1991	5-year
0.2	5.1	8.9	6.5	10.8	35.3

INVESTMENT PORTFOLIO

Total Assets (mil.)	Expense Ratio	Turnover Ratio
$145	0.50%	43%

FEDERATED SHORT INTERMEDIATE MUNICIPAL TRUST

Federated Securities
1001 Liberty Avenue
Pittsburgh, PA 15222
800-245-2423

Minimum: $25,000
Front-End Load: None
12b-1: None
Redemption Fee: None
Ticker Symbol: FSHIX

TOTAL RETURNS (%)

1987	1988	1989	1990	1991	5-year
2.3	5.6	6.5	6.3	7.3	31.2

INVESTMENT PORTFOLIO

Total Assets (mil.)	Expense Ratio	Turnover Ratio
$161	0.46%	40%

FEDERATED TAX-FREE INCOME FUND

Federated Securities
1001 Liberty Avenue
Pittsburgh, PA 15222
800-356-2805

Minimum: $500
Front-End Load: 4.50%
12b-1: None
Redemption Fee: 0.50%
Ticker Symbol: FTFRX

TOTAL RETURNS (%)

1987	1988	1989	1990	1991	5-year
-0.1	11.3	10.4	5.8	12.5	46.1

INVESTMENT PORTFOLIO

Total Assets (mil.)	Expense Ratio	Turnover Ratio
$574	0.90%	45%

FIDELITY AGGRESSIVE TAX FREE PORTFOLIO

Fidelity Distributors Corporation
82 Devonshire Street, Mail Zone L7b
Boston, MA 02109
800-544-8888

Minimum: $2,500
Front-End Load: None
12b-1: None
Redemption Fee: 1.00%
Ticker Symbol: FATFX

TOTAL RETURNS (%)

1987	1988	1989	1990	1991	5-year
1.4	13.4	9.5	7.5	11.8	51.3

INVESTMENT PORTFOLIO

Total Assets (mil.)	Expense Ratio	Turnover Ratio
$638	0.67%	46%

FIDELITY CALIFORNIA TAX FREE HIGH YIELD

Fidelity Distributors Corporation
82 Devonshire Street, Mail Zone L7b
Boston, MA 02109
800-544-8888

Minimum: $2,500
Front-End Load: None
12b-1: None
Redemption Fee: None
Ticker Symbol: FCTFX

TOTAL RETURNS (%)

1987	1988	1989	1990	1991	5-year
-3.7	11.8	9.7	7.0	10.2	39.1

INVESTMENT PORTFOLIO

Total Assets (mil.)	Expense Ratio	Turnover Ratio
$539	0.58%	15%

FIDELITY CALIFORNIA TAX FREE INSURED PORTFOLIO

Fidelity Distributors Corporation
82 Devonshire Street, Mail Zone L7b
Boston, MA 02109
800-544-8888

Minimum: $2,500
Front-End Load: None
12b-1: None
Redemption Fee: None
Ticker Symbol: FCXIX

TOTAL RETURNS (%)

1987	1988	1989	1990	1991	5-year
-4.5	11.6	8.8	7.0	11.0	37.7

INVESTMENT PORTFOLIO

Total Assets (mil.)	Expense Ratio	Turnover Ratio
$155	0.73%	14%

FIDELITY HIGH YIELD TAX FREE PORTFOLIO

Fidelity Distributors Corporation
82 Devonshire Street, Mail Zone L7b
Boston, MA 02109
800-544-8888

Minimum: $2,500
Front-End Load: None
12b-1: None
Redemption Fee: None
Ticker Symbol: FHIGX

TOTAL RETURNS (%)

1987	1988	1989	1990	1991	5-year
-2.8	12.2	11.4	8.5	10.2	45.2

INVESTMENT PORTFOLIO

Total Assets (mil.)	Expense Ratio	Turnover Ratio
$1,986	0.58%	58%

FIDELITY INSURED TAX FREE PORTFOLIO

Fidelity Distributors Corporation
82 Devonshire Street, Mail Zone L7b
Boston, MA 02109
800-544-8888

Minimum: $2,500
Front-End Load: None
12b-1: None
Redemption Fee: None
Ticker Symbol: FMUIX

TOTAL RETURNS (%)

1987	1988	1989	1990	1991	5-year
-2.1	11.2	9.4	7.1	11.6	42.4

INVESTMENT PORTFOLIO

Total Assets (mil.)	Expense Ratio	Turnover Ratio
$288	0.68%	66%

FIDELITY LIMITED TERM MUNICIPALS

Fidelity Distributors Corporation
82 Devonshire Street, Mail Zone L7b
Boston, MA 02109
800-544-8888

Minimum: $2,500
Front-End Load: None
12b-1: None
Redemption Fee: None
Ticker Symbol: FLTMX

TOTAL RETURNS (%)

1987	1988	1989	1990	1991	5-year
1.1	8.2	7.8	7.0	11.2	40.4

INVESTMENT PORTFOLIO

Total Assets (mil.)	Expense Ratio	Turnover Ratio
$665	0.68%	72%

FIDELITY MASSACHUSETTS TAX FREE HIGH YIELD

Fidelity Distributors Corporation
82 Devonshire Street, Mail Zone L7b
Boston, MA 02109
800-544-8888

Minimum: $2,500
Front-End Load: None
12b-1: None
Redemption Fee: None
Ticker Symbol: FDMMX

TOTAL RETURNS (%)

1987	1988	1989	1990	1991	5-year
-1.3	10.7	9.2	7.4	11.3	42.7

INVESTMENT PORTFOLIO

Total Assets (mil.)	Expense Ratio	Turnover Ratio
$968	0.57%	29%

FIDELITY MICHIGAN TAX FREE PORTFOLIO

Fidelity Distributors Corporation
82 Devonshire Street, Mail Zone L7b
Boston, MA 02109
800-544-8888

Minimum: $2,500
Front-End Load: None
12b-1: None
Redemption Fee: None
Ticker Symbol: FMHTX

TOTAL RETURNS (%)

1987	1988	1989	1990	1991	5-year
-2.8	13.0	10.2	5.1	12.0	42.6

INVESTMENT PORTFOLIO

Total Assets (mil.)	Expense Ratio	Turnover Ratio
$367	0.65%	18%

FIDELITY MINNESOTA TAX FREE PORTFOLIO

Fidelity Distributors Corporation
82 Devonshire Street, Mail Zone L7b
Boston, MA 02109
800-544-8888

Minimum: $2,500
Front-End Load: None
12b-1: None
Redemption Fee: None
Ticker Symbol: FIMIX

TOTAL RETURNS (%)

1987	1988	1989	1990	1991	5-year
-3.8	12.6	9.2	7.2	8.5	37.6

INVESTMENT PORTFOLIO

Total Assets (mil.)	Expense Ratio	Turnover Ratio
$216	0.77%	29%

FIDELITY MUNICIPAL BOND PORTFOLIO

Fidelity Distributors Corporation
82 Devonshire Street, Mail Zone L7b
Boston, MA 02109
800-544-8888

Minimum: $2,500
Front-End Load: None
12b-1: None
Redemption Fee: None
Ticker Symbol: FMBDX

TOTAL RETURNS (%)

1987	1988	1989	1990	1991	5-year
-1.6	12.3	9.6	6.9	11.9	44.9

INVESTMENT PORTFOLIO

Total Assets (mil.)	Expense Ratio	Turnover Ratio
$1,133	0.55%	49%

FIDELITY NEW YORK TAX FREE INSURED PORTFOLIO

Fidelity Distributors Corporation
82 Devonshire Street, Mail Zone L7b
Boston, MA 02109
800-544-8888

Minimum: $2,500
Front-End Load: None
12b-1: None
Redemption Fee: None
Ticker Symbol: FNTIX

TOTAL RETURNS (%)

1987	1988	1989	1990	1991	5-year
-3.2	11.2	9.1	6.2	12.5	40.3

INVESTMENT PORTFOLIO

Total Assets (mil.)	Expense Ratio	Turnover Ratio
$285	0.65%	33%

FIDELITY OHIO TAX FREE PORTFOLIO

Fidelity Distributors Corporation
82 Devonshire Street, Mail Zone L7b
Boston, MA 02109
800-544-8888

Minimum: $2,500
Front-End Load: None
12b-1: None
Redemption Fee: None
Ticker Symbol: FOHFX

TOTAL RETURNS (%)

1987	1988	1989	1990	1991	5-year
-2.4	12.9	10.0	7.5	11.4	45.3

INVESTMENT PORTFOLIO

Total Assets (mil.)	Expense Ratio	Turnover Ratio
$315	0.67%	12%

FINANCIAL TAX FREE INCOME SHARES

INVESCO Funds Group
P. O. Box 2040
Denver, CO 80201
800-525-8085

Minimum: $250
Front-End Load: None
12b-1: None
Redemption Fee: None
Ticker Symbol: FTIFX

TOTAL RETURNS (%)

1987	1988	1989	1990	1991	5-year
-4.0	15.1	11.7	7.1	12.5	48.7

INVESTMENT PORTFOLIO

Total Assets (mil.)	Expense Ratio	Turnover Ratio
$238	0.76%	27%

FIRST INVESTORS INSURED TAX EXEMPT FUND

First Investors Management
10 Woodbridge Center Drive
Woodbridge, NJ 07095
800-423-4026

Minimum: $2,000
Front-End Load: 6.90%
12b-1: 0.30%
Redemption Fee: None
Ticker Symbol: FITAX

TOTAL RETURNS (%)

1987	1988	1989	1990	1991	5-year
2.3	10.6	8.7	6.0	10.3	43.9

INVESTMENT PORTFOLIO

Total Assets (mil.)	Expense Ratio	Turnover Ratio
$1,187	1.15%	28%

FIRST INVESTORS MULTI-STATE INSURED TAX FREE CALIFORNIA

First Investors Management
10 Woodbridge Center Drive
Woodbridge, NJ 07095
800-423-4026

Minimum: $2,000
Front-End Load: 6.90%
12b-1: None
Redemption Fee: None
Ticker Symbol: None

TOTAL RETURNS (%)

1987	1988	1989	1990	1991	5-year
NA	12.9	10.3	6.7	11.3	NA

INVESTMENT PORTFOLIO

Total Assets (mil.)	Expense Ratio	Turnover Ratio
$12	0.08%	27%

FIRST INVESTORS MULTI-STATE INSURED TAX FREE MASSACHUSETTS

First Investors Management
10 Woodbridge Center Drive
Woodbridge, NJ 07095
800-423-4026

Minimum: $2,000
Front-End Load: 6.90%
12b-1: None
Redemption Fee: None
Ticker Symbol: None

TOTAL RETURNS (%)

1987	1988	1989	1990	1991	5-year
NA	13.4	10.4	6.8	11.4	NA

INVESTMENT PORTFOLIO

Total Assets (mil.)	Expense Ratio	Turnover Ratio
$17	0.06%	22%

FIRST INVESTORS MULTI-STATE INSURED TAX FREE MICHIGAN

First Investors Management
10 Woodbridge Center Drive
Woodbridge, NJ 07095
800-423-4026

Minimum: $2,000
Front-End Load: 6.90%
12b-1: None
Redemption Fee: None
Ticker Symbol: None

TOTAL RETURNS (%)

1987	1988	1989	1990	1991	5-year
NA	13.7	11.0	6.8	11.3	NA

INVESTMENT PORTFOLIO

Total Assets (mil.)	Expense Ratio	Turnover Ratio
$14	0.10%	11%

FIRST INVESTORS MULTI-STATE INSURED TAX FREE MINNESOTA

First Investors Management
10 Woodbridge Center Drive
Woodbridge, NJ 07095
800-423-4026

Minimum: $2,000
Front-End Load: 6.90%
12b-1: None
Redemption Fee: None
Ticker Symbol: None

TOTAL RETURNS (%)

1987	1988	1989	1990	1991	5-year
NA	11.5	9.8	6.7	10.8	NA

INVESTMENT PORTFOLIO

Total Assets (mil.)	Expense Ratio	Turnover Ratio
$4	0.15%	22%

FIRST INVESTORS MULTI-STATE INSURED TAX FREE OHIO

First Investors Management
10 Woodbridge Center Drive
Woodbridge, NJ 07095
800-423-4026

Minimum: $2,000
Front-End Load: 6.90%
12b-1: None
Redemption Fee: None
Ticker Symbol: None

TOTAL RETURNS (%)

1987	1988	1989	1990	1991	5-year
NA	14.0	11.1	7.1	11.5	NA

INVESTMENT PORTFOLIO

Total Assets (mil.)	Expense Ratio	Turnover Ratio
$9	0.07%	31%

FIRST INVESTORS NEW YORK INSURED TAX FREE FUND

First Investors Management
10 Woodbridge Center Drive
Woodbridge, NJ 07095
800-423-4026

Minimum: $2,000
Front-End Load: 6.90%
12b-1: 0.30%
Redemption Fee: None
Ticker Symbol: FNYFX

TOTAL RETURNS (%)

1987	1988	1989	1990	1991	5-year
-1.2	10.2	9.4	5.8	11.0	39.7

INVESTMENT PORTFOLIO

Total Assets (mil.)	Expense Ratio	Turnover Ratio
$159	1.24%	33%

FIRST TRUST TAX-FREE BOND FUND INCOME SERIES

Clayton Brown & Associates
500 West Madison Street, Suite 3000
Chicago, IL 60606
800-848-8222

Minimum: $1,000
Front-End Load: 4.50%
12b-1: None
Redemption Fee: None
Ticker Symbol: FTICX

TOTAL RETURNS (%)

1987	1988	1989	1990	1991	5-year
-0.5	12.7	11.2	6.1	11.9	47.9

INVESTMENT PORTFOLIO

Total Assets (mil.)	Expense Ratio	Turnover Ratio
$23	1.16%	0%

FIRST TRUST TAX-FREE BOND INSURED SERIES

Clayton Brown & Associates
500 West Madison Street, Suite 3000
Chicago, IL 60606
800-848-8222

Minimum: $1,000
Front-End Load: 4.50%
12b-1: None
Redemption Fee: None
Ticker Symbol: FTISX

TOTAL RETURNS (%)

1987	1988	1989	1990	1991	5-year
-2.4	12.5	10.9	6.2	11.4	44.0

INVESTMENT PORTFOLIO

Total Assets (mil.)	Expense Ratio	Turnover Ratio
$24	0.91%	0%

FLAGSHIP ARIZONA DOUBLE TAX EXEMPT FUND

Flagship Financial
One First National Plaza, Suite 910
Dayton, OH 45402
800-227-4648

Minimum: $3,000
Front-End Load: 4.20%
12b-1: 0.40%
Redemption Fee: None
Ticker Symbol: FAZTX

TOTAL RETURNS (%)

1987	1988	1989	1990	1991	5-year
-1.0	12.3	9.9	5.5	12.3	44.7

INVESTMENT PORTFOLIO

Total Assets (mil.)	Expense Ratio	Turnover Ratio
$43	0.79%	18%

FLAGSHIP GEORGIA DOUBLE TAX EXEMPT FUND

Flagship Financial
One First National Plaza, Suite 910
Dayton, OH 45402
800-227-4648

Minimum: $3,000
Front-End Load: 4.20%
12b-1: 0.40%
Redemption Fee: None
Ticker Symbol: FGATX

TOTAL RETURNS (%)

1987	1988	1989	1990	1991	5-year
-1.6	12.5	8.6	6.5	11.7	43.0

INVESTMENT PORTFOLIO

Total Assets (mil.)	Expense Ratio	Turnover Ratio
$56	0.73%	24%

FLAGSHIP MICHIGAN TRIPLE TAX EXEMPT FUND

Flagship Financial
One First National Plaza, Suite 910
Dayton, OH 45402
800-227-4648

Minimum: $3,000
Front-End Load: 4.20%
12b-1: 0.40%
Redemption Fee: None
Ticker Symbol: FMITX

TOTAL RETURNS (%)

1987	1988	1989	1990	1991	5-year
-1.0	12.5	10.2	5.3	11.6	44.3

INVESTMENT PORTFOLIO

Total Assets (mil.)	Expense Ratio	Turnover Ratio
$155	0.95%	23%

FLAGSHIP NORTH CAROLINA TRIPLE TAX EXEMPT FUND

Flagship Financial
One First National Plaza, Suite 910
Dayton, OH 45402
800-227-4648

Minimum: $3,000
Front-End Load: 4.20%
12b-1: 0.40%
Redemption Fee: None
Ticker Symbol: FLNCX

TOTAL RETURNS (%)

1987	1988	1989	1990	1991	5-year
-2.9	12.6	10.1	5.8	11.7	42.1

INVESTMENT PORTFOLIO

Total Assets (mil.)	Expense Ratio	Turnover Ratio
$120	1.00%	12%

FLAGSHIP OHIO DOUBLE TAX EXEMPT FUND

Flagship Financial
One First National Plaza, Suite 910
Dayton, OH 45402
800-227-4648

Minimum: $3,000
Front-End Load: 4.20%
12b-1: 0.40%
Redemption Fee: None
Ticker Symbol: FOHTX

TOTAL RETURNS (%)

1987	1988	1989	1990	1991	5-year
-0.9	13.1	9.7	6.2	11.8	46.0

INVESTMENT PORTFOLIO

Total Assets (mil.)	Expense Ratio	Turnover Ratio
$296	1.03%	14%

FLAGSHIP PENNSYLVANIA TRIPLE TAX EXEMPT FUND

Flagship Financial
One First National Plaza, Suite 910
Dayton, OH 45402
800-227-4648

Minimum: $3,000
Front-End Load: 4.20%
12b-1: 0.40%
Redemption Fee: None
Ticker Symbol: FPNTX

TOTAL RETURNS (%)

1987	1988	1989	1990	1991	5-year
-1.9	13.2	9.5	5.1	11.8	42.9

INVESTMENT PORTFOLIO

Total Assets (mil.)	Expense Ratio	Turnover Ratio
$36	0.92%	23%

FLAGSHIP VIRGINIA DOUBLE TAX EXEMPT FUND

Flagship Financial
One First National Plaza, Suite 910
Dayton, OH 45402
800-227-4648

Minimum: $3,000
Front-End Load: 4.20%
12b-1: 0.40%
Redemption Fee: None
Ticker Symbol: FVATX

TOTAL RETURNS (%)

1987	1988	1989	1990	1991	5-year
-1.1	12.7	9.2	6.5	11.8	45.0

INVESTMENT PORTFOLIO

Total Assets (mil.)	Expense Ratio	Turnover Ratio
$54	0.92%	22%

FRANKLIN CALIFORNIA INSURED TAX-FREE INCOME

Franklin Distributors
777 Mariners Island Blvd., 6th Floor
San Mateo, CA 94404
800-342-5236

Minimum: $100
Front-End Load: 4.00%
12b-1: None
Redemption Fee: None
Ticker Symbol: FRCIX

TOTAL RETURNS (%)

1987	1988	1989	1990	1991	5-year
-5.4	11.8	9.8	6.1	10.5	36.0

INVESTMENT PORTFOLIO

Total Assets (mil.)	Expense Ratio	Turnover Ratio
$644	0.58%	4%

FRANKLIN CALIFORNIA TAX-FREE INCOME FUND

Franklin Distributors
777 Mariners Island Blvd., 6th Floor
San Mateo, CA 94404
800-342-5236

Minimum: $100
Front-End Load: 4.00%
12b-1: None
Redemption Fee: None
Ticker Symbol: FKTFX

TOTAL RETURNS (%)

1987	1988	1989	1990	1991	5-year
-0.8	11.6	8.3	6.3	10.7	41.1

INVESTMENT PORTFOLIO

Total Assets (mil.)	Expense Ratio	Turnover Ratio
$12,303	0.49%	16%

FRANKLIN FEDERAL TAX-FREE INCOME FUND

Franklin Distributors
777 Mariners Island Blvd., 6th Floor
San Mateo, CA 94404
800-342-5236

Minimum: $100
Front-End Load: 4.00%
12b-1: None
Redemption Fee: None
Ticker Symbol: FKTIX

TOTAL RETURNS (%)

1987	1988	1989	1990	1991	5-year
-3.0	13.5	8.7	5.2	12.9	42.2

INVESTMENT PORTFOLIO

Total Assets (mil.)	Expense Ratio	Turnover Ratio
$4,862	0.55%	29%

FRANKLIN INSURED TAX-FREE INCOME FUND

Franklin Distributors
777 Mariners Island Blvd., 6th Floor
San Mateo, CA 94404
800-342-5236

Minimum: $100
Front-End Load: 4.00%
12b-1: None
Redemption Fee: None
Ticker Symbol: FTFIX

TOTAL RETURNS (%)

1987	1988	1989	1990	1991	5-year
-3.4	12.4	9.7	6.3	11.1	40.6

INVESTMENT PORTFOLIO

Total Assets (mil.)	Expense Ratio	Turnover Ratio
$1,030	0.54%	10%

FRANKLIN MASSACHUSETTS INSURED TAX FREE INCOME

Franklin Distributors
777 Mariners Island Blvd., 6th Floor
San Mateo, CA 94404
800-342-5236

Minimum: $100
Front-End Load: 4.00%
12b-1: None
Redemption Fee: None
Ticker Symbol: FMISX

TOTAL RETURNS (%)

1987	1988	1989	1990	1991	5-year
-3.4	12.0	8.8	4.8	11.2	37.3

INVESTMENT PORTFOLIO

Total Assets (mil.)	Expense Ratio	Turnover Ratio
$201	0.75%	11%

FRANKLIN MICHIGAN INSURED TAX-FREE INCOME

Franklin Distributors
777 Mariners Island Blvd., 6th Floor
San Mateo, CA 94404
800-342-5236

Minimum: $100
Front-End Load: 4.00%
12b-1: None
Redemption Fee: None
Ticker Symbol: FTTMX

TOTAL RETURNS (%)

1987	1988	1989	1990	1991	5-year
-3.3	12.5	9.2	5.8	10.7	39.1

INVESTMENT PORTFOLIO

Total Assets (mil.)	Expense Ratio	Turnover Ratio
$627	0.62%	4%

FRANKLIN MINNESOTA INSURED TAX-FREE INCOME

Franklin Distributors
777 Mariners Island Blvd., 6th Floor
San Mateo, CA 94404
800-342-5236

Minimum: $100
Front-End Load: 4.00%
12b-1: None
Redemption Fee: None
Ticker Symbol: FMINX

TOTAL RETURNS (%)

1987	1988	1989	1990	1991	5-year
-3.5	12.9	9.2	5.5	10.6	38.7

INVESTMENT PORTFOLIO

Total Assets (mil.)	Expense Ratio	Turnover Ratio
$332	0.68%	9%

FRANKLIN NEW YORK TAX-FREE INCOME FUND

Franklin Distributors
777 Mariners Island Blvd., 6th Floor
San Mateo, CA 94404
800-342-5236

Minimum: $100
Front-End Load: 4.00%
12b-1: None
Redemption Fee: None
Ticker Symbol: FNYTX

TOTAL RETURNS (%)

1987	1988	1989	1990	1991	5-year
-2.2	12.0	9.3	4.4	13.3	41.6

INVESTMENT PORTFOLIO

Total Assets (mil.)	Expense Ratio	Turnover Ratio
$3,373	0.55%	19%

FRANKLIN OHIO INSURED TAX-FREE INCOME FUND

Franklin Distributors
777 Mariners Island Blvd., 6th Floor
San Mateo, CA 94404
800-342-5236

Minimum: $100
Front-End Load: 4.00%
12b-1: None
Redemption Fee: None
Ticker Symbol: FTOIX

TOTAL RETURNS (%)

1987	1988	1989	1990	1991	5-year
-3.8	13.4	9.0	6.4	10.6	39.9

INVESTMENT PORTFOLIO

Total Assets (mil.)	Expense Ratio	Turnover Ratio
$372	0.66%	4%

FRANKLIN PUERTO RICO TAX-FREE INCOME FUND

Franklin Distributors
777 Mariners Island Blvd., 6th Floor
San Mateo, CA 94404
800-342-5236

Minimum: $100
Front-End Load: 4.00%
12b-1: None
Redemption Fee: None
Ticker Symbol: FPRTX

TOTAL RETURNS (%)

1987	1988	1989	1990	1991	5-year
-2.2	11.8	9.5	5.1	12.0	40.8

INVESTMENT PORTFOLIO

Total Assets (mil.)	Expense Ratio	Turnover Ratio
$116	0.75%	6%

GIT TAX FREE TRUST HIGH YIELD PORTFOLIO

Bankers Finance Investment Management
1655 Fort Myer Drive
Arlington, VA 22209
800-336-3063

Minimum: $2,500
Front-End Load: None
12b-1: None
Redemption Fee: None
Ticker Symbol: GTFHX

TOTAL RETURNS (%)

1987	1988	1989	1990	1991	5-year
0.2	8.5	7.3	5.4	10.2	35.4

INVESTMENT PORTFOLIO

Total Assets (mil.)	Expense Ratio	Turnover Ratio
$40	1.25%	41%

IDS CALIFORNIA TAX EXEMPT FUND

IDS Financial Services
1000 Roanoke Building
Minneapolis, MN 55402
800-328-8300

Minimum: $2,000
Front-End Load: 5.00%
12b-1: 0.02%
Redemption Fee: None
Ticker Symbol: ICALX

TOTAL RETURNS (%)

1987	1988	1989	1990	1991	5-year
-1.7	10.5	10.1	5.7	11.0	40.3

INVESTMENT PORTFOLIO

Total Assets (mil.)	Expense Ratio	Turnover Ratio
$202	0.65%	6%

IDS HIGH YIELD TAX EXEMPT FUND

IDS Financial Services
1000 Roanoke Building
Minneapolis, MN 55402
800-328-8300

Minimum: $2,000
Front-End Load: 5.00%
12b-1: 0.02%
Redemption Fee: None
Ticker Symbol: INHYX

TOTAL RETURNS (%)

1987	1988	1989	1990	1991	5-year
0.3	9.9	11.4	5.2	12.0	44.7

INVESTMENT PORTFOLIO

Total Assets (mil.)	Expense Ratio	Turnover Ratio
$5,291	0.65%	22%

IDS INSURED TAX EXEMPT FUND

IDS Financial Services
1000 Roanoke Building
Minneapolis, MN 55402
800-328-8300

Minimum: $2,000
Front-End Load: 5.00%
12b-1: 0.02%
Redemption Fee: None
Ticker Symbol: IINSX

TOTAL RETURNS (%)

1987	1988	1989	1990	1991	5-year
-0.3	9.7	10.4	6.0	11.7	42.9

INVESTMENT PORTFOLIO

Total Assets (mil.)	Expense Ratio	Turnover Ratio
$235	0.70%	24%

IDS MASSACHUSETTS TAX EXEMPT FUND

IDS Financial Services
1000 Roanoke Building
Minneapolis, MN 55402
800-328-8300

Minimum: $2,000
Front-End Load: 5.00%
12b-1: 0.03%
Redemption Fee: None
Ticker Symbol: NA

TOTAL RETURNS (%)

1987	1988	1989	1990	1991	5-year
NA	8.6	7.4	5.9	12.1	NA

INVESTMENT PORTFOLIO

Total Assets (mil.)	Expense Ratio	Turnover Ratio
$34	0.85%	25%

IDS MICHIGAN TAX EXEMPT FUND

IDS Financial Services
1000 Roanoke Building
Minneapolis, MN 55402
800-328-8300

Minimum: $2,000
Front-End Load: 5.00%
12b-1: 0.03%
Redemption Fee: None
Ticker Symbol: INMIX

TOTAL RETURNS (%)

1987	1988	1989	1990	1991	5-year
NA	10.6	10.4	4.8	11.3	NA

INVESTMENT PORTFOLIO

Total Assets (mil.)	Expense Ratio	Turnover Ratio
$47	0.81%	5%

IDS MINNESOTA TAX EXEMPT FUND

IDS Financial Services
1000 Roanoke Building
Minneapolis, MN 55402
800-328-8300

Minimum: $2,000
Front-End Load: 5.00%
12b-1: 0.03%
Redemption Fee: None
Ticker Symbol: IMNTX

TOTAL RETURNS (%)

1987	1988	1989	1990	1991	5-year
-1.6	9.3	10.8	5.4	10.6	38.9

INVESTMENT PORTFOLIO

Total Assets (mil.)	Expense Ratio	Turnover Ratio
$265	0.66%	8%

IDS NEW YORK TAX EXEMPT FUND

IDS Financial Services
1000 Roanoke Building
Minneapolis, MN 55402
800-328-8300

Minimum: $2,000
Front-End Load: 5.00%
12b-1: 0.03%
Redemption Fee: None
Ticker Symbol: INYKX

TOTAL RETURNS (%)

1987	1988	1989	1990	1991	5-year
-3.4	10.4	10.0	5.2	12.5	38.9

INVESTMENT PORTFOLIO

Total Assets (mil.)	Expense Ratio	Turnover Ratio
$86	0.67%	1%

IDS OHIO TAX EXEMPT FUND

IDS Financial Services
1000 Roanoke Building
Minneapolis, MN 55402
800-328-8300

Minimum: $2,000
Front-End Load: 5.00%
12b-1: 0.03%
Redemption Fee: None
Ticker Symbol: IOHIX

TOTAL RETURNS (%)

1987	1988	1989	1990	1991	5-year
NA	9.8	9.1	5.4	11.6	NA

INVESTMENT PORTFOLIO

Total Assets (mil.)	Expense Ratio	Turnover Ratio
$38	0.82%	10%

IDS TAX EXEMPT BOND FUND

IDS Financial Services
1000 Roanoke Building
Minneapolis, MN 55402
800-328-8300

Minimum: $2,000
Front-End Load: 5.00%
12b-1: 0.02%
Redemption Fee: None
Ticker Symbol: INTAX

TOTAL RETURNS (%)

1987	1988	1989	1990	1991	5-year
-0.5	8.2	11.7	6.6	10.1	41.2

INVESTMENT PORTFOLIO

Total Assets (mil.)	Expense Ratio	Turnover Ratio
$1,188	0.62%	112%

KEMPER CALIFORNIA TAX-FREE FUND

Kemper Financial Services
120 South LaSalle Street, 20th Floor
Chicago, IL 60603
800-621-1048

Minimum: $1,000
Front-End Load: 4.50%
12b-1: None
Redemption Fee: None
Ticker Symbol: KCTFX

TOTAL RETURNS (%)

1987	1988	1989	1990	1991	5-year
4.2	7.5	11.5	6.7	11.4	48.5

INVESTMENT PORTFOLIO

Total Assets (mil.)	Expense Ratio	Turnover Ratio
$1,031	0.65%	15%

KEMPER MUNICIPAL BOND FUND

Kemper Financial Services
120 South LaSalle Street, 20th Floor
Chicago, IL 60603
800-621-1048

Minimum: $1,000
Front-End Load: 4.50%
12b-1: None
Redemption Fee: None
Ticker Symbol: KPMBX

TOTAL RETURNS (%)

1987	1988	1989	1990	1991	5-year
3.1	8.6	11.3	6.7	12.8	49.9

INVESTMENT PORTFOLIO

Total Assets (mil.)	Expense Ratio	Turnover Ratio
$2,507	0.50%	30%

KEYSTONE AMERICA TAX FREE INCOME FUND

Keystone Distributors
99 High Street, 29th Floor
Boston, MA 02110
800-633-4900

Minimum: $1,000
Front-End Load: 4.75%
12b-1: 0.75%
Redemption Fee: 2.00%
Ticker Symbol: KATIX

TOTAL RETURNS (%)

1987	1988	1989	1990	1991	5-year
NA	10.8	8.8	5.4	11.4	NA

INVESTMENT PORTFOLIO

Total Assets (mil.)	Expense Ratio	Turnover Ratio
$136	1.67%	42%

KEYSTONE TAX EXEMPT TRUST

Keystone Distributors
99 High Street, 29th Floor
Boston, MA 02110
800-633-4900

Minimum: $10,000
Front-End Load: None
12b-1: 1.14%
Redemption Fee: 4.00%
Ticker Symbol: KSTEX

TOTAL RETURNS (%)

1987	1988	1989	1990	1991	5-year
-2.8	12.3	8.9	5.3	10.9	38.9

INVESTMENT PORTFOLIO

Total Assets (mil.)	Expense Ratio	Turnover Ratio
$624	1.85%	73%

KEYSTONE TAX FREE FUND

Keystone Distributors
99 High Street, 29th Floor
Boston, MA 02110
800-633-4900

Minimum: $1,000
Front-End Load: None
12b-1: 0.55%
Redemption Fee: 4.00%
Ticker Symbol: KSTFX

TOTAL RETURNS (%)

1987	1988	1989	1990	1991	5-year
-0.1	10.9	9.1	6.7	10.8	42.9

INVESTMENT PORTFOLIO

Total Assets (mil.)	Expense Ratio	Turnover Ratio
$1,094	1.18%	64%

LORD ABBETT CALIFORNIA TAX-FREE INCOME FUND

Lord Abbett & Company
767 Fifth Avenue
New York, NY 10153
800-874-3733

Minimum: $1,000
Front-End Load: 4.75%
12b-1: 0.25%
Redemption Fee: None
Ticker Symbol: LCFIX

TOTAL RETURNS (%)

1987	1988	1989	1990	1991	5-year
-1.2	11.3	9.8	7.3	12.7	46.0

INVESTMENT PORTFOLIO

Total Assets (mil.)	Expense Ratio	Turnover Ratio
$164	0.62%	38%

LORD ABBETT TAX FREE INCOME—NATIONAL SERIES

Lord Abbett & Company
767 Fifth Avenue
New York, NY 10153
800-874-3733

Minimum: $1,000
Front-End Load: 4.75%
12b-1: 0.17%
Redemption Fee: None
Ticker Symbol: LANSX

TOTAL RETURNS (%)

1987	1988	1989	1990	1991	5-year
0.7	12.6	9.5	7.3	12.5	49.8

INVESTMENT PORTFOLIO

Total Assets (mil.)	Expense Ratio	Turnover Ratio
$420	0.62%	43%

LORD ABBETT TAX FREE INCOME—NEW YORK SERIES

Lord Abbett & Company
767 Fifth Avenue
New York, NY 10153
800-874-3733

Minimum: $1,000
Front-End Load: 4.75%
12b-1: 0.17%
Redemption Fee: None
Ticker Symbol: LANYX

TOTAL RETURNS (%)

1987	1988	1989	1990	1991	5-year
0.8	12.0	9.3	6.3	13.7	49.2

INVESTMENT PORTFOLIO

Total Assets (mil.)	Expense Ratio	Turnover Ratio
$242	0.65%	28%

LUTHERAN BROTHERHOOD MUNICIPAL BOND

Lutheran Brotherhood Securities
625 Fourth Avenue South
Minneapolis, MN 55415
800-328-4552

Minimum: $500
Front-End Load: 5.00%
12b-1: None
Redemption Fee: None
Ticker Symbol: LUBMX

TOTAL RETURNS (%)

1987	1988	1989	1990	1991	5-year
1.4	10.8	9.9	6.7	10.3	45.4

INVESTMENT PORTFOLIO

Total Assets (mil.)	Expense Ratio	Turnover Ratio
$433	0.86%	68%

MACKENZIE CALIFORNIA MUNICIPAL FUND

Mackenzie Investment Management
P. O. Box 5007
Boca Raton, FL 33431
800-456-5111

Minimum: $250
Front-End Load: 4.75%
12b-1: 0.25%
Redemption Fee: None
Ticker Symbol: MCCAX

TOTAL RETURNS (%)

1987	1988	1989	1990	1991	5-year
NA	NA	10.4	6.5	10.9	NA

INVESTMENT PORTFOLIO

Total Assets (mil.)	Expense Ratio	Turnover Ratio
$37	1.08%	55%

MACKENZIE NATIONAL MUNICIPAL FUND

Mackenzie Investment Management
P. O. Box 5007
Boca Raton, FL 33431
800-456-5111

Minimum: $250
Front-End Load: 4.75%
12b-1: 0.25%
Redemption Fee: None
Ticker Symbol: MCNMX

TOTAL RETURNS (%)

1987	1988	1989	1990	1991	5-year
NA	NA	9.2	6.0	10.6	NA

INVESTMENT PORTFOLIO

Total Assets (mil.)	Expense Ratio	Turnover Ratio
$32	1.08%	97%

MACKENZIE NEW YORK MUNICIPAL FUND

Mackenzie Investment Management
P. O. Box 5007
Boca Raton, FL 33431
800-456-5111

Minimum: $250
Front-End Load: 4.75%
12b-1: 0.25%
Redemption Fee: None
Ticker Symbol: MCNYX

TOTAL RETURNS (%)

1987	1988	1989	1990	1991	5-year
NA	NA	9.5	5.1	12.0	NA

INVESTMENT PORTFOLIO

Total Assets (mil.)	Expense Ratio	Turnover Ratio
$31	1.08%	41%

MAINSTAY TAX FREE BOND FUND

NYLIFE Securities
51 Madison Avenue, Room 117
New York, NY 10010
800-522-4202

Minimum: $500
Front-End Load: None
12b-1: 0.50%
Redemption Fee: 5.00%
Ticker Symbol: MKTBX

TOTAL RETURNS (%)

1987	1988	1989	1990	1991	5-year
0.5	9.4	7.4	4.7	10.9	37.1

INVESTMENT PORTFOLIO

Total Assets (mil.)	Expense Ratio	Turnover Ratio
$196	1.45%	44%

MERRILL LYNCH CALIFORNIA MUNICIPAL BOND FUND B

Merrill Lynch Funds Distributor
P. O. Box 9011
Princeton, NJ 08543
800-637-3863

Minimum: $1,000
Front-End Load: None
12b-1: 0.50%
Redemption Fee: 4.00%
Ticker Symbol: MRCTX

TOTAL RETURNS (%)

1987	1988	1989	1990	1991	5-year
-1.3	9.3	9.7	5.5	10.3	37.8

INVESTMENT PORTFOLIO

Total Assets (mil.)	Expense Ratio	Turnover Ratio
$701	1.16%	120%

MERRILL LYNCH MUNICIPAL BOND HIGH YIELD A

Merrill Lynch Funds Distributor
P. O. Box 9011
Princeton, NJ 08543
800-637-3863

Minimum: $1,000
Front-End Load: 4.00%
12b-1: None
Redemption Fee: None
Ticker Symbol: MLHYX

TOTAL RETURNS (%)

1987	1988	1989	1990	1991	5-year
-5.8	18.1	9.1	5.8	12.6	44.7

INVESTMENT PORTFOLIO

Total Assets (mil.)	Expense Ratio	Turnover Ratio
$1,245	0.56%	75%

MERRILL LYNCH MUNICIPAL BOND INSURED A

Merrill Lynch Funds Distributor
P. O. Box 9011
Princeton, NJ 08543
800-637-3863

Minimum: $1,000
Front-End Load: 4.00%
12b-1: None
Redemption Fee: None
Ticker Symbol: MLMBX

TOTAL RETURNS (%)

1987	1988	1989	1990	1991	5-year
0.9	10.9	9.5	7.1	12.1	47.0

INVESTMENT PORTFOLIO

Total Assets (mil.)	Expense Ratio	Turnover Ratio
$2,029	0.46%	33%

MERRILL LYNCH MUNICIPAL BOND LIMITED MATURITY

Merrill Lynch Funds Distributor
P. O. Box 9011
Princeton, NJ 08543
800-637-3863

Minimum: $1,000
Front-End Load: 0.75%
12b-1: None
Redemption Fee: None
Ticker Symbol: MLLMX

TOTAL RETURNS (%)

1987	1988	1989	1990	1991	5-year
3.2	5.9	6.9	6.1	7.4	33.1

INVESTMENT PORTFOLIO

Total Assets (mil.)	Expense Ratio	Turnover Ratio
$449	0.45%	93%

MERRILL LYNCH MUNICIPAL INCOME FUND B

Merrill Lynch Funds Distributor
P. O. Box 9011
Princeton, NJ 08543
800-637-3863

Minimum: $1,000
Front-End Load: None
12b-1: 0.30%
Redemption Fee: 2.00%
Ticker Symbol: MRMFX

TOTAL RETURNS (%)

1987	1988	1989	1990	1991	5-year
-0.9	6.4	7.7	5.1	10.9	32.6

INVESTMENT PORTFOLIO

Total Assets (mil.)	Expense Ratio	Turnover Ratio
$97	1.23%	236%

MERRILL LYNCH NEW YORK MUNICIPAL BOND FUND B

Merrill Lynch Funds Distributor
P. O. Box 9011
Princeton, NJ 08543
800-637-3863

Minimum: $1,000
Front-End Load: None
12b-1: 0.50%
Redemption Fee: 4.00%
Ticker Symbol: MRNKX

TOTAL RETURNS (%)

1987	1988	1989	1990	1991	5-year
-0.6	9.9	8.9	4.3	12.8	39.9

INVESTMENT PORTFOLIO

Total Assets (mil.)	Expense Ratio	Turnover Ratio
$567	1.19%	54%

MFS LIFETIME MANAGED MUNICIPAL BOND TRUST

Massachusetts Financial Services
500 Boylston Street
Boston, MA 02116
800-225-2606

Minimum: $1,000
Front-End Load: None
12b-1: 1.00%
Redemption Fee: 6.00%
Ticker Symbol: LTMMX

TOTAL RETURNS (%)

1987	1988	1989	1990	1991	5-year
-4.3	12.9	9.2	3.5	11.4	36.1

INVESTMENT PORTFOLIO

Total Assets (mil.)	Expense Ratio	Turnover Ratio
$409	2.06%	91%

MFS MANAGED CALIFORNIA MUNICIPAL BOND TRUST

Massachusetts Financial Services
500 Boylston Street
Boston, MA 02116
800-225-2606

Minimum: $1,000
Front-End Load: 4.75%
12b-1: None
Redemption Fee: 1.00%
Ticker Symbol: MCFTX

TOTAL RETURNS (%)

1987	1988	1989	1990	1991	5-year
-1.0	10.9	9.8	6.4	11.8	43.3

INVESTMENT PORTFOLIO

Total Assets (mil.)	Expense Ratio	Turnover Ratio
$151	0.88%	102%

MFS MANAGED HIGH YIELD MUNICIPAL BOND TRUST

Massachusetts Financial Services
500 Boylston Street
Boston, MA 02116
800-225-2606

Minimum: $1,000
Front-End Load: 4.75%
12b-1: None
Redemption Fee: None
Ticker Symbol: MMHYX

TOTAL RETURNS (%)

1987	1988	1989	1990	1991	5-year
1.6	9.1	10.7	3.2	10.4	39.7

INVESTMENT PORTFOLIO

Total Assets (mil.)	Expense Ratio	Turnover Ratio
$644	0.66%	23%

MFS MANAGED MULTI-STATE MUNICIPAL BOND MARYLAND

Massachusetts Financial Services
500 Boylston Street
Boston, MA 02116
800-225-2606

Minimum: $1,000
Front-End Load: 4.75%
12b-1: 0.35%
Redemption Fee: None
Ticker Symbol: MFSMX

TOTAL RETURNS (%)

1987	1988	1989	1990	1991	5-year
-0.1	10.8	9.0	6.3	10.1	41.3

INVESTMENT PORTFOLIO

Total Assets (mil.)	Expense Ratio	Turnover Ratio
$114	1.18%	41%

MFS MANAGED MULTI-STATE MUNICIPAL BOND MASSACHUSETTS

Massachusetts Financial Services
500 Boylston Street
Boston, MA 02116
800-225-2606

Minimum: $1,000
Front-End Load: 4.75%
12b-1: 0.35%
Redemption Fee: None
Ticker Symbol: MFSSX

TOTAL RETURNS (%)

1987	1988	1989	1990	1991	5-year
-0.3	10.4	8.0	6.5	11.8	41.6

INVESTMENT PORTFOLIO

Total Assets (mil.)	Expense Ratio	Turnover Ratio
$234	1.08%	43%

MFS MANAGED MULTI-STATE MUNICIPAL BOND NORTH CAROLINA

Massachusetts Financial Services
500 Boylston Street
Boston, MA 02116
800-225-2606

Minimum: $1,000
Front-End Load: 4.75%
12b-1: 0.35%
Redemption Fee: None
Ticker Symbol: MSNCX

TOTAL RETURNS (%)

1987	1988	1989	1990	1991	5-year
0.0	9.7	9.1	6.3	10.4	40.5

INVESTMENT PORTFOLIO

Total Assets (mil.)	Expense Ratio	Turnover Ratio
$300	1.10%	44%

MFS MANAGED MULTI-STATE MUNICIPAL BOND SOUTH CAROLINA

Massachusetts Financial Services
500 Boylston Street
Boston, MA 02116
800-225-2606

Minimum: $1,000
Front-End Load: 4.75%
12b-1: 0.35%
Redemption Fee: None
Ticker Symbol: MFSCX

TOTAL RETURNS (%)

1987	1988	1989	1990	1991	5-year
2.8	10.9	9.1	6.4	10.7	46.5

INVESTMENT PORTFOLIO

Total Assets (mil.)	Expense Ratio	Turnover Ratio
$96	1.19%	47%

MFS MANAGED MULTI-STATE MUNICIPAL BOND VIRGINIA

Massachusetts Financial Services
500 Boylston Street
Boston, MA 02116
800-225-2606

Minimum: $1,000
Front-End Load: 4.75%
12b-1: 0.35%
Redemption Fee: None
Ticker Symbol: MSVAX

TOTAL RETURNS (%)

1987	1988	1989	1990	1991	5-year
1.2	11.2	9.4	6.8	10.4	45.1

INVESTMENT PORTFOLIO

Total Assets (mil.)	Expense Ratio	Turnover Ratio
$320	1.12%	38%

MFS MANAGED MULTI-STATE MUNICIPAL BOND WEST VIRGINIA

Massachusetts Financial Services
500 Boylston Street
Boston, MA 02116
800-225-2606

Minimum: $1,000
Front-End Load: 4.75%
12b-1: 0.35%
Redemption Fee: None
Ticker Symbol: MFWVX

TOTAL RETURNS (%)

1987	1988	1989	1990	1991	5-year
0.0	11.6	9.2	7.0	10.4	44.0

INVESTMENT PORTFOLIO

Total Assets (mil.)	Expense Ratio	Turnover Ratio
$77	1.22%	37%

MFS MANAGED MUNICIPAL BOND TRUST

Massachusetts Financial Services
500 Boylston Street
Boston, MA 02116
800-225-2606

Minimum: $1,000
Front-End Load: 4.75%
12b-1: None
Redemption Fee: None
Ticker Symbol: MMBFX

TOTAL RETURNS (%)

1987	1988	1989	1990	1991	5-year
1.8	11.7	9.7	6.3	12.8	49.5

INVESTMENT PORTFOLIO

Total Assets (mil.)	Expense Ratio	Turnover Ratio
$1,725	0.65%	160%

NEW ENGLAND TAX EXEMPT INCOME FUND

TNE Investment Services
399 Boylston Street, 8th Floor
Boston, MA 02116
800-343-7104

Minimum: $1,000
Front-End Load: 4.50%
12b-1: 0.25%
Redemption Fee: None
Ticker Symbol: NELTX

TOTAL RETURNS (%)

1987	1988	1989	1990	1991	5-year
-3.0	11.5	9.7	5.5	11.6	39.7

INVESTMENT PORTFOLIO

Total Assets (mil.)	Expense Ratio	Turnover Ratio
$159	0.98%	85%

NUVEEN CALIFORNIA TAX FREE FUND INSURED BOND

Nuveen (John) & Company
333 West Wacker Drive
Chicago, IL 60606
800-621-7227

Minimum: $1,000
Front-End Load: 4.75%
12b-1: None
Redemption Fee: None
Ticker Symbol: NCIBX

TOTAL RETURNS (%)

1987	1988	1989	1990	1991	5-year
-3.7	11.0	10.4	6.7	11.5	40.4

INVESTMENT PORTFOLIO

Total Assets (mil.)	Expense Ratio	Turnover Ratio
$91	0.69%	29%

NUVEEN CALIFORNIA TAX FREE FUND SPECIAL BOND

Nuveen (John) & Company
333 West Wacker Drive
Chicago, IL 60606
800-621-7227

Minimum: $1,000
Front-End Load: 4.75%
12b-1: None
Redemption Fee: None
Ticker Symbol: NCSPX

TOTAL RETURNS (%)

1987	1988	1989	1990	1991	5-year
-2.2	10.2	11.7	6.2	11.1	41.9

INVESTMENT PORTFOLIO

Total Assets (mil.)	Expense Ratio	Turnover Ratio
$122	0.70%	15%

NUVEEN INSURED TAX FREE BOND MASSACHUSETTS PORTFOLIO

Nuveen (John) & Company
333 West Wacker Drive
Chicago, IL 60606
800-621-7227

Minimum: $1,000
Front-End Load: 4.75%
12b-1: None
Redemption Fee: None
Ticker Symbol: NIMAX

TOTAL RETURNS (%)

1987	1988	1989	1990	1991	5-year
-1.0	10.7	8.9	6.5	11.8	41.9

INVESTMENT PORTFOLIO

Total Assets (mil.)	Expense Ratio	Turnover Ratio
$24	0.85%	6%

NUVEEN INSURED TAX FREE BOND NATIONAL PORTFOLIO

Nuveen (John) & Company
333 West Wacker Drive
Chicago, IL 60606
800-621-7227

Minimum: $1,000
Front-End Load: 4.75%
12b-1: None
Redemption Fee: None
Ticker Symbol: NITNX

TOTAL RETURNS (%)

1987	1988	1989	1990	1991	5-year
0.5	12.8	10.6	6.7	12.8	50.9

INVESTMENT PORTFOLIO

Total Assets (mil.)	Expense Ratio	Turnover Ratio
$264	0.85%	53%

NUVEEN INSURED TAX FREE BOND NEW YORK PORTFOLIO

Nuveen (John) & Company
333 West Wacker Drive
Chicago, IL 60606
800-621-7227

Minimum: $1,000
Front-End Load: 4.75%
12b-1: None
Redemption Fee: None
Ticker Symbol: NINYX

TOTAL RETURNS (%)

1987	1988	1989	1990	1991	5-year
-4.0	10.7	9.8	5.3	13.4	39.4

INVESTMENT PORTFOLIO

Total Assets (mil.)	Expense Ratio	Turnover Ratio
$141	0.74%	13%

NUVEEN MUNICIPAL BOND FUND

Nuveen (John) & Company
333 West Wacker Drive
Chicago, IL 60606
800-621-7227

Minimum: $1,000
Front-End Load: 4.75%
12b-1: None
Redemption Fee: None
Ticker Symbol: NUVBX

TOTAL RETURNS (%)

1987	1988	1989	1990	1991	5-year
2.1	10.3	10.9	6.3	11.3	47.8

INVESTMENT PORTFOLIO

Total Assets (mil.)	Expense Ratio	Turnover Ratio
$1,721	0.63%	8%

NUVEEN TAX FREE BOND MASSACHUSETTS PORTFOLIO

Nuveen (John) & Company
333 West Wacker Drive
Chicago, IL 60606
800-621-7227

Minimum: $1,000
Front-End Load: 4.75%
12b-1: None
Redemption Fee: None
Ticker Symbol: NBMAX

TOTAL RETURNS (%)

1987	1988	1989	1990	1991	5-year
-3.7	10.1	10.1	5.4	12.4	38.4

INVESTMENT PORTFOLIO

Total Assets (mil.)	Expense Ratio	Turnover Ratio
$31	0.76%	23%

NUVEEN TAX FREE BOND FUND NEW YORK PORTFOLIO

Nuveen (John) & Company
333 West Wacker Drive
Chicago, IL 60606
800-621-7227

Minimum: $1,000
Front-End Load: 4.75%
12b-1: None
Redemption Fee: None
Ticker Symbol: NTNYX

TOTAL RETURNS (%)

1987	1988	1989	1990	1991	5-year
-1.1	9.3	10.8	4.0	13.8	41.9

INVESTMENT PORTFOLIO

Total Assets (mil.)	Expense Ratio	Turnover Ratio
$59	0.76%	51%

NUVEEN TAX-FREE BOND OHIO PORTFOLIO

Nuveen (John) & Company
333 West Wacker Drive
Chicago, IL 60606
800-621-7227

Minimum: $1,000
Front-End Load: 4.75%
12b-1: None
Redemption Fee: None
Ticker Symbol: NXOHX

TOTAL RETURNS (%)

1987	1988	1989	1990	1991	5-year
0.3	10.0	12.4	6.2	12.0	47.5

INVESTMENT PORTFOLIO

Total Assets (mil.)	Expense Ratio	Turnover Ratio
$82	0.74%	38%

OPPENHEIMER TAX-FREE BOND FUND

Oppenheimer Fund Management
P. O. Box 300
Denver, CO 80201
800-255-2755

Minimum: $1,000
Front-End Load: 4.75%
12b-1: 0.11%
Redemption Fee: None
Ticker Symbol: OPTAX

TOTAL RETURNS (%)

1987	1988	1989	1990	1991	5-year
0.0	9.5	9.5	5.9	12.1	42.3

INVESTMENT PORTFOLIO

Total Assets (mil.)	Expense Ratio	Turnover Ratio
$382	0.90%	29%

PACIFIC HORIZON CALIFORNIA TAX EXEMPT BOND

Security Pacific National Bank
333 South Hope Street
Los Angeles, CA 90071
800-332-3863

Minimum: $1,000
Front-End Load: 4.50%
12b-1: 0.18%
Redemption Fee: None
Ticker Symbol: PHCTX

TOTAL RETURNS (%)

1987	1988	1989	1990	1991	5-year
-1.4	8.6	9.3	6.2	11.1	38.2

INVESTMENT PORTFOLIO

Total Assets (mil.)	Expense Ratio	Turnover Ratio
$138	0.99%	33%

PAINEWEBBER CALIFORNIA TAX FREE INCOME A

PaineWebber
1285 Avenue of the Americas, 18th Floor
New York, NY 10019
800-647-1568

Minimum: $1,000
Front-End Load: 4.00%
12b-1: 0.25%
Redemption Fee: None
Ticker Symbol: PCIAX

TOTAL RETURNS (%)

1987	1988	1989	1990	1991	5-year
0.6	10.2	9.1	6.7	10.8	43.1

INVESTMENT PORTFOLIO

Total Assets (mil.)	Expense Ratio	Turnover Ratio
$232	0.68%	23%

PAINEWEBBER TAX EXEMPT INCOME FUND

PaineWebber
1285 Avenue of the Americas, 18th Floor
New York, NY 10019
800-647-1568

Minimum: $1.000
Front-End Load: 4.00%
12b-1: 0.25%
Redemption Fee: None
Ticker Symbol: PWTEX

TOTAL RETURNS (%)

1987	1988	1989	1990	1991	5-year
1.2	10.6	9.1	6.3	10.5	43.4

INVESTMENT PORTFOLIO

Total Assets (mil.)	Expense Ratio	Turnover Ratio
$383	0.94%	24%

PIONEER MUNICIPAL BOND FUND

Pioneer Funds Distributor
60 State Street
Boston, MA 02109
800-225-6292

Minimum: $1,000
Front-End Load: 4.50%
12b-1: 0.23%
Redemption Fee: None
Ticker Symbol: PMBFX

TOTAL RETURNS (%)

1987	1988	1989	1990	1991	5-year
-3.9	12.8	9.8	6.4	11.2	40.7

INVESTMENT PORTFOLIO

Total Assets (mil.)	Expense Ratio	Turnover Ratio
$43	0.67%	8%

PRINCOR TAX-EXEMPT BOND FUND

Principal Financial Group
711 High Street
Des Moines, IA 50309
800-247-4123

Minimum: $1,000
Front-End Load: 5.00%
12b-1: 0.20%
Redemption Fee: None
Ticker Symbol: PTBDX

TOTAL RETURNS (%)

1987	1988	1989	1990	1991	5-year
-2.5	14.3	10.7	5.6	12.1	45.9

INVESTMENT PORTFOLIO

Total Assets (mil.)	Expense Ratio	Turnover Ratio
$64	1.12%	3%

PUTNAM CALIFORNIA TAX EXEMPT INCOME FUND

Putnam Financial Services
One Post Office Square, 12th Floor
Boston, MA 02109
800-634-1590

Minimum: $500
Front-End Load: 4.75%
12b-1: None
Redemption Fee: None
Ticker Symbol: PCTEX

TOTAL RETURNS (%)

1987	1988	1989	1990	1991	5-year
0.4	12.4	10.0	6.8	11.4	47.8

INVESTMENT PORTFOLIO

Total Assets (mil.)	Expense Ratio	Turnover Ratio
$2,377	0.53%	33%

PUTNAM MASSACHUSETTS TAX EXEMPT INCOME FUND

Putnam Financial Services
One Post Office Square, 12th Floor
Boston, MA 02109
800-634-1590

Minimum: $500
Front-End Load: None
12b-1: 0.75%
Redemption Fee: 2.50%
Ticker Symbol: PTMAX

TOTAL RETURNS (%)

1987	1988	1989	1990	1991	5-year
-1.0	10.5	8.3	4.6	12.2	39.0

INVESTMENT PORTFOLIO

Total Assets (mil.)	Expense Ratio	Turnover Ratio
$79	1.65%	125%

PUTNAM MICHIGAN TAX EXEMPT INCOME FUND

Putnam Financial Services
One Post Office Square, 12th Floor
Boston, MA 02109
800-634-1590

Minimum: $500
Front-End Load: None
12b-1: 0.75%
Redemption Fee: 2.50%
Ticker Symbol: PTMCX

TOTAL RETURNS (%)

1987	1988	1989	1990	1991	5-year
-2.7	12.8	9.6	4.8	10.9	39.8

INVESTMENT PORTFOLIO

Total Assets (mil.)	Expense Ratio	Turnover Ratio
$44	1.54%	105%

PUTNAM MINNESOTA TAX EXEMPT INCOME FUND

Putnam Financial Services
One Post Office Square, 12th Floor
Boston, MA 02109
800-634-1590

Minimum: $500
Front-End Load: None
12b-1: 0.75%
Redemption Fee: 2.50%
Ticker Symbol: PTMNX

TOTAL RETURNS (%)

1987	1988	1989	1990	1991	5-year
-3.7	12.8	9.1	4.9	7.3	33.2

INVESTMENT PORTFOLIO

Total Assets (mil.)	Expense Ratio	Turnover Ratio
$33	1.57%	70%

PUTNAM NEW YORK TAX EXEMPT INCOME FUND

Putnam Financial Services
One Post Office Square, 12th Floor
Boston, MA 02109
800-634-1590

Minimum: $500
Front-End Load: 4.75%
12b-1: None
Redemption Fee: None
Ticker Symbol: PTEIX

TOTAL RETURNS (%)

1987	1988	1989	1990	1991	5-year
0.5%	12.7	9.4	3.9	14.3	47.2

INVESTMENT PORTFOLIO

Total Assets (mil.)	Expense Ratio	Turnover Ratio
$1,659	0.57%	17%

PUTNAM OHIO TAX EXEMPT INCOME FUND

Putnam Financial Services
One Post Office Square, 12th Floor
Boston, MA 02109
800-634-1590

Minimum: $500
Front-End Load: None
12b-1: 0.75%
Redemption Fee: 2.50%
Ticker Symbol: PTOHX

TOTAL RETURNS (%)

1987	1988	1989	1990	1991	5-year
-2.4	12.4	9.3	5.7	10.0	39.4

INVESTMENT PORTFOLIO

Total Assets (mil.)	Expense Ratio	Turnover Ratio
$102	1.60%	77%

PUTNAM TAX EXEMPT INCOME FUND

Putnam Financial Services
One Post Office Square, 12th Floor
Boston, MA 02109
800-634-1590

Minimum: $500
Front-End Load: 4.75%
12b-1: None
Redemption Fee: None
Ticker Symbol: PTAEX

TOTAL RETURNS (%)

1987	1988	1989	1990	1991	5-year
-1.2	13.1	10.9	4.9	12.7	46.5

INVESTMENT PORTFOLIO

Total Assets (mil.)	Expense Ratio	Turnover Ratio
$1,542	0.55%	74%

PUTNAM TAX-FREE HIGH YIELD FUND

Putnam Financial Services
One Post Office Square, 12th Floor
Boston, MA 02109
800-634-1590

Minimum: $500
Front-End Load: None
12b-1: 1.00%
Redemption Fee: 5.00%
Ticker Symbol: PTHYX

TOTAL RETURNS (%)

1987	1988	1989	1990	1991	5-year
0.3	11.2	8.7	3.7	11.7	40.4

INVESTMENT PORTFOLIO

Total Assets (mil.)	Expense Ratio	Turnover Ratio
$789	1.67%	47%

PUTNAM TAX-FREE INSURED FUND

Putnam Financial Services
One Post Office Square, 12th Floor
Boston, MA 02109
800-634-1590

Minimum: $500
Front-End Load: None
12b-1: 1.00%
Redemption Fee: 5.00%
Ticker Symbol: PTFIX

TOTAL RETURNS (%)

1987	1988	1989	1990	1991	5-year
-0.4	11.1	9.8	5.3	11.1	42.1

INVESTMENT PORTFOLIO

Total Assets (mil.)	Expense Ratio	Turnover Ratio
$383	1.64%	86%

SAFECO MUNICIPAL BOND FUND

SAFECO Securities
4333 Brooklyn Avenue N.E.
Seattle, WA 98185
800-426-6730

Minimum: $1,000
Front-End Load: None
12b-1: None
Redemption Fee: None
Ticker Symbol: SFCOX

TOTAL RETURNS (%)

1987	1988	1989	1990	1991	5-year
0.2	13.9	10.1	6.7	13.8	52.4

INVESTMENT PORTFOLIO

Total Assets (mil.)	Expense Ratio	Turnover Ratio
$394	0.57%	39%

SCUDDER MANAGED MUNICIPAL BOND

Scudder Stevens & Clark
175 Federal Street, 12th Floor
Boston, MA 02110
800-225-2470

Minimum: $1,000
Front-End Load: None
12b-1: None
Redemption Fee: None
Ticker Symbol: SCMBX

TOTAL RETURNS (%)

1987	1988	1989	1990	1991	5-year
0.9	12.3	11.2	6.8	12.2	51.0

INVESTMENT PORTFOLIO

Total Assets (mil.)	Expense Ratio	Turnover Ratio
$774	0.63%	90%

SCUDDER TAX FREE TARGET 1993

Scudder Stevens & Clark
175 Federal Street, 12th Floor
Boston, MA 02110
800-225-2470

Minimum: $1,000
Front-End Load: None
12b-1: None
Redemption Fee: None
Ticker Symbol: STTFX

TOTAL RETURNS (%)

1987	1988	1989	1990	1991	5-year
3.1	5.6	7.3	6.4	7.5	33.6

INVESTMENT PORTFOLIO

Total Assets (mil.)	Expense Ratio	Turnover Ratio
$38	0.90%	61%

SCUDDER TAX FREE TARGET 1996

Scudder Stevens & Clark
175 Federal Street, 12th Floor
Boston, MA 02110
800-225-2470

Minimum: $1,000
Front-End Load: None
12b-1: None
Redemption Fee: None
Ticker Symbol: STSIX

TOTAL RETURNS (%)

1987	1988	1989	1990	1991	5-year
2.0	7.5	8.0	6.6	9.3	38.0

INVESTMENT PORTFOLIO

Total Assets (mil.)	Expense Ratio	Turnover Ratio
$33	1.03%	98%

SHEARSON CALIFORNIA MUNICIPAL

Shearson Lehman Brothers
Two World Trade Center
New York, NY 10048
800-451-2010

Minimum: $500
Front-End Load: 5.00%
12b-1: None
Redemption Fee: None
Ticker Symbol: SHRCX

TOTAL RETURNS (%)

1987	1988	1989	1990	1991	5-year
-1.1	11.8	9.5	6.8	11.5	44.2

INVESTMENT PORTFOLIO

Total Assets (mil.)	Expense Ratio	Turnover Ratio
$354	0.66%	53%

SHEARSON INCOME PORTFOLIO TAX EXEMPT

Shearson Lehman Brothers
Two World Trade Center
New York, NY 10048
800-451-2010

Minimum: $500
Front-End Load: None
12b-1: 0.75%
Redemption Fee: 5.00%
Ticker Symbol: SXMTX

TOTAL RETURNS (%)

1987	1988	1989	1990	1991	5-year
0.3	11.8	9.1	5.0	11.3	42.8

INVESTMENT PORTFOLIO

Total Assets (mil.)	Expense Ratio	Turnover Ratio
$671	1.48%	29%

SHEARSON MANAGED MUNICIPALS

Shearson Lehman Brothers
Two World Trade Center
New York, NY 10048
800-451-2010

Minimum: $500
Front-End Load: 5.00%
12b-1: None
Redemption Fee: None
Ticker Symbol: SHMMX

TOTAL RETURNS (%)

1987	1988	1989	1990	1991	5-year
0.4	10.9	10.2	5.2	14.2	47.5

INVESTMENT PO

Total Assets (mil.)	Expense Ratio
$1,566	0.59%

SHEARSON NEW YORK MUNICIPALS

Shearson Lehman Brothers
Two World Trade Center
New York, NY 10048
800-451-2010

Minimum: $500
Front-End Load: 5.00%
12b-1: None
Redemption Fee: None
Ticker Symbol: SHNYX

TOTAL RETURNS (%)

1987	1988	1989	1990	1991	5-year
-1.1	11.9	9.1	5.4	13.0	43.6

INVESTMENT PORTFOLIO

Total Assets (mil.)	Expense Ratio	Turnover Ratio
$459	0.65%	18%

SIT NEW BEGINNING TAX-FREE INCOME FUND

SIT Investment Associates
4600 Norwest Center, 90 S. 7th Street
Minneapolis, MN 55402
800-332-5580

Minimum: $2,000
Front-End Load: None
12b-1: None
Redemption Fee: None
Ticker Symbol: SNTIX

TOTAL RETURNS (%)

1987	1988	1989	1990	1991	5-year
NA	NA	8.4	7.3	9.3	NA

INVESTMENT PORTFOLIO

Total Assets (mil.)	Expense Ratio	Turnover Ratio
$124	0.85%	74%

SPARTAN PENN MUNICIPAL HIGH YIELD PORTFOLIO

Fidelity Distributors Corporation
82 Devonshire Street, Mail Zone L7b
Boston, MA 02109
800-544-8888

Minimum: $2,500
Front-End Load: None
12b-1: None
Redemption Fee: 0.50%
Ticker Symbol: FPXTX

TOTAL RETURNS (%)

1987	1988	1989	1990	1991	5-year
-5.7	14.2	9.8	7.2	12.5	42.6

INVESTMENT PORTFOLIO

Total Assets (mil.)	Expense Ratio	Turnover Ratio
$190	0.65%	8%

SPARTAN SHORT INTERMEDIATE MUNICIPAL BOND

Fidelity Distributors Corporation
82 Devonshire Street, Mail Zone L7b
Boston, MA 02109
800-544-8888

inimum: $10,000
ont-End Load: None
-1: None
emption Fee: None
er Symbol: FSTFX

TOTAL RETURNS (%)

1987	1988	1989	1990	1991	5-year
0.3	4.9	6.3	6.4	7.6	28.0

INVESTMENT PORTFOLIO

Total Assets (mil.)	Expense Ratio	Turnover Ratio
$267	0.55%	76%

STEIN ROE HIGH-YIELD MUNICIPALS

Stein Roe & Farnham
P. O. Box 1162
Chicago, IL 60690
800-338-2550

Minimum: $1,000
Front-End Load: None
12b-1: None
Redemption Fee: None
Ticker Symbol: SRMFX

TOTAL RETURNS (%)

1987	1988	1989	1990	1991	5-year
1.6	13.7	11.4	7.7	9.8	52.2

INVESTMENT PORTFOLIO

Total Assets (mil.)	Expense Ratio	Turnover Ratio
$395	0.71%	261%

STEIN ROE INTERMEDIATE MUNICIPALS

Stein Roe & Farnham
P. O. Box 1162
Chicago, IL 60690
800-338-2550

Minimum: $1,000
Front-End Load: None
12b-1: None
Redemption Fee: None
Ticker Symbol: SRIMX

TOTAL RETURNS (%)

1987	1988	1989	1990	1991	5-year
3.2	6.1	8.1	7.5	10.7	40.9

INVESTMENT PORTFOLIO

Total Assets (mil.)	Expense Ratio	Turnover Ratio
$136	0.85%	141%

STEIN ROE MANAGED MUNICIPALS

Stein Roe & Farnham
P. O. Box 1162
Chicago, IL 60690
800-338-2550

Minimum: $1,000
Front-End Load: None
12b-1: None
Redemption Fee: None
Ticker Symbol: SRMMX

TOTAL RETURNS (%)

1987	1988	1989	1990	1991	5-year
0.9	10.9	10.6	7.0	11.9	48.2

INVESTMENT PORTFOLIO

Total Assets (mil.)	Expense Ratio	Turnover Ratio
$701	0.67%	95%

STRONG MUNICIPAL BOND

Strong/Corneliuson Capital Management
100 Heritage Reserve
Menomonee Falls, WI 53051
800-368-3863

Minimum: $2,500
Front-End Load: None
12b-1: None
Redemption Fee: None
Ticker Symbol: SXFIX

TOTAL RETURNS (%)

1987	1988	1989	1990	1991	5-year
-1.7	7.6	7.1	4.6	13.3	34.3

INVESTMENT PORTFOLIO

Total Assets (mil.)	Expense Ratio	Turnover Ratio
$88	0.30%	586%

SUN AMERICA TAX FREE CALIFORNIA MUNICIPAL BOND

Sun America Capital Services
10 Union Square East, 2nd Floor
New York, NY 10003
800-821-5100

Minimum: $500
Front-End Load: 4.75%
12b-1: None
Redemption Fee: None
Ticker Symbol: None

TOTAL RETURNS (%)

1987	1988	1989	1990	1991	5-year
NA	NA	9.9	5.4	10.5	NA

INVESTMENT PORTFOLIO

Total Assets (mil.)	Expense Ratio	Turnover Ratio
$14	0.20%	5%

SUN AMERICA TAX FREE

Sun America Capital Services
10 Union Square East, 2nd Floor
New York, NY 10003
800-821-5100

Minimum: $500
Front-End Load: 4.75%
12b-1: 0.35%
Redemption Fee: None
Ticker Symbol: STSRX

TOTAL RETURNS (%)

1987	1988	1989	1990	1991	5-year
0.6	11.3	8.1	5.8	8.7	39.2

INVESTMENT PORTFOLIO

Total Assets (mil.)	Expense Ratio	Turnover Ratio
$95	1.32%	0%

T. ROWE PRICE CALIFORNIA TAX FREE BOND

T. Rowe Price Investor Services
100 East Pratt Street
Baltimore, MD 21202
800-638-5660

Minimum: $2,500
Front-End Load: None
12b-1: None
Redemption Fee: None
Ticker Symbol: PRXCX

TOTAL RETURNS (%)

1987	1988	1989	1990	1991	5-year
-6.8	9.5	8.5	5.8	12.1	31.5

INVESTMENT PORTFOLIO

Total Assets (mil.)	Expense Ratio	Turnover Ratio
$106	0.73%	193%

T. ROWE PRICE TAX FREE HIGH YIELD

T. Rowe Price Investor Services
100 East Pratt Street
Baltimore, MD 21202
800-638-5660

Minimum: $2,500
Front-End Load: None
12b-1: None
Redemption Fee: None
Ticker Symbol: PRFHX

TOTAL RETURNS (%)

1987	1988	1989	1990	1991	5-year
0.2	11.2	10.5	7.1	11.7	47.4

INVESTMENT PORTFOLIO

Total Assets (mil.)	Expense Ratio	Turnover Ratio
$606	0.85%	51%

T. ROWE PRICE TAX FREE INCOME

T. Rowe Price Investor Services
100 East Pratt Street
Baltimore, MD 21202
800-638-5660

Minimum: $2,500
Front-End Load: None
12b-1: None
Redemption Fee: None
Ticker Symbol: PRTAX

TOTAL RETURNS (%)

1987	1988	1989	1990	1991	5-year
-4.2	7.9	9.2	5.9	12.2	34.0

INVESTMENT PORTFOLIO

Total Assets (mil.)	Expense Ratio	Turnover Ratio
$1,220	0.63%	80%

T. ROWE PRICE TAX FREE SHORT INTERMEDIATE

T. Rowe Price Investor Services
100 East Pratt Street
Baltimore, MD 21202
800-638-5660

Minimum: $2,500
Front-End Load: None
12b-1: None
Redemption Fee: None
Ticker Symbol: PRFSX

TOTAL RETURNS (%)

1987	1988	1989	1990	1991	5-year
2.2	5.0	6.9	6.0	7.9	31.2

INVESTMENT PORTFOLIO

Total Assets (mil.)	Expense Ratio	Turnover Ratio
$302	0.75%	190%

TAX-EXEMPT BOND FUND OF AMERICA

American Funds Distributor
333 South Hope Street, 52nd Floor
Los Angeles, CA 90071
800-421-9900

Minimum: $1,000
Front-End Load: 4.75%
12b-1: 0.20%
Redemption Fee: None
Ticker Symbol: AFTEX

TOTAL RETURNS (%)

1987	1988	1989	1990	1991	5-year
0.1	9.3	9.5	6.2	10.8	40.9

INVESTMENT PORTFOLIO

Total Assets (mil.)	Expense Ratio	Turnover Ratio
$746	0.73%	25%

TAX-EXEMPT FUND OF CALIFORNIA

American Funds Distributor
333 South Hope Street, 52nd Floor
Los Angeles, CA 90071
800-421-9900

Minimum: $1,000
Front-End Load: 4.75%
12b-1: 0.18%
Redemption Fee: None
Ticker Symbol: TAFTX

TOTAL RETURNS (%)

1987	1988	1989	1990	1991	5-year
-2.5	8.5	10.0	5.6	9.9	34.9

INVESTMENT PORTFOLIO

Total Assets (mil.)	Expense Ratio	Turnover Ratio
$117	0.86%	34%

TAX-EXEMPT FUND OF MARYLAND

American Funds Distributor
333 South Hope Street, 52nd Floor
Los Angeles, CA 90071
800-421-9900

Minimum: $1,000
Front-End Load: 4.75%
12b-1: 0.20%
Redemption Fee: None
Ticker Symbol: TMMDX

TOTAL RETURNS (%)

1987	1988	1989	1990	1991	5-year
-1.2	9.0	10.4	5.9	9.8	38.2

INVESTMENT PORTFOLIO

Total Assets (mil.)	Expense Ratio	Turnover Ratio
$39	1.00%	22%

TAX-EXEMPT FUND OF VIRGINIA

American Funds Distributor
333 South Hope Street, 52nd Floor
Los Angeles, CA 90071
800-421-9900

Minimum: $1,000
Front-End Load: 4.75%
12b-1: 0.21%
Redemption Fee: None
Ticker Symbol: TFVAX

TOTAL RETURNS (%)

1987	1988	1989	1990	1991	5-year
-0.1	8.8	9.0	5.7	11.0	39.0

INVESTMENT PORTFOLIO

Total Assets (mil.)	Expense Ratio	Turnover Ratio
$44	1.00%	35%

THOMSON TAX EXEMPT FUND B

Thomson Securities
1 Station Place
Stamford, CT 06902
800-628-1237

Minimum: $1,000
Front-End Load: None
12b-1: 1.00%
Redemption Fee: 1.00%
Ticker Symbol: TTEBX

TOTAL RETURNS (%)

1987	1988	1989	1990	1991	5-year
-1.4	9.4	10.5	4.7	10.0	37.3

INVESTMENT PORTFOLIO

Total Assets (mil.)	Expense Ratio	Turnover Ratio
$45	1.75%	48%

TRANSAMERICA SPECIAL HIGH YIELD TAX FREE

TransAmerica Distributors
1000 Louisiana, Suite 6000
Houston, TX 77002
800-343-6840

Minimum: $1,000
Front-End Load: None
12b-1: 0.98%
Redemption Fee: 6.00%
Ticker Symbol: TSHTX

TOTAL RETURNS (%)

1987	1988	1989	1990	1991	5-year
-3.6	12.9	8.0	3.8	12.2	37.0

INVESTMENT PORTFOLIO

Total Assets (mil.)	Expense Ratio	Turnover Ratio
$53	1.14%	35%

TRANSAMERICA TAX-FREE BOND

TransAmerica Distributors
1000 Louisiana, Suite 6000
Houston, TX 77002
800-343-6840

Minimum: $1,000
Front-End Load: 4.75%
12b-1: 0.15%
Redemption Fee: None
Ticker Symbol: TAMBX

TOTAL RETURNS (%)

1987	1988	1989	1990	1991	5-year
NA	NA	NA	NA	14.8	NA

INVESTMENT PORTFOLIO

Total Assets (mil.)	Expense Ratio	Turnover Ratio
$76	1.25%	64%

TWENTIETH CENTURY TAX-EXEMPT INTERMEDIATE TERM BOND

Twentieth Century Investors
4500 Main Street, P. O. Box 418210
Kansas City, MO 64111
800-345-2021

Minimum: None
Front-End Load: None
12b-1: None
Redemption Fee: None
Ticker Symbol: TWTIX

TOTAL RETURNS (%)

1987	1988	1989	1990	1991	5-year
NA	6.0	6.7	6.3	10.1	NA

INVESTMENT PORTFOLIO

Total Assets (mil.)	Expense Ratio	Turnover Ratio
$47	1.00%	102%

TWENTIETH CENTURY TAX-EXEMPT LONG TERM BOND

Twentieth Century Investors
4500 Main Street, P. O. Box 418210
Kansas City, MO 64111
800-345-2021

Minimum: None
Front-End Load: None
12b-1: None
Redemption Fee: None
Ticker Symbol: TWTLX

TOTAL RETURNS (%)

1987	1988	1989	1990	1991	5-year
NA	10.4	9.5	6.2	11.2	NA

INVESTMENT PORTFOLIO

Total Assets (mil.)	Expense Ratio	Turnover Ratio
$40	1.00%	144%

UNIFIED INDIANA BOND FUND

Unified Management
429 North Pennsylvania Street
Indianapolis, IN 46204
800-862-7283

Minimum: $1,000
Front-End Load: 4.50%
12b-1: None
Redemption Fee: None
Ticker Symbol: UNMIX

TOTAL RETURNS (%)

1987	1988	1989	1990	1991	5-year
0.2	10.3	9.7	6.4	9.3	41.1

INVESTMENT PORTFOLIO

Total Assets (mil.)	Expense Ratio	Turnover Ratio
$14	0.59%	25%

UNITED SERVICE FUNDS—TAX FREE

United Services Advisors
P. O. Box 29467
San Antonio, TX 78229
800-873-8637

Minimum: $1,000
Front-End Load: None
12b-1: None
Redemption Fee: None
Ticker Symbol: USUTX

TOTAL RETURNS (%)

1987	1988	1989	1990	1991	5-year
-0.2	12.0	8.2	6.0	9.9	40.9

INVESTMENT PORTFOLIO

Total Assets (mil.)	Expense Ratio	Turnover Ratio
$7	1.94%	54%

USAA TAX EXEMPT HIGH YIELD FUND

USAA Investment Management
USAA Building
San Antonio, TX 78288
800-531-8181

Minimum: $3,000
Front-End Load: None
12b-1: None
Redemption Fee: None
Ticker Symbol: USTEX

TOTAL RETURNS (%)

1987	1988	1989	1990	1991	5-year
-1.9	12.5	10.6	6.6	12.4	46.1

INVESTMENT PORTFOLIO

Total Assets (mil.)	Expense Ratio	Turnover Ratio
$1,596	0.45%	91%

USAA TAX EXEMPT INTERMEDIATE-TERM

USAA Investment Management
USAA Building
San Antonio, TX 78288
800-531-8181

Minimum: $3,000
Front-End Load: None
12b-1: None
Redemption Fee: None
Ticker Symbol: USATX

TOTAL RETURNS (%)

1987	1988	1989	1990	1991	5-year
1.0	8.7	9.2	6.7	11.1	42.2

INVESTMENT PORTFOLIO

Total Assets (mil.)	Expense Ratio	Turnover Ratio
$781	0.44%	66%

USAA TAX EXEMPT SHORT-TERM FUND

USAA Investment Management
USAA Building
San Antonio, TX 78288
800-531-8181

Minimum: $3,000
Front-End Load: None
12b-1: None
Redemption Fee: None
Ticker Symbol: USSTX

TOTAL RETURNS (%)

1987	1988	1989	1990	1991	5-year
2.8	6.1	7.4	5.9	7.7	33.5

INVESTMENT PORTFOLIO

Total Assets (mil.)	Expense Ratio	Turnover Ratio
$602	0.55%	96%

VALUE LINE TAX EXEMPT HIGH YIELD PORTFOLIO

Value Line Securities
711 Third Avenue
New York, NY 10017
800-223-0818

Minimum: $1,000
Front-End Load: None
12b-1: None
Redemption Fee: None
Ticker Symbol: VLHYX

TOTAL RETURNS (%)

1987	1988	1989	1990	1991	5-year
0.1	11.0	8.4	6.6	12.2	43.9

INVESTMENT PORTFOLIO

Total Assets (mil.)	Expense Ratio	Turnover Ratio
$295	0.65%	122%

VANGUARD CALIFORNIA TAX FREE FUND—INSURED LONG TERM

Vanguard Group
Vanguard Financial Center
Valley Forge, PA 19482
800-662-7447

Minimum: $3,000
Front-End Load: None
12b-1: None
Redemption Fee: None
Ticker Symbol: VCITX

TOTAL RETURNS (%)

1987	1988	1989	1990	1991	5-year
-3.9	12.1	10.5	7.0	11.0	41.4

INVESTMENT PORTFOLIO

Total Assets (mil.)	Expense Ratio	Turnover Ratio
$629	0.27%	6%

VANGUARD MUNICIPAL BOND HIGH YIELD

Vanguard Group
Vanguard Financial Center
Valley Forge, PA 19482
800-662-7447

Minimum: $3,000
Front-End Load: None
12b-1: None
Redemption Fee: None
Ticker Symbol: VWAHX

TOTAL RETURNS (%)

1987	1988	1989	1990	1991	5-year
-1.6	13.8	11.1	5.9	14.8	51.2

INVESTMENT PORTFOLIO

Total Assets (mil.)	Expense Ratio	Turnover Ratio
$1,282	0.26%	58%

VANGUARD MUNICIPAL BOND INTERMEDIATE TERM

Vanguard Group
Vanguard Financial Center
Valley Forge, PA 19482
800-662-7447

Minimum: $3,000
Front-End Load: None
12b-1: None
Redemption Fee: None
Ticker Symbol: VWITX

TOTAL RETURNS (%)

1987	1988	1989	1990	1991	5-year
1.6	10.0	10.0	7.2	12.2	47.9

INVESTMENT PORTFOLIO

Total Assets (mil.)	Expense Ratio	Turnover Ratio
$2,323	0.26%	27%

VANGUARD MUNICIPAL BOND LONG TERM

Vanguard Group
Vanguard Financial Center
Valley Forge, PA 19482
800-662-7447

Minimum: $3,000
Front-End Load: None
12b-1: None
Redemption Fee: None
Ticker Symbol: VWLTX

TOTAL RETURNS (%)

1987	1988	1989	1990	1991	5-year
-1.1	12.2	11.5	6.8	13.5	50.1

INVESTMENT PORTFOLIO

Total Assets (mil.)	Expense Ratio	Turnover Ratio
$848	0.26%	62%

VANGUARD MUNICIPAL BOND SHORT TERM

Vanguard Group
Vanguard Financial Center
Valley Forge, PA 19482
800-662-7447

Minimum: $3,000
Front-End Load: None
12b-1: None
Redemption Fee: None
Ticker Symbol: VWSTX

TOTAL RETURNS (%)

1987	1988	1989	1990	1991	5-year
4.1	5.6	7.1	6.6	7.2	34.5

INVESTMENT PORTFOLIO

Total Assets (mil.)	Expense Ratio	Turnover Ratio
$873	0.26%	104%

VANGUARD MUNICIPAL LIMITED TERM MATURITY

Vanguard Group
Vanguard Financial Center
Valley Forge, PA 19482
800-662-7447

Minimum: $3,000
Front-End Load: None
12b-1: None
Redemption Fee: None
Ticker Symbol: VMLTX

TOTAL RETURNS (%)

1987	1988	1989	1990	1991	5-year
NA	6.4	8.1	7.0	9.5	NA

INVESTMENT PORTFOLIO

Total Assets (mil.)	Expense Ratio	Turnover Ratio
$517	0.25%	57%

VANGUARD NEW YORK INSURED TAX FREE FUND

Vanguard Group
Vanguard Financial Center
Valley Forge, PA 19482
800-662-7447

Minimum: $3,000
Front-End Load: None
12b-1: None
Redemption Fee: None
Ticker Symbol: VNYTX

TOTAL RETURNS (%)

1987	1988	1989	1990	1991	5-year
-3.4	12.0	10.4	6.2	12.8	43.0

INVESTMENT PORTFOLIO

Total Assets (mil.)	Expense Ratio	Turnover Ratio
$408	0.32%	17%

VANGUARD PENNSYLVANIA TAX FREE INSURED LONG TERM

Vanguard Group
Vanguard Financial Center
Valley Forge, PA 19482
800-662-7447

Minimum: $3,000
Front-End Load: None
12b-1: None
Redemption Fee: None
Ticker Symbol: VPAIX

TOTAL RETURNS (%)

1987	1988	1989	1990	1991	5-year
-1.3	12.3	10.6	6.9	12.3	47.2

INVESTMENT PORTFOLIO

Total Assets (mil.)	Expense Ratio	Turnover Ratio
$828	0.26%	9%

VAN KAMPEN MERRITT INSURED TAX FREE INCOME FUND

Van Kampen Merritt
17W110 22nd Street
Oakbrook Terrace, IL 60181
800-225-2222

Minimum: $1,500
Front-End Load: 4.90%
12b-1: 0.17%
Redemption Fee: None
Ticker Symbol: VKMTX

TOTAL RETURNS (%)

1987	1988	1989	1990	1991	5-year
0.3	11.5	9.4	7.1	10.6	44.8

INVESTMENT PORTFOLIO

Total Assets (mil.)	Expense Ratio	Turnover Ratio
$807	0.88%	108%

VAN KAMPEN MERRITT TAX FREE HIGH INCOME FUND

Van Kampen Merritt
17W110 22nd Street
Oakbrook Terrace, IL 60181
800-225-2222

Minimum: $1,500
Front-End Load: 4.90%
12b-1: 0.14%
Redemption Fee: None
Ticker Symbol: VKMHX

TOTAL RETURNS (%)

1987	1988	1989	1990	1991	5-year
2.9	10.7	9.7	3.2	8.5	39.9

INVESTMENT PORTFOLIO

Total Assets (mil.)	Expense Ratio	Turnover Ratio
$621	0.95%	66%

VENTURE MUNICIPAL PLUS

Venture Advisers
P. O. Box 1688
Santa Fe, NM 87501
800-279-0279

Minimum: $1,000
Front-End Load: None
12b-1: 1.25%
Redemption Fee: 5.00%
Ticker Symbol: VMPIX

TOTAL RETURNS (%)

1987	1988	1989	1990	1991	5-year
0.1	11.0	11.0	2.8	11.7	41.7

INVESTMENT PORTFOLIO

Total Assets (mil.)	Expense Ratio	Turnover Ratio
$95	2.45%	29%

Index

Dr. Gerald Perritt's *The* ***Mutual Fund Letter***

"One of America's Most Widely Read Mutual Fund Advisory Newsletters"

As a subscriber to *The Mutual Fund Letter* you'll receive top-notch, up-to-date information every month:

- Investment Outlook & Strategy
- Investment Ideas and Portfolio Management Strategies
- Model Portfolios for Five Investment Objectives
- Buy-Hold-Sell Advice for Specific Funds
- Fund Family Reports
- ***and Much More!***

Heard Through the Grapevine...

"If you're the type to follow a newsletter's advice to a T, then you might try ***The Mutual Fund Letter****... among the top-ranked fund letters for the past three years."*

—USA Today

" A lot of stuff packed in here."

—Kiplinger's Changing Times

"Gerald W. Perritt has been crusading for better informed investing for more than a decade—first as a college professor, then as director of a nonprofit group, and now as a newsletter publisher and author of books on investing."

—St. Petersburg Times

Over, please